# Biology

for Cambridge IGCSE™

COURSEBOOK

Mary Jones & Geoff Jones

# CAMBRIDGE
## UNIVERSITY PRESS

University Printing House, Cambridge CB2 8BS, United Kingdom

One Liberty Plaza, 20th Floor, New York, NY 10006, USA

477 Williamstown Road, Port Melbourne, VIC 3207, Australia

314–321, 3rd Floor, Plot 3, Splendor Forum, Jasola District Centre, New Delhi – 110025, India

79 Anson Road, #06–04/06, Singapore 079906

Cambridge University Press is part of the University of Cambridge.

It furthers the University's mission by disseminating knowledge in the pursuit of education, learning and research at the highest international levels of excellence.

www.cambridge.org
Information on this title: www.cambridge.org/9781108936767

© Cambridge University Press 2021

This publication is in copyright. Subject to statutory exception and to the provisions of relevant collective licensing agreements, no reproduction of any part may take place without the written permission of Cambridge University Press.

First edition 2002
Second edition 2010
Third edition 2014
Fourth edition 2021

20 19 18 17 16 15 14 13 12 11 10 9 8 7 6 5 4 3 2 1

*Printed in Dubai by Oriental Press*

*A catalogue record for this publication is available from the British Library*

ISBN 978-1-108-93676-7 Coursebook with Digital Access (2 Years)
ISBN 978-1-108-97028-0 Digital Coursebook (2 Years)
ISBN 978-1-108-94744-2 Coursebook eBook

Additional resources for this publication at www.cambridge.org/go

Illustrations by Eleanor Jones

---

NOTICE TO TEACHERS IN THE UK

It is illegal to reproduce any part of this work in material form (including photocopying and electronic storage) except under the following circumstances:

(i) where you are abiding by a licence granted to your school or institution by the Copyright Licensing Agency;

(ii) where no such licence exists, or where you wish to exceed the terms of a licence, and you have gained the written permission of Cambridge University Press;

(iii) where you are allowed to reproduce without permission under the provisions of Chapter 3 of the Copyright, Designs and Patents Act 1988, which covers, for example, the reproduction of short passages within certain types of educational anthology and reproduction for the purposes of setting examination questions.

NOTICE TO TEACHERS

Cambridge International copyright material in this publication is reproduced under licence and remains the intellectual property of Cambridge Assessment International Education.

Exam-style questions and sample answers have been written by the authors. In examinations, the way marks are awarded may be different. References to assessment and/or assessment preparation are the publisher's interpretation of the syllabus requirements and may not fully reflect the approach of Cambridge Assessment International Education.

# DEDICATED TEACHER AWARDS

## Teachers play an important part in shaping futures. Our Dedicated Teacher Awards recognise the hard work that teachers put in every day.

Thank you to everyone who nominated this year; we have been inspired and moved by all of your stories. Well done to all of our nominees for your dedication to learning and for inspiring the next generation of thinkers, leaders and innovators.

### Congratulations to our incredible winner and finalists!

**WINNER**

- **Patricia Abril** — New Cambridge School, Colombia
- **Stanley Manaay** — Salvacion National High School, Philippines
- **Tiffany Cavanagh** — Trident College Solwezi, Zambia
- **Helen Comerford** — Lumen Christi Catholic College, Australia
- **John Nicko Coyoca** — University of San Jose-Recoletos, Philippines
- **Meera Rangarajan** — RBK International Academy, India

For more information about our dedicated teachers and their stories, go to
**dedicatedteacher.cambridge.org**

# Contents

| | | |
|---|---|---|
| How to use this series | | vi |
| How to use this book | | viii |
| Introduction | | x |

## 1 Characteristics and classification of living organisms
| | | |
|---|---|---|
| 1.1 | Characteristics of organisms | 3 |
| 1.2 | The biological classification system | 5 |
| 1.3 | Keys | 7 |
| 1.4 | Kingdoms | 10 |
| 1.5 | Groups within the animal and plant kingdoms | 15 |
| 1.6 | Viruses | 24 |

## 2 Cells
| | | |
|---|---|---|
| 2.1 | Animal and plant cells | 33 |
| 2.2 | Bacterial cells | 40 |
| 2.3 | Specialised cells | 41 |
| 2.4 | Sizes of specimens | 42 |

## 3 Movement into and out of cells
| | | |
|---|---|---|
| 3.1 | Diffusion | 51 |
| 3.2 | Osmosis | 55 |
| 3.3 | Active transport | 61 |

## 4 Biological molecules
| | | |
|---|---|---|
| 4.1 | Carbohydrates, fats and proteins | 70 |
| 4.2 | The structure of DNA | 77 |

## 5 Enzymes
| | | |
|---|---|---|
| 5.1 | Biological catalysts | 84 |
| 5.2 | Factors that affect enzymes | 86 |

## 6 Plant nutrition
| | | |
|---|---|---|
| 6.1 | Making carbohydrates using light energy | 99 |
| 6.2 | Leaves | 103 |
| 6.3 | Factors affecting photosynthesis | 107 |

## 7 Human nutrition
| | | |
|---|---|---|
| 7.1 | Diet | 128 |
| 7.2 | The human digestive system | 132 |
| 7.3 | Digestion | 136 |
| 7.4 | Absorption and assimilation | 140 |

## 8 Transport in plants
| | | |
|---|---|---|
| 8.1 | Xylem and phloem | 149 |
| 8.2 | Transport of water | 152 |
| 8.3 | Translocation of sucrose and amino acids | 159 |

## 9 Transport in animals
| | | |
|---|---|---|
| 9.1 | Circulatory systems | 170 |
| 9.2 | The heart | 172 |
| 9.3 | Blood vessels | 178 |
| 9.4 | Blood | 182 |

## 10 Diseases and immunity
| | | |
|---|---|---|
| 10.1 | Transmission of pathogens | 195 |
| 10.2 | The immune response | 203 |

## 11 Respiration and gas exchange
| | | |
|---|---|---|
| 11.1 | Respiration | 217 |
| 11.2 | Gas exchange in humans | 220 |

## 12 Coordination and response
| | | |
|---|---|---|
| 12.1 | The human nervous system | 236 |
| 12.2 | Sense organs | 241 |
| 12.3 | Hormones | 246 |
| 12.4 | Coordination in plants | 247 |

## 13 Excretion and homeostasis
| | | |
|---|---|---|
| 13.1 | Excretion | 262 |
| 13.2 | Homeostasis | 266 |

## 14 Reproduction in plants
| | | |
|---|---|---|
| 14.1 | Asexual and sexual reproduction | 283 |
| 14.2 | Sexual reproduction in flowering plants | 286 |
| 14.3 | Advantages and disadvantages of different methods of reproduction | 293 |

## 15 Reproduction in humans
| | | |
|---|---|---|
| 15.1 | The human reproductive systems | 304 |
| 15.2 | Sexually transmitted infections | 312 |

## 16 Chromosomes, genes and proteins
| | | |
|---|---|---|
| 16.1 | Chromosomes and cell division | 322 |
| 16.2 | Inheriting genes | 326 |
| 16.3 | Genes and protein synthesis | 337 |

## 17 Variation and selection
| | | |
|---|---|---|
| 17.1 | Variation | 348 |
| 17.2 | Selection | 352 |

## 18 Organisms and their environment
| | | |
|---|---|---|
| 18.1 | Energy flow and food webs | 372 |
| 18.2 | Nutrient cycles | 379 |
| 18.3 | Populations | 382 |

## 19 Human influences on ecosystems
| | | |
|---|---|---|
| 19.1 | Human pressures on ecosystems | 396 |
| 19.2 | Conservation | 411 |

## 20 Biotechnology and genetic modification
| | | |
|---|---|---|
| 20.1 | Biotechnology | 427 |
| 20.2 | Genetic modification | 434 |

## Glossary 446

## Index 458

## Acknowledgements 467

CAMBRIDGE IGCSE™ BIOLOGY: COURSEBOOK

# > How to use this series

We offer a comprehensive, flexible array of resources for the Cambridge IGCSE™ Biology syllabus. We provide targeted support and practice for the specific challenges we've heard that students face: learning science with English as a second language; learners who find the mathematical content within science difficult; and developing practical skills.

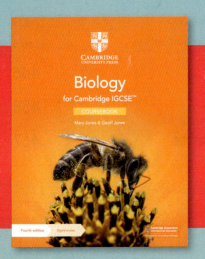

This coursebook provides coverage of the full Cambridge IGCSE Biology syllabus. Each chapter explains facts and concepts, and uses relevant real-world examples of scientific principles to bring the subject to life. Together with a focus on practical work and plenty of active learning opportunities, the coursebook prepares learners for all aspects of their scientific study. At the end of each chapter, examination-style questions offer practice opportunities for learners to apply their learning.

The digital teacher's resource contains detailed guidance for all topics of the syllabus, including common misconceptions identifying areas where learners might need extra support, as well as an engaging bank of lesson ideas for each syllabus topic. Differentiation is emphasised with advice for identification of different learner needs and suggestions of appropriate interventions to support and stretch learners. The teacher's resource also contains support for preparing and carrying out all the investigations in the practical workbook, including a set of sample results for when practicals aren't possible.

The teacher's resource also contains scaffolded worksheets and unit tests for each chapter. Answers for all components are accessible to teachers for free on the Cambridge GO platform.

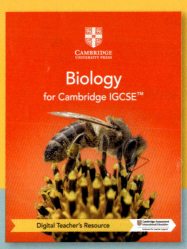

# How to use this series

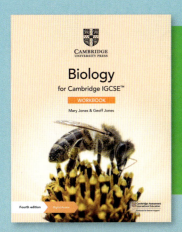

The skills-focused workbook has been carefully constructed to help learners develop the skills that they need as they progress through their Cambridge IGCSE Biology course, providing further practice of all the topics in the coursebook. A three-tier, scaffolded approach to skills development enables students to gradually progress through 'focus', 'practice' and 'challenge' exercises, ensuring that every learner is supported. The workbook enables independent learning and is ideal for use in class or as homework.

The practical workbook provides learners with additional opportunities for hands-on practical work, giving them full guidance and support that will help them to develop their investigative skills. These skills include planning investigations, selecting and handling apparatus, creating hypotheses, recording and displaying results, and analysing and evaluating data.

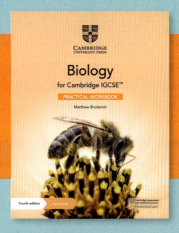

Mathematics is an integral part of scientific study, and one that learners often find a barrier to progression in science. The Maths Skills for Cambridge IGCSE Biology write-in workbook has been written in collaboration with the Association of Science Education, with each chapter focusing on several maths skills that students need to succeed in their Biology course.

Our research shows that English language skills are the single biggest barrier to students accessing international science. This write-in English language skills workbook contains exercises set within the context of IGCSE Biology topics to consolidate understanding and embed practice in aspects of language central to the subject. Activities range from practising using 'effect' and 'affect' in the context of enzymes, to writing about expiration with a focus on common prefixes.

CAMBRIDGE IGCSE™ BIOLOGY: COURSEBOOK

# How to use this book

Throughout this book, you will notice lots of different features that will help your learning. These are explained below.

### LEARNING INTENTIONS

These set the scene for each chapter, help with navigation through the coursebook and indicate the important concepts in each topic.

> In the learning intentions table, the summary table and the exam-style questions, Supplement content is indicated with a large arrow and a darker background, as in the example here.

### GETTING STARTED

This contains questions and activities on subject knowledge you will need before starting this chapter.

### SCIENCE IN CONTEXT

This feature presents real-world examples and applications of the content in a chapter, focussing on topics that go beyond the syllabus. There are discussion questions at the end, which look at some of the benefits and problems of these applications, and encourage you to look further into the topics.

### EXPERIMENTAL SKILLS

This feature focuses on developing your practical skills. They include lists of equipment required and any safety issues, step-by-step instructions so you can carry out the experiment, and questions to help you think about what you have learnt.

### KEY WORDS

Key vocabulary is highlighted in the text when it is first introduced, and definitions are given in boxes near the vocabulary. You will also find definitions of these words in the Glossary at the back of this book.

## Questions

Appearing throughout the text, questions give you a chance to check that you have understood the topic you have just read about. The answers to these questions are accessible to teachers for free on the Cambridge GO site.

### ACTIVITY

Activities give you an opportunity to check and develop your understanding throughout the text in a more active way, for example by creating presentations, posters or role plays. When activities have answers, teachers can find these for free on the Cambridge GO site.

### COMMAND WORDS

Command words that appear in the syllabus and might be used in exams are highlighted in the exam-style questions. In the margin, you will find the Cambridge International definition. You will also find these definitions in the Glossary at the back of the book with some further explanation on the meaning of these words.

> **Supplement content:** Where content is intended for students who are studying the Supplement content of the syllabus as well as the Core, this is indicated using the arrow and the bar, as on the left here. You may also see the teal text with just an arrow (and no bar), in boxed features such as the Key Words or the Getting Started.

viii

# How to use this book

> **REFLECTION**
>
> These activities ask you to think about the approach that you take to your work, and how you might improve this in the future.

> **SELF/PEER ASSESSMENT**
>
> At the end of some activities and experimental skills boxes, you will find opportunities to help you assess your own work, or that of your classmates, and consider how you can improve the way you learn.

> These boxes tell you where information in the book is extension content, and is not part of the syllabus.

> **SUMMARY**
>
> There is a summary of key points at the end of each chapter.

> **PROJECT**
>
> Projects allow you to apply your learning from the whole chapter to group activities such as making posters or presentations, or taking part in debates. They may give you the opportunity to extend your learning beyond the syllabus if you want to.

> **EXAM-STYLE QUESTIONS**
>
> Questions at the end of each chapter provide more demanding exam-style questions, some of which may require use of knowledge from previous chapters. The answers to these questions are accessible to teachers for free on the Cambridge GO site.

> **SELF-EVALUATION CHECKLIST**
>
> The summary checklists are followed by 'I can' statements which relate to the Learning intentions at the beginning of the chapter. You might find it helpful to rate how confident you are for each of these statements when you are revising. You should revisit any topics that you rated 'Needs more work' or 'Almost there'.
>
> | I can | See Topic... | Needs more work | Almost there | Confident to move on |
> |---|---|---|---|---|
> | Core | | | | |
> | Supplement | | | | |

# Introduction

This is the fourth edition of our Cambridge IGCSE™ Biology Coursebook, and it provides everything that you need to support your course for Cambridge IGCSE Biology (0610/0970). It provides full coverage of the syllabus for examination from 2023 onwards.

The chapter order generally follows the same sequences as the topics in the syllabus with some exceptions where appropriate.

The various features that you will find in these chapters are explained in the previous two pages.

Many of the questions you will meet during your course test if you have a deep understanding of the facts and concepts you have learnt. It is therefore not enough just to learn words and diagrams that you can repeat in answer to questions; you need to ensure that you really understand each concept fully. Trying to answer the questions that you find within each chapter, and at the end of each chapter, should help you to do this.

Although you will study your biology as a series of different topics, it is important to appreciate that all of these topics link up with each other. You need to make links between different areas of the syllabus to answer some questions.

As you work through your course, make sure that you keep reflecting on the work that you did earlier and how it relates to the current topic that you are studying. The reflection boxes throughout the chapters ask you to think about *how* you learn, to help you to make the very best use of your time and abilities as your course progresses. You can also use the self-evaluation checklists at the end of each chapter to decide how well you have understood each topic in the syllabus, and whether or not you need to do more work on each one.

Practical skills are an important part of your biology course. You will develop these skills as you do experiments and other practical work related to the topics you are studying.

# Chapter 1
# Characteristics & classification of living organisms

**IN THIS CHAPTER YOU WILL:**

- learn about the seven characteristics of living organisms
- find out how the binomial system is used to name organisms
- practise using and constructing keys
- describe how to classify vertebrates and arthropods
- describe the features of the five kingdoms of organisms
- describe how to classify ferns and flowering plants
- outline the features of viruses.

# CAMBRIDGE IGCSE™ BIOLOGY: COURSEBOOK

## GETTING STARTED

1 The list below contains some features of living organisms. With your partner, discuss which of these features are found in *all* living organisms.

**breathing    excretion    a blood system    a nervous system    sensitivity**

**growth    reproduction    movement    nutrition    respiration**

2 When you have made your decisions, write a very short description of each of the features you have chosen.

Be ready to share your ideas.

## THE PUZZLE OF THE PLATYPUS

In 1799, a dead specimen of a strange animal was taken to England from Australia. The animal had a beak and webbed feet, like a duck. It had fur, like a mole. No one knew whether it laid eggs or gave birth to live young. So, was it a bird? Was it a mammal? No one could decide.

It was studied by Dr George Shaw. To begin with, he thought it was a hoax. He looked to see if the beak was stitched onto the head, but no – the beak was clearly a genuine part of the animal.

Dr Shaw gave the animal a Latin name, *Platypus anatinus*. 'Platypus' means 'flat-footed' and 'anatinus' means 'like a duck'. However, someone then pointed out that the name *Platypus* had already been taken and belonged to a species of beetle. So, another name was suggested – *Ornithorhynchus paradoxus*. The first word means 'nose like a bird' and the second means 'puzzling'. The name has now changed back again, to *Platypus anatinus*.

Later, proof was found that platypuses lay eggs, rather than giving birth to live young. However, they feed their young on milk, which is a characteristic feature of mammals. Scientists eventually decided to classify the platypus as a mammal. It was put into a new group of mammals, called monotremes, which also includes the echidnas (spiny anteaters).

**Figure 1.1:** A platypus is adapted for hunting prey under water.

### Discussion questions

1 Scientists give every species on Earth a two-word name that is used by everyone, all over the world. Do you think this is a good idea? Why do you think this?

2 Scientific names for organisms are in Latin, which is a language that no one speaks now. This naming system was invented in the 18th century. Do you think using Latin is a good idea?

# 1.1 Characteristics of organisms

Biology is the study of organisms. An **organism** is a complete living thing – such as yourself, a platypus, a bacterium or a mango tree. There are very many different kinds of organism on Earth, but all of them share seven characteristics (Figure 1.2). Some non-living things have some of these characteristics, but no non-living thing has all of them.

> **KEY WORDS**
>
> **organism:** a living thing
>
> **movement:** an action by an organism or part of an organism causing a change of position or place

**Movement** is the ability of an organism, or part of it, to change position or place. It is easy to see most animals moving, but less easy to see a plant move.

**Growth** All organisms begin small and get larger, by the growth of their cells and by adding new cells to their bodies.

**Movement** All organisms are able to move to some extent. Most animals can move their whole body from place to place, and plants can slowly move parts of themselves.

**Sensitivity** All organisms pick up information about changes in their environment, and react to the changes.

**Excretion** All organisms produce unwanted or toxic waste products as a result of their metabolic reactions, and these must be removed from the body.

**Reproduction** Organisms are able to make new organisms of the same species as themselves.

**Nutrition** Organisms take substances from their environment and use them to provide energy or materials to make new cells.

**Respiration** All organisms break down glucose and other substances inside their cells, to release energy that they can use.

**Figure 1.2:** Characteristics of living organisms.

**Figure 1.3:** This fly is about to be caught in a trap. The Venus flytrap leaves will close together, trapping the fly inside. The plant will digest the fly and absorb nutrients from it.

**Figure 1.4:** When a pufferfish detects a threat, it swallows water and inflates (puffs up) its spiny body so that predators cannot easily eat it.

A few plants can move parts of themselves quite quickly (Figure 1.3). And in almost any plant, if you look at the cells under the microscope, you can see chloroplasts moving about inside them.

Respiration is the way that organisms obtain energy from nutrients – usually from glucose. Respiration is a chemical reaction that happens inside every living cell. You will find out much more about respiration in Chapter 11. Organisms use the energy that they obtain from respiration to make other chemical reactions in their cells happen. All of these chemical reactions – including respiration – are called metabolism.

> **KEY WORDS**
>
> **respiration:** the chemical reactions in cells that break down nutrient molecules and release energy for metabolism
>
> **metabolism:** the chemical reactions that take place in living organisms
>
> **sensitivity:** the ability to detect and respond to changes in the internal or external environment
>
> **growth:** a permanent increase in size and dry mass
>
> **dry mass:** the mass of an organism after it has been killed and all water removed from it
>
> **reproduction:** the processes that make more of the same kind of organism

Sensitivity is the ability to detect changes in the environment and respond to them. These changes may be in the internal environment (such as the temperature of the blood) or the external environment (such as the intensity of sunlight). For example, you use your ears to detect someone talking to you. Plants detect the direction that light is coming from and can turn their flowers to face the sun.

Growth can be defined as a permanent increase in size and dry mass. All organisms can grow. Some organisms – such as a pufferfish – can get bigger just for a short time to help to deter (put off) predators (Figure 1.4). This is not growth, because the fish goes back to its original size when the threat has gone away. Plants and animals grow by producing new cells. If you are studying the Supplement, you will find out how they do this in Chapter 16.

We can measure growth in many ways. One method is to find the dry mass. This involves finding the mass of several organisms of the same type over a period of time. An organism is killed and dried (so this method is more often used for plants than for animals). The mass of its body without any water is then found. After a particular period of time – for example, one day – the dry mass of another of the organisms is found. This is repeated with several organisms for the growth period being observed.

Reproduction means making more organisms of the same kind. Not every individual organism can reproduce, but at least some individuals of each kind of organism can do so. You can find out more about reproduction in Chapters 14 and 15.

There are many different chemical reactions going on inside every living cell. Some of the products that are formed in these reactions are not needed by the cells. These waste products are removed from the organism, in a process called *excretion*. Excretion also removes substances in excess of requirements – for example, extra water. You can find out about excretion in humans in Chapter 13.

*Nutrition* is the last of the seven characteristics of all organisms. All living organisms need chemicals to build their cells, and also as a source of energy. Nutrition means taking in materials that provide these things. Plants and animals have very different methods of nutrition, and you will find out about this in Chapters 6 and 7.

> **KEY WORDS**
>
> **excretion:** the removal of the waste products of metabolism and substances in excess of requirements
>
> **nutrition:** taking in materials for energy, growth and development

> **ACTIVITY 1.1**
>
> **Matching the characteristics of living things with their descriptions**
>
> Work in a group of four or five for this activity.
>
> **You will need:**
> - 14 pieces of blank card, all exactly the same.
>
> 1 Write the seven characteristics of living things on seven of the pieces of card.
>
> 2 Write descriptions of each of the seven characteristics on the other seven cards.
>
> 3 Shuffle each set of cards. Place them face down in two rows of seven.
>
> 4 One person then selects a card from each row and turns them face up. If the name and description match, this person keeps the two cards. If they do not match, they place them face down again in the same positions.
>
> 5 Now the next person does the same.
>
> 6 Keep taking turns until all the cards have been taken by someone. The winner is the person with most cards at the end.

## 1.2 The biological classification system

Classification means putting things into groups. There are many possible ways that we could classify organisms. For example, we could put all the animals with legs into one group, and all the other organisms into different groups. But this would mean that insects went into the same group as vertebrates. This would not make much sense, because we can easily see that insects and vertebrates are very different kinds of animal (Figure 1.5).

Biologists try to classify organisms according to how closely they think they are related. Long ago – perhaps 4.5 billion years ago – the first living organism appeared on Earth. It would have been a single cell. Since then, over a very long period of time, this cell gave rise to more complex organisms. For example, we think that all mammals descended from a species that lived more than 200 million years ago. This species was the **common ancestor** of mammals. All mammals are related because they all share a relatively recent common ancestor.

> **KEY WORDS**
>
> **common ancestor:** a species that lived in the past, and is thought to have given rise to several different species alive today; for example, all mammals share a common ancestor

When we classify organisms, we look for features that they share with others, which suggest that they are related to one another. This is a useful way of classifying things, because it helps us to understand how an organism 'works'. If we find a new animal that has hair and feeds its young on milk, we know that it is a mammal. We already know a lot about it, even before we can study it in detail.

# CAMBRIDGE IGCSE™ BIOLOGY: COURSEBOOK

Figure 1.5: Although they both have legs these two animals are not closely related. The ant is an insect, so it belongs to the arthropod group. The chameleon is a reptile, and belongs to the vertebrate group.

## Species

The smallest group into which biologists classify living organisms is the **species**. (Species is an unusual word, because the singular and plural are exactly the same – one species and many species.) A species is a group of organisms that can reproduce with each other to produce offspring that can also reproduce. The offspring are **fertile**.

For example, horses belong to the species *Equus caballus*. Members of this species can reproduce with each other. The offspring are also horses. They belong to the same species, and they can reproduce again to produce more horses.

Donkeys belong to a different species, *Equus asinus*. Donkeys reproduce with each other to produce fertile donkeys. But donkeys can also reproduce with horses. If a male donkey reproduces with a female horse, the offspring is a mule. Mules 'work' very well – they are usually strong, healthy organisms (Figure 1.6), but they cannot reproduce. They are **infertile**.

> **KEY WORDS**
>
> **species:** a group of organisms that can reproduce to produce fertile offspring
>
> **fertile:** able to reproduce
>
> **infertile:** not able to reproduce

Figure 1.6 a: Horses and donkeys belong to different species. b: Mules are the result of reproduction between horses and donkeys. They are infertile.

## The binomial naming system

You have seen that the 'official' names for the species that horses and donkeys belong to are written in a special way. This is the way that biologists name each species on Earth.

These scientific names always have two words. The naming system is therefore called the **binomial system**. 'Bi' means two, and 'nomial' means to do with names.

The first name in the binomial is the name of the **genus** that the organism belongs to. A genus is a group of species that are related to one another. If you look at Figure 1.6, you can see that horses and donkeys share a lot of features. They are obviously different species, but they belong to the same genus.

In the two-word name, the genus is always written with a capital letter. The second name tells us which species the organism belongs to, and this is written with a small letter. When the binomial is printed, it is in italics. You cannot do that when you are writing, but instead you can underline the binomial.

## Questions

1. Yaks have the scientific name *Bos grunniens*. Explain what this tells us about the groups into which yaks are classified.
2. A yakolo is the offspring of a yak and a buffalo. Yakolos are unable to reproduce.
   Explain how this suggests that yaks and buffalo belong to different species.

## 1.3 Keys

If you want to identify an organism whose name you do not know, you may be able to find a picture of it in a book. However, not every organism may be pictured, or your organism may not look exactly like any of the pictures. If this happens, you can use a **dichotomous key** to work out what your organism is.

'Dichotomous' means branching (dividing) into two. A dichotomous key is a way of leading you through to the name of your organism by giving you two descriptions at a time and asking you to choose between them. Each choice you make then leads you on to another pair of descriptions, until you end up with the name of your organism. Here is a key that you could use to identify the organisms shown in Figure 1.7.

| 1 | jointed limbs | 2 |
| | no jointed limbs | earthworm |
| 2 | more than 5 pairs of jointed limbs | centipede |
| | 5 or fewer pairs of jointed limbs | 3 |
| 3 | first pair of limbs form large claws | crab |
| | no large claws | 4 |
| 4 | 3 pairs of limbs | locust |
| | 4 pairs of limbs | spider |

> **KEY WORDS**
>
> **binomial system:** a system of naming species that is internationally agreed, in which the scientific name is made up of two parts showing the genus and the species
>
> **genus:** a group of species that share similar features and a common ancestor
>
> **dichotomous key:** a way of identifying an organism, by working through pairs of statements that lead you to its name

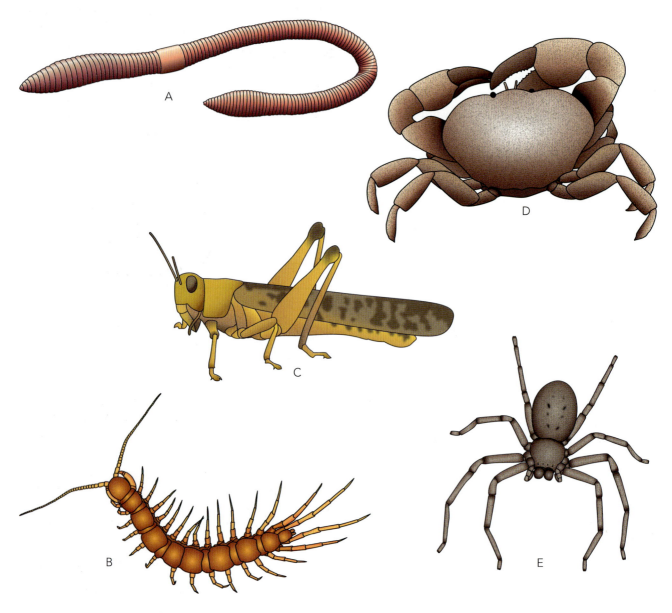

**Figure 1.7:** Five organisms for practising using a key.

To use the key:

- Choose **one** of the animals that you are going to identify. Let's say you choose organism B.
- Look at the first pair of statements in the key. Decide which description in step 1 matches your organism. It has jointed limbs, so the key tells us to go to step 2.
- Look at the descriptions in step 2. Decide which describes organism B. It has more than 5 pairs of jointed limbs, so it is a centipede.

Now try working through the key to identify the other four animals.

Notice that, in the key, each pair of statements are 'opposites' of one another. In 1, for example, the two statements are about whether the organism has jointed limbs or not. Remember this when you are writing your own keys. Don't mix different ideas into a pair of statements.

# 1 Characteristics & classification of living organisms

## ACTIVITY 1.2

### Constructing a key

Using a key is quite easy, but writing your own key is much more of a challenge.

Work with a partner for this activity.

You are going to write a key to enable someone to identify each of the four flowers in Figure 1.8.

**Figure 1.8:** Four flowers for identification using a key.

First, make a list of features that clearly differ between the flowers. They should be features that cannot possibly be mistaken. Remember that the person using the key will probably only have one of the flowers to look at, so they cannot necessarily compare it with another kind of flower. Therefore, the number of petals or the colour is a good choice, but the size (large or small) is not, because different people might have different ideas about what is 'large' or 'small'.

Choose one of the features that can split the flowers into two groups. The two groups don't have to be the same size – you could have two in one group and two in the other, or perhaps one in one group and the other three flowers in the second group.

Write down the two statements for this feature. Remember that the two statements need to be 'opposites' of one another.

Next, concentrate on a group that contains more than one flower. Choose another feature that will allow you to split the flowers into two further groups. Keep doing this until each 'group' contains only one flower.

Go back to your key and make changes to improve it. Think carefully about the wording of each pair of statements. Make sure that each pair is made up of two clear alternatives. Try to reduce your key to the smallest possible number of statement pairs.

Finally, try your key out on a friend. If they have any problems with it, then try to reword or restructure your key to make it easier to use.

### Self-assessment

Rate yourself according to the following scheme for each of the points listed.

- ☺ if you did it really well
- 😐 if you made a good attempt at it and partly succeeded
- ☹ if you did not try to do it, or did not succeed

- I had my own ideas, but I also listened to my partner's ideas.
- We wrote the descriptions in the key very clearly.
- We chose descriptions that other people could easily use.
- The two statements in each pair were 'opposites' of one another.
- Our key had no more than three pairs of statements.
- When we asked other people to try our key, they found it easy to use.

> **REFLECTION**
>
> Describe one thing that you think you did very well when you worked on constructing your key.
>
> Now describe one thing that you will try to do better, next time you construct a key.

## 1.4 Kingdoms

We have seen that the species is the smallest group into which living organisms are classified. Now we will look at the largest groups. These are the **kingdoms** of living organisms.

The kingdoms with which we are most familiar are the animal kingdom and the plant kingdom.

## The animal kingdom

Animals (Figure 1.9) are usually easy to recognise. Most animals can move actively, looking for food. Under the microscope, we can see that their cells have no cell walls.

**Figure 1.9:** Jellyfish, birds and butterflies all belong to the animal kingdom.

Characteristic features of animals:

- Their cells have a nucleus, but no cell walls or chloroplasts.
- They feed on **organic substances** made by other living organisms.

## The plant kingdom

The plants that are most familiar to us are the flowering plants, which include most kinds of trees. These plants have leaves, stems, roots and flowers (Figures 1.10 and 1.11). However, there are other types of plants – including ferns and mosses – that do not have flowers. What all of them have in common is the green colour, caused by a pigment called **chlorophyll**. This pigment absorbs energy from sunlight, and the plant can use this energy to make sugars, by the process of photosynthesis.

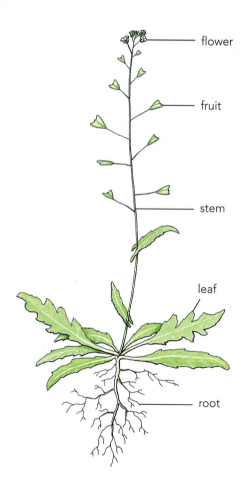

**Figure 1.10:** Many kinds of plant have roots, stems and leaves. Some also have flowers.

# 1 Characteristics & classification of living organisms

**Figure 1.11:** Moss, saguaro cacti and coconut palms belong to the plant kingdom.

Because they do not need to move around to get their food, plants are adapted to remain in one place. They often have a spreading shape, enabling them to capture as much sunlight energy as possible. Under the microscope we can see that the cells of plants have cell walls.

Characteristic features of plants:

- Their cells have a nucleus and cell walls made of **cellulose** and often contain chloroplasts.
- They feed by photosynthesis.
- They may have roots, stems and leaves (but some plants do not have these organs).

### KEY WORDS

**kingdom:** one of the major groups into which all organisms are classified

**organic substances:** substances whose molecules contain carbon; in biology, we normally consider organic compounds to be ones that are made by living things

**chlorophyll:** a green pigment (coloured substance) that absorbs energy from light; the energy is used to combine carbon dioxide with water and make glucose

**cellulose:** a carbohydrate that forms long fibres, and makes up the cell walls of plants

## Questions

3   Figure 1.12 shows a sea anemone, which belongs to the animal kingdom.

**Figure 1.12:** A sea anemone.

  a   In the past, people used to think that sea anemones were plants. Suggest why.
  b   Explain how using a microscope could help you to confirm that sea anemones are animals.

4   Figure 1.13 shows part of a plant called a liverwort. Liverworts do not have roots or flowers. Suggest how you could show that a liverwort belongs to the plant kingdom.

**Figure 1.13:** Part of a liverwort.

## The five kingdoms

As well as the animal kingdom and the plant kingdom, there are three other kingdoms into which organisms are classified. These are the **fungus**, **prokaryote** and **protoctist** kingdoms.

### The fungus kingdom

For a very long time, fungi were classified as plants. However, we now know that they are really very different, and belong in their own kingdom. Figure 1.14 shows some of the features of fungi.

> **KEY WORDS**
>
> **fungus:** an organism whose cells have cell walls, but that does not photosynthesise
>
> **prokaryote:** an organism whose cells do not have a nucleus
>
> **protoctist:** a single-celled organism, or one with several very similar cells
>
> **hyphae:** microscopic threads, made of cells linked in a long line, that make up the body of a fungus

Mushrooms and toadstools are fungi, and they can be colourful and easy to spot (Figure 1.15). However, the main body of most fungi, including mushrooms and toadstools, is made up of microscopic threads called **hyphae**. These are made of many cells joined end to end. The cells have cell walls, but these are not made of cellulose.

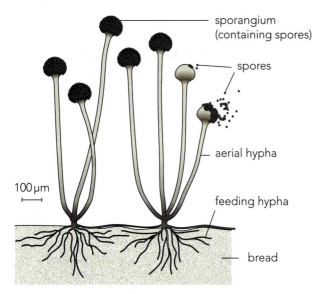

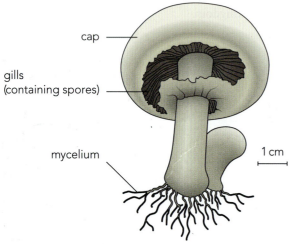

Figure 1.14: Two examples of fungi.

Figure 1.15 **a:** These toadstools are feeding on dead wood. Their hyphae grow through the wood, taking up nutrients from it. **b:** The mould on this strawberry is a fungus.

# 1 Characteristics & classification of living organisms

Fungi do not have chlorophyll and do not photosynthesise. Instead they feed saprophytically, or parasitically, on organic material such as faeces, human foods and dead plants or animals. Many fungi are **decomposers**, breaking down waste material from other organisms and dead organisms. This helps to return nutrients to the soil that other organisms can use for their growth.

Fungi reproduce by forming **spores**. These are tiny groups of cells with a tough, protective outer covering. They can be spread by the wind or animals, and grow to form a new fungus.

We have found many different uses to make of fungi. We eat them as mushrooms. We use the single-celled fungus, yeast, to make ethanol and bread – you can find out about this in Chapter 20. We obtain antibiotics such as penicillin from various different fungi.

Some fungi, however, are harmful. Some of these cause food decay, while a few cause diseases, including ringworm and athlete's foot.

Characteristic features of fungi:

- They are usually **multicellular** (many-celled), but some such as yeast are **unicellular** (single-celled).
- They have nuclei and cell walls, but the walls are not made of cellulose.
- They do not have chlorophyll.
- They feed by digesting waste organic material and absorbing it into their cells.

> ### KEY WORDS
>
> **decomposers:** organisms that break down organic substances outside their bodies, releasing nutrients from them that other organisms can use
>
> **spores:** very small groups of cells surrounded by a protective wall, used in reproduction
>
> **multicellular:** made of many cells
>
> **unicellular:** made of a single cell

Figure 1.17: This photograph shows some pond water seen through a microscope. All of the organisms are protictists. Some are unicellular, and some are multicellular. Some have cells like animal cells, while others have cells like plant cells.

## The protoctist kingdom

The kingdom Protoctista (Figures 1.16 and 1.17) contains a mixed collection of organisms. They all have cells with a nucleus, but some have plant-like cells with chloroplasts and cellulose cell walls, while others have animal-like cells without these features. Most protoctists are unicellular (made of just a single cell) but some, such as seaweeds, are multicellular.

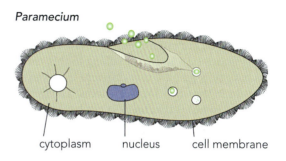

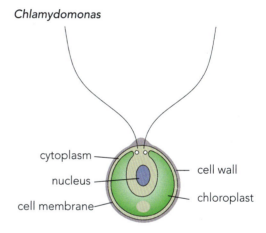

Figure 1.16: Two examples of protoctists. *Paramecium* has animal-like cells, while *Chlamydomonas* has plant-like cells.

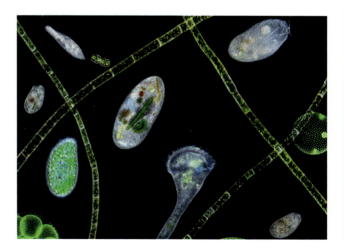

Characteristic features of protoctists:

- They are multicellular or unicellular.
- Their cells have a nucleus and may or may not have a cell wall and chloroplasts.
- Some feed by photosynthesis and others feed on organic substances made by other organisms.

## The prokaryote kingdom

The prokaryote kingdom contains a huge number of organisms, but we are often completely unaware of them. Bacteria (Figures 1.18 and 1.19) belong to this kingdom. Bacteria have cells that are very different from the cells of organisms in the other four kingdoms. The most important difference is that they do not have a nucleus.

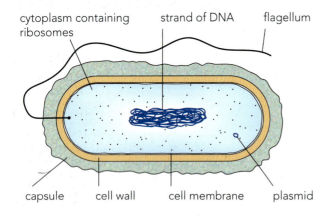

Figure 1.18: The structure of a prokaryotic cell.

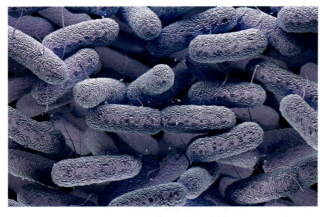

Figure 1.19: This photograph was taken using an electron microscope and shows bacteria that can live in the alimentary canal, and can make you feel ill. It has been magnified approximately 10 000 times.

You will meet bacteria at various stages in your biology course. Some of them are harmful to us and cause diseases such as cholera. Many more, however, are helpful. You will find out about their useful roles in the carbon cycle and the nitrogen cycle in Chapter 18, and their uses in biotechnology in Chapter 20.

Some bacteria can carry out photosynthesis. The oldest fossils belong to this kingdom, so we think that they were among the first kinds of organism to appear on Earth. Recently, biologists have discovered bacteria living in rocks more than 3 km beneath the Earth's surface.

Most organisms belonging to this kingdom are unicellular, and so their characteristic features are to do with the structure of their cells. This is described in more detail in Chapter 2, where you will find explanations of some of the terms below that may be unfamiliar (for example: mitochondria, plasmids).

Characteristic features of prokaryotes:

- They are usually unicellular (single-celled).
- They have no nucleus.
- They have cell walls, not made of cellulose.
- They have no mitochondria.
- They have a circular loop of DNA, which is free in the cytoplasm.
- They often have plasmids.

## Questions

5 *Staphylococcus aureus* is a bacterium that is often found on human skin.
   a Name the genus to which this bacterium belongs.
   b Name the kingdom to which this bacterium belongs.
   c Describe **two** ways in which the structure of *Staphylococcus aureus* differs from the structure of a plant cell.

6 Figure 1.20 shows part of a fungus. The photograph was taken with an electron microscope.
   a Name the structure labelled A.
   b Explain how the cells in this structure differ from the cells of an organism belonging to the animal kingdom.
   c The structure labelled B contains spores. What is the function of this structure?

# 1 Characteristics & classification of living organisms

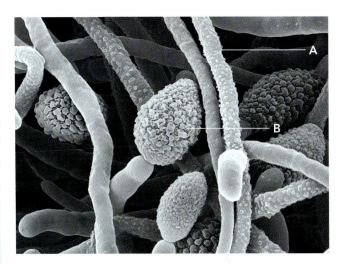

Figure 1.20: Part of a fungus.

## ACTIVITY 1.3

### Making a display about a kingdom of organisms

Work in a group of three or four for this activity.

In your group, choose one of the kingdoms of organisms. Try to make sure that at least one group is working on each kingdom.

Make a poster or other type of display, to describe the features of this kingdom. Include photographs or drawings of several different organisms that belong to this kingdom.

## 1.5 Groups within the animal and plant kingdoms

Within each kingdom, biologists classify organisms into smaller groups. In the animal kingdom, these groups include vertebrates and arthropods. If you are studying the Supplement, you also need to know about some of the groups in the plant kingdom.

### Vertebrates

Vertebrates are animals that have backbones. These are the most familiar animals – fish, amphibians, reptiles, birds and mammals.

### Fish

Fish (Figures 1.21 and 1.22) all live in water, apart from a few species such as mudskippers that are able to come onto land for short periods of time.

Figure 1.21 **a:** A great white shark. **b:** Masked butterfly fish.

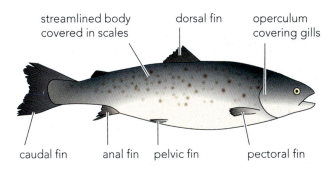

Figure 1.22: A fish.

Characteristic features of fish:
- They are vertebrates with scaly skin.
- They have gills throughout their life.
- They have fins.
- Their eggs have no shells and are laid in water.

## Amphibians

Most adult amphibians live on land. However, they always go back to the water to breed. The larvae are called tadpoles, and they spend the first part of their life in water. They then undergo a major change in the shape of their body, called **metamorphosis**, as they become an adult. Frogs, toads and salamanders are amphibians (Figures 1.23 and 1.24).

Characteristic features of amphibians:

- They are vertebrates with skin with no scales.
- Their eggs have no shells and are laid in water.
- The tadpoles live in water, but adults often live on land.
- The tadpoles have gills for gas exchange, but adults have lungs.

> **KEY WORD**
>
> **metamorphosis:** changing from a larva with one body form to an adult with a different body form

## Reptiles

These are the crocodiles, lizards, snakes, turtles and tortoises (Figures 1.25 and 1.26). Reptiles all have scales on their skin. Unlike amphibians, reptiles do not need to go back to the water to breed because their eggs have a soft but waterproof shell which stops them from drying out.

**Figure 1.23:** Two examples of amphibians: **a:** a salamander **b:** a toad.

**Figure 1.25 a:** This Nile crocodile has just hatched from its soft-shelled egg. **b:** Dinosaurs, including *Tyrannosaurus rex*, are a group of reptiles that became extinct about 65 million years ago, but we know a lot about them from fossils.

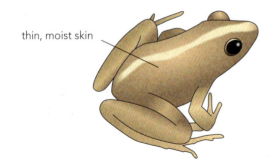

thin, moist skin

**Figure 1.24:** A frog, an example of an amphibian.

# 1 Characteristics & classification of living organisms

Figure 1.26: A snake, an example of a reptile.

Characteristic features of reptiles:
- They are vertebrates with scaly skin.
- They lay eggs with soft shells.

## Birds

Birds evolved from dinosaurs, and some biologists consider that they are 'dinosaurs with feathers'. Birds are easy to identify, because they are the only animals with feathers (Figures 1.27 and 1.28). However, they sometimes do have scales – like reptiles – but generally only on their legs. The other very distinctive feature is their beak.

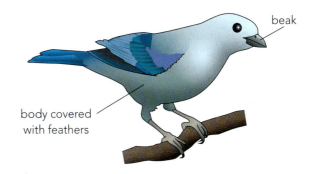

Figure 1.28: A bird.

Characteristic features of birds:
- They have feathers (and also sometimes a few scales).
- They have a beak.
- Their front two limbs are wings (though not all birds can fly).
- They lay eggs with hard shells.

Figure 1.27 a: Although ostriches have wings, they cannot fly. b: The oriental dwarf kingfisher lives in forests in India and south east Asia. Despite its name, it eats small frogs and crickets rather than fish.

## Mammals

The mammals are the most familiar vertebrates, and people who have not studied biology often use the word 'animal' to mean 'mammal'. Humans, of course, are mammals.

Some of the features of mammals are shared with birds. For example, both mammals and birds control their body temperature (see Chapter 13) and have a heart with four chambers (compartments) (see Chapter 9). Mammals also give birth to live young, but this is not helpful in identifying them, because many fish and reptiles also do this.

The easiest way to identify a mammal is that its skin has hair (Figures 1.29 and 1.30). Looking more closely, we find that their ears have a **pinna** (ear flap) on the outside, and that they have different kinds of teeth. But it is their method of reproduction and caring for their young that is most distinctive. Only mammals have a uterus and **placenta** (Chapter 15), and only mammals have **mammary glands** that produce milk to feed their young.

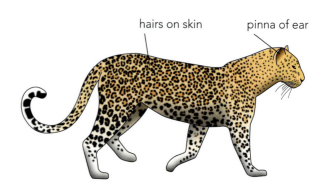

**Figure 1.30:** Some of the visible external features of a mammal.

Characteristic features of mammals:

- They have hair on their skin.
- Their young develop in a uterus, attached to the mother by a placenta.
- The females have mammary glands, which produce milk to feed their young.
- They have different kinds of teeth (incisors, canines, premolars and molars).
- They have a pinna (ear flap) on the outside of the body.
- They have sweat glands in the skin.
- They have a **diaphragm**.

**Figure 1.29:** Two examples of mammals: **a:** A pangolin may look like a reptile at first glance, but if you look closely you can see hairs on its face and feet. **b:** A baby sperm whale sucks milk from its mother's mammary glands.

### KEY WORDS

**pinna:** a flap on the outside of the body that directs sound into the ear

**placenta:** an organ that connects the growing fetus to its mother, in which the blood of the fetus and mother are brought close together so that materials can be exchanged between them

**mammary glands:** organs found only in mammals, which produce milk to feed young

**diaphragm:** a muscle that separates the chest cavity from the abdominal cavity in mammals; it helps with breathing

# 1 Characteristics & classification of living organisms

## Questions

7  Name the kingdom to which mammals belong.
8  List **two** differences between amphibians and reptiles.
9  List **a** two *external* and **b** two *internal* features of mammals that are not found in other groups of vertebrates.

## Arthropods

**Arthropods** are animals with jointed legs, but no backbone. They are a very successful group, because they have a waterproof **exoskeleton**. An exoskeleton is on the outside of the body, rather than on the inside like yours. The exoskeleton supports arthropod bodies, and also allows these animals to live on land without drying out. There are more kinds of arthropod in the world than all the other kinds of animal put together.

Characteristic features of all arthropods:

- They have several pairs of jointed legs.
- They have an exoskeleton.

There are several different groups of arthropods, including insects, crustaceans, arachnids and myriapods.

### Insects

Insects (Figures 1.31 and 1.32) are a very successful group of arthropods. Their success is mostly due to their exoskeleton and tracheae, which are very good at stopping water from evaporating from the insects' bodies, so they can live in very dry places. They are mainly **terrestrial** (land-living).

Characteristic features of insects:

- They are arthropods with three pairs of jointed legs.
- They have two pairs of wings (one or both may be **vestigial**).
- They breathe through tubes called tracheae.
- Their body is divided into a head, thorax and abdomen.
- They have one pair of antennae.

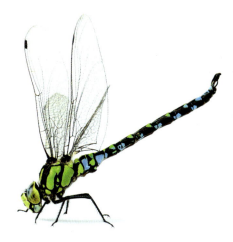

**Figure 1.31:** A dragonfly, an example of an insect.

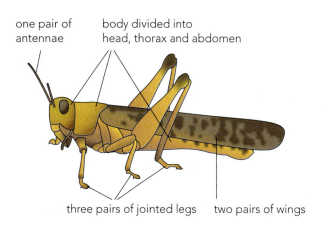

**Figure 1.32:** Features of a typical insect.

### KEY WORDS

**arthropod:** an animal with jointed legs, but no backbone

**exoskeleton:** a supportive structure on the outside of the body

**terrestrial:** living on land

**vestigial:** description of a structure that has evolved to become so small that it is no longer useful

## Crustaceans

These are the crabs, lobsters and woodlice (Figures 1.33 and 1.34). They breathe through gills, so most of them live in wet places and many are **aquatic** (live in water).

Characteristics:

- They are arthropods with more than four pairs of jointed legs.
- They have two pairs of antennae.

## Arachnids

These are the spiders, ticks and scorpions (Figures 1.35 and 1.36). Arachnids are generally land-dwelling organisms.

Characteristics:

- They are arthropods with four pairs of jointed legs.
- They have no antennae.
- Their body is divided into two parts – a cephalothorax and abdomen.

**Figure 1.33:** A lobster, an example of a crustacean. You can clearly see the two pairs of antennae on its head.

**Figure 1.35:** A scorpion, an example of an arachnid.

**Figure 1.34:** Features of a crustacean.

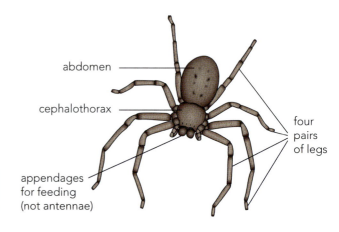

**Figure 1.36:** Features of an arachnid.

> **KEY WORD**
>
> **aquatic:** living in water

1 Characteristics & classification of living organisms

## Myriapods

These are the centipedes and millipedes (Figures 1.37 and 1.38).

Characteristics:

- Their body consists of many similar segments.
- Each of their body segments has jointed legs.
- They have one pair of antennae.

**Figure 1.37:** A giant African millipede, an example of a myriapod.

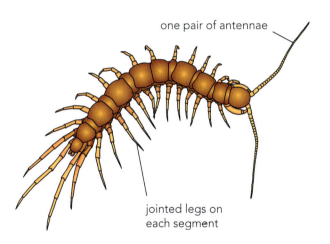

**Figure 1.38:** Features of a myriapod.

## Questions

10  a  List **two** features that are shared by myriapods and arachnids.

  b  Describe **two** differences between myriapods and arachnids.

11  Fleas are insects, but they do not have wings. Suggest **two** features of fleas that would show that they should be classified as insects.

### ACTIVITY 1.4

#### Classifying animals

In this activity, you practise identifying the classification groups to which animals belong.

> **You will need:**
> - pictures or specimens of different vertebrates and arthropods, arranged around the room
> - (optional) a clipboard.

Work with a partner for this activity.

First, read ahead to find out what you are going to do. On a sheet of paper, draw a table in which you can fill in your answers.

Look carefully at the first specimen. Discuss with your partner whether it is a vertebrate or an arthropod, and then decide which smaller group it belongs to within these two large groups.

Write down your decision, and the reasons for it.

Repeat for as many of the other specimens as you have time for.

### REFLECTION

How are you going to try to remember the features of the four groups of arthropods? Which of these ideas, or a combination of them, do you think might work best for you?

- looking at labelled diagrams and reading lists of features
- trying to write your own list of features
- writing features on cards and then sorting them to match each group
- testing a friend or asking them to test you.

## Ferns

Ferns are plants with leaves called fronds (Figures 1.39 and 1.40). They do not produce flowers, but instead reproduce by means of spores produced on the underside of the fronds. Most ferns are quite small, but some species can be as much as 20 m tall.

Characteristic features of ferns:

- They are plants with roots, stems and leaves (fronds).
- They do not produce flowers.
- They reproduce by spores produced on the undersides of their fronds.

Figure 1.39: Tree ferns in Bali, Indonesia.

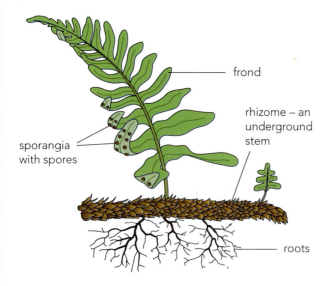

Figure 1.40: Features of a fern.

## Flowering plants

These are the plants that are most familiar to us. As their name suggests, they reproduce by producing flowers (Figure 1.41). You will find out about their transport systems and method of reproduction in Chapters 8 and 14.

Characteristic features of flowering plants:

- They are plants with roots, stems and leaves.
- They reproduce using flowers and seeds.
- Their seeds are produced inside an ovary, in the flower.

Flowering plants can be divided into two main groups – **dicotyledons** and **monocotyledons**. These names refer to the structure of their seeds. The seeds of flowering plants contain 'seed leaves' or cotyledons. Monocotyledons (monocots for short) have only one cotyledon in their seeds, whereas dicotyledons (dicots) have two (Figures 1.41, 1.42 and 1.43).

Characteristic features of dicots:

- They have seeds with two cotyledons.
- They usually have a main root with side roots coming out from it.
- Their leaves have a network of veins.
- They have flower parts (e.g. petals) in multiples of four or five.
- They have vascular bundles in the stem, arranged in a ring (see Chapter 8).

Characteristic features of monocots:

- They have seeds with one cotyledon.
- Their roots grow out directly from the stem.
- Their leaves have parallel veins.
- They have flower parts in multiples of three.
- They have vascular bundles in the stem, arranged randomly.

### KEY WORDS

**dicotyledons:** plants with two cotyledons in their seeds

**monocotyledons:** plants with only one cotyledon in their seeds

# 1 Characteristics & classification of living organisms

Figure 1.41: Two examples of flowering plants. **a:** An iris, an example of a monocot plant. **b:** Hibiscus, an example of a dicot plant.

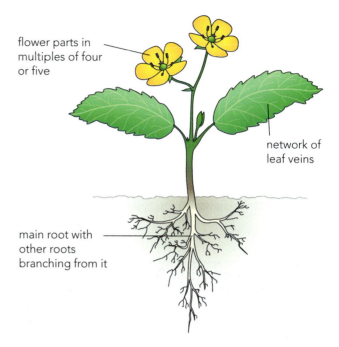

Figure 1.43: Features of a dicot plant.

## Questions

12  Describe **two** differences between ferns and flowering plants.

13  In your local area, find two examples of monocotyledons and two examples of dicotyledons. Explain how you were able to decide which group each plant belonged to.

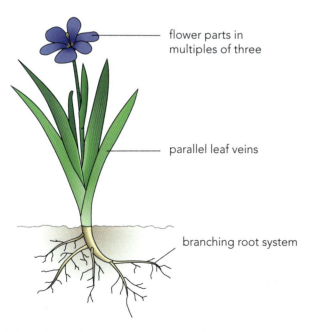

Figure 1.42: Features of a monocot plant.

ACTIVITY 1.5

**Classifying animals and plants**

In this activity, you practise identifying the classification groups to which organisms belong.

You will need:
- pictures or specimens of organisms belonging to the animal, plant, fungus, prokaryote and protoctist kingdoms, arranged around the room
- pictures of ferns and flowering plants – some dicotyledons and some monocotyledons, also arranged around the room
- (optional) a clipboard.

Work with a partner for this activity.

First, read ahead to find out what you are going to do. On a sheet of paper, draw a table in which you can fill in your answers.

Look carefully at the first specimen. Discuss with your partner which group it belongs to.

Write down your decision, and the reasons for it.

Repeat for as many of the other specimens as you have time for.

# 1.6 Viruses

You have almost certainly had an illness caused by a virus. Viruses cause common diseases such as colds and influenza, and also more serious ones such as AIDS.

Viruses are not normally considered to be living organisms because they cannot do anything other than just exist until they get inside a living cell. They then take over the cell's machinery to make multiple copies of themselves. These new viruses burst out of the cell and invade others, where the process is repeated. The host cell is usually killed when this happens. On their own, viruses cannot move, feed, excrete, show sensitivity, grow or reproduce. They do not display the seven characteristics of living things.

Figure 1.44 shows one kind of virus. It is not made of a cell – it is simply a piece of genetic material surrounded by a protein coat. It is hugely magnified in this diagram. The scale bar represents a length of 10 nanometres. One nanometre is $1 \times 10^{-9}$ m. In other words, you could line up more than 15 000 of these viruses between two of the millimetre marks on your ruler.

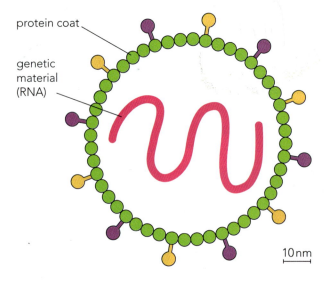

**Figure 1.44:** The structure of a virus.

## Question

14  Figure 1.45 shows a virus. With reference to the diagram, and your own knowledge, discuss whether or not viruses can be considered to be living organisms.

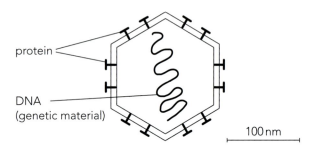

**Figure 1.45:** A virus.

# 1 Characteristics & classification of living organisms

## SUMMARY

All organisms show seven characteristics: movement, respiration, sensitivity, growth, reproduction, excretion and nutrition.

Organisms are classified into groups according to features that they share.

Classification systems reflect evolutionary relationships between organisms.

The binomial system of naming organisms shows the genus and species. The name of the genus has a capital letter, followed by the name of the species with a small letter.

Dichotomous keys are used to identify organisms. They are made up of pairs of contrasting statements or questions. Taking one organism at a time, you work through the key until it leads you to the name of the organism.

When constructing a dichotomous key, it is important to make sure that a person using the key can make a decision looking at only one organism. Comparative or subjective descriptions (e.g. large, taller) are not suitable.

Organisms belonging to the plant kingdom have cells with cell walls made of cellulose, and some of their cells have chloroplasts. Organisms belonging to the animal kingdom have cells that do not have these features.

Vertebrates are animals with backbones. They are classified in five main groups: fish, amphibians, reptiles, birds and mammals, each with their own set of distinguishing features.

Arthropods are animals with an exoskeleton and jointed legs. They include insects, arachnids, crustaceans and myriapods, which can be distinguished from each other by the number of legs and antennae.

As well as the animal and plant kingdoms, organisms are classified into the fungus, prokaryote and protoctist kingdoms. They differ in the structure of their cells.

Ferns and flowering plants are two groups within the plant kingdom. Flowering plants can be classified as monocots or dicots, which differ in the patterns of veins in their leaves, the structure of their root systems, the number of flower parts and the distribution of vascular bundles in their stems.

Viruses are not classified in any of the five kingdoms, as they do not show the characteristics of living organisms. They do not have cells, and consist of genetic material surrounded by a protein coat.

# CAMBRIDGE IGCSE™ BIOLOGY: COURSEBOOK

## PROJECT

### A new species

Each year, biologists discover new species. Some of these are small (insects, small plants) while others are surprisingly large (mammals, trees).

Work in a group of three or four. Use the internet to search for some examples of newly discovered species and select one to research in detail.

Decide how you will share the results of your research with others. For example, you could give an illustrated talk, or produce a poster. Decide how you will share out the tasks between you.

Try to find information about some or all of these issues:

- Where and how was the new species discovered? Why had it not been discovered before?

- How did biologists decide that it really was a new species?

- How was the binomial for the new species chosen? What does its name mean?

- Biologists will want to find out more about the new species, but if it is rare they will not want to take many specimens from the wild, or disturb it in its habitat. How have these conflicts been resolved?

**Figure 1.46:** The tree *Dinizia jueirana-facao* is a species that was recently discovered in Brazil.

# 1 Characteristics & classification of living organisms

## EXAM-STYLE QUESTIONS

1 Which characteristic is **not** shown by all living organisms?
   A  excretion
   B  movement
   C  photosynthesis
   D  respiration [1]

2 Which feature is found in all vertebrates and all arthropods?
   A  a backbone
   B  an exoskeleton
   C  antennae
   D  cells without cell walls [1]

3 The binomial of the okapi is *Okapia johnstoni*.
   What genus does the okapi belong to?
   A  animals
   B  *johnstoni*
   C  mammals
   D  *Okapia* [1]

4 Which are features of monocotyledons?
   A  flower parts in multiples of four or five, one cotyledon in seeds
   B  one cotyledon in seeds, vascular bundles in a ring
   C  vascular bundles in a ring, network of veins in leaf
   D  parallel veins in leaf, flower parts in multiples of three [1]

5 What two features do all viruses possess?
   A  cell membrane, cell wall
   B  cytoplasm, nucleus
   C  genetic material, protein coat
   D  ribosomes, plasmids [1]

> **TIP**
> The mark allocation for a question will often indicate the number of points that you should make, in order to fully answer that question.

## CONTINUED

6

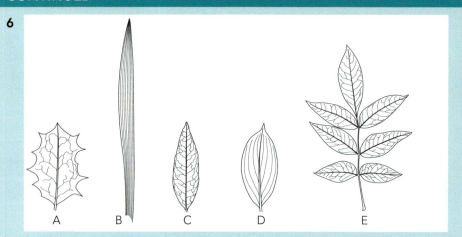

a The diagram above shows five leaves. Use the key to **identify** the species of plant that each of these leaves came from.

| 1 | (a) | veins are parallel | go to 2 |
| --- | --- | --- | --- |
| | (b) | veins are branching | go to 3 |
| 2 | (a) | the leaf is more than 5 times as long as it is wide | *Iris germanica* |
| | (b) | the leaf is less than 5 times as long as it is wide | *Tricyrtis hirta* |
| 3 | (a) | leaf has a prickly edge | *Ilex aquifolium* |
| | (b) | leaf does not have a prickly edge | go to 4 |
| 4 | (a) | leaf is divided into many leaflets | *Fraxinus excelsior* |
| | (b) | leaf is not divided into many leaflets | *Buddleia davidii* |

[4]

b i **Explain** the meaning of the term *species*. [2]

ii Biologists give each species a two-word Latin name. What is the term used to describe this naming system? [1]

[Total: 7]

### COMMAND WORDS

**identify:** name / select / recognise

**explain:** set out purposes or reasons / make the relationships between things evident / provide why and/or how and support with relevant evidence

7 The table shows features of three animals.

| Animal | Exoskeleton | Number of jointed legs | Number of antennae |
| --- | --- | --- | --- |
| P | yes | four pairs | none |
| Q | yes | three pairs | one pair |
| R | yes | more than five pairs | one pair |

a Name the major group that **all** of these animals belong to. [1]

b Each animal is classified into a smaller group within this major group. Name the smaller group into which each animal is classified. [3]

c List **two** features, other than those shown in the table, that animal Q has, which are **not** shared with animals P and R. [2]

[Total: 6]

# 1 Characteristics & classification of living organisms

## CONTINUED

8 Three species of tree have the following Latin names:
  - *Carpodiptera africana*
  - *Commiphora africana*
  - *Commiphora angolensis*

  a Which **two** species do biologists consider to be the most closely related? Explain your answer. [2]

  b *Commiphora africana* is a dicotyledon.
    State **two** features that it shares with all other dicotyledons, but **not** with monocotyledons. [2]

  [Total: 4]

9 All living organisms are classified into five kingdoms. These include the plant, animal and fungus kingdoms.

  a Name the other two kingdoms. [2]
  b Describe **two** ways in which the cells of fungi differ from those of plants. [2]
  c The diagram below shows a virus.

  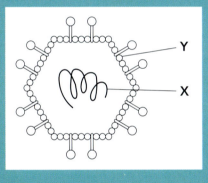

  i Name parts **X** and **Y**. [2]
  ii Explain why viruses are not generally classified into any of the five kingdoms. [2]

  [Total: 8]

29

## SELF-EVALUATION CHECKLIST

After studying this chapter, think about how confident you are with the different topics. This will help you to see any gaps in your knowledge and help you to learn more effectively.

| I can | See Topic… | Needs more work | Almost there | Confident to move on |
|---|---|---|---|---|
| describe the seven characteristics of living organisms | 1.1 | | | |
| explain that organisms are classified according to features that they share | 1.2 | | | |
| explain that biologists classify organisms according to their evolutionary relationships | 1.2 | | | |
| describe and use the binomial naming system | 1.2 | | | |
| construct and use dichotomous keys | 1.3 | | | |
| state the main features of the animal and plant kingdoms | 1.4 | | | |
| state the main features of the fungus, prokaryote and protoctist kingdoms | 1.4 | | | |
| state the main features of the five groups of vertebrates – fish, amphibians, reptiles, birds and mammals | 1.5 | | | |
| state the main features of the four groups of arthropods – insects, crustacea, arachnids and myriapods | 1.5 | | | |
| state the main features of two groups of plants – ferns and flowering plants, including dicots and monocots | 1.5 | | | |
| state the main features of viruses | 1.6 | | | |

# Chapter 2
# Cells

**IN THIS CHAPTER YOU WILL:**
- find out about the structure of the cells of animals, plants and bacteria
- learn about the functions of each of the parts of these cells
- describe how the structures of some specialised cells are related to their functions
- practise using the magnification equation.

# CAMBRIDGE IGCSE™ BIOLOGY: COURSEBOOK

## GETTING STARTED

Organisms that belong to different kingdoms have different kinds of cells.

With a partner, think about the answers to these questions:

1 If you have a microscope, how can you distinguish between a cell of an organism belonging to the plant kingdom, and one belonging to the animal kingdom?

2 Still using your microscope, how could you tell if a cell belongs to an organism from the prokaryote kingdom?

## CELLS FROM DEEP TIME

Despite its inviting blue colour, you would not want to get into the water in this hot spring. The temperature of the water can be as high as 90 °C in Yellowstone National Park, USA.

But there are organisms that can live in this hot water. They are called extremophiles, meaning 'organisms that like extreme conditions'. They produce the colours around the edge of the pool.

Many of these organisms are bacteria. Bacteria are made of single cells. Their cells are much less complex than animal or plant cells – for example, they do not have a nucleus.

Scientists think that bacteria like these first evolved more than 3.5 billion years ago, when conditions on Earth were quite similar to conditions in some hot springs today. This was long before animals and plants first appeared on Earth. Despite their simple structure, bacteria are clearly very successful. They have survived on Earth almost unchanged, through an unimaginably long period of time.

### Discussion questions

1 What evidence might lead scientists to think that bacteria evolved more than 3.5 billion years ago?

2 We tend to think of complex organisms such as humans as being 'more advanced' than simple ones such as bacteria. But bacteria have lived on Earth for 3.5 billion years, and are still here and doing well. Do you think that humans really are 'more advanced' than bacteria?

## 2 Cells

## 2.1 Animal and plant cells

All organisms are made of **cells**. Cells are very small, so large organisms contain millions of cells. They are multicellular. Some organisms are unicellular, which means that they are made of just a single cell. Bacteria and yeast are examples of single-celled organisms.

All cells are made from existing cells. New cells are formed when a fully grown cell divides. You can read about how cells divide in Chapter 16.

> **KEY WORD**
>
> **cells:** the smallest units from which all organisms are made

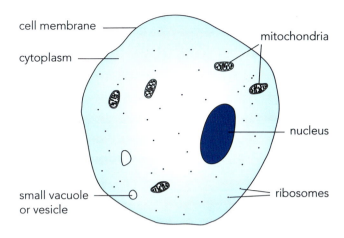

**Figure 2.2:** An animal cell as it appears through a light microscope.

## Microscopes

To see cells clearly, you need to use a microscope (Figure 2.1). The kind of microscope used in a school laboratory is called a light microscope. This is because it shines light through the piece of animal or plant you are looking at. It uses glass lenses to magnify and focus the image. A very good light microscope can magnify about 1500 times, so that all the structures in Figures 2.2 and 2.3 can be seen.

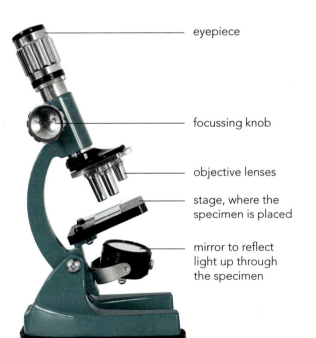

**Figure 2.1:** A light microscope.

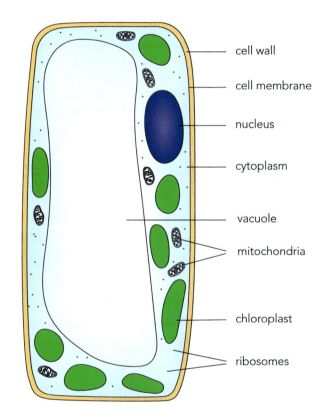

**Figure 2.3:** A plant cell as it appears through a light microscope.

A photograph taken using a light microscope is called a photomicrograph. Figure 2.4 is a photomicrograph of some animal cells, and Figure 2.5 is a photomicrograph of some plant cells.

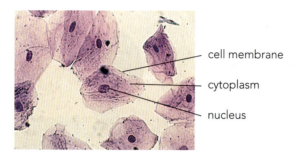

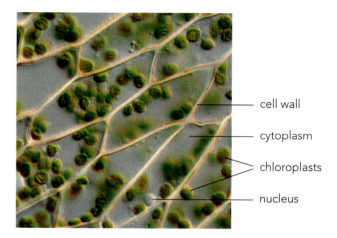

Figure 2.4: These are cells from the trachea (windpipe) of a mammal. They have been stained (coloured) with a dye that makes the nucleus look darker than the cytoplasm.

Figure 2.5: These are cells from a moss plant. You cannot see the cell membranes because they are pressed tightly against the inside of the cell walls.

To see smaller things inside a cell, an electron microscope is used. A picture taken with an electron microscope is called an **electron micrograph**. This type of microscope uses a beam of electrons instead of light and can magnify things up to 500 000 times. This means that a lot more detail can be seen inside a cell. We can see many structures more clearly and can see some structures that cannot be seen at all with a light microscope (Figure 2.6).

> **KEY WORDS**
>
> **electron micrograph:** an image made using an electron microscope

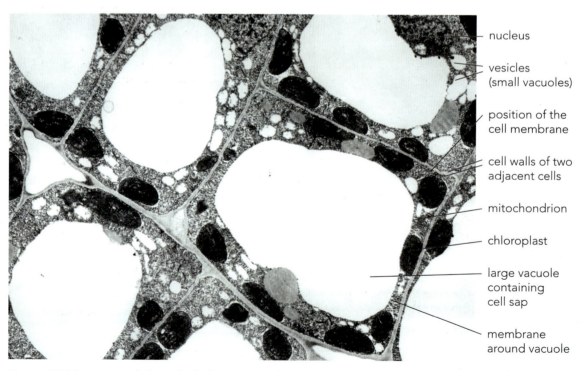

Figure 2.6: These are cells from the leaf of a maize plant, seen using an electron microscope. Electron microscopes do not provide images that show the colours of the different parts. Often, colour is added to the image afterwards.

## Questions

1. Explain the difference between a unicellular organism and a multicellular organism, giving one example of each.
2. Look at the micrographs in Figures 2.4 and 2.5. Suggest why a stain has been added to the animal cells, but we can easily see the plant cells without using a stain.

## Cell membrane

Every cell has a **cell membrane** around the outside. The cell membrane is a very thin layer of protein and fat. It is very important to the cell because it controls what goes in and out of it. It is said to be **partially permeable**, which means that it will let some substances through but not others. The cell membrane separates the contents of the cell from its environment (surroundings).

It is difficult to see the cell membrane in a plant cell, because it is pressed tightly against the inside of the cell wall.

## Cell wall

All plant cells are surrounded by a **cell wall** made mainly of cellulose. Paper, which is made from cell walls, is also made of cellulose. Animal cells never have cell walls.

Cellulose belongs to a group of substances called polysaccharides, which are described in Chapter 4. Cellulose forms fibres which criss-cross over one another to form a very strong covering to the cell (Figure 2.7). This helps to protect and support the cell. If the cell absorbs a lot of water and swells, the cell wall stops it bursting.

**Figure 2.7:** This photograph of a plant cell wall was taken with a kind of electron microscope that shows surfaces in three dimensions. You can see how the fibres of cellulose criss-cross over one another.

Because of the spaces between fibres, even very large molecules are able to go through the cellulose cell wall. It is described as **fully permeable**.

## Cytoplasm

**Cytoplasm** is a clear jelly. It is nearly all water; about 70% is water in many cells. It contains many substances dissolved in it, especially proteins. Many different **metabolic reactions** (the chemical reactions of life) take place in the cytoplasm.

## Vacuole

A **vacuole** is a fluid-filled space inside a cell which is surrounded by its own membrane. Plant cells have very large, permanent vacuoles, which contain a solution of sugars and other substances called **cell sap**. When the vacuole is full, it presses outwards on the rest of the cell, and helps it to keep its shape. Animal cells have much smaller vacuoles, called **vesicles**, which also contain solutions.

> ### KEY WORDS
>
> **cell membrane:** a very thin layer surrounding the cytoplasm of every cell; it controls what enters and leaves the cell
>
> **partially permeable:** allows some molecules and ions to pass through, but not others
>
> **cell wall:** a tough layer outside the cell membrane; found in the cells of plants, fungi and bacteria
>
> **fully permeable:** allows all molecules and ions to pass through it
>
> **cytoplasm:** the jelly-like material that fills a cell
>
> **metabolic reactions:** chemical reactions that take place in living organisms
>
> **vacuole:** a fluid-filled space inside a cell, separated from the cytoplasm by a membrane
>
> **cell sap:** the fluid that fills the large vacuoles in plant cells
>
> **vesicle:** a very small vacuole

## Nucleus

The **nucleus** (plural: nuclei) is where the genetic information is stored. The information is kept on the **chromosomes**, which are inherited from the organism's parents. The chromosomes are made of **DNA**. The information carried on the DNA determines the kinds of proteins that are made in the cell. You can find much more about this in Chapter 16.

Chromosomes are very long, but so thin that they cannot easily be seen even using an electron microscope. However, when the cell is dividing, they become short and thick, and can be seen with a good light microscope (Figure 2.8).

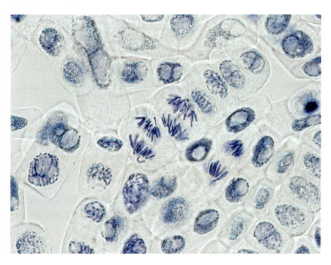

**Figure 2.8:** This photomicrograph shows some plant cells dividing. The nuclei of the cells have been coloured with a blue stain. The things that look like spider legs are chromosomes. We can normally only see chromosomes when a cell is dividing.

> **KEY WORDS**
>
> **nucleus:** a structure containing DNA in the form of chromosomes
>
> **chromosome:** a length of DNA, found in the nucleus of a cell; it contains genetic information in the form of many different genes
>
> **DNA:** a molecule that contains genetic information, in the form of genes, that controls the proteins that are made in the cell

## Chloroplasts

**Chloroplasts** are never found in animal cells, but most of the cells in the green parts of plants have them. They contain the green colouring or pigment called chlorophyll.

Chlorophyll absorbs energy from sunlight, and this energy is then used in making food for the plant by photosynthesis (Chapter 6). Chloroplasts often contain **starch grains**, which have been made by photosynthesis (Figure 2.9). Animal cells never contain starch grains.

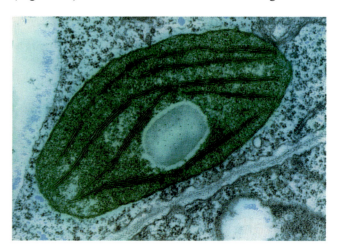

**Figure 2.9:** This electron micrograph shows a chloroplast from a cell in a pea plant. The large blue structure inside the chloroplast is a starch grain. The black stripes inside the chloroplast are membranes where the chlorophyll is kept.

> **KEY WORDS**
>
> **chloroplasts:** small structures found inside some plant cells, inside which photosynthesis takes place
>
> **starch grains:** tiny pieces of starch, made of thousands of starch molecules, that are stored in some plant cells

## Mitochondria

All the structures we have looked at so far – cell membrane, cell wall, cytoplasm, vacuoles, nucleus and chloroplasts – can be seen with a good light microscope. But there are some smaller structures inside cells that we cannot see clearly unless we use an electron microscope. These include **mitochondria** (singular: **mitochondrion**).

Mitochondria are found in almost all plant and animal cells. Figure 2.10 is an electron micrograph of a mitochondrion, and Figure 2.11 shows what one might look like if we could cut it open and see it in three dimensions.

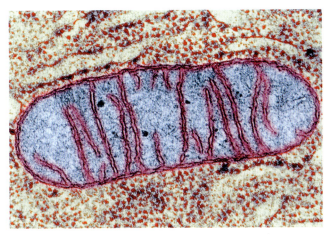

**Figure 2.10:** An electron micrograph of a mitochondrion. The pink lines are membranes, which separate the inside of the mitochondrion from the rest of the cell.

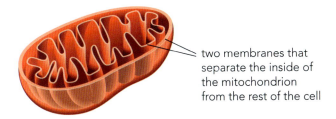

two membranes that separate the inside of the mitochondrion from the rest of the cell

**Figure 2.11:** A drawing of a mitochondrion, cut open to show the membrane inside it.

Mitochondria are the parts of the cell where **aerobic respiration** happens. This is how energy is released from glucose. You can read about aerobic respiration in Chapter 11.

Aerobic respiration is the main way in which cells get the energy that they need to stay alive. The more energy a cell needs, the more mitochondria it has. Muscle cells, for example, are packed full of mitochondria.

## Ribosomes

**Ribosomes** are tiny structures found in almost all animal cells and plant cells. They are so small that we can only see them with an electron microscope.

Ribosomes are where the cell makes proteins. The instructions on the DNA molecules are used to link together long chains of amino acids in a particular sequence. You can read more about protein molecules in Chapter 4, and more about how a cell makes them in Chapter 16.

> **KEY WORDS**
>
> **mitochondrion:** a small structure in a cell, where aerobic respiration releases energy from glucose
>
> **aerobic respiration:** chemical reactions that take place in mitochondria, which use oxygen to break down glucose and other nutrient molecules to release energy for the cell to use
>
> **ribosomes:** very small structures in a cell that use information on DNA to make protein molecules

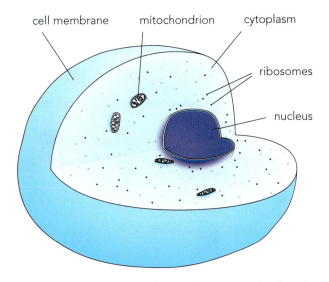

**Figure 2.12:** This diagram shows what an animal cell might look like if we cut it open.

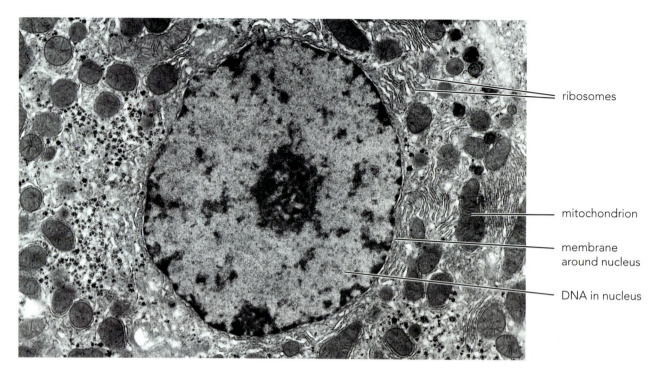

**Figure 2.13:** An electron micrograph showing the central part of an animal cell.

## Questions

3 Name the part of a cell which has each of these functions:
   a  making proteins
   b  containing the information about which proteins to make
   c  photosynthesis
   d  preventing the cell bursting when it takes up water
   e  storing a solution of sugars and other solutes
   f  controlling what enters and leaves the cell.

4 Which of the structures that you have named in Question 3 are found in both animal and plant cells?

### ACTIVITY 2.1

#### Comparing animal cells and plant cells

Work in a group of three or four for this activity.

You are going to make a display to compare the structures of animal cells and plant cells.

Decide how you will do this. You could perhaps use annotated drawings, construct a large comparison table, or make a presentation.

You can use the information in this chapter to make your comparison. You might also like to look for some more pictures on the internet.

## 2 Cells

### ACTIVITY 2.2

**Functions of the parts of a plant cell**

You could work on your own or in a pair for this activity.

> **You will need:**
> - a large sheet of paper, at least A4 and larger if possible
> - a pencil, marker pens and a ruler.

1. On your large sheet of paper, make a drawing of a plant cell. You could copy the one in Figure 2.3. Leave plenty of space around your drawing.
2. Use the information in this chapter to find the function of one part of the cell – for example, the cell wall.
3. Draw a label line, using a ruler, to this part of the cell. Write the name of the part, and then a short summary of what it does.
4. Repeat steps 2 and 3 for each part of the cell.

You could think about:

- whether the drawing is as large and clear as possible
- how well they have described the function of each part.

**Peer assessment**

Exchange your diagram with a partner.

Look at your partner's diagram and assess how well they have carried out the task.

Rate them a mark according to the following scheme.

**Green**    if they did it really well

**Amber**    if they made a good attempt at it and partly succeeded

**Red**    if they did not try to do it, or did not succeed

### REFLECTION

Now that you have studied your partner's diagram, is there anything you would like to change on yours?

## 2.2 Bacterial cells

**Bacteria** (singular: bacterium) are unicellular organisms. Bacterial cells are rather different from the cells of animals and plants. Figure 2.14 is a diagram of a bacterium.

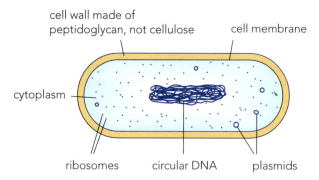

Figure 2.14: A bacterial cell.

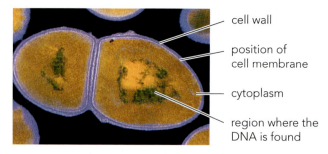

**Figure 2.15:** This picture was taken with an electron microscope, after which the colours were added to it. It shows a bacterium called *Enterococcus faecalis* dividing into two. This is the way that bacteria reproduce.

Bacterial cells always have a cell wall. Unlike plant cells, this cell wall is not made of cellulose. But the function is the same as in plant cells – the bacterial cell wall helps to support the cell, and stops it bursting if the cell takes up a lot of water.

A partially permeable cell membrane is pressed tightly against the inside of the bacterial cell wall. As in plant and animal cells, the cell membrane controls what enters and leaves the cell.

Bacterial cells have cytoplasm and ribosomes, which have the same functions as in animal and plant cells. They do not have mitochondria or chloroplasts.

The most important difference between a bacterial cell and animal or plant cells is that bacteria do not have a nucleus. Bacterial cells are also known as **prokaryotic cells**. 'Pro' means 'before', and 'karyotic' means 'nucleus'. Prokaryotic cells appeared on Earth millions of years before cells with nuclei appeared.

Instead of chromosomes inside a nucleus, bacteria have a circle of DNA. This is sometimes called a bacterial chromosome. The DNA has exactly the same function as in other cells – it provides instructions for making proteins.

Bacterial cells often have one or more smaller circles of DNA, called **plasmids**. Scientists can use plasmids in the genetic modification of cells and organisms, which you can read about in Chapter 20.

### KEY WORDS

**bacteria:** unicellular organisms whose cells do not contain a nucleus

**prokaryotic cells:** cells with no nucleus; bacteria have prokaryotic cells

**plasmids:** small, circular molecules of DNA, found in many prokaryotic cells in addition to the main, much larger circle of DNA

## Question

5   Construct a table to compare the structure of a bacterial cell with animal and plant cells. Remember to include similarities as well as differences.

### REFLECTION

How will you try to learn the names of the parts of animal, plant and bacterial cells, and their functions? Think about which of these ideas might work for you:

- looking at diagrams and reading about the structures
- practising drawing your own diagrams and labelling them
- getting a friend to test you by asking questions
- making some revision cards for yourself, with the name of a structure on one side and its function on the other side

What other ideas might you try?

## 2.3 Specialised cells

Multicellular organisms, such as humans or plants, may contain many millions of cells. Not all of these cells are alike. For example, in a human body almost all of our cells have the same features that are found in most animal cells – a cell membrane, cytoplasm, mitochondria, ribosomes, and a nucleus. But most of our cells have a particular function to perform, and their structure is modified to help them to carry out that function effectively. They are said to be specialised. The same is true in a flowering plant, where all the cells have the basic characteristics of plant cells, but then have slightly different structures that relate to their specific functions.

You will meet many examples of specialised cells as you continue through your biology course. Table 2.1 lists seven of these (five from animals and two from plants) and indicates where you can find out more about each one.

### Tissues

Often, cells that specialise in the same activity are found together. A group of cells like this is called a **tissue**. An example of a tissue is a layer of cells lining your stomach. These cells make enzymes to help to digest your food (Figure 2.16).

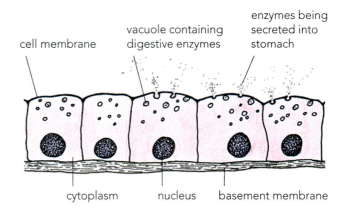

**Figure 2.16:** Cells lining the stomach – an example of a tissue.

The stomach also contains other tissues. For example, there is a layer of muscle in the stomach wall, made of cells which can move. This muscle tissue makes the wall of the stomach move in and out, churning the food and mixing it up with enzymes.

Plants also have tissues. You may already have looked at some epidermis tissue from an onion bulb. Inside a leaf, a layer of cells makes up the palisade tissue – these cells are specialised to carry out photosynthesis.

> **KEY WORD**
>
> **tissue:** a group of similar cells that work together to perform a particular function

| Specialised cell | Where it is found | Function | Where you can find out more |
|---|---|---|---|
| ciliated cell | lining the trachea and bronchi of animals | cilia move mucus upwards | Topic 11.2 |
| neurone | in the nervous system of animals | conducting electrical impulses | Topic 12.1 |
| red blood cell | in the blood of mammals | transporting oxygen | Topic 9.4 |
| sperm cell | produced in the testes of mammals | the male gamete in sexual reproduction | Topic 15.1 |
| egg cell | produced in the ovaries of mammals | the female gamete in reproduction | Topic 15.1 |
| root hair cell | near the tips of the roots of flowering plants | absorption of water and mineral ions | Topic 8.2 |
| palisade mesophyll cell | in the leaves of flowering plants | photosynthesis | Topic 6.2 |

**Table 2.1:** Examples of specialised cells.

## Organs

A group of different tissues that carry out a function together is called an **organ**. The stomach is an organ. Other organs include the heart, the kidneys and the lungs. In a plant, an onion bulb is an organ. A leaf is another example of a plant organ.

The stomach is only one of the organs which help in the digestion of food. The mouth, the intestines and the stomach are all part of an **organ system** called the digestive system. The heart is part of the circulatory system, while each kidney is part of the excretory system.

The way in which organisms are built up can be summarised like this: cells make up tissues, which make up organs, which make up organ systems, which make up organisms.

## 2.4 Sizes of specimens

Many of the structures that biologists study are very small. Cells, for example, are so small that we cannot see them without a microscope. The photographs and diagrams of cells in this chapter are all much larger than actual cells.

We can tell someone how much bigger the image is than the actual object by giving its **magnification**. The magnification of an object is how many times larger it is than the real object.

$$\text{magnification} = \frac{\text{size of image}}{\text{size of actual object}}$$

For example, try measuring the length of the spider's body in Figure 2.17.

Figure 2.17: A spider.

You should find that it is 40 mm long.

The real spider was 8 mm long. So, we can work out how much the diagram is magnified:

$$\text{magnification} = \frac{\text{length of body in the drawing}}{\text{length of body of the real spider}}$$

$$= \frac{40}{8}$$

$$= \times 5$$

There are two very important things to remember when you are calculating a magnification:

- Make sure that all the numbers in your calculation have the same units. It is often a good idea to convert everything to millimetres, mm, before you do anything else.

- Magnification is always written with a multiplication sign in front of it, ×. Magnification does not have units.

> **KEY WORDS**
>
> **organ:** a group of tissues that work together to perform a particular function
>
> **organ system:** several organs that work together to perform a particular function
>
> **magnification:** how many times larger an image is than the actual object.

Some of the objects that we study in biology are so small that even millimetres are not a suitable unit to use for measuring them. Instead, we use micrometres. The symbol for a micrometre is µm.

$$1 \, \mu m = 1 \times 10^{-6} \, m$$

$$1 \, m = 10^6 \, \mu m$$

## Questions

6   How many micrometres are there in 1 mm?

7   The mitochondrion in Figure 2.10 is magnified 20 000 times.

   a   Using a ruler, carefully measure the maximum length of the mitochondrion. Record your measurement in mm (millimetres).

   b   Convert your answer to µm (micrometres).

**c** Use this formula to calculate the real size of the mitochondrion in μm:

$$\text{real size in μm} = \frac{\text{size of image in μm}}{\text{magnification}}$$

**d** How many of these mitochondria could you line up end to end between two of the mm marks on your ruler?

## ACTIVITY 2.3

### Practising using the magnification equation

Work on your own for the first part of this activity, and then pair up with someone else for the second part.

> **You will need:**
> - several small objects that are easy to measure and draw – for example an eraser, a paper clip, a button
> - a ruler that can measure in mm
> - some plain paper, a good pencil and an eraser.

### First part – work on your own for this

1. Measure each object carefully and write down the measurements. Don't let anyone else see these measurements at this point.
2. Make a magnified drawing of your objects. Calculate the magnification of each one and write it next to your drawings. Try to use different magnifications for each object. (You could even try drawing some objects smaller than they really are, so that the magnification is less than 1.)

## CONTINUED

### Second part – work with a partner

3. Exchange your drawings with a partner. Each of you uses the drawings and magnifications to work out the size of the actual object.
4. Check your answers with your partner – did you correctly calculate the actual sizes of the objects they had drawn? Did your partner calculate the actual sizes of the objects that you had drawn?

### Self-assessment

Did you calculate the magnifications of your drawings correctly, so that your partner could work out the actual size of each drawing?

If not, where did you go wrong?

Were you able to calculate the actual size of the objects your partner had drawn? If not, where did you (or they) go wrong?

## REFLECTION

What are the most important things that you need to remember when you use the magnification equation?

What can you do to help you to remember the equation and how to use it?

## SUMMARY

| |
|---|
| All organisms are made of cells. New cells are always made by the division of existing cells. |
| Animal and plant cells contain cytoplasm, a cell membrane, ribosomes, mitochondria and a nucleus containing DNA in the form of chromosomes. Plant cells also contain a cell wall, a large vacuole and sometimes chloroplasts. |
| Bacterial cells have cytoplasm, a cell membrane, a cell wall and ribosomes. They do not have a nucleus. Their DNA is circular. They may have extra, small circles of DNA called plasmids. |
| The cell membrane of all cells is partially permeable and controls what enters and leaves the cell. The cell wall is fully permeable and allows all molecules and ions to pass through it. |
| Ribosomes are the site of protein synthesis in a cell. |
| Mitochondria release energy from glucose and other nutrients, by aerobic respiration. |
| Chloroplasts are the site of photosynthesis. |
| Cells may be specialised for specific functions. |
| Magnification can be calculated using the equation $$\text{magnification} = \frac{\text{size of image}}{\text{size of actual object}}$$ |

## PROJECT

### Making a model cell

It is best to work in a group of three or four for this project.

Discuss different ideas about how you can make a model cell. What kind of cell will it be – an animal cell, a plant cell or a bacterial cell?

How can you construct your cell? What materials will you need?

If you are short of ideas, you could search on the internet. However, even if you do find some good suggestions there, it is important to make the model cell your own, using some of your own ideas that make it different from everyone else's models.

As you build your model, you will almost certainly make some changes to your original plans, so be prepared to source some extra materials as you work.

After you have completed your model, you can compare it with the models that other groups have made. This might give you ideas about how you could make an even better model if you did it again.

2 Cells

EXAM-STYLE QUESTIONS

1 The diagram below shows a cell from a plant leaf.

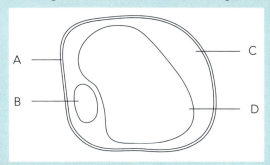

Which labelled part contains DNA? [1]

2 Which structure is **not** found in both animal and bacterial cells?
A cell membrane
B cytoplasm
C mitochondrion
D ribosome [1]

3 A diagram of a flower is 8 cm across. The magnification of the diagram is ×4. What is the actual width of the flower?

A 3.2 mm    B 20 mm    C 0.5 cm    D 32 cm    [1]

4 This diagram shows a group of palisade cells from a plant leaf.

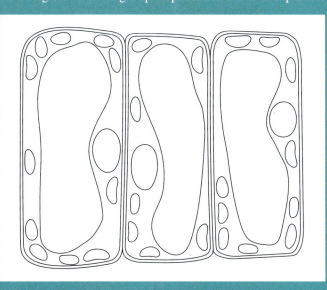

The width of the diagram is 60 mm. The mean width of an actual palisade cell is 40 µm.
What is the magnification of the diagram?

A ×1.5    B ×500    C ×667    D ×50    [1]

45

## CONTINUED

5 This is a photograph taken through a light microscope. It shows a group of plant cells.

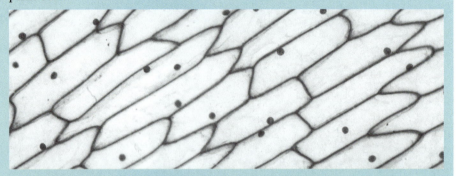

    a  i  **State** one way you can tell that these are plant cells and not animal cells. [1]

        ii  State one way you can tell that these are **not** bacterial cells. [1]

        iii  Name **one** cell structure that these cells do **not** contain, which you would expect to find in a palisade cell. [1]

    b  **Outline** the function of each of these parts of a plant cell.

        i  the nucleus [2]

        ii  ribosomes [2]

[Total: 7]

### COMMAND WORDS

**state:** express in clear terms

**outline:** set out main points

6 The photograph shows a jellyfish. A jellyfish belongs to the animal kingdom.

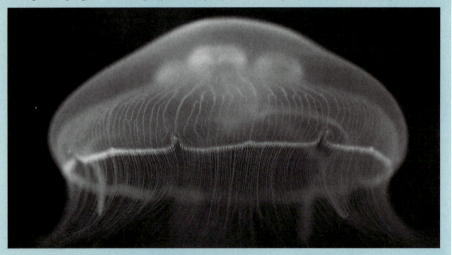

    a  The actual jellyfish is 50 mm in diameter.
        **Calculate** the magnification of the photograph. [3]

    b  Name **three** parts that you would find in a cell in a jellyfish **and** outline the function of each part. [6]

    c  Some of the cells in the jellyfish are neurones.
        State the function of a neurone. [1]

[Total: 10]

### COMMAND WORD

**calculate:** work out from given facts, figures or information

## CONTINUED

**7** This is an electron micrograph of a small part of a cell from the pancreas. This cell makes large quantities of protein molecules, which are stored in vesicles before being exported from the cell.

vesicle containing protein molecules made by the cell

a Structure **A** contains molecules that determine the type of proteins made in the cell. Identify structure **A**. [1]

b Use the information above to explain why the cell has large numbers of structures **B** and **C**. [6]

[Total: 7]

# CAMBRIDGE IGCSE™ BIOLOGY: COURSEBOOK

## SELF-EVALUATION CHECKLIST

After studying this chapter, think about how confident you are with the different topics. This will help you to see any gaps in your knowledge and help you to learn more effectively.

| I can | See Topic… | Needs more work | Almost there | Confident to move on |
|---|---|---|---|---|
| describe and compare the structure of an animal cell with a plant cell | 2.1 | | | |
| describe the functions of each of the structures found in an animal cell and a plant cell | 2.1 | | | |
| identify the parts of cells in diagrams, and in images taken using a light microscope or an electron microscope | 2.1 | | | |
| describe the structure of a bacterial cell, and the functions of each of its parts | 2.2 | | | |
| name some specialised cells and their functions | 2.3 | | | |
| remember the magnification equation, and use it to calculate magnifications or actual sizes of objects shown in images | 2.4 | | | |
| convert measurements between millimetres and micrometres | 2.4 | | | |

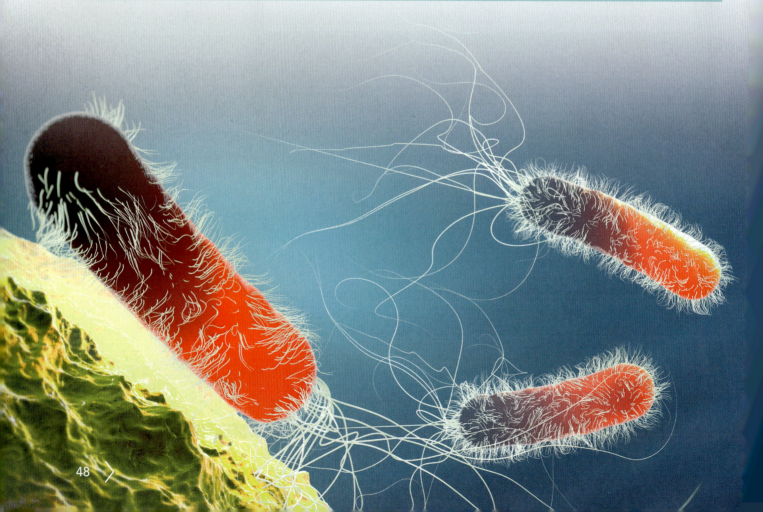

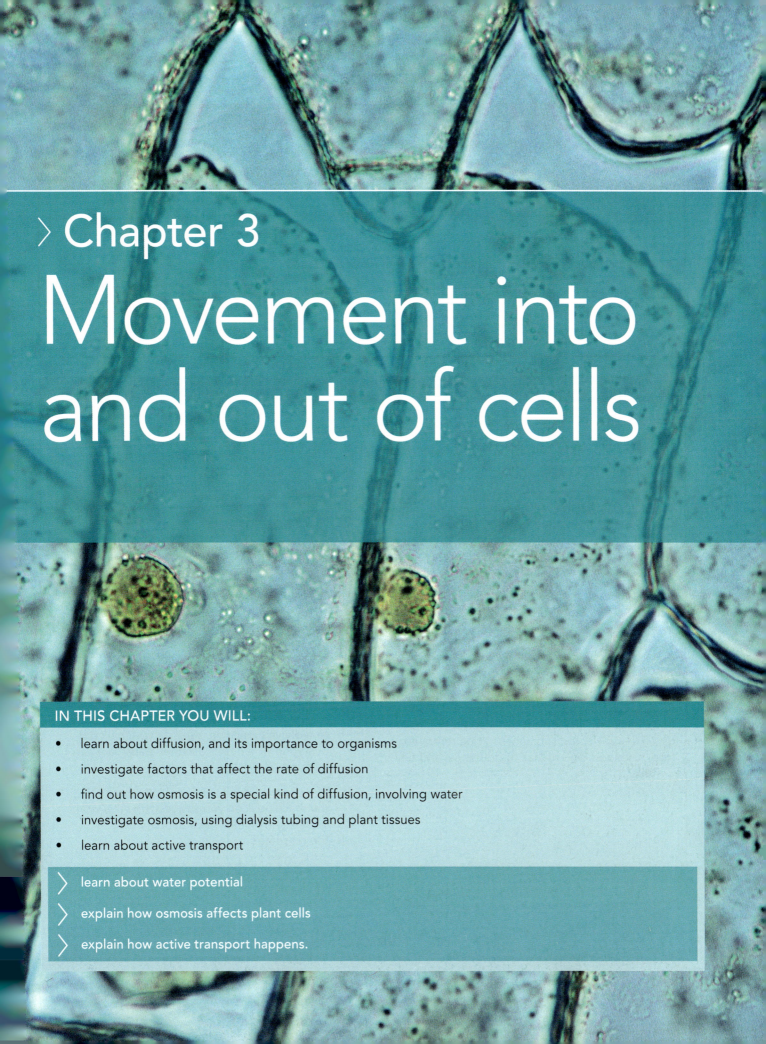

# Chapter 3
# Movement into and out of cells

**IN THIS CHAPTER YOU WILL:**

- learn about diffusion, and its importance to organisms
- investigate factors that affect the rate of diffusion
- find out how osmosis is a special kind of diffusion, involving water
- investigate osmosis, using dialysis tubing and plant tissues
- learn about active transport

> learn about water potential
> explain how osmosis affects plant cells
> explain how active transport happens.

# CAMBRIDGE IGCSE™ BIOLOGY: COURSEBOOK

## GETTING STARTED

The particle theory helps us to explain how matter behaves.

Here are six statements about particles. Some of them describe solids, some describe liquids and some describe gases. Which are which?

- The particles are far apart and rarely collide with each other.
- The particles vibrate on the spot.
- The particles are close to one another but can move around.
- The particles move freely in all directions.
- The particles stay in contact and slide past one another as they move.
- The particles are in fixed positions, close to one another.

## USING DIFFUSION TO CLEAN THE BLOOD

We each have two kidneys whose function is to remove unwanted substances from the blood. The kidneys produce a solution of the unwanted substances, which is removed from the body as urine.

However, sometimes kidneys stop working. When this happens, the unwanted substances build up in the blood. Some of them can be quite dangerous so it is important to find another way to remove them.

The boy in Figure 3.1 is attached to a dialysis machine. The blood from a vein in his arm flows into the machine. Inside the machine, a liquid called dialysis fluid flows past his blood. There is a very thin membrane between his blood and the dialysis fluid. The unwanted substances in his blood diffuse through the membrane into the dialysis fluid, which then flows away. His cleaned blood flows back into his body. It takes several hours for all the unwanted substances to be removed from his blood, and he has to do this several times a week.

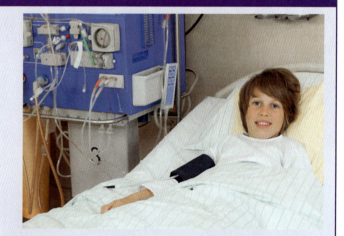

Figure 3.1: A patient undergoing dialysis.

### Discussion questions

1   If the boy could have a kidney transplant, he would not have to spend time attached to a dialysis machine. Why do you think not everyone who needs a kidney transplant can have one?

2   The dialysis fluid flows constantly through the machine. Can you suggest why this works better than just having stationary fluid in the machine?

# 3.1 Diffusion

Everything – including living cells – is made of atoms, molecules and ions. These **particles** are always moving. The higher the temperature, the faster they move. This is because the particles have more **kinetic energy** at higher temperatures. The more kinetic energy they have, the faster they move.

In a solid substance, the particles cannot move very far, because they are held together by attractive forces between them. They simply vibrate around a fixed position. In a liquid they can move more freely but stay in contact with one another. They bump into one another and rebound. In a gas they are freer still, with no attractive forces between the molecules or atoms. When molecules and ions are in a solution, they can move as freely as when they are liquid.

## Diffusion down a concentration gradient

When they can move freely, particles tend to spread themselves out as evenly as they can. This happens with gases, solutions, and mixtures of liquids.

Imagine, for example, a rotten egg full of hydrogen sulfide gas in one corner of a room. Hydrogen sulfide gas is *very* smelly. To begin with, there is a high concentration of the gas near the egg but none in the rest of the room (Figure 3.2). The hydrogen sulfide molecules quickly spread through the air in the whole room. Soon, you cannot tell where the smell first came from – the whole room smells of rotten egg!

The hydrogen sulfide molecules have spread out through the air. This spreading out is called **diffusion**. Diffusion happens because the molecules move randomly. They do not purposefully move from one place to another. Each molecule just moves by chance, changing direction when it bumps into another molecule. Some molecules might even go back into the rotten egg again. But, overall, the molecules spread fairly evenly across the room.

We call this the **net movement** of the molecules. Some go from the egg into the room, and a few from the room back into the egg – but overall, most of them go from the egg into the room.

A place where a lot of the molecules are quite close together has a high concentration of molecules. In this example, the rotten egg had the highest concentration of hydrogen sulfide molecules. The rest of the room had a low concentration of hydrogen sulfide molecules. Overall, the random movements of the molecules caused them to spread out evenly throughout all of the space they could get to.

One way of thinking about this is to imagine a slope. The place with the high concentration (the rotten egg) is at the top of the slope. The place with the low concentration (the rest of the room) is at the bottom of the slope. The molecules move 'down the slope' from where there is a high concentration to where there is a low concentration. Another word for 'slope' is 'gradient'. We can therefore say that there is a **concentration gradient** from the rotten egg to the rest of the room. The overall result of diffusion is that the hydrogen sulfide molecules move 'down' this concentration gradient.

a 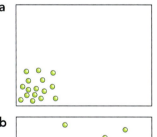 There is a high concentration of hydrogen sulfide molecules in one corner.

b 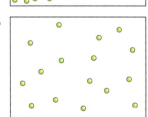 Given time, the molecules spread evenly through the space available.

**Figure 3.2:** The random movements of gas molecules result in them spreading evenly through all the space available.

> ### KEY WORDS
>
> **particles:** (in this context) the smallest pieces of which a substance is made; particles can be molecules, atoms or ions
>
> **kinetic energy:** energy of moving objects
>
> **diffusion:** the net movement of particles from a region of their higher concentration to a region of their lower concentration (i.e. down a concentration gradient), as a result of their random movement
>
> **net movement:** overall or average movement
>
> **concentration gradient:** an imaginary 'slope' from a high concentration to a low concentration

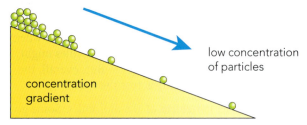

**Figure 3.3:** This diagram shows how we can use the analogy of a slope to think about a concentration gradient. We can imagine particles moving down the slope, from a high concentration to a low concentration.

### ACTIVITY 3.1

**Modelling diffusion**

In this activity, you will model diffusion using people to represent particles.

> **You will need:**
> - a fairly big, empty space to move around in – e.g. a playground or a large hall.

Work as a whole class for this activity.

Each person in the class represents a particle in a gas.

Start with most people in one corner of the room or space. Don't crowd too closely – remember that gas particles do not touch one another. Face any way that you like.

Each person now starts to move in a straight line in the direction they are facing. (Real gas particles move very quickly, but it's best if you don't move too fast, or there might be uncomfortable collisions.)

Keep going in your straight line until you hit something. This might be another particle, or it might be the wall of your 'container'. When you collide, change direction and keep going in your new straight line.

### CONTINUED

Continue doing this for a few minutes. Then stop and look around you.

#### Questions

1. What has happened to the 'particles'? Are they still concentrated in one corner?
2. Try to explain why this happened.

### REFLECTION

You have now used two different models of diffusion. The first one was the picture of a slope in Figure 3.3, and the second model used moving people to represent particles.

Do either of these models help you to understand diffusion? Why do you think that is?

## Diffusion in living organisms

Living organisms get many of the substances they need by diffusion. They also get rid of many of their waste products in this way. For example, plants need carbon dioxide for photosynthesis. This diffuses from the air into the leaves, through the stomata. It does this because there is a lower concentration of carbon dioxide inside the leaf, as the cells are using it up. Outside the leaf in the air, there is a higher concentration. Carbon dioxide molecules therefore diffuse into the leaf, as a result of their random movement, down this concentration gradient.

Oxygen, which is a waste product of photosynthesis, diffuses out in the same way. There is a higher concentration of oxygen inside the leaf, because it is being made there. Oxygen therefore diffuses out through the stomata into the air.

Diffusion is also important in gas exchange for respiration in animals and plants (Figure 3.4). Cell membranes are freely permeable to oxygen and carbon dioxide, so these gases easily diffuse into and out of cells.

# 3 Movement into and out of cells

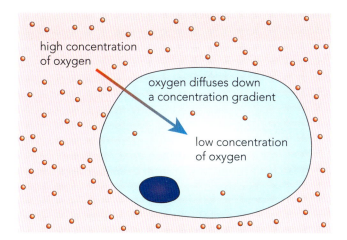

**Figure 3.4:** Some substances, such as oxygen and carbon dioxide, move into and out of cells by diffusion through the cell membrane.

Oxygen and carbon dioxide are both gases, but living organisms also rely on diffusion of solutes. A solute is a substance that has dissolved in a liquid, which is called a solvent. In organisms, the solvent is always water. For example, the cytoplasm of all cells contains many solutes, such as glucose molecules or sodium ions. These particles are free to move through the cytoplasm, so they diffuse, spreading to all parts of the cytoplasm.

## Questions

1. Look at the definition of diffusion in the Key words box.

   Explain what each of these words in the definition means:

   a  net movement

   b  concentration gradient

   c  random movement

2. When substances diffuse into and out of cells, which part of the cell must they move through?

3. Describe **three** examples of diffusion in organisms. For each example, state whether the substance that is diffusing is a gas or a solute.

4. Where does the energy for diffusion come from?

### EXPERIMENTAL SKILLS 3.1

#### Investigating how surface area affects diffusion

In this investigation, you will use pieces of agar jelly to represent cells. You will follow instructions to investigate how the surface area of the 'cells' affects the diffusion of a substance through them.

#### You will need:
- a dish containing agar jelly, made with a little bit of a weak alkali such as ammonium hydroxide, and coloured with a dye called cresol red
- a sharp knife to cut the jelly into pieces
- some plastic or blunt-ended forceps (tweezers)
- a ruler to measure in mm
- two large test-tubes or other large glass tubes, more than 1 cm in diameter
- a stopwatch
- some dilute hydrochloric acid.

**Safety:** Take care with the acid. Wear safety glasses in case of splashes. If you spill it, clean up the spills immediately, using plenty of cold water.

Take care with the sharp blade. Cut with the blade facing away from you. Place the jelly on a firm surface before you start to cut it.

#### Method

1. Cut two cubes of agar jelly, with sides of 1 cm.

2. Cut one of the cubes into four smaller cubes, each with sides of 0.5 cm.

3. Put the large cube into a test-tube. Put the four small cubes into the other test-tube.

4. Add equal volumes of dilute hydrochloric acid to each tube, making sure that all of the cubes are covered with acid.

5. Start the stopwatch. Time how many seconds it takes for the cubes in each test-tube to become fully yellow.

53

## CONTINUED

### Questions

1  The jelly cubes contained a weak alkali and cresol red, which is an indicator. Explain why the cubes changed colour.

2  How did the volume of the four small cubes compare with the volume of the one larger cube? Was it greater, smaller, or the same?

3  How did the total surface area of the four small cubes compare with the surface area of the one larger cube? Was it greater, smaller, or the same?

4  Copy and complete these sentences, choosing the correct words.

   The time taken for the four small cubes to completely change colour was **greater / smaller** than the one single cube.

   This is because the **surface area / volume** of the small cubes was **greater / smaller** than for the single cube.

5  Write a conclusion for your experiment. Include the words **diffusion** and **surface area** in your conclusion.

## EXPERIMENTAL SKILLS 3.2

### Investigating how temperature, concentration gradient or distance affect diffusion

In the last experiment, you used cubes of alkaline agar jelly and an indicator, so that you could measure the time taken for an acid to diffuse through the cubes. Now you are going to plan how you can use this technique to investigate other factors. You may be able to do the experiment that you plan.

1  As well as surface area, diffusion is also affected by:
   - temperature
   - concentration gradient
   - distance.

   Choose **one** of these variables to investigate.

2  The variable that you change in your experiment is called the **independent variable**. What is the independent variable in your experiment?

3  Think about how you can change your independent variable. Decide how many different values you will have.

4  The variable that you measure, as you collect your results, is the **dependent variable**. What is the dependent variable in your experiment?

5  Describe how you will measure your dependent variable.

6  It is important that no variables, other than the one you are investigating, affect your experiment. Which variables will you standardise (keep the same) in your experiment? How will you do this?

7  Write a short, clear description of how you will do your experiment.

8  Draw a results chart that you could use to fill in your results. Include headings, but do not put in any results (unless you are able to actually do your experiment, of course).

9  Predict what you would expect to find in your experiment.

### KEY WORDS

**independent variable:** the variable that you change in an experiment

**dependent variable:** the variable that you measure, as you collect your results

## Questions

5 Using what you know about how diffusion happens, explain each of these statements:

   a  Diffusion happens faster at higher temperatures.

   b  The greater the difference in concentration between two solutions, the faster diffusion happens.

   c  In a kidney dialysis machine, many small tubes containing dialysis fluid are used, rather than one big one.

   d  In a kidney dialysis machine, the membrane separating the blood and the dialysis fluid is very thin.

# 3.2 Osmosis

Water is one of the most important **compounds** in living organisms. It can make up around 80% of some organisms' bodies. It has many functions, including acting as a solvent for many different substances. For example:

- when we swallow food, some of it dissolves in water in the alimentary canal, where it can be acted on by enzymes which are also dissolved in water (Chapter 7)
- the kidneys excrete urea dissolved in water, to form urine (Chapter 13)
- substances are transported around the body dissolved in the water in blood plasma (Chapter 9).

Every cell in an organism's body has water inside it and outside it. Many different substances are dissolved in this water, and their concentrations may be different inside and outside the cell. This creates concentration gradients, down which water and solutes will diffuse, if they are able to pass through the membrane.

It's easiest to think about this if we consider a simple situation involving just one solute. Figure 3.5 illustrates a concentrated sugar solution, separated from a dilute sugar solution by a membrane. The membrane has holes or pores in it which are very small. An example of a membrane like this is dialysis tubing.

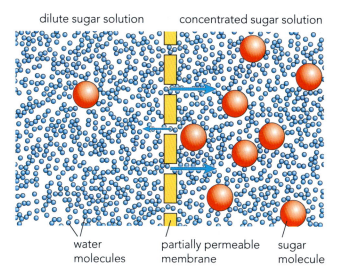

**Figure 3.5:** How osmosis happens. It is important to think about the diffusion of each kind of molecule separately.

Water molecules are also very small. Each one is made of two hydrogen atoms and one oxygen atom. Sugar molecules are many times larger than this.

In dialysis tubing, the holes are big enough to let the water molecules through, but not the sugar molecules. Dialysis tubing is called a **partially permeable membrane** because it will let some molecules through but not others.

There is a higher concentration of sugar molecules on the right-hand side of the membrane in Figure 3.5, and a lower concentration on the left-hand side. If the membrane was not there, the sugar molecules would diffuse from the concentrated solution into the dilute one until they were evenly spread out. However, they cannot do this because the holes in the membrane are too small for them to get through.

There is also a concentration gradient for the water molecules. On the left-hand side of the membrane, there is a high concentration of water molecules. On the right-hand side, the concentration of water molecules is lower because a lot of space is taken up by sugar molecules.

> **KEY WORDS**
>
> **compound:** a substance formed by the chemical combination of two or more elements in fixed proportions
>
> **partially permeable membrane:** a membrane (very thin layer) that lets some particles move through it, but prevents others passing through

Because there are more water molecules on the left-hand side, at any one moment more of them will 'hit' a hole in the membrane and move through to the other side than will go the other way (right to left). Over time, there will be an overall, or net, movement of water from left to right. This is called **osmosis**.

You can see that osmosis is really just a kind of diffusion. It is the diffusion of water molecules in a situation where the water molecules but not the solute molecules can pass through a membrane.

> ### KEY WORD
>
> **osmosis:** the diffusion of water molecules through a partially permeable membrane

> ### KEY WORDS
>
> **osmosis (in terms of water potential):** the net movement of water molecules from a region of higher water potential (dilute solution) to a region of lower water potential (concentrated solution) through a partially permeable membrane
>
> **high water potential:** an area where there are a lot of water molecules – a dilute solution
>
> **low water potential:** an area where there are not many water molecules – a concentrated solution
>
> **water potential gradient:** a difference in water potential between two areas

## Water potential

It can be confusing to talk about the 'concentration' of water molecules, because the term *concentration* is normally used to mean the concentration of the solute dissolved in the water. It is much better to use a different term. We say that a dilute solution (where there is a lot of water) has a **high water potential**. A concentrated solution (where there is less water) has a **low water potential**.

In Figure 3.6, there is a high water potential on the left-hand side and a low water potential on the right-hand side. There is a **water potential gradient** between the two sides. The water molecules diffuse down this gradient, from a high water potential to a low water potential.

Water potential and osmosis are of great importance to organisms because they affect how and when organisms take up and lose water. You will find out about the uptake and loss of water by plants in Chapter 8. The uptake of water by humans is described in Chapter 7.

## Questions

These questions are about the diagram in Figure 3.5.

6  What is the solvent in the sugar solution? What is the solute?

7  Explain why water molecules can move from one side of the membrane to the other, but sugar molecules cannot.

8  In which direction is the net movement of water molecules?

9  Where does the energy come from, to cause this movement?

10 In Figure 3.5, which solution has the higher water potential? Explain your answer.

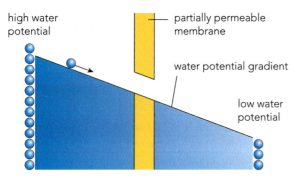

Figure 3.6: We can think of a water potential gradient as a 'slope'. Water molecules have a tendency to move down the slope, from a high water potential to a low water potential.

# 3 Movement into and out of cells

## EXPERIMENTAL SKILLS 3.3

### Using dialysis tubing to investigate osmosis

In this investigation, you will watch osmosis happen. You can also use the apparatus to investigate how differences in concentration of the solutions affect the rate at which osmosis happens.

> You will need:
> - the apparatus shown in Figure 3.7
> - a dropper pipette
> - a stopwatch
> - at least two different concentrations of sugar solution.

It is best to do this experiment with a partner, as you often need at least three hands to do some of the steps successfully.

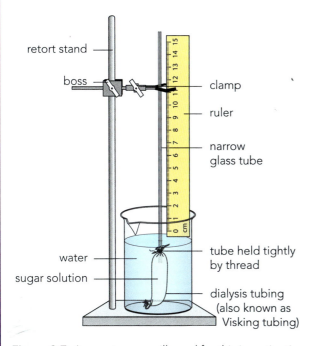

**Figure 3.7:** Apparatus you will need for this investigation.

### Method

1. Collect a piece of dialysis tubing. Put a few drops of water on it to soften it, and rub it gently between your fingers until it opens. Tie one end of it around itself in a tight knot.

2. Use a dropper pipette to carefully fill the piece of tubing with the most concentrated sugar solution.

3. Place a long, narrow glass tube into the dialysis tubing, as shown in Figure 3.7. Use some strong thread to tie the dialysis tubing very tightly around the glass tube.

4. Place the dialysis tubing inside a beaker of water, as shown in Figure 3.7. Support the glass tube using a retort stand, boss and clamp.

5. Mark the level of the liquid inside the glass tube.

6. Every two minutes, record the level of liquid inside the glass tube.

7. You can now try repeating your experiment, but this time use a different concentration of sugar solution. This is quite tricky to do, because you will need to take your apparatus apart to change the sugar solution. Record your results using the new sugar solution.

8. On a large sheet of graph paper, draw a line graph for your first set of results. Remember that the independent variable goes on the x-axis, and the dependent variable goes on the y-axis.

9. If you were able to repeat the experiment with a different sugar solution, plot another graph on the same pair of axes.

> **CONTINUED**
>
> **Questions**
>
> 1 Explain why the liquid moved up the glass tube.
>
> 2 Use your graph for the first set of results to work out the mean rate at which the liquid moved up the tube, in mm per second.
>
> 3 If you were able to repeat the experiment with a different sugar solution, compare the two sets of results. Can you explain any differences between them?
>
> 4 Imagine you are able to use dialysis tubing with ridges on it, instead of a smooth surface. Predict how this might affect your results. Explain your prediction.
>
> 5 Suggest how you could modify this experiment to find out how temperature affects the rate of osmosis. Predict the results you would expect.

# Osmosis and animal cells

You have seen that osmosis happens when two solutions (or a solution and pure water) are separated from each other by a partially permeable membrane. The membrane lets water molecules through, but not the other molecules that are dissolved in the water.

Cell membranes are partially permeable. They let water through easily, but other molecules and ions often cannot get through. This means that osmosis happens across cell membranes.

Figure 3.8 shows an animal cell in pure water. The cytoplasm inside the cell is a fairly concentrated solution. The proteins and many other substances dissolved in it are too large to get through the cell membrane. However, water molecules can get through the membrane.

If you compare this situation with Figure 3.5, you will see that they are similar. The dilute solution in Figure 3.5 and the pure water in Figure 3.8 are each separated from a concentrated solution by a partially permeable membrane. In Figure 3.8, the concentrated solution is the cytoplasm and the partially permeable membrane is the cell membrane. Therefore, osmosis will occur.

Water molecules will diffuse from the dilute solution into the concentrated solution. As more and more water enters the cell, it swells. The cell membrane has to stretch as the cell gets bigger, until eventually the strain is too much, and the cell bursts.

Figure 3.9 shows an animal cell in a concentrated solution. If this solution is more concentrated than the cytoplasm, then water molecules will diffuse out of the cell. Look at Figure 3.5 to see why. As the water molecules go out through the cell membrane, the cytoplasm shrinks, so the cell gets smaller.

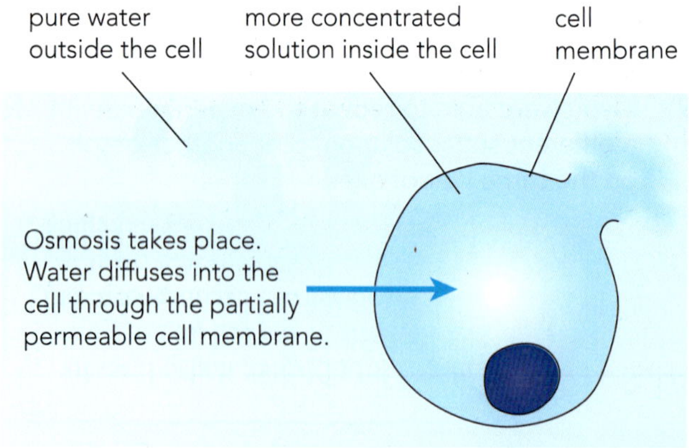

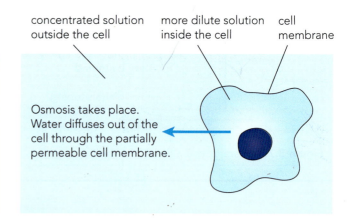

**Figure 3.8:** If an animal cell is placed in pure water, water enters the cell by osmosis. The cell swells and bursts.

**Figure 3.9:** If an animal cell is placed in a concentrated solution, water leaves the cell by osmosis. The cell shrinks.

## 3 Movement into and out of cells

# Osmosis and plant cells

Plant cells do not burst in pure water. Figure 3.10 shows a plant cell in pure water. Plant cells are surrounded by a cell wall. This is fully permeable, which means that it will let any molecules go through it.

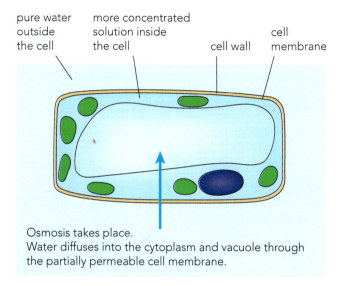

**Figure 3.10:** If a plant cell is placed in pure water, water enters the cell by osmosis. The cell swells but does not burst, because of its strong cell wall.

Although it is not easy to see, a plant cell also has a cell membrane just like an animal cell. The cell membrane is partially permeable. A plant cell in pure water will take in water by osmosis through its partially permeable cell membrane in the same way as an animal cell. As the water goes in, the cytoplasm and vacuole will swell.

However, the plant cell has a very strong cell wall around it. The cell wall is much stronger than the cell membrane and it stops the plant cell from bursting. The cytoplasm presses out against the cell wall, but the wall resists and presses back on the contents.

In a plant leaf, cells that have plenty of water are all in this state. In each one, the cytoplasm presses out on the cell walls. The pressure of the water pushing outwards on the cells' walls keeps the whole group of cells strong and firm. This helps to support plant leaves.

A plant cell in this state is rather like a blown-up tyre – tight and firm. It is said to be **turgid**. The pressure of the water pushing outwards on the cell wall is called **turgor pressure**. Turgor pressure helps a plant that has no wood in it to stay upright, and keeps the leaves firm. Plant cells are usually turgid.

> **KEY WORDS**
>
> **turgid:** a description of a plant cell that is tight and firm
>
> **turgor pressure:** the pressure of the water pushing outwards on a plant cell wall

Now imagine that a plant cell is placed in a solution that is more concentrated than its cytoplasm. Water leaves the cell by osmosis. The cytoplasm and vacuole shrink. But the cell wall is strong and stays in position. The cytoplasm therefore pulls away from the cell wall. This pulls the membrane away from the cell wall, too. The cell now looks like the diagram in Figure 3.11 and the photographed cells in Figure 3.12.

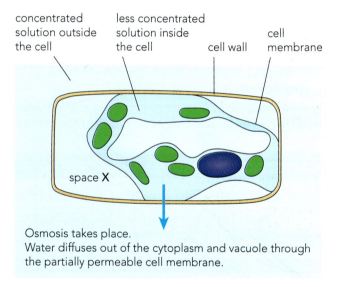

**Figure 3.11:** If a plant cell is placed in a concentrated solution, water moves out of it by osmosis. The cytoplasm and vacuole shrink, and the cell membrane pulls away from the cell wall.

When a plant cell loses a lot of water, it also loses its turgor pressure. The contents of the cell do not push outwards on the cell wall, so the cell becomes soft and floppy. It is said to be **flaccid**. If the cells in a plant become flaccid, the plant loses its firmness and begins to wilt.

> **KEY WORD**
>
> **flaccid:** a description of a plant cell that is soft

59

When the cell membrane tears away from the cell wall, the cell is said to be **plasmolysed**. Plasmolysis can kill a plant cell because the cell membrane is damaged as it tears away from the cell wall.

> **KEY WORD**
>
> **plasmolysed:** a description of a cell in which the cell membrane tears away from the cell wall

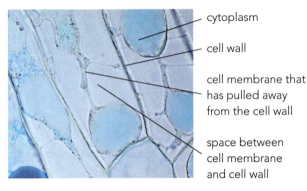

**Figure 3.12:** These onion cells have been placed in a concentrated solution. The cytoplasm has lost so much water, and shrunk so much, that it has pulled away from the cell wall.

## Questions

11 Copy and complete this sentence:

   When an animal cell is placed in pure water, water _____ the cell by _____ through the partially permeable cell _____.

12 Animal cells burst if they are placed in pure water, but plant cells do not. Explain why.

13 Here are some descriptions of what happens to a plant cell when it is placed in a concentrated solution. They are in the wrong order. Write the descriptions in the correct order.

   - The cytoplasm and vacuole shrink.
   - The cell membrane is pulled away from the cell wall.
   - Water moves out of the cell through the partially permeable cell membrane.

14 Look at Figure 3.11. What fills space X? Explain your answer.

15 A group of plant cells has been placed in a concentrated solution, and the cells are plasmolysed. Predict what will happen if the cells are now placed in pure water. Explain your answer, using the term *water potential*.

---

### EXPERIMENTAL SKILLS 3.4

**Investigating the effect of osmosis on potato strips**

In this investigation, you will place pieces of plant tissue into different solutions and measure the effect on their length.

> **You will need:**
> - a large potato
> - a sharp knife or other way to peel the potato
> - a cork borer to cut cylinders from the potato (or you can use the knife to cut strips)
> - a ruler to measure in mm
> - three containers such as small beakers
> - some distilled water, a dilute sugar solution and a concentrated sugar solution.

**Method**

1 Peel the potato. Use a cork borer to cut six cylinders from the potato. Cut the ends from each cylinder so that each one is the same length – 40 mm is a good length to use. Record this length. If you do not have a cork borer, you can cut rectangular pieces from the potato instead (see Figure 3.13).

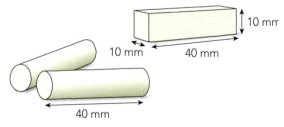

**Figure 3.13:** You can cut either cylinders or rectangular blocks from the potato.

# 3 Movement into and out of cells

## CONTINUED

2. Pour the distilled water into one beaker, and the two sugar solutions into the other two beakers. Label each beaker with the concentration of the solution.

3. Place two potato strips into each liquid, making sure they are completely covered.

4. Leave the potato strips in their liquids for about 20 minutes. While you are waiting, construct a results chart. You can fill in the original lengths of the strips.

5. After 20 minutes, take the potato strips out of their solutions. Measure the length of each one again. Record the new lengths.

6. Calculate the change in length of each strip. Remember to say whether it has got longer (a positive change) or shorter (a negative change).

### Questions

1. What happened to the length of the potato strips that were placed in the distilled water?

2. Use your knowledge of osmosis to explain why this happened.

3. What happened to the length of the potato strips that were placed in the concentrated solution?

4. Use your knowledge of osmosis to explain why this happened.

### Peer assessment

When you have completed your results table, exchange it with a partner.

Look at your partner's work, and give them a score for each of the following features:

**0 marks** not done at all, or very poor

**1 mark** quite well done

**2 marks** really good

- The results table is drawn with a ruler.
- There are clear headings for all the columns, with units.
- There are no units written anywhere except in the headings.
- It is really easy to understand the results table.
- The changes in length are shown in the results table.
- The changes in length have been correctly calculated, and say whether the strips increased or decreased in length.

Add up the marks you will give to your partner. If you have not given them full marks, make sure you can explain why.

## 3.3 Active transport

There are many occasions when cells need to take in substances which are only present in small quantities around them. If the substance has a lower concentration outside the cell than inside, then we would expect the substance to diffuse out of the cell.

If the cell needs this substance, then it has to do something to make it go *into* the cell instead of diffusing out of it. Cells can use energy to make substances move across their membranes, *up* the concentration gradient. This process is called **active transport**. The energy needed to do this is provided by respiration. Aerobic respiration, in mitochondria in the cell, releases energy for the cell to use. Some of this energy is used for active transport, moving substances against their concentration gradients.

### KEY WORDS

**active transport:** the movement of molecules or ions through a cell membrane from a region of lower concentration to a region of higher concentration (i.e. against a concentration gradient) using energy from respiration

In plants, for example, root hair cells take in nitrate ions from the soil. The concentration of nitrate ions inside the root hair cell is usually higher than their concentration in the soil. The diffusion gradient for the nitrate ions is out of the root hair, and into the soil. But the root hair cells are still able to take nitrate ions in, using active transport. Figure 3.14 shows how they do this.

There are special **carrier proteins** in the cell membrane of the root hair cells. These proteins pick up nitrate ions from outside the cell, and then change shape so that they push the nitrate ions through the cell membrane and into the cytoplasm of the cell. Energy – provided by the mitochondria, which carry out aerobic respiration – is needed to produce the shape change in the carrier protein.

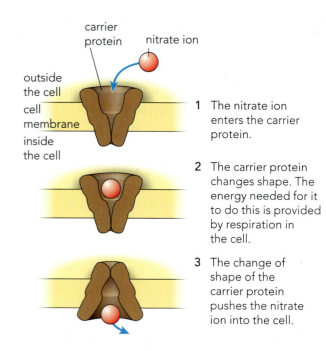

1. The nitrate ion enters the carrier protein.
2. The carrier protein changes shape. The energy needed for it to do this is provided by respiration in the cell.
3. The change of shape of the carrier protein pushes the nitrate ion into the cell.

Figure 3.14: How active transport happens.

> **KEY WORDS**
>
> **carrier proteins** (or **protein carriers**): protein molecules in cell membranes that can use energy to change shape and move ions or molecules into or out of a cell

## SUMMARY

| |
|---|
| Diffusion is the net movement of molecules or ions from a high concentration to a lower concentration, as a result of their random movement and kinetic energy. |
| Oxygen and carbon dioxide enter and leave cells by diffusion through the cell membranes, down a concentration gradient. |
| An increase in temperature, concentration gradient or surface area speeds up diffusion into a cell. This can be investigated using pieces of agar jelly. |
| Water is important in organisms as a solvent, for example in digestion, excretion and transport. |
| Water diffuses through partially permeable membranes, including cell membranes, by osmosis. |
| Dialysis tubing is partially permeable and can be used to investigate osmosis. |
| Animal cells burst in pure water and shrink when placed in a concentrated solution. Plant cells do not burst in pure water because their cell wall stops this happening. |
| A solution containing a lot of water has a high water potential; in osmosis, water diffuses down a water potential gradient. |

## 3 Movement into and out of cells

### CONTINUED

> A plant cell in pure water takes up water by osmosis and becomes turgid, as its contents exert outward pressure on the cell wall. A plant cell in a concentrated solution loses water by osmosis and becomes flaccid and may plasmolyse.

Active transport is the movement of particles across a cell membrane, up the concentration gradient, using energy from respiration.

> Protein carriers in cell membranes change shape to move substances across the cell membrane during active transport.

### PROJECT

#### Making a good cup of tea

Tea leaves are dried leaves from a camellia plant (*Camellia sinensis* is the tea plant). When hot water is added to tea leaves, colour and flavour molecules diffuse out of the tea leaves and into the water.

You are going to investigate some factors that make a really good cup of tea.

Here are some ideas for questions to investigate. You might also think of some questions of your own.

- Does the temperature of the water affect the rate at which the molecules diffuse out of the tea bag?
- Does the temperature of the water affect the flavour of the tea?
- Do different kinds of tea bag affect the diffusion of substances out of the tea leaves and into the water?
- Does adding milk to the cup before you add the water affect the diffusion of molecules out of the tea leaves?

Work in a group of three or four.

Start by deciding on a question to investigate. Then plan how you will do your experiment. Remember to change only one variable – your independent variable. Think carefully about how you will measure your dependent variable, and how you will try to standardise other variables.

You could try to predict the results you would expect to get. Think about how you will record them, and how you will use them to answer the question you are investigating.

## EXAM-STYLE QUESTIONS

1 Diffusion is a result of the movement of particles. How does each particle move?
   A down a concentration gradient
   B in one direction only
   C randomly
   D up a concentration gradient [1]

2 Where does the energy for diffusion come from?
   A glucose
   B kinetic energy of molecules and ions
   C respiration in mitochondria
   D sunlight [1]

3 Which change would increase the rate at which a substance diffuses across a membrane?
   A a decrease in concentration gradient
   B a decrease in the surface area of the membrane
   C an increase in distance across the membrane
   D an increase in temperature [1]

4 The table shows information about diffusion, osmosis and active transport. Which row is correct?

|   | Diffusion | Osmosis | Active transport |
|---|---|---|---|
| A | uses energy from respiration | always involves a partially permeable membrane | uses protein carriers in membranes |
| B | uses kinetic energy of molecules and ions | uses kinetic energy of water molecules | involves movement up a concentration gradient |
| C | uses protein carriers in membranes | involves movement up a concentration gradient | always involves a partially permeable membrane |
| D | always involves a partially permeable membrane | uses protein carriers in membranes | uses energy from respiration |

[1]

5 Which process involves active transport?
   A the uptake of carbon dioxide by a cell in a plant leaf
   B the uptake of magnesium ions by a root hair cell
   C the uptake of oxygen by an animal cell
   D the uptake of water by a root hair cell [1]

# 3 Movement into and out of cells

## CONTINUED

**6** A learner investigated how temperature affected the rate at which a dye moved through a piece of agar jelly.

She filled seven test-tubes with a solution of red dye. She placed each tube into a water-bath at a different temperature and left them for ten minutes.

She cut seven cubes of jelly. She placed each cube into one of the tubes containing the red dye. She measured the time taken for the cubes to change colour.

This graph shows her results.

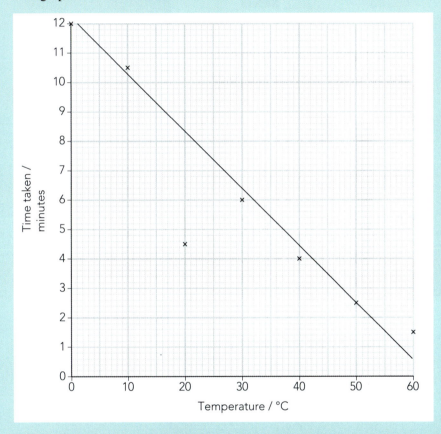

**a** Name **and describe** the process by which the dye moved through the jelly. [3]
**b** **Suggest** why the learner left the tubes of red dye in the water-baths for ten minutes. [1]
**c** List **two** variables that the learner should standardise (keep the same) in her experiment. [2]
**d i** One of the learner's results is anomalous. **Identify** this result and **explain** why you think it is anomalous. [2]
  **ii** Describe the trend or pattern shown by the results. [1]
  **iii** Use your knowledge of diffusion to explain the results. [2]

[Total: 11]

> **COMMAND WORDS**
>
> **describe:** state the points of a topic / give characteristics and main features
>
> **suggest:** apply knowledge and understanding to situations where there are a range of valid responses in order to make proposals/ put forward considerations
>
> **identify:** name/ select/recognise
>
> **explain:** set out purposes or reasons / make the relationships between things evident / provide why and/or how and support with relevant evidence

## CONTINUED

7 a Describe what is meant by osmosis. [3]

b Compare the effect of immersing an animal cell and a plant cell in pure water. Explain the reasons for any differences that you describe. [6]

[Total: 9]

8 This bar chart shows the concentration of potassium ions and sodium ions in a sample of pond water, and in the cells of a plant growing in the water.

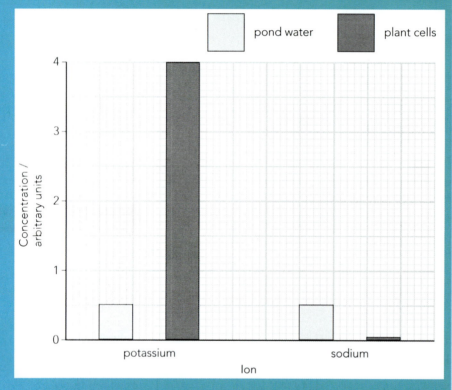

a Describe the differences between the concentrations of the ions in the pond water and in the plant cells. [3]

b Use the data in the graph to suggest how the ions move between the pond water and the plant cells. Explain your answer. [2]

c Describe how the process you have described in your answer to b takes place. [4]

[Total: 9]

## 3 Movement into and out of cells

### SELF-EVALUATION CHECKLIST

After studying this chapter, think about how confident you are with the different topics. This will help you to see any gaps in your knowledge and help you to learn more effectively.

| I can | See Topic… | Needs more work | Almost there | Confident to move on |
|---|---|---|---|---|
| describe diffusion, referring to particles and kinetic energy | 3.1 | | | |
| explain what is meant by a diffusion gradient | 3.1 | | | |
| explain why diffusion is important to organisms | 3.1 | | | |
| describe how to investigate factors that affect diffusion | 3.1 | | | |
| describe osmosis, referring to diffusion of water through a partially permeable membrane | 3.2 | | | |
| describe how to investigate osmosis using dialysis tubing | 3.2 | | | |
| describe what happens when animal or plant cells are immersed in solutions of different concentrations | 3.2 | | | |
| explain how water in their cells helps to support plants | 3.2 | | | |
| describe osmosis, using the term *water potential* | 3.2 | | | |
| explain what happens when animal or plant cells are immersed in solutions of different concentrations | 3.2 | | | |
| describe active transport | 3.3 | | | |
| explain how active transport happens, including the role of protein carriers in membranes | 3.3 | | | |

# Chapter 4
# Biological molecules

**IN THIS CHAPTER YOU WILL:**

- find out about the components of carbohydrates, proteins and lipids
- use food tests to detect the presence of different biological molecules
- learn about the structure of DNA.

# 4 Biological molecules

## GETTING STARTED

Work with a partner.

Can you answer these questions about elements, compounds, atoms and molecules?

1. Oxygen gas is made up of pairs of oxygen atoms combined together.
   - a What is the formula for oxygen gas?
   - b What do we call a particle made up of two or more atoms combined together?
   - c Is oxygen an element or a compound?

2. Glucose is made up of the elements that have the symbols C, H and O.
   - a What do C, H and O stand for?
   - b One molecule of glucose contains 6 atoms of carbon, 12 atoms of hydrogen and 6 atoms of oxygen. Can you write the formula for glucose?
   - c Is glucose an element, a compound or a mixture?

## HOW DID LIFE ON EARTH START?

One of the greatest mysteries of life on Earth is how it began. Today, all living things are formed from other living things. But how did it all begin? How did non-living substances on Earth first form life?

Living cells are made up of special types of molecules that are not often found in non-living things. Scientists think that these molecules may have formed from simpler substances when the Earth was still very young, perhaps 4 billion years ago. The mixture of chemicals that we know existed in the seas and atmosphere at that time, and the energy provided by volcanic eruptions and lightning strikes, could possibly explain how these molecules of life were first produced.

Another possibility is that at least some of these molecules arrived on Earth from outer space. Meteorites are rocks that arrive on Earth from space. They come from the asteroid belt, far away towards the edge of the solar system. Some meteorites contain amino acids, which are what proteins are made of. Did amino acids, delivered to Earth from space, perhaps contribute to the origin of life?

Many scientists are researching these questions. If we can understand how life first arose on Earth, this can help us to answer another important question – is there life anywhere else in the universe?

### Discussion questions

1. Most scientists think that all life on Earth today comes from other life. Suggest why scientists think it is unlikely that life could arise from non-living things today.

2. Recent discoveries on Mars suggest that there used to be liquid water there. It is possible that simple life once existed on Mars. In your opinion, what precautions should we take if we send humans to Mars one day?

# 4.1 Carbohydrates, fats and proteins

What is a human made of? The most abundant compound in our bodies is water, which makes up around 62% of our total body mass. About 16% is protein, another 16% is fat, and around 1% is carbohydrate. The remaining 6% is calcium and phosphorus (mostly in bones) and some other elements such as potassium, sodium, phosphate and chloride ions. DNA makes up less than 1% of our mass.

In this chapter, you will find out about the three main organic compounds – carbohydrates, fats and proteins – that make up the bodies of all living things. If you are studying the Supplement, you also need to know about DNA.

## Carbohydrates

**Carbohydrates** include starch, cellulose and sugar. Carbohydrate molecules are made from three elements – carbon, hydrogen and oxygen. One molecule of carbohydrate contains about twice as many hydrogen atoms as carbon or oxygen atoms.

The simplest types of carbohydrate, with the smallest molecules, are **sugars**. Sugars taste sweet. They are soluble in water.

One type of sugar is **glucose**. A glucose molecule is made of six carbon atoms, twelve hydrogen atoms and six oxygen atoms. Its formula is $C_6H_{12}O_6$. These atoms are arranged to form a hexagon shape (Figure 4.1).

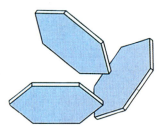

**Figure 4.1:** Glucose molecules are quite small and have a hexagon shape.

Glucose is the way that carbohydrates are transported around the human body. Glucose dissolves in blood plasma, which delivers it to every cell. Cells need glucose for energy.

Glucose molecules can link together in chains, to form much larger molecules. In animals, the large molecules that are formed are **glycogen**. The liver helps to keep the concentration of glucose in the blood constant – you can read about this in Chapter 13. If there is too much glucose in the blood, the liver links glucose molecules together to make glycogen. Glycogen is stored in the liver cells. It can be broken down to form glucose again when the body needs it.

In plants, glucose molecules are linked together in a slightly different way, to make **starch** (Figure 4.2). Starch is stored in plant cells. It can be broken down to form glucose again when the plant needs it.

> **KEY WORDS**
>
> **carbohydrates:** substances that include sugars, starch and cellulose; they contain carbon, hydrogen and oxygen
>
> **sugars:** carbohydrates that have relatively small molecules; they are soluble in water and they taste sweet
>
> **glucose:** a sugar that is used in respiration to release energy
>
> **glycogen:** a carbohydrate that is used as an energy store in animal cells
>
> **starch:** a carbohydrate that is used as an energy store in plant cells

Plants also make another carbohydrate, called cellulose. Cellulose molecules are also made of many glucose molecules linked in a chain, but they form straight lines instead of coiling into a spiral. Cellulose is used for making plant cell walls.

## 4 Biological molecules

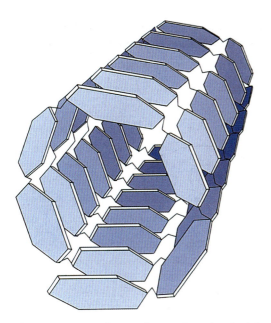

**Figure 4.2:** This is a small part of a starch molecule. It is made from many glucose molecules linked together in a long chain, which coils into a spiral shape.

You can detect the presence of starch using **iodine solution**. This changes from brown to blue-black if starch is present (Figure 4.3).

**Figure 4.3:** The black colour shows that starch is present in the potato.

Most sugars can be detected using **Benedict's solution**. Benedict's solution is blue, and it changes to orange-red when it is heated with **reducing sugars** such as glucose. The colour change is gradual, so the blue solution becomes green and yellow before finally turning orange-red (Figure 4.4).

**Figure 4.4:** Positive results of the Benedict's test. The tube on the left contains a small amount of reducing sugar – the blue Benedict's solution has changed to green. The tube on the right contains a large amount of reducing sugar.

### KEY WORDS

**iodine solution:** a solution of iodine in potassium iodide; it is orange-brown, and turns blue-black when mixed with starch

**Benedict's solution:** a blue liquid that turns orange-red when heated with reducing sugar

**reducing sugars:** sugars such as glucose, which turn Benedict's solution orange-red when heated together

## Questions

1. Give **two** similarities and **one** difference between a molecule of starch and a molecule of cellulose.
2. Name **one** carbohydrate that is found in both plants and animals.

71

## EXPERIMENTAL SKILLS 4.1

### Testing for carbohydrates

You are going to test several different foods to find out if they contain starch or sugar.

> **You will need:**
> - a selection of foods to test, kept separate from one another
> - a knife to cut the foods into small pieces
> - a white tile
> - a small bottle of iodine solution, with a dropper
> - a water-bath set at about 80 °C (you can use an electric one or you can make your own water-bath by heating water in a beaker over a burner – see Figure 4.5)
> - a thermometer to check the temperature of the water-bath
> - several large test-tubes (boiling tubes), and a beaker to stand them in
> - some Benedict's solution, with a dropper.

### Method: Testing for starch

1. Read through the instructions, and decide which foods you are going to test for starch.

2. Construct a results chart ready to fill in as you work. You will need a column for the food, another column for your observations, and a third column for your conclusion.

> When you record your results, make sure that you state the colour that you see. Do not write "no change".

2. Take a small piece of the first food and place it on the white tile. Add a drop or two of iodine solution. If the iodine solution stays brown, there is no starch in the food. If you see a dark blue or black colour, then starch is present.

3. Repeat with several other samples of different foods.

### Method: Testing for reducing sugars

1. Read through the instructions and construct a results chart.

2. Take some of your first food and cut it into very small pieces. Put the pieces into a boiling tube and add a little water. Shake the tube to try to dissolve any sugar in the food.

3. Add some Benedict's solution – enough to cover the food. Shake to mix.

4. If you are using an electric water-bath, take a beaker and fill it with water from the water-bath. Stand the beaker in the water-bath. Stand the test-tube in the beaker. If you have made your own water-bath, simply stand the test-tube in the beaker of hot water (Figure 4.5).

5. Watch as the mixture of food and Benedict's solution heats up. If it stays blue, there is no reducing sugar in the food. If it changes to red, there is sugar in the food.

6. Repeat with several other samples of different foods.

Figure 4.5: Heating a mixture of Benedict's solution and food in a water-bath, to test for reducing sugar.

### Questions

1. Make a list of the foods that contained starch, and the foods that contained reducing sugar.

2. Do these foods come from plants, or from animals?

## ACTIVITY 4.1

### Comparing reducing sugar content

Work in a group of two or three for this activity.

When you tested foods for reducing sugar, you probably noticed that the red colour took a few minutes to appear.

The less time it takes for the red colour to appear, the more reducing sugar there is in the food.

Discuss how you could use this fact to compare the quantity of reducing sugar in three different foods. Write a list of instructions that someone could follow that would make it easy for them to make this comparison.

### Peer assessment

When your group has completed the instructions, exchange the instructions with another group.

How well have they written their instructions? Would they be easy to follow? Would they give a correct indication of which food contained the most reducing sugar?

Give feedback to the group about what they have done well, and also one or two things that could be improved.

When you get your own feedback, think about it carefully. If you were asked to plan a similar experiment in future, what would you do differently?

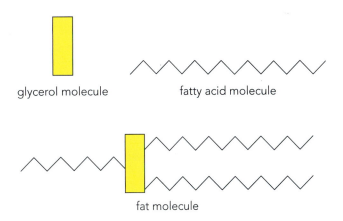

**Figure 4.6:** A fat molecule is made from a glycerol molecule and three fatty acid molecules combined together.

## Fats and oils

**Fats** and **oils** are also known as **lipids**. A fat is a lipid that is solid at room temperature, and an oil is a lipid that is liquid at room temperature.

Fats and oils contain the three elements carbon, hydrogen and oxygen. You may remember that carbohydrates also contain these elements. However, in fats, each molecule contains much less oxygen than is found in a carbohydrate molecule.

Fat molecules are made of two kinds of smaller molecule – glycerol and fatty acids. Figure 4.6 shows how these are joined together to make a fat molecule.

Fats are important for making cell membranes. They are also used as energy stores. Mammals often have a layer of cells containing fat droplets beneath the skin. This fat-containing tissue is both an energy store and a heat insulating layer.

Fats and oils do not dissolve in water. However, they do dissolve in ethanol. We can use this to detect their presence in food. First, the food is shaken with ethanol, to allow any fats in it to dissolve in the ethanol. Next, the ethanol is poured into a clean tube containing water. If there are fats in the ethanol, they form tiny droplets in the water, which give it a milky appearance (Figure 4.7). The mixture of tiny droplets in water is called an **emulsion**, so this test is called the ethanol emulsion test.

### KEY WORDS

**fats:** lipids that are solid at room temperature

**oils:** lipids that are liquid at room temperature

**lipids:** substances containing carbon, hydrogen and oxygen; they are insoluble in water and are used as energy stores in organisms

**emulsion:** a liquid containing two substances that do not fully mix; one of them forms tiny droplets dispersed throughout the other

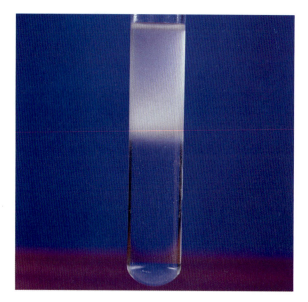

Figure 4.7: This milky appearance is what you see when you get a positive result using the ethanol emulsion test for fats and oils.

## Questions

3  Animals that live in very cold places often have especially thick layers of fat underneath the skin (Figure 4.8). Suggest why.

4  Fat stores contain more energy per gram than carbohydrate stores. Suggest why birds that are about to go on long migrations build up stores of fat before they fly.

Figure 4.8: Bearded seals have a really thick layer of fat underneath their skin.

### EXPERIMENTAL SKILLS 4.2

**Testing for fats and oils**

You are going to test a selection of different foods to find out if they contain fats or oils.

**You will need:**
- a selection of foods to test, kept separate from one another
- a knife to cut the foods into small pieces
- several very clean test-tubes
- a small bottle of ethanol, with a dropper
- some distilled water.

**Method**

1  Read through the instructions and construct a results chart.

2  Take some of your first food and cut it into very small pieces. Put the pieces into a very clean test-tube and add a little ethanol. Shake the tube to try to dissolve any fats or oils in the food.

3  Take another clean test-tube and put some distilled water into it. Very carefully, pour the ethanol from the first tube into the distilled water. Do not let any of the food go in! If you see a milky white colour appearing, this shows that there was fat in the food.

# 4 Biological molecules

## Proteins

**Protein** molecules contain four elements – carbon, hydrogen, oxygen and nitrogen. Some proteins, but not all, also contain a small quantity of the element sulfur.

A protein molecule is made of a long chain of smaller molecules, called **amino acids** (Figure 4.9). There are 20 different kinds of amino acid. Each kind of protein has different amino acids linked together in a precise order. If even one amino acid is changed or moves into a different place in the protein molecule, then we get a different protein. So, there is an almost infinite number of different kinds of protein that can be made.

Proteins have many different functions in organisms. All enzymes are proteins. (You will study enzymes in the next chapter.) **Antibodies**, which help to protect the body against **pathogens**, are proteins. So is haemoglobin, the red pigment that transports oxygen in mammalian blood. Proteins are also important for forming cell membranes in all organisms. In humans, hair and fingernails are made from a protein called **keratin**.

**Figure 4.10:** These are negative and positive results of the biuret test. The tube on the left has no protein, but the one on the right does contain protein.

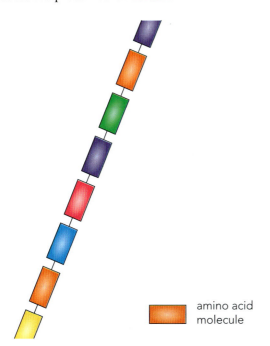

**Figure 4.9:** A small part of a protein molecule. Proteins are made of long chains of amino acid molecules.

To test for proteins, we use **biuret reagent**. This is blue, and it changes to violet when in contact with proteins (Figure 4.10).

### KEY WORDS

**protein:** a substance whose molecules are made of many amino acids linked together; each different protein has a different sequence of amino acids

**amino acids:** substances with molecules containing carbon, hydrogen, oxygen and nitrogen; there are 20 different amino acids found in organisms

**antibodies:** molecules secreted by white blood cells, which bind to pathogens and help to destroy them

**pathogens:** microorganisms that cause disease, such as bacteria

**keratin:** the protein that forms hair

**biuret reagent:** a blue solution that turns purple when mixed with amino acids or proteins

## Questions

5 Which element is found in all proteins, but not in carbohydrates and fats?

6 Some proteins are soluble in water, but some are not. Do you think that the protein keratin is soluble in water? Explain your answer.

## EXPERIMENTAL SKILLS 4.3

### Testing for proteins

You are going to test a selection of different foods to find out if they contain proteins.

You may find it helpful to start by testing something that you know contains protein, such as cooked egg white. Keep a tube showing a negative result (biuret reagent added to water, which will be blue) with the tube showing a positive result (violet) in a test-tube rack, so you can refer to these to decide whether you have a negative or positive result in each of your food tests.

#### You will need:
- a selection of foods to test, kept separate from one another
- a knife to cut the foods into small pieces
- several clean test-tubes
- a small bottle of biuret solution with a dropper.

### Method

1. Read through the instructions and construct a results chart.
2. Take some of your first food and cut it into very small pieces. Put the pieces into a clean test-tube and add some biuret solution. Shake to mix.
3. Look for a change from blue to violet.

### KEY WORD

**DCPIP:** a purple liquid that becomes colourless when mixed with vitamin C

## EXPERIMENTAL SKILLS 4.4

### Testing for vitamin C

Vitamin C is not a carbohydrate, fat or protein. We can test for it using a purple solution called **DCPIP**. DCPIP loses its colour when vitamin C is mixed with it.

#### You will need:
- some purple DCPIP solution, kept covered (if it mixes with oxygen from the air, it gradually loses its colour)
- two or more dropper pipettes
- several test-tubes
- some foods to test for vitamin C – for example lemon juice and other fruit juices, milk, potatoes, cooked rice
- a pestle and mortar to crush any non-liquid foods (such as the potato or rice).

### Method

1. Choose the foods you are going to test, and then construct a results chart.
2. Put about 1 cm depth of DCPIP into a test-tube. Use a dropper pipette to add lemon juice to the DCPIP. Lemon juice contains a lot of vitamin C, so this should make the DCPIP lose its colour.
3. Now test at least four other kinds of food. If the food is solid, you will need to mash it up first, and then mix it with distilled water, before adding it to DCPIP.

### REFLECTION

With a partner, discuss good ways of remembering the different reagents used for the four tests you have met in this topic. Which methods do you think are likely to work best for you?

## 4.2 The structure of DNA

> DNA stands for deoxyribonucleic acid. You do not need to remember this long name.

DNA is the material that makes up our genes and chromosomes. The nucleus of every cell in the body (apart from red blood cells, which do not have a nucleus) contains DNA. We inherit our DNA from our parents.

DNA is an amazing molecule. It carries a 'code', which instructs the cell which amino acids to link together, in which sequence, to make proteins. The sequence of bases in the DNA molecule determines the sequence of the amino acids that are used to build a protein. You will find out more about this in Chapter 16.

Because proteins have so many different functions in organisms, DNA determines almost everything about an organism's body structure, and how its metabolic reactions take place.

DNA is made of smaller molecules called **nucleotides**. Each nucleotide contains a **base**. There are four bases, A, C, G and T.

A DNA molecule contains two chains of nucleotides, coiled around one another (Figure 4.11). This shape is called a double helix. The two chains or strands are held together by bonds that form between the bases of opposite strands. A always forms bonds with T, and C with G. This is called **complementary base pairing**.

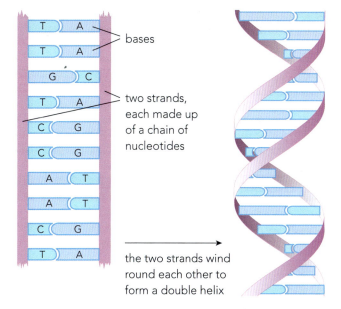

**Figure 4.11:** Part of a DNA molecule.

### KEY WORDS

**nucleotides:** molecules that are linked together into long chains, to make up a DNA molecule

**base:** one of the components of DNA; there are four bases, A, C, G and T, and their sequence determines the proteins that are made in a cell

**complementary base pairing:** the way in which the bases of the two strands of DNA pair up; A always pairs with T, and C with G

### SUMMARY

| |
|---|
| Carbohydrates are made of the elements C, H and O. Sugars, such as glucose, have relatively small molecules. Starch, glycogen and cellulose are made of many glucose molecules linked in a long chain. |
| Starch can be detected using the iodine test. Benedict's solution is used to test for reducing sugars. |
| Fats and oils are also made of the elements C, H and O. Another name for fats and oils is lipids. A lipid molecule is made of three fatty acid molecules combined with one glycerol molecule. |
| The ethanol emulsion test is used to detect the presence of fats and oils. |
| Proteins contain the elements C, H, O and N. A protein molecule is made of many amino acid molecules combined in a long chain. There are 20 different amino acids, and their specific sequence in the molecule determines the specific protein that is formed. |

## CONTINUED

Biuret reagent is used to test for proteins.

The DCPIP test is used to test for vitamin C.

DNA is made of two strands of nucleotides coiled to form a double helix.

The two strands are held together by bonds between pairs of bases. A pairs with T and C with G.

## PROJECT

### Modelling biological molecules

You are going to make models of some biological molecules.

Work in a group of three or four. Try to organise the class so that different groups work on different molecules.

Make your models using paper and card.

Different groups could make models of:

- starch and cellulose molecules – both made of glucose molecules linked in chains, but starch is coiled while cellulose is straight
- protein molecules – made of 20 different amino acids in different sequences
- fats and oils – made of glycerol and fatty acids
- DNA – made of two strands of nucleotides linked by bases

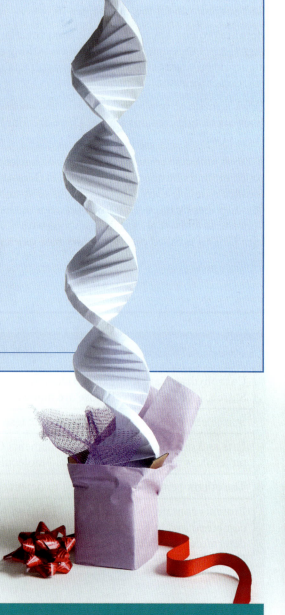

Figure 4.12: Modelling biological molecules.

## EXAM-STYLE QUESTIONS

1. Which liquid is used to test for proteins?
   A Benedict's solution
   B biuret reagent
   C DCPIP
   D iodine solution [1]

2. Which substance is made by linking amino acids together?
   A cellulose
   B fat
   C protein
   D vitamin C [1]

3. Which elements are contained in cellulose?
   A carbon and hydrogen only
   B carbon, hydrogen and oxygen
   C carbon, hydrogen and nitrogen
   D carbon, oxygen and nitrogen [1]

4. The table shows the results of tests on four samples of food.
   Which food contains **only** fat?

   |   | Iodine test | Benedict's test | Ethanol emulsion test | DCPIP test |
   |---|---|---|---|---|
   | A | brown | blue | milky white | purple |
   | B | blue-black | red | colourless | colourless |
   | C | brown | blue | colourless | purple |
   | D | blue-black | red | milky white | colourless |

   [1]

5. Which diagram shows part of a DNA molecule? [1]

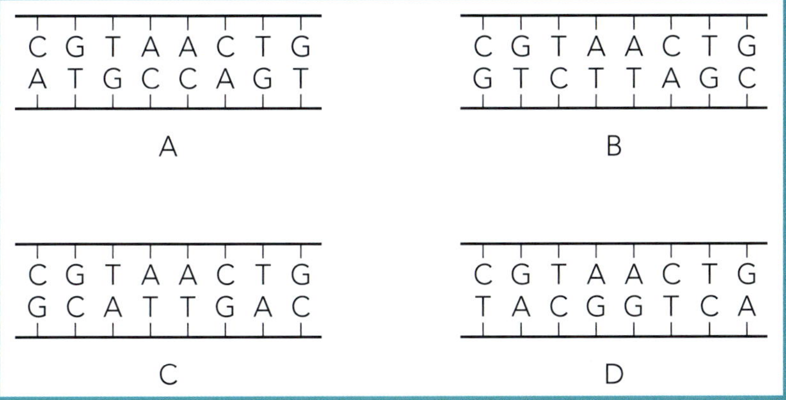

   ```
   C G T A A C T G          C G T A A C T G
   A T G C C A G T          G T C T T A G C
          A                        B

   C G T A A C T G          C G T A A C T G
   G C A T T G A C          T A C G G T C A
          C                        D
   ```

## CONTINUED

**6** Glucose, starch, glycogen and cellulose are carbohydrates.
  **a** Which of these substances are found in plants only, and not in animals? [1]
  **b** List the elements that the molecules of all these substances contain. [1]
  **c** Describe the structure of a starch molecule. [2]
  **d** Glucose is a reducing sugar. Describe how you could test a liquid to find out if it contains glucose. [3]
  [Total: 7]

> **COMMAND WORD**
>
> **describe:** state the points of a topic / give characteristics and main features

**7 a** Biuret reagent is used to test for proteins.
  These statements about the biuret test are incorrect. Write corrected versions of each statement.
  **i** To carry out the biuret test, add biuret solution to the food and heat gently. [1]
  **ii** If a food contains protein, biuret reagent turns from purple to blue. [1]
  **b** Ethanol is used to test for fats and oils.
  **i** Describe how you would carry out the ethanol test. [3]
  **ii** Describe what you would see if the test gives a positive result. [1]
  [Total: 6]

**8** Fruit juice can be tested to find out if it contains vitamin C by adding the juice to DCPIP. The less juice that has to be added to the DCPIP to make it lose its colour, the more vitamin C is contained in the juice.
Describe how you could compare the vitamin C content of fresh lemon juice and preserved lemon juice. [6]

**9** A sample of DNA was tested to find out which bases were present.
It was found that 30% of the bases were T.
  **a** What percentage of the bases would you expect to be A? Explain your answer. [2]
  **b** What percentage of the bases in the DNA would you expect to be C? Explain your answer. [2]
  **c** Outline the function of DNA in a cell. [3]
  [Total: 7]

# 4 Biological molecules

## SELF-EVALUATION CHECKLIST

After studying this chapter, think about how confident you are with the different topics. This will help you to see any gaps in your knowledge and help you to learn more effectively.

| I can | See Topic… | Needs more work | Almost there | Confident to move on |
|---|---|---|---|---|
| list the chemical elements that make up carbohydrates, fats and proteins | 4.1 | | | |
| state that starch, cellulose and glycogen are made from glucose | 4.1 | | | |
| state that fats and oils are made from fatty acids and glycerol | 4.1 | | | |
| state that proteins are made from amino acids | 4.1 | | | |
| describe how to use the Benedict's test for reducing sugars | 4.1 | | | |
| describe how to use the iodine test for starch | 4.1 | | | |
| describe how to use the biuret test for proteins | 4.1 | | | |
| describe how to use the ethanol emulsion test for fats and oils | 4.1 | | | |
| describe how to use the DCPIP test for vitamin C | 4.1 | | | |
| describe the structure of a DNA molecule, including reference to base pairing between A and T, C and G | 4.2 | | | |

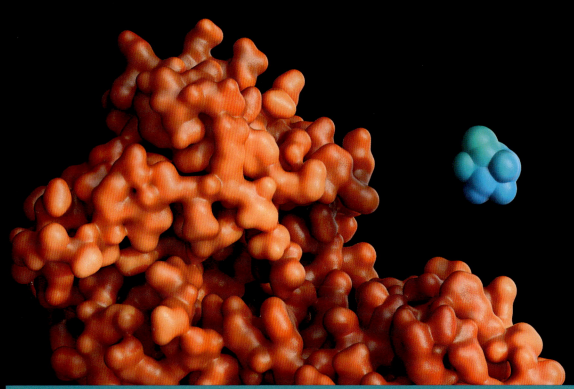

# Chapter 5
# Enzymes

**IN THIS CHAPTER YOU WILL:**

- learn about enzymes, and how they work as catalysts
- investigate how temperature and pH affect the activity of enzymes
- > find out why enzymes are specific, and why temperature and pH affect them.

# 5 Enzymes

## GETTING STARTED

Work with a partner.

Here are some statements about chemical reactions. Two of them are not correct.

Can you identify these incorrect statements? When you think you have identified them, make changes to each of them to correct them.

In a chemical reaction:

- one or more substances are changed to one or more new substances.
- a large molecule may be split into smaller molecules.
- atoms of one element are rearranged to make atoms of other elements.
- small molecules may combine to form larger molecules.
- products are changed to reactants.

## LACTOSE INTOLERANCE

All mammals feed their young on milk (Figure 5.1). Milk is an excellent food – it contains carbohydrates, fats, proteins, minerals and vitamins.

Humans are mammals and we feed on milk as babies. To help babies digest the carbohydrates in milk, they produce an enzyme called lactase. This enzyme breaks a sugar called lactose into smaller molecules, which can be absorbed into the blood.

Most people stop making lactase once they are old enough to take in food other than milk. But, in a few parts of the world, including Europe, people continue to make lactase all their lives. They can drink milk and eat dairy products (foods made from milk), with no problems. In Europe, dairy products are a normal part of many people's diets.

For everyone else, though, eating these foods makes them feel ill. They are intolerant to lactose, because they do not make lactase. The lactose is not broken down in their digestive system. It stays inside the **alimentary canal** (the tube that food passes through). This makes water move into the canal by osmosis. All this extra water in the alimentary canal can give a person diarrhoea. Also, the lactose provides food for the bacteria that live in the alimentary canal. As the bacteria feed on the lactose, they produce gases as a waste product. This can give the person abdominal pain, and cause flatulence.

What is the solution to lactose intolerance? The simplest solution is not to eat foods containing lactose. Another approach is to take pills that contain the enzyme lactase. If a lactose-intolerant person swallows one of these pills before eating dairy products, they may avoid these unpleasant symptoms.

### Discussion questions

1. If most people stop making lactase when they are adults, there must be some advantage in this. Discuss what this might be.

2. Use your knowledge of osmosis to explain why having undigested lactose in the intestines can give someone diarrhoea.

**Figure 5.1:** Young guanacos feed on milk from their mother, just like all young mammals.

## 5.1 Biological catalysts

Many chemical reactions can be speeded up by substances called catalysts. A **catalyst** alters the rate of a chemical reaction, without being changed itself.

Within any living organism, chemical reactions are taking place all the time. These reactions are called metabolic reactions. Almost every metabolic reaction is controlled by catalysts called **enzymes**. Without enzymes, the reactions would take place very slowly or not at all. Enzymes ensure that the rates of metabolic reactions are great enough to sustain life.

For example, inside the intestines, large molecules are broken down to smaller ones in the process of digestion. These reactions are speeded up by enzymes. A different enzyme is needed for each kind of nutrient. For example, starch is digested to a sugar called maltose by an enzyme called **amylase**. Proteins are digested to amino acids by **protease**.

These enzymes are also found in plants – for example, in germinating seeds they digest the food stores for the growing seedling. Many seeds contain stores of starch. As the seed soaks up water, the enzyme amylase becomes active. Amylase catalyses the reaction in which starch breaks down to maltose. Starch is insoluble, but maltose is soluble. So, maltose can easily be transported to the embryo in the seed. The embryo uses it to provide energy for growth.

Maltose can be broken down to provide glucose molecules that can be linked together to make cellulose molecules. Cellulose is necessary for the cell walls of the new cells produced as the embryo grows.

Another enzyme which speeds up the breakdown of a substance is **catalase**. Catalase works inside all the cells of living organisms. It breaks down hydrogen peroxide to water and oxygen. This is necessary because hydrogen peroxide is produced by many of the chemical reactions which take place inside cells. Hydrogen peroxide is a very dangerous substance and must be broken down immediately.

$$\text{hydrogen peroxide} \xrightarrow{\text{catalase}} \text{water} + \text{oxygen}$$

Not all enzymes help to break things down. Many enzymes help to make large molecules from small ones. For example, enzymes help to link amino acids together to make proteins inside cells.

Many industries now use enzymes, and the production of enzymes on a large scale is becoming a very profitable major industry (Figure 5.2). You can find out about some of these industrial uses of enzymes in Chapter 20.

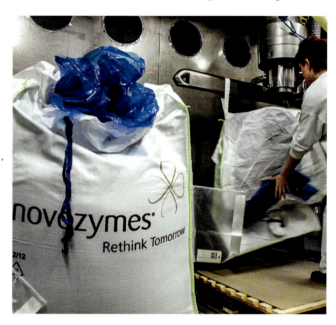

**Figure 5.2:** If you see 'zyme' on the end of a word, it is almost certainly an enzyme. This factory produces huge quantities of enzymes for other industries to use.

> ### KEY WORDS
>
> **alimentary canal:** the part of the digestive system through which food passes as it moves from the mouth to the anus
>
> **catalyst:** a substance that increases the rate of a chemical reaction and is not changed by the reaction
>
> **enzymes:** proteins that are involved in all metabolic reactions, where they function as biological catalysts
>
> **amylase:** an enzyme that catalyses the breakdown of starch to maltose
>
> **protease:** an enzyme that catalyses the breakdown of protein to amino acids
>
> **catalase:** an enzyme that catalyses the breakdown of hydrogen peroxide to water and oxygen

## Naming enzymes

Enzymes are named according to the reaction that they catalyse. Their names often end in -ase. For example, enzymes that catalyse the breakdown of carbohydrates are called **carbohydrases**. If they break down proteins, they are proteases. If they break down fats and oils (lipids) they are **lipases**.

Sometimes, enzymes are given more specific names than this. For example, we have seen that the carbohydrase that breaks down starch is called amylase. A carbohydrase that breaks down maltose is called **maltase**. A carbohydrase that breaks down sucrose is called **sucrase**.

The substance that an enzyme changes is called its **substrate**. The substrate of amylase is starch. The substrate of lipase is lipids.

Notice how careful you have to be to spell the name of the enzyme and its substrate correctly, and to write clearly. *Maltose* and *maltase* can look almost the same if you do not write carefully.

> **KEY WORDS**
>
> **carbohydrases:** enzymes that break down carbohydrates
>
> **lipases:** enzymes that break down lipids (fats and oils)
>
> **maltase:** an enzyme that catalyses the breakdown of maltose to glucose
>
> **sucrase:** an enzyme that breaks down sucrose
>
> **substrate:** the substance that an enzyme causes to react

## Questions

1. Explain why enzymes are called *biological catalysts*.
2. You read about the enzyme lactase at the start of this chapter.
   a. What type of enzyme is lactase?
   b. Name the substrate of lactase.

## How enzymes work

Each type of enzyme has molecules with a very specific shape. The enzyme molecule has a 'dent' in it, called the **active site** (Figure 5.3).

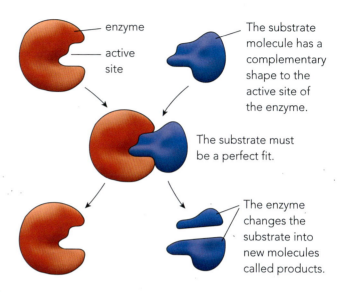

**Figure 5.3:** How an enzyme catalyses a reaction.

An enzyme works by allowing a molecule of its substrate to fit into the active site, where the substrate and the enzyme bind together. For this to happen, the fit has to be perfect. We say that the shape of the enzyme and the shape of the substrate are **complementary** to one another.

When the substrate is in the active site and bound to the enzyme, the enzyme makes the substrate change into a new substance called the **product**. Then the product breaks away from the enzyme. Now the enzyme is free, and ready to bind with another substrate molecule.

In Figure 5.3, the substrate is a single molecule, and it is broken into two product molecules. Enzymes can also catalyse reactions where two substrate molecules bind with its active site and are joined together to form a single product molecule.

> **KEY WORDS**
>
> **active site:** the part of an enzyme molecule to which the substrate temporarily binds
>
> **complementary:** with a perfect mirror-image shape
>
> **product:** the new substance formed by a chemical reaction

You have probably taken a few minutes to read about how enzymes work, and to look at the diagram in Figure 5.3. In that time, a single enzyme molecule could have catalysed millions of reactions. The enzyme catalase is the fastest enzyme known. One catalase molecule can break down an almost unbelievable 44 million hydrogen peroxide molecules in one second.

The short-lived structure that forms as the substrate slots into the enzyme's active site has its own name. It is called the **enzyme–substrate complex**.

> ### ACTIVITY 5.1
>
> #### Enzyme specificity
>
> Each enzyme can only catalyse reactions with one type of substrate. This is described as enzyme **specificity**.
>
> Take a minute or two to think about why enzymes are specific. Then turn to a partner and discuss your ideas together.
>
> Be ready to share your ideas with the rest of the class.

> ### KEY WORDS
>
> **enzyme–substrate complex:** the short-lived structure formed as the substrate binds temporarily to the active site of an enzyme
>
> **specificity:** of enzymes, only able to act on a particular (specific) substrate

## 5.2 Factors that affect enzymes

We have seen that enzymes act very quickly. Each enzyme molecule can change many substrate molecules to products every second.

But there are some factors that can affect this speed of action. Enzymes are very sensitive to temperature and pH. Each kind of enzyme has a particular temperature and pH at which it works fastest (Figures 5.4 and 5.5). These are called the **optimum** temperature, and the optimum pH, for that enzyme.

> ### KEY WORD
>
> **optimum:** best; for example, the optimum temperature of an enzyme is the temperature at which its activity is greatest

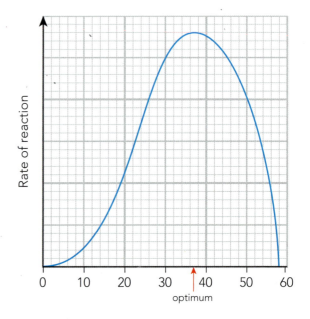

**Figure 5.4:** The effect of temperature on enzyme activity.

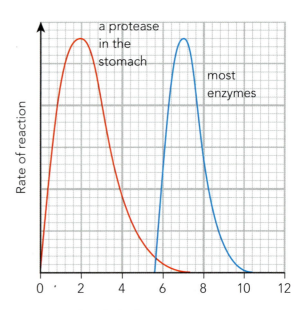

**Figure 5.5:** The effect of pH on enzyme activity.

## Questions

3 Look at Figure 5.4. Describe what is shown on the graph. ('Describe' means state the main points in words; give main features that you can see. When you are describing a graph it is a good idea to quote figures, with units.)

4 Look at Figure 5.5.
   a What is the optimum pH of the protease in the stomach?
   b What is the optimum pH of most enzymes?
   c What is the **range** of pH values at which most enzymes are able to work?

### EXPERIMENTAL SKILLS 5.1

**Investigating the effect of pH on the activity of catalase**

You are going to find out how changing the pH affects the rate at which catalase breaks down hydrogen peroxide to water and oxygen.

You will change the pH using **buffer solutions**. A buffer solution is a liquid that has a particular pH. It keeps this pH the same, even if chemical reactions take place.

> **KEY WORDS**
>
> **range:** the lowest to the highest value
>
> **buffer solution:** a liquid that has a known pH, and that keeps that pH steady all the time

You will use catalase from celery or any other plant such as a potato, or some leaves. You can mash up the celery in water, so that the catalase forms a solution in the water. It's best if this is done once for the whole class.

> **You will need:**
> - a blender or liquidiser, or a pestle and mortar
> - some fresh plant material such as celery
> - distilled water
> - muslin or a sieve, and a filter funnel
> - some 3% hydrogen peroxide solution
> - five 50 cm$^3$ beakers
> - small measuring cylinders or syringes, to measure 5 cm$^3$ and 10 cm$^3$
> - five buffer solutions, each with a different pH
> - 15 small squares of filter paper, all the same size (about 5 mm × 5 mm)
> - forceps (tweezers)
> - a stopwatch or timer.

**Before you start**

Practise using the forceps to pick up the little pieces of filter paper – it isn't easy!

**Method**

1 Cut up some celery and put it into a blender. Add water and blend. If you don't have a blender, cut the celery into small pieces and grind it with water using a pestle and mortar.

2 Pour the mixture of celery and water through some muslin, using a filter funnel, or through a sieve. (It takes too long if you use filter paper.) This will separate out most of the bits of celery from the liquid.

3 You now have a liquid containing catalase. Label a beaker 'catalase solution' and pour some of this liquid into it.

4 Copy the results table below.

| pH | Time taken for paper to rise to top / s | | | |
|---|---|---|---|---|
| | 1st try | 2nd try | 3rd try | Mean |
| | | | | |
| | | | | |
| | | | | |
| | | | | |
| | | | | |

## CONTINUED

5 Find out which buffer solutions you will be using. Write them into your results chart. Label each of the small beakers with the pH of one of the buffer solutions.

6 Measure 5 cm³ of hydrogen peroxide solution into each labelled beaker.

7 Measure 10 cm³ of the appropriate buffer solution into each beaker.

8 Use forceps to pick up one of the little squares of filter paper. Dip the paper into the liquid containing catalase (Figure 5.6).

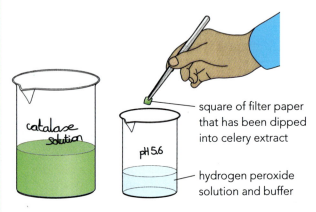

**Figure 5.6:** The filter paper has been soaked in the catalase solution, and is ready to put into the hydrogen peroxide solution.

9 Get your stopwatch ready. Still using the forceps, push the paper to the bottom of the hydrogen peroxide solution in one of the small beakers. Let it go, and time how long it takes for the paper to rise to the top of the liquid (Figure 5.7). Record this in your results table.

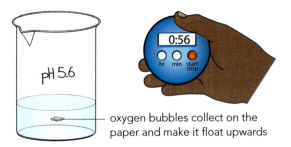

**Figure 5.7:** The catalase on the filter paper breaks down the hydrogen peroxide in the beaker, producing oxygen.

10 Repeat Steps 8 and 9 twice more, using the hydrogen peroxide solution in the same small beaker.

11 Now repeat Steps 8, 9 and 10 for the other small beakers.

12 Collect a sheet of graph paper. Draw a line graph to display your results. Put pH on the x-axis, and mean time to rise to top on the y-axis. Join your points with ruled straight lines.

### Questions

1 Write the word equation for the chemical reaction that took place in the small beakers.

2 Explain, in your own words, why the pieces of filter paper rose to the top of the liquid in the beaker.

3 Describe the relationship between the pH and the time taken for the filter paper to rise to the top of the liquid.

4 Did you have any anomalous results? If so, explain why you decided that these results were anomalous. Explain how you dealt with these results when you drew your graph.

5 Use your results to estimate the optimum pH of the catalase that you used.

6 Suggest what you could do to get a more precise value for the optimum pH of this enzyme.

7 Evaluate your experiment by identifying the main sources of error. Suggest how you could improve the experiment, to reduce these sources of error and give you more confidence that your results are correct.

# 5 Enzymes

## EXPERIMENTAL SKILLS 5.2

### Investigating the effect of temperature on the activity of lipase

Lipase is an enzyme that catalyses the breakdown of lipids (fats and oils).

$$\text{lipid} \xrightarrow{\textit{lipase}} \text{fatty acids and glycerol}$$

Fatty acids are acids, so they decrease the pH. You will use an indicator called thymolphthalein to detect their presence. Thymolphthalein is blue in alkaline conditions and loses its colour when the pH becomes less alkaline.

**You will need:**

- fresh milk
- lipase solution, with a concentration of about 5%
- sodium carbonate solution, with a concentration of $0.05 \, \text{mol} \, \text{dm}^{-3}$
- a small bottle of thymolphthalein indicator, with a dropper
- five test-tubes and a rack to stand them in
- a test-tube holder
- a syringe or measuring cylinder to measure $10 \, \text{cm}^3$
- a small syringe to measure $1 \, \text{cm}^3$
- a stopwatch or timer
- one or more glass rods
- water-baths at five different temperatures (see note)
- a thermometer
- a waterproof marker to label the test-tubes.

**Note about water-baths:** You may be able to use electric water-baths, which can be set to temperatures above room temperature (Figure 5.8). If you do not have these, you can make your own water-bath by heating water in a beaker over a burner. You can also make a water-bath with a temperature of 0 °C by filling a beaker with crushed ice. In this case, you can monitor the temperature of the water with a thermometer, and either heat with a burner or add cold water to try to keep the temperature fairly constant.

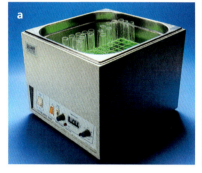 

**Figure 5.8 a:** An electronic water-bath, which you can set to a particular temperature. **b:** A water-bath over a burner.

**Safety:** Take care not to knock over the beaker of water if you have made your own water-bath. Stand up while you are working, so that if something does get knocked over you can quickly move out of the way.

If the water-bath is very hot, do not touch the hot water, or a hot test-tube, with your hands. Use a test-tube holder.

## REFLECTION

The instructions for these experiments are quite long and complicated. How did you deal with that? What can you do in the future, to help you to understand complicated instructions and follow them successfully?

## CONTINUED

### Method

1. Read through the instructions and draw a results chart that you can fill in as you work.
2. Label your test-tubes with your initials.
3. Measure 5 cm³ of milk into each test-tube (Figure 5.9).
4. Measure 7 cm³ of sodium carbonate solution into each test-tube.
5. Add 5 drops of thymolphthalein indicator to each test-tube. This will make the liquid go blue. Stir the contents using the glass rod.

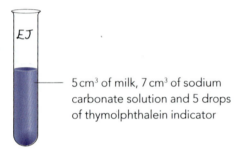

5 cm³ of milk, 7 cm³ of sodium carbonate solution and 5 drops of thymolphthalein indicator

**Figure 5.9:** One of the tubes, ready to go into the water-bath.

6. Stand each test-tube in a water-bath at a different temperature. Leave the test-tubes for a few minutes, so that the contents come to the same temperature as the water-bath. Measure this temperature and record it.
7. Using the small syringe, add 1 cm³ of lipase to the first test-tube. Start timing immediately. Stir with a clean glass rod, to mix the lipase into the milk.
8. Record the time taken for the blue colour to disappear. Measure the time to the nearest second.
9. Repeat for the other four temperatures.
10. Use your results to draw a line graph. Put temperature on the *x*-axis and time taken on the *y*-axis. Join the points with ruled lines between them.

### Questions

1. Explain why the liquid containing the milk was blue at the start of the experiment.
2. Explain why the liquid in some of the tubes became colourless.
3. Describe how temperature affected the time taken for the liquid to become colourless.
4. According to your results, what is the optimum temperature for lipase?
5. Your timer probably measured to 0.1 or even 0.01 seconds. Suggest why it is sensible to record the times to the nearest second.
6. Evaluate your experiment, by identifying the main sources of error. How could you improve the experiment, so that you have more confidence in your results?

### Self-assessment

How well did you construct and complete your results chart? Rate yourself for each of the following statements using:

- ☺ if you did it really well
- 😐 if you made a good attempt at it and partly succeeded
- ☹ if you did not try to do it or did not succeed

- I drew the results chart using a ruler for all the rows and columns.
- I included the units (s for the time measurements, and °C for the temperature measurements) in the headings of the table.
- I did not write the units again with the individual results in the table.
- I recorded each temperature reading to the nearest whole degree or 0.5 degree.
- I recorded each time reading to the nearest second.
- A friend confirms that my results chart is very easy to understand.

# 5 Enzymes

## Denaturation

We have seen that enzymes have an optimum temperature, at which they work fastest. Enzymes from the human body generally have an optimum temperature of about 37 °C. Enzymes from plants may have optimum temperatures much lower than this. Some bacteria, especially those that live in hot springs, may have really high optimum temperatures – up to 80 °C in some cases.

For many enzymes, a temperature above about 60 °C completely stops them working. This is because the high temperature damages the enzyme. The enzyme is said to be denatured. It cannot catalyse its reaction anymore.

Enzymes also have an optimum pH. For most enzymes, this is around pH 7. However, there are some enzymes that work best in a much higher or lower pH than this. For example, in Chapter 7, you will find out about an enzyme that works best in the acidic conditions in the human stomach – at a pH of about 2.

When an enzyme is placed in a liquid with a pH that is not its optimum pH, it is damaged. The enzyme is denatured and cannot catalyse its reaction.

## Explaining how temperature and pH affect enzyme activity

Look at the graph in Figure 5.4. You can see that at 0 °C, the enzyme has no activity. At this temperature, molecules have very little kinetic energy – they are moving only slowly. As they are moving only slowly, the substrate molecules rarely collide with the enzyme. So, they rarely enter its active site, and very few substrate molecules are converted to product.

As the temperature increases, the kinetic energy of the enzyme and substrate molecules increases. They move faster and collide with each other more frequently and with more energy. Effective collisions are more frequent. Each second, more substrate molecules collide with an active site and are converted to product. This is why the graph shows enzyme activity increasing as temperature increases.

However, as temperature increases above the optimum, the kinetic energy of the enzyme begins to shake it apart. Its molecules begin to lose their shape, so that the active site is no longer a true complementary shape to the substrate. When a substrate molecule collides with an active site, it may not fit. It cannot form an enzyme–substrate complex and is not converted to product. The activity of the enzyme therefore decreases. When the temperature reaches 60 °C, the active site is so out of shape that the enzyme has completely stopped working. It is completely denatured.

Something similar happens when pH changes. Each enzyme molecule has a very specific shape, with the active site being the best fit for the substrate at its optimum pH. A pH well above or below this value causes the enzyme molecule to lose its shape (denature), so it can no longer bind with the substrate.

## Questions

5 Look at the graph that you drew from your results in Experimental skills 5.2 Investigating the effect of temperature on the activity of lipase. In your own words, explain the shape of the graph. ('Explain' means using your biological knowledge and understanding to give reasons for the shape of the graph.)

6 Use your own words to explain the shapes of the curve for most enzymes, in Figure 5.5.

---

### SUMMARY

| |
|---|
| Enzymes are proteins that function as biological catalysts and increase the rate of metabolic reactions. |
| Without enzymes, these reactions would not take place fast enough to sustain life. |
| Each enzyme has an active site that has a complementary shape to its substrate. |
| When the substrate binds with the active site of the enzyme, the substrate is converted to product. The enzyme is unchanged. |
| The binding of substrate to the active site of the enzyme forms an enzyme–substrate complex. |

# CAMBRIDGE IGCSE™ BIOLOGY: COURSEBOOK

## CONTINUED

Enzymes have an optimum temperature and pH at which they work most quickly. Higher temperatures or a very different pH cause the enzyme to change shape and denature.

As temperature increases, the kinetic energy of enzyme and substrate molecules increases, and they collide more frequently. This increases the rate of activity of the enzyme. However, above the optimum temperature, the enzyme begins to lose its shape, until it can no longer combine with the substrate. The shape of the active site is no longer complementary to the shape of the substrate.

A pH that is well below or above an enzyme's optimum pH also causes it to denature, and therefore to stop working.

## PROJECT

### An enzyme demonstration

It is best if you work in a group of three for this project.

You are going to use your knowledge of enzymes to produce a short demonstration to explain what enzymes are and how they work. Your demonstration could be 'live' with a commentary, or you could make a video with a voiceover.

Imagine that your audience do not know anything about enzymes. Your task is to make them interested in enzymes, and begin to understand what enzymes are and what they do. Work with your group to plan what you will do.

**Figure 5.10:** Raw liver contains a lot of catalase, which breaks down hydrogen peroxide and releases oxygen very quickly.

The best enzyme to use in your demonstration is catalase, because it is easy to see it working. Catalase is present in all animal and plant tissues. When catalase breaks down hydrogen peroxide, it releases oxygen. If you use an animal tissue such as liver, the reaction can be quite spectacular (Figure 5.10). Although this is fun, it might be better to use something that behaves a little more quietly, such as potato (Figure 5.11).

**Figure 5.11:** If hydrogen peroxide is added to raw potato, the catalase in the potato breaks it down and releases oxygen, which forms a white froth.

**Safety:** It is extremely important to consider safety as you plan. What are the risks that you need to be aware of? How will you reduce these risks?

## 5 Enzymes

### EXAM-STYLE QUESTIONS

1. Which statement is **not** true for **all** catalysts?
   - A They are enzymes.
   - B They are not used up in the reaction.
   - C They increase the rate of a chemical reaction.
   - D They remain unchanged at the end of a reaction. [1]

2. What are the smaller molecules from which an enzyme molecule is made?
   - A amino acids
   - B fatty acids
   - C glucose
   - D glycerol [1]

3. A solution containing an enzyme and no other substance was tested. Which test would give a positive result?
   - A Benedict's test
   - B biuret test
   - C ethanol test
   - D iodine test [1]

4. What explains why a reaction controlled by an enzyme happens more slowly as temperature decreases?
   - A The enzyme and substrate molecules have less kinetic energy.
   - B The enzyme is denatured.
   - C The enzyme is killed by the low temperature.
   - D The substrate changes shape and cannot fit into the active site. [1]

5. a Copy and complete the sentences about enzymes. Use words from the list. You may use each word once, more than once or not at all.

   active   carbohydrate   catalysts   chemical
   complementary   identical   metabolic   proteins

   Enzymes are _____ that function as biological _____. They are involved in all _____ reactions.
   The part of an enzyme where a substrate binds is called its _____ site. The shape of this site, and the shape of the substrate, are _____. [5]

   b **Describe** why enzymes are important to all living organisms. [2]

   [Total: 7]

> **COMMAND WORD**
>
> **describe:** state the points of a topic / give characteristics and main features

## CONTINUED

6 The figure below shows some stages in an enzyme-controlled reaction. What are P, Q, R and S?

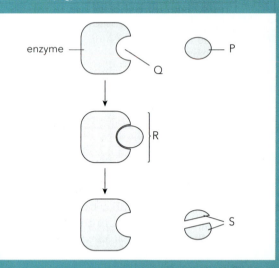

|   | P | Q | R | S |
|---|---|---|---|---|
| A | active site | product | substrate | enzyme–substrate complex |
| B | enzyme–substrate complex | substrate | active site | product |
| C | substrate | active site | enzyme–substrate complex | product |
| D | product | enzyme-substrate complex | substrate | active site |

[1]

7 Amylase is an enzyme that breaks down starch to maltose.

a A student put some starch solution into a test-tube. He took a small sample of starch from the tube and added it to a drop of iodine solution on a white tile.

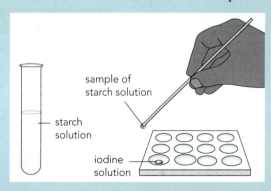

### CONTINUED

Next, he added some amylase solution to the starch solution. After five minutes, he took another sample from the tube, and tested it with iodine solution.

The table shows his results.

|  | Result of iodine test |
|---|---|
| At start | blue-black |
| After adding amylase solution | brown |

**Explain** the student's results. [3]

**COMMAND WORD**

**explain:** set out purposes or reasons / make the relationships between things evident / provide why and/or how and support with relevant evidence

b The student investigated the effect of pH on the activity of amylase.

He placed the same volume of starch solution in five tubes. He added different buffer solutions to each tube. He then added amylase solution to each tube. He took samples of the mixture from each tube and measured the time for all the starch to disappear.

His results are shown in the table.

| pH | Time for starch to disappear / minutes |
|---|---|
| 4 | did not disappear |
| 6 | 8 |
| 7 | 4 |
| 9 | 14 |
| 11 | did not disappear |

i Use the student's results to describe the effect of pH on the activity of amylase. [3]

ii The student kept the volume of starch solution the same in each tube. **State** three other variables that the student should have kept the same in his experiment. [3]

[Total: 9]

**COMMAND WORD**

**state:** express in clear terms

8 The graph below shows how the activity of two enzymes, A and B, is affected by temperature.

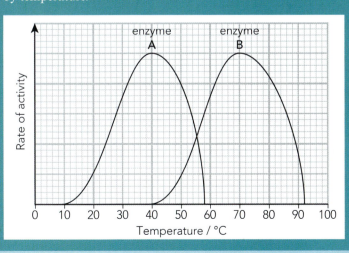

> ## CONTINUED
>
> a  Compare the effect of temperature on enzyme **A** and enzyme **B**. [5]
> b  Explain the effect of temperature on enzyme B from:
>    i   0 to 60 °C [3]
>    ii  70 to 90 °C [4]
>
> [Total: 12]

## SELF-EVALUATION CHECKLIST

After studying this chapter, think about how confident you are with the different topics. This will help you to see any gaps in your knowledge and help you to learn more effectively.

| I can | See Topic… | Needs more work | Almost there | Confident to move on |
|---|---|---|---|---|
| explain what a catalyst is | 5.1 | | | |
| explain why enzymes are said to be biological catalysts, and why they are important to sustain life | 5.1 | | | |
| describe how enzymes work, using the terms *active site*, *substrate*, *complementary shape* and *product* | 5.1 | | | |
| use the term *enzyme–substrate complex* | 5.1 | | | |
| explain why enzymes are specific | 5.1 | | | |
| describe how to investigate the effect of temperature and pH on enzyme activity, and describe these effects, using the words *optimum* and *denaturation* | 5.2 | | | |
| explain the effect of temperature on enzyme activity, using the words *kinetic energy*, *frequency of effective collision*, *complementary shape* and *denaturation* | 5.2 | | | |
| explain the effect of pH on enzyme activity, using the words *complementary shape* and *denaturation* | 5.2 | | | |

# Chapter 6
# Plant nutrition

**IN THIS CHAPTER YOU WILL:**

- learn about photosynthesis and the equation for it
- find out how plants use the carbohydrates made in photosynthesis
- learn how the structure of a leaf is adapted for photosynthesis
- investigate the need for chlorophyll, light and carbon dioxide in photosynthesis
- investigate how light, carbon dioxide and temperature affect the rate of photosynthesis

> find out what a limiting factor is, and how limiting factors affect photosynthesis.

# CAMBRIDGE IGCSE™ BIOLOGY: COURSEBOOK

> ## GETTING STARTED
>
> Work with a partner. Discuss the answers to the questions below, and be ready to share your ideas with the rest of the class.
>
> 1. What types of nutrient does your body use to obtain energy?
> 2. Energy cannot be created or destroyed. Where did the energy in the nutrients come from originally?
> 3. How did the energy get into the nutrients?

## USING SOLAR ENERGY TO MAKE FUELS

As the human population continues to grow, we are using more and more fuel to provide energy for our homes, industries and vehicles. Good progress is being made in using more renewable energy sources, such as wind and solar power, but a lot of this energy still comes from fossil fuels.

Burning fossil fuels produces carbon dioxide and the quantity of carbon dioxide in the atmosphere is increasing. This contributes to global warming. We urgently need to find alternative ways of providing energy.

Can we take a lesson from plants? Plants use energy from sunlight to make carbohydrates, which provide energy for their cells. This way of providing useful energy does not produce carbon dioxide – it uses it up. Already, in many parts of the world, plants are being grown to provide us with biofuels that can be burnt to produce electricity, or to move vehicles. But this takes up a large amount of land that may be needed to grow food crops, or that would be better left as natural forests or other habitats for wildlife.

So scientists are looking into ways in which we might use a kind of 'artificial photosynthesis' to make fuels (Figure 6.1).

Plants contain a substance called chlorophyll, which captures energy from sunlight and helps to transfer this energy into carbohydrates. Research into artificial photosynthesis is exploring other substances that might be able to perform the same role. One laboratory is using tiny particles of gold as a substitute for chlorophyll. It works – but only very slowly. Researchers think it will be at least 2030 before we are able to use artificial photosynthesis to produce significant quantities of fuel for the human population to use.

### Discussion questions

1. How might the large-scale use of artificial photosynthesis help to reduce the pace of climate change?
2. Why might artificial photosynthesis be a better option for the environment than growing crops for biofuel production?

**Figure 6.1:** So far, most attempts to mimic photosynthesis to make fuels are still small-scale.

# 6.1 Making carbohydrates using light energy

## Plant nutrition

All living organisms need to take many different substances – nutrients – into their bodies. Some of these may be used to make new parts or to repair old parts. Others may be used to release energy. Taking in useful substances is called nutrition.

In Chapter 4, you saw that there are several important groups of biological molecules. These include proteins, fats, carbohydrates and DNA. These are all organic substances. Animals are not able to make organic substances themselves but must take them in as nutrients when they feed.

Plants, however, can make these organic nutrients from inorganic substances. They use carbon dioxide, water and mineral ions, which they take in from the air and soil. The process by which they make carbohydrates is called **photosynthesis**, which means 'making with light'.

> **KEY WORD**
>
> **photosynthesis:** the process by which plants synthesise carbohydrates from raw materials using energy from light

## Chlorophyll

In the chloroplasts of a plant's leaves, water and carbon dioxide react together to make carbohydrates and oxygen. In other circumstances, you could shine light on a mixture of carbon dioxide and water for ever, and no carbohydrates or oxygen would ever appear. What is special about a plant's leaves is that they contain a green pigment called chlorophyll.

Chlorophyll is able to capture energy from sunlight (Figure 6.2). When it has done this, it immediately passes the energy on (transfers it) to water molecules and carbon dioxide molecules. The energy makes these substances react, producing a kind of carbohydrate called glucose.

**Figure 6.2:** A forest is a giant carbohydrate factory, using sunlight as fuel and carbon dioxide and water as its raw materials.

The glucose that is made in the leaves contains some of the energy that was originally in the sunlight. Chlorophyll has transferred some of the energy in the sunlight into energy in carbohydrates.

## The photosynthesis equation

We have seen that, in photosynthesis, water and carbon dioxide react together to produce glucose and oxygen. They will only do this in the presence of sunlight and chlorophyll.

We can write this reaction as a word equation:

$$\text{carbon dioxide} + \text{water} \xrightarrow{\text{sunlight and chlorophyll}} \text{glucose} + \text{oxygen}$$

Like all reactions in organisms, photosynthesis depends on enzymes to help it take place.

We can also write a balanced chemical equation, which includes the chemical formula for each of the reactants and products. It also provides information about how many molecules of each are involved in the reaction.

$$6CO_2 + 6H_2O \rightarrow C_6H_{12}O_6 + 6O_2$$

The formula $CO_2$ represents carbon dioxide, and it tells us that one molecule of carbon dioxide contains one atom of carbon, C, and two atoms of oxygen, O. The formula $C_6H_{12}O_6$ represents glucose. It tells us that one molecule of glucose contains six atoms of carbon, twelve atoms of hydrogen and six atoms of oxygen. So, six carbon dioxide molecules are needed to make one glucose molecule. There are the same number of atoms on each side of the equation.

## Questions

1 Explain why animals are dependent on plants for their supply of energy.

2 Explain how chlorophyll helps photosynthesis to happen.

3 How many glucose molecules can be made from 12 molecules of carbon dioxide and 12 molecules of water?

### ACTIVITY 6.1

#### Modelling photosynthesis

Work in a group of four or five for this activity.

**You will need:**
- egg cartons cut into:

  six shapes like Figure 6.3a

  six shapes like Figure 6.3b

  six shapes like Figure 6.3c

- one complete egg carton that can hold 12 eggs, labelled like Figure 6.3d
- 36 small balls that fit into the egg cartons – for example, table tennis balls
- red, black and blue pens to write on the balls.

a   b   c

d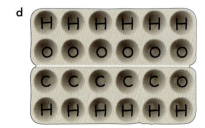

Figure 6.3: How to cut up and label your egg cartons.

1 The small balls represent atoms.

Use the red pen to label 18 of them 'O' or 'oxygen'.

Use the black pen to label 6 of them 'C' or 'carbon'.

Use the blue pen to label the other 12 'H', or 'hydrogen'.

2 Take the balls representing one oxygen and two hydrogens, and put them into an angled box to make a water molecule (Figure 6.4).

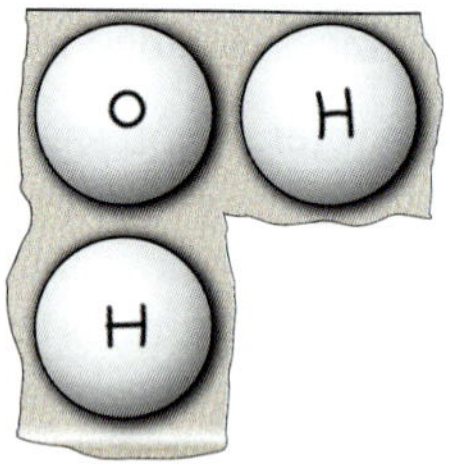

3 Make five more water molecules.

Figure 6.4: Modelling a water molecule.

4 Use the remaining balls to make six carbon dioxide molecules. (Make sure you choose the correct egg carton shapes for this.)

5 Now use your water molecules and carbon dioxide molecules to make a glucose molecule, by putting the balls into the correct holes in the base and lid of the 12-hole egg carton. To do this, use oxygen from the water only. Do **not** use oxygen from the carbon dioxide.

6 Use your leftover balls to make oxygen molecules.

7 If you have time, take apart your glucose molecule and the oxygen molecules, and turn them back into carbon dioxide and water again.

#### Questions

1 Explain how this model represents the balanced equation for photosynthesis.

2 Suggest how you could modify the model, or the way that you use the model, to show how energy in sunlight helps the reaction to take place.

3 You may hear people say that 'photosynthesis changes carbon dioxide into oxygen'. Use your model to explain why this is not correct.

> **REFLECTION**
>
> Some people find using a model like this, where you handle objects and move them around, helps them to understand. Did this model help you to understand the photosynthesis equation?
>
> If it did, can you explain how it helped?
>
> If it did not, is there a different method you might suggest people like you could use, to help them to understand?

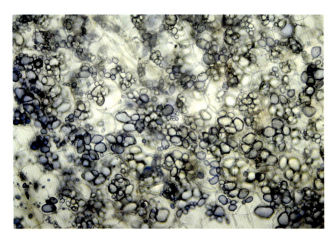

**Figure 6.5:** This is a photomicrograph of cells from a potato tuber. Iodine solution has been added so the starch grains are stained blue. You can see some cell walls if you look closely.

## How a plant uses carbohydrates

We have seen that there are two products of photosynthesis – glucose and oxygen. The oxygen is released into the atmosphere (or into the water if the plant is aquatic). The glucose is used for many different purposes.

### Releasing useful energy

Some of the glucose is used by the plant to provide energy for various activities that its cells need to undertake. For example, energy is needed to move mineral ions into the root hairs, by active transport. Energy is also needed to build protein molecules from amino acids, for growth.

The energy is released from glucose by respiration. You will find out about respiration in Chapter 11.

### Storing, to use later

Plants usually make much more glucose than they need to use for energy immediately. They store it by turning it into starch.

In Chapter 4, you saw that starch molecules are made by linking many glucose molecules together, to make a long, spiral chain. Millions of these molecules clump together to make starch grains (Figure 6.5). Starch molecules are not soluble in water, so they do not get involved in the chemical reactions taking place inside the plant cells. They also do not affect the concentration of the solutions inside the cell, so they do not cause water to enter or leave by osmosis. The starch molecules can quickly and easily be broken down to glucose molecules again when the plant needs them.

### Making sucrose, for transport

Plants can only make glucose in the parts that contain chlorophyll, which usually means the leaves. All the other parts of the plant have glucose delivered to them. Plants, however, do not actually transport glucose. They first change it into a sugar with larger molecules, called **sucrose**. The sucrose is carried from one part of the plant to another inside tubes called phloem tubes. You can find more about this in Chapter 8.

When the sucrose reaches its destination, it can be changed back to glucose again, and used in respiration to release energy.

> **KEY WORD**
>
> **sucrose:** a sugar whose molecules are made of glucose and another similar molecule (fructose) linked together

### Making cellulose, to build cell walls

As plants grow, they make new cells. Every cell needs a cell wall, so a growing plant must make cellulose molecules to form these walls. Cellulose is made by linking glucose molecules in long chains, in a different way from starch, so the chains stay straight rather than coiling up into spirals.

## Making nectar, to attract pollinators

Many plants reproduce sexually, producing male and female gametes in flowers. Unlike animal gametes, the male gametes of flowers cannot move themselves from place to place. Instead, they rely on insects, bats or birds to carry them, inside pollen grains, from one flower to another (Figure 6.6). No animal is going to do this for a plant unless it gets a reward, so flowers produce **nectar** that animals can feed on. Nectar contains different kinds of sugar, all made from the glucose that the plant has made by photosynthesis.

**Figure 6.6:** Insects are attracted to flowers to collect the carbohydrate-rich nectar, and protein-rich pollen. Unknown to the insects, they help the flower by pollinating it.

> **KEY WORD**
>
> **nectar:** a sweet liquid secreted by many insect-pollinated flowers, to attract their pollinators

## Making amino acids, to make proteins

Plants use some of the glucose made in photosynthesis to make amino acids. These amino acids can then be used to make proteins, for growth.

You may remember that proteins contain not only carbon, hydrogen and oxygen, but also nitrogen. So, in order to make amino acids from glucose, plants need a source of nitrogen. They get this from the soil, in the form of nitrate ions. Usually, these ions are taken in by active transport, through the root hairs. The ions can be transported to all parts of the plant, where they can be combined with glucose to make amino acids.

If a plant cannot get enough nitrate ions, it will not be able to synthesise proteins effectively, and so will not grow quickly or strongly.

## Making other substances, e.g. chlorophyll

Glucose can also be used to make chlorophyll. Chlorophyll is not a protein, but it does contain nitrogen. It also contains magnesium. Plants therefore need to take in magnesium ions, as well as nitrate ions, to make chlorophyll. Without these ions, the plant's leaves will look yellow rather than the green we would expect when there is plenty of chlorophyll present (Figure 6.7). If a plant cannot make lots of chlorophyll, it will not be able to photosynthesise well, and therefore will not grow well.

**Figure 6.7:** These leaves are on an orange tree, growing in soil that does not contain enough magnesium ions. The tree cannot make enough chlorophyll, so the leaves are not completely green.

# Questions

4. Starch can easily be broken down to glucose by the enzyme amylase, which is found in plants. Cellulose is much more difficult to break down to glucose. Suggest how these differences between starch and cellulose relate to their functions in a plant.
5. Animals do not make or store starch. What is the substance that animals store, which is made of chains of glucose molecules?
6. Explain why some parts of a plant must have sucrose delivered to them.

7 Copy and complete this table.

| Element | _____ | magnesium |
|---|---|---|
| Mineral salt | nitrate ions | magnesium ions |
| Why needed | to make _____, and then proteins | _____ |
| Deficiency | weak growth, yellow leaves | yellowing of leaves, often especially between the veins |

8 Making nectar costs a plant energy because it uses up glucose that the plant has made. Explain why the expense is worthwhile.

## 6.2 Leaves

Photosynthesis happens inside chloroplasts. This is where the enzymes and chlorophyll are that catalyse and supply energy for the reaction. In a typical plant, most chloroplasts are in the cells in the leaves. A leaf is a factory for making carbohydrates.

It is therefore not surprising that most plants have leaves that are perfectly adapted to help photosynthesis to take place as quickly and efficiently as possible.

### The structure of a leaf

A leaf consists of a broad, flat part (Figure 6.8), which is joined to the rest of the plant by a leaf stalk. Inside the leaf stalk are collections of parallel tubes called **vascular bundles**, which also form the veins in the leaf. The tubes in the vascular bundles carry substances to and from the leaf (Chapter 8).

Photosynthesis happens inside chloroplasts in the leaf cells. This is where the chlorophyll is found. The chlorophyll is spread out on membranes, so that a lot of sunlight can reach it.

> **KEY WORDS**
>
> **vascular bundles:** collections of xylem tubes and phloem vessels running side by side, which form the veins in a leaf

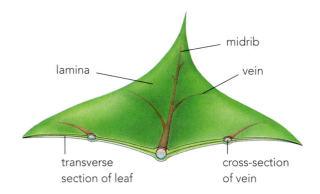

Figure 6.8: The structure of a leaf.

You will remember that the raw materials for photosynthesis are carbon dioxide and water, and that sunlight is needed to provide energy. Most – but not all – leaves have a large surface area and are very thin. The large surface area allows large amounts of sunlight to fall onto the leaf. The large surface area also increases the rate at which carbon dioxide can diffuse into the leaf from the air. Only 0.04% of the air is carbon dioxide, so the structure of a leaf must ensure that it can move in really easily.

Being thin means that sunlight can pass right through the leaf, allowing many cells inside it to photosynthesise. The thinness also helps carbon dioxide to reach all the cells quite quickly by diffusion.

Water is brought to the leaf from the soil, in tubes called xylem (pronounced zi-lem) vessels. These run in the vascular bundles, which form the veins in the leaf. You can often see many tiny veins in a leaf if you look closely. You may remember that dicot plants have veins arranged in a network, while monocots have veins arranged parallel to one another (Figures 6.9 and 6.10).

Figure 6.9: The network of veins in this dicot leaf carries water to all parts of it.

103

# Tissues in a leaf

Although a leaf is thin, it is made up of several layers of cells. You can see these if you look at a transverse section (TS) of a leaf under a microscope (Figures 6.11, 6.12 and 6.13).

Each tissue in a leaf has its own function. We will work from the top down, considering each one in turn.

On the top of the leaf is the upper **epidermis**. The cells in this layer are packed tightly together, to reduce the quantity of water vapour escaping from the leaf. They do not contain chloroplasts, so they cannot photosynthesise. These cells **secrete** (make and release) a waxy substance, which forms a thin, transparent, waterproof covering called the **cuticle**.

The next layer down is the **palisade mesophyll**. This is made up of tall, narrow cells containing very large numbers of chloroplasts. Their main function is photosynthesis. As they are close to the top of the leaf, they get plenty of sunlight. The transparent epidermis cells above them let the light through easily.

**Figure 6.10:** In monocots, the veins usually run parallel to one another, rather than forming a network.

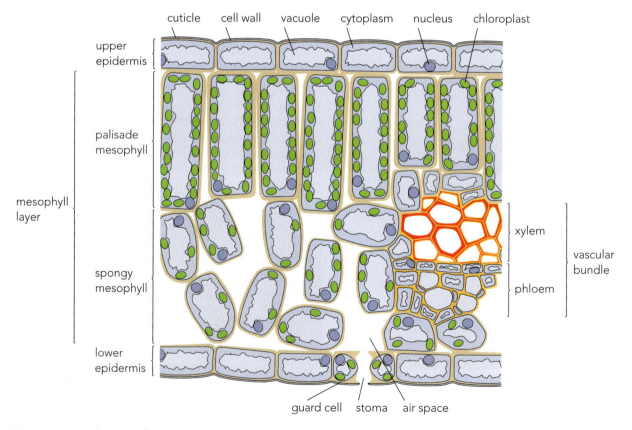

**Figure 6.11:** A diagram of a transverse section (TS) through a leaf.

# 6 Plant nutrition

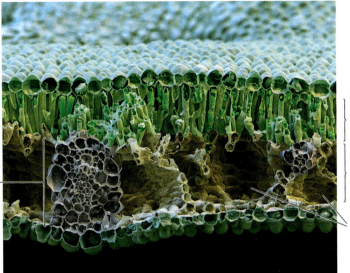

upper epidermis, made of tightly packed cells

vascular bundle, containing xylem vessels (top) and phloem tubes (below)

lower epidermis, made of tightly packed cells

palisade mesophyll layer, made of tall, narrow cells containing many chloroplasts

spongy mesophyll layer, made of more rounded cells, with fewer chloroplasts

air spaces between the spongy mesophyll cells

Figure 6.12: A scanning electron micrograph of a section through a leaf from a taro plant (×400).

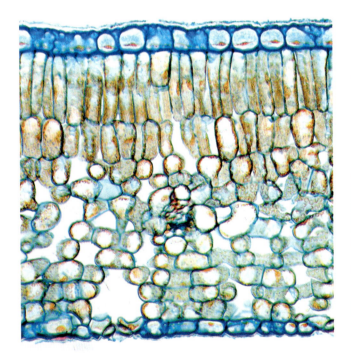

Figure 6.13: A photomicrograph of a small part of a leaf from a tea plant (×400). Can you identify some of the tissues labelled in Figure 6.11?

Beneath the palisade mesophyll is the **spongy mesophyll**. The cells in this tissue also contain chloroplasts, but not as many as in the palisade cells. They are not as tightly packed, either. There are many air spaces between them. These spaces allow carbon dioxide and oxygen to diffuse between the air and the cells inside the leaf. The spaces also allow vapour to move from the surface of the cells to the outside of the leaf. You will learn more about this in Chapter 8.

### KEY WORDS

**epidermis:** the outer layer of tissue on a plant; also the outer layer of an animal's skin

**secrete:** make a useful substance and then send it out of the cell where it is made, to be used in another part of the body

**cuticle:** a thin layer of wax that covers the upper surface of a leaf

**palisade mesophyll:** the layer of cells immediately beneath the upper epidermis, where most photosynthesis happens

**spongy mesophyll:** the layer of cells immediately beneath the palisade mesophyll, where some photosynthesis happens; this tissue contains a lot of air spaces between the cells

The bottom of the leaf is covered by a tissue similar to the upper epidermis, called the lower epidermis. On some leaves, this tissue makes a cuticle, but usually it does not. This is because the underside of the leaf does not often have sunlight falling onto it, so it does not get as hot and therefore does not lose as much water vapour.

There are openings in the lower epidermis called **stomata** (singular: **stoma**). Each stoma is surrounded by a pair of **guard cells** (Figure 6.14). The guard cells, unlike the other cells in the epidermis, contain chloroplasts. The guard cells can change their shape, which can open and close the stomata. The stomata allow diffusion of carbon dioxide and oxygen in and out of the leaf. Water vapour also diffuses out of the leaf through the stomata.

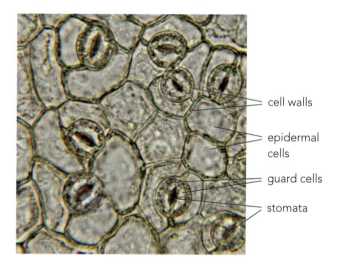

**Figure 6.14:** This photograph of the lower epidermis of a leaf was taken using a light microscope (×350).

> **KEY WORDS**
>
> **stomata** (singular: **stoma**): openings in the surface of a leaf, most commonly in the lower surface; they are surrounded by pairs of guard cells, which control whether the stomata are open or closed
>
> **guard cells:** a pair of cells that surrounds a stoma and controls its opening; guard cells are the only cells in the epidermis that contain chloroplasts

Figure 6.15 summarises how the raw materials for photosynthesis – carbon dioxide and water – travel to a chloroplast in a palisade cell.

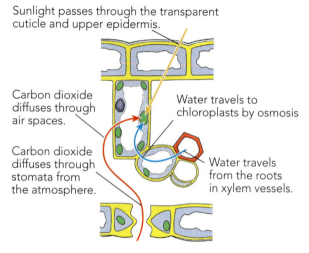

**Figure 6.15:** How the raw materials for photosynthesis get into a palisade cell.

# Chloroplasts

You have seen that the palisade mesophyll cells, spongy mesophyll cells and guard cells in a leaf all contain chloroplasts. It is inside chloroplasts that photosynthesis happens.

Figure 6.16 shows the structure of a chloroplast. Many chloroplasts are found in a cell, and the palisade cells contain most of them. Chloroplasts can move around inside the palisade cells, to ensure that they get the best quantity of sunlight.

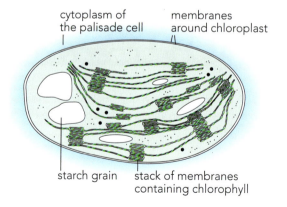

**Figure 6.16:** One of the chloroplasts in a palisade cell.

## Questions

9  Explain briefly how each of these features of a leaf are adaptations for photosynthesis:
   a  having a large surface area
   b  being thin

10 Explain how a palisade mesophyll cell is adapted for its function.

11 Suggest why the cells in the lower epidermis of a leaf (apart from the guard cells) do not contain chloroplasts.

12 Look at the photographs in Figure 6.12 and Figure 6.13. One is taken using a scanning electron microscope (and then artificially coloured), and one with a light microscope. The magnification is almost the same for each one.

   What differences can you see in the type of image these two kinds of microscope produce?

## 6.3 Factors affecting photosynthesis

The rate at which photosynthesis happens is affected by several environmental factors. These include:

- the supply of the raw materials – carbon dioxide and water
- the quantity of sunlight, which provides energy for the reactions
- the temperature, because this affects the activity of enzymes.

As well as these environmental factors, the quantity of the chlorophyll in the leaf also helps to determine how fast photosynthesis can take place.

In this section, you will investigate how each of these factors affects the rate of photosynthesis. If you are studying the Supplement, you will also find out about limiting factors.

### EXPERIMENTAL SKILLS 6.1

#### Testing a leaf for starch

Leaves turn some of the glucose that they make in photosynthesis into starch. If we find starch in a leaf, that tells us if it has been photosynthesising. In this experiment, you will practise working safely, making careful observations and drawing conclusions.

**You will need:**

- a 250 cm$^3$ beaker
- a burner, tripod and gauze
- a boiling tube
- some iodine solution, with a dropper
- forceps
- a glass rod
- some alcohol (methylated spirits) – collect this only when you are ready to use it
- a fresh green leaf that has been photosynthesising
- a white tile.

**Safety:** Alcohol is flammable (burns easily). Do not collect the alcohol until you have turned out your burner.

If your alcohol (or someone else's) does start to burn, put a damp cloth over it immediately.

#### Method

1  Boil some water in a beaker (Figure 6.17). Take a green leaf from a healthy plant and drop it into the boiling water. This breaks down the cell membranes in the leaf. Leave the leaf in the boiling water for about 30 s.

2  Turn out the flame.

3  Put some alcohol into a boiling tube. Stand the tube of alcohol in the hot water.

4  Use the forceps to remove the softened leaf from the hot water. Drop it into the tube of alcohol. Chlorophyll is soluble in alcohol, so it will come out of the leaf. Leave the leaf in the alcohol until all the chlorophyll has come out of the leaf.

## CONTINUED

5 The leaf will now be brittle (it will break easily). Carefully remove it from the alcohol, and dip it into hot water again to soften it.

6 Spread out the leaf on a white tile and cover it with iodine solution. A blue-black colour shows that the leaf contains starch.

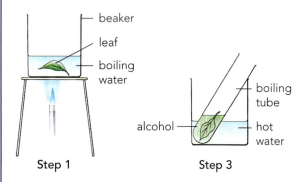

Figure 6.17: Testing a leaf for starch.

### Questions

1 Describe the results of your experiment. What conclusion can you make?

2 Cell membranes are partially permeable. They will not allow starch or iodine molecules to pass through them. Use this information to explain why it was necessary to boil the leaf.

3 Suggest why it is a good idea to remove the chlorophyll from the leaf, before adding iodine solution to it.

## EXPERIMENTAL SKILLS 6.2

### Investigating the necessity for chlorophyll for photosynthesis

In this investigation, you will use the starch test again. A variegated leaf is one that has some white areas and some green areas (Figure 6.18). You will practise recording your observations with a labelled drawing.

**You will need:**
- the same apparatus as for Experimental skills 6.1 Testing a leaf for starch
- a fresh variegated leaf, taken from a plant that has been photosynthesising.

**Safety:** Alcohol is flammable (burns easily). Do not collect the alcohol until you have turned out your burner.

If your alcohol (or someone else's) does start to burn, put a damp cloth over it immediately.

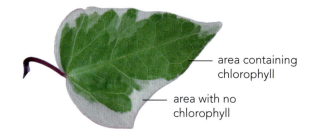

Figure 6.18: A variegated leaf.

### Method

1 Make a drawing of your variegated leaf. Do not colour it. Label the parts that are green and the parts that are white.

2 Test the leaf for starch, following the procedure described in Experimental skills 6.1.

3 Record your results by drawing and labelling the leaf after you have added iodine solution to it.

### Questions

1 Which parts of the leaf contained starch?

2 Write a brief conclusion for your experiment.

# 6 Plant nutrition

### EXPERIMENTAL SKILLS 6.3

#### Investigating the necessity for light for photosynthesis

In this investigation, you will use the starch test to compare the starch content of parts of a leaf that have and have not received light. This is another chance to practise recording results using a labelled drawing, and to write a short conclusion.

> **You will need:**
> - a healthy plant growing in a pot, which has been in a dark cupboard for two days
> - some black paper, scissors and paper clips
> - (after one day) the same apparatus as for Experimental skills 6.1 Testing a leaf for starch.

**Safety:** Alcohol is flammable (burns easily). Do not collect the alcohol until you have turned out your burner.

If your alcohol (or someone else's) does start to burn, put a damp cloth over it immediately.

#### Method

1. Cut out a shape from the black paper, which you can attach to a leaf. If you like, you can cut your initials into the paper (Figure 6.19).
2. Attach the paper to a leaf on the potted plant. Do not take the leaf off the plant!
3. Put the plant into a place where it gets plenty of light. Leave it until the next day.

**Figure 6.19:** Using black paper to block light from reaching part of a leaf.

4. Now remove the leaf from the plant. Remove the black paper from the leaf.
5. Test the leaf for starch.
6. Record your results by drawing and labelling the leaf after you have added iodine solution to it.

#### Questions

1. The potted plant was put into a cupboard to make sure it used it up all its starch stores and had no light to be able to make more. This is called **destarching**. Suggest why this was a necessary part of this experiment.
2. Explain why, in this experiment, the leaf had to remain attached to the plant for a day, after you put the black paper onto it.
3. Use your results to write a short conclusion to your experiment.

## Controls

In Experimental skills 6.3, you wanted to find out whether light was needed for photosynthesis. To do this, you needed to be able to compare a part of a leaf that did have light with a part that did not have light.

The part of the leaf that you did not cover was the **control** in your experiment. You could compare the part that did not have light with this normal part.

> ### KEY WORDS
>
> **destarching:** leaving a plant in the dark for long enough for it to use up its starch stores
>
> **control:** a standard sample that you use as a comparison, to find the effect of changing a variable

If you had covered all the leaf, and found that none of it photosynthesised, you would not be sure that the reason was because it had no light. It could have been because the whole plant was not photosynthesising.

In Experimental skills 6.2, you wanted to find out whether chlorophyll was needed for photosynthesis. The white parts of the leaf had no chlorophyll, and you could compare these with the normal, green parts. These green parts were the control in this experiment.

### EXPERIMENTAL SKILLS 6.4

**Investigating the necessity for carbon dioxide for photosynthesis**

In this investigation, you will compare the ability of two leaves on the same plant – one with carbon dioxide and one without – to make starch. This is not an easy experiment to set up, so you will probably just use one set of apparatus for the whole class.

**You will need:**

- a healthy plant growing in a pot, which has been destarched (see Experimental skills 6.3)
- two transparent containers, e.g. conical flasks
- two rubber bungs to fit the flasks, each with a slit in one edge in which a leaf stalk can fit
- petroleum jelly
- a method of supporting the transparent containers
- some potassium hydroxide solution
- some distilled water
- (after one day) the same apparatus as for Experimental skills 6.1 Testing a leaf for starch.

**Safety:** Alcohol is flammable (burns easily). Do not collect the alcohol until you have turned hout your burner.

If your alcohol (or someone else's) does start to burn, put a damp cloth over it immediately.

**Method**

1. Set up the apparatus as shown in Figure 6.20. Note that you will have to find a way of supporting the flasks so that they don't pull on the leaves – you could use a retort stand and clamps. Once you have that organised, put the liquids into the two flasks. Next, hold one of the leaf stalks carefully, and slot it into one of the rubber bungs. Then gently push the flask over the bung and into its support. Repeat with the other leaf and flask.

2. Rub petroleum jelly over the rubber bungs, to try to prevent any air entering or leaving the flask.

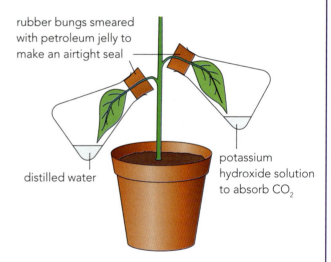

**Figure 6.20:** Using potassium hydroxide solution to remove carbon dioxide from around a leaf.

3. Place the apparatus in a light place and leave it for at least one day.
4. Test both leaves for starch.
5. Record your results.

# 6 Plant nutrition

## CONTINUED

### Questions

1 What was the control in this experiment?

2 Suggest why distilled water was added to one flask, rather than just leaving it empty.

3 Write a short conclusion for your experiment.

## EXPERIMENTAL SKILLS 6.5

### Investigating the effect of varying light intensity on the rate of photosynthesis

In this experiment, you will use an aquatic plant – that is, one that lives in water. This makes it easy to measure the rate of photosynthesis, because we can see bubbles of oxygen being released into the water. In order to measure a rate, we need to measure how much oxygen is given off in unit time – that is, a definite length of time such as one minute.

**You will need:**
- a healthy aquatic plant, which has been in the light and has been photosynthesising
- the apparatus shown in Figure 6.21
- a paperclip
- a lamp
- a ruler to measure the distance between the lamp and the plant
- a stopwatch or timer.

**Safety:** Keep water away from the lamp.

### Before you start

Check that you know how to use your stopwatch or timer, and that it is working properly.

### Method

1 Collect a piece of aquatic plant. Cut off a piece about 7 to 9 cm long. Work out which way up it is. Attach a paperclip to the top of it.

2 Set up the apparatus as in the diagram. The paperclip will hold the top of the plant down, so that its cut end floats upwards.

3 Place the lamp as close as possible to the beaker. Measure the distance, and record it in a results table like this:

| Distance of lamp from beaker / cm | Number of bubbles produced in one minute | | | |
|---|---|---|---|---|
| | 1st try | 2nd try | 3rd try | Mean |
| | | | | |
| | | | | |

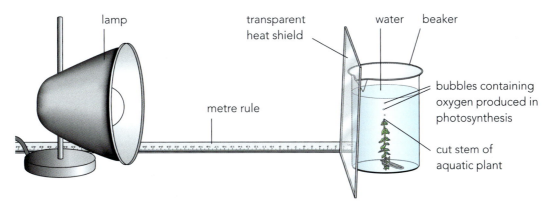

Figure 6.21: Apparatus for Experimental skills 6.5.

## CONTINUED

4  Start the stopwatch or timer and count the number of bubbles released from the cut end of the stem in one minute. Record this, and then repeat two more times.

5  Move the lamp a little bit further from the plant. Measure the new distance, and repeat step 4.

6  Repeat step 5 several times, until you have bubble counts for at least five different distances. Do more if you have time.

7  Plot your results as a line graph, with distance on the x-axis and mean number of bubbles on the y-axis. Make sure that the two axes are labelled fully, and that you choose suitable scales. Join the points using ruled, straight lines between the points.

### Questions

1  Explain why an aquatic plant was used in this experiment.

2  Light intensity decreases as the distance of the lamp from the beaker increases. Write a conclusion to summarise what your results show about the effect of light intensity on the rate of photosynthesis.

3  Lamps produce heat as well as light. Explain why you would be unable to draw a conclusion about light intensity, if you did not use a heat shield.

4  It is possible to collect the gas given off by the plant and measure its volume. Suggest why this would be an improvement on the method you have used here.

### Self-assessment

Give yourself a mark according to the following scheme for each of the features of your graph listed below.

**2 marks**  if you did it really well

**1 mark**   if you made a good attempt at it and partly succeeded

**0 marks**  if you did not try to do it, or did not succeed

- The axes are both fully labelled, including units.
- The scales on both axes go up in even steps.
- The scales use at least half of the graph paper.
- The points are plotted as small, neat crosses in exactly the right place.
- The lines between the points are drawn with a ruler, and exactly meet the centres of the crosses.

How many marks do you give yourself out of 10? What will you do next time you draw a line graph, to increase your score?

### 6 Plant nutrition

## EXPERIMENTAL SKILLS 6.6

### Investigating the effect of carbon dioxide concentration or temperature on the rate of photosynthesis

In this experiment, you will use a similar method to Experimental skills 6.5. This time, however, your independent variable will be either carbon dioxide concentration or temperature. You are going to plan your own experiment.

**You will need:**
- the apparatus used in Experimental skills 6.5
- *if you are going to investigate the effect of carbon dioxide concentration:* sodium hydrogencarbonate and a spatula
- *if you are going to investigate the effect of temperature:* electronic water-baths, or access to ice and hot water, and a thermometer.

### Method

1. Decide which variable you will investigate – carbon dioxide concentration or temperature. If possible, make sure that different groups in your class investigate different variables.

2. Think about how you will vary your chosen variable.

   You can vary carbon dioxide concentration by adding different masses of sodium hydrogencarbonate to the water that the plant is in.

   You can vary temperature by standing the beaker in a water-bath at different temperatures, or by adding ice and hot water to the water around the plant

   You should aim to have at least five values of your independent variable.

3. Think about other variables that you should try to keep constant, and how you will do this.

4. Write out your plan. You could structure it like this:
   - Independent variable and how you will vary it
   - Values of the independent variable you will use
   - Variables that you will keep constant, and how you will do this
   - The variable that you will measure, and how you will do this
   - Possible safety risks, and how you will minimise them
   - An outline results chart, ready to complete as you work

5. If possible, exchange your plan with another person in your class who is investigating the other variable. Give them feedback on their plan. Use their feedback to you to make improvements to your own plan.

6. When you are ready, carry out your experiment and record your results.

### Questions

1. Plot a line graph to display your results.
2. Write a short conclusion.
3. You probably encountered some difficulties or problems as you did your experiment. What were they, and how did you overcome them?
4. If you could start again, and had lots of time available, what improvements would you make to your experiment?

# EXPERIMENTAL SKILLS 6.7

## Investigating the effect of light and darkness on gas exchange in an aquatic plant

In this investigation, you will use a liquid called hydrogencarbonate indicator to look for changes in carbon dioxide concentration in the water around an aquatic plant. You will make careful observations of colour changes, and then use your results and your own knowledge to try to explain them.

### You will need:
- four very clean large test-tubes (boiling tubes) and airtight bungs to fit them
- some hydrogencarbonate indicator solution
- two pieces of aquatic plant
- some black paper and sticky tape
- a rack or beaker to stand the tubes in.

**Note:** Hydrogencarbonate indicator changes colour according to how much carbon dioxide there is. The colours are:

- 🟣 purple when there is no carbon dioxide
- 🔴 red when there is a little carbon dioxide (as in ordinary air)
- 🟡 yellow when there is a lot of carbon dioxide.

### Method

1. Pour hydrogencarbonate indicator into each of the four tubes, to the same depth in each one. About a third full works well. Record the colour of the indicator in each tube.

2. Place a piece of aquatic plant in the indicator in two tubes. Try to use similar sizes of plant in each.

3. Use black paper to wrap around one of the tubes with a plant in it, and one without. Make sure the tubes are completely covered (Figure 6.22).

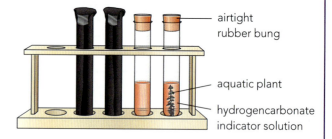

**Figure 6.22:** Using hydrogencarbonate indicator to investigate the effect of light and dark on an aquatic plant.

4. Stand all four tubes in the light and leave them for at least one hour – preferably longer.

5. When the indicator has changed colour in at least one of the tubes without a covering, remove the black paper from the two covered tubes. Record the colour of the indicator in each tube.

### Questions

1. Use the information about the colour of hydrogencarbonate indicator to compare the concentration of carbon dioxide in the four tubes.

2. Plants, like all living organisms, respire. They do this all the time. Respiration uses oxygen and produces carbon dioxide.

   In bright light, plants photosynthesise as well as respiring. They photosynthesise faster than they respire.

   Use this information to explain your results.

# 6 Plant nutrition

## Limiting factors

If a plant is given plenty of sunlight, carbon dioxide and water, the limit on the rate at which it can photosynthesise is its own ability to absorb these materials and make them react. However, quite often plants do not have unlimited supplies of these materials, and so their rate of photosynthesis is not as high as it might be. A factor that is in short supply, and that therefore limits how quickly the plant can photosynthesise, is called a **limiting factor**.

> **KEY WORDS**
>
> **limiting factor:** a factor that is in short supply, which stops an activity (such as photosynthesis) happening at a faster rate

## Light intensity

In the dark, a plant cannot photosynthesise at all. In dim light, it can photosynthesise slowly. As light intensity increases, the rate of photosynthesis increases, until the plant is photosynthesising as fast as it can. At this point, even if the light becomes brighter, the plant cannot photosynthesise any faster (Figure 6.23).

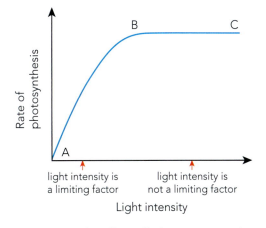

**Figure 6.23:** The effect of light intensity on the rate of photosynthesis.

Over the first part of the curve in Figure 6.23, between A and B, light is a limiting factor. The low light intensity is preventing the plant from photosynthesising any faster. The plant is limited in how fast it can photosynthesise because it does not have enough light. You can tell that this is so because the rising line on the graph shows that as the light intensity increases, the rate of photosynthesis increases.

Between B and C, however, light is **not** a limiting factor. You can see this because, even when the light intensity increases, the rate of photosynthesis stays the same. The graph shows that increasing the light intensity beyond B does not increase the rate of photosynthesis. The plant already has as much light as it can use.

## Carbon dioxide

Carbon dioxide can also be a limiting factor (Figure 6.24). The more carbon dioxide a plant is given, the faster it can photosynthesise. But once the carbon dioxide concentration reaches a certain level, there is no further increase in the rate of photosynthesis.

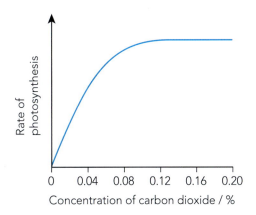

**Figure 6.24:** The effect of carbon dioxide concentration on the rate of photosynthesis.

## Temperature

The chemical reactions of photosynthesis can only take place slowly at low temperatures, so a plant can photosynthesise faster on a warm day than on a cold one.

Some of the reactions involved in photosynthesis are catalysed by enzymes, and therefore temperature affects the rate of photosynthesis in the same way as any enzyme-catalysed reaction. A graph of rate of photosynthesis against temperature would look quite similar to Figure 5.4. The main difference is that most plant enzymes have an optimum temperature that is much lower than that of mammalian enzymes. The curve would therefore lie to the left of the curve in Figure 5.4.

## Stomata

Carbon dioxide diffuses into the leaf through the stomata. If the stomata are closed, photosynthesis cannot take place because the plant lacks one of its raw materials. Stomata often close if the weather is very hot and sunny, to prevent too much water being lost. This means that on a really hot or bright day photosynthesis may slow down.

## Questions

13  Compare Figure 6.23 with the graph that you drew for your investigation into the effect of light intensity on the rate of photosynthesis. Are they similar in any way? What differences are there? Can you explain these differences?

14  Look at Figure 6.24.

   Between which values of carbon dioxide concentration is carbon dioxide a limiting factor? Explain how you can tell.

Sometimes, you may be asked to think about two limiting factors at once. The graph in Figure 6.25 shows how light intensity affects the rate of photosynthesis, at two different carbon dioxide concentrations.

First, look at the curve labelled **A**. As light intensity increases, up to a value of 25 a.u. (**arbitrary units**), the rate of photosynthesis increases. So, we know that light intensity is a limiting factor over this range. But if light intensity increases above 25 a.u, there is no change in the rate of photosynthesis. So light intensity is not a limiting factor now – it is not lack of light that is stopping the plant from photosynthesising faster.

But the graph does show a way of helping the plant to photosynthesise faster, at these high light intensities. We can give it more carbon dioxide. Curve **B** shows the results for a plant that was given a higher concentration of carbon dioxide. Clearly, it is photosynthesising faster than the one with a low concentration. So, for curve **A** at high light intensities, carbon dioxide is a limiting factor.

> ### KEY WORDS
>
> **arbitrary units:** these are sometimes used on a graph scale to represent quantitative differences between values, instead of 'real' units such as seconds or centimetres; this is usually because the real units would be very complicated to use

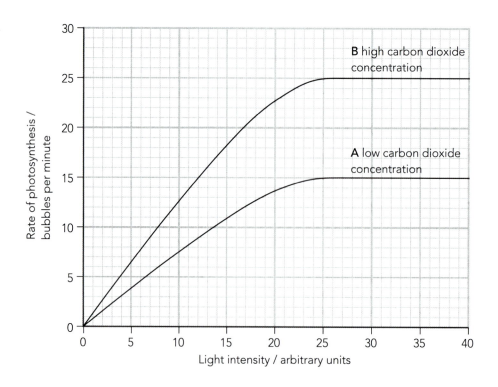

Figure 6.25: The effect of light intensity and carbon dioxide concentration on the rate of photosynthesis.

# 6 Plant nutrition

## SUMMARY

Photosynthesis is a reaction in which plants make carbohydrates from carbon dioxide and water, using light as a source of energy.

The word equation for photosynthesis is:
carbon dioxide + water → glucose + oxygen

The balanced equation is:
$6CO_2 + 6H_2O \rightarrow C_6H_{12}O_6 + 6O_2$

Chlorophyll is present in the chloroplasts of some plant cells. It transfers energy from light into energy in carbohydrates.

The carbohydrate glucose is made in photosynthesis, and this can be used to release energy in respiration. Glucose can be used to make starch for storage of energy, cellulose for cell walls, sucrose for transport and other sugars to make nectar.

Glucose can be used to make amino acids and proteins, using nitrogen obtained from nitrate ions. It can also be used to make chlorophyll, using nitrogen and also magnesium ions.

Leaves have a large surface area, to capture energy from sunlight and to increase absorption of carbon dioxide from the air. Stomata on the lower surface allow carbon dioxide to diffuse into the air spaces, and then to the cells in the palisade mesophyll layer, where most photosynthesis takes place.

To test a leaf for starch, it is first boiled to break down cell membranes, then heated in alcohol to remove the chlorophyll, and finally iodine solution is added.

We can use the starch test to show that leaves, or parts of a leaf, that do not have light, chlorophyll or carbon dioxide are not able to photosynthesise and make starch. Controls are needed so that we can compare the results with them.

We can use an aquatic plant to measure the rate of photosynthesis, by counting the number of bubbles given off in unit time, or by measuring the volume of gas given off in unit time.

This method, using an aquatic plant, can be used to investigate the effect of altering light intensity, temperature or carbon dioxide concentration on the rate of photosynthesis.

An environmental factor that is in short supply, and is preventing a plant from photosynthesising any faster, is called a limiting factor. We can recognise a limiting factor because if the plant is given more of it, the plant photosynthesises faster.

Light intensity, carbon dioxide concentration and temperature can all be limiting factors for photosynthesis.

## PROJECT

### Designing a glasshouse

Work in a group of three or four for this activity. You might like to assign different roles to different people (e.g. organiser, researcher, communicator and so on).

You are going to design a glasshouse (Figure 6.26) to grow a crop in your country. The glasshouse will provide ideal conditions to help the plants to photosynthesise quickly and grow fast, so that they will provide a high yield for the grower. Your group will then give a presentation to the rest of the class.

Here are some things to think about and research:

- What crop will you grow in the glasshouse?
- What conditions does this crop need to grow well?
- How can a glasshouse provide better conditions for the crop, than if it was grown outside?
- How will you control temperature in the glasshouse? In your country, will you need to heat the glasshouse or cool it – or do both at different times?
- How will you control light in the glasshouse? In your country, will you need to give extra light, or might you need to shade the glasshouse sometimes?
- How will you provide carbon dioxide in the glasshouse? Providing carbon dioxide costs money, so what might be a suitable concentration to aim for, that will give you a good return for your expenditure?

You can make your presentation as a video, use PowerPoint or make models and draw diagrams – or all of these methods if you like.

**Figure 6.26:** Pepper plants growing in a glasshouse in the Netherlands. These plants are growing with their roots in a liquid containing just the right quantities of the mineral ions that they need, rather than in soil.

# 6 Plant nutrition

## EXAM-STYLE QUESTIONS

1 What are the raw materials required for photosynthesis?
   A carbon dioxide and oxygen
   B oxygen and glucose
   C glucose and water
   D water and carbon dioxide [1]

2 A student investigated the necessity of light for photosynthesis. He covered a leaf with black paper to prevent light reaching it. What is an appropriate control for his experiment?
   A a leaf that has been destarched
   B a leaf that is not covered with black paper
   C a leaf that is partly white and partly green
   D a leaf that has no carbon dioxide provided [1]

3 Which ions does a plant require to make amino acids from glucose?
   A calcium
   B iron
   C magnesium
   D nitrate [1]

4 In photosynthesis, how many glucose molecules can be made from 30 carbon dioxide molecules and 30 water molecules?
   A 5
   B 6
   C 30
   D 60 [1]

5 The graph shows how two variables affect the rate of photosynthesis in a plant. At which value of carbon dioxide concentration is carbon dioxide **not** a limiting factor? [1]

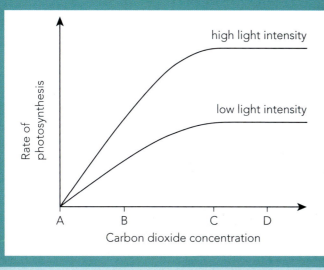

## CONTINUED

**6** The diagram shows a three-dimensional drawing of a section through a leaf.

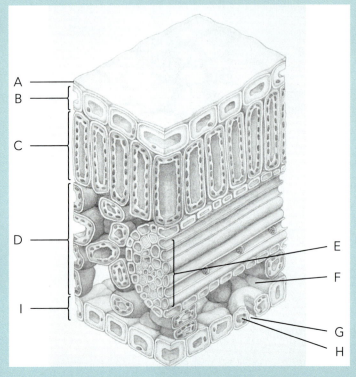

- **a**  **i**  Name the tissue labelled C. [1]
-    **ii** **Outline** how this tissue is adapted for its function. [3]
- **b** **Give** the letters of **two** cells or tissues that do **not** contain chloroplasts. [2]
- **c** **Describe** the function of the cell labelled H. [2]
- **d** Use the letters on the diagram to describe how water reaches a chloroplast in the leaf. [2]

[Total: 10]

### COMMAND WORDS

**outline:** set out main points

**give:** produce an answer from a given source or recall/memory

**describe:** state the points of a topic / give characteristics and main features

# 6 Plant nutrition

## CONTINUED

**7** The bar chart shows the mean number of chloroplasts in four different types of cell in a leaf.

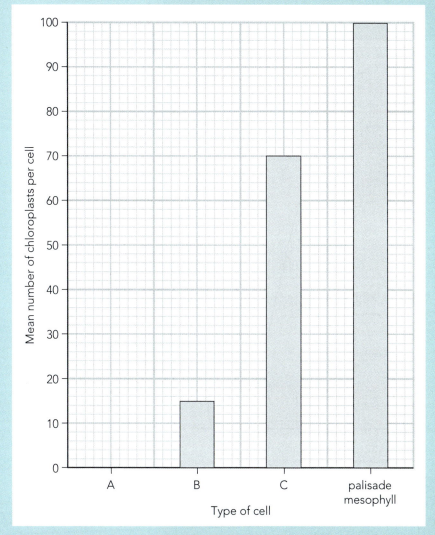

a **Explain** why palisade mesophyll cells have so many chloroplasts. [2]
b Which cell could be a cell in the upper epidermis? Explain your answer. [2]
c Guard cells contain chloroplasts, but not as many as spongy mesophyll cells. Which cell could be a guard cell? [1]
d Chloroplasts contain chlorophyll. Describe the function of chlorophyll in photosynthesis. [2]

[Total: 7]

**8** a Describe how plants synthesise carbohydrates. [4]
b Outline **two** subsequent uses of the carbohydrates made in photosynthesis. [4]

[Total: 8]

> **COMMAND WORD**
>
> **explain:** set out purposes or reasons / make the relationships between things evident / provide why and/or how and support with relevant evidence

## CONTINUED

9 An experiment was carried out to measure the rate of photosynthesis of a plant at different temperatures. The experiment was carried out first in normal air, and then in air enriched with carbon dioxide.

The results are shown in the graph.

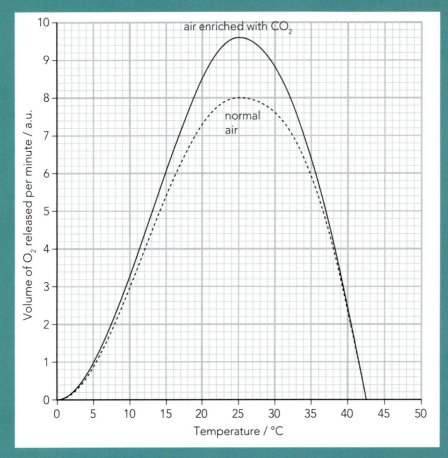

a Use the graph to describe the effect of increasing temperature on the rate of photosynthesis in normal air. [4]

b Explain the differences between the two curves between a temperature of 0 °C and 25 °C. Use the term *limiting factor* in your explanation. [3]

c Suggest why the optimum temperature of 25 °C is the same for both curves. [2]

d Explain the shape of the curves above 25 °C. [3]

[Total: 12]

## CONTINUED

**10** Two students carried out an experiment to investigate the effect of carbon dioxide concentration on the rate of photosynthesis of an aquatic plant. The photograph shows some of the apparatus that they used.

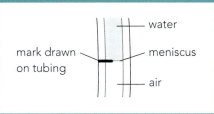

- The students filled five syringes with five different concentrations of sodium hydrogencarbonate solution. This provides carbon dioxide.
- They placed a piece of aquatic plant in each syringe.
- They attached a long transparent tube to the nozzle of each syringe.
- They pushed the plunger of each syringe in a little way, to force some of the sodium hydrogencarbonate into the tubing.
- They then pulled each plunger out a little way, to introduce some air into the tubing.
- They marked the position of the meniscus on each piece of tubing, as shown in the diagram.

## CONTINUED

All five syringes were then placed in bright sunshine. As the plants photosynthesised, they released oxygen. The oxygen gas collected above the liquid in the syringe, pushing the liquid down the tube.

The students recorded the distance moved by the meniscus in each piece of apparatus after 30 minutes.

a  Identify the independent variable and the dependent variable in this investigation. [2]

b  Explain why the five syringes were placed in bright sunshine. [2]

The table shows the results of the experiment.

| | Percentage concentration of sodium hydrogencarbonate solution | | | | |
|---|---|---|---|---|---|
| Distance moved by meniscus after 30 minutes / mm | 0 | 0.1 | 0.2 | 0.3 | 0.4 |
| | 5 | 8 | 12 | 14 | 17 |

c  Draw a line graph to display these results. Join the points with ruled straight lines. [5]

d  Is carbon dioxide a limiting factor at any of the concentrations of sodium hydrogencarbonate used in this investigation? Explain your answer. [2]

e  i  Suggest **two** possible sources of error in this investigation. [2]

   ii  Suggest how the investigation could be modified to reduce these sources of error. [2]

[Total: 15]

# 6 Plant nutrition

## SELF-EVALUATION CHECKLIST

After studying this chapter, think about how confident you are with the different topics. This will help you to see any gaps in your knowledge and help you to learn more effectively.

| I can | See Topic… | Needs more work | Almost there | Confident to move on |
|---|---|---|---|---|
| state the word equation for photosynthesis | 6.1 | | | |
| write the balanced equation for photosynthesis | 6.1 | | | |
| describe the role of chlorophyll in transferring energy from light to carbohydrates, in photosynthesis | 6.1 | | | |
| outline the uses of starch, cellulose, sucrose and nectar, made from the carbohydrates made in photosynthesis | 6.1 | | | |
| state the functions of nitrate ions and magnesium ions in a plant | 6.1 | | | |
| describe the structure of a leaf, and name the different cell types and layers | 6.2 | | | |
| explain how the features of a leaf are adaptations for photosynthesis | 6.2 | | | |
| describe how to investigate the necessity for chlorophyll, light and carbon dioxide for photosynthesis | 6.3 | | | |
| explain what a control is, in an experiment | 6.3 | | | |
| describe how to investigate the effect of varying light intensity, carbon dioxide concentration and temperature on the rate of photosynthesis of an aquatic plant | 6.3 | | | |
| describe how to use hydrogencarbonate indicator to investigate the effect of light and dark on an aquatic plant | 6.3 | | | |
| explain what a limiting factor is | 6.3 | | | |
| explain how light intensity, temperature and carbon dioxide concentration can act as limiting factors for photosynthesis | 6.3 | | | |
| use information presented on graphs to identify limiting factors | 6.3 | | | |

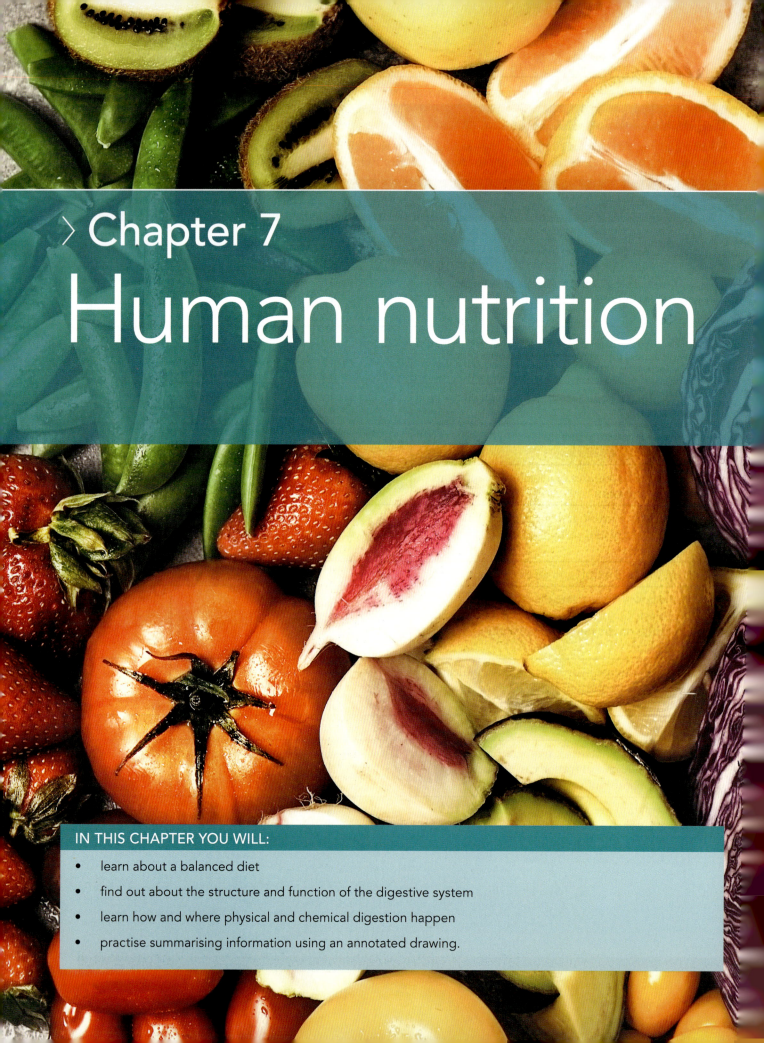

# Chapter 7
# Human nutrition

**IN THIS CHAPTER YOU WILL:**

- learn about a balanced diet
- find out about the structure and function of the digestive system
- learn how and where physical and chemical digestion happen
- practise summarising information using an annotated drawing.

# 7 Human nutrition

## GETTING STARTED

First, think on your own about the answers to these questions about biological molecules.

Then discuss your ideas with a partner.

Be ready to share your ideas.

1. What type of biological molecule is starch?
2. What are the smaller units that a starch molecule is made of?
3. What are the smaller units that a protein molecule is made of?
4. Lipase is an enzyme that digests fats. What are the products of this reaction?
5. What type of biological molecule is lipase?

## STOMACH ACID

The photograph in Figure 7.1 shows the inside of a healthy human stomach. The picture was taken using a tiny camera on the end of a tube that can be passed down the oesophagus and into the stomach.

The stomach is a very important part of the digestive system. It has strong, muscular walls, which help to break up food that you have swallowed and mix it with liquids. The folded walls of the stomach produce a liquid called gastric juice. This juice contains hydrochloric acid and enzymes that break down protein molecules.

The hydrochloric acid in your stomach has a concentration of about $0.1\,\text{mol}\,\text{dm}^{-3}$. Hydrochloric acid is a strong acid. If you dipped a piece of blue litmus paper into this acid, it would go red. The acid helps us by killing many of the microorganisms in the food that we swallow.

The stomach does not produce acid all the time. It starts to do it when we smell, taste, see or think about eating food.

### Discussion questions

1. The stomachs of some carnivorous animals, such as lions and hyenas, secrete more concentrated acid than we do. Can you suggest how this may help them to survive?
2. Suggest why it is not good for the stomach to secrete acid all the time.

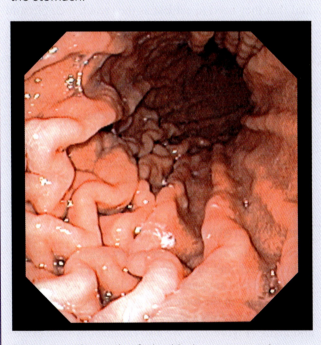

Figure 7.1: The inside of a healthy human stomach.

## 7.1 Diet

The food an animal eats every day is called its **diet**. Humans need six types of nutrient in their diet. These are:

- carbohydrates
- proteins
- fats
- vitamins
- minerals
- water.

In addition, the diet should contain fibre (roughage). This is not really a nutrient, as it is not absorbed into the body. It just passes straight through the digestive system and is passed out in the faeces.

A diet which contains all of these things, in the correct amounts and proportions, is called a **balanced diet**.

> **KEY WORDS**
>
> **diet:** the food eaten in one day
>
> **balanced diet:** a diet that contains all of the required nutrients, in suitable proportions, and the right amount of energy

### Energy needs

Every day, a person uses up energy. The amount you use partly depends on how old you are, which sex you are and what job you do. A few examples are shown in Figure 7.2.

The energy you use each day comes from the food you eat. If you eat too much food, some of the extra will probably be stored as fat. If you eat too little, you may not be able to obtain as much energy as you need. This will make you feel tired.

All food contains some energy. Scientists have worked out how much energy there is in particular kinds of food. You can look up this information on the internet. One gram of fat contains about twice as much energy as one gram of protein or carbohydrate.

A person's diet may need to change at different times of their life. For example, a woman will need to eat a little more each day when she is pregnant, and make sure that she has extra calcium and iron in her diet, to help to build her baby's bones, teeth and blood. She will also need to eat more while she is breast feeding. Most people find that they need to eat less as they reach their 50s and 60s, because their metabolism slows down.

### Nutrients

As well as providing you with energy, food is needed for many other reasons. To make sure that you eat a balanced diet, you must eat foods containing carbohydrate, fat and protein. You also need each kind of vitamin and mineral, fibre and water. If your diet doesn't contain all of these substances, your body will not be able to work properly.

#### Carbohydrates

Carbohydrates are needed for energy. Carbohydrates include starch and sugar. In most countries, there is a staple food that supplies much of the carbohydrate in people's diets, in the form of starch. Staple foods include potatoes, wheat (often made into bread or pasta), rice and maize (Figure 7.3). We also eat carbohydrate in sweet foods, which contain sugar.

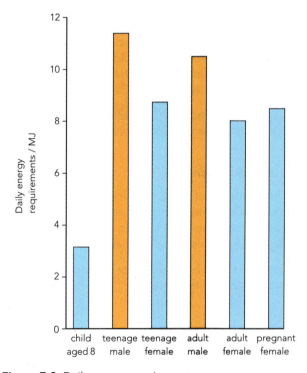

Figure 7.2: Daily energy requirements.

# 7 Human nutrition

**Figure 7.3:** Some good sources of carbohydrate.

## Fats and oils

Fats and oils are needed for energy, and to make cell membranes. We store excess fat and oil under the skin, in adipose tissue. Here, it acts as an insulator, reducing heat loss from the body to the air. It can also form a layer around body organs such as the kidneys, providing mechanical protection for them. We obtain fat from cooking oils, meat, eggs, dairy products and oily fish (Figure 7.4).

## Proteins

Proteins are needed to build new cells, for growth. They are also used to make proteins, including haemoglobin, insulin (a hormone) and antibodies (which help to destroy pathogens). We get protein from meat, fish, eggs, dairy products, peas and beans, nuts and seeds (Figure 7.5).

**Figure 7.4:** Some good sources of fats and oils.

**Figure 7.5:** Some good sources of protein.

## Vitamins

Vitamins are organic substances which are only needed in tiny amounts. If you do not have enough of a vitamin, you may get a deficiency disease. Table 7.1 shows information about sources and uses in the body of vitamins C and D.

| Vitamin | Foods that contain it | Why it is needed | Deficiency disease |
|---|---|---|---|
| C | citrus fruits (such as oranges, limes), raw vegetables | to make the stretchy protein collagen, found in skin and other tissues; keeps tissues in good repair | scurvy, which causes pain in joints and muscles, and bleeding from gums and other places; this used to be a common disease of sailors, who had no fresh vegetables during long voyages |
| D | butter, egg yolk (but most of our vitamin D is made by the skin when sunlight falls on it) | helps calcium to be absorbed, for making bones and teeth | rickets, in which the bones become soft and deformed; this disease was common in young children in industrial areas, who rarely got out into the sunshine |

**Table 7.1:** Vitamins C and D.

## Minerals

Minerals are inorganic substances. Once again, only small amounts of them are needed in the diet. Table 7.2 gives information about the sources and uses of two of the most important ones.

| Mineral ion | Foods that contain it | Why it is needed | Deficiency disease |
|---|---|---|---|
| calcium | milk and other dairy products, bread | for bones and teeth; for blood clotting | brittle bones and teeth; poor blood clotting |
| iron | liver, red meat, egg yolk, dark green vegetables | for making haemoglobin, the red pigment in blood which carries oxygen | anaemia, in which there are not enough red blood cells so the tissues do not get enough oxygen delivered to them |

**Table 7.2:** Calcium and iron.

## Fibre

Fibre helps to keep the alimentary canal working properly. The alimentary canal is the part of the digestive system through which food passes as it moves from the mouth to the anus. Food moves through the alimentary canal (see Topic 7.2) because the muscles contract and relax to squeeze it along. This is called **peristalsis**. The muscles are stimulated to do this when there is food in the alimentary canal. Soft foods do not stimulate the muscles very much. The muscles work more strongly when there is harder, less digestible food, like fibre, in the alimentary canal. Fibre keeps the digestive system in good working order and helps to prevent constipation.

All plant foods, such as fruits and vegetables, contain fibre (Figure 7.6). This is because plant cells have cellulose cell walls. Humans cannot digest cellulose.

One excellent source of fibre is the outer husk of cereal grains, such as oats, wheat and barley. This is called bran. Some of this husk is found in wholemeal bread. Brown or unpolished rice is also a good source of fibre.

> **KEY WORD**
>
> **peristalsis:** rhythmical muscular contractions that move food through the alimentary canal

**Figure 7.6:** Some good sources of fibre (roughage).

## Water

More than 60% of the human body is water. Water is an important solvent. Cytoplasm is a solution of many substances in water. The spaces between our cells are also filled with a watery liquid.

Inside our cells, chemical reactions are happening all the time. These are called metabolic reactions. They can only take place if the chemicals that are reacting are in solution. If a cell dries out, then the reactions stop, and the cell dies.

The liquid part of blood, plasma (Chapter 9), is also mostly water. It contains many substances dissolved in it, which are transported around the body in the blood. Water is also needed to dissolve enzymes and nutrients in the alimentary canal, so that digestion can take place (Topic 7.3).

We also need water to get rid of waste products. As you will see in Chapter 13, the kidneys remove a waste product called urea from the blood. The urea is dissolved in water to form urine.

We get most of our water by drinking fluids, but some foods such as fruit also contain a lot of water.

> **ACTIVITY 7.1**
>
> **A balanced diet in your country**
>
> You are going to work as a group to construct a balanced diet, by thinking about foods that are commonly eaten in your country.
>
> In your group, discuss the foods that people eat in your country. Decide which ones are good sources of each kind of nutrient.
>
> Construct a simple menu for the meals someone will eat in a day, ensuring that all the different nutrients are contained in the food. Don't forget to include drinks as well.
>
> If you can, collect these foods together and take photographs of the meals, or the ingredients from which they would be made.

## Questions

1. Too much animal fat in the diet can increase the risk of heart disease. Explain why, despite this, we still need to eat some fat or oil.
2. Too much sugar in the diet can increase the risk of tooth decay and diabetes. Explain how we can avoid these risks but still eat plenty of carbohydrate.
3. Construct a table showing the main dietary sources of carbohydrate, fat and protein, and their uses in the body.

> ### REFLECTION
>
> Some people find that summarising facts in a table – as in Question 3 – helps them to learn and remember the information. Does that work for you? Is it better if you construct the table yourself or if you just learn a table that is given to you?

## 7.2 The human digestive system

You may remember that a body system, such as the **digestive system**, is a group of organs that work together to perform a particular function. The human digestive system includes the alimentary canal and also the **liver** and the **pancreas**. All of these work together to break down the food that we eat, so that it can be **absorbed** into the blood and delivered to all body cells.

> ### KEY WORDS
>
> **digestive system:** the group of organs that carries out digestion of food
>
> **liver:** a large, dark red organ that carries out many different functions, including production of bile and the regulation of blood glucose concentration
>
> **pancreas:** a creamy-white organ lying close to the stomach, which secretes pancreatic juice; it also secretes the hormones insulin and glucagon, which are involved in the control of blood glucose concentration
>
> **absorbed:** soaked up; nutrients are absorbed from the alimentary canal into the blood, through the walls of the small intestine

The digestive system deals with the food in a series of processes (Figure 7.7). These are:

- **ingestion** – This means taking food and drink into the mouth. We do this using the lips, teeth and tongue.
- **digestion** – The food that we eat contains large pieces and large molecules. The large pieces have to be broken down to small pieces (**physical digestion**) and the large molecules must be broken down to small molecules (**chemical digestion**). The small molecules can then get through the walls of the intestines and into the blood.
- **absorption** – This is the movement of the small nutrient molecules and mineral ions through the walls of the intestines and into the blood.
- **assimilation** – This is what happens to the nutrients as they become part of the body. They are absorbed by individual cells and used for energy or to make new substances.
- **egestion** – There is always some material in our food that we cannot digest. Much of this is fibre. This is not absorbed. It remains in the intestines and eventually passes out as faeces.

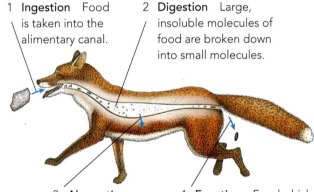

1. **Ingestion** Food is taken into the alimentary canal.
2. **Digestion** Large, insoluble molecules of food are broken down into small molecules.
3. **Absorption** The small molecules are absorbed into the blood.
4. **Egestion** Food which could not be digested or absorbed is removed from the body.

**Figure 7.7:** How the digestive system of a fox deals with food. The human digestive system works in a similar way.

The processes of chemical digestion and physical digestion are described in Topic 7.3. Absorption is described in Topic 7.4. To begin with, we will look at the structure of the alimentary canal, and outline what happens in each part.

## 7 Human nutrition

> **KEY WORDS**
>
> **ingestion:** the taking of food and drink into the body
>
> **digestion:** the breakdown of food
>
> **physical digestion:** the breakdown of food into smaller pieces, without making any chemical changes to the molecules in the food
>
> **chemical digestion:** the breakdown of large molecules in food into smaller molecules, so that they can be absorbed
>
> **absorption:** the movement of nutrients from the alimentary canal into the blood
>
> **assimilation:** the uptake and use of nutrients by cells
>
> **egestion:** the removal of undigested food from the body as faeces

## Questions

These questions are about Figure 7.8.

4   Explain the difference between the alimentary canal and the digestive system.

5   Name **two** parts of the digestive system that food does **not** pass through.

> **KEY WORDS**
>
> **anus:** the exit from the alimentary canal, through which faeces are removed
>
> **sphincter muscles:** rings of muscle that can contract to close a tube
>
> **lubricated:** made smooth and slippery, to reduce friction
>
> **mucus:** a smooth, viscous fluid secreted by many different organs in the body
>
> **goblet cells:** cells found in the lining (epithelium) of the respiratory passages and digestive system, which secrete mucus

## The alimentary canal

The alimentary canal is a long tube which runs from the mouth to the **anus**. It is part of the digestive system. As we have seen, the digestive system also includes the liver and the pancreas.

The wall of the alimentary canal contains muscles, which contract and relax to make food move along. These muscular contractions are called peristalsis.

Sometimes, it is necessary to keep the food in one part of the alimentary canal for a while, before it is allowed to move to the next part. Special muscles can close the tube completely in certain places. They are called **sphincter muscles**.

To help the food to slide easily through the alimentary canal, it is **lubricated** with **mucus**. Mucus is made in **goblet cells** which are found in the lining of the alimentary canal, along its entire length.

Each section of the alimentary canal has its own part to play in the digestion, absorption and egestion of food. Figure 7.8 shows the main organs of the digestive system.

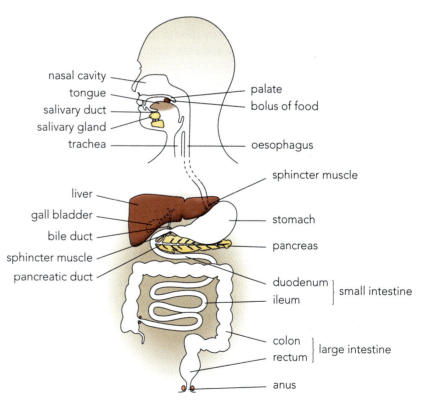

Figure 7.8: The human digestive system.

133

## The mouth

Food is ingested using the teeth, lips and tongue. The teeth then bite or grind the food into smaller pieces, increasing its surface area. This begins physical digestion. You can find much more about teeth in Topic 7.3.

The tongue mixes the food with saliva and forms it into a little ball that can be swallowed.

The **salivary glands** make saliva. This is a mixture of water, mucus and the enzyme amylase. The water helps to dissolve substances in the food, allowing us to taste them. The mucus helps the chewed food to bind together to form a small ball, and lubricates it so that it slides easily down the **oesophagus** when it is swallowed. Amylase begins to digest starch – see Topic 7.3 for much more about this, and all the other examples of digestion mentioned here.

## The oesophagus

There are two tubes leading down from the back of the mouth. The one in front is the **trachea** or windpipe, which takes air down to the lungs. Behind the trachea is the oesophagus, which takes food down to the **stomach**.

The 'hole' in the centre of the oesophagus, down which food can pass, is called a **lumen**. This word is used to describe the space in the middle of any tube in the body. There is a lumen in all parts of the alimentary canal. All blood vessels also have a lumen.

The entrance to the stomach from the oesophagus is closed by a sphincter muscle. The muscle relaxes to let food pass into the stomach, then contracts to close the entrance again.

## The stomach

The stomach (Figures 7.1 and 7.9) has strong, muscular walls. The muscles contract and relax to mix the food with the enzymes and mucus.

Like all parts of the alimentary canal, the stomach wall contains goblet cells which secrete mucus. It also contains other cells which produce enzymes and others which make hydrochloric acid. The enzymes produced in the stomach digest proteins, so they are proteases.

The hydrochloric acid produces a low pH, of about pH 2, in the stomach, which kills harmful microorganisms in the food. This pH is also the optimum pH for the protease enzymes that act in the stomach.

The stomach can store food for quite a long time. After one or two hours, the sphincter at the bottom of the stomach opens and lets the partly digested food move into the **duodenum**.

> ### KEY WORDS
>
> **salivary glands:** groups of cells close to the mouth, which secrete saliva into the salivary ducts
>
> **oesophagus:** the tube leading from the mouth to the stomach
>
> **trachea:** the tube through which air travels to the lungs; it has rings of cartilage in its walls, to support it
>
> **stomach:** a wide part of the alimentary canal, in which food can be stored for a while, and where the digestion of protein begins
>
> **lumen:** the space in the centre of a tube, through which substances can move
>
> **duodenum:** the first part of the small intestine, into which the pancreatic duct and bile duct empty fluids

## The small intestine

The **small intestine** is the part of the alimentary canal between the stomach and the **colon**. It is about 5 m long. It is called the small intestine because it is quite narrow. Different parts of the small intestine have different names. The first part, nearest to the stomach, is the duodenum. The last part, nearest to the colon, is the **ileum**.

The pancreas is a cream-coloured gland, lying just underneath the stomach. A tube called the **pancreatic duct** leads from the pancreas into the duodenum.

Pancreatic juice is a fluid made by the pancreas. It flows along the pancreatic duct into the duodenum. Pancreatic juice contains many different enzymes, so chemical digestion continues in the duodenum.

The ileum is where all the digested nutrients are absorbed into the blood. This is described in Topic 7.4. Water is also absorbed into the blood at this stage.

# 7 Human nutrition

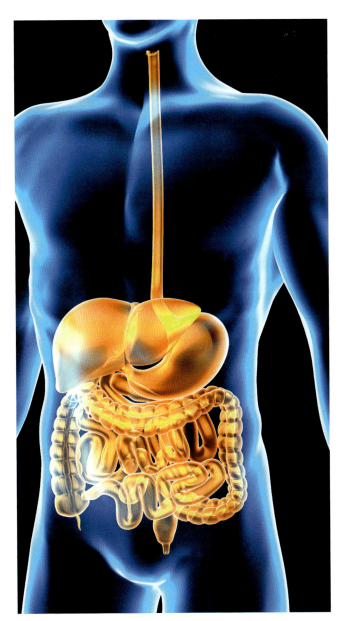

Figure 7.9: This artwork shows where some of the organs of the digestive system are positioned in the body. Can you name any of them?

## The pancreas and liver

The pancreas and liver are important organs in the digestive system, but they are not part of the alimentary canal. Food does not pass through them.

We have seen that the pancreas secretes a fluid containing enzymes, which help with digestion of food in the duodenum. The liver also secretes a fluid that helps with digestion. This fluid is called **bile**.

The bile that has been made by the liver is stored in the **gall bladder**. When food enters the duodenum, the bile flows along the **bile duct** and is mixed with the food in the duodenum.

Bile is a yellowish green, alkaline, watery liquid, which helps to neutralise the acidic mixture from the stomach.

> **KEY WORDS**
>
> **small intestine:** a long, narrow part of the alimentary canal, consisting of the duodenum and ileum
>
> **colon:** the first part of the large intestine
>
> **ileum:** the second part of the small intestine; most absorption takes place here
>
> **pancreatic duct:** the tube that carries pancreatic fluid from the pancreas to the duodenum
>
> **large intestine:** a relatively wide part of the alimentary canal, consisting of the colon and rectum
>
> **rectum:** the second part of the large intestine, where faeces are produced and stored
>
> **bile:** an alkaline fluid produced by the liver, which helps with fat digestion
>
> **gall bladder:** a small organ that stores bile, before the bile is released into the duodenum
>
> **bile duct:** the tube that carries bile from the gall bladder to the duodenum

## The large intestine

The final part of the alimentary canal is the **large intestine**. It is made up of the colon and **rectum**. The colon absorbs much of the water that still remains in the food. The rectum stores undigested food as faeces. These are then egested from the body through the anus.

## Questions

6  List, in order, all the parts of the digestive system through which food passes as it moves from the mouth to the anus.

7  a  Which of the parts you have named in Question 6 are involved in ingestion?

   b  Which parts are involved in digestion?

   c  Which parts are involved in absorption?

   d  Which parts are involved in egestion?

# 7.3 Digestion

The food that we eat usually contains large molecules of starch (a type of carbohydrate), protein and fat. These large molecules are too big to get through the walls of the intestines and into the blood. They must be broken down into much smaller molecules, allowing them to be absorbed. As you have seen, this process is called digestion.

Digestion takes place in two stages:

- **Physical digestion:** First, large pieces of food are broken down into smaller pieces. This is mostly done by the teeth, but the churning movements of the stomach also help. This physical digestion does not change the chemical components of the food in any way.

- **Chemical digestion:** Next, the large molecules in the food are broken apart into smaller molecules. This involves chemical reactions, and they are catalysed by enzymes. These smaller molecules are soluble in water, which makes it easier for them to be absorbed into cells.

Table 7.3 summarises what happens to each of the large molecules of starch, protein and fat as a result of digestion. The molecules of vitamins and water are already small enough to be absorbed, and this is also the case for mineral ions. So, none of those need to be chemically digested.

| Large molecule | Enzyme that breaks it down | Small molecules produced |
|---|---|---|
| starch | amylase | simple reducing sugars |
| protein | protease | amino acids |
| fat | lipase | fatty acids and glycerol |

**Table 7.3:** The effect of digestion on starch, protein and fat.

## Teeth

Teeth help with the ingestion and mechanical digestion of the food we eat.

Teeth can be used to bite off pieces of food. They then chop, crush or grind the pieces into smaller pieces. This gives the food a larger surface area, which makes it easier for enzymes to work on the food in the digestive system. It also helps any soluble molecules or ions in the food to dissolve in the watery saliva in the mouth.

The structure of a tooth is shown in Figure 7.10. The tooth is embedded in the gum. The part of the tooth above the gum is covered with **enamel**. Enamel is the hardest substance made by animals. It is very difficult to break or chip it. However, it can be dissolved by acids. Bacteria feed on sweet foods left on the teeth. These bacteria produce acids, which dissolve the enamel and cause decay.

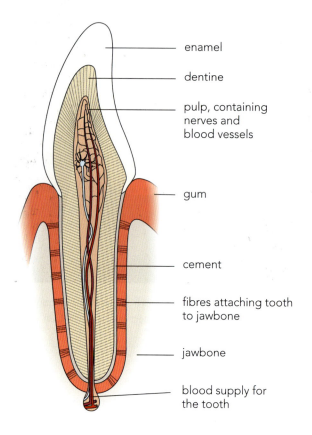

**Figure 7.10:** The structure of an incisor tooth.

# 7 Human nutrition

Under the enamel is a layer of dentine, which is rather like bone. Dentine is quite hard, but not as hard as enamel. It has channels in it which contain living cytoplasm.

In the middle of the tooth, there are nerves and blood vessels. The blood vessels supply the cytoplasm in the dentine with nutrients and oxygen.

The part of the tooth that is embedded in the gum is covered with cement. This has fibres growing out of it. These attach the tooth to the bone in the jaw but allow it to move slightly when biting or chewing.

Most mammals have four kinds of teeth (Figure 7.11). **Incisors** are the sharp-edged, chisel-shaped teeth at the front of the mouth. They are used for biting off pieces of food. **Canines** are the more pointed teeth at either side of the incisors. **Premolars** and **molars** are the large teeth towards the back of the mouth. They are used for chewing food. In humans, the ones right at the back are sometimes called wisdom teeth. They do not grow until much later in the person's development than the others.

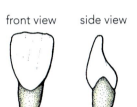
front view   side view

Incisors are chisel shaped for biting off pieces of food.

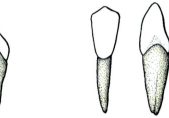
Canines are very similar to incisors in humans.

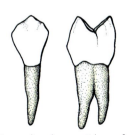
Premolars have wide surfaces, for grinding food.

Molars, like premolars, are used for grinding.

**Figure 7.11:** The four types of mammalian teeth.

> ## KEY WORDS
>
> **enamel:** the very strong material that covers the surface of a tooth
>
> **dentine:** a living tissue that lies just beneath the enamel of a tooth
>
> **cement:** the material that holds a tooth in the gum
>
> **incisors:** chisel-shaped teeth at the front of the mouth, used for biting off pieces of food
>
> **canines:** pointed teeth at either side of the incisors, used in a similar way to incisors; in carnivores, they are used for killing prey
>
> **premolars:** teeth with broad, ridged surfaces, found between the canines and molars; they are used for grinding food to increase its surface area
>
> **molars:** teeth similar to premolars but usually larger, with broad, ridged surfaces, found towards the back of the mouth; they are used for grinding food to increase its surface area

> ## ACTIVITY 7.2
>
> ### Counting your own teeth
>
> You can work on your own for this activity, using a mirror to look at your own teeth. Alternatively, you could work with a partner and count each other's teeth.
>
> Count the total number of teeth on your upper jaw. Then count how many of these are incisors, canines or premolars and molars. (You cannot tell the different between premolars and molars, so just count these together.)
>
> Now do the same for your lower jaw.
>
> Does everyone in your class have the same number of teeth as you? If not, suggest reasons for any differences.

## Chemical digestion

The actions of the teeth and stomach help to break food into smaller pieces, increasing its surface area. This means enzymes can more easily make contact with the molecules in the food and start to break them apart.

Table 7.4 summarises where each type of enzyme is made, and where it works in the human digestive system.

| Enzyme | Where it is secreted | Where it acts |
|---|---|---|
| amylase | by the salivary glands | in the mouth |
|  | by the pancreas | in the duodenum |
| protease | by the walls of the stomach | in the stomach |
|  | by the pancreas | in the duodenum |
| lipase | by the pancreas | in the duodenum |

**Table 7.4:** The sites of secretion and action of digestive enzymes.

In Chapter 5, we saw that enzymes are affected by temperature and pH. The digestive enzymes in the human digestive system all work best at a temperature of about 38 °C, which is our normal body temperature.

The digestive enzymes vary in the pH at which they work best. The stomach walls secrete hydrochloric acid to kill bacteria, so the protease that works in the stomach has to be able to work in these conditions. It has an optimum pH of about 2. The enzymes that work in the duodenum require a pH of just above 7 to work at their fastest. This higher pH is provided by bile and pancreatic juice, which contain alkaline substances that neutralise the acidic mixture that passes into the duodenum from the stomach.

## Questions

8   Teeth are involved in physical digestion.
    a   How do they do this?
    b   Explain how physical digestion helps chemical digestion to happen faster.
9   Describe how the structure of a molar tooth adapts it for its function.
10  State **two** places in the human digestive system where starch is broken down to simple reducing sugars.
11  State **two** places in the human digestive system where proteins are digested.

## Enzymes in the human digestive system

In this topic, we will look in more detail at the way that digestive enzymes break down large food molecules.

We have seen that amylase is secreted into the mouth and the duodenum. The amylase in these two parts of the digestive system does the same thing – it breaks starch molecules down to a sugar called **maltose**. You may be able to taste this sugar if you chew starchy food for a long time, as the amylase in your saliva breaks the starch down.

Each maltose molecule is made of two glucose molecules linked together. Although maltose molecules are much smaller than starch molecules, they are still too big to be absorbed. Another enzyme, maltase, breaks the maltose molecules apart to produce glucose molecules. Maltase is secreted by the cells lining the small intestine. This lining tissue is called an **epithelium**. The maltase does not go into the lumen of the small intestine, but remains attached to the epithelial cells, sitting on their cell membranes. So, maltose is digested on the surface of these epithelial cells.

We can summarise this two-step process like this:

starch $\xrightarrow{amylase}$ maltose $\xrightarrow{maltase}$ glucose

> **KEY WORDS**
>
> **maltose:** a reducing sugar made of two glucose molecules joined together
>
> **epithelium:** a tissue that covers a surface in an animal; for example, an epithelium covers the inside of the wall of the human alimentary canal

Protease is secreted into the stomach and the duodenum. The protease that is produced in the stomach is called **pepsin**. Pepsin is secreted from the stomach walls, in a liquid called **gastric juice**. Gastric juice also contains hydrochloric acid, to kill harmful microorganisms in food. Pepsin has an optimum pH of 2, so it is perfectly suited to working in these very acidic conditions.

7 Human nutrition

The protease that is produced in the pancreas, and works in the duodenum, is called **trypsin**. Pepsin and trypsin both break protein molecules apart, producing amino acids. Amino acids are small enough to be absorbed.

Trypsin has an optimum pH just above 7. As we have seen, this means that the acidic contents of the stomach must be neutralised, and this is done by the alkaline substances in bile and pancreatic juice.

Bile has another important function. Fats and oils are insoluble in water, so any fat or oil in the food that you eat stays as little drops that do not fully mix into the watery fluids inside the digestive system. Bile acts rather like liquid detergent. It breaks up large drops of fat or oil into tiny droplets, which can disperse among the watery liquids. A mixture of tiny, floating droplets of one liquid in another is called an emulsion. So, bile **emulsifies** fats.

> **KEY WORDS**
>
> **pepsin:** a protease enzyme secreted in gastric juice; it has an optimum pH of 2
>
> **gastric juice:** a liquid secreted by the walls of the stomach; it contains pepsin and hydrochloric acid
>
> **trypsin:** a protease enzyme secreted by the pancreas; it works in the duodenum
>
> **emulsifies:** breaks down large drops of fat or oil into smaller droplets, increasing their surface area and allowing them to mix with watery liquids

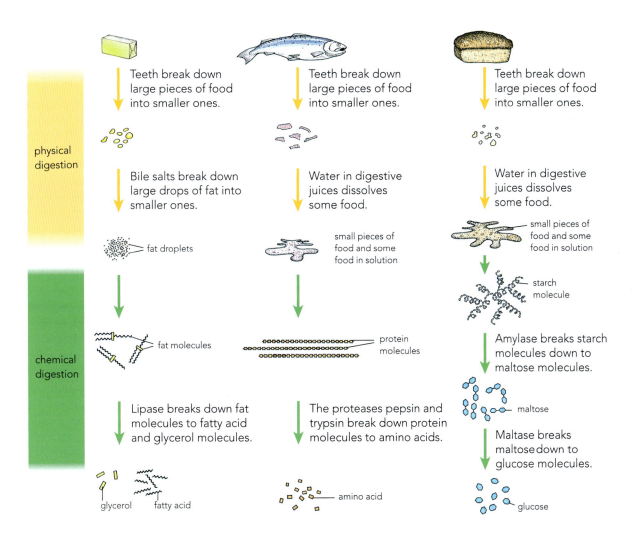

Figure 7.12: A summary of physical and chemical digestion in the human digestive system.

Notice that bile does not actually do anything to the individual fat molecules. Emulsification is physical digestion, not chemical digestion. Emulsification increases the surface area of the fat droplets. So, the emulsified fats are much easier for the fat-digesting enzyme, lipase, to access. Lipase can now chemically digest the fats, breaking them apart into fatty acids and glycerol.

Figure 7.12 summarises the physical and chemical digestion of fats, proteins and carbohydrates in the human digestive system.

## Questions

12 Name the part of the digestive system where each of these events occurs.
   a  Amylase breaks down starch to maltose
   b  Maltase breaks down maltose to glucose

13 a  From which part of the digestive system is lipase secreted?
   b  In which part of the digestive system does lipase act?

14 a  Where is pepsin secreted?
   b  Explain why pepsin stops working when the contents of the stomach pass into the duodenum.

15 Bile emulsifies fats. Explain what this means, and why it is an important part of fat digestion.

> ### ACTIVITY 7.3
>
> **Functions of organs in the digestive system**
>
> You can work in a group of two or three for this activity.
>
> On a large sheet of paper, make a very big drawing of the human digestive system.
>
> Leave plenty of space around your drawing, for labels and annotations.
>
> Label each part. To each label, add a description of what happens in that part.
>
> You could use different pens to colour code your written descriptions. For example, you could use one colour to represent physical digestion and a different colour to represent chemical digestion.

> ### CONTINUED
>
> **Note:** After you have learnt about absorption, in the next topic in this chapter, you may like to return to your drawing and add some more information about the small intestine. So, try to leave a little bit of space for this.
>
> **Peer assessment**
>
> Exchange your finished drawing with another group.
>
> Compare your drawing with theirs.
>
> Which one is clearer?
>
> Which contains more information?
>
> Which is the more interesting?

## 7.4 Absorption and assimilation

By the time food has passed through the duodenum, most of the large molecules have been fully digested to small ones. Carbohydrates have been broken down to glucose, proteins to amino acids, and fats to fatty acids and glycerol. These small, soluble molecules are now able to pass through the walls of the small intestine and into the blood. This process is called absorption.

There are also several other small molecules and ions in the food, which were already small enough to be absorbed and did not need to be digested. Mineral ions (including iron and calcium ions), vitamins and water are all absorbed into the blood from the small intestine. A smaller quantity of water is also absorbed in the colon.

# Villi

The inner wall of the small intestine is covered with tiny projections. They are called **villi** (singular: **villus**). Each villus is about 1 mm long. Figure 7.13 shows the lining of the small intestine with thousands of villi.

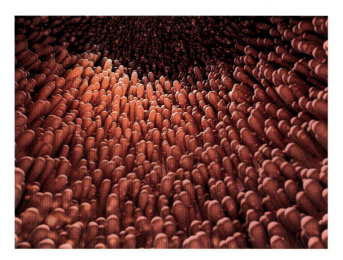

**Figure 7.13:** The villi that line the small intestine greatly increase its internal surface area.

Figure 7.14 shows the structure of a single villus.

The cell membrane on the surface of each villus is folded to form many tiny **microvilli**. It is on these membranes that maltase acts, breaking down maltose into glucose molecules. It is also through these membranes that glucose, amino acids, fatty acids, glycerol, vitamins, mineral ions and water are absorbed.

Most of these substances pass into the blood capillaries inside the villus. The blood capillaries from all the villi link up to join a vein, called the **hepatic portal vein**, which takes all of these substances to the liver.

> **KEY WORDS**
>
> **villi** (singular: **villus**): very small finger-like projections that line the inner surface of the small intestine, greatly increasing its surface area
>
> **microvilli**: tiny folds on the surfaces of the cells of the epithelium of the villi in the small intestine
>
> **hepatic portal vein**: the blood vessel that carries blood from the small intestine to the liver

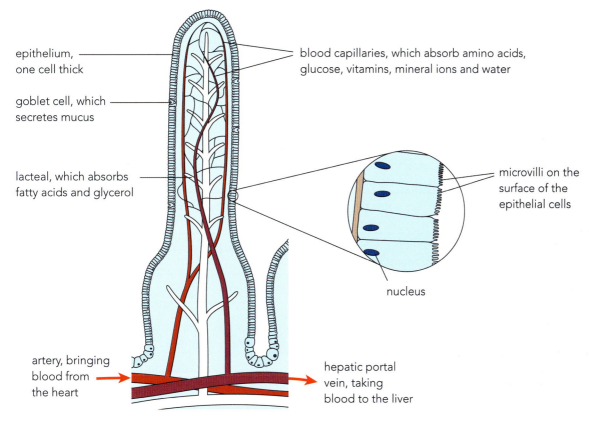

**Figure 7.14:** The structure of a villus.

The liver cells absorb and assimilate these substances. Glucose may be changed by the liver cells to glycogen for storage; you can read more about this in Chapter 13. Amino acids are used by the liver cells to make many different kinds of proteins, some of which are then returned to the blood to be transported to other parts of the body. If there are more amino acids than the body requires, they may be broken down in the liver to form urea, which is excreted. This is also described in Chapter 13.

The fatty acids and glycerol pass into the **lacteals**. The contents of the lacteals are eventually emptied into the blood.

You can see from the image in Figure 7.13 that the villi hugely increase the surface area of the lining of the small intestine. And as each villus is covered with thousands of microvilli, the total surface area is increased even more. This greatly speeds up the rate at which absorption happens.

> **KEY WORD**
>
> **lacteals:** small vessels that absorb fatty acids and glycerol in the small intestine; their contents are eventually emptied into the blood

## SUMMARY

| |
|---|
| A balanced diet contains some of all six nutrients – proteins, carbohydrates, fats, minerals, vitamins and water – in suitable amounts and proportions. It also contains fibre. |
| Scurvy is caused by a lack of vitamin C, and rickets by a lack of vitamin D. |
| The digestive system is made up of the mouth, oesophagus, stomach, duodenum and ileum (small intestine), colon and rectum (large intestine), the liver, gall bladder and pancreas. |
| Food is first ingested; this is followed by digestion, absorption and assimilation. Food that cannot be absorbed is egested. |
| Physical digestion is done by the teeth and stomach. It involves breaking large pieces of food to small ones. |
| Chemical digestion is done by enzymes in the mouth, stomach and small intestine. It involves breaking down large molecules of nutrients to small ones, so that they can be absorbed. |
| Teeth help in physical digestion, grinding food into smaller pieces to increase its surface area. This allows subsequent chemical digestion to happen faster. Humans have four types of teeth – incisors, canines, premolars and molars. |
| In chemical digestion: amylase breaks down starch to simpler reducing sugars; protease breaks down proteins to amino acids: lipase breaks down fats to fatty acids and glycerol. |
| Hydrochloric acid in the stomach provides a low pH for enzymes to work, and also kills harmful microorganisms in food. |
| Amylase breaks down starch to maltose in the mouth and duodenum. Maltase breaks down maltose to glucose, on the surface of the villi in the small intestine. |
| The protease in the stomach is called pepsin, and it requires a low pH which is supplied by the hydrochloric acid secreted in gastric juice. The pancreas secretes a protease called trypsin. This requires a higher pH, which is provided by alkaline substances in bile. |
| Bile is secreted by the liver and stored in the gall bladder before being released into the duodenum. It emulsifies fats, which makes it easier for lipase to digest them. |
| Nutrients, including water, are absorbed into the blood from the small intestine. More water is absorbed from the colon. |
| Villi and microvilli increase the surface area of the small intestine, which speeds up absorption. |

## 7 Human nutrition

> **PROJECT**
>
> **Make a model of the human alimentary canal**
>
> You are going to work in a group to make a model of the human digestive system.
>
> You can use whatever materials you can find. For example, you may like to use cardboard tubes of various sizes, balloons – whatever you think will work well for you. Be imaginative!
>
> First, discuss in your group how you will construct your model. Think about the materials that you will need.
>
> Gather your materials together and make your model. You will almost certainly make some changes to your original plan as you work – that is fine.
>
> When everyone has completed their models, they can be displayed around the room. One or two people from each group should stay with their model and explain it to others as they walk around the display. Then swap over, so that everyone has a chance to see all the other models, and to help to explain their own model.

**Figure 7.15:** Students planning how to model the human digestive system.

> **EXAM-STYLE QUESTIONS**
>
> 1 What causes scurvy?
>   - **A** a lack of calcium in the diet
>   - **B** a lack of vitamin C in the diet
>   - **C** too much carbohydrate in the diet
>   - **D** too much fat in the diet [1]
>
> 2 Where in the digestive system are protease enzymes secreted?
>   - **A** mouth and stomach
>   - **B** stomach and pancreas
>   - **C** pancreas and liver
>   - **D** liver and mouth [1]
>
> 3 From which part of the digestive system is most water absorbed into the blood?
>   - **A** large intestine
>   - **B** mouth
>   - **C** small intestine
>   - **D** stomach [1]

## CONTINUED

4 What is assimilation?
  A the breakdown of large molecules into small molecules
  B the movement of small molecules from the intestine into the blood
  C the movement of small molecules into cells, where they are used
  D the taking of food into the mouth [1]

5 What is a function of bile?
  A chemically digesting fats
  B emulsifying proteins
  C killing harmful microorganisms
  D increasing pH [1]

6 The diagram shows the human digestive system.

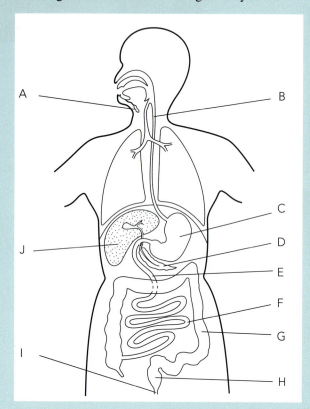

  a Name the parts labelled G and J. [2]
  b **Give** the letters of **two** parts where amylase is secreted. [2]
  c Give the letter of **one** part where lipase acts. [1]
  d **Describe** how part C helps in digestion. [6]
  [Total: 11]

### COMMAND WORDS

**give:** produce an answer from a given source or recall/memory

**describe:** state the points of a topic / give characteristics and main features

# 7 Human nutrition

## CONTINUED

**7** The diagram shows the teeth in the upper jaw of a human.

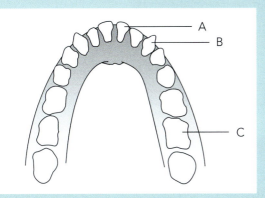

a Name the types of tooth labelled A, B and C. [3]
b **Outline** the functions of tooth A and tooth C. [4]
c Draw and label a diagram to show the internal structure of the tooth labelled C. [6]

[Total: 13]

**COMMAND WORD**

**outline:** set out main points

**8** a State **two** principal sources of carbohydrate in a balanced diet. [1]
b Outline the importance of carbohydrate in the diet. [2]
c Describe how and where carbohydrates are chemically digested in the human digestive system. [6]

[Total: 9]

**9** The photograph shows a section through two villi from the human digestive system.

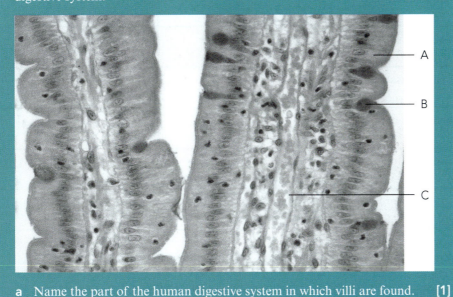

a Name the part of the human digestive system in which villi are found. [1]
b Name the part of the villus labelled A and describe its functions. [4]

## CONTINUED

c  The cell labelled B secretes mucus. Suggest the function of mucus in this part of the digestive system. [1]

d  The part labelled C is a blood capillary. Name **two** nutrients that are absorbed into the blood capillaries in a villus. [2]

e  Some nutrients are not absorbed into blood capillaries. Name the structures into which these nutrients are absorbed. [1]

[Total: 9]

## SELF-EVALUATION CHECKLIST

After studying this chapter, think about how confident you are with the different topics. This will help you to see any gaps in your knowledge and help you to learn more effectively.

| I can | See Topic… | Needs more work | Almost there | Confident to move on |
|---|---|---|---|---|
| explain what is meant by a balanced diet | 7.1 | | | |
| give examples of good sources of each type of nutrient, and the importance of each nutrient | 7.1 | | | |
| identify the main organs of the digestive system | 7.2 | | | |
| describe the functions of each of the organs in the digestive system | 7.2 | | | |
| explain the difference between physical digestion and chemical digestion | 7.3 | | | |
| explain why digestion has to happen before nutrients can be absorbed | 7.3 | | | |
| describe the different types of teeth, the structure of a tooth, and the functions of teeth | 7.3 | | | |
| state where amylase, protease and lipase act, and what they do | 7.3 | | | |
| describe the function of hydrochloric acid in the stomach | 7.3 | | | |
| describe where amylase, maltase, pepsin and trypsin act, and what they do | 7.3 | | | |
| explain the functions of bile, including providing an alkaline pH and emulsifying fats | 7.3 | | | |
| state that the small intestine is where most nutrients are absorbed, including water, and that more water is absorbed in the colon | 7.4 | | | |
| describe the structure of a villus, and explain how villi and microvilli speed up absorption | 7.4 | | | |

# Chapter 8
# Transport in plants

**IN THIS CHAPTER YOU WILL:**

- learn about the functions of xylem and phloem, and where they are found
- describe the pathway taken by water as it moves through a plant
- investigate the movement of water through stem and leaves
- find out what transpiration is, why it happens, and conditions that affect its rate
- learn about translocation of sucrose and amino acids in plants.

## GETTING STARTED

Work in a group of three.

In your group, think of a way to complete each of these sentences. Try to include some good scientific information in your sentence.

Plants take up water _____

Water gets to the leaves of plants _____

When each group has completed the sentences, share the different ideas from all the groups. Work together to combine everyone's ideas into two sentences summarising what you already know about how leaves obtain water.

## THE WORLD'S TALLEST TREES

Is there any limit to the height to which a tree can grow? The world's tallest trees are the coastal redwoods, *Sequoia sempervirens*, that can be found in some parts of California in the USA (Figure 8.1). The tallest one is 116 m tall, growing in the Redwood National Park. This tree is probably 2500 years old.

Scientists think that it is impossible for a tree to grow taller than about 130 m. This is because of the xylem that makes up most of a tree's trunk.

Xylem is the tissue that wood is made of. It contains dead, empty cells joined end to end, called xylem vessels. These long tubes run all the way up through a tree's trunk and out into its branches. Xylem vessels have walls made of a very strong substance called lignin. These vessels have two functions – they help to hold the tree up, and they provide a pathway for water to flow from the roots all the way up to the leaves at the top of the tree.

### Discussion questions

1. Small plants, such as mosses, do not have xylem vessels to transport water. How might water get to all the different cells of a moss plant?

2. It takes about 10 minutes for water to move by osmosis through a cylinder of potato that is 1 cm in diameter. What does this suggest about the possibility of using osmosis alone to supply the leaves at the top of a giant redwood tree?

Figure 8.1: Resistance to fire has allowed redwood trees to live for thousands of years.

## 8.1 Xylem and phloem

### Plant transport systems

All organisms need to obtain substances from their environment. For plants, these substances are carbon dioxide and water for photosynthesis, and mineral ions which they absorb from the ground.

Plants have branching shapes. This gives them a large surface area in relation to their volume. It means that most cells are close to the surface. As we saw in Chapter 6, leaves are adapted to ensure that no cell is far away from the air, so carbon dioxide can simply diffuse in through the stomata and air spaces, easily reaching the photosynthesising mesophyll cells.

Water comes from further away. Plants absorb water through their roots, and this water must be transported up to the leaves. The transport system that does this is made up of a tissue called **xylem**. Mineral ions are also transported in xylem.

Plants also have a second transport system, made up of a tissue called **phloem**. Phloem transports sucrose and amino acids from the leaves where they are made, to other parts of the plant such as its roots and flowers.

> **KEY WORDS**
>
> **xylem:** a plant tissue made up of dead, empty cells joined end to end; it transports water and mineral ions and helps to support the plant
>
> **phloem:** a plant tissue made up of living cells joined end to end; it transports substances made by the plant, such as sucrose and amino acids

> **KEY WORD**
>
> **lignin:** a hard, strong, waterproof substance that forms the walls of xylem vessels

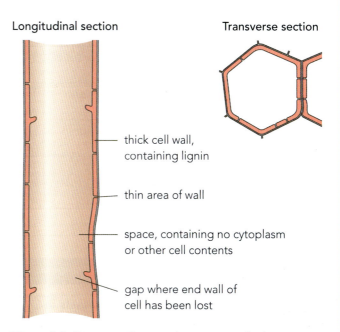

Figure 8.2: Diagrams showing the structure of xylem vessels.

### Xylem

A xylem vessel is like a long drainpipe (Figures 8.2 and 8.3). It is made of many hollow, dead cells, joined end to end. The end walls of the cells have disappeared, so a long, open tube is formed. Xylem vessels run from the roots of the plant, right up through the stem. They branch out into every leaf.

Xylem vessels contain no cytoplasm or nuclei. Their walls are made of cellulose and **lignin**. Lignin is very strong, so xylem vessels help to keep plants upright. Wood is made almost entirely of lignified xylem vessels.

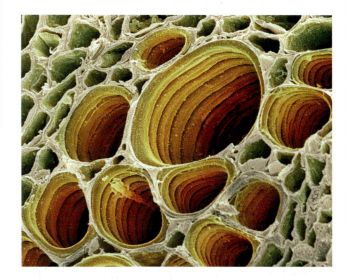

Figure 8.3: This scanning electron micrograph shows xylem vessels in a plant stem. The parts coloured orange are made of lignin. The biggest xylem vessel is about 100 μm in diameter.

Table 8.1 summarises how the structure of xylem vessels is related to their functions.

| Function | Feature | Explanation |
|---|---|---|
| Support | The walls of vessels contain lignin. | Lignin is very strong and can support the great weight of even a heavy tree.<br><br>In leaves, xylem vessels in vascular bundles help the leaf to be held flat, to provide a large surface area to absorb sunlight. |
| Transport | The cells are dead, with no contents. | Water can flow easily through the tube. |
|  | There are no cross walls between the dead cells. | There is a continuous tube for water to flow through, all the way from the roots to the leaves. |
|  | The walls of vessels contain lignin. | Lignin is solid and makes sure the vessels stay open and do not collapse, allowing water to flow through easily. |
|  | The diameter of the vessels is between about 15 μm and 200 μm. | This is narrow enough to make sure the column of water inside them does not break; but wide enough to allow a lot of water to flow through. |

**Table 8.1:** Structure and function of xylem vessels.

### ACTIVITY 8.1

#### Identifying the positions of xylem vessels in stems, roots and leaves

You are going to use micrographs (photographs taken using microscopes) to make simple diagrams. Your diagrams will show the position of xylem vessels in a stem, a root and a leaf.

1 Look at Figure 8.4. It shows a plant stem, cut across. The xylem vessels have been coloured blue.

2 Draw a circle (not a perfect one) to represent the section across the stem. Then draw triangles (not perfect ones) to show where the xylem vessels are found. Label the xylem on your drawing.

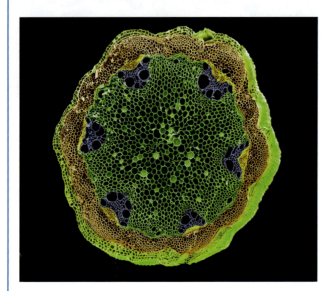

**Figure 8.4:** Scanning electron micrograph of a section across a plant stem.

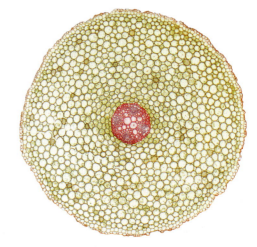

**Figure 8.5:** Photomicrograph of a section across a plant root.

# 8 Transport in plants

## CONTINUED

3   Look at Figure 8.5. It shows a plant root, cut across. The xylem vessels are the big, empty cells with red walls in the centre. The walls are red because a red stain has been used to make the lignin show up clearly.

4   Draw a diagram, similar to the one that you drew of the stem, to show the position of xylem vessels in a root.

5   Look at Figure 8.6. It shows part of a plant leaf, cut across. A stain has been used to colour the cell walls. The xylem vessels are the empty cells with purple walls, arranged in a semi-circle.

6   Draw a diagram, similar to the ones that you drew of the stem and root, to show the position of xylem vessels in a leaf.

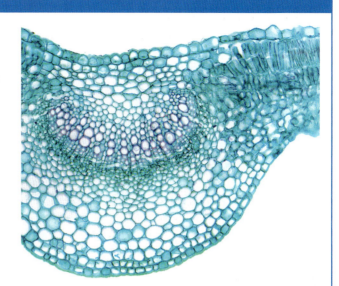

**Figure 8.6:** Photomicrograph of a section across a plant leaf.

### Self-assessment

How well did you achieve each of these goals?

Rate yourself according to the following scheme for each of the features of your drawing listed opposite.

☺   if you did it really well

😐   if you made a good attempt at it and partly succeeded

☹   if you did not try to do it or did not succeed

- Your drawings are large – bigger than the size of the micrographs.
- You used a sharp pencil for your drawings.
- The lines in your drawings are single and unbroken.
- You showed the position of the xylem correctly and clearly.
- You labelled the xylem with a label line drawn with a ruler, touching the xylem.

## Vascular bundles

Xylem vessels and phloem tubes are usually found close together. A group of xylem vessels and phloem tubes is called a vascular bundle.

The positions of vascular bundles in roots and stems are shown in Figures 8.7 and 8.8. In a root, vascular tissue is found at the centre. In a stem, vascular bundles are arranged in a ring near the outside edge. Vascular bundles are also found in leaves (Figures 6.11, 6.12 and Figure 8.6). They help to support the leaves, holding them out flat to capture sunlight.

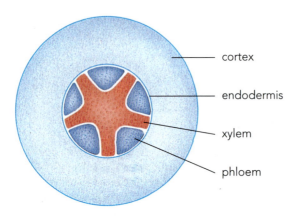

Figure 8.7: Diagram of a transverse section of a root.

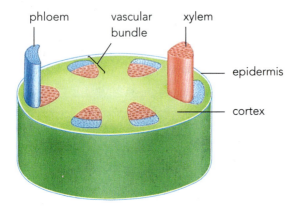

Figure 8.8: Diagram of a stem cut across, to show the positions of xylem and phloem tissue.

## Questions

1. State the **two** functions of xylem.
2. Name the substance that makes up the cell walls of xylem vessels.
3. State the function of phloem.
4. Use your diagrams from Activity 8.1, and the diagrams in Figures 8.7, 8.8 and 6.11, to describe **in words** the positions of xylem and phloem in roots, stems and leaves.
5. Explain **two** ways in which the structure of xylem vessels is related to their functions.

## 8.2 Transport of water

### Water uptake

Plants take in water from the soil, through their root hairs. Figure 8.9 shows the end of a root, magnified. At the very tip is a protective cap, to protect the root as it grows through the soil. The rest of the root is covered by a layer of cells called the epidermis. The root hairs are formed from some of the cells in the epidermis.

You can see in Figure 8.9 that there are no root hairs at the very tip of the root – they start a little way behind it. Each root hair is a long epidermal cell (Figures 8.10 and 8.11). Root hairs do not live for very long. As the root grows, they get damaged by the soil particles, and are replaced by new ones.

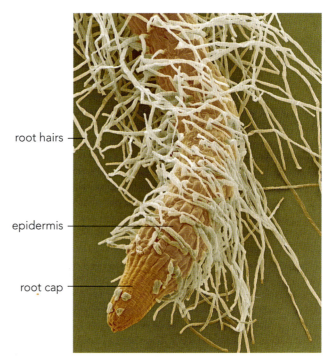

Figure 8.9: A micrograph of the tip of a root, magnified 70 times.

The function of root hairs is to absorb water and mineral ions from the soil. We have seen that water moves into a root hair by osmosis. The cytoplasm and cell sap inside the root hair are quite concentrated solutions. The water in the soil is normally a more dilute solution.

# 8 Transport in plants

Water therefore diffuses into the root hair, down its concentration gradient, through the partially permeable cell surface membrane (Chapter 3, Topic 3.2). The long, thin root hairs have a large surface area, which increases the uptake of water and mineral ions.

## The pathway of water through a plant

The root hairs are on the edge of the root. The xylem vessels are in the centre. Before the water can be taken to the rest of the plant, it must travel across the root to these xylem vessels.

The path that the water takes is shown in Figure 8.11. The water travels by osmosis through the cortex, from cell to cell. Some of it may also just seep through the spaces between the cells, or through the cell walls, never actually entering a cell at all. Eventually it reaches the xylem vessels in the middle of the root. These transport it all the way up through the stem and into the leaves.

When water reaches the xylem, it moves up xylem vessels in the same way that a drink moves up a straw when you suck it. When you suck a straw, you reduce the pressure at the top of the straw. The liquid at the bottom of the straw is at a higher pressure, so the liquid flows up the straw into your mouth.

The same thing happens with the water in xylem vessels. The pressure at the top of the vessels is lowered, while the pressure at the bottom stays high. Water therefore flows up the xylem vessels.

In the next topic, we will see what causes the reduction in pressure at the top of the xylem vessels.

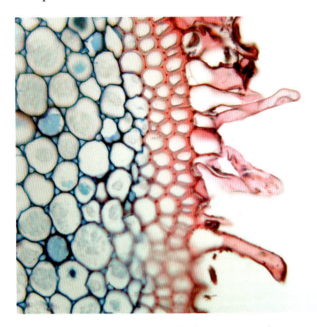

**Figure 8.10:** A photomicrograph showing part of a transverse section of a root (×100). You can see several root hairs on the right-hand side.

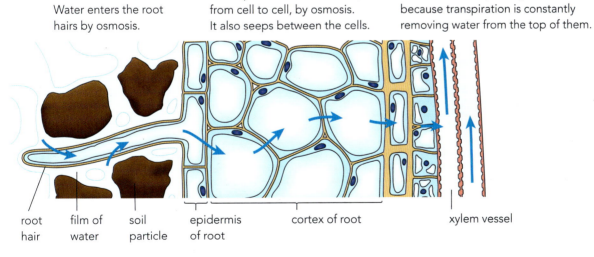

**Figure 8.11:** How water moves from the soil to the xylem vessels in a root.

153

## Questions

6  What are the functions of root hairs?

7  Explain how the structure of a root hair helps it to carry out its function.

8  Use your knowledge of osmosis to explain how water moves from the soil into a root hair.

9  Use your understanding of water potential to explain how water moves from the soil and across the root cortex.

## Transpiration

**Transpiration** is the loss of water vapour from a plant. Most of this loss takes place from the leaves (Figure 8.12).

You may remember that there are openings on the surface of the leaf called stomata (Figure 8.13). There are usually more stomata on the underside of the leaf, in the lower epidermis. The mesophyll cells inside the leaf are each covered with a thin film of moisture. Some of this film of moisture evaporates from the cells into the air spaces. This water vapour diffuses out of the leaf through the stomata. Water from the xylem vessels in the leaf then travels to the mesophyll cells by osmosis to replace it.

Water is constantly being taken from the top of the xylem vessels, to supply the cells in the leaves. This reduces the effective pressure at the top of the xylem vessels, so that water flows up them. This process is known as the transpiration stream (Figure 8.12).

> **KEY WORD**
>
> **transpiration:** the loss of water vapour from leaves

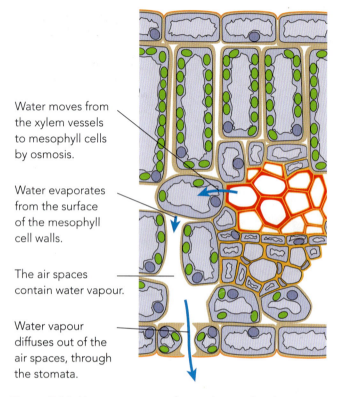

Figure 8.13: How water moves from xylem to the air, through a plant leaf.

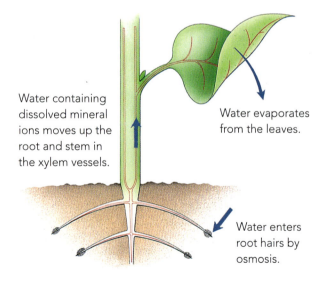

Figure 8.12: The transpiration stream.

# EXPERIMENTAL SKILLS 8.1

### Investigating the pathway of water through the above-ground parts of a plant

In this investigation, you will use a coloured liquid to trace the path of water as it moves through a plant stalk and leaf. You will practise following instructions, observing carefully and drawing conclusions. You can also try planning another experiment using the technique you have just used.

**You will need:**
- a celery stalk, with some leaves attached
- a small beaker
- some water with a coloured dye added, such as eosin
- a sharp knife or scalpel
- a surface on which you can cut the stalk (for example, a white tile)
- a hand lens.

**Safety:** Take care with the sharp knife or scalpel. Try not to get the dye on your skin or clothes, as it will be very difficult to wash off.

### Method

1. Put a small quantity of the coloured water into a beaker.
2. Stand the celery in the coloured water. Leave it for at least an hour – longer if you can.
3. Remove the celery from the water. Place it on a tile and cut it across. Study the cut end with a hand lens. It may look like the one in Figure 8.14.
4. Make a labelled drawing of the surface of your celery stalk.
5. Look at the leaves. Can you see the dye in the leaves? If so, describe which part contains the dye.

### Questions

1. From the position of the coloured areas in the stalk in Figure 8.14, and in your own celery stalk, which tissue in the stalk do you think contains the coloured water?

2. Did the coloured water get into the leaves? If so, which part of the leaf contains the coloured water?

3. Suggest how you could use this technique to test this hypothesis:

   Water moves more quickly through a plant when the temperature is higher.

   Think about:
   - the variable you will change and how you will do this
   - the variables you will try to keep constant, and how you will do this
   - how and when you will measure your results
   - any safety risks in your experiment, and how you will minimise them.

**Figure 8.14:** A cut celery stalk that has been standing in a solution of a red dye.

## ACTIVITY 8.2

### How can we use a balance to estimate rate of transpiration?

Figure 8.15 shows two plants in pots. One plant has a transparent plastic bag covering the whole plant and pot, the other plant has a transparent plastic bag covering only the soil and pot.

**Figure 8.15:** Using pot plants to measure the rate of transpiration.

In your group, discuss how you could use these plants and a balance (scale) to measure how quickly a plant is losing water vapour by transpiration.

Be ready to share your ideas with the rest of the class.

## Transpiration pull

The spongy mesophyll tissue in a plant leaf is very important in helping to keep water moving through the plant. The combined surface area of all the spongy mesophyll cells is very large, and this surface is in contact with the air spaces in the leaf. Liquid water moves into the mesophyll cells from the xylem vessels by osmosis. A lot of this water then evaporates from the cell walls, ending up as water vapour in the interconnecting air spaces.

As we have seen, the water vapour then diffuses out through the stomata and into the air surrounding the leaf. The rate at which this water vapour diffuses out of the leaf is generally greater in leaves where there are many open stomata.

This constant movement of water from the xylem, through the mesophyll cells, into the air spaces and through the stomata into the air means that water is removed from the upper ends of the xylem vessels. This reduces the pressure in the vessels. The pressure at the top of the xylem vessels is therefore less than the pressure at the bottom, in the roots. This pressure difference causes water to flow upwards, from higher pressure at the bottom to the lower pressure at the top. The pressure difference is called **transpiration pull**, because it is caused by the loss of water vapour by transpiration.

You can think of transpiration pull as similar to sucking a drink through a straw. As you suck at the top of the straw, you reduce the pressure. The pressure at the bottom of the straw is greater than at the top, so the drink flows up the straw and into your mouth.

The drink in the straw, and the water in the xylem, can flow upwards like this because water molecules have a strong tendency to stick to each other. There is a force of attraction between them. As one water molecule moves upwards, others stick with it and move up as well. The water therefore stays together as one continuous column and does not break apart.

### KEY WORDS

**transpiration pull:** a force produced by the loss of water vapour from a leaf, which reduces the pressure at the top of xylem vessels

## Questions

10  Put these words in order, to describe the sequence in which water moves through a plant.

mesophyll cells     root cortex cells
root hair cells     xylem

11  State whether water is in the form of a liquid or a gas, in each of these places:
   a   as it moves from the soil into root hairs
   b   as it moves through xylem vessels
   c   as it moves out of plant leaves into the air

12  Explain the importance of the large surface area of the mesophyll cells, in helping water to move through a plant.

13  Explain, in your own words, why water moves up through xylem vessels in an unbroken column.

8 Transport in plants

> **REFLECTION**
>
> It can be tricky to explain why water moves through a plant, because the process that causes it – transpiration – happens at the *end* of the pathway, not at the beginning.
>
> Do you find it easier to describe and explain this movement by starting at the top with transpiration, or starting at the bottom with root hairs?
>
> Try to decide *why* you find one way easier than the other. Use your decision to plan how you would manage if a question asks you to describe it the other way round.

## Measuring transpiration rates

It is not easy to measure how much water is lost from the leaves of a plant. It is much easier to measure how fast the plant takes up water. The rate at which a plant takes up water depends on the rate of transpiration – the faster a plant transpires, the faster it takes up water.

Figure 8.16 illustrates apparatus which can be used to compare the rate of transpiration in different conditions.

It is called a potometer, which simply means 'water measurer'. By recording how fast the air/water meniscus moves along the capillary tube, you can compare how fast the plant takes up water in different conditions. (A capillary tube is a glass tube with a very narrow hole.)

There are many different kinds of potometer, so yours may not look like Figure 8.16. The simplest kind is just a long glass tube which you can fill with water. A piece of rubber tubing slid over one end allows you to fix the cut end of a shoot into it, making an air-tight connection (Figure 8.17). This works just as well as the one in Figure 8.16 but is much harder to refill with water.

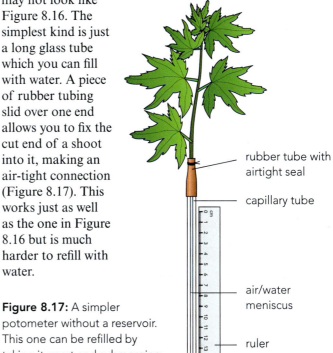

**Figure 8.17:** A simpler potometer without a reservoir. This one can be refilled by taking it apart and submerging the tube in water.

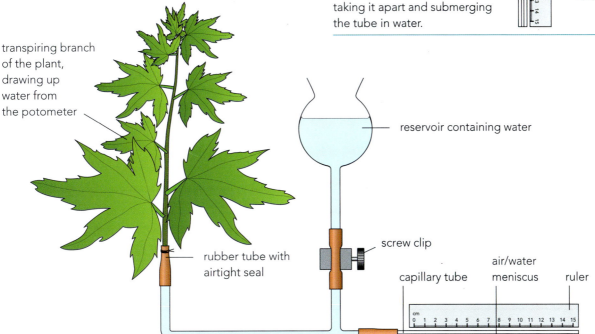

**Figure 8.16:** A potometer with a reservoir, which makes it easy to refill.

## EXPERIMENTAL SKILLS 8.2

### Using a potometer to investigate the effects of different variables on the rate of transpiration

In this investigation, you will use a potometer to measure how fast a plant shoot takes up water in different conditions. You will practise handling apparatus carefully, making accurate measurements, recording results and drawing conclusions. You will also evaluate your method and think about possible improvements.

> **You will need:**
> - a potometer, like the ones in Figure 8.16 or 8.17
> - a retort stand, boss and clamp to support the potometer
> - a fresh, leafy shoot
> - a sharp blade to cut the end of the shoot so that it fits into the potometer
> - a timer
> - a fan
> - access to places with different temperatures – for example a warm room and a fridge.

**Safety:** Take care with the sharp blade. In step 2, put the plant shoot onto a non-slip surface such as a cork board to cut it. Cut away from you, not towards you.

### Before you start

Look carefully at your potometer and check you know how it works and how to use it.

### Method

1. Fill the potometer with water. If you have a potometer like the one in Figure 8.16, you can simply open the clip and then close it once the tubes are all full of water. If it is like the one in Figure 8.17, submerge it in a big container of water (such as a big sink).

2. Cut a plant shoot, making a slanting cut. Push the shoot into the potometer. If your potometer is like the one in Figure 8.17, do this while the tube is still completely under water.

3. If you have submerged your potometer in water, take it out of the water and stand it on the bench. Check that your potometer is airtight and that there are no air bubbles. (If you suspect it is not airtight, you can smear petroleum jelly over anywhere that you think might be leaky.)

4. Now leave the apparatus in a light, airy place. Fix the ruler close to the tube, to act as a scale. As the plant transpires, the water it loses is replaced by water taken up through the cut end of the stem. Air will be drawn in at the end of the capillary tube.

5. When the air/water meniscus reaches the scale, begin to record the position of the meniscus every two minutes for ten minutes.

6. Repeat the investigation, but with the apparatus in a different situation. You could try each of these:
   - blowing it with a fan
   - putting it in a refrigerator.

### Questions

1. a  Did you have any difficulties setting up the potometer and getting the meniscus to move? If so, explain what you think caused the difficulties.

   b  Did you manage to overcome the difficulties? If so, describe how you did this.

2. Explain why the air/water meniscus moves along the scale.

3. Use your results to draw line graphs, so that you can easily compare the rate of movement in different conditions.

## Conditions that affect transpiration rate

The rate at which water vapour diffuses out of a plant's leaves is affected by the environment. Transpiration happens faster when the temperature is high and when it is windy.

The higher the temperature, the greater the kinetic energy of water molecules. This means that water evaporates faster from the surface of the mesophyll cells, and the water vapour diffuses out of the leaf into the air more quickly.

On a windy day, the air around the leaf – which contains a lot of water vapour that has just diffused out of the leaf – is quickly moved away. This means that there is always a diffusion gradient for the water vapour, because there is less of it outside the leaf than in the air spaces inside the leaf. So, water vapour diffuses out of the leaf faster on a windy day than on a day when the air is still.

Transpiration rate is also affected by **humidity**. Humidity means the moisture content of the air. The higher the humidity, the less water vapour will diffuse out from the leaves. This is because there is not much of a diffusion gradient for the water between the air spaces inside the leaf, and the wet air outside it. Transpiration decreases as humidity increases.

If the temperature is high, it is windy and the air is very dry, then transpiration will happen very quickly. The plant may lose water from its leaves faster than it can take it up from its roots. The individual cells in the plant lose so much water that they become flaccid (Chapter 3, Topic 3.2). The tissues in the leaves are no longer supported by the turgid cells pushing outwards against one another. The leaves become soft and floppy. This is called **wilting** (Figure 8.18).

**Figure 8.18:** These pictures, taken over a period of one hour, show a plant that is gradually losing more water by transpiration than it can take up into its roots.

## Questions

14 Copy and complete this sentence:
Transpiration happens faster when temperature is _____ and wind speed is _____.

15 To measure transpiration rate using a potometer, we need to record two values. One is the distance moved by the meniscus. What is the other?

16 Explain why a plant is more likely to wilt on a hot day than on a cold day.

17 Look at the wilted plant in Figure 8.18. Suggest how wilting might help a plant to survive the shortage of water that has caused it to wilt.

# 8.3 Translocation of sucrose and amino acids

Leaves make carbohydrates by photosynthesis. They also use some of these carbohydrates to make amino acids, proteins, fats and oils and other organic substances.

Some of the substances made in the leaves, especially sucrose and amino acids, are transported to other parts of the plant in the phloem tubes. This is called **translocation**.

## Sources and sinks

The part of a plant from which sucrose and amino acids are being translocated is called a **source**. The part of the plant to which they are being translocated is called a **sink**.

> **KEY WORDS**
>
> **humidity:** how much water vapour is present in air
>
> **wilting (of a plant):** losing more water than it can take up, so the cells lose their turgidity
>
> **translocation:** the movement of sucrose and amino acids in phloem from sources to sinks
>
> **source:** part of a plant that releases sucrose or amino acids, to be transported to other parts
>
> **sink:** part of a plant to which sucrose or amino acids are being transported, and where they are used or stored

When a plant is actively photosynthesising and growing, the leaves are generally the major sources of translocated material. They are constantly producing sucrose, which is carried in the phloem to all other parts of the plant. These 'receiving' parts – the sinks – include the roots and flowers.

The roots may change some of the sucrose to starch and store it. The flowers use the sucrose to make fructose (an especially sweet-tasting sugar found in nectar). Later, when the fruits are developing, sucrose may be used to produce sweet, juicy fruits ready to attract animals.

But many plants have a time of year when they wait in a state of reduced activity for harsh conditions to end. In a hot climate, this may be during the hottest, driest season. In temperate countries, it may be during the winter.

During these difficult times, the plant does not photosynthesise. It survives by using its stores of starch, oils and other materials in its roots. The stored materials are converted to sucrose and transported to other parts of the plant. So, these storage areas have now become sources.

For example, baobab trees (Figure 8.19) grow in tropical countries such as Madagascar. In the wet season, their leaves photosynthesise and make sucrose. This is transported to the trunk and roots, where it is stored as starch. In the dry season, the baobab drops its leaves. When it rains again, the stores of starch are changed to sucrose, and transported to the growing buds, helping them to grow and form new leaves.

You can see from this example that phloem can transfer sucrose in either direction – up or down the plant. This isn't true for the transport of water in the xylem vessels. That can only go upwards, because transpiration always happens at the leaf surface, and it is this that provides the 'pull' to draw water up the plant.

## Questions

18 In the wet season, which part of a baobab is a source, and which parts are sinks?

19 As the dry season comes to an end, which part of a baobab becomes a source, and which parts are sinks?

20 Phloem tubes can transport sucrose both up and down a plant. Explain why xylem can only transport water up a plant and not down it.

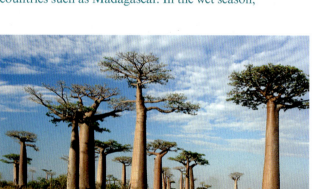

Figure 8.19: Baobab trees in the wet season, when the leaves are sources of sucrose.

Figure 8.20: In the dry season, the stems and roots store starch, ready to supply the leaves with sucrose when they begin to grow in a few months time.

## SUMMARY

In plants, xylem transports water and mineral ions and supports the plant. Phloem transports sucrose and amino acids.

In roots, xylem and phloem are found in the centre, but in stems they are arranged in groups close to the outer edge. In leaves, they are found in the veins.

## CONTINUED

| |
|---|
| Xylem vessels have thick, strong walls containing lignin, and no cell contents. Their cells are joined end to end with no cross walls. These features help them to carry out their functions of support and water transport. |
| The large surface area of root hair cells helps them to absorb water and mineral ions. |
| Water moves from root hair cells through the root cortex, through the xylem and into the mesophyll cells in leaves. |
| Transpiration is the movement of water vapour from the air spaces in a leaf into the air outside the leaf, through stomata. |
| The water vapour in the air spaces comes from the mesophyll cells, as it evaporates from their cell walls. |
| The loss of water vapour from the leaves reduces the pressure at the top of xylem vessels, and water moves up the xylem as a result of this transpiration pull. Attractive forces between water molecules help the water to move in a continuous column. |
| High temperatures and high wind speeds increase the rate of transpiration. |
| High temperature increases kinetic energy of molecules, which speeds up evaporation and diffusion. High wind speed and low humidity increase the diffusion gradient for water vapour from the air spaces into the surrounding air. |
| Plants wilt if they lose water faster than they can absorb it, so that cells lose their turgidity. |
| Translocation is the transport of sucrose and amino acids from sources to sinks, in phloem tubes. |

## PROJECT

### Making a display about using eucalyptus trees to find gold

You are going to research information on the internet and use your findings to contribute to a display.

Scientists have discovered that some eucalyptus trees have nanoparticles (very small particles) of gold in their leaves (Figure 8.21). The gold is present in the leaves that are growing on living trees, and also in the dead leaves that fall to the ground.

In your group, use the internet to find out more about this discovery. Choose one or more of these issues to research. Once you begin, you may also find another interesting issue that you would like to research, that is not in this list.

- Where in the world has this discovery been made, and how was the discovery made?
- Where does the gold come from?
- How do the trees absorb the gold?
- How is the gold transported to the leaves of the trees?
- Why are mining companies very interested in this discovery?
- How might the discovery eventually affect the environment where the trees grow?

Try to share out the different areas of research between different groups, and plan how each group will contribute to the final display.

Figure 8.21: Eucalyptus trees are helping mining companies to find gold that is deep underground.

# CAMBRIDGE IGCSE™ BIOLOGY: COURSEBOOK

## EXAM-STYLE QUESTIONS

1. What is a function of phloem but **not** xylem?
   - A supporting the plant
   - B transporting amino acids
   - C transporting mineral ions
   - D transporting water [1]

2. Which word best completes the sentence?
   Water evaporates from the _____ cells in the leaves and then diffuses out of the stomata.
   - A epidermal
   - B guard
   - C mesophyll
   - D xylem [1]

3. The diagrams show a transverse section through a root and a stem.

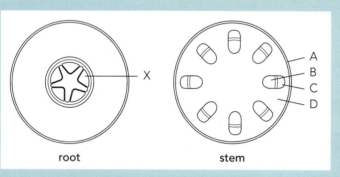

   Which label on the diagram of the stem indicates the same tissue as X? [1]

4. The diagram shows an experiment set up by a learner.

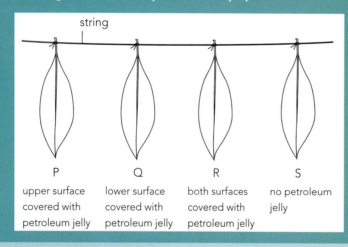

## CONTINUED

Which sequence shows the order of loss of mass by the leaves after one hour?

⟶ increasing loss of mass

A  P, Q, R, S
B  Q, R, P, S
C  R, Q, P, S
D  S, P, Q, R     [1]

5  The diagram shows a plant that has had a ring of tissue removed from its stem.

After two days, the concentration of sucrose at X was much greater than at Y. What explains this?

A  The phloem has been removed, so sucrose cannot move from the sink to the source.
B  The phloem has been removed, so sucrose cannot move from the source to the sink.
C  The xylem has been removed, so water cannot move down the stem and transport the sucrose.
D  The xylem has been removed, so water cannot move up the stem and dilute the sucrose.     [1]

### CONTINUED

**6 a** Name the tissue that transports water from the roots to the leaves of a plant. [1]

A student set up the apparatus shown in the diagram.

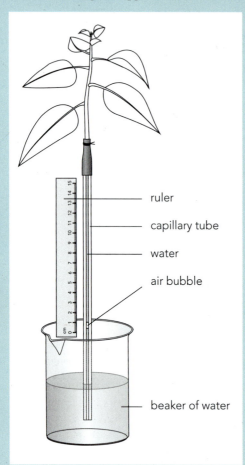

The student recorded the position of the air bubble every two minutes for ten minutes. She then switched on a fan and recorded the position every two minutes for the next ten minutes.

The table shows her results.

| Time / minutes | Position of air bubble / mm | |
| --- | --- | --- |
| | No fan | With fan |
| 0 | 8 | 10 |
| 2 | 11 | 14 |
| 4 | 15 | 19 |
| 6 | 18 | 24 |
| 8 | 21 | 29 |
| 10 | 25 | 34 |

# 8 Transport in plants

## CONTINUED

**b** **Explain** why the air bubble moved up the capillary tube. [2]

**c** With no fan, the mean rate of movement of the bubble was 1.7 mm per minute.
**Calculate** the mean rate of movement of the bubble with the fan blowing. Show your working. [2]

**d** **State** **one** factor, other than wind speed, that could increase the rate of movement of the bubble. [2]

[Total: 7]

**7** The figure below is a photomicrograph of the centre of a root.

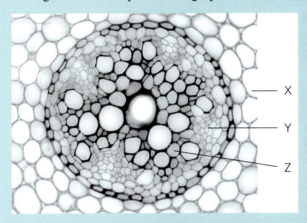

**a** **Identify** the tissues labelled X, Y and Z. [3]
**b** **Describe** how water is taken up into a root hair from the soil. [2]
**c** **Outline** the pathway taken by water from the root hair to the leaves. [3]

[Total: 8]

**8 a** Leaves lose water vapour through their stomata.
The micrograph shows a surface view of the lower epidermis of a leaf.

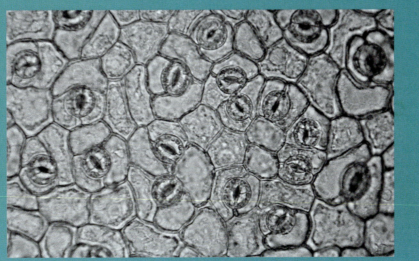

### COMMAND WORDS

**explain:** set out purposes or reasons / make the relationships between things evident / provide why and/or how and support with relevant evidence

**calculate:** work out from given facts, figures or information

**state:** express in clear terms

### COMMAND WORDS

**identify:** name/select/recognise

**describe:** state the points of a topic / give characteristics and main features

**outline:** set out main points

## CONTINUED

The area of the leaf shown in the micrograph is $0.06\,mm^2$.

Calculate the mean number of stomata per $mm^2$ of the surface of the lower epidermis.

Give your answer to the nearest whole number. [2]

b Explain the importance of each of the following in the movement of water through a plant.

   i   Root hairs have a large surface area. [2]

   ii  There are many interconnecting air spaces between the mesophyll cells in a leaf. [3]

   iii There are forces of attraction between water molecules. [2]

c Describe **two** ways in which transport in phloem differs from transport in xylem. [2]

[Total: 11]

9 Stomata open to allow carbon dioxide to diffuse into leaves. However, if the plant is short of water, stomata may close to prevent loss of water vapour.

a Explain why it is important to a plant to allow carbon dioxide to diffuse into its leaves. [2]

b Water vapour diffuses out of a plant's leaves. Explain where this water vapour comes from. [2]

c The cells in the leaves of a plant growing in hot conditions can become partly dehydrated. This means that they contain less water than normal. The graph shows how the percentage hydration of a plant's leaves, and the hydration of the soil, changed during a period of five days without any rainfall.

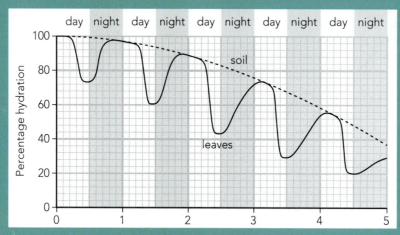

   i   Use the data in the graph to describe how the hydration of the leaves changes during the five days without rainfall. [5]

   ii  Suggest an explanation for the trend and pattern you have described in your answer to i. [4]

   iii Predict the appearance of the plant on day 5. Explain your prediction. [3]

[Total: 16]

# 8 Transport in plants

## SELF-EVALUATION CHECKLIST

After studying this chapter, think about how confident you are with the different topics. This will help you to see any gaps in your knowledge and help you to learn more effectively.

| I can | See Topic… | Needs more work | Almost there | Confident to move on |
|---|---|---|---|---|
| state the functions of xylem and phloem | 8.1 | | | |
| identify the positions of xylem and phloem in roots, stems and leaves | 8.1 | | | |
| relate the structure of xylem vessels to their functions | 8.1 | | | |
| identify root hair cells, state their functions, and explain how their structure is related to their functions | 8.2 | | | |
| describe the pathway taken by water from soil to leaves | 8.2 | | | |
| investigate the pathway of water through the above-ground parts of a plant | 8.2 | | | |
| explain what transpiration is, and how it happens | 8.2 | | | |
| investigate and describe the effects of variation of temperature and wind speed on transpiration rate | 8.2 | | | |
| explain the importance of the large surface area of the mesophyll cells | 8.2 | | | |
| explain the mechanism that causes water to move up through xylem vessels | 8.2 | | | |
| explain how temperature, wind speed and humidity affect transpiration rate | 8.2 | | | |
| explain how and why wilting occurs | 8.2 | | | |
| explain what is meant by translocation | 8.3 | | | |
| explain why some parts of a plant may act as sources and sinks at different times | 8.3 | | | |

> # Chapter 9
> # Transport in animals

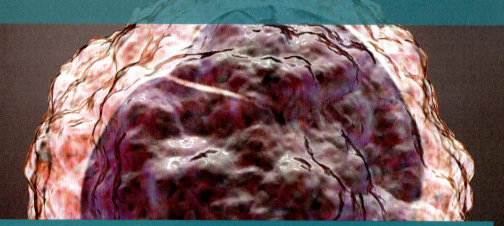

### IN THIS CHAPTER YOU WILL:

- find out about the human circulatory system
- learn about the structure and function of the heart
- think about factors that increase the risk of developing heart disease
- investigate how exercise affects heart rate
- compare the structure and function of arteries, veins and capillaries
- find out about the components of blood, and what they do

> explain how the structures of arteries, veins and capillaries are related to their functions.

9 Transport in animals

> **GETTING STARTED**
>
> Draw a very simple diagram of a human (animal) cell, showing its nucleus, cell membrane and cytoplasm.
>
> Draw arrows pointing into the cell, and label them to show what the cell needs to take in to stay alive.
>
> Draw arrows pointing out of the cell, and label them to show what the cell has to get rid of.
>
> Think about how these substances are brought to the cell and taken away from it.
>
> Share your ideas with the rest of the class.

## BLOOD TRANSFUSIONS

Every day, thousands of people worldwide need to be given a blood transfusion. This could be because they have had an injury and lost a lot of blood, or perhaps they have a disease that has caused a problem with their blood.

The blood that is used for transfusions is given by blood donors. In most countries, donors give their blood for free, but in some countries, hospitals pay people for their donated blood. The donor is tested carefully beforehand, to make sure that their blood does not contain anything harmful, such as viruses.

**Figure 9.1:** A nurse takes blood from a blood donor. Collecting the blood takes about 10 minutes, but testing and checking the donor and their blood involves about another 20 minutes.

The donor is also tested to find their blood group. There are four main blood groups – A, B, AB and O. Blood group O can be safely given to anyone, but in general it is best to match the donated blood to the blood group of the recipient. Although donated blood can be stored at low temperature for a while, there is sometimes a shortage of particular blood types.

For a long time, scientists have been trying to produce artificial blood, which could be safely given to anyone to keep them alive at least until there is enough 'real' blood available for them. Progress is being made, and perhaps by the time you are reading this, artificial blood may be used in some countries.

### Discussion questions

1   Do you think it is a good idea to pay donors for their blood or is it better for blood to be given for free?

2   What might be the advantages of using artificial blood, rather than blood taken from donors?

## 9.1 Circulatory systems

The main transport system of all mammals, including humans, is the blood system. It is also known as the **circulatory system**. It is a network of tubes, called blood vessels. A pump, the heart, keeps blood flowing through the vessels. **Valves** in the heart and blood vessels make sure the blood flows in the correct direction.

> **KEY WORDS**
>
> **circulatory system:** a system of blood vessels with a pump and valves to ensure one-way flow of blood
>
> **valves:** structures that allow a liquid to flow in one direction only

Figure 9.2 shows the general layout of the human blood system. The arrows show the direction of blood flow. Put your finger on the position of the lungs, at the top of the diagram, and then follow the arrows. You can see that blood flows from the lungs into the left-hand side of the heart, and then out to the rest of the body. It then flows back to the right-hand side of the heart, before travelling to the lungs again.

## Oxygenating the blood

The blood in the left-hand side of the heart has come from the lungs. It contains oxygen, which was picked up in the capillaries surrounding the alveoli. It is called **oxygenated blood**.

This oxygenated blood is then sent around the body. Some of the oxygen is taken up by the body cells, which need oxygen for respiration (Chapter 11). When this happens, the blood becomes deoxygenated. The **deoxygenated blood** is brought back to the right-hand side of the heart. It then goes to the lungs, where it becomes oxygenated once more.

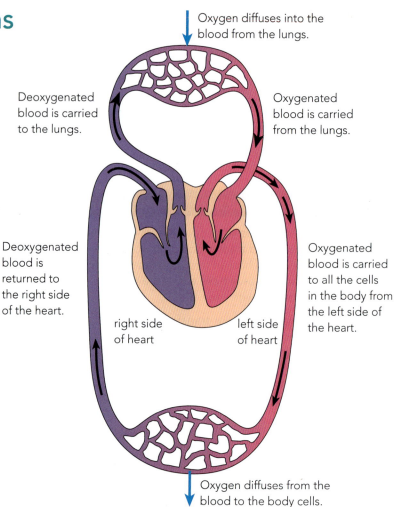

**Figure 9.2:** The general layout of the circulatory system of a human, as seen from the front.

> **KEY WORDS**
>
> **oxygenated blood:** blood containing a lot of oxygen
>
> **deoxygenated blood:** blood containing only a little oxygen

## Double and single circulatory systems

The circulatory system shown in Figure 9.2 is a **double circulatory system**. This means that the blood passes through the heart twice on one complete circuit of the body.

We can think of the double circulatory system being made up of two parts – the blood vessels that take the blood to the lungs and back, called the pulmonary system, and the blood vessels that take the blood to the rest of the body and back, called the systemic system.

Double circulatory systems are found in all mammals, and in birds and reptiles. However, fish have a circulatory system in which the blood passes through the heart only once on a complete circuit. This is called a **single circulatory system** and is shown in Figure 9.3.

> ### KEY WORDS
>
> **double circulatory system:** a system in which blood passes through the heart twice on one complete circuit of the body
>
> **single circulatory system:** a system in which blood passes through the heart only once on one complete circuit of the body

Double circulatory systems have some advantages over single circulatory systems. When blood flows through the tiny blood vessels in a fish's gills or a mammal's lungs, it loses a lot of the pressure that was given to it by the pumping of the heart. In a mammal, this low-pressure blood is delivered back to the heart, which raises its pressure again before sending it off to the rest of the body.

In a fish, the low-pressure blood just continues around the fish's body. This means that blood travels much more slowly to a fish's body organs than it does in a mammal.

This is particularly important when you think about the delivery of oxygen for respiration. Any tissues that are metabolically very active need a lot of oxygen delivered to them as quickly as possible, and this delivery is much more effective in a mammal than in a fish.

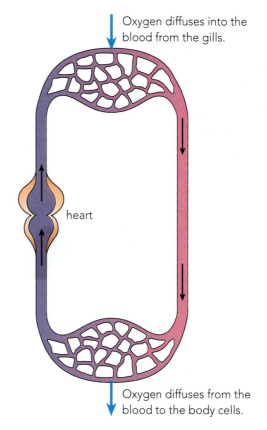

**Figure 9.3:** The single circulatory system of a fish.

## Questions

1. Look at Figure 9.2. Which side of the heart contains oxygenated blood, and which contains deoxygenated blood?
2. Explain how, and where, blood becomes deoxygenated.
3. Explain why a double circulatory system can provide respiring cells with oxygen more quickly than a single circulatory system.

## 9.2 The heart

The function of the heart is to pump blood around the body. It is made of a special type of muscle that contracts and relaxes regularly, throughout life.

Figure 9.4 is a section through a heart. The heart is divided into four spaces, called chambers. The two upper chambers are called **atria** (singular: **atrium**). The two lower chambers are **ventricles**. The chambers on the left-hand side are completely separated from the ones on the right-hand side by a **septum**.

If you look at Figures 9.2 and 9.4, you will see that blood flows into the heart at the top, into the atria. Both of the atria receive blood. The left atrium receives blood from the **pulmonary veins**, which come from the lungs. The right atrium receives blood from the rest of the body, arriving through the big veins called the **venae cavae** (singular: **vena cava**).

From the atria, the blood flows into the ventricles. The muscles in the walls of the ventricles contract. This pumps the blood out of the heart. The muscle contracts strongly, producing a large force that squeezes inwards on the blood inside the heart and pushes it out. The blood in the left ventricle is pumped into the **aorta**. This is a big artery that takes the blood around the body. The right ventricle pumps blood into the **pulmonary artery**, which takes it to the lungs.

> **KEY WORDS**
>
> **atria** (singular: **atrium**): the thin-walled chambers at the top of the heart, which receive blood
>
> **ventricles**: the thick-walled chambers at the base of the heart, which pump out blood
>
> **septum**: the structure that separates the left and right sides of the heart, keeping oxygenated blood separate from deoxygenated blood

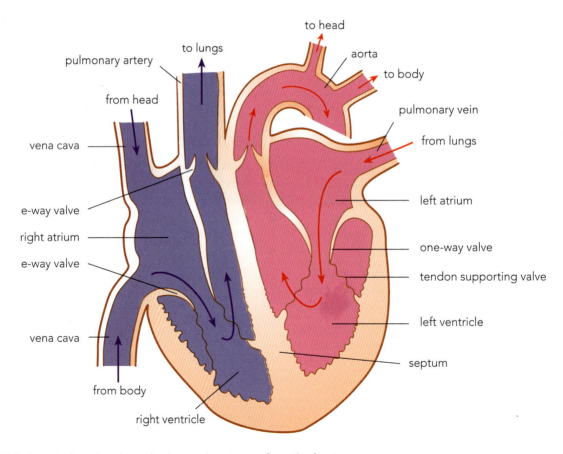

**Figure 9.4:** A vertical section through a human heart, seen from the front.

> **KEY WORDS**
>
> **pulmonary veins:** the veins that carry oxygenated blood from the lungs to the left atrium of the heart
>
> **venae cavae** (singular: **vena cava**): the large veins that bring deoxygenated blood to the right atrium
>
> **aorta:** the largest artery in the body, which receives oxygenated blood from the left ventricle and delivers it to the body organs
>
> **pulmonary artery:** the artery that carries deoxygenated blood from the right ventricle to the lungs

## Valves

Look again at the one-way valves in Figure 9.4. The valves between the atria and the ventricles are called **atrioventricular valves**. They allow blood to flow from the atria into the ventricles but prevent it from going in the opposite direction.

The valves in the entrances to the aorta and the pulmonary artery are called **semilunar valves**. This name means 'half-moon' and refers to their shape. These valves allow blood to flow from the ventricles into the arteries, but stop it going the other way.

> **KEY WORDS**
>
> **atrioventricular valve:** a valve between an atrium and a ventricle in the heart, which allows blood to flow from the atrium to the ventricle but not in the opposite direction
>
> **semilunar valves:** valves close to the entrances to the aorta and pulmonary artery, which prevent backflow of blood from the arteries to the ventricles

## Differences in muscle wall thickness

The function of the ventricles is different from the function of the atria. The atria simply receive blood, from either the lungs or the body, and supply it to the ventricles. The ventricles pump blood out of the heart and all around the body. To help them do this, the ventricles have much thicker, more muscular walls than the atria.

There is also a difference in the thickness of the walls of the right and left ventricles. The right ventricle pumps blood to the lungs, which are very close to the heart. The left ventricle, however, pumps blood to the rest of the body. The left ventricle has an especially thick wall of muscle to enable it to do this. The blood flowing to the lungs in the pulmonary artery has a much lower pressure than the blood in the aorta.

## Questions

4  Look at Figure 9.2 and Figure 9.4. List, in order, the parts of the heart that blood flows through on one complete journey around the circulatory system.

5  Which parts of the heart contain oxygenated blood?

6  Do arteries carry blood towards or away from the heart?

7  Do veins carry blood towards or away from the heart?

8  Describe how blood is pushed out of the heart.

9  Which structure keeps oxygenated blood and deoxygenated blood separate from one another in the heart? Suggest why it is important for them to be kept separate.

10 If you have a diagram of a vertical section of the heart in your notebook, add labels to it to show which of the one-way valves are atrioventricular valves, and which are semilunar valves.

11 Explain, in your own words, why the walls of the atria are thinner than the walls of the ventricles.

## Coronary arteries

Figure 9.5 shows the external structure of a human heart. You can see that there are blood vessels on the outside of the heart. They are called the **coronary arteries**. These vessels supply blood to the heart muscles.

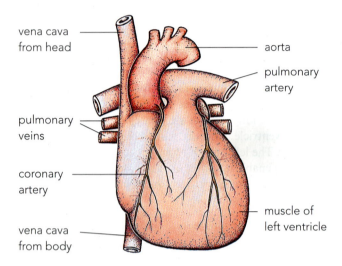

**Figure 9.5:** External appearance of a human heart.

It may seem odd that this is necessary, when the heart is full of blood. However, the muscle of the heart is so thick that the nutrients and oxygen in the blood inside the heart would not be able to diffuse to all the muscle quickly enough. The heart muscle needs a constant supply of nutrients and oxygen, so that it can undergo aerobic respiration. This releases energy that the muscle uses to contract. The coronary arteries supply the nutrients and oxygen that the muscle needs.

Coronary arteries can get blocked. In some people, cholesterol deposits build up inside the walls of arteries, including the coronary arteries (Figure 9.6). These deposits make the artery wall stiffer and the lumen narrower, so it is more difficult for blood to flow through. Blood clots can form. If the coronary artery is blocked, the cardiac muscle does not get any oxygen. The muscle cells cannot respire aerobically, so they cannot obtain energy to allow them to contract. The heart therefore stops beating.

Blockage of the coronary arteries is called **coronary heart disease**, or CHD for short. It is a very common cause of illness and death, especially in developed countries. We know several factors that increase a person's risk of getting coronary heart disease.

> **KEY WORDS**
>
> **coronary arteries:** vessels that deliver oxygenated blood to the heart muscle
>
> **coronary heart disease (CHD):** disease caused by blockage of the coronary arteries

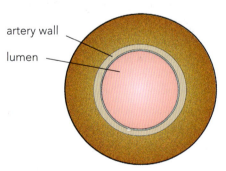

1 This is a transverse section across a normal coronary artery.

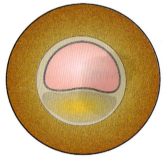

2 Cholesterol deposits make the lumen of the artery narrower. This increases the blood pressure. It also makes the wall of the artery much stiffer.

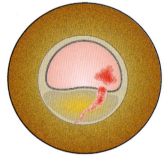

3 Blood clots can form. If one breaks away, it may get stuck in a smaller blood vessel and stop the blood from getting through.

**Figure 9.6:** How coronary heart disease is caused.

## 9 Transport in animals

## Preventing CHD

CHD is the one of the commonest causes of death in many countries. No one can completely eliminate the risk of developing CHD, but there is a lot that can be done to reduce this risk.

The most obvious thing you can do is not to smoke cigarettes. Smoking greatly increases the chances of developing CHD, as well as many other unpleasant and dangerous health problems.

Taking care over your diet is also a good thing to do. A diet that is high in saturated fats is linked with an increase in the concentration of cholesterol in a person's blood, and this in turn increases the risk of CHD. Meat is higher in saturated fats than plant-based foods, so one simple way to reduce the risk of CHD is to substitute animal fats with plant oils when you are cooking. Fast foods are often high in animal fat, so these should be eaten in moderation.

Regular exercise has a very beneficial effect on many parts of the body, including the heart (Figure 9.7). Most people can find some kind of exercise that they enjoy. Exercise helps to keep you fit, prevents excessive weight gain and decreases blood pressure. It also has a 'feel-good' effect, by helping to clear your mind of things that may be worrying you and causing the release of chemicals in the brain that increase feelings of well-being.

**Figure 9.7:** Regular exercise can decrease the risk of developing CHD.

## Heartbeat

You may be able to feel your heart beating if you put your hand on your chest. Most people's hearts beat about 60 to 75 times a minute when they are resting. If you put your head against a friend's chest or use a stethoscope, you can also hear the sounds of the valves closing with each heartbeat. They sound rather like 'lub-dub'. Each complete 'lub-dub' represents one heartbeat.

A good way to measure the rate of your heartbeat is to take your **pulse rate**. A pulse is the expansion and relaxation of an artery, caused by the heart pushing blood through it. Your pulse rate is therefore the same as your heart rate. You can find a pulse wherever there is an artery fairly near to the surface of the skin. Two good places are inside your wrist, and just to the side of the big tendons in your neck. There are also phone apps and smart watches that can automatically record your pulse rate.

In a hospital, the activity of the heart can be recorded as an **ECG**. This stands for electrocardiograph. Little electrodes are stuck onto the person's body, and the electrical activity in the heart is recorded (Figure 9.8). The activity is recorded as a graph. An example of a normal ECG is shown in Figure 9.9.

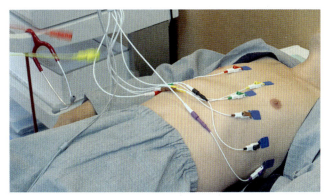

**Figure 9.8:** The electrodes fixed to the man's body will record the activity of his heart.

> ### KEY WORDS
>
> **pulse rate:** the number of times an artery expands and recoils in one minute; it is a measure of heart rate
>
> **ECG:** a graph showing the electrical activity of the heart plotted against time

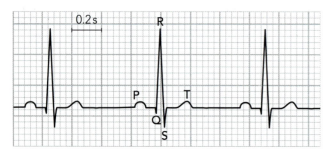

Figure 9.9: A normal ECG. You can think of it as a graph with time on the x-axis and electrical activity on the y-axis. The points labelled P, Q, R, S and T represent different stages in one heartbeat.

## How the heart beats

The heart beats as the muscles in its walls contract and relax. When they contract, the heart becomes smaller, squeezing blood out (Figure 9.10). When they relax, the heart becomes larger, allowing blood to flow into the atria and ventricles.

We have seen that there is an atrioventricular valve between the left atrium and the left ventricle, and another between the right atrium and ventricle. The valve on the left-hand side of the heart is made of two parts and is called the bicuspid valve or the mitral valve. The valve on the right-hand side has three parts and is called the tricuspid valve.

As the walls of the atria contract, they increase the pressure of the blood in the atria. This pushes down on the atrioventricular valves, swinging them open like doors and allowing blood to flow through, down into the ventricles. But when the ventricles contract, the valves are pushed closed again by the pressure of the blood in the ventricles. The tendons attached to them stop them from swinging up too far – they have to stop in the 'closed' position.

## Questions

12 Describe where you would find coronary arteries and explain their function.

13 Explain why coronary arteries can sometimes become blocked.

14 List **three** different ways you can measure your heart rate.

15 Look at the ECG in Figure 9.9.
   a  Use the scale to find the mean time between two Q spikes.
   b  Use your answer to a to calculate the person's heart rate in beats per minute.

16 Explain how the septum and the bicuspid valve help to ensure that fully oxygenated blood leaves the heart in the aorta at high pressure.

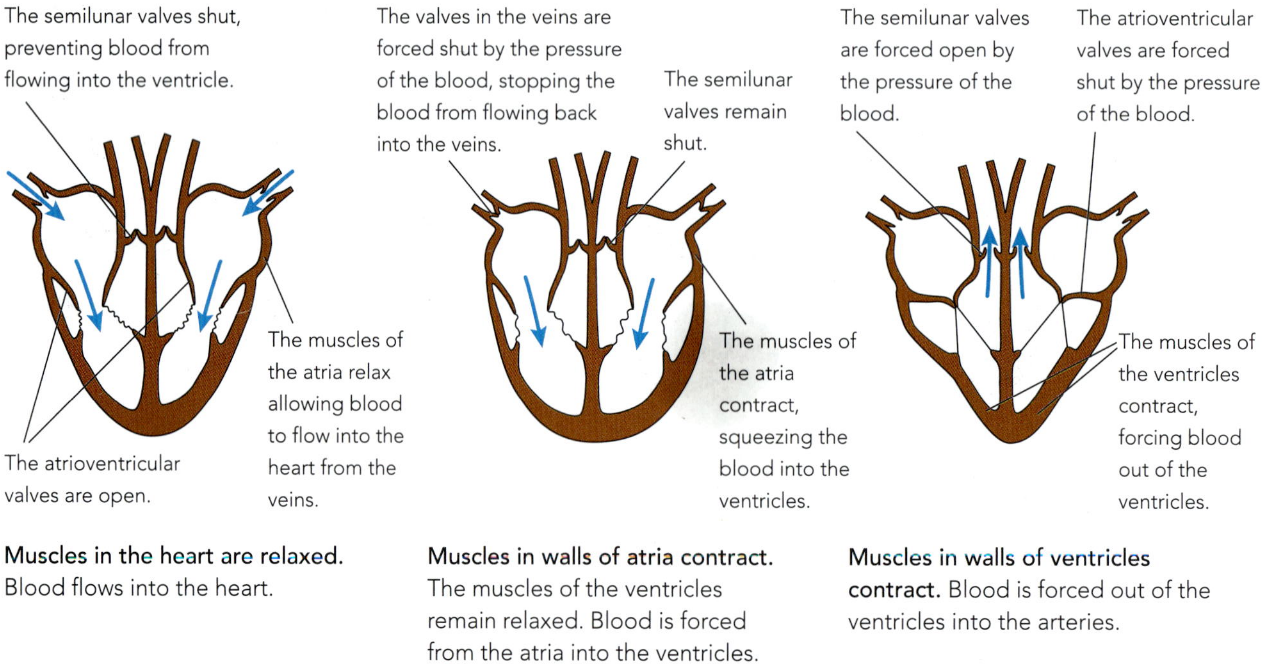

---

The semilunar valves shut, preventing blood from flowing into the ventricle.

The valves in the veins are forced shut by the pressure of the blood, stopping the blood from flowing back into the veins.

The muscles of the atria relax allowing blood to flow into the heart from the veins.

The atrioventricular valves are open.

**Muscles in the heart are relaxed.** Blood flows into the heart.

The semilunar valves remain shut.

The muscles of the atria contract, squeezing the blood into the ventricles.

**Muscles in walls of atria contract.** The muscles of the ventricles remain relaxed. Blood is forced from the atria into the ventricles.

The semilunar valves are forced open by the pressure of the blood.

The atrioventricular valves are forced shut by the pressure of the blood.

The muscles of the ventricles contract, forcing blood out of the ventricles.

**Muscles in walls of ventricles contract.** Blood is forced out of the ventricles into the arteries.

Figure 9.10: How the heart beats.

## EXPERIMENTAL SKILLS 9.1

### Investigating the effect of physical activity on heart rate

In this investigation, you will measure your pulse rate before and after exercise. You will practise measuring carefully, recording results clearly and using them to draw a line graph.

> **You will need:**
> - a timer, or a smart watch that can measure pulse rate.

**Safety:** If you are worried that doing exercise might make you ill, do not do it! You can measure someone else's pulse rate instead.

### Before you start

Practise measuring pulse rate. Try placing two fingers on your own neck – rest them gently closely to one of the big tendons and try to feel the beating of your pulse (Figure 9.11). When you are confident that you can feel the pulse, try to find it on your partner's neck. If you are going to use a smart watch to measure pulse rate, make sure that you know how to use it.

Now practise counting how many pulses there are in 30 seconds. You may find it helpful to have a partner to call out 'start counting' and 'stop counting'. You can multiply the number of pulses you have counted by two, to find the pulse rate in beats per minute.

Figure 9.11: Feeling the pulse in the neck.

### Method

Work with a partner.

1. Read through the method and construct a table to fill in your results.

2. Ask your partner to sit very still and relax. After a few minutes, measure your partner's pulse rate. Do this three times. Record the three values.

3. Ask your partner to do some exercise, such as raising their arms over their head vigorously for one minute or running on the spot. When they stop, measure and record their pulse rate again. Do this, every two minutes, until their pulse rate goes back to the resting value.

### Questions

1. Use your results to draw a line graph. Put time (minutes) on the x-axis, and pulse rate (beats per minute) on the y-axis. Mark on the x-axis where exercise began and ended. Use a ruler to join the points with straight lines.

2. Use your table or graph to describe, in words, how exercise affected your partner's pulse rate.

3. Explain why the pulse rate increases when you exercise. Think about:

    - what your muscles do when you exercise
    - how the muscles get the energy to do this
    - how the muscles are supplied with their needs.

    (When you have studied respiration, in Chapter 11, you will also be able to explain why the pulse rate does not go back to normal immediately after stopping exercise.)

## 9.3 Blood vessels

There are three main kinds of blood vessel: **arteries**, **capillaries** and **veins** (Figure 9.12).

Arteries carry blood away from the heart. They divide again and again, and eventually form very tiny vessels called capillaries (Figure 9.13). Capillaries deliver blood containing oxygen and nutrients close to every cell in the body.

The capillaries gradually join up with one another to form large vessels called veins (Figure 9.13). Veins carry blood towards the heart. They have valves to help to keep the blood flowing in the correct direction.

> **KEY WORDS**
>
> **artery:** a thick-walled vessel that takes high-pressure blood away from the heart
>
> **capillary:** a tiny vessel with walls only one cell thick, that takes blood close to body cells
>
> **vein:** a thin-walled vessel that takes low-pressure blood back to the heart

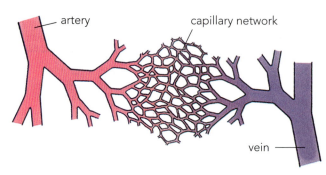

Figure 9.13: Arteries divide to form capillaries, which join up again to form veins.

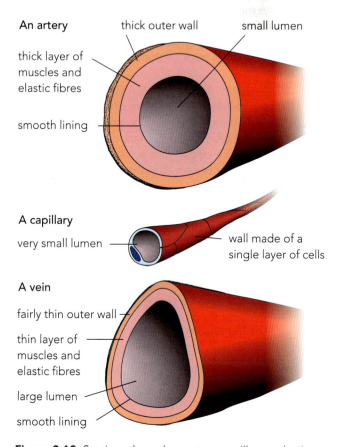

Figure 9.12: Sections through an artery, capillary and vein. The drawings are not to scale – in reality, capillaries are much smaller than either arteries or veins.

## Arteries

When blood flows out of the heart, it enters the arteries. This blood is at high pressure, because it has just been forced out of the heart by the contraction of the muscles of the ventricles. Arteries need very strong walls to withstand the high pressure of the blood flowing through them.

The blood does not flow smoothly through the arteries. It pulses through. The pressure of the blood is high when the muscles in the ventricles contract, and reduces as these muscles relax. The arteries have elastic tissue in their walls which can stretch and recoil (bounce back) with the force of the blood. This helps to make the flow of blood smoother. You can feel your arteries stretch and recoil when you feel your pulse in your neck or wrist.

## Capillaries

The arteries gradually divide to form smaller and smaller vessels. These are the capillaries. The capillaries are very small and penetrate to every part of the body (Figure 9.14). No cell is very far away from a capillary.

The function of the capillaries is to take nutrients, oxygen and other materials to all the cells in the body, and to take away their waste materials. To do this, their walls must be very thin so that substances can get in and out of the capillaries easily. The walls of the smallest capillaries are only one cell thick (Figure 9.12).

Figure 9.14: A capillary, shown in blue, makes its way through muscle tissue (×600).

## Veins

The capillaries gradually join up again to form veins. By the time the blood gets to the veins, it is at a much lower pressure than it was in the arteries. The blood flows more slowly and smoothly than it did in the arteries. There is no need for veins to have such thick, strong, elastic walls.

If the veins were narrow, this would slow down the blood even more. To help keep the blood moving easily through them, the space inside the veins – the lumen – is much wider than the lumen of the arteries.

Veins have valves in them to stop the blood flowing backwards (Figure 9.15). Valves are not needed in the arteries, because the pressure produced by the heart keeps blood moving forwards through them.

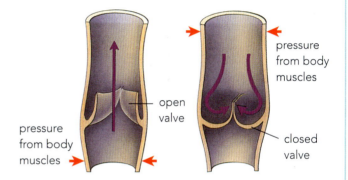

Figure 9.15: Valves in a vein. The veins are like pockets set into the wall of the vein.

Blood is also kept moving in the veins by the contraction of muscles around them (Figure 9.15). The large veins in your legs are squeezed by your leg muscles when you walk. This helps to push the blood back up to your heart.

Table 9.1 summarises the structure and function of arteries, capillaries and veins.

| Blood vessel | Function | Structure of wall | Width of lumen | How structure fits function |
|---|---|---|---|---|
| arteries | carry blood away from the heart | thick and strong, containing muscle and elastic tissue | relatively narrow; it varies with heartbeat, because the walls can stretch and recoil | strength and elasticity needed to withstand the high pressure and pulsing of the blood as it is pumped through the arteries by the heart |
| capillaries | supply all cells with their requirements, and take away waste products | very thin, only one cell thick | very narrow, just wide enough for a red blood cell to pass through | no need for strong walls, as most of the blood pressure has been lost; thin walls and narrow lumen bring blood into close contact with body tissues |
| veins | return blood to the heart | quite thin, containing far less muscle and elastic tissue than arteries | wide; contains valves | no need for strong walls, as most of the blood pressure has been lost; wide lumen offers less resistance to blood flow; valves prevent backflow |

Table 9.1: Structure and functions of arteries, capillaries and veins.

# Naming blood vessels

Figures 9.16 illustrates the positions of the main arteries and veins in the body.

Each organ of the body, except the lungs, is supplied with oxygenated blood from an artery. Deoxygenated blood is taken away by a vein. The artery and vein are named according to the organ with which they are connected. For example, the blood vessels of the kidneys are the renal artery and vein.

The liver has two blood vessels supplying it with blood. The first is the **hepatic artery**, which supplies oxygen. The second is the hepatic portal vein. This vein brings blood from the digestive system (Figure 9.17), so that the liver can process the food which has been absorbed, before it travels to other parts of the body. All the blood leaves the liver in the **hepatic veins**.

> ### KEY WORDS
>
> **hepatic artery:** the blood vessel that supplies oxygenated blood to the liver
>
> **hepatic veins:** the blood vessels that carry blood away from the liver

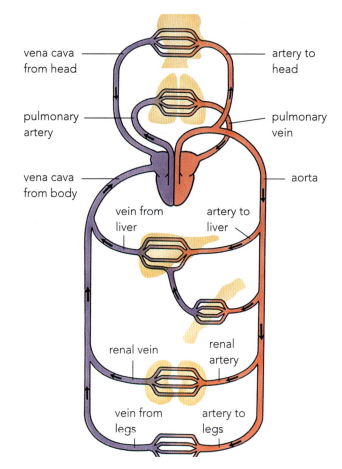

Figure 9.16: Plan of the main blood vessels in the human body. Red represents oxygenated blood, and purple represents deoxygenated blood.

9 Transport in animals

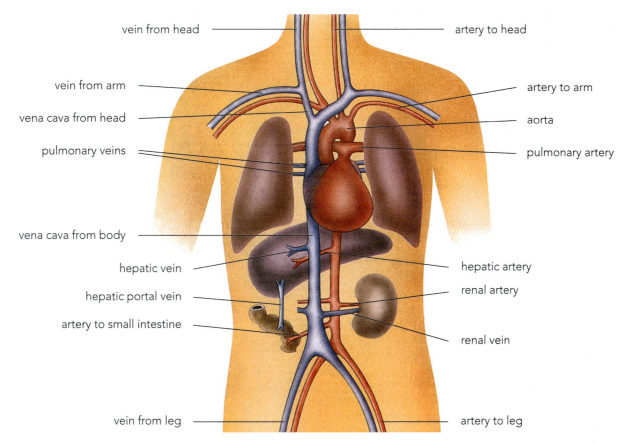

Figure 9.17: The main arteries and veins of the human body.

### ACTIVITY 9.1

**Comparing plant and animal transport systems**

Work in a group of two, three or four for this activity.

In Chapter 8, you learnt about how xylem and phloem are involved in transporting substances in plants. Now, you also know how blood vessels transport substances in animals.

In your group, think of at least **two** similarities between the transport system of a plant and the transport system of a human.

Now think of at least **two** differences between them.

Work with the other groups in your class to combine all of your ideas to produce a comparison between the transport systems in a plant and in a human. Perhaps this can go on display in your classroom.

### REFLECTION

Think about how you worked to construct your comparison.

How well do you think you contributed to your group's work? Did other people in the group help you in any way? Did you help others?

Do you think that working in a group like this helps you to understand or remember information better than working on your own?

181

## Questions

17 Name the type of blood vessel that:
   a  has the thickest wall
   b  has the thinnest wall
   c  contains valves

18 Look at Figure 9.16.
   a  Where does deoxygenated blood become oxygenated?
   b  Where does oxygenated blood become deoxygenated?
   c  Most arteries carry oxygenated blood. Name **one** artery that carries deoxygenated blood.

19 Explain why the walls of arteries need to contain more elastic tissue than the walls of veins.

20 Outline how the supply of blood to the liver differs from the supply of blood to other body organs.

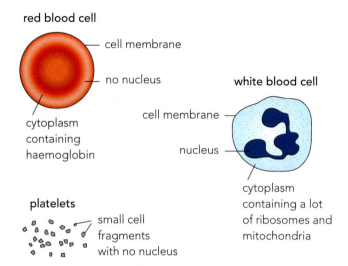

Figure 9.18: The components of blood. These cells and cell fragments float in a pale yellow liquid called plasma.

## 9.4 Blood

Blood is a liquid that contains cells. The liquid part of blood is called **plasma**. Most of the cells that are carried in this liquid are **red blood cells**. A much smaller number are **white blood cells**. There are also small cell fragments called **platelets**; they are formed from special cells in the bone marrow (Figures 9.18 and 9.19).

> **KEY WORDS**
>
> **plasma:** the liquid part of blood
>
> **red blood cells:** biconcave blood cells with no nucleus, which transport oxygen
>
> **white blood cells:** blood cells with a nucleus, which help to defend against pathogens
>
> **platelets:** tiny cell fragments present in blood, which help with clotting

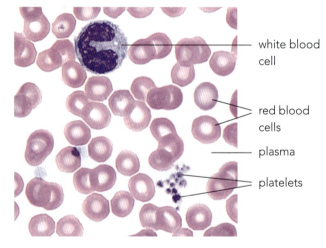

Figure 9.19: A photomicrograph of blood. The blood has been coloured with a stain to make the different kinds of cell show up clearly (×1500).

## Red blood cells

Red blood cells are red because they contain the pigment (coloured substance) **haemoglobin**. This carries oxygen. Haemoglobin is a protein, and contains iron. It is this iron that readily combines with oxygen where the oxygen concentration is high. This happens where blood capillaries take the blood close to the alveoli in the lungs. Haemoglobin that is combined with oxygen is called oxyhaemoglobin.

Oxyhaemoglobin readily releases its oxygen where the oxygen supply is low. This happens when the blood passes through capillaries close to cells that are respiring, using up oxygen.

Red blood cells are unusual because they do not possess a nucleus or mitochondria. The lack of a nucleus in a red blood cell means that there is more space for packing in millions of molecules of haemoglobin.

Another unusual feature of red blood cells is their shape. They are biconcave discs – like a flat disc that has been pinched in on both sides. This, together with their small size, gives them a relatively large surface area compared with their volume. This high surface area to volume ratio speeds up the rate at which oxygen can diffuse in and out of the red blood cell.

The small size of the red blood cell is also useful in enabling it to squeeze through even the tiniest capillaries. This means that oxygen can be taken very close to every cell in the body.

> **KEY WORD**
>
> **haemoglobin:** a red pigment found in red blood cells, which can combine reversibly with oxygen; it is a protein

## White blood cells

White blood cells are easily recognised, because – unlike red blood cells – they have a nucleus. The nucleus is often quite large.

Many white blood cells can move around. They can squeeze out through the walls of blood capillaries into all parts of the body. Their function is to fight pathogens (disease-causing microorganisms), and to clear up any dead body cells.

Some white blood cells destroy pathogens by engulfing them (taking them into their cytoplasm) and digesting them, in a process called **phagocytosis** (Figure 9.20).

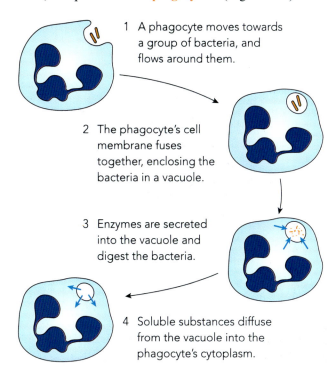

1. A phagocyte moves towards a group of bacteria, and flows around them.
2. The phagocyte's cell membrane fuses together, enclosing the bacteria in a vacuole.
3. Enzymes are secreted into the vacuole and digest the bacteria.
4. Soluble substances diffuse from the vacuole into the phagocyte's cytoplasm.

**Figure 9.20:** How a white blood cell destroys bacteria by phagocytosis.

Other white blood cells produce molecules called antibodies. These molecules fix onto pathogens and help to destroy them. If you are studying the Supplement, you will find out more about antibodies in Chapter 10.

> **KEY WORD**
>
> **phagocytosis:** taking bacteria or other small structures into a cell's cytoplasm, and digesting them with enzymes

White blood cells that destroy pathogens by phagocytosis are called **phagocytes**. Most phagocytes have a lobed nucleus, like the ones in Figures 9.19 and 9.20.

White blood cells that produce antibodies are called **lymphocytes**. They usually have a large, round nucleus that almost fills the cell (Figure 9.21).

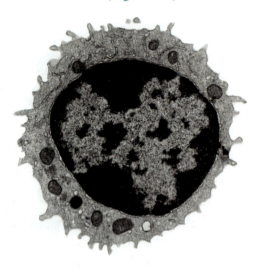

Figure 9.21: Electron micrograph of a lymphocyte ×5000.

> ### KEY WORDS
>
> **phagocytes:** white blood cells that destroy pathogens by phagocytosis
>
> **lymphocytes:** white blood cells that secrete antibodies

## Platelets

Platelets are small fragments of cells, with no nucleus. They are made in the red bone marrow, and they are involved in blood clotting.

Blood clotting stops pathogens getting into the body through breaks in the skin. Normally, your skin provides a very effective barrier against the entry of bacteria and viruses. Blood clotting also prevents too much blood loss.

Blood plasma contains a soluble protein called **fibrinogen**. When a blood vessel is broken, the platelets release a substance that makes the fibrinogen change. The soluble fibrinogen becomes an insoluble protein called **fibrin**. This forms fibres, which pile up on top of each other to make a mesh-like structure that helps to seal the wound. Red blood cells get trapped in the mesh.

The platelets stick together to form clumps. The fibres, the trapped red blood cells and the clumps of platelets form a blood clot (Figures 9.22 and 9.23).

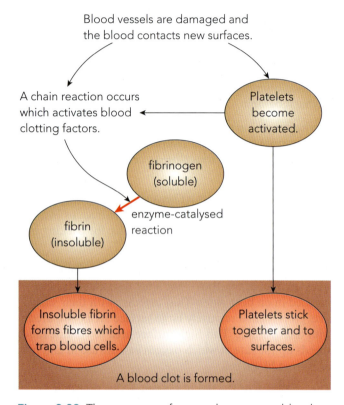

Figure 9.22: The sequence of events that causes a blood clot to form.

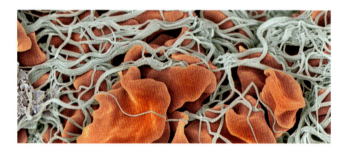

Figure 9.23: This scanning electron micrograph shows red blood cells trapped in a tangle of fibrin fibres.

> ### KEY WORDS
>
> **fibrinogen:** a soluble protein, present in blood plasma
>
> **fibrin:** an insoluble protein that is formed from fibrinogen when a blood vessel is damaged

# Plasma

Blood plasma is mostly water. Many substances are dissolved in it. Soluble nutrients such as glucose, amino acids, and mineral ions are carried in the plasma.

Plasma also transports hormones such as adrenaline (Chapter 12) and waste products, including carbon dioxide and urea (Chapters 11 and 13).

Table 9.2 summarises some of the substances that are transported in blood plasma.

| Component | Source | Destination | Notes |
|---|---|---|---|
| Water | Absorbed in small intestine and colon. | All cells. | Excess is removed by the kidneys. |
| Various proteins (including fibrinogen and antibodies) | Fibrinogen is made in the liver. Antibodies are made by lymphocytes. | Remain in the blood. | Fibrinogen helps in blood clotting. Antibodies kill invading pathogens. |
| Lipids including cholesterol and fatty acids | Absorbed in the ileum. Also derived from fat reserves in the body. | To the liver, for breakdown. To adipose tissue, for storage. To respiring cells, as an energy source. | Breakdown of fats yields energy – heart muscle depends largely on fatty acids for its energy supply. High cholesterol levels in the blood increase the risk of developing heart disease. |
| Carbohydrates, especially glucose | Absorbed in the ileum. Also produced by the breakdown of glycogen in the liver. | To all cells, for energy release by respiration. | Excess glucose is converted to glycogen and stored in the liver. |
| Excretory substances, e.g. urea | Produced by amino acid deamination in the liver. | To kidneys for excretion. | Most of the urea is removed by the kidneys, dissolved in water to form urine. |
| Mineral ions, e.g. $Na^+$, $Cl^-$ | Absorbed in the ileum and colon. | To all cells. | Excess ions are excreted by the kidneys. |
| Hormones | Secreted into the blood by endocrine glands. | To all parts of the body. | Hormones only affect their target cells. Hormones are broken down by the liver, and their remains are excreted by the kidneys. |
| Dissolved gases, e.g. carbon dioxide | Carbon dioxide is released by all cells as a waste product of respiration. | To the lungs for excretion. | Most carbon dioxide is carried as hydrogencarbonate ions ($HCO_3^-$) in the blood plasma. |

Table 9.2: Some of the main components of blood plasma.

### ACTIVITY 9.2

**Summarising the functions of blood components**

Work in a group of three or four for this activity.

You will need a large sheet of paper, to make an illustrated table that can be displayed.

In your group, discuss what your table will look like. You might like to have three columns – one for the component of blood, one for a description or picture of the structure of this component, and a third for a description of its functions.

Try to make your table:

- really easy to understand
- colourful and eye-catching
- full of relevant and clearly explained information.

**Peer assessment**

When all the groups have completed their tables, they can all be displayed on the wall.

Take some time to look carefully at the tables that other groups have produced. Make a note of at least one good point about each table, and at least one thing that could be improved.

Share your ideas with the other groups, and listen to their ideas about your table.

Is there anything that another group has done that you wish you had thought of?

What do other groups like about your table?

What do other groups suggest you could have done better?

## Questions

21 State how you can distinguish a white blood cell from a red blood cell in a photomicrograph.

22 Write **one** sentence that explains, in your own words, what blood plasma is.

23 Outline **two** roles of blood clotting.

24 Explain how you can tell the difference between a phagocyte and a lymphocyte, in a photomicrograph.

25 Blood plasma and platelets both play important parts in forming a blood clot. Describe how they do this.

### SUMMARY

| The mammalian circulatory system has blood vessels, a pump and valves. |
|---|
| Fish have a single circulation, but mammals have a double circulation, where blood passes through the heart twice on one complete circuit. |
| The heart has a muscular wall, a septum, left and right ventricles and atria, one-way valves and coronary arteries. |
| The walls of the ventricles are thicker than those of the atria. The wall of the left ventricle is thicker than that of the right ventricle. The thicker walls contain more muscle and can produce more force when it contracts. |
| Atrioventricular and semilunar valves keep blood flowing in the correct direction. |
| Blood is pumped away from the heart in arteries and returns to the heart in veins. |

## CONTINUED

| |
|---|
| Pulse rate, the sounds of valves closing, and ECGs can be used to monitor the activity of the heart. |
| Coronary heart disease is caused when the coronary arteries become blocked. Risk factors for CHD include diet, sedentary lifestyle, stress, smoking, genes, age and gender. |
| Arteries have a thicker wall than veins and a smaller lumen. Veins have valves. Capillaries have very thin walls. |
| The differences between the structures of arteries and veins are related to the higher and more fluctuating pressure of blood in arteries than in veins. |
| Each body organ is supplied with blood by an artery, and blood is taken away in a vein. Pulmonary vessels supply the lungs and renal vessels supply the kidneys. |
| Blood is made up of plasma, red blood cells, white blood cells and platelets. |
| Red blood cells transport oxygen. White blood cells protect against pathogens, by phagocytosis and producing antibodies. Platelets help with blood clotting. Plasma transports blood cells, ions, nutrients, urea, hormones and carbon dioxide. |
| Phagocytes carry out phagocytosis, while lymphocytes produce antibodies. |
| When blood clots, soluble fibrinogen is converted to insoluble fibrin, which forms a mesh and traps red blood cells. |

## PROJECT

### Decreasing the risk of coronary heart disease

Work in a group of three or four for this activity.

You are going to produce a leaflet that can help people to reduce their risk of developing coronary heart disease.

Here are some things to think about as you design the leaflet.

- Who will read your leaflet?
- How will the leaflet be distributed to people?
- Keep it simple. People get confused if they are given too much information at once.
- Make it look attractive. A carefully thought-out picture or diagram can be much more interesting and easier to understand than a lot of words.
- Keep it positive. Do not make people feel hopeless about their present lifestyle. Try to help them to feel that they can easily make small changes that will make a difference.
- Be informative. People are much more likely to take action if they understand the reasons why it is important to do so.

You can produce your leaflet by hand, or you can construct it using a computer or tablet.

**Figure 9.24:** A care worker talking a patient through a leaflet.

## EXAM-STYLE QUESTIONS

1. What is a function of all arteries?
   A  to deliver oxygen close to every cell in the body
   B  to ensure that blood flows in one direction only
   C  to pump blood around the body
   D  to transport blood away from the heart [1]

2. Which component of blood transports dissolved carbon dioxide?
   A  plasma
   B  platelets
   C  red blood cells
   D  white blood cells [1]

3. The diagram shows a section through the heart.

   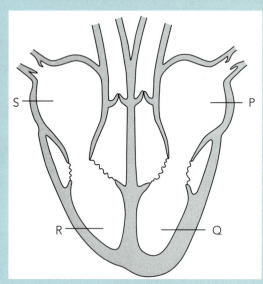

   Which two areas contain deoxygenated blood?
   A  P and Q
   B  Q and R
   C  R and S
   D  S and P [1]

# 9 Transport in animals

## CONTINUED

4 The diagram shows some of the blood vessels supplying organs in the abdomen.

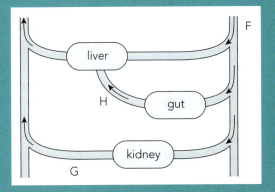

What are blood vessels F, G and H?

| | vessel F | vessel G | vessel H |
|---|---|---|---|
| A | aorta | renal vein | hepatic portal vein |
| B | hepatic artery | vena cava | aorta |
| C | vena cava | renal artery | hepatic vein |
| D | renal vein | hepatic vein | vena cava |

[1]

5 What happens when blood clots?
   A Insoluble fibrin is converted to fibrinogen.
   B Insoluble fibrinogen is converted to fibrin.
   C Soluble fibrin is converted to insoluble fibrinogen.
   D Soluble fibrinogen is converted to insoluble fibrin. [1]

6 The figure shows a white blood cell and a red blood cell.

   a **State two** features of the white blood cell that differ from the red blood cell. [2]
   b The diameter of a red blood cell is 0.007 mm.
     Measure the diameter of the red blood cell in the figure.
     Use your measurement to **calculate** the magnification of the diagram.
     Show your working. [2]

> **COMMAND WORDS**
>
> **state:** express in clear terms
>
> **calculate:** work out from given facts, figures or information

## CONTINUED

c  Red blood cells transport oxygen.
   **Explain** how red blood cells take up oxygen, and how they transport it to respiring cells. [3]

d  **Outline** the function of white blood cells. [2]

[Total: 9]

7  a  Outline **two** ways in which the activity of the heart can be monitored. [2]

   b  **Describe** how the activity of the heart changes when a person exercises and then rests. [3]

   c  The coronary arteries supply the muscle of the heart with oxygen. Describe the problems that occur if these arteries become blocked **and** discuss how a person can reduce the risk of this happening. [6]

[Total: 11]

8  The graph below shows how the volume of the left ventricle changes over a time period of 1.2 seconds.

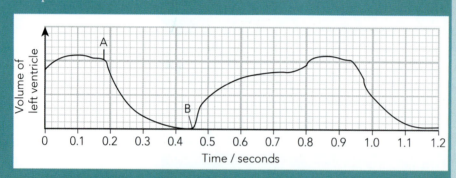

a  Describe what the muscle in the wall of the left ventricle is doing at points **A** and **B** on the graph. [2]

b  Use the graph to determine the time for one complete heartbeat. [1]

c  Use your answer to **b** to calculate the heart rate in beats per minute. [2]

d  The atrioventricular valves close at point **A**. Explain how this helps the blood to circulate correctly. [2]

e  Make a copy of the graph. On your copy, sketch a line to show the volume of the right ventricle during this 1.2 second period. [2]

[Total: 9]

---

### COMMAND WORDS

**explain:** set out purposes or reasons / make the relationships between things evident / provide why and/or how and support with relevant evidence

**outline:** set out main points

**describe:** state the points of a topic / give characteristics and main features

## CONTINUED

9 The diagram shows a red blood cell inside a capillary.

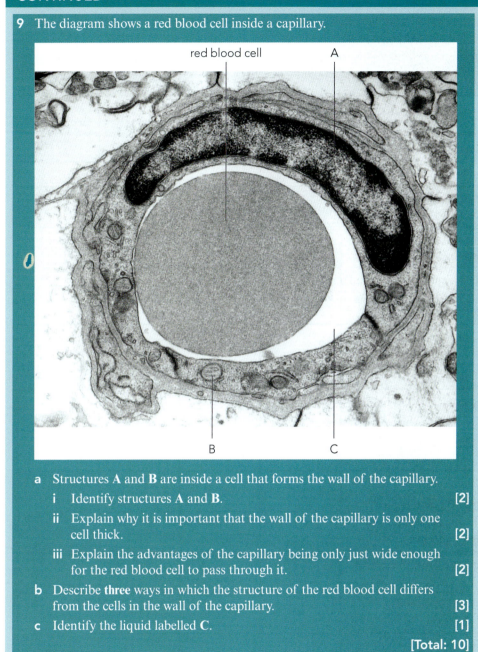

a Structures **A** and **B** are inside a cell that forms the wall of the capillary.
  i  Identify structures **A** and **B**. [2]
  ii Explain why it is important that the wall of the capillary is only one cell thick. [2]
  iii Explain the advantages of the capillary being only just wide enough for the red blood cell to pass through it. [2]
b Describe **three** ways in which the structure of the red blood cell differs from the cells in the wall of the capillary. [3]
c Identify the liquid labelled **C**. [1]

[Total: 10]

# CAMBRIDGE IGCSE™ BIOLOGY: COURSEBOOK

## SELF-EVALUATION CHECKLIST

After studying this chapter, think about how confident you are with the different topics. This will help you to see any gaps in your knowledge and help you to learn more effectively.

| I can | See Topic… | Needs more work | Almost there | Confident to move on |
|---|---|---|---|---|
| describe the structure of the circulatory system | 9.1 | | | |
| explain the advantages of a double circulatory system compared with a single circulatory system | 9.1 | | | |
| describe the structure of the heart | 9.2 | | | |
| explain the relative thickness of the walls of the atria and ventricles, and the left and right ventricles | 9.2 | | | |
| describe the functioning of the heart in terms of the contraction of muscles and the action of valves | 9.2 | | | |
| state that the activity of the heart can be monitored by measuring pulse rate, using ECGs and listening to the valves closing | 9.2 | | | |
| investigate and describe how exercise affects heart rate | 9.2 | | | |
| explain how exercise affects heart rate | 9.2 | | | |
| describe coronary heart disease (CHD) and list factors that increase the risk of developing CHD | 9.2 | | | |
| describe the structures of arteries, veins and capillaries | 9.3 | | | |
| identify and name the main blood vessels to and from the heart, lungs and kidneys | 9.3 | | | |
| explain how the structures of arteries, veins and capillaries are related to their functions | 9.3 | | | |
| identify the hepatic artery, hepatic portal vein and hepatic vein | 9.3 | | | |
| identify red blood cells, white blood cells and platelets in micrographs and diagrams | 9.4 | | | |
| identify lymphocytes and phagocytes in micrographs and diagrams, and describe their functions | 9.4 | | | |
| describe the functions of plasma, red blood cells, white blood cells and platelets | 9.4 | | | |
| state the function of blood clotting | 9.4 | | | |
| describe how fibrinogen is involved in the process of blood clotting | 9.4 | | | |

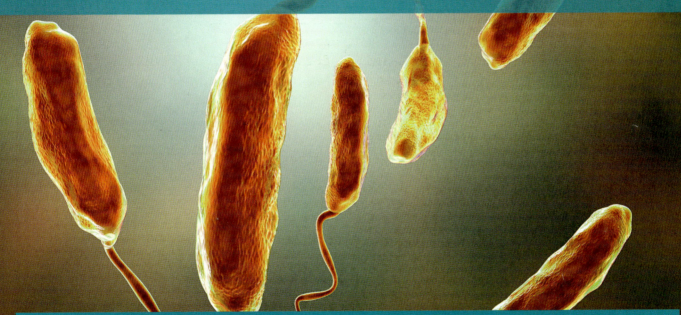

# Chapter 10
# Diseases and immunity

**IN THIS CHAPTER YOU WILL:**

- find out how pathogens are transmitted from one host to another
- learn how the body defends itself against pathogens
- explain what immunity is, and how it is produced naturally and through vaccination.

## GETTING STARTED

Here is a list of words that you have already used in your biology course.

**antibody    bacterium    pathogen    virus    white blood cell**

Try to write a sentence that includes all of those words. You can use plurals instead of singular words, if you like. If you can't fit all the words into one sentence, try writing two sentences.

Take turns with others to read out your sentence or sentences.

Who has written the best sentence? What makes this the best sentence?

## GLOBAL OUTBREAKS OF MEASLES

Measles used to be a very common disease, particularly of young children. Although many people who get measles recover fully, it can lead to serious complications – and even death.

In most countries, children are vaccinated against measles. The vaccine gives almost complete protection, and cases of measles fell dramatically when the vaccine first began to be used in the late 1960s and 1970s. However, in 2019 there was a significant increase in numbers of measles cases, with serious outbreaks happening in Ukraine, the Democratic Republic of the Congo (DRC), Madagascar, Angola, Cameroon, Chad, Kazakhstan, Nigeria, Philippines, South Sudan, Sudan, and Thailand. Numbers of cases also increased in developed countries such as the USA, which had its highest number of cases for 25 years. Worldwide, three times more cases of measles were reported in 2019 than in 2018.

What happened? The virus that causes measles is very easily spread from one person to another. If at least 95% of people in a community are vaccinated against measles, then even the ones who are not vaccinated are unlikely to get the disease, because there are not enough 'hosts' for the measles virus to live in. This helps to protect vulnerable children and adults, such as those who have a weak immune system. But not every country manages to vaccinate this percentage of children. And, increasingly, some parents are choosing not to have their children vaccinated.

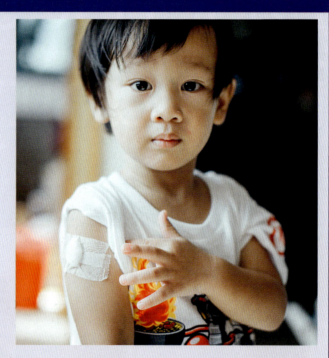

**Figure 10.1:** This boy has just been vaccinated against a number of common childhood diseases, including measles.

### Discussion questions

1. Why might some parents choose not to have their children vaccinated against measles?

2. Some schools refuse to allow children who have not been vaccinated to come to classes. Do you think this is a good idea?

## 10.1 Transmission of pathogens

A **pathogen** is a microorganism (a tiny organism that can only be seen with a microscope) that causes disease. Many diseases are caused by pathogens that get into our bodies and breed there (Figure 10.2). Table 10.1 shows the four kinds of microorganism that can act as pathogens, and some of the diseases that they cause.

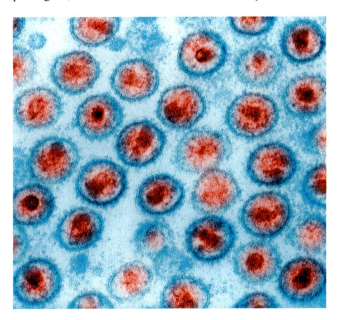

**Figure 10.2:** An electron micrograph of human immunodeficiency viruses (HIV). The colours are not real – they have been added to make the viruses show up more clearly. The blue circles are the protein coats, and the genetic material is contained in the red areas. Each virus is about 0.1 µm across.

| Group to which pathogen belongs | Examples of diseases which they cause |
|---|---|
| viruses | influenza, common cold, poliomyelitis, measles, AIDS |
| bacteria | cholera, syphilis, whooping cough, tuberculosis, tetanus |
| protoctists | malaria, amoebic dysentery |
| fungi | athlete's foot, ringworm |

**Table 10.1:** Types of pathogen.

A person or other animal in which the pathogen lives and breeds is called a **host**. Diseases that are caused by pathogens can usually be passed from one host to another. They are called **transmissible diseases**.

> ### KEY WORDS
>
> **pathogen:** a microorganism that causes disease
>
> **host:** an organism in which a pathogen lives and reproduces
>
> **transmissible disease:** a disease that can be passed from one host to another; transmissible diseases are caused by pathogens

Once inside the body, some pathogens damage our cells by living in them and using up their resources. Others cause harm to cells and body systems by producing waste products, called **toxins**, which spread around the body and cause **symptoms** such as high temperature and rashes and make you feel ill. Some toxins produced by pathogens are among the most dangerous poisons in the world – for example, the one produced by the bacterium *Clostridium botulinum*.

> ### KEY WORDS
>
> **toxin:** a poisonous substance; a chemical that damages cells
>
> **symptoms:** features that you experience when you have a disease

### How pathogens enter the body

The movement of a pathogen from one host to another is called **transmission**. The entry of the pathogen into the body is known as **infection**. There are several ways in which transmission and infection can happen.

> ### KEY WORDS
>
> **transmission:** the movement of a pathogen from one host to another
>
> **infection:** the entry of a pathogen into the body of a host

## Direct contact

Some pathogens pass from one person to another when there is direct contact between an infected person and an uninfected one. Diseases transmitted like this are known as transmissible diseases (sometimes called contagious diseases). For example, the virus that causes AIDS, called HIV (the human immunodeficiency virus) can be transmitted when an infected person's blood comes into contact with another person's blood. The fungus that causes the skin infection, athlete's foot, can be passed on by sharing a towel with an infected person.

## Indirect transmission

Most pathogens are transmitted indirectly. This can happen through:

- breathing in droplets containing pathogens
- touching a surface that someone with the pathogen has touched
- eating food or drinking water that contains pathogens
- contact with animals that are carrying pathogens.

Cold, influenza and Covid-19 viruses are carried in the air in tiny droplets of moisture. Every time someone with these illnesses speaks, coughs or sneezes, millions of viruses are propelled into the air (Figure 10.3). If you breathe in the droplets, you may become infected. You can also pick up these viruses if you touch a surface on which they are present, and then put your hands to your face.

Bacteria such as *Salmonella* can enter your alimentary canal with the food that you eat. If you eat a large number of these bacteria, you may get food poisoning. Fresh foods, such as fruit and vegetables, should be washed in clean water before you eat them. Cooking usually destroys bacteria, so eating recently cooked food is generally safe. Food bought from street stalls is safe if it is hot and has just been cooked, but you need to take care with anything that has been kept warm for a while, as this gives any bacteria on it a chance to breed (Figure 10.4). Many governments make sure that food sellers are checked regularly to make sure that they are using good hygiene, and that their food is safe to eat.

**Figure 10.4:** This food from a street stall is safe to eat because it has just been cooked, and the seller has reduced the risk of contaminating it with harmful bacteria by wearing gloves to protect the food.

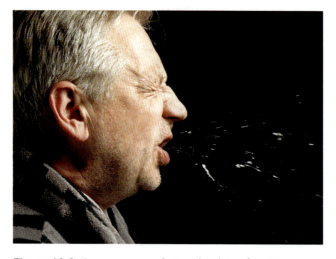

**Figure 10.3:** A sneeze propels tiny droplets of moisture, containing millions of viruses, into the air. Catch your sneeze in a tissue!

**Figure 10.5:** Contaminated water such as this almost certainly contains pathogens that would cause disease if they got into a person's body.

Many pathogens, including the virus that causes poliomyelitis and the bacterium that causes cholera, are transmitted in water. If you swim in water that contains these pathogens, or drink water containing them, you run the risk of catching these diseases (Figure 10.5). These pathogens can also get onto your hands if you touch anything that contains them, and then be passed into your body when you eat food that you have touched, or touch your mouth with your fingers.

### ACTIVITY 10.1

#### Transmissible diseases

To start with, work on your own.

Think about any transmissible diseases that you, or someone you know, may have had. Make a list.

What kind of pathogen do you think caused each disease?

How do you think that pathogen got into the body?

Now share your ideas with your partner. Are there any transmissible diseases that you have both listed? Do you agree about the kinds of pathogen that caused these diseases? Do you agree about how the pathogen got into the body? If you do not agree, use the internet to check who is right.

### REFLECTION

When you are searching for reliable information on the internet, what tactics do you use? How do you decide on your search terms?

How do you decide whether you can trust the information on a particular web site?

## Body defences

The human body has many natural defences against pathogens. Some of them prevent pathogens from getting to parts of the body where they could breed. Figure 10.6 shows some of these defences.

Pathogens that manage to get through all of these defences are usually destroyed by white blood cells. In Chapter 9, we saw that some of these cells take in and digest the pathogens by phagocytosis, while others produce chemicals called antibodies that incapacitate or directly kill the pathogens.

## Questions

1 Explain what is meant by a transmissible disease.
2 The pathogens that cause some transmissible diseases are transmitted by direct contact. How does the skin help to protect us against the entry of these pathogens?
3 How does stomach acid protect us against transmissible diseases?

Skin prevents pathogens from entering the body. If the skin is broken, a blood clot forms to seal the wound and stop pathogens getting in.

Hairs in the nose help to filter out particles from the air, which could contain pathogens.

If we smell or taste food that is bad, we don't want to eat it, or it might make us sick.

Mucus in the airways traps bacteria. Then they are swept up to the back of the throat and swallowed, rather than being allowed to get into the lungs.

The stomach contains hydrochloric acid, which kills a lot of the bacteria in our food.

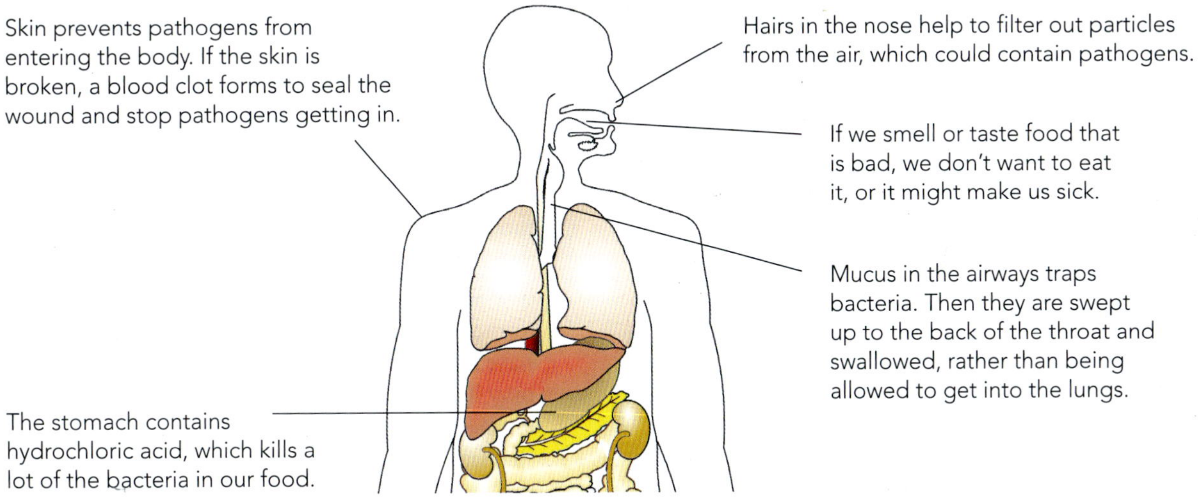

Figure 10.6: Body defences against the entry of pathogens.

## A clean water supply

We use water for many different purposes each day, especially for drinking, washing and in preparing food. Water that has not been made safe to drink – for example, from a dirty container or from a river or lake – can contain many different pathogens. Some of these are very dangerous, such as the bacterium that causes cholera (Topic 10.2) or the virus that causes polio.

A clean water supply is one of the most basic health needs. In many countries, clean, safe water is supplied to homes and industries by a network of pipes. Before entering the pipes, the water is filtered to remove dirt, and then treated with chlorine to kill all the microorganisms in it. Where there is no piped water supply, people may be able to collect clean water from a communal source, such as a tap or deep well (Figure 10.7).

**Figure 10.7:** Where clean water is not supplied through pipes, a deep well can be the best source of water. It is even better if the water is boiled before use, to kill any pathogens it might contain.

## Food hygiene

Good food hygiene makes it much less likely that someone eating the food you have prepared will get ill. Most food poisoning is caused by bacteria, so understanding the conditions that bacteria need for growth and reproduction can help us to keep them under control. A few simple rules can prevent you, or anyone else eating food you have prepared, from getting food poisoning.

1. Keep your own bacteria and viruses away from food. Always wash your hands before touching or eating food or putting your hands into your mouth for any reason. Keep your hair out of food. People working in food preparation environments often wear uniforms that cover their clothes and hair (Figure 10.8). Never cough or sneeze over food.

**Figure 10.8:** Preparing food in a hospital kitchen.

2. Keep animals away from food. Animals are even more likely to have harmful bacteria on them than you are, so they should never be allowed to come into contact with food.

   Some are particularly dangerous. Houseflies usually have harmful bacteria on their feet because they may have been walking on rubbish, faeces or dead animals. And when flies feed, they spit saliva onto the food (Figure 10.9). Rats and mice often carry pathogens. Covering food to keep flies and other animals from touching it is always a good idea.

# 10 Diseases and immunity

Figure 10.9: Houseflies can transmit pathogens to food, on their feet and in their saliva.

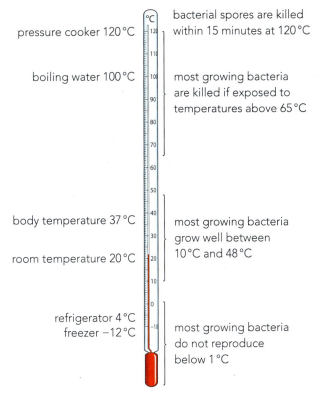

Figure 10.10: The effect of temperature on bacterial growth.

3   Do not keep foods at room temperature for long periods. Figure 10.10 shows how bacterial growth and reproduction are affected by temperature. If there are even just a few harmful bacteria on food, these can reproduce and form large populations if the temperature is right for them. Keeping food in the fridge slows down bacterial growth. Cooking food at a high temperature will kill most bacteria. If cooked food is reheated, it should be made really hot, not just warmed.

4   Keep raw meat away from other foods. Raw meat often contains bacteria. This is not a problem if the meat is to be cooked, because these bacteria will be killed. However, if the bacteria get onto other foods that might be eaten raw, then they might breed there. In any case, foods such as salads and vegetables that are to be eaten raw should be washed in clean water before eating, unless they have been packaged so that they cannot be contaminated with bacteria.

## Personal hygiene

Personal hygiene means keeping your body clean. This can greatly reduce the risk of getting, or passing on, transmissible diseases. We have already seen how important this is when preparing or eating food.

Human skin makes an oil that helps to keep it supple and waterproof. If the skin is not washed regularly, this oil can build up, as can dirt from things that we have touched.

When we are hot, we produce sweat from sweat glands in the skin. The evaporation of water from the sweat helps us to keep our body temperature from rising too high. If oil, dirt and sweat are left on the skin for long, they provide breeding grounds for bacteria. These can produce substances that smell unpleasant. Washing regularly, using soap and shampoo to help to remove oils, prevents this from happening (Figure 10.11).

**Figure 10.11:** Washing with soap reduces the risk of transferring pathogens.

**Figure 10.12:** Waste – especially food waste – left in the street encourages rats and other animals, which can spread pathogens.

There are also millions of bacteria inside our mouths. Most of these are harmless and may even be beneficial to us. But some of them can cause bad breath and tooth decay. Brushing teeth twice a day, and perhaps also using a mouthwash, can keep these harmful bacteria under control.

# Waste disposal

We produce an enormous amount of rubbish each year. Waste food, cardboard and paper packaging, bottles and cans, newspapers and magazines, plastic bags, old tyres – anything that we have finished with and no longer want to use – are all thrown away.

Sometimes, this waste simply accumulates close to where people live and work (Figure 10.12). Animals such as houseflies, rats and stray dogs may forage for food in the rubbish. Bacteria breed in the waste food. Dangerous chemicals seep out of the rubbish, polluting the ground and waterways.

In many countries, waste is regularly collected and taken to landfill sites. In some places, nothing is done to make the landfill site safe, but good management can avoid risk of infection and pollution. Figure 10.13 shows a well-designed landfill site. Only licensed operators are allowed to add material to the site, and the rubbish is checked as it is brought in, to make sure that nothing really dangerous is included. The rubbish is added in even layers and is compacted (pressed down) to reduce the space it takes up.

Some of the rubbish in the landfill site is rotted by decomposers, especially bacteria. This produces a gas called methane, which is flammable and could cause explosions if it is allowed to build up. Placing pipes in the rubbish can allow the methane to escape harmlessly into the air. Better still, the methane can be collected and used as a fuel.

Eventually, when the landfill site is full, it can be covered over with soil and grass, and trees allowed to grow.

## Sewage treatment

Sewage is waste liquid that has come from houses, industry and other parts of villages, towns and cities. Some of it has just run off streets into drains when it rains. Some of it has come from toilets, bathrooms and kitchens in people's houses and offices. Some of it has come from factories. Sewage is mostly water, but also contains many other substances. These include urine and faeces, toilet paper, detergents, oil and many other chemicals.

Sewage should not be allowed to run into rivers or the sea before it has been treated (Figure 10.14). This is because it can harm people and the environment. Untreated sewage is called raw sewage.

# 10 Diseases and immunity

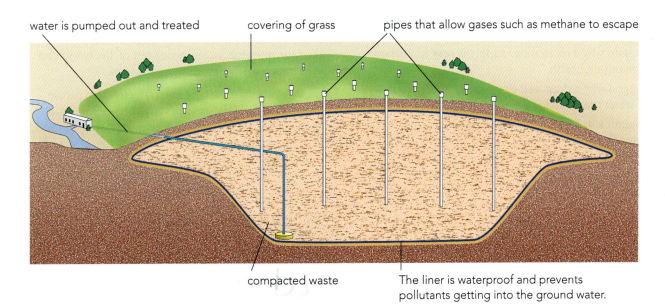

Figure 10.13: A well-constructed landfill site.

Figure 10.14: This open drainage canal contains rubbish and raw sewage – a major health risk to people living in this area.

Raw sewage contains many bacteria and other microorganisms, some of which are likely to be pathogens. People who come into contact with raw sewage may get ill, especially if it gets into their mouths. Poliomyelitis and cholera are just two of the serious diseases that can be transmitted through water polluted with raw sewage.

### ACTIVITY 10.2

#### Controlling the spread of disease

Work in a group of three or four for this activity.

Your task is to summarise the importance of a clean water supply, hygienic food preparation, personal hygiene, and safe disposal of sewage and other waste. Your summary should be in a form which can be shared with others.

Decide on the form that your summary could take. It could be a series of slides, a video presentation, a poster or an illustrated summary table.

You can use the information in this book, or you may like to research more information on the internet.

#### Peer assessment

Share your summary with another group or groups.

Look at their summary and decide on at least **two** things that they have done very well. Then suggest **two** things that would improve their summary.

Then consider the feedback that the other group gives to you. Do you agree with it? If you can, use their suggestions to improve your summary.

# CAMBRIDGE IGCSE™ BIOLOGY: COURSEBOOK

## Questions

4   Explain why a clean water supply is very important to maintain health.

5   Suggest why a deep well can provide a safer source of water than a river or lake.

6   Explain why food that is not going to be eaten immediately should be:
   a   kept covered
   b   kept in a fridge.

## Cholera

Cholera is a serious transmissible disease caused by a bacterium (Figure 10.15). Cholera bacteria can be spread through water and food that has been contaminated with faeces from an infected person. In places where people are forced to live in unhygienic conditions, such as in refugee camps, cholera can spread very rapidly. A very serious cholera outbreak happened in Haiti in 2010, following a major earthquake that displaced thousands of people from their homes. At least 8000 people were killed by this disease.

Cholera bacteria live and breed in the small intestine, and produce a toxin (poison) that stimulates the cells lining the intestine to secrete chloride ions (Figure 10.16). These ions accumulate in the lumen of the small intestine. This increases the concentration of the fluid in the lumen, lowering its water potential.

Once this water potential becomes lower than the water potential of the blood flowing through the vessels in the walls of the intestine, water moves out of the blood and into the lumen of the intestine, by osmosis.

This is why cholera is so dangerous. The infected person suffers severe diarrhoea, in which large quantities of water are lost from the body in watery faeces. Without treatment, death may occur from dehydration and the loss of chloride ions from the blood. However, so long as enough fluids can be given to replace these losses, almost every person suffering from cholera will eventually recover.

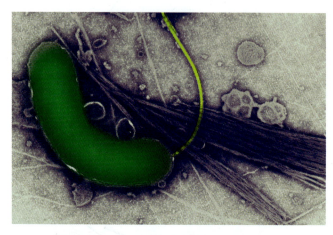

Figure 10.15: This scanning electron micrograph shows a cholera bacterium. The long yellow-green thread is called a flagellum, and the bacterium uses this to move itself through a liquid.

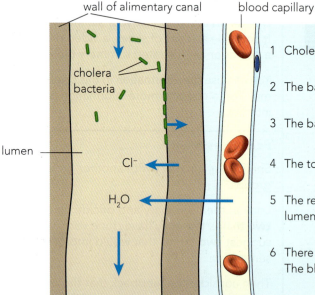

1   Cholera bacteria are ingested and multiply.

2   The bacteria attach to the wall of the alimentary canal.

3   The bacteria release toxin.

4   The toxin causes Cl⁻ ions to be released.

5   The release of ions causes water to move into the lumen by osmosis.

6   There is now a lot of water in the canal (watery diarrhoea). The blood contains too little Cl⁻ and water.

Figure 10.16: How the cholera toxin causes diarrhoea.

## Questions

7 Explain why cholera outbreaks are most likely to occur when people are displaced from their homes.

8 People with cholera can be successfully treated by giving them drinks containing water, glucose and salt (sodium chloride). This is called rehydration therapy. Use the information in Figure 10.16 to suggest how these drinks can help them to survive.

## 10.2 The immune response

In Chapter 9, we saw that one type of white blood cell – lymphocytes – produces molecules called antibodies. Antibodies help to destroy pathogens.

### Antibodies

In your body, you have thousands of different kinds of lymphocyte. Each kind is able to produce a different sort of antibody.

An antibody is a protein molecule with a particular shape. This shape is complementary to the shape of another molecule, which is a called an **antigen**.

Many antigens are molecules found on the outside of a pathogen. Each pathogen has its own antigens, which have specific shapes. To destroy a particular pathogen, antibody molecules must be made which are a perfect complementary shape to the antigens on the pathogen.

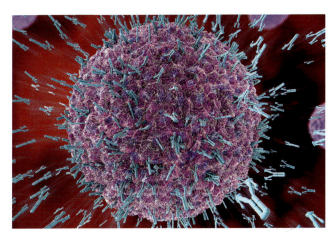

**Figure 10.17:** This drawing shows antibodies binding to their antigens on a virus. The antibody molecules are the Y-shaped blue structures.

The antibody molecules bind with the antigen (Figure 10.17). In some cases, this directly kills the pathogen. In other cases, the antigens stick the pathogens together. This stops the pathogens dividing or moving, making it easier for phagocytes to destroy them.

Most of the time, most of your lymphocytes do not produce antibodies. It would be a waste of energy and materials if they did. Instead, each lymphocyte waits for a signal that a pathogen which can be destroyed by its particular antibody is in your body.

If a pathogen enters the body, it is likely to meet a large number of lymphocytes. One of these may recognise the pathogen as being something that its antibody can destroy. This lymphocyte will start to divide rapidly by mitosis, making a clone of lymphocytes just like itself. These lymphocytes then secrete their antibody, destroying the pathogen (Figure 10.18).

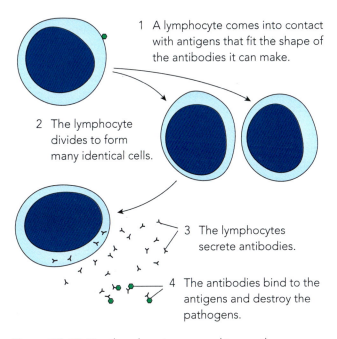

1 A lymphocyte comes into contact with antigens that fit the shape of the antibodies it can make.

2 The lymphocyte divides to form many identical cells.

3 The lymphocytes secrete antibodies.

4 The antibodies bind to the antigens and destroy the pathogens.

**Figure 10.18:** How lymphocytes respond to a pathogen.

> **KEY WORD**
>
> **antigen:** a chemical that is recognised by the body as being 'foreign' – that is, it is not part of the body's normal set of chemical substances – and stimulates the production of antibodies

This takes time. It may take a while for the 'right' lymphocyte to recognise the pathogen, and then a few days more for it to produce enough identical lymphocytes to make enough antibodies to kill the pathogen. In the meantime, the pathogen breeds, making you ill. Eventually, however, the lymphocytes, antibodies and phagocytes usually manage to destroy the pathogen, and you get better.

Lymphocytes are a very important part of your immune system. The way in which they respond to pathogens, by producing antibodies, is called the **immune response**.

## Memory cells

When a lymphocyte makes copies of itself (clones), not all of the new cells make antibodies. Some of them simply remain in the blood and other parts of the body, living for a very long time. They are called **memory cells**.

If the same kind of pathogen gets into the body again, these memory cells will be ready and waiting for them. They will be able to make enough antibodies, very quickly, to kill the pathogens before they have time to produce a large population and do any harm. The person has become immune to that type of pathogen.

Figure 10.19 shows how numbers of bacteria and antibodies in the body change after infection with a pathogen that your immune system has not met before, and when it infects you a second time.

> ### KEY WORDS
>
> **immune response:** the reaction of the body to the presence of an antigen; it involves the production of antibodies
>
> **memory cells:** long-lived cells produced by the division of lymphocytes that have contacted their antigen; memory cells are able to respond quickly to subsequent contact with the same antigen

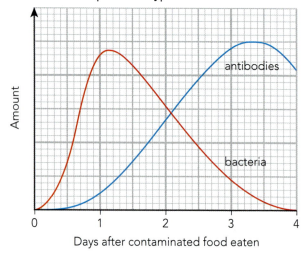

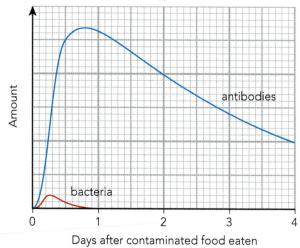

**Figure 10.19:** Changes in the amount of antibodies and number of bacteria after a first and second infection.

## Questions

9  Explain the difference between an antigen and an antibody.

10  A learner wrote that antibodies are the same shape as their specific antigens. What is wrong with that statement?

11 Look at the first graph in Figure 10.19.
   a  Infection happens at time 0. Explain why the number of antibodies does not begin to rise until some hours after this.
   b  Describe and explain what happens to the number of bacteria over the four-day period.
12 Look at the second graph in Figure 10.19.
   Describe and explain what happens to the number of bacteria the second time a person comes into contact with the bacteria.
13 Predict and explain what would happen if the person is infected with a different kind of bacterium, after an immune response like the one in Figure 10.19.

> **Peer assessment**
>
> Exchange your answer to Question 13 with a partner.
>
> Has your partner made a clear *prediction* about what would happen?
>
> Have they given a clear *explanation* of what they predict would happen?
>
> Give feedback to your partner about how well you think they have done this. Listen to their feedback to you, and make changes to your answer if necessary.

## Vaccination

In most countries, children are given vaccinations at various ages as they grow up. This is to immunise children against diseases caused by pathogens. Adults can also be given vaccinations if they are at risk of getting particular diseases.

A **vaccine** may contain weakened or dead viruses or bacteria that normally cause disease. Some vaccines don't contain complete viruses or bacteria, but only their antigens.

When the weakened pathogens or their antigens are introduced into the body, they are recognised by the lymphocytes that can make antibodies that have a complementary shape to their antigens. These lymphocytes multiply and produce antibodies just as they would after a 'real' infection. They also make memory cells, which give long-term immunity. So, if the 'normal' viruses or bacteria get into the body one day, they will be attacked and destroyed immediately.

Some diseases require two vaccinations to provide really good, long-lasting immunity. After the first dose, the body makes enough antibodies and memory cells to provide partial protection against the pathogen. A second vaccination given a few weeks afterwards, sometimes called a booster, stimulates the lymphocytes and memory cells to make even more antibodies and even more memory cells.

## Active and passive immunity

A person has **active immunity** to a disease if their body has made its own antibodies and memory cells that protect against that disease. These memory cells can last in the body for many years. You can develop active immunity by:

- having the disease and recovering from it
- being vaccinated.

Active immunity can last a long time – sometimes an entire lifetime. The memory cells that were made during the infection or after the vaccination can spring into action at a moment's notice to make antibodies and stop an invading pathogen in its tracks.

We can also be given a different kind of immunity, called **passive immunity**. A person has passive immunity to a disease if they have been given ready-made antibodies that have been made by another organism (Figure 10.20).

Babies get passive immunity by breast feeding. Breast milk contains antibodies from the mother, which are passed on to her baby. This is useful because a young baby's immune system is not well developed, and so the mother's antibodies can protect it against any diseases to which she is immune, for the first few months of its life.

> **KEY WORDS**
>
> **vaccine:** a harmless preparation of dead or inactivated pathogens that is injected into the body to induce an immune response
>
> **active immunity:** long-term defence against a pathogen by antibody production in the body
>
> **passive immunity:** short-term defence against a pathogen by antibodies acquired from another individual, such as from mother to infant

Another way of getting passive immunity is to be injected with antibodies that have been made by another organism. For example, if a person is bitten by an animal that might have rabies, they can be given antibodies against the rabies virus. These can destroy the virus immediately, whereas waiting for the body to make its own antibodies will take too long and the person is unlikely to recover.

Active immunity is usually very long-lasting. Passive immunity, however, only lasts for a short time. This is because the antibodies will eventually break down. No lymphocytes have been stimulated to make clones of themselves. The body has not made memory cells, so any infection will be treated as a first-time one.

**Active immunity**
Immunity is developed after contacting pathogens inside the body. The body's own lymphocytes make antibodies and memory cells.

in an infection — by injection of live or dead pathogen

**Passive immunity**
Immunity is provided by antibodies from outside the body.

antibodies from a mother in breast milk or across the placenta during pregnancy — by injection of antibodies

Figure 10.20: Active and passive immunity.

# Controlling disease by vaccination

Smallpox is a serious, often fatal, disease caused by a virus. It is transmitted by direct contact. If a person survives smallpox, they are often left with badly scarred skin, and may be made blind.

In 1956, the World Health Organization (WHO) began a campaign to try to completely eradicate smallpox. They wanted to make the smallpox virus extinct. They set up systems to get as many people as possible, all over the world, vaccinated against smallpox. The campaign was a success. More than 80% of people in the world who were at risk from the disease were vaccinated. The very last case of smallpox happened in 1977, in Somalia. By 1980, three years had gone by with no more cases, and the WHO were able to declare that smallpox had been eradicated.

Currently, attempts are being made to eradicate some other very serious diseases caused by viruses. One of these is poliomyelitis (polio for short) (Figure 10.21). Polio can infect children, and usually leaves them with permanent paralysis of parts of their body. Eradicating this virus is proving difficult, as people in some countries are resisting efforts to vaccinate children. Polio is now very rare in most parts of the world, but cases are still occurring in a small number of countries.

Figure 10.21: A child being vaccinated for polio. The polio vaccine is unusual because it can be given by mouth – no injection is needed.

The control of many other serious infectious diseases relies on vaccination of children. For example, we saw in the Science in Context at the start of this chapter that, in most countries, children are vaccinated against measles. Measles is spread by airborne droplets. It causes a skin rash and fever, and there can be very severe complications, such as blindness and brain damage.

Vaccinating children against measles protects not only the children that are vaccinated, but also those that are not. This is sometimes called 'herd immunity' – vaccinating enough individuals protects the whole 'herd' of people, even the ones who have not been vaccinated. 'Herd immunity' works because there are fewer places for the measles viruses to replicate – they can only do so if they enter the body of an unvaccinated person.

> ### ACTIVITY 10.3
>
> **Vaccinations in your country**
>
> Work with a partner, or in a small group.
>
> Use the internet to find out what vaccinations are given to young children in your country.
>
> Do any of the vaccinations need to be given more than once, to provide good immunity?
>
> At what ages are the vaccinations given?

## Questions

14 Outline **two** ways in which active immunity can be gained.
15 Outline **two** ways in which passive immunity can be gained.
16 Describe **one** difference between active immunity and passive immunity, other than the different ways that they are gained.
17 Explain how vaccination can help to control the spread of a transmissible disease.

## Covid-19

In December 2019, a new infection was detected. Scientists discovered that the pathogen that caused it was a new virus, which they named SARS-CoV-2. This stands for Severe Acute Respiratory Syndrome Coronavirus 2.

Coronaviruses are spherical viruses (Figure 10.22), with protein spikes sticking out. These spikes help the virus to attach to human cells. We already live with many different coronaviruses, which cause colds and flu. But this one is different – the illness it causes can often be very severe, and even fatal.

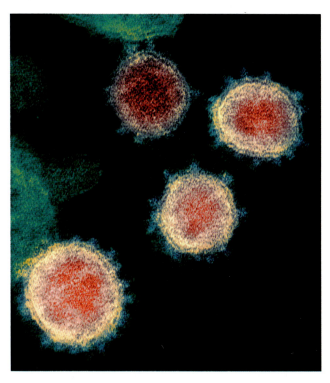

**Figure 10.22:** This electron micrograph shows four SARS-CoV-2 coronavirus particles. The protein coat with its spikes has been artificially coloured blue in this image ×200 000.

The disease caused by SARS-CoV-2 has become named Covid-19. You may like to try to work out what the letters and number in that name refer to.

## Learning about Covid-19

It took a little while for scientists to learn important facts about Covid-19. In particular, people needed to know how it is transmitted. This would help countries to plan how they could reduce the transmission. They also needed to find out how the virus affects the body, which would help to find ways to treat the disease.

- The virus is very easily transmitted from one person to another. It can be passed on in droplets, when a person coughs, sneezes or talks. It can remain on a surface – such as a door handle – for several days, and then get into another person's respiratory system if they touch the surface and then their mouth. Because the virus spreads so easily, it quickly caused a pandemic – a disease that is present all over the world.

- The virus can even be transmitted from a person who does not have any symptoms. People can be completely unaware that they could be passing the virus on.

- In most people, the virus causes only mild symptoms. But in others, the lungs can be so badly affected that the person has great difficulty breathing. Even with excellent medical treatment, some of these people die.

Scientists from many different countries worked together to discover all they could about the virus – how it is transmitted, what it does to the body and how we could stop it. Medical staff across the globe focused their attention on finding ways to treat people who were suffering severe symptoms. Mathematical modellers used the information that different countries were providing – about numbers of people infected with the virus, how many of them were ill enough to be admitted to hospital, how many of them died – and tried to predict what would happen next, and how different strategies might help to keep the numbers of infected and seriously ill people to a minimum.

Many countries asked people to stay at home and not travel. Tests were developed to find out who had the virus, and some governments asked people who tested positive to isolate themselves for 14 days. In many countries, people who did go out were asked to wear masks (Figure 10.23).

> ### ACTIVITY 10.4
>
> #### Researching Covid-19
>
> Covid-19 is a new disease. You are going to research the current understanding of this disease, and how people are affected by it.
>
> In your group, choose **one** of these topics to research. If you are not studying the Supplement, then Topic 1 is the best choice. Select websites carefully, ensuring that they are providing you with good scientific information. Use your findings to contribute to a display to put on the wall of the laboratory or your classroom.
>
> **Topic 1** *How did your country respond to the fight against Covid-19?*
>
> What did your country do to try to stop this disease spreading when it first appeared? How does this compare with what other countries did? Why did different countries take different steps? Which worked best? How can we use this information to make better decisions if another pandemic arises in future?
>
> **Topic 2** *What does the virus do in the body?*
>
> How does the virus infect cells? How does the immune system respond to infection with this virus? What have scientists learnt about why some people are more likely to become very ill than others? What treatments have proved to be most effective, and why?
>
> **Topic 3** *A vaccine against Covid-19*
>
> Producing and testing vaccines was done much more quickly than usual – how was this achieved? Have any vaccines proved to be successful? How do the vaccines work? Who is able to be vaccinated? How does this affect the lives of people in different countries of the world?

# 10 Diseases and immunity

**Figure 10.23:** Research shows that wearing a mask not only reduces the risk of passing a virus to someone else, but also reduces the person's risk of inhaling it themselves.

## SUMMARY

| |
|---|
| Transmissible diseases are caused by pathogens, which can be passed from one host to another. |
| Pathogens can be transmitted through direct contact with blood or other body fluids, or indirectly through contaminated surfaces, food, from animals or through the air. |
| The body has defences to prevent the entry of pathogens, including skin, hairs in the nose, mucus and stomach acid. White blood cells destroy pathogens that get through these defences and enter the body. |
| Each pathogen has its own antigens, which have specific shapes. |
| Lymphocytes produce antibodies, which are proteins with specific shapes that are complementary to specific antigens. Antibodies bind with their antigens and either destroy the pathogen directly or make it easier for phagocytes to destroy the pathogen. |
| Lymphocytes that have made contact with their antigen divide to form clones of memory cells. These remain in the body for long periods of time and can quickly respond to entry of pathogens with the same antigen at a later date. |
| The production of antibodies and memory cells from the body's own lymphocytes leads to active immunity. This is long-lasting. |
| Active immunity can result from having a disease and recovering from it or from vaccination. |
| Immunity can also be gained by being given ready-made antibodies. Babies obtain antibodies from their mother when they feed on breast milk. Antibodies can also be given by injection. This is called passive immunity and is not long-lasting because no memory cells are produced. |
| Vaccination of a high percentage of a population helps to stop the spread of disease, because there are only a few unvaccinated hosts in which a pathogen can reproduce. |

## PROJECT

### Finding a vaccine for malaria

Malaria is a serious disease that kills thousands of people each year, mostly children. The first malaria vaccine to be used on a widespread scale was launched in Kenya, Ghana and Malawi in 2019.

You are going to help to write a short play about the introduction of this vaccine, and then perhaps take part in the play.

First, do some research about the first vaccine that was used in 2019. You could search on the following websites to begin with but do look for others as well.

- World Health Organization website, and search for malaria vaccine
- The History of Vaccines website, and search for malaria
- The Zero Malaria Africa website

When you feel that you have collected enough information, begin to think about your play.

It could involve characters like some of the following people:

- a philanthropist who is giving money to support the production and use of the malaria vaccine
- doctors who will be involved in the malaria vaccine campaign

- health workers who will be administering the vaccines
- parents who are wondering whether to let their child be given the vaccine

- children and/or adults who are going to be given the vaccine
- anyone else who might be involved in the project.

- scientists trying to develop a malaria vaccine or who have developed one that is now going to be used on a large scale for the first time

## 10 Diseases and immunity

### EXAM-STYLE QUESTIONS

1  What is the correct term for a microorganism that causes disease?
   A  antibody
   B  host
   C  pathogen
   D  vector                                                                        [1]

2  Which disease is **not** transmissible?
   A  AIDS, caused by HIV
   B  coronary heart disease, caused by blockage in the coronary arteries
   C  influenza, caused by a virus
   D  malaria, caused by a single-celled organism                                   [1]

3  What is a function of mucus in the passages leading to the lungs?
   A  making it easy for air to move in and out of the lungs
   B  providing a low pH that kills pathogens
   C  secreting enzymes to kill bacteria
   D  trapping microorganisms before they reach the lungs                           [1]

4  Which statement about an antibody is correct?
   A  It is a protein.
   B  It is found on the surface of a pathogen.
   C  It is secreted by phagocytes.
   D  It is the same shape as a specific antigen.                                   [1]

5  Which statements about active and passive immunity are correct?

   |   | Active immunity | Passive immunity |
   |---|---|---|
   | A | antibodies are secreted by lymphocytes | antibodies are obtained from outside the body |
   | B | cannot be gained by vaccination | can be gained by vaccination |
   | C | lasts for a short time only | lasts for a long time |
   | D | no memory cells produced | memory cells are produced |
   
   [1]

6  a  Choose words from the list to complete the sentences about diseases.

      bacteria    enzymes    host    mucus    pathogens    viruses

      All transmissible diseases are caused by _____,
      which are passed from one _____ to another.
      The lining of the respiratory passages helps to prevent this from
      happening by producing _____.                                         [3]
   b  **Describe** how the body defences help to prevent bacteria entering:
      i   through the skin                                                          [2]
      ii  in food                                                                   [3]

      [Total: 8]

> **COMMAND WORD**
>
> **describe:** state the points of a topic / give characteristics and main features

## CONTINUED

**7 a** Explain how vaccination produces active immunity in a child. [5]

**b** The graph shows the number of cases of measles in the USA between 1944 and 2004. Measles is caused by a virus. Vaccination for measles was introduced in the USA in 1963.

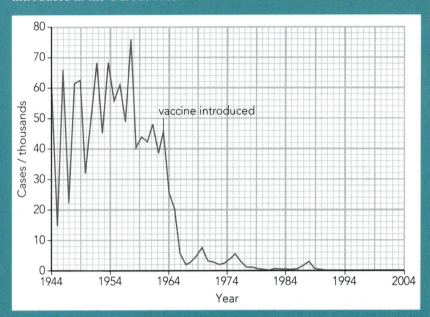

  **i** Describe how the number of cases of measles in the USA changed between 1945 and 1958. [3]

  **ii** Describe **and** explain the effect of the introduction of vaccination. [4]

[Total: 12]

**8 a** For each of the following events, decide whether it produces active immunity or passive immunity.
- having a disease and recovering from it
- feeding a baby on breast milk
- being injected with antibodies
- being vaccinated with weakened viruses [2]

**b** An aid worker is asked to travel immediately to an area where a disaster has taken place. There is a high risk of her being exposed to pathogens that cause serious diseases. Her doctor recommends that she should have an injection of antibodies, rather than a vaccination of weakened pathogens, before she travels.
Suggest an explanation for the doctor's recommendation. [3]

**c** Describe how antibodies help to destroy pathogens. [4]

[Total: 9]

## CONTINUED

**9** The electron micrograph shows a group of influenza viruses.

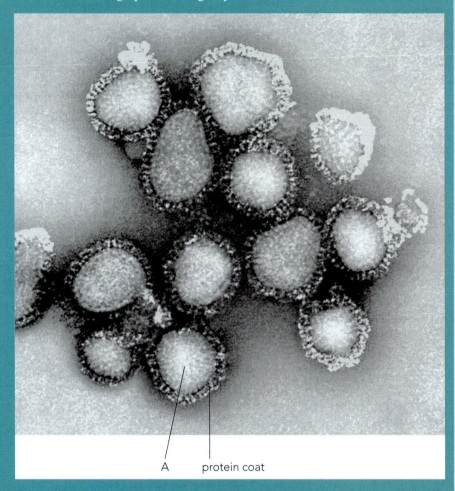

A    protein coat

**a** Identify the part of the virus labelled **A**. [1]

**b** New strains of the influenza virus frequently occur. The new strains have different proteins in their coats.

Explain why a person who has recovered from influenza in one year may not be immune to influenza in the future. [5]

[Total: 6]

# CAMBRIDGE IGCSE™ BIOLOGY: COURSEBOOK

## SELF-EVALUATION CHECKLIST

After studying this chapter, think about how confident you are with the different topics. This will help you to see any gaps in your knowledge and help you to learn more effectively.

| I can | See Topic… | Needs more work | Almost there | Confident to move on |
|---|---|---|---|---|
| explain what a pathogen is | 10.1 | | | |
| describe how pathogens can be transmitted through direct contact, or indirectly | 10.1 | | | |
| describe how the skin, hairs in the nose, mucus, stomach acid and white blood cells help to defend against pathogens | 10.1 | | | |
| explain the importance of clean water, hygienic food preparation, personal hygiene, waste disposal and sewage treatment in controlling the spread of disease | 10.1 | | | |
| explain what an antigen is, and state that each pathogen has its own antigens with a specific shape | 10.2 | | | |
| describe antibodies as proteins secreted by lymphocytes, which bind to specific antigens with a complementary shape | 10.2 | | | |
| outline how antibodies destroy pathogens, or help phagocytes to destroy them | 10.2 | | | |
| explain what active immunity is, and how it is gained by an infection or vaccination | 10.2 | | | |
| describe how memory cells are produced, and what they do | 10.2 | | | |
| outline how vaccination can provide long-term immunity | 10.2 | | | |
| explain how vaccination can help to control the spread of transmissible diseases | 10.2 | | | |
| explain what passive immunity is, how it is gained and how it differs from active immunity | 10.2 | | | |

> Chapter 11

# Respiration and gas exchange

**IN THIS CHAPTER YOU WILL:**

- find out how the body uses energy, and how aerobic and anaerobic respiration supply this energy
- learn the equations for aerobic respiration and anaerobic respiration
- describe how gas exchange happens in the lungs, and the features of gas exchange surfaces
- investigate the differences in composition between inspired and expired air

> explain the differences in composition between inspired and expired air
> explain how breathing happens
> explain how activity affects breathing rate.

# CAMBRIDGE IGCSE™ BIOLOGY: COURSEBOOK

## GETTING STARTED

Sit quietly. Rest one hand against your sternum (breastbone) like the girl in the photo below. Think about the breathing movements you can feel.

Now stand up and take four or five steps on the spot. Feel your breathing movements again.

What happened? Why did this happen?

## SLEEP APNOEA

Most of the time we breathe regularly without even thinking about it. If you count your breathing movements, perhaps feeling the movements of your thorax (chest) as you breathe (Figure 11.1), you will probably find that you breathe in and out between 12 and 22 times each minute. Breathing moves air into and out of the lungs, providing oxygen that can be transported to all the cells in the body in the blood.

Breathing is an automatic process, which happens even when we are asleep. But for some people, sleeping greatly disrupts their pattern of breathing. They seem to hold their breath for a long time, and then suddenly breathe in – sometimes with a snorting, gasping noise. People often wake themselves up when they do this. This condition is called sleep apnoea. If it is severe, it can cause health problems.

A person with severe sleep apnoea can be helped by using a small machine to pump air into a mask that they wear over the mouth or nose while asleep. This helps to keep their breathing more regular, so that they can get a better night's sleep. Serious sleep apnoea is more common in people who are very overweight, so losing weight can also help. It may also be helpful if they sleep on their side, rather than on their back. Stopping smoking is also a good idea.

### Discussion questions

1 Breathing happens automatically, but we can also at least partly control it consciously. In contrast, we cannot control our heartbeat consciously. Can you suggest any reasons for these two processes being different in this respect?

2 Statistics show that people with untreated sleep apnoea are more likely to have car accidents. Can you suggest why?

**Figure 11.1:** You can feel your breathing movements by resting your hand just below the collarbone.

# 11.1 Respiration

## Using energy

Every living cell needs energy. In humans, our cells need energy for:

- contracting muscles, so that we can move parts of the body
- making protein molecules (protein synthesis) by linking together amino acids into long chains
- cell division, so that we can repair damaged tissues and can grow
- active transport, so that we can move substances across cell membranes up their concentration gradients
- growth, by building new cells which can then divide to form new cells
- transmitting nerve impulses, so that we can transfer information quickly from one part of the body to another
- producing heat inside the body, to keep the body temperature constant even if the environment is cold.

All of this energy comes from the food that we eat. The food is digested – that is, broken down into smaller molecules – which are absorbed from the small intestine into the blood. The blood transports the nutrients to all the cells in the body. The cells take up the nutrients that they need.

The main nutrient used to provide energy in cells is glucose. Glucose contains a lot of chemical energy. In order to make use of this energy, cells have to break down the glucose molecules and release the energy from them. They do this in a series of metabolic reactions called respiration. Like all metabolic reactions, respiration involves the action of enzymes.

## Aerobic respiration

Most of the time, our cells release energy from glucose by combining it with oxygen. This is called **aerobic respiration**.

This happens in a series of small steps, each one controlled by enzymes. Most of the steps in aerobic respiration take place inside mitochondria.

We can summarise the reactions of aerobic respiration as an equation:

glucose + oxygen → carbon dioxide + water

The balanced equation is:

$$C_6H_{12}O_6 + 6O_2 \rightarrow 6CO_2 + 6H_2O$$

## Anaerobic respiration

It is possible to release energy from glucose without using oxygen. It is not such an efficient process as aerobic respiration and not much energy is released per glucose molecule. This is called **anaerobic respiration** ('an' means without). Anaerobic respiration happens in the cytoplasm of a cell, not in mitochondria.

Yeast, a single-celled fungus, often respires anaerobically. It breaks down glucose to alcohol.

glucose → alcohol + carbon dioxide

$$C_6H_{12}O_6 \rightarrow 2C_2H_5OH + 2CO_2$$

You can see from the equation that carbon dioxide is made in this process. Plants can also respire anaerobically like this, but only for short periods of time.

Some of the cells in your body, particularly muscle cells, can also respire anaerobically for a short time. But they do not do this in the same way as yeast. They make lactic acid instead of alcohol and no carbon dioxide is produced. This happens when you do vigorous exercise, and your lungs and heart cannot supply oxygen to your muscles as quickly as they are using it. The muscle cells are able to release at least some energy from glucose without using oxygen, just to keep them going until oxygen is available again.

glucose → lactic acid

> **KEY WORDS**
>
> **aerobic respiration:** chemical reactions that take place in mitochondria, which use oxygen to break down glucose and other nutrient molecules to release energy for the cell to use
>
> **anaerobic respiration:** chemical reactions in cells that break down nutrient molecules to release energy, without using oxygen

> ### REFLECTION
>
> There are several equations to learn here – three word equations if you are studying the Core only, plus two balanced equations if you are studying the Supplement. You have already learnt the equation for photosynthesis in Chapter 6.
>
> How will you try to remember all of these equations, and not get them mixed up?

Table 11.1 compares aerobic and anaerobic respiration.

| Aerobic respiration | Anaerobic respiration |
|---|---|
| involves chemical reactions in cells that break down glucose to release energy | involves chemical reactions in cells that break down glucose to release energy |
| uses oxygen | does not use oxygen |
| no alcohol or lactic acid made | alcohol (in yeast and plants) or lactic acid (in animals) is made |
| large amount of energy released from each molecule of glucose | much less energy released from each molecule of glucose |
| carbon dioxide made | carbon dioxide is made by yeast and plants, but not by animals |

**Table 11.1:** A comparison of aerobic and anaerobic respiration.

## Questions

1. Look at the equation for aerobic respiration (either the word equation, or the balanced equation). How does this compare with the equation for photosynthesis, which you learnt in Chapter 6?
2. In which cells in your body does respiration happen?
3. In respiration, energy is released from glucose. Think back to your earlier work, and explain how the energy became incorporated into the glucose molecules.

> ### ACTIVITY 11.1
>
> **Predicting the results of an experiment**
>
> Work with a partner for this activity.
>
> Look at Experimental skills 11.1, Investigating the effect of temperature on respiration in yeast.
>
> Using what you have learnt about respiration in this chapter, predict how temperature is likely to affect respiration in yeast. Hint: you may like to remind yourself of some of the information in Chapter 5.
>
> Sketch a graph to show your prediction.
>
> With your partner, write a sentence or two to justify your prediction.

# 11 Respiration and gas exchange

## EXPERIMENTAL SKILLS 11.1

### Investigating the effect of temperature on respiration in yeast

In this investigation, you will measure the rate of respiration in yeast by counting how many bubbles of gas it releases in unit time. You will practise handling apparatus carefully, making measurements, recording results and displaying them in a suitable graph.

> **You will need:**
> - the apparatus shown in Figure 11.2
> - retort stands, bosses and clamps to support it (or you can stand the tubes in beakers)
> - a timer
> - electronically controlled water-baths or make your own using beakers of water that you can heat or cool (see Experimental skills 5.2)
> - a thermometer.

**Safety:** Take care when using hot water – water at 80 °C is hot enough to burn skin.

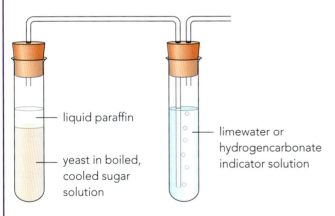

**Figure 11.2:** Apparatus for investigating respiration in yeast.

### Before you start

Find out whether you will be using electronically controlled water-baths or making your own. If you are going to make your own, make sure you know how you will do this.

Whichever type of water-bath you use, practise moving your apparatus into and out of a water-bath without any of the tubes coming loose. Only the tube on the left in the diagram needs to be in the water-bath.

### Method

1. Set up the apparatus shown in Figure 11.2.

2. Check the temperature of the electronically controlled water-baths or set up your own water-bath. If you are making your own, decide on the temperatures you will use. If possible, use five different temperatures – perhaps 0 °C (using ice) as your lowest and 80 °C as the highest, and three more in between.

3. Stand the tube with the yeast in it in the water-bath at the first temperature. (The other tube in your apparatus does not need to be in the water-bath, and it will be easier to see the bubbles if you keep it outside.) Leave the apparatus in the water-bath for at least three or four minutes, to give time for the yeast and glucose mixture to come to the correct temperature.

4. Now start your timer and count how many bubbles of gas are released into the liquid in the right-hand tube in one minute. Repeat twice more at this temperature.

5. Repeat steps 3 and 4 at the four other temperatures you have chosen.

6. Record all of your results in a suitable chart. Remember to calculate the mean number of bubbles produced at each temperature and include that in your results chart.

7. Plot a line graph with temperature on the x-axis and mean number of bubbles per minute on the y-axis.

> **CONTINUED**
>
> **Questions**
>
> 1. Did you have any anomalous results – that is, results that did not fit the general pattern? If so, what did you do about them?
> 2. Describe the shape of your graph.
> 3. Use your knowledge of enzymes to explain the shape of your graph.
> 4. How well did the results of your experiment match the prediction that you made in Activity 11.1? If they were not the same, can you suggest why?
> 5. Explain why we cannot tell if the yeast was respiring aerobically or anaerobically during this experiment.
> 6. If the experiment is continued for a long time, no more bubbles are produced. Suggest why this happens.
>
> **Self-assessment**
>
> How well did you manage this experiment? Rate yourself for each of the statements using:
>
> ☺ if you did it really well
>
> 😐 if you made a good attempt at it and partly succeeded
>
> ☹ if you did not try to do it or did not succeed
>
> - I used at least five different temperatures.
> - I managed the water-baths well (if you made your own).
> - I moved the apparatus into and out of the water-baths without letting anything fall apart.
> - I counted the bubbles accurately.
> - I kept myself and others safe while doing the experiment.

## 11.2 Gas exchange in humans

### Gas exchange surfaces

If you look back at the aerobic respiration equation near the beginning of this chapter, you will see that two substances are needed. They are glucose and oxygen. The way in which cells obtain glucose is described in Chapters 6 and 7. Animals get sugars such as glucose from carbohydrates which they eat. Plants make theirs by photosynthesis.

Oxygen is obtained in a different way. Animals and plants get their oxygen directly from their surroundings – either from the air for terrestrial (land-living) organisms or from oxygen dissolved in water for aquatic (water-living) ones.

If you look again at the aerobic respiration equation, you can see that carbon dioxide is made. This is a waste product and it must be removed from the organism.

In organisms, there are special areas where the oxygen enters and carbon dioxide leaves. One gas is entering, and the other leaving, so these are surfaces for **gas exchange**. The **gas exchange surfaces** have to be permeable, so that oxygen and carbon dioxide can move easily through them. They have other characteristics which help the process to be quick and efficient:

- They are thin to allow gases to diffuse across them quickly.
- They are close to an efficient transport system to take gases to and from the exchange surface.
- They have a large surface area, so that a lot of gas can diffuse across at the same time.
- They have a good supply of oxygen.

> **KEY WORDS**
>
> **gas exchange:** the diffusion of oxygen and carbon dioxide into and out of an organism's body
>
> **gas exchange surface:** a part of the body where gas exchange between the body and the environment takes place

# 11 Respiration and gas exchange

## The human breathing system

Figure 11.3 shows the structures which are involved in gas exchange in a human. The most obvious are the two lungs. Each lung is filled with many tiny air spaces called air sacs or **alveoli**. It is here that oxygen diffuses into the blood, so the surface of the alveoli is the gas exchange surface. Because they are so full of air spaces, lungs feel very light and spongy to touch. The lungs are supplied with air through the windpipe or **trachea**.

> **KEY WORDS**
>
> **alveoli:** tiny air-filled sacs in the lungs where gas exchange takes place
>
> **trachea:** the tube through which air travels to the lungs; it has rings of cartilage in its walls, to support it

## The nose and mouth

Air can enter the body through either the nose or mouth. Hairs in the nose trap dust particles in the air.

Inside the nose are some thin bones which are covered with a thin layer of cells. Some of these cells, called **goblet cells**, make a liquid containing water and mucus (Figure 11.4). The water in this liquid evaporates into the air in the nose and moistens it.

Other cells have very tiny hair-like projections called **cilia**. The cilia are always moving, and bacteria or particles of dust get trapped in them and in the mucus. Cilia are found all along the trachea and bronchi, too. They sweep the mucus, containing bacteria and dust particles, up to the back of the throat, so that it does not block the lungs.

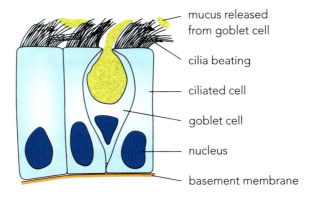

Figure 11.4: Part of the lining of the respiratory passages.

> **KEY WORDS**
>
> **goblet cells:** cells found in the lining (epithelium) of the respiratory passages and digestive system, which secrete mucus
>
> **cilia:** tiny projections from some of the cells in the lining of the respiratory passages; the cilia of many adjacent cells beat rhythmically in unison

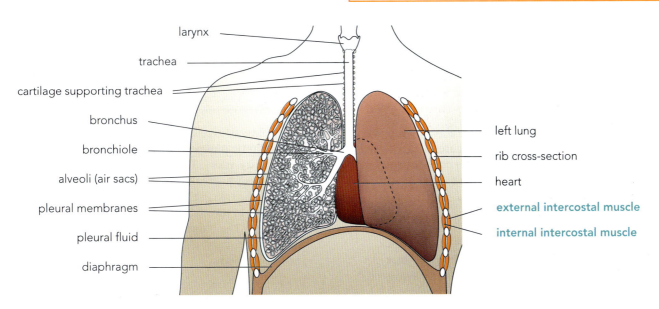

Figure 11.3: The human gas exchange system.

## The trachea

From the nose or mouth, the air then passes into the windpipe or trachea. Just below the epiglottis is the voice box or larynx. This contains the vocal cords. The vocal cords can be tightened by muscles so that they make sounds when air passes over them.

The trachea has rings of cartilage around it. As you breathe in and out, the pressure of the air in the trachea increases and decreases. The cartilage helps to prevent the trachea collapsing at times when the air pressure inside is lower than the pressure of the air outside it.

## The bronchi

The trachea goes down through the neck and into the **thorax**. The thorax is the upper part of your body from the neck down to the bottom of the ribs and diaphragm. In the thorax, the trachea divides into two. The two branches are called the right and left bronchi (singular: **bronchus**). One bronchus goes to each lung and then branches out into smaller tubes called **bronchioles**.

> ### KEY WORDS
>
> **thorax:** the chest; the part of the body from the neck down to the diaphragm
>
> **bronchus:** one of the two tubes that takes air from the trachea into the lungs
>
> **bronchiole:** a small tube that takes air from a bronchus to every part of the lungs

## Alveoli

There are many tiny air sacs or alveoli at the end of each bronchiole (Figure 11.5). This is where gas exchange takes place.

As we have seen, the walls of the alveoli are the gas exchange surface. Tiny capillaries are closely wrapped around the outside of the alveoli (Figure 11.6). Oxygen diffuses across the walls of the alveoli into the blood. Carbon dioxide diffuses the other way.

The walls of the alveoli have several features which make them an efficient gas exchange surface:

- They are very thin. They are only one cell thick. The capillary walls are also only one cell thick. An oxygen molecule only has to diffuse across this small thickness to get into the blood.

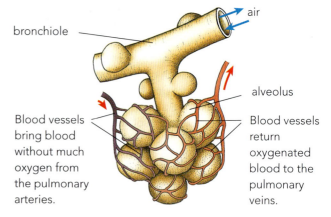

Figure 11.5: Alveoli in the lungs, and the blood vessels that are associated with them.

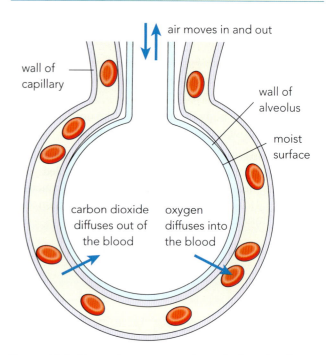

Figure 11.6: Gas exchange across the wall of an alveolus.

- They have an excellent transport system. Blood is constantly pumped to the lungs along the pulmonary artery. This branches into thousands of capillaries which take blood to all parts of the lungs. Carbon dioxide in the blood can diffuse out into the air spaces in the alveoli and oxygen can diffuse into the blood. The blood is then taken back to the heart in the pulmonary vein, ready to be pumped to the rest of the body.

- They have a large surface area. In fact, the surface area is enormous. The total surface area of all the alveoli in your lungs is over $100\,m^2$.

- They have a good supply of oxygen. Your breathing movements keep your lungs well supplied with oxygen. This is called **ventilation**.

> **KEY WORD**
>
> **ventilation:** the movement of air into and out of the lungs, by breathing movements

## Questions

4  List, in order, all of the structures that a molecule of oxygen passes through as it moves from the air, down into the lungs, and into the blood.

5  In Figure 11.6, look carefully at the arrows showing the movement of oxygen into the blood, and carbon dioxide out of the blood. Apart from going in different directions, what other difference can you see between them? Explain this difference.

6  Look at Figure 11.6 again. Some of the movement indicated by the arrows is mass flow, where a lot of air all moves in the same direction. Some of the movement is by diffusion, where individual molecules move randomly. Which arrows represent which type of movement?

7  People who smoke cigarettes often develop an illness called emphysema, where the walls of the alveoli break down. Instead of having millions of tiny air spaces in their lungs, they have fewer larger ones. Predict how this might affect the person's ability to do exercise. Explain your prediction.

### EXPERIMENTAL SKILLS 11.2

**Investigating the difference in composition between inspired and expired air**

In this investigation, you will use limewater to compare how much carbon dioxide there is in the air you breathe in and the air you breathe out. You will practise observing carefully, and then use your observations to draw a conclusion.

> **You will need:**
> - the apparatus shown in Figure 11.7.

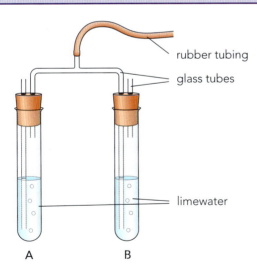

**Figure 11.7:** Apparatus for comparing the carbon dioxide concentration in inspired and expired air.

**Safety:** Limewater is an irritant. Do not get it in your mouth. Wear safety goggles when breathing in and out through the tubing. Make sure that you do not suck hard through the rubber tubing.

Take care that the rubber tubing is really clean before you put your mouth over it. Use a new piece of tubing for each person who uses the apparatus.

**Method**

1  Look carefully at the apparatus – especially at the lengths of the glass tubes. When someone breathes gently into the rubber tubing, in which test-tube do you predict bubbles will appear?

2  Breathe gently into and out of the rubber tubing. Take care not to suck too hard – you want to make bubbles appear in the limewater, not suck limewater into your mouth. Keep doing this until the limewater in one of the test-tubes becomes cloudy.

3  Continue breathing in and out for a while. You may find that the limewater in the other test-tube also becomes cloudy.

**Questions**

1  Explain why bubbles appeared in different test-tubes when you breathed in and when you breathed out.

2  Explain why the limewater went cloudy more quickly in one of the test-tubes.

## Comparing inspired air and expired air

Table 11.2 summarises the differences between the composition of inspired air and expired air.

| Component | Percentage in inspired air | Percentage in expired air |
|---|---|---|
| oxygen | 21 | 16 |
| carbon dioxide | 0.04 | 4 |
| water vapour | variable | usually very high |

**Table 11.2:** A comparison of inspired air and expired air.

The air that we breathe in usually has an oxygen content of about 20 to 21%. There is less oxygen in the air that we breathe out, because cells in the body use oxygen in respiration. However, expired air does still contain a significant amount of oxygen, usually about 16%. The main reason for this is that our expired air mixes with normal air in the bronchi and trachea, so that what we actually breathe out is a mixture of the air in the alveoli, and atmospheric air.

The air we breathe in contains only a very small percentage of carbon dioxide, usually about 0.04%. Body cells produce carbon dioxide in aerobic respiration, and this carbon dioxide diffuses out of the blood and into the alveoli. Extra carbon dioxide is therefore present in the air that we breathe out, increasing its concentration to about 4%.

## Breathing movements

To make air move in and out of the lungs, you must change the volume of your thorax. First, you make it large so that air is sucked in. Then you make it smaller again so that air is squeezed out. This is called **breathing**.

Muscles in two parts of the body help you to breathe. Some of them, called the **intercostal muscles**, are between the ribs (Figure 11.8). The others are in the **diaphragm**. The diaphragm is a large sheet of muscle and elastic tissue which stretches across your body, underneath the lungs and heart.

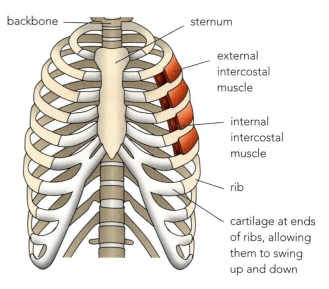

**Figure 11.8:** The rib cage and intercostal muscles.

> **KEY WORDS**
>
> **breathing:** using the muscles in the diaphragm, and the intercostal muscles, to change the volume of the thorax so that air is drawn into and pushed out of the lungs
>
> **intercostal muscles:** muscles between the ribs, which raise and lower the rib cage when they contract and relax
>
> **diaphragm:** a muscle that separates the chest cavity from the abdominal cavity in mammals; it helps with breathing

### Breathing in (inspiration)

When breathing in, the muscles of the diaphragm contract. This pulls the diaphragm downwards, which increases the volume in the thorax (Figure 11.9). At the same time, the external intercostal muscles contract. This pulls the rib cage upwards and outwards. This also increases the volume of the thorax.

As the volume of the thorax increases, the pressure inside it falls below atmospheric pressure. Air therefore flows in along the trachea and bronchi into the lungs.

## Breathing out (expiration)

When breathing out, the muscles of the diaphragm relax. The diaphragm springs back up into its domed shape because it is made of elastic tissue. This decreases the volume in the thorax. The external intercostal muscles also relax. The rib cage drops down again into its normal position. This also decreases the volume of the thorax.

Usually, relaxing the external intercostal muscles and the muscles of the diaphragm is all that is needed for breathing out. Sometimes, though, you breathe out more forcefully – when coughing, for example. Then the internal intercostal muscles contract strongly, making the rib cage drop down even further. The muscles of the abdomen wall also contract, helping to squeeze extra air out of the thorax.

## Questions

8   Suggest why the quantity of water vapour in expired air is always high.

9   Nitrogen is soluble in water, and molecules of nitrogen gas can pass easily through cell membranes. Body cells cannot use nitrogen gas. Inspired air contains about 78% nitrogen. Predict the percentage of nitrogen in expired air and explain your prediction.

10  Construct a table to show what the diaphragm, external intercostal and internal intercostal muscles do when you are breathing in, and when you are breathing out.

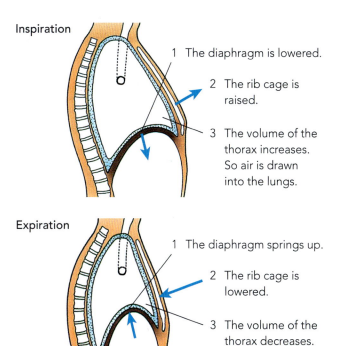

**Figure 11.9:** How breathing movements change the volume of the thorax.

### ACTIVITY 11.2

**Explaining the meanings of terms**

Many people use the words *breathing*, *respiration* and *gas exchange* as though they mean the same thing.

Work in a small group to discuss the meaning of these three terms. Try to write a short, clear description of each one, which makes clear the differences between them.

Share your ideas with other groups. Use the best ideas from all the groups in your class to write a really clear description that you think will help everyone to use the words correctly.

### EXPERIMENTAL SKILLS 11.3

**Investigating the effect of physical activity on rate and depth of breathing**

In this experiment, you will investigate how exercise affects your breathing. You will plan your own experiment, using the experience you gained when you did Experimental skills 9.1, Investigating the effect of physical activity on heart rate.

This investigation gives you practice in planning an experiment where you change one variable, measure another and try to keep other important variables the same.

**You will need:**
- a timer.

**Safety:** If you are worried that doing exercise might make you ill, do not do it! You can measure someone else's breathing rate instead.

**Before you start**

Practise measuring breathing rate and depth. Work with a partner, and decide how you will count how many breaths you take per minute. For breathing depth, you may need to just observe any changes, rather than trying to measure them. Make a firm decision about how you will do this.

**Method**

1. Make a plan of what you will do. Think about how you will change your independent variable (activity). You may find it helpful to look at the instructions for Experimental skills 9.1 Investigating the effect of physical activity on heart rate. Or, think about how you did that investigation.

2. Construct a results table.

3. Do your experiment and record your results in your table. Be prepared to make changes to your original plan, if you realise that this would improve your experiment.

**Questions**

1. Use your results to draw a line graph. Put time/minutes on the x-axis and breathing rate/breaths per minute on the y-axis. Mark on the x-axis where exercise began and ended. Use a ruler to join the points with straight lines.

2. Use your table or graph to describe, in words, how exercise affected breathing rate.

3. Evaluate the reliability of your results. Do you think you would get the same results if you did your experiment again tomorrow? Explain why you think this.

## Exercise and breathing rate

All the cells in your body need oxygen for respiration and all of this oxygen is supplied by the lungs. The oxygen is carried by the blood to every part of the body.

Sometimes, cells may need a lot of oxygen very quickly. Imagine you are running in a race. The muscles in your legs contract much harder and more frequently than usual, so they require more energy. The cells in the muscles combine oxygen with glucose as fast as they can, to release extra energy for muscle contraction.

A lot of oxygen is needed to work as hard as this. You breathe deeper and faster to get more oxygen into your blood. Your heart beats faster to get the oxygen to the leg muscles as quickly as possible.

Eventually a limit is reached. The heart and lungs cannot supply oxygen to the muscles any faster. But the muscles continue to contract quickly, requiring more energy. How can that extra energy be found?

Extra energy can be provided by anaerobic respiration. The muscle cells continue to respire aerobically with the oxygen they have, but they also break down some glucose without combining it with oxygen.

$$\text{glucose} \rightarrow \text{lactic acid} + \text{energy}$$

As you saw in Topic 11.1, anaerobic respiration does not release very much energy, but a little extra might make all the difference.

When you stop running, you will have quite a lot of lactic acid in your muscles and your blood. This lactic acid must be broken down by combining it with oxygen in the liver. This is done by aerobic respiration in the liver cells. So, even though you no longer need extra energy, you continue to breathe faster and more deeply

## 11 Respiration and gas exchange

than normal, and your heart rate continues to be high. You are taking in and transporting extra oxygen to break down the lactic acid. The faster heart rate also helps to transport lactic acid as quickly as possible from the muscles to the liver.

While you were running, you built up an **oxygen debt**. You 'borrowed' some extra energy, without 'paying' for it with oxygen. Now, as the lactic acid is combined with oxygen, you are paying off the debt. Not until all the lactic acid has been used up, do your breathing rate and heart rate return to normal (Figure 11.10).

> **KEY WORDS**
>
> **oxygen debt:** extra oxygen that is needed after anaerobic respiration has taken place, in order to break down the lactic acid produced

**Figure 11.10:** Runners in a 400 m race use anaerobic respiration, as well as aerobic respiration, to provide energy to their muscles. After the race, they have to pay back their oxygen debt.

### Control of breathing rate

The rate at which your breathing muscles work – and therefore your breathing rate – is controlled by the brain. The brain constantly monitors the pH of the blood that flows through it. If there is a lot of carbon dioxide or lactic acid in the blood, this causes the pH to fall. When the brain senses this, it sends nerve impulses to the diaphragm and the intercostal muscles, stimulating them to contract harder and more often. The result is a faster breathing rate and deeper breaths.

### SUMMARY

| |
|---|
| Organisms need energy for muscle contraction, protein synthesis, cell division, active transport, growth, transmitting nerve impulses and maintaining a constant body temperature. |
| Respiration is a metabolic reaction that takes place in all living cells, and releases energy from glucose and other nutrient molecules. |
| Respiration, like all metabolic reactions, is controlled by enzymes. In yeast, an increase in temperature causes an increase in the rate of respiration, but at temperatures above about 40 °C, enzymes are denatured and so the rate decreases. |
| Aerobic respiration happens in mitochondria. Oxygen is combined with glucose, releasing a lot of energy and producing carbon dioxide and water. |
| Anaerobic respiration happens in the cytoplasm. Glucose is broken down without using oxygen, releasing a small amount of energy. In humans, lactic acid is produced. In yeast, carbon dioxide and ethanol are produced. |
| The place where oxygen enters an organism's body and carbon dioxide leaves is called the gas exchange surface. In terrestrial animals, these surfaces have a large surface area, a thin surface, a good blood supply and good ventilation with air. |
| In humans, the gas exchange surface is the alveoli in the lungs. Air moves to them through the trachea, bronchi and bronchioles. |

> ## CONTINUED
>
> | |
> |---|
> | Inspired air contains more oxygen and less carbon dioxide than expired air. |
> | The intercostal muscles and the diaphragm cause breathing movements, which ventilate the lungs. When breathing in, the diaphragm and external intercostal muscles contract, which increases the volume of the thorax and therefore reduces the air pressure in the lungs. To breathe out, these muscles all relax. |
> | Physical activity causes the rate and depth of breathing to increase, in order to supply extra oxygen to muscles. |
> | The depth and rate of breathing is controlled by the brain, which detects a decrease in the pH of the blood when it contains more carbon dioxide or lactic acid than usual. During exercise, faster aerobic respiration by muscles produces more carbon dioxide, and therefore results in an increase in breathing depth and rate. |
> | During intense physical activity, muscles may use anaerobic respiration as well as aerobic respiration, to supply extra energy. After exercise has finished, the lactic acid produced is broken down in the liver by aerobic respiration, which requires extra oxygen. This is called an oxygen debt. |

## PROJECT

### Scientific and everyday usage of terms

The terms *respiration* and *breathing* are often used in everyday life in ways that do not always match their scientific meaning. For example, we talk about 'artificial respiration'. We say that frogs 'breathe' through their skin. Neither of these are correct usages of the words in their scientific sense.

You are going to explore this issue, and contribute to a display about the scientific meaning, and the everyday usage, of these two words.

Work in a group of three for this project.

Choose one of these three issues to investigate. If possible, different groups should research different issues, so that you can combine your findings to make one display for the whole class.

Before you begin to investigate your chosen issue, make sure that you are absolutely certain about the scientific meanings of *respiration* and *breathing*. Check back to the work you did in Activity 11.2.

### Issue 1: Do all languages have different words for respiration and breathing?

This would be a good choice for a group containing people who can speak different languages. You could also use the internet to search for these words in other languages.

### Issue 2: Is the word *respiration* always used in its correct scientific sense?

Here are some suggestions for how you might investigate this issue.

- Construct some questions or conversation openers that you could use to talk to people, and listen to how they use this word. You could perhaps make a recording of your questions and their answers.

- Look at magazines, newspapers and social media to find examples of this word. Remember to look for other forms of the word – respire, respires, respired and respiring as well as respiration.

### Issue 3: Is the word *breathing* always used in its correct scientific sense?

You could use the same approach as described above for Issue 2. Again, remember to look for different forms of the word – breathe, breathes and breathed as well as breathing.

## EXAM-STYLE QUESTIONS

1 What are the products of anaerobic respiration in human muscle cells?
   A carbon dioxide only
   B carbon dioxide and water
   C lactic acid only
   D lactic acid and water [1]

2 What is the approximate concentration of carbon dioxide in expired air?
   A 0.16%
   B 0.4%
   C 4%
   D 16% [1]

3 Which process in living organisms does **not** use energy released in respiration?
   A cell division to make new cells for growth
   B diffusion of oxygen from the alveoli into the blood
   C maintaining a constant body temperature
   D passage of impulses along a nerve cell [1]

4 This equation for anaerobic respiration in yeast is not balanced.
$$C_6H_{12}O_6 \rightarrow XC_2H_5OH + YCO_2$$
What numbers do X and Y represent, to balance the equation?

|   | X | Y |
|---|---|---|
| A | 1 | 1 |
| B | 2 | 2 |
| C | 2 | 3 |
| D | 3 | 2 |

[1]

5 Which statement describes what happens when the diaphragm muscles contract?
   A The volume of the thorax decreases, so the pressure decreases, and air moves into the lungs.
   B The volume of the thorax decreases, so the pressure increases, and air moves out of the lungs.
   C The volume of the thorax increases, so the pressure decreases, and air moves into the lungs.
   D The volume of the thorax increases, so the pressure increases, and air moves out of the lungs. [1]

## CONTINUED

**6 a** Write the **word** equation for aerobic respiration. [2]

**b** Aerobic respiration releases energy that can be used by cells in the body. List **three** ways in which the body uses this energy. [3]

**c** Yeast is a fungus that can use anaerobic respiration to release energy. Name the **two** products of anaerobic respiration in yeast. [2]

[Total: 7]

**7** A girl breathed into apparatus that recorded the volume of air she breathed in and out. The results were recorded as a graph of volume against time.
The graphs below show the results obtained when she was resting and when she was exercising.

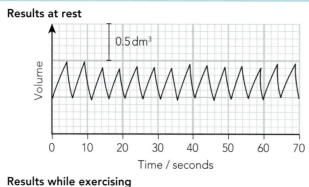

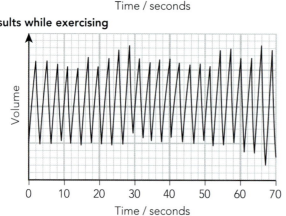

**a** Use the first graph to find:

**i** how many breaths per minute the girl took while she was resting [1]

**ii** the volume of the first breath she took while she was resting. [1]

**b** Use the second graph to find:

**i** how many breaths per minute she took while exercising [1]

**ii** the volume of the second breath she took while exercising. [1]

**c** Explain how the brain was involved in the change in the girl's breathing when she exercised. [4]

**d** Explain how these changes in her breathing helped the girl to do the exercise. [5]

[Total: 13]

## CONTINUED

**8 a** Copy and complete the table, to summarise what happens during breathing.

|  | Breathing in | Breathing out |
|---|---|---|
| External intercostal muscles |  |  |
| Internal intercostal muscles |  |  |
| Muscles in diaphragm |  |  |
| Volume change in thorax |  |  |
| Pressure change in thorax |  |  |

[5]

**b** The graph below shows how a learner's breathing rate changed during and after exercise.

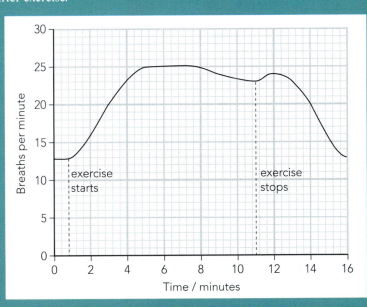

**i** Calculate how long it took, after he finished exercising, for his breathing rate to return to normal. [1]

**ii** Explain why the learner's breathing rate did not return to normal immediately after exercise stopped. [5]

[Total: 11]

## CONTINUED

9 The figure below is an electron micrograph of part of a cell.

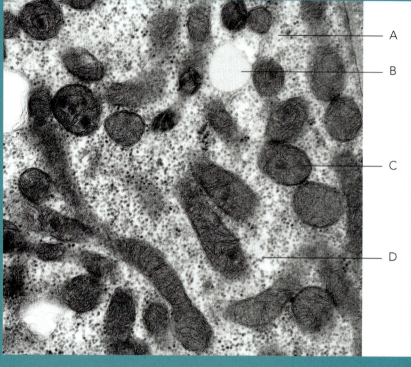

a  i   Give the letter of the label that indicates a ribosome. [1]
   ii  Give the letter of the label that indicates a mitochondrion. [1]
   iii Explain why it is **not** possible to determine whether this cell is from an animal or from a plant. [2]
b  Name and describe the metabolic reaction that happens inside mitochondria. [4]
c  Suggest why each of the following cell types contains large quantities of mitochondria.
   i   muscle cells [1]
   ii  cells in the pancreas that produce enzymes [1]
d  Red blood cells do not contain mitochondria. Suggest a reason for this. [2]

[Total: 12]

# 11 Respiration and gas exchange

## SELF-EVALUATION CHECKLIST

After studying this chapter, think about how confident you are with the different topics. This will help you to see any gaps in your knowledge and help you to learn more effectively.

| I can | See Topic… | Needs more work | Almost there | Confident to move on |
|---|---|---|---|---|
| state the uses of energy in living organisms | 11.1 | | | |
| investigate and describe the effect of temperature on respiration in yeast | 11.1 | | | |
| describe aerobic respiration, and write the word equation for it | 11.1 | | | |
| describe anaerobic respiration in human muscles and in yeast, and write the word equations for them | 11.1 | | | |
| write the balanced equations for aerobic respiration, and for anaerobic respiration in yeast | 11.1 | | | |
| describe the features of gas exchange surfaces in humans | 11.2 | | | |
| identify the organs in the respiratory system in diagrams and images | 11.2 | | | |
| explain the role of goblet cells, mucus and ciliated cells in protecting the gas exchange system from pathogens and particles | 11.2 | | | |
| investigate the differences in carbon dioxide content between inspired air and expired air, using limewater | 11.2 | | | |
| explain the roles of ribs, and the external and internal intercostal muscles, in breathing, and how changes in volume and pressure in the thorax produce air movements | 11.2 | | | |
| explain the differences in composition between inspired air and expired air | 11.2 | | | |
| investigate and describe the effect of physical activity on rate and depth of breathing | 11.2 | | | |
| explain the effects of physical activity on rate and depth of breathing, including reference to lactic acid and oxygen debt, and the control of breathing rate by the brain | 11.2 | | | |

# Chapter 12
# Coordination and response

## IN THIS CHAPTER YOU WILL:

- learn about the human nervous system
- find out how different types of neurone are involved in reflex actions
- learn about the structure of the eye, as an example of a sense organ
- find out about hormones, and compare nervous and hormonal control in humans
- learn about tropic responses in plants

> describe how nerve impulses cross a synapse

> explain how the eye focuses light.

# 12 Coordination and response

## GETTING STARTED

You probably remember that one of the characteristics of organisms is the ability to detect changes in the environment and respond to them.

Sit quietly. Think about the different ways in which your body is detecting information about your environment.

For example, what are your eyes detecting? When you close your eyes, what other features of the environment can you sense, and with which parts of your body?

Share your ideas with the rest of the class and try to build a list of the different sense organs, and what they sense, in the human body.

## REACTION TIMES

Having a fast reaction time is important in many sports, but in a short sprint event it could make the difference between a gold medal and a silver one.

Sprint races are started with a gun. Because sound takes time to travel, it is considered not to be fair for the starter to stand at one end of the starting line and simply fire the gun – the sound would take longer to reach the runner furthest away from him. Instead, the firing of the gun is silent, and is transmitted as an electrical signal along wires to individual speakers in each runner's starting blocks. Each runner should hear the sound of the gun at exactly the same moment.

**Figure 12.1:** Sensors in the starting blocks measure the time between the gun being fired and each athlete's feet pushing back on the blocks.

In the men's 100 m final in the 2016 Olympics in Rio de Janeiro, Usain Bolt's reaction time between hearing the gun and pushing off from his blocks was 0.155 s. Despite this relatively slow reaction time, Bolt won gold, completing the race in 9.81 s. The athletes who won silver and bronze medals – Justin Gatlin and Andre de Grasse – had reaction times of 0.152 s and 0.141 s, and completed the race in 9.89 and 9.91 s respectively. However, these were not the fastest reaction times in that race; the fastest of all was that of Akani Simbine, which was only 0.128 s.

Most people's reaction times are longer than this, often around 0.2 s or more. Sprinters whose 'reaction time' is measured at less than 0.1 s are judged to have pushed off before the gun was fired – and disqualified. In the photograph below, you can see the start of one of the semi-finals of the men's 100 m in Rio. The athlete in red was disqualified for a false start.

### Discussion questions

1   How do you think the figure of 'less than 0.1 s reaction time', to determine a false start, was decided? Do you think this is fair?

2   Sound travels at 330 m per second in air. An Olympic athletics track usually has nine lanes, each 1.22 m wide. Estimate how long it would take sound to travel from the inside of the track to reach the runner in the outside lane. Would this make a significant difference to his or her chance of winning the race?

## 12.1 The human nervous system

Changes in an organism's environment are called **stimuli** (singular: **stimulus**) and are sensed by specialised cells called **receptors**. The organism responds using **effectors**. Muscles are effectors and may respond to a stimulus by contracting. Glands can also be effectors. For example, if you smell good food cooking, your salivary glands may respond by secreting saliva.

Animals need fast and efficient communication systems between their receptors and effectors. This is partly because most animals move in search of food. Many animals need to be able to respond very quickly to catch their food or to avoid predators.

To make sure that the right effectors respond at the right time, there needs to be some kind of communication system between receptors and effectors. If you touch something hot, pain receptors on your fingertips send an electrical impulse to your arm muscles to make them contract, pulling your hand away from the hot surface. The way in which receptors detect stimuli, and then pass information on to effectors, is called **coordination**.

Most animals have two methods of sending information from receptors to effectors. The fastest is by means of **nerves**. The receptors and nerves make up the animal's nervous system. A slower method, but still a very important one, is by means of chemicals called hormones. Hormones are part of the endocrine system, and this is described in Topic 12.3 in this chapter.

> **KEY WORDS**
>
> **stimuli** (singular: **stimulus**): changes in the environment that can be detected by organisms
>
> **receptors**: cells or groups of cells that detect stimuli
>
> **effectors**: parts of the body that respond to a stimulus; muscles and glands are effectors
>
> **coordination**: ensuring that the actions of different parts of the body work together
>
> **nerve**: a group of neurone axons lying together (like an electrical cable containing many wires)

## Neurones

The human nervous system is made of special cells called **neurones**. Figure 12.2 illustrates a particular type of neurone called a **motor neurone**.

Neurones contain the same basic parts as any animal cell. Each has a nucleus, cytoplasm, and a cell membrane. However, their structure is specially adapted to be able to carry electrical signals very quickly.

To enable them to do this, they have long, thin fibres of cytoplasm stretching out from the cell body. The longest fibre in a neurone is called an **axon** (see Figure 12.2). Axons can be more than a metre long. The shorter fibres are called **dendrites**.

The dendrites pick up electrical signals from other neurones lying nearby. These signals are called **nerve impulses**. The signal passes to the cell body, then along the axon, which might pass it to another neurone.

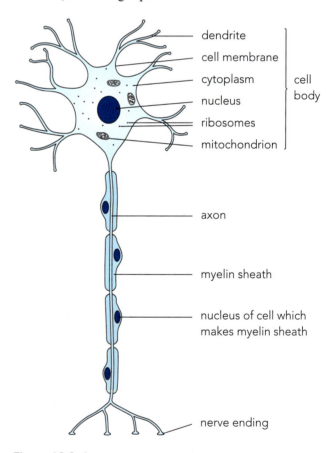

Figure 12.2: A motor neurone.

## 12 Coordination and response

> **KEY WORDS**
>
> **neurone:** a cell that is specialised for conducting electrical impulses rapidly
>
> **motor neurone:** a neurone that transmits electrical impulses from the central nervous system to an effector
>
> **axon:** a long, thin, fibre of cytoplasm that extends from the cell body of a neurone
>
> **dendrites:** short fibres of cytoplasm in a neurone
>
> **nerve impulse:** an electrical signal that passes rapidly along an axon

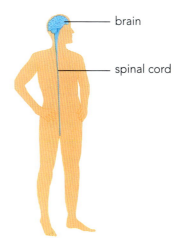

**Figure 12.3:** The human central nervous system.

> **Myelin**
>
> Some of the nerve fibres of active animals such as mammals are wrapped in a layer of fat and protein called myelin. Every now and then, there are narrow gaps in this myelin sheath.
>
> We have seen that the signals that neurones transmit are in the form of electrical impulses. Myelin insulates the nerve fibres, so that they can carry these impulses much faster. For example, a myelinated nerve fibre in a cat's body can carry impulses at up to 100 metres per second. A fibre without myelin can only carry impulses at about 5 metres per second.

## The central nervous system

All mammals (and many other animals) have a **central nervous system** (CNS) and a **peripheral nervous system** (PNS). The CNS is made up of the brain and spinal cord (Figure 12.3). Like the rest of the nervous system, the CNS is made up of neurones. Its role is to coordinate the electrical impulses travelling through the nervous system.

The peripheral nervous system is made up of nerves that spread out from the CNS. Each nerve contains hundreds of neurones. The peripheral nervous system also includes the receptors in our sense organs.

When a receptor detects a stimulus, it sends an electrical impulse along a neurone to the brain or spinal cord. The brain or spinal cord receives the impulse, and sends an impulse on, along the appropriate nerve fibres, to the appropriate effector.

## Reflex arcs

Figures 12.4 and 12.5 show how these electrical impulses travel. If your hand touches a hot plate, a sensory receptor in your finger detects this. The receptor starts off an electrical impulse, which travels to the spinal cord along the axon from the receptor cell. This cell is called a **sensory neurone**, because it is carrying an impulse from a sensory receptor (Figures 12.4 and 12.6).

In the spinal cord, the neurone passes the electrical impulse to several other neurones. Only one is shown in Figure 12.4. These neurones are called **relay neurones**, because they relay the impulse on to other neurones. The relay neurones pass the impulse on to the brain. They also pass it on to a motor neurone to pass to an effector.

In this case, the effectors are the muscles in your arm. The electrical impulse travels to the muscle along the axon of a motor neurone. The muscle then contracts, so that your hand is pulled away.

> **KEY WORDS**
>
> **central nervous system (CNS):** the brain and spinal cord
>
> **peripheral nervous system (PNS):** the nerves outside the brain and spinal cord
>
> **sensory neurone:** a neurone that transmits electrical impulses from a receptor to the central nervous system
>
> **relay neurone:** a neurone that transmits electrical impulses within the central nervous system

237

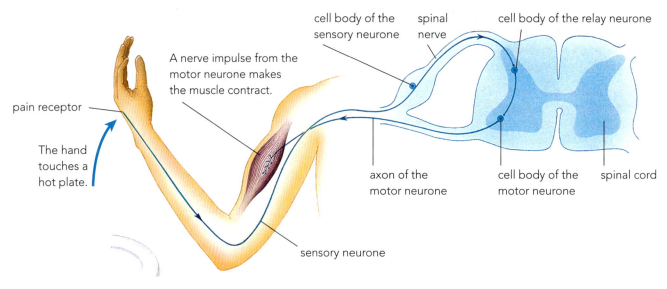

Figure 12.4: A reflex arc.

The pathway along which the nerve impulse passes – the sensory neurone, relay neurones and motor neurone – is called a **reflex arc**.

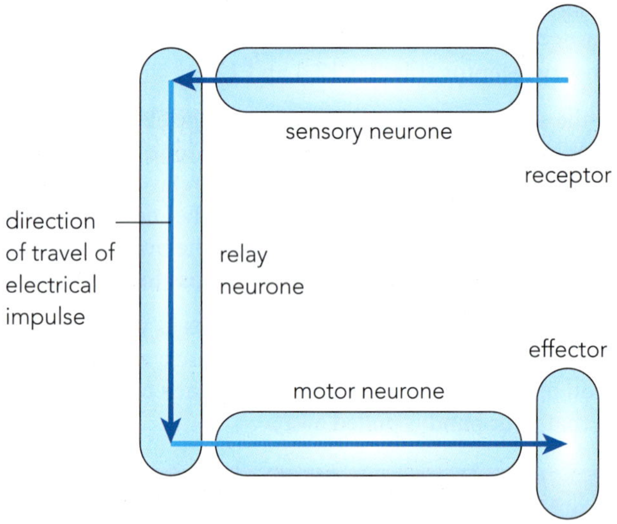

The three types of neurone that are involved in a reflex arc have different shapes. They are shown in Figure 12.6.

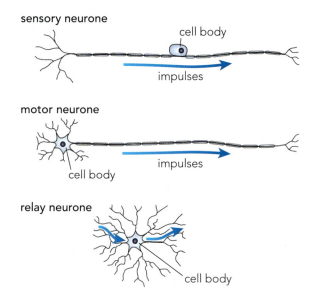

Figure 12.5: Schematic diagram of a reflex arc.

Figure 12.6: The structure of sensory, motor and relay neurones.

> ### KEY WORDS
>
> **reflex arc:** a series of neurones (sensory, relay and motor) that transmit electrical impulses from a receptor to an effector

The reaction that happens after the impulse has sped around the reflex arc is called a **reflex action**. You do not need to think about reflex actions. Your brain is made aware of the action, but you only consciously realise what is happening after the electrical impulse has been sent on to your muscles.

# 12 Coordination and response

Reflex actions are very useful because information gets from the receptor to the effector as quickly as possible. You do not waste time in thinking about what to do. Reflex actions are automatic actions. They help to coordinate our actions. If you receive more than one stimulus at once – such as the sound of a roar and the sight of a lion leaping towards you – these stimuli will be integrated (combined) to produce electrical impulses in sensory neurones, which will travel very quickly around a reflex arc and produce an appropriate and very fast response.

> **KEY WORDS**
>
> **reflex action:** a means of automatically and rapidly integrating and coordinating stimuli with the responses of effectors

Figure 12.7 shows a man's reflex actions being tested – you may have had this test yourself. Another reflex action – the response of the muscles in the iris to changes in light intensity – is described later in this chapter.

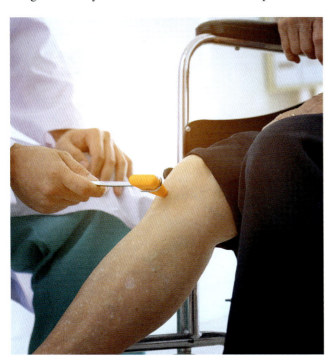

**Figure 12.7:** The knee jerk reflex is an example of a reflex action. A sharp tap just below the knee stimulates a receptor. This sends impulses along a sensory neurone into the spinal cord. The impulse then travels along a motor neurone to the thigh muscle, which quickly contracts and raises the lower leg.

## Questions

1. Describe **three** ways in which neurones are similar to other animal cells.
2. Describe **one** way in which neurones are specialised to carry out their function of transmitting electrical impulses very quickly.
3. Outline the function of the central nervous system.
4. Look at Figure 12.4. Describe where the cell bodies of each of these types of neurone are found:
   a  sensory neurone
   b  relay neurone
   c  motor neurone
5. Look at Figure 12.6. Describe, in words, the differences in structure between sensory neurones, relay neurones and motor neurones.
6. Describe two reflex actions, other than pulling your hand away from a hot plate, or the knee jerk reflex. For each one, say what the stimulus is, where the receptor is and what the response is.
7. Many of the actions that we take (such as you reading and answering these questions) are not reflex actions. Suggest the advantages and disadvantages of reflex actions.

> ### ACTIVITY 12.1
>
> **Estimating the mean reaction time in your class**
>
> 1. Get as many people as possible to stand in a big circle, holding hands.
> 2. One person lets go of his or her neighbour with their left hand and holds a stopwatch in it. When everyone is ready, this person simultaneously starts the stopwatch, and squeezes his or her neighbour's hand with the right hand.
> 3. As soon as each person's left hand is squeezed, he or she squeezes his or her neighbour with the right hand. The message of squeezes goes all round the circle.
> 4. While the message is going round, the person with the stopwatch puts it into the right hand and holds his or her neighbour's hand with the left hand. When the squeeze arrives, he or she should stop the watch.

> **CONTINUED**
>
> 5 Keep repeating this, until the squeeze is going round as fast as possible. Record the time taken, and also the number of people in the circle.
>
> 6 Now try again, but this time make the squeezes go the other way around the circle.
>
> **Questions**
>
> 1 Using the fastest time you obtained, work out the mean time it took for one person to respond to the stimulus they received.
>
> 2 Did people respond faster as the experiment went on? Why might this happen?
>
> 3 Did the squeeze travel as quickly when you changed direction? Explain your answer.
>
> 4 Search the internet for a site that allows you to measure your reaction time. Try it out. Do you think the website gives you more reliable results than the 'circle' method? Compare the results you obtain and suggest the advantages and disadvantages of each method.

## Synapses

If you look carefully at Figure 12.4, you will see that the three neurones involved in the reflex arc do not quite connect to each other. There is a small gap between each pair. These gaps are called **synaptic gaps**. The ends of the two neurones on either side of the gap, plus the gap itself, is called a **synapse**.

Figure 12.8 shows a synapse between a sensory neurone and a relay neurone in more detail. Inside the sensory neurone's axon are hundreds of tiny vacuoles, or **vesicles**. These each contain huge numbers of molecules of a chemical called a **neurotransmitter**.

When an electrical impulse arrives along the axon of the sensory neurone, it causes these vesicles to move to the cell membrane of the sensory neurone. They fuse with the membrane and empty their contents – the neurotransmitter molecules – into the synaptic gap.

The neurotransmitter quickly diffuses across the tiny gap. The molecules of neurotransmitter attach to **receptor proteins** in the cell membrane of the relay neurone.

This happens because the shape of the neurotransmitter molecules is complementary to the shape of the receptor proteins.

The binding of the neurotransmitter with the receptors triggers an electrical impulse in the relay neurone. This impulse sweeps along the relay neurone, until it reaches the next synapse. Here, a similar process occurs to transmit the impulse to the motor neurone.

Synapses act like one-way valves. There is only neurotransmitter on one side of the synapse, so the impulses can only go across from that side. Synapses ensure that nerve impulses travel only in one direction.

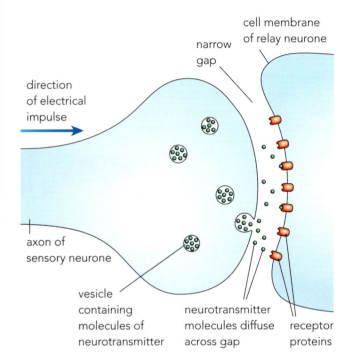

Figure 12.8: A synapse between a sensory neurone and a relay neurone.

## Questions

8 We can say that information travels along a neurone in an electrical form but travels between neurones in a chemical form. Explain this statement.

9 Explain what is meant by a 'complementary shape', and why it is important that the receptor proteins have a complementary shape to the neurotransmitter molecules.

## 12 Coordination and response

> **KEY WORDS**
>
> **synaptic gap:** a tiny gap between two neurones, at a synapse
>
> **synapse:** a junction between two neurones
>
> **vesicle:** a very small vacuole
>
> **neurotransmitter:** a chemical stored in vesicles at the end of neurones, which can be released to diffuse across the synaptic gap and set up an electrical impulse in the next neurone
>
> **receptor proteins:** proteins on the membrane of the second neurone at a synapse, which have a complementary shape to the molecules of neurotransmitter

## 12.2 Sense organs

The parts of an organism's body that detect stimuli, the receptors, may be specialised cells or just the endings of sensory neurones. In animals, the receptors are often part of a **sense organ** (Figure 12.9). A sense organ is a group of receptor cells that respond to a particular stimulus. Your eye, for example, is a sense organ, and contains receptor cells in the retina. These receptor cells are sensitive to light.

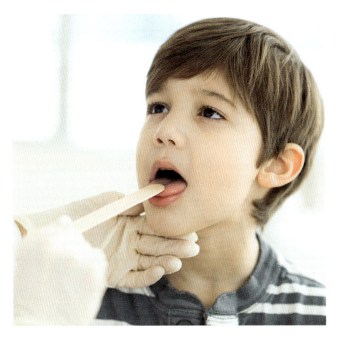

**Figure 12.9:** Which sense organs can you see in this photo?

## The structure of the eye

Figure 12.10 shows the internal structure of the eye. The part of the eye that contains the receptor cells is the **retina**. This is the part which is actually sensitive to light. The rest of the eye simply helps to protect the retina, or to focus light onto it.

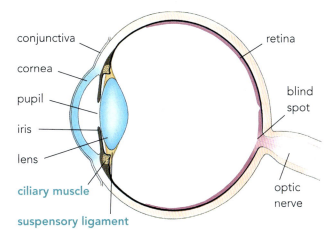

**Figure 12.10:** A section through the eye. Note: you only need to learn about the ciliary muscle and the suspensory ligament if you are studying the Supplement.

Each eye is set in a bony socket in the skull, which protects the eye. Only the very front of the eye is not surrounded by bone (Figure 12.11). The eye is filled with fluid, which helps to keep it in shape.

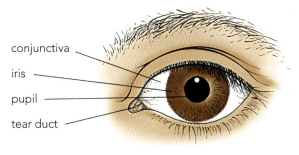

**Figure 12.11:** The eye seen from the front.

> **KEY WORDS**
>
> **sense organ:** a group of receptor cells that are able to respond to a specific stimulus
>
> **retina:** a tissue at the back of the eye that contains receptor cells that respond to light

> The front of the eye is covered by a thin, transparent membrane called the conjunctiva, which helps to protect the parts behind it.
>
> You do not need to remember this word, but you may have heard of conjunctivitis, when this membrane becomes sore and inflamed.

The surface of the eye is always kept moist by a fluid made in the tear glands. This fluid contains an enzyme called lysozyme, which can kill bacteria.

The fluid is washed across your eye by your eyelids when you blink. The eyelids, eyebrows and eyelashes also help to stop dirt from landing on the surface of your eyes.

## The retina

The retina is at the back of the eye. This is where the receptor cells are. When light falls on a receptor cell in the retina, the cell sends an electrical impulse along the **optic nerve** to the brain. The brain uses the impulses from each receptor cell to build up an image. Some of these receptor cells are sensitive to light of different colours, enabling us to see coloured images.

There are no receptor cells where the optic nerve leaves the retina. This part is called the **blind spot**. If light falls on this place, no impulses will be sent to the brain.

### KEY WORDS

**optic nerve:** the nerve that carries electrical impulses from the retina to the brain

**blind spot:** the part of the retina where the optic nerve leaves, and where there are no receptor cells

## Rods and cones

The closer together the receptor cells are, the clearer the image the brain can produce. The part of the retina where the receptor cells are packed most closely together is called the **fovea**. This is the part of the retina where light is focused when you look straight at an object.

We have two kinds of receptor cells in the retina (Figure 12.13). **Rods** are sensitive to quite dim light, but they do not respond to colour. **Cones** are able to distinguish between the different colours of light, but they only function when the light is quite bright. We have three different kinds of cones, sensitive to red, green and blue light.

Rods therefore allow us to see in dim light but only in black and white, while cones give us colour vision.

The fovea contains almost entirely cones, packed tightly together. When we look directly at an object, we use our cones to produce a sharp image, in colour. Rods are found further out on the retina and are less tightly packed. They show us a less detailed image.

### ACTIVITY 12.2

**Can you always see the image?**

Figure 12.12 shows two shapes, with a space between them.

**Figure 12.12:** Testing your blind spot.

Hold this page about 45 cm from your face.

Close your left eye and look at the cross with your right eye.

Gradually bring the page closer to you.

What happens? Can you explain it?

### KEY WORDS

**fovea:** the part of the retina where cone cells are very tightly packed; this is where light is focused when you look directly at an object

**rods:** receptor cells in the retina that respond to dim light, but do not detect colour

**cones:** receptor cells in the retina that are sensitive to light of different colours, but only function in bright light

# 12 Coordination and response

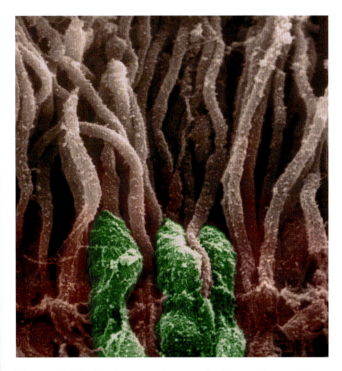

**Figure 12.13:** An electron micrograph of a small part of the retina, showing rods and cones. Colour has been added to the micrograph to make it clearer. The tall, pink cells are rods, and the green ones are cones.

## The iris

In front of the lens is a circular piece of tissue called the **iris**. This is the coloured part of your eye. The iris contains pigments, which absorb light and stop it passing through. In the middle of the iris is a gap called the **pupil**.

The size of the pupil can be adjusted. The wider the pupil is, the more light can get through to the retina. In high light intensity, the iris closes in, and makes the pupil small. This stops too much light getting in and damaging the retina. In low light intensity, the iris pulls back from the pupil, so that the pupil becomes larger. This allows more light to reach the retina.

> ### KEY WORDS
>
> **iris:** the coloured part of the eye; it contains muscles that can alter the size of the pupil
>
> **pupil:** a circular gap in the middle of the iris, through which light can pass

To allow it to adjust the size of the pupil, the iris contains muscles. Circular muscles are arranged in circles around the pupil. When they contract, they make the pupil get smaller. Radial muscles run outwards from the edge of the pupil. When they contract, they make the pupil dilate, or get larger (Figure 12.14). This is called the **iris reflex** or the **pupil reflex**.

The circular muscles and radial muscles are **antagonistic muscles**. They work together to control an action and have opposite effects. When one muscle contracts, the other relaxes.

These responses of the iris are examples of a reflex action. Although the nerve impulses go into the brain, we do not need to think consciously about what to do. The response of the iris to light intensity (the stimulus) is fast and automatic. Like many reflex actions, this is very advantageous: it prevents damage to the retina that could be caused by very bright light falling onto it.

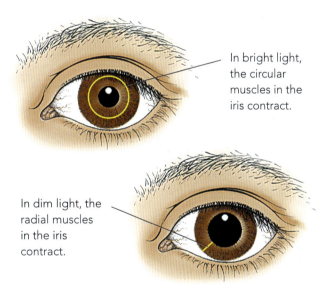

**Figure 12.14:** The iris (pupil) reflex.

> ### KEY WORDS
>
> **iris reflex (pupil reflex):** an automatic response to a change in light intensity; the receptors are in the retina, and the effector is the muscles in the iris
>
> **antagonistic muscles:** a pair of muscles whose contraction has opposite effects; when one contracts, the other relaxes

## ACTIVITY 12.3

### Looking at human eyes

It is best to do this activity with a partner, although you could manage by using a mirror to look at your own eyes.

1 Identify the structures shown in Figure 12.11.

2 Make a simple, clear diagram of the front view of the eye and label each of these structures on it.

3 Ask your partner to close his or her eyes, and cover them with something dark to cut out as much light as possible. (Alternatively, you may be able to darken the whole room.) After about three or four minutes, quickly remove the cover (or switch on the lights) and look at your partner's eyes as they adapt to the light. What happens? What is the purpose of this change?

### Peer assessment

Exchange your drawing from step 2 with a partner.

How well have they drawn and labelled the eye? Look for:

- a drawing that shows all the visible parts of the eye in the correct positions and proportions
- lines that are clean and clear, with no fuzzy parts or breaks
- no shading has been used
- all the parts in Figure 12.11 have been labelled, using ruled label lines and with the labels not written over the drawing.

## KEY WORDS

**refraction:** bending light rays

**cornea:** a transparent layer near the front of the eye, which refracts light rays entering the eye

**lens:** a transparent structure in the eye, which changes shape to focus light rays onto the retina

Figure 12.15 shows how the cornea and lens focus light onto the retina. The image on the retina is upside down. The brain interprets this so that you see it the right way up.

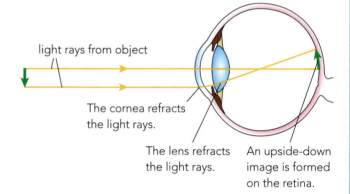

Figure 12.15: How an image is focused onto the retina.

## Adjusting the focus

Not all light rays need bending by the same amount to focus them onto the retina. Light rays coming from an object in the distance are only diverging slightly. They do not need much bending (Figure 12.16).

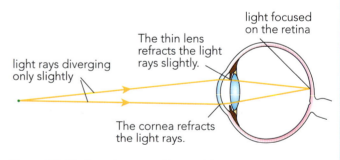

Figure 12.16: Focusing on a distant object.

# Focusing light

For the brain to see a clear image, there must be a clear image focused on the retina. Light rays must be bent so that they focus exactly onto the retina. Bending light rays is called **refraction**.

Most refraction of the light entering the eye is done by the **cornea**. The **lens** makes fine adjustments.

# 12 Coordination and response

Light rays coming from a nearby object are going away from one another or diverging. They need to be bent inwards quite strongly (Figure 12.17).

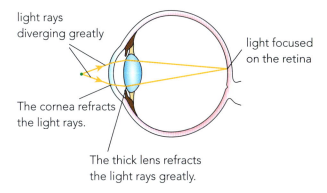

Figure 12.17: Focusing on a nearby object.

The shape of the lens is altered, to make it bend light rays by different amounts. The thicker the lens, the more it bends the light rays. The thinner it is, the less it bends them. This adjustment in the shape of the lens, to focus light coming from different distances, is called **accommodation**.

Figure 12.18 shows how the shape of the lens is changed. It is held in position by a ring of **suspensory ligaments**. The tension on the suspensory ligaments, and thus the shape of the lens, is altered by means of the **ciliary muscle**. When this muscle contracts, the suspensory ligaments are loosened. When it relaxes, they are pulled tight.

When the suspensory ligaments are tight, the lens is pulled thin. When they are loosened, the lens gets thicker.

> **KEY WORDS**
>
> **accommodation:** changing the shape of the lens to focus on objects at different distances from the eye
>
> **suspensory ligaments:** strong, inelastic fibres that hold the lens in position; when they are under tension, they pull the lens into a thinner shape
>
> **ciliary muscle:** a circle of muscle surrounding the lens, and joined to it by the suspensory ligaments; when it contracts, it slackens the ligaments so that the lens becomes fatter

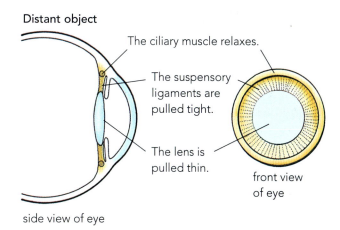

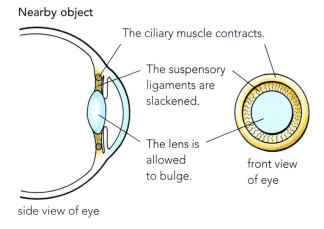

Figure 12.18: How the shape of the lens is changed.

## Questions

10 Name three different sense organs in the human body, and state the stimulus that they detect.

11 Outline the function of each of these parts of the eye:
   a  cornea
   b  iris
   c  lens
   d  retina
   e  optic nerve

12 Look at the electron micrograph in Figure 12.13. Which part of the retina is shown in the micrograph? Explain your answer.

13 Copy and complete this table, to summarise how accommodation is achieved.

| Focusing | Ciliary muscle | Suspensory ligaments | Lens |
|---|---|---|---|
| on a distant object | | | |
| on a near object | | | |

> **REFLECTION**
>
> People often confuse the iris (pupil) reflex with accommodation. Why do you think people confuse these two actions? What can you do to avoid confusing them?

## 12.3 Hormones

So far in this chapter, we have seen how nerves can carry electrical impulses very quickly from one part of an animal's body to another. Animals also use chemicals to transmit information from one part of the body to another.

The chemicals are called **hormones**. Hormones are made in special glands called **endocrine glands**. The hormones pass from the gland into the blood and are carried around the body in the blood plasma. Each hormone has particular organs that it affects, called its **target organs**. The hormone alters the activity of these target organs.

> **KEY WORDS**
>
> **hormones:** chemicals that are produced by a gland and carried in the blood, which alter the activities of their specific target organs
>
> **endocrine glands:** glands that secrete hormones
>
> **target organs:** organs whose activity is altered by a hormone

Figure 12.19 shows the positions of some endocrine glands in the human body. Table 12.1 summarises their functions.

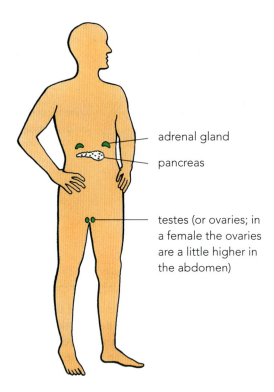

**Figure 12.19:** The positions of some endocrine glands in the body.

| Gland | Hormone that it secretes | Function of hormone |
|---|---|---|
| adrenal gland | adrenaline | prepares body for vigorous action |
| pancreas | insulin | reduces the concentration of glucose in the blood |
| | glucagon | increases the concentration of glucose in the blood |
| testis | testosterone | causes the development of male secondary sexual characteristics |
| ovary | oestrogen | causes the development of female secondary sexual characteristics, and helps in the control of the menstrual cycle |

**Table 12.1:** Some important endocrine glands and their functions.

## Adrenaline

There are two adrenal glands, one above each kidney. They make a hormone called **adrenaline**. When you are frightened, excited or keyed up, your brain sends impulses along a nerve to your adrenal glands. This makes them secrete adrenaline into the blood.

Adrenaline has several effects which are designed to help you to cope with danger. These effects are known as the 'fight or flight' response. For example, your heart beats faster, supplying oxygen to your brain and muscles more quickly. This allows your muscles to carry out aerobic respiration more quickly, giving them more energy for fighting or running away. Your breathing rate increases, so that more oxygen can enter the blood in the lungs. Adrenaline also causes the pupils in the eye to widen. This allows more light into the eye, which might help you to see the danger more clearly.

> Adrenaline causes the liver to release glucose into the blood. This extra glucose for the muscles, along with the extra oxygen provided by the increased breathing rate and heart rate, allows the muscles to increase their metabolic activity. You can read more about the control of blood glucose concentration in Chapter 13.

Table 12.2 compares the nervous and endocrine systems.

| Nervous system | Endocrine system |
|---|---|
| made up of neurones | made up of glands |
| information transmitted in the form of electrical impulses | information transmitted in the form of chemicals called hormones |
| impulses transmitted along neurones | chemicals carried in the blood plasma |
| impulses travel very quickly, so action is fast | chemicals travel more slowly, so action is slower |
| effect of a nerve impulse usually only lasts for a very short time | effect of a hormone may last longer |

**Table 12.2:** A comparison of the nervous and endocrine systems of a mammal.

## Questions

14 Name three endocrine glands, and the hormone that each secretes.

15 Describe how hormones are transported around the body.

16 Describe two situations in which adrenaline is likely to be secreted.

17 Explain how adrenaline helps to prepare the body for action.

# 12.4 Coordination in plants

Like animals, plants are able to respond to their environment, although usually with much slower responses than those of animals.

In general, plants respond to stimuli by changing their rate or direction of growth. They may grow either towards or away from a stimulus. Growth towards a stimulus is said to be a positive response, and growth away from a stimulus is a negative response. These growth responses are called **tropisms**.

Two important stimuli for plants are light and gravity. Growth responses to light are called **phototropism**. Growth responses to gravity are called **gravitropism**.

Shoots normally grow towards light. They are positively phototropic (Figure 12.20). Roots do not usually respond to light, but in some plants, the root grows away from light.

> **KEY WORDS**
>
> **adrenaline:** a hormone secreted by the adrenal glands, which prepares the body for fight or flight
>
> **tropism:** a growth response by a plant, in which the direction of growth is related to the direction of the stimulus
>
> **phototropism:** a response in which part of a plant grows towards or away from the direction from which light is coming
>
> **gravitropism:** a response in which part of a plant grows towards or away from gravity

Figure 12.20: The shoots of these young seedlings are growing towards the light. This maximises the amount of light that falls onto their leaves, so they can photosynthesise more.

Shoots generally grow away from the pull of gravity, so they are negatively gravitropic. Roots generally grow towards the pull of gravity, so they are positively gravitropic (Figure 12.21).

Figure 12.21: As this maize seed germinates, its shoot grows upward, away from gravity, and its root grows downward.

These responses help the plant to survive. Shoots must grow upwards, away from gravity and towards the light, so that the leaves are held out into the sunlight. The more light they have, the better they can photosynthesise. Flowers, too, need to be held up in the air, where insects, birds or the wind can pollinate them.

Roots, though, need to grow downwards, into the soil in order to anchor the plant in the soil, and to absorb water and minerals from between the soil particles.

## 12 Coordination and response

### EXPERIMENTAL SKILLS 12.1

**Investigating how shoots respond to light**

In this investigation, you will find out how the shoots of young seedlings respond to light from one direction. You will practise observing carefully and drawing conclusions.

> **You will need:**
> - three Petri dishes or other suitable containers
> - cotton wool or filter paper
> - seeds – for example, peas or beans
> - a cardboard box with a small hole or slit in one side
> - another cardboard box with no hole.

**Method**

1. Label three Petri dishes A, B and C. Line each with moist cotton wool or filter paper and put about six peas or beans in each (Figure 12.22).
2. Leave all three dishes in a warm place for a day or two, until the seeds begin to germinate. Check that they do not dry out.
3. Now put dish A into a light-proof box with a slit in one side, so that the seedlings get light from one side only.
4. Put dish B in the light. Organise your group to make sure that someone turns the dish three or four times a day, so that the light is not always falling onto the seedlings from the same direction. (You may be lucky enough to have an electrical instrument with a platform that turns around slowly, which does this task for you. This is sometimes called a clinostat.)
5. Put dish C into a completely light-proof box.
6. Leave all the dishes for a week, checking that they do not dry out.
7. Make labelled drawings of one seedling from each dish.

**Questions**

1. Describe how the seedlings in dish A responded to light from one side. What is the name for this response?
2. Explain the purpose of dish B in this experiment.
3. Describe what happened to the seedlings in dish C.

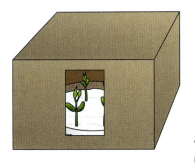
Dish A

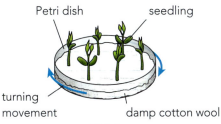
Dish B

Dish C

**Figure 12.22:** Method for investigating how light affects shoot growth.

### EXPERIMENTAL SKILLS 12.2

#### Investigating how shoots respond to gravity

In this investigation, you will find out how the shoots of a plant growing in a pot respond to gravity.

> **You will need:**
> - two similar plants in pots, both well watered
> - a dark cupboard or a large cardboard box.

#### Method

1. Stand both pots in a place where they do not get any light – for example in a cupboard, or underneath a cardboard box.
2. Lie one pot on its side.
3. Leave both pots for a day or so.

Figure 12.23 shows what is likely to happen to the plant placed on its side.

before

after

**Figure 12.23:** How a plant shoot responds to being placed on its side.

#### Questions

1. What is the response shown by the shoot that was placed on its side? Use two of these words in your answer:

   **gravitropism**   **negative**

   **phototropism**   **positive**

2. What is the control in this experiment?
3. Explain why the pots were left in the dark.

## 12 Coordination and response

### EXPERIMENTAL SKILLS 12.3

#### Investigating how roots respond to gravity

In this investigation, you will use bean seedlings to investigate the gravitropic response of roots.

**You will need:**
- several bean seeds that have been soaked in water for a few hours
- a glass jar such as a jam jar or a gas jar
- a piece of filter paper or strong paper towel that you can roll into a cylinder and stand in the jar.

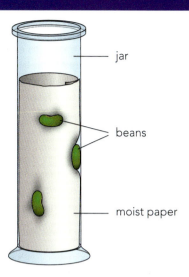

Figure 12.24: Method for investigating gravitropic responses in roots.

#### Method

1. Stand the roll of paper in the jar (Figure 12.24). Pour a little water into the jar, and let it soak up into the paper.
2. Carefully place the bean seeds between the moist paper and the wall of the jar. You should find that they stay in place. Arrange the beans in different positions.
3. Place the jar in a dark place.
4. Leave the beans in their jars for a few days, to allow their roots to grow.

#### Questions

1. Describe your results. You could include labelled diagrams if you like.
2. Use two of these words to describe the responses of the roots to gravity:

   **gravitropism    negative**

   **phototropism    positive**

3. Explain why this response is advantageous to the young bean seedlings.

### EXPERIMENTAL SKILLS 12.4

**Investigating how roots respond to light**

This experiment is much easier to do if you have an electrically powered turntable that revolves automatically. If you don't have one, you can turn the beans by hand every few hours.

> **You will need:**
> - two Petri dishes or other suitable containers with lids, each with a layer of folded, damp blotting paper or filter paper in them (Figure 12.25)
> - several bean seeds that have been soaked in water for a few hours
> - pins
> - if possible, an electrically powered turntable (a clinostat).

**Method**

1. Pin some soaked bean seeds onto the blotting paper in each container. Arrange them so that they are lying in different directions.

2. If possible, put one of the containers onto a clinostat (Figure 12.25) and switch the clinostat on. (If you do not have a clinostat, you can turn the dish yourself every few hours. You can leave it overnight, as there is no light then anyway.)

3. Cover both dishes with a box, with a hole in one side.

**Questions**

1. Describe your results. You could include labelled drawings if you like.

2. Did the roots respond to light coming from one direction? Explain your answer.

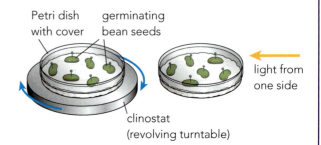

Figure 12.25: Method for investigating the response of roots to light.

## Auxin

We have seen that for an organism to respond to a stimulus, there must be a receptor to detect the stimulus, an effector to respond to it, and some kind of communication system in between. In mammals, the receptor is often part of a sense organ, and the effector is a muscle or gland. Information is sent between them as electrical impulses along nerve cells, or sometimes by means of hormones.

But plants do not have complex sense organs, muscles or nervous systems. So how do they manage to respond to stimuli like light and gravity?

Plants use chemicals to transfer information between one part of their body and another. These chemicals are sometimes called plant hormones. One important plant hormone is **auxin**. Auxin is being made all the time by the cells in the tip of a shoot. The auxin diffuses downwards from the tip, into the rest of the shoot.

Auxin makes the cells just behind the tip get longer (elongate). The more auxin there is, the faster they elongate. Without auxin, they will not grow.

When light shines onto a shoot from all around, auxin is distributed evenly around the tip of the shoot. The cells all elongate at about the same rate, so the shoot grows straight upwards. This is what normally happens in plants growing outside.

But when light shines onto a shoot from one side, the auxin at the tip concentrates on the shady side (Figure 12.26). This makes the cells on the shady side grow faster than the ones on the bright side, so the shoot bends towards the light. This is how auxin controls positive phototropism in shoots.

> **KEY WORD**
>
> **auxin:** a plant hormone made in the tips of shoots, which causes cells to elongate

Auxin also helps to control gravitropism. If a shoot is placed on its side, as in Figure 12.23, the auxin concentrates on the lower side of the shoot. The cells on this side therefore elongate faster than the ones on the upper surface. So, the shoot bends upwards as it grows.

## Questions

18 Copy and complete these sentences:
   Shoots grow towards _____, so they show _____ _____. Shoots grow away from _____, so they show _____ _____.

19 Write two similar sentences, to describe the tropic responses of roots.

20 Read the information about how auxin controls gravitropism. Draw and label a diagram, similar to the one in Figure 12.26, to explain how auxin controls gravitropism in shoots.

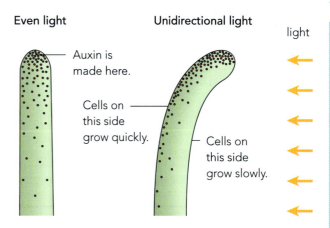

Figure 12.26: How auxin controls positive phototropism in a shoot.

### SUMMARY

| |
|---|
| In mammals, the nervous system is made up of the central nervous system and the peripheral nervous system. The nervous system coordinates and helps to regulate body functions. |
| Neurones transmit information in the form of electrical impulses. |
| A reflex arc consists of a sensory neurone, relay neurone and motor neurone. An impulse produced in a receptor passes along the sensory neurone, into the relay neurone, then the motor neurone, and then to an effector. The effector takes action, bringing about a reflex action. Reflex actions are fast and automatic. |
| A place where two neurones meet is called a synapse. |
| The arrival of an electrical impulse in the first neurone at a synapse stimulates it to release molecules of neurotransmitter into the synaptic gap. The neurotransmitter diffuses across the gap and binds with receptor proteins on the membrane of the second neurone. This stimulates an electrical impulse in the second neurone. |
| As there is neurotransmitter on only one side at a synapse, the impulse can only cross the synapse in one direction. |
| Sense organs are groups of receptor cells that respond to specific stimuli. |
| In the eye, the cornea refracts (bends) light and the lens helps to focus light onto the retina, where receptor cells are found. Some of these receptor cells are sensitive to light of different colours. They produce electrical impulses that pass along the optic nerve to the brain. |
| Cones are tightly packed in the fovea, while rods are further out on the retina. Cones respond only to bright light and give colour vision. Rods respond to dimmer light and do not respond to colour. |

## CONTINUED

| |
|---|
| The iris (pupil) reflex controls the diameter of the pupil, and therefore how much light passes through. |
| The radial and circular muscles in the iris are an example of antagonistic muscles. |
| Accommodation is the change of shape of the lens to focus light from distant or near objects. To focus on a near object, the ciliary muscle contracts and loosens the suspensory ligaments, allowing the lens to become fat. To focus on a distant object, the ciliary muscle relaxes and pulls on the suspensory ligaments, which pull on the lens and make it thinner. |
| Hormones are chemicals that are secreted by glands and travel in the blood. They alter the activity of target organs. |
| The adrenal glands secrete adrenaline, which prepares the body for fight or flight by increasing breathing rate, heart rate and the diameter of the pupil. |
| Adrenaline increases metabolic activity, increasing blood glucose concentration and the supply of glucose and oxygen to body organs, by increasing heart rate and breathing rate |
| Nervous control acts more quickly than hormonal control but lasts for a shorter time. |
| Plants respond to stimuli by growth. Gravitropism is a growth response to gravity, and phototropism is a growth response to light. Usually, shoots are positively phototropic and negatively gravitropic. Roots are positively gravitropic and do not usually respond to light. |
| Tropic responses are controlled by auxin, which is secreted by cells in the tip of a shoot. Auxin concentrates on the shady or lower side of a shoot, making the cells in those areas elongate faster than on the other side. This causes the shoot to bend towards light or away from gravity as it grows. |

## PROJECT

### Using photography to record plant responses

Plants respond to stimuli just as we do – but much more slowly.

You are going to make a time-lapse sequence of photographs, to show a plant responding to a stimulus (Figure 12.27).

You will need a digital camera – the camera on a phone is ideal – to take photographs.

The photographs should be taken from exactly the same position, at regular time intervals. You may be able to leave the camera in place, and then just press the button to take a photograph whenever you decide to do so. If you cannot do that, then you will need to devise a way of ensuring that the camera is placed in the same position each time you take a photograph.

Here are three ideas. You can use these ideas or different ideas of your own.

- Sow some cress or other small seeds in damp cotton wool in a Petri dish. When they have germinated, take a photograph of the seedlings then cover the dish with an upside-down box with a hole in one side. Every two hours, remove the box and take a photograph, then replace the box in the same position. In this way, you will record how the seedlings respond to light coming from one side. If you have a camera with flash, you might be able to take your photographs through the hole in the box.

## CONTINUED

- Take a potted plant and lie it on its side. If you like, you can cover the plant with a dark box, to make sure it is responding to gravity and not to light. Take photographs of the plant at the start, and then every two hours, to show how the shoot responds to gravity.

- Germinate some broad bean (fava bean) seeds on damp cotton wool. Pin the germinating seeds to a cork or other surface and arrange them in different positions. If you like, you can cover them with a dark box, to make sure they are responding to gravity and not to light. Photograph them every two hours, to record how the roots respond to gravity.

When you have your set of photographs, make a slide show to show how the plants responded. You may be able to merge the photos into a time-lapse video sequence.

Record a voice commentary that can be played as the slide show or time-lapse sequence plays. Your commentary should explain what the stimulus is, which part of the plant is responding, and how it responds.

**Figure 12.27:** This plant shoot has grown away from gravity.

## EXAM-STYLE QUESTIONS

1 What does the peripheral nervous system consist of?
   A the brain and spinal cord
   B the brain and nerves
   C the nerves outside the brain and spinal cord
   D the spinal cord only [1]

2 Which two parts of the eye refract light?
   A the cornea and lens
   B the lens and iris
   C the iris and pupil
   D the pupil and cornea [1]

3 What is the response of a shoot to gravity?
   A negative gravitropism
   B negative phototropism
   C positive gravitropism
   D positive phototropism [1]

## CONTINUED

4 Where are receptor proteins found at a synapse, and what shape do they have?

　A in the synaptic gap, same shape as the neurotransmitter molecules

　B in the vesicles in the first neurone, complementary shape to the neurotransmitter molecules

　C on the cell membrane of the first neurone, same shape as the neurotransmitter molecules

　D on the cell membrane of the second neurone, complementary shape to the neurotransmitter molecules [1]

5 Where is auxin made, and what is its effect on cells?

|   | Where it is made | Effect |
|---|---|---|
| A | at the shoot tip | makes cells elongate |
| B | in all parts of the shoot | makes cells divide |
| C | on the shady side of a shoot | makes cells shrink |
| D | on the lower side of a shoot | makes cells bend |

[1]

6 a Adrenaline and insulin are examples of hormones.

　　i **Explain** what is meant by the word *hormone*. [3]

　　ii Name the gland that secretes adrenaline. [1]

　　iii Name the gland that secretes insulin. [1]

　b The diagram shows the eye of a person who is relaxed.

　　i **Describe** how the appearance of the eye would change if the person is frightened, and adrenaline is secreted in their body. [1]

　　ii Describe **one** other stimulus that would cause the same change that you have described in i. [1]

　c **Outline** two ways in which control by hormones such as adrenaline and insulin differs from control by nerves. [2]

[Total: 9]

7 Humans and plants can both respond to light.

　a Name the sense organ in humans that responds to light. [1]

　b Describe the position of the receptor cells that respond to light. [1]

### COMMAND WORDS

**explain:** set out purposes or reasons / make the relationships between things evident / provide why and/or how and support with relevant evidence

**describe:** state the points of a topic / give characteristics and main features

**outline:** set out main points

## CONTINUED

c Explain how information from these receptor cells is transmitted to the brain. [2]

d Plant shoots show positive phototropism.
 i Explain what is meant by positive phototropism. [2]
 ii **Suggest** how positive phototropism helps a plant to survive. [2]

e The diagram shows some germinating bean seeds.

Name the response that is being shown by the roots of the seedlings. [2]

[Total: 10]

> **COMMAND WORD**
>
> **suggest:** apply knowledge and understanding to situations where there are a range of valid responses in order to make proposals / put forward considerations

8 a Copy and complete these sentences about accommodation in the eye.
When focusing on a near object, the ciliary muscles _____. This _____ the tension on the suspensory ligaments. The lens becomes _____, so that it refracts light rays _____ and focuses them onto the retina. [4]

b The photograph shows a tarsier.

Tarsiers are nocturnal animals. They have pupils that can open wider than in most animals, and many more rods than cones in their retinas. Explain how these features help to adapt tarsiers for a nocturnal lifestyle. [4]

[Total: 8]

## CONTINUED

9 The diagram shows a synapse.

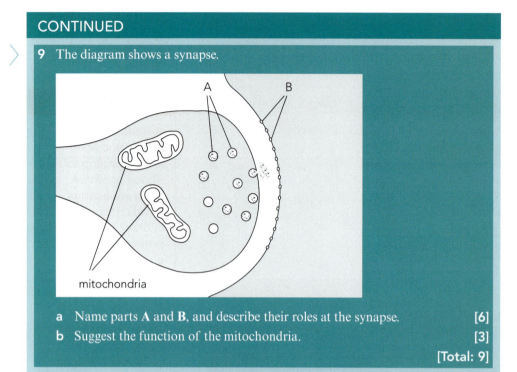

mitochondria

a Name parts **A** and **B**, and describe their roles at the synapse. [6]
b Suggest the function of the mitochondria. [3]

[Total: 9]

## SELF-EVALUATION CHECKLIST

After studying this chapter, think about how confident you are with the different topics. This will help you to see any gaps in your knowledge and help you to learn more effectively.

| I can | See Topic… | Needs more work | Almost there | Confident to move on |
|---|---|---|---|---|
| state that electrical impulses travel along neurones | 12.1 | | | |
| state what the central nervous system and the peripheral nervous system consist of and what they do | 12.1 | | | |
| describe a simple reflex arc, including the positions and roles of sensory, relay and motor neurones; and explain how this arc transmits an impulse from a receptor to an effector | 12.1 | | | |
| describe a reflex action as a means of automatically and rapidly integrating and coordinating stimuli and responses | 12.1 | | | |
| describe a synapse as a junction between two neurones | 12.1 | | | |

## 12 Coordination and response

CONTINUED

| I can | See Topic… | Needs more work | Almost there | Confident to move on |
|---|---|---|---|---|
| describe the structure of a synapse, including vesicles containing neurotransmitter molecules, the synaptic gap and receptor proteins on the membrane of the second neurone | 12.1 | | | |
| describe the events at a synapse, and explain how synapses allow impulses to pass in one direction only | 12.1 | | | |
| describe sense organs as groups of receptor cells that respond to the stimuli of light, sound, touch, temperature and chemicals | 12.2 | | | |
| describe the structure of the eye | 12.2 | | | |
| describe the functions of the cornea, iris, lens, retina and optic nerve | 12.2 | | | |
| state the distribution of rods and cones in the retina (including reference to the fovea), and describe their function | 12.2 | | | |
| explain how the iris (pupil) reflex controls the diameter of the pupil in different light intensities | 12.2 | | | |
| explain how the antagonistic muscles in the iris bring about the iris (pupil) reflex | 12.2 | | | |
| explain accommodation to focus on objects at different distances from the eye, including the roles of the ciliary muscle and suspensory ligaments | 12.2 | | | |
| explain what a hormone is and list the hormones produced by the adrenal glands, pancreas, testes and ovaries | 12.3 | | | |
| describe how adrenaline prepares the body for fight or flight | 12.3 | | | |
| compare nervous and hormonal control | 12.3 | | | |
| explain what is meant by positive and negative gravitropism and phototropism, and state which of these are shown by shoots and roots | 12.4 | | | |
| investigate gravitropism and phototropism in shoots and roots | 12.4 | | | |
| explain how auxin controls phototropism and gravitropism in shoots | 12.4 | | | |

# Chapter 13
# Excretion and homeostasis

### IN THIS CHAPTER YOU WILL:

- learn about the main excretory products of humans, and where they are lost from the body
- describe homeostasis

> find out how the kidneys excrete urea and other waste substances

> explain how negative feedback is involved in the maintenance of constant blood glucose concentration and body temperature.

# 13 Excretion and homeostasis

> **GETTING STARTED**
>
> In this chapter, you will find out how blood glucose concentration is controlled.
>
> Think about these questions on your own for a few minutes. Then turn to the person next to you and discuss your ideas together.
>
> - What do cells use glucose for?
> - Where does the glucose come from?
> - If a cell was put into a concentrated solution of glucose, what would happen to the water in the cell, and why?

> **BIRD DROPPINGS**
>
> It's probable that, at some time in your life, a bird dropping has landed on you. You may not realise that bird droppings contain their urine as well as faeces. Birds excrete urine as a white paste, rather than as a liquid (Figure 13.1).
>
> Think about how young birds develop. They grow inside a shelled egg. If they produced liquid urine, the egg would quickly become filled with it. Instead, they produce a concentrated, paste-like urine, which collects into one small area of the egg where it is kept away from the growing bird. If you are ever able to watch a chick hatch from an egg, look for this little package of waste material that is left behind, inside the egg shell.
>
> Excreting urine as a paste rather than a liquid uses less water. However, the body has to use more energy to make this semi-solid urine than it does to make liquid urine.
>
> **Discussion questions**
>
> 1. How does excreting urine as a paste help to adapt birds for their lifestyle?
> 2. Birds evolved from reptiles. Would you expect reptiles to excrete paste-like urine or liquid urine? Find out if you are correct.
>
> **Figure 13.1:** This parent bird is removing a little package of waste from one of its babies. The parent will take the waste away from the nest.

## 13.1 Excretion

In Chapter 1, we saw that one of the characteristics of all living things is that they remove waste products of metabolism from their bodies. This is called **excretion**.

All living cells have many metabolic reactions going on inside them. For example, the reactions of respiration (Chapter 11) provide energy for the cell. Metabolic reactions often produce other substances as well, which the cells do not need. Some of these substances may be toxic, so they must be removed.

For example, respiration provides energy but also water and carbon dioxide. Animal cells need the energy and may be able to make use of the water. But they do not need the carbon dioxide. The carbon dioxide is a waste product.

In mammals, the carbon dioxide from respiration is excreted from the lungs. If it were allowed to remain in the body, it would be toxic to cells. Carbon dioxide dissolves to form a weak acid, which would lower the pH of cells and the blood. The way in which carbon dioxide is removed from cells and then removed from the body in the alveoli of the lungs, is described in Chapter 11.

Plants are living things, so they also excrete waste materials. During daylight hours, plant cells can use the carbon dioxide that they produce in respiration for photosynthesis, so it is not a waste product for them at that time. However, at night, plants cannot photosynthesise but they continue to respire, so the carbon dioxide is a waste product. Plants excrete carbon dioxide through their stomata.

## Urea

**Urea** is a waste product that is produced in the liver in humans. Too much urea in the blood is toxic. Urea is removed from the blood by the kidneys (Figure 13.2). The kidneys also remove excess water and excess ions from the blood, and produce **urine**. The urine flows down the **ureters** and into the bladder, where it is stored. When the sphincter muscle at the entrance to the urethra relaxes, the urine flows out of the body through the **urethra**.

> **KEY WORDS**
>
> **excretion:** the removal of the waste products of metabolism and substances in excess of requirements
>
> **urea:** a waste product produced in the liver, from the breakdown of excess amino acids
>
> **urine:** a solution of urea and other waste materials in water, produced by the kidneys
>
> **ureter:** one of a pair of tubes that carries urine from the kidneys to the bladder
>
> **urethra:** the tube that carries urine from the bladder to the outside

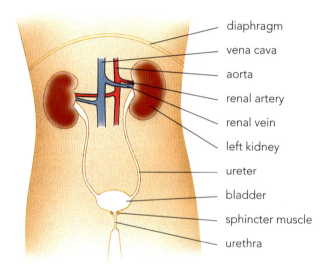

Figure 13.2: The human excretory system.

## Questions

1. Explain why the removal of carbon dioxide from the body is an example of excretion.
2. During the day, plants photosynthesise faster than they respire. What waste gas will they excrete, and how does this gas leave their bodies?
3. Copy and complete this sentence.

   Urea is made in the _____ and excreted by the _____.
4. Explain the difference between urea and urine.
5. Explain the difference between a ureter and a urethra.

## How urea is produced

We have seen that urea is formed in the liver. The liver makes urea from excess proteins and amino acids. Animals – including humans – are not able to store proteins or amino acids in their bodies. Any that are surplus to requirements are broken down to form urea.

Figure 13.3 shows how this happens. When you eat proteins, digestive enzymes in your stomach, duodenum and ileum break them down into amino acids. The amino acids are absorbed into the blood capillaries in the villi in your ileum. These blood capillaries all join up to form the hepatic portal vein, which takes the amino acids to the liver.

The liver allows some of the amino acids to carry on, in the blood, to other parts of your body. But if you have eaten more than you need, then some of them must be removed from the body.

It would be very wasteful to excrete the extra amino acids just as they are. They contain energy which, if it is not needed straight away, might be needed later. So enzymes in the liver split up each amino acid molecule. The part containing the energy is kept, turned into carbohydrate and stored. The rest, which is the part that contains nitrogen, is turned into urea. This process is called **deamination**.

The urea dissolves in the blood plasma and is taken to the kidneys to be excreted.

> **KEY WORD**
>
> **deamination:** the removal of the nitrogen-containing part of amino acids to form urea

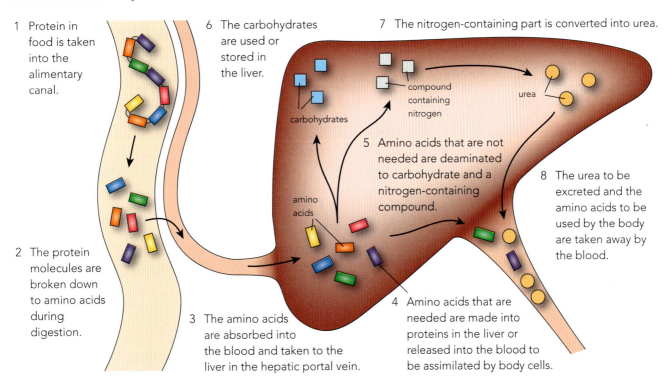

Figure 13.3: How urea is made in the liver.

# The kidneys

Urea is toxic. If too much builds up in the blood, you would get very ill. As we have seen, the kidneys constantly remove urea from the blood, excreting it in urine.

Figure 13.4 shows a longitudinal section through a kidney. It has two main parts – the **cortex** and the **medulla**. Leading from the kidney is a tube called the ureter. The ureter carries urine that the kidney has made to the bladder.

> **KEY WORDS**
>
> **cortex:** the tissue making up the outer layer in a kidney
>
> **medulla:** the tissue making up the inner layers in a kidney

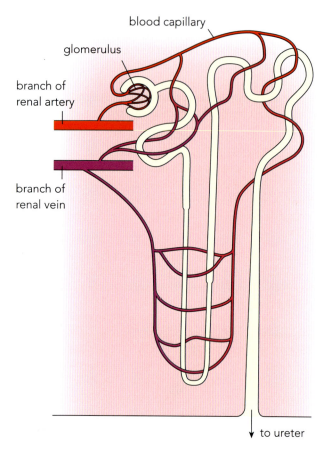

Figure 13.5: A nephron.

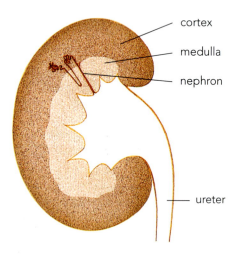

Figure 13.4: A longitudinal section through a kidney.

## Nephrons

Although they seem solid, kidneys are actually made up of thousands of tiny tubules called **nephrons** (Figures 13.4 and 13.5). Each nephron begins in the cortex, loops down into the medulla, back into the cortex, and then goes down again through the medulla. The nephrons join up with the ureter.

## Urine formation

Blood flows into the kidney from the renal artery. This divides to form many tiny, coiled capillaries, called **glomeruli** (singular: **glomerulus**).

As the blood flows through a glomerulus, it is filtered. Small molecules can pass through the filter, but large molecules and blood cells cannot. The filtrate (the substances that pass through the filter) includes water, urea, glucose, and ions. These all move into the nephron (Figure 13.6).

> **KEY WORDS**
>
> **nephron:** one of the thousands of microscopic tubes inside a kidney, where urine is made
>
> **glomeruli** (singular: **glomerulus**): a little 'network' of blood capillaries, where the blood is filtered in a kidney

**Filtration**
Small molecules, such as water, glucose, ions and urea, are filtered out of the blood into the nephron.

**Reabsorption**
Any useful substances, such as water and glucose, are taken back into the blood.

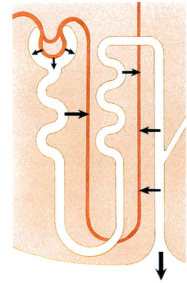

The remaining liquid, called urine, flows into the ureter.

**Figure 13.6:** How urine is made in a kidney nephron.

Some of these filtrate substances need to be lost from the body. The urea is a toxic waste product and some of the water and ions may be in excess to requirements. These substances all continue through the nephron.

However, some of the substances are not waste. The glucose in particular, is needed by the body. So is a lot of the water, and probably some of the ions, too. All of the glucose, most of the water and some of the ions are taken back into the blood as the fluid flows through the nephron. This process is called **reabsorption**. You can see, in Figures 13.5 and 13.6, how the blood capillaries come close to the nephron, making it easy for these substances to move back into the blood. Figure 13.7 shows some of the cells in the wall of the nephron, where reabsorption takes place.

> **KEY WORD**
>
> **reabsorption:** in a kidney nephron, taking back required substances into the blood

### ACTIVITY 13.1

#### Interpreting a scanning electron micrograph

Work with a partner, or in a group of three, for this activity.

Figure 13.7 is a scanning electron micrograph, or SEM for short. SEMs show surfaces in three dimensions, at a very high magnification. The colour in an SEM is not 'real'; it is added to make the picture look clearer.

This SEM shows the cells in the wall of a nephron. The cells have been cut through, so you can see inside them. The top of the picture shows the lumen of the nephron, where the filtrate flows through. The bottom of the picture is the outer edge of the cells, close to where the blood capillaries lie.

Think about the following questions on your own for a few minutes. Then discuss your ideas with your partner, or the rest of your group.

#### Questions

1  What do you think the large, rounded, brown structures inside the cells might be?

**Figure 13.7:** A scanning electron micrograph of cells in the wall of a nephron.

2  Look at the yellow objects at the top of the picture. Think about what you have learnt about the cells that line the small intestine. What might these structures in the nephron be? What could their function be?

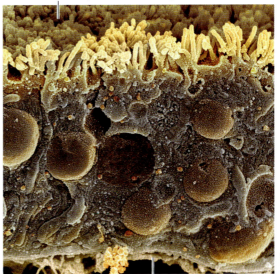

inside of the nephron containing the filtrate

magnification ×3300

outer edge of the nephron close to blood capillaries

Reabsorption happens in this direction.

> REFLECTION

You may sometimes be given an electron micrograph to interpret in a question. This can be quite scary, because at first glance everything looks completely unfamiliar. But you will usually be given some information to get you started.

How can you approach a task like that, to give yourself the best chance of being able to identify some of the features on the micrograph?

The final liquid that flows out of the nephron is a solution of urea and salts in water. As we have seen, this liquid is called urine and it flows out of the kidneys, along the ureters and into the bladder. It is stored in the bladder for a while, before being released from the body through the urethra.

The kidneys are very efficient at reabsorbing water. Over 99% of the water entering the tubules is reabsorbed. In humans, the two kidneys filter about 170 dm$^3$ of water per day, yet only about 1.5 dm$^3$ of urine are produced in the same period.

The volume of urine that is produced depends on how much excess water there is in the body. If a person has drunk more liquid than they need, then they will excrete large volumes of dilute urine. If they have not drunk very much, or have lost a lot of water by sweating, then they will produce smaller volumes of concentrated urine. More concentrated urine looks darker, so the colour of urine is a good indication of how well hydrated the body is (Figure 13.8).

**Figure 13.8:** A well-hydrated person has a lot of excess water to be excreted in urine, so the urine is dilute and pale – as on the right in this picture. Very dark urine indicates that there is not enough water in the body, and the person needs to drink more.

## Questions

6 Outline how the liver helps with the assimilation of amino acids. (If you have forgotten the meaning of 'assimilation', look back at Chapter 7.)

7 Explain what deamination is, and where it happens.

8 The body does not want to lose glucose, but it is filtered from the blood into the nephron. Explain:
   a where and why glucose moves from the blood into the nephron
   b what happens to make sure that glucose is not excreted in urine.

9 A nephron is long and narrow. It is surrounded by many blood capillaries, in quite close contact with it. Explain how these features help reabsorption to take place effectively.

# 13.2 Homeostasis

We have seen how the kidneys remove urea from the body, as well as excess water and ions. By doing this, the kidneys are helping to keep the quantities of these substances in the blood at the correct level. This is important to help the cells in the body to work efficiently.

The environment (surroundings) of a living organism is always changing. Think about your own environment. The temperature of the air around you changes. For example, if you live in a temperate country, it might be −10 °C outside on a cold day in winter, and 23 °C indoors. If you live in the tropics, the outside temperature can be over 40 °C.

The cells inside your body, however, do not have a changing environment. Your body keeps the environment inside you almost the same, all the time. In the body, the temperature and the quantity of water in the blood are kept almost the same, all the time. So is the concentration of glucose in the blood. Keeping this **internal environment** constant is called **homeostasis**.

> **KEY WORDS**
>
> **internal environment:** the conditions inside the body
>
> **homeostasis:** the maintenance of a constant internal environment

Homeostasis helps your cells to work as efficiently as possible. Keeping a constant temperature of around 37 °C helps enzymes to work at the optimum rate. Keeping a constant amount of water means that your cells are not damaged by absorbing or losing too much water by osmosis. Keeping a constant concentration of glucose means that there is always enough fuel for respiration.

In this topic, you will see how homeostasis occurs in humans. It involves the nervous system, as well as hormones.

## Controlling blood glucose concentration

The control of the concentration of glucose in the blood is a very important part of homeostasis. Cells need a steady supply of glucose to allow them to respire; without this, they cannot release the energy they need. Brain cells are especially dependent on glucose for respiration, and they die quite quickly if they are deprived of it.

On the other hand, too much glucose in the blood is not good either. It can cause water to move out of cells and into the blood by osmosis. This leaves the cells with too little water for them to carry out their normal metabolic processes.

Blood glucose concentration is controlled by hormones, secreted by the pancreas. If the blood glucose concentration gets too high – for example, after you have eaten a meal with a lot of sugar in it – the pancreas secretes a hormone called **insulin**. Insulin reduces the concentration of glucose in the blood.

> ### KEY WORD
>
> **insulin:** a hormone secreted by the pancreas, which decreases blood glucose concentration

The pancreas is two glands in one. Most of it is an ordinary gland with a duct. It makes pancreatic juice, which flows along the pancreatic duct into the duodenum (Chapter 7). Scattered through the pancreas, however, are groups of cells called islets (because they look like little 'islands' among a 'sea' of all the other cells).

These cells do not make pancreatic juice. They make two hormones – insulin and **glucagon**. These hormones help the liver to control the amount of glucose in the blood.

As we have seen, insulin has the effect of lowering blood glucose concentration. Glucagon does the opposite.

If you eat a meal that provides a lot of glucose, the concentration of glucose in the blood goes up. The islets in the pancreas detect this and secrete insulin into the blood (Figure 13.9). When insulin reaches the liver, it causes the liver to absorb glucose from the blood. Some is used for respiration, but some is converted into the insoluble polysaccharide, glycogen. This is stored in the liver.

If the blood glucose concentration falls too low, the pancreas secretes glucagon. This causes liver cells to break down glycogen to glucose and release it into the blood.

## Negative feedback and set points

In practice, our blood glucose concentration does not stay absolutely constant. A normal concentration is somewhere between 0.8 and 1.1 mg per $cm^3$ of blood. As we have around 5 $dm^3$ of blood in our body, this means we usually have a minimum of 4 g of glucose circulating in the bloodstream at any one time.

This range of normal values is called the **set point** for blood glucose concentration. The pancreas and liver work together to try to keep the values within this range.

Various things can push the blood concentration above or below its set point. For example, you might eat a lot of sweets or ice cream, loading your blood with sugars that are absorbed from the ileum. Your blood glucose levels could rise well above the set point. Alternatively, you might forget to eat breakfast and then do some energetic sport in the morning. By lunchtime, your blood glucose concentration could have fallen below the set point.

> ### KEY WORDS
>
> **glucagon:** a hormone secreted by the pancreas, which increases blood glucose concentration
>
> **set point:** the normal value or range of values for a particular parameter – for example, the normal range of blood glucose concentration or the normal body temperature

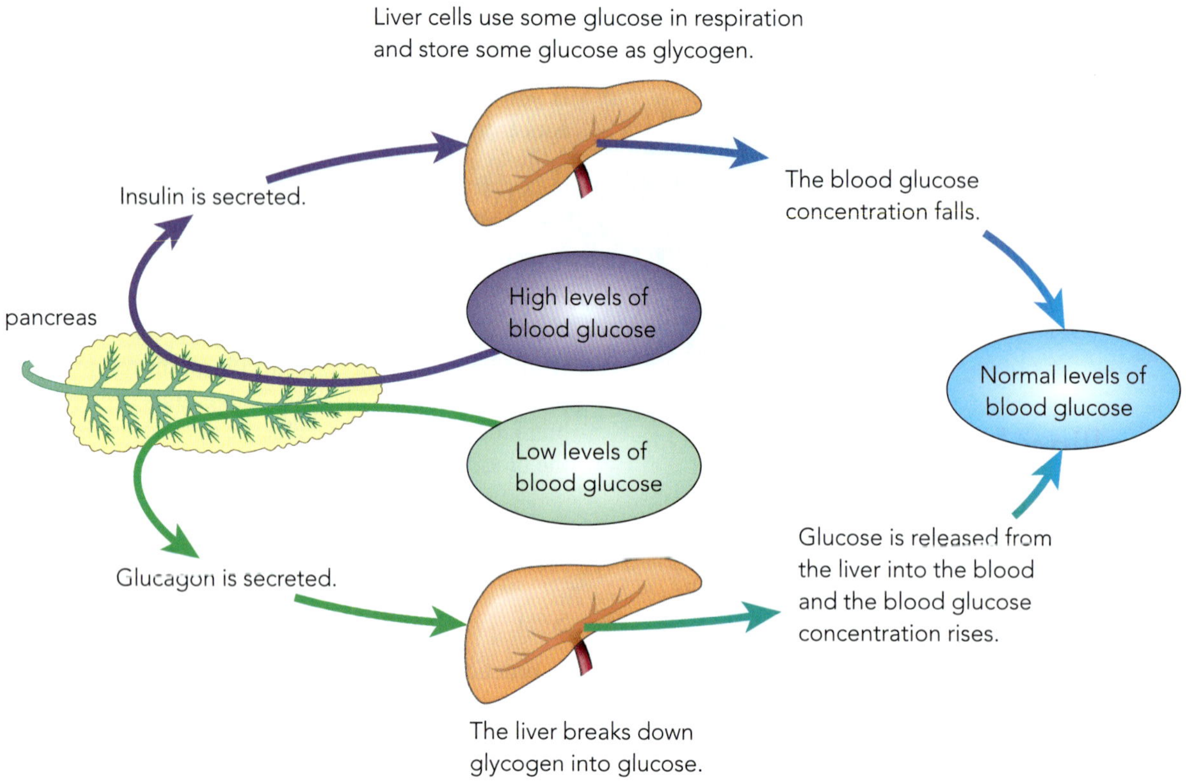

**Figure 13.9:** How blood glucose concentration is regulated. Start in the middle at either high or low levels of blood glucose and follow the arrows around.

In either case, cells in the pancreas detect that the blood glucose concentration is outside its normal limits. If it has gone too high, they secrete insulin. If it has fallen too low, they secrete glucagon.

The secretion of insulin causes the liver to absorb glucose from the blood, which reduces its concentration. The liver can use up some of this glucose in respiration, breaking it down to carbon dioxide and water. It can also change some of it to glycogen, linking many glucose molecules together into a long chain to make glycogen molecules. These can be stored in the liver cells.

The secretion of glucagon causes the liver to break down its glycogen stores. The glucose molecules that are produced move out of the liver and into the blood, increasing the blood glucose concentration so that it goes back towards normal.

This is an example of **negative feedback**. In negative feedback:

- There is a set point – a normal level that the system tries to maintain.
- There is a 'measuring device' that keeps track of whether the level is within the range of the set point.
- If the level goes outside the set point, this triggers events to happen that bring the level back into line again.

These things do not happen instantaneously. For example, if your blood glucose concentration goes too high, it takes a short while for the cells in the pancreas to detect it. Then more time is needed for them to secrete insulin, for the insulin to get to the liver, and for the liver to take up glucose from the blood. Only then does the blood glucose concentration start to fall. This time lag means that the blood glucose concentration often goes up and down, around the set point, rather than staying absolutely steady.

### KEY WORDS

**negative feedback:** a mechanism that detects a move away from the set point, and brings about actions that take the value back towards the set point

# Questions

10  Explain how both insulin and glucagon fit the definition of a hormone.

11  The graph shows the blood glucose concentration in a healthy person. She ate a meal containing starch at time 0.

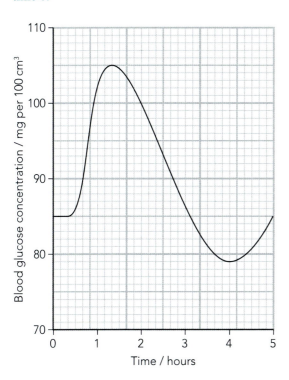

Figure 13.10: Blood glucose concentration in a healthy person.

a  Describe the changes in the girl's blood glucose concentration between 0 and 5 hours.
b  Explain why the blood glucose concentration did not begin to rise until about 20 minutes after she ate her meal.
c  Explain what happened to make the blood glucose concentration fall.
d  Suggest why the blood glucose concentration fell below its starting value, before increasing again.

12  Insulin and glucagon are proteins. Explain why the cells in the islets of the pancreas contain many mitochondria and ribosomes.

# Diabetes

In some people, the cells that secrete insulin die. This is called **type 1 diabetes**. It is not certain exactly what causes this disease, but it is thought to result from the body's own immune system attacking and destroying the cells in the pancreas that secrete insulin. This type of diabetes usually develops when a person is a young child.

When a person eats a meal containing a lot of carbohydrate, the concentration of glucose in the blood increases. Normally, this would trigger the secretion of insulin from the pancreas, but in a person with type 1 diabetes this does not happen. The blood glucose concentration goes up above the set point and remains high. This usually makes the person feel unwell – they may have a dry mouth, blurred vision and feel very thirsty. Their heart rate and breathing rate may increase.

On the other hand, not eating carbohydrate for a long time will cause the blood glucose concentration to drop very low. Because no insulin has been secreted, the liver has not built up stores of glycogen that can now be broken down to produce glucose. Cells do not have a supply of glucose to release energy by respiration, so the person feels very tired and may show confusion and irrational behaviour. Eventually, they can become unconscious. People with diabetes usually become very good at recognising when this series of events is beginning and know that they need to eat something sweet to get their blood glucose concentration up towards normal.

> **KEY WORDS**
>
> **type 1 diabetes:** a condition in which insufficient insulin is secreted by the pancreas, so that blood glucose concentration is not controlled

## Treating type 1 diabetes

Having blood glucose concentrations that swing very high and very low can, over long periods of time, damage many different body organs. It is important that a person with type 1 diabetes tries to keep their blood glucose concentration within reasonably normal limits.

Most people with diabetes get into the habit of checking their blood glucose concentration regularly, using a simple sensor (Figure 13.11). They can also test their urine for glucose, using a simple dipstick (Figure 13.12). Urine should not contain any glucose, but if a person's blood glucose concentration rises very high, then the kidneys are not able to reabsorb it all from the filtrate in the nephron, and some remains in the urine that is excreted.

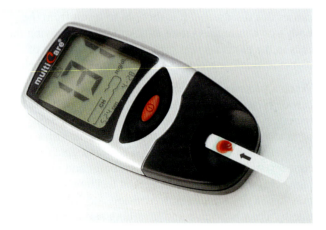

**Figure 13.11:** To use this sensor, a person puts a tiny drop of blood onto a special stick, and places it in the sensor. The sensor then gives a reading of blood glucose concentration in mg per 100 cm³.

**Figure 13.12:** This dipstick has been dipped into a urine sample. The colour on the stick can be matched against a chart, showing whether the urine contains glucose, and how much. This test is showing a lot of glucose in the urine.

Eating little and often, and particularly avoiding large amounts of carbohydrate, can help to stop blood glucose concentration fluctuating too widely. A person with type 1 diabetes can learn how much carbohydrate they need to eat, to balance out with the amount of glucose that is broken down in respiration. For example, if they do a lot of sport on one morning, they may need to eat more carbohydrate than usual for breakfast and lunch.

Most people with type 1 diabetes will also need to inject themselves with insulin. There are several different types of insulin, and each person needs to discuss their treatment plan with their doctor. For example, most people with type 1 diabetes will need to take rapid-acting insulin just before or after they eat a meal. They will need to judge how much carbohydrate they are going to eat (or have eaten) and adjust the dose accordingly.

They may also need to take long-acting insulin. This is taken once a day, at the same time each day. It provides a 'background' dose of insulin.

## Questions

13 Explain why the urine of a person who does not have diabetes does not contain glucose.

14 Look at Figures 13.11 and 13.12. Suggest why the sensor in Figure 13.11 is a better tool for a person with diabetes to use, than the dipstick in Figure 13.12.

15 Insulin is a protein. Explain why it has to be taken by injection, and not as a pill that can be swallowed.

## Controlling body temperature

Some animals – including ourselves – are very good at controlling their body temperature. They can keep their temperature almost constant, even though the temperature of their environment changes. This has great advantages. If the internal body temperature can be kept at around 37 °C, enzymes can always work very efficiently, no matter what the outside temperature is. Metabolism can keep going, even when it is cold outside. In cold weather or at night, the animal can be active when other animals are too cold to move.

### The structure of human skin

One of the most important organs involved in temperature regulation in mammals is the skin. Figure 13.13 shows a section through human skin.

The skin is covered with a layer of dead cells, which form a tough, impermeable barrier that prevents water evaporating from the living cells below. It also prevents pathogens getting into the body.

Underneath this protective layer, many different types of living tissue are present. On the right-hand side of Figure 13.13, you can see a **sweat gland**. Sweat glands extract water and ions from the blood and produce

# 13 Excretion and homeostasis

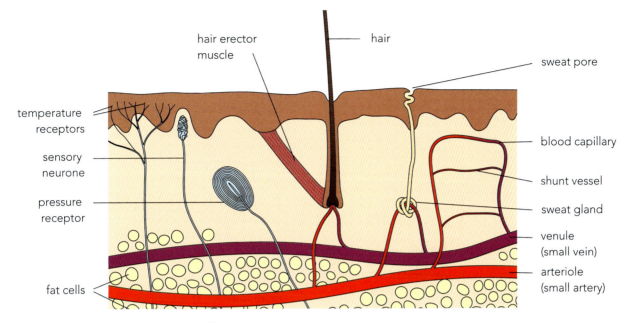

Figure 13.13: A section through human skin.

the liquid that we call sweat. The sweat travels up the sweat duct to the skin surface and is released through a pore. As you will see, this plays an important part in temperature regulation.

You can see some blood vessels to the right of the sweat gland in the diagram. Arterioles bring oxygenated blood to the skin. These divide to form capillaries, which take blood up to just below the skin surface, before joining together again to form venules. You can also see 'short-cut' vessels that the blood can travel through without having to go all the way up to the skin surface.

Further to the left on the diagram, you will see a hair. Each hair has a tiny muscle attached to it, called a hair erector muscle. When this muscle contracts, it pulls the hair up straight.

On the left of the diagram, you can pick out two kinds of receptor. Some of these are sensitive to temperature, and they send electrical impulses along sensory neurones if the temperature of the environment changes. Others are sensitive to pressure.

Underneath all of these structures is a layer of fat. This fatty tissue is made up of cells that contain large drops of oil. This layer helps to insulate your body against heat loss, and also acts as an energy reserve.

## The hypothalamus

A part of the brain called the **hypothalamus** is at the centre of the control mechanism that keeps internal temperature constant. The hypothalamus coordinates the activities of the parts of the body that can help to keep the temperature of the blood at its set point.

### KEY WORDS

**sweat gland:** a structure found in the skin of mammals, which secretes a watery fluid onto the skin surface to reduce body temperature

**hypothalamus:** part of the brain that is involved in the control of body temperature

The hypothalamus acts like a thermostat. It contains temperature receptors that sense the temperature of the blood running through it. If this is above or below 37 °C, then the hypothalamus sends electrical impulses, along neurones, to the parts of the body which have the function of regulating your body temperature.

Notice that we have two different sets of temperature receptors. There are the ones in the hypothalamus, which sense the temperature of the blood. There are also temperature receptors near the surface of the skin, which sense the temperature of the air or water around us. These can give us 'early warning' that the body temperature might be going to change. For example, if the receptors in the skin detect a very low temperature around us, this suggests that the body might be about to lose a lot of heat, making the body temperature fall. These receptors can send electrical impulses that help to prevent this happening, even before the temperature of the blood has changed.

## When temperature falls

The set point for the internal body temperature of a human is about 37 °C. If the temperature of the blood flowing through the hypothalamus drops below 37 °C, the hypothalamus sends electrical impulses along motor neurones to the skin, muscles and liver. This causes the following things to happen (Figure 13.14).

- **Muscles contract** – Muscles in some parts of the body contract and relax very quickly, in a process called shivering. They get the energy for this from respiration, and some of the energy is released as heat. The heat generated in the muscles warms the blood as it flows through them. The blood distributes this heat all over the body.

- **Metabolism may increase** – The speed of chemical reactions in other tissues, not only muscles, may increase. For example, the liver cells may respire faster. This also releases more heat.

- **Hairs stand up** – The erector muscles in the skin contract, pulling the hairs up on end. In humans, this does not do anything very useful – it just produces 'goose pimples'. But in a hairy animal, such as a cat, it traps a thicker layer of warm air next to the skin. This prevents the skin from losing more warmth. It acts as an insulator.

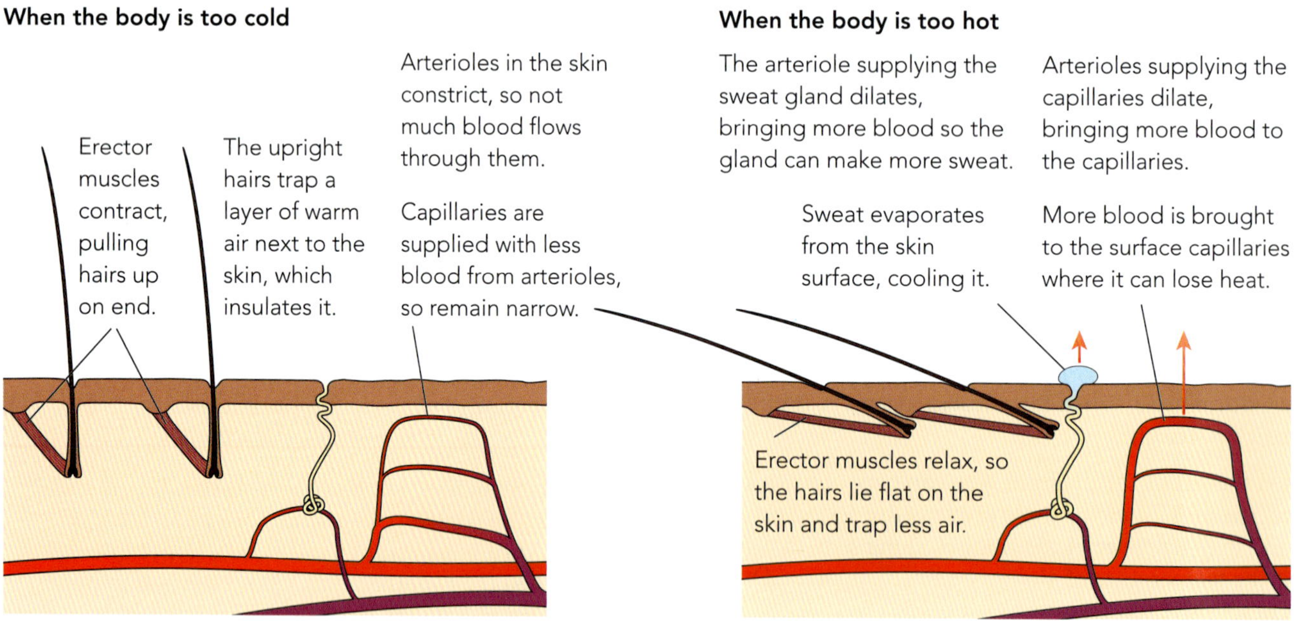

**When the body is too cold**

Erector muscles contract, pulling hairs up on end.

The upright hairs trap a layer of warm air next to the skin, which insulates it.

Arterioles in the skin constrict, so not much blood flows through them.

Capillaries are supplied with less blood from arterioles, so remain narrow.

**When the body is too hot**

The arteriole supplying the sweat gland dilates, bringing more blood so the gland can make more sweat.

Sweat evaporates from the skin surface, cooling it.

Erector muscles relax, so the hairs lie flat on the skin and trap less air.

Arterioles supplying the capillaries dilate, bringing more blood to the capillaries.

More blood is brought to the surface capillaries where it can lose heat.

Figure 13.14: How skin helps with temperature regulation.

- **Vasoconstriction** – The arterioles that supply the blood capillaries near to the surface of the skin become narrower (constricted). This is called **vasoconstriction**. Only a very little blood can flow in the surface capillaries. The blood flows through the deep-lying capillaries instead. Because these are deep under the skin, beneath the insulating fatty tissue, the blood does not lose so much heat to the air.
- **Sweat glands reduce secretion** – Sweat glands reduce the quantity of sweat that they produce. As you will see, sweat helps to cool the body down, so it is not required when you want to warm up.

## When temperature rises

When a rise in blood temperature is detected by the receptors in the hypothalamus, electrical impulses are sent along neurones to cause the following responses (Figure 13.14).

- **Hairs lie flat** – The erector muscles in the skin relax, so that the hairs lie flat on the skin. This allows heat to leave the skin through radiation into the air.
- **Vasodilation** – The arterioles supplying the capillaries near the surface of the skin get wider – they become dilated. This is called **vasodilation**. More blood therefore flows through these capillaries near the surface. Because a lot of blood is so near the surface of the skin, heat is readily lost from the blood into the air.
- **Sweat production increases** – The sweat glands secrete more sweat. The sweat lies on the surface of the hot skin. The water in it then evaporates, taking heat from the skin with it, thus cooling the body.

### KEY WORDS

**vasoconstriction:** narrowing of arterioles, caused by the contraction of the muscle in their walls

**vasodilation:** widening of arterioles, caused by the relaxation of the muscle in their walls

### ACTIVITY 13.2

**Comparing the control of temperature regulation with blood glucose concentration**

Work in a group of three for this activity.

Look again at the descriptions of negative feedback and the control of blood glucose concentration. Think about similarities between that process, and the way that body temperature is controlled.

For example:

- They both have receptors that detect changes. Where are these, and what do they detect?
- They both involve set points. What is this for each of them?
- They both involve negative feedback. How does this happen, in each of them?

Now try constructing a diagram, similar to the one in Figure 13.9, to summarise and illustrate the control of body temperature.

**Peer assessment**

Exchange your diagram with another group.

How well do you think they have succeeded? Does the diagram 'work' – that is, if you follow the arrows around, does the sequence of events make sense?

How can you improve your own group's diagram?

## SUMMARY

Carbon dioxide is excreted from the lungs. Urea, excess water and excess ions are excreted by the kidneys.

Urine is a solution of urea and ions in water. It flows from the kidneys in the ureters, into the bladder, and then is released out of the body through the urethra.

Urea is made in the liver by the deamination of excess amino acids.

A kidney has an outer cortex and an inner medulla. It contains thousands of tiny tubules, called nephrons.

Blood passes through a coiled capillary called a glomerulus. The blood is filtered into the nephron. Water, glucose and ions are present in the filtrate that passes into the lumen of the nephron.

As the filtrate flows along the nephron, all of the glucose, most of the water and some of the ions are reabsorbed into the blood.

Homeostasis is the maintenance of a constant internal environment.

Insulin is secreted by the pancreas when blood glucose concentration is too high. It decreases blood glucose concentration.

In homeostasis, negative feedback helps to keep a value close to its set point.

Blood glucose concentration is controlled by a negative feedback loop involving the pancreas and liver.

When blood glucose concentration rises above its set point, insulin is secreted by the pancreas. This causes the liver to take up glucose from the blood, and to use some in respiration and also convert some to glycogen and store it.

When blood glucose concentration falls below its set point, glucagon is secreted by the pancreas. This causes the liver to break down some of its glycogen stores, and release glucose into the blood.

Temperature is controlled by a negative feedback loop involving receptors in the skin and hypothalamus in the brain, and effectors in the skin and muscles.

When body temperature rises above its set point, the hypothalamus sends electrical impulses along motor neurones to the skin. This causes arterioles supplying the skin surface capillaries to dilate, in a process called vasodilation. More blood flows close to the surface and more heat is lost to the air. Also, the sweat glands secrete more sweat, which evaporates from the skin surface, producing a cooling effect.

When body temperature falls below its set point, the hypothalamus sends electrical impulses along motor neurones to the skin. This causes arterioles supplying the skin surface capillaries to get narrower, in a process called vasoconstriction. Blood is diverted to capillaries deeper in the skin, so that less heat is lost to the air.

Fatty tissue underneath the skin helps to insulate the body, reducing heat loss to the air.

## PROJECT

### Teaching about how negative feedback works

Negative feedback can be a tricky topic to understand. In this project, you will work in a small group to plan and present a short lesson to help people understand how negative feedback works in homeostasis.

Your lesson should:

- last no more than 8 to 10 minutes
- include some active learning for your pupils – where they have to do something and think for themselves, rather than just listening to you
- concentrate on one example of negative feedback in homeostasis
- not try to do too much – your lesson should not be a full-length lesson done at top speed, but just a small part of a lesson done properly.

Your lesson could also:

- use other examples of negative feedback to help people to understand – for example, how a thermostat works in a heating or cooling system in a house
- use a slide show or video clip that you have constructed yourself
- use other IT if you have it, such as tablets.

First, work as a group to plan your lesson. Think about these issues:

1. How do you plan to explain negative feedback? How can you make this easy for people to understand?
2. How will you start your lesson? How will you get everyone's attention right at the beginning?
3. What resources do you need? You might want to use drawings, handouts, slides or video clips, for example.
4. How will you check that your class understands your explanation? What questions will you ask, to find out how well they understand?

When every group has planned their lesson, each group should give their lesson to the rest of the class.

Be ready to give feedback to each group. How interesting and helpful was their lesson? What has the group done well? What could they do better?

## EXAM-STYLE QUESTIONS

1  This figure shows part of the human excretory system.

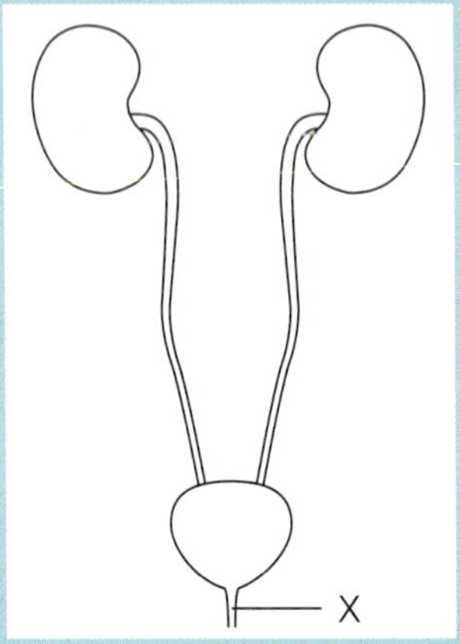

   What is the structure labelled X?
   A  bladder
   B  kidney
   C  urethra
   D  ureter  [1]

2  Which is a definition of homeostasis?
   A  the excretion of urea by the kidneys
   B  the maintenance of a constant internal environment
   C  the reduction of blood glucose concentration by insulin
   D  the removal of carbon dioxide from the lungs  [1]

3  Where is urea produced and excreted?

   |   | Produced | Excreted |
   |---|----------|----------|
   | A | kidney   | kidney   |
   | B | kidney   | liver    |
   | C | liver    | kidney   |
   | D | liver    | liver    |

   [1]

4  How does the liver help to assimilate amino acids?
   A  by converting them to urine
   B  by deaminating them to produce urea
   C  by digesting them
   D  by using them to synthesise proteins  [1]

5  In negative feedback, a receptor detects when a value has moved outside a set point.
   Where is the receptor that detects when blood glucose concentration is outside its set point?
   A  in the brain
   B  in the kidneys
   C  in the liver
   D  in the pancreas  [1]

## CONTINUED

**6 a** A boy ate some rice, which contains starch.
  **i** **Describe** how and where the starch is broken down to glucose in his body. [3]
  **ii** Name the part of the digestive system where the glucose is absorbed into the blood. [1]
**b** Use your knowledge of osmosis to explain how a high concentration of glucose in the blood could harm body cells. [2]
**c** Shortly after the boy ate the rice, the quantity of insulin in his blood increased.
  **i** Name the gland that secretes insulin. [1]
  **ii** **State** the effect of insulin on blood glucose concentration. [1]

[Total: 8]

> **COMMAND WORDS**
>
> **describe:** state the points of a topic / give characteristics and main features
>
> **state:** express in clear terms

**7** This figure is an electron micrograph of parts of three cells in the pancreas. The cell on the left produces enzymes. The two cells on the right produce insulin.

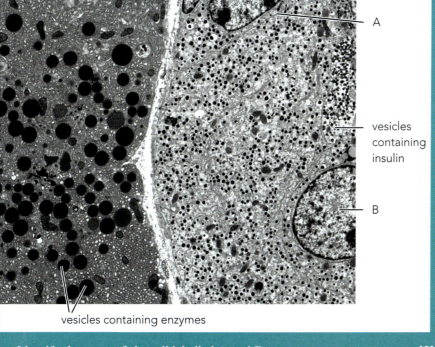

**a** Identify the parts of the cell labelled **A** and **B**. [2]
**b** Outline how the enzymes produced in the left-hand cell travel to their final destination. [3]
**c** Outline how the insulin produced in the right-hand cell travels to its target organ. [3]

[Total: 8]

## CONTINUED

**8 a** Explain why body cells need a constant supply of glucose. [3]

**b** In healthy humans, the blood normally contains about 90 mg of glucose per 100 cm³ of blood.

Name the gland that secretes the hormones that help to keep this concentration fairly constant. [1]

**c** The graph shows the changes in concentration of blood glucose after a meal containing starch.

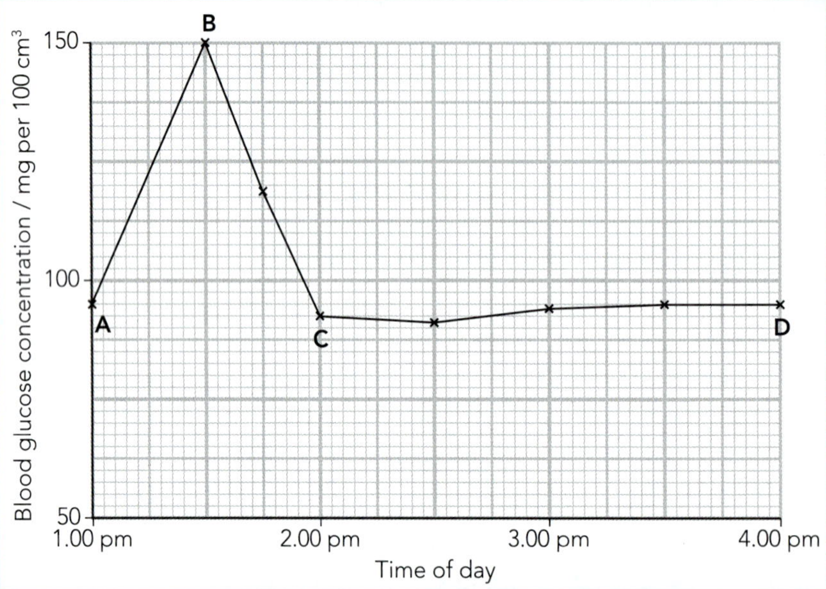

[Graph: Blood glucose concentration / mg per 100 cm³ vs Time of day. Point A at ~1.00 pm at ~90, rising to B at ~1.30 pm at 150, falling to C at ~2.00 pm at ~85, then roughly constant to D at 4.00 pm at ~90.]

   **i** Explain why the concentration of glucose in the blood rises between **A** and **B**. [3]

   **ii** Explain why the concentration of glucose in the blood falls between **B** and **C**. [4]

**d** The graph shows that the blood glucose concentration remains fairly constant between **C** and **D**. Explain the role of negative feedback in keeping blood glucose concentration constant. [3]

**e i** Make a copy of the graph. On your graph, sketch a curve to show how you would expect the blood glucose concentration of a person with type 1 diabetes to change, if they ate the same meal at the same time. [3]

   **ii** Explain your answer to e (i). [2]

[Total: 19]

## CONTINUED

**9** When a person is submerged in cold water, their body temperature can drop very quickly. This is because heat is transferred quickly, by conduction, from the warm body into the cold water.

An experiment was carried out to see if it is better to stay still if you fall into cold water or to try to swim.

- Two men sat for 30 minutes, in air at a temperature of 15 °C.
- They then got into a swimming pool, where the water was also at a temperature of 15 °C.
- Person **A** swam for the next 30 minutes. Person **B** lay still in the water.

The body temperatures of both men were measured at 10-minute intervals throughout the experiment. The results are shown below.

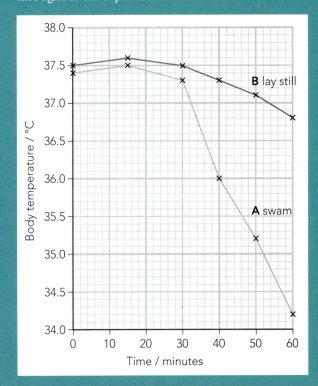

- **a** State the body temperatures of both men at the start of the experiment. [2]
- **b** Explain why their body temperatures remained roughly constant for the first 30 minutes of the experiment. [4]
- **c** Explain why the body temperatures of both men dropped between 30 minutes and 60 minutes. [2]
- **d** Suggest why person **A**'s temperature dropped faster than person **B**'s temperature during this time period. [3]

[Total: 11]

# CAMBRIDGE IGCSE™ BIOLOGY: COURSEBOOK

## SELF-EVALUATION CHECKLIST

After studying this chapter, think about how confident you are with the different topics. This will help you to see any gaps in your knowledge and help you to learn more effectively.

| I can | See Topic… | Needs more work | Almost there | Confident to move on |
|---|---|---|---|---|
| state where carbon dioxide, urea, excess water and ions are excreted | 13.1 | | | |
| identify the kidneys, ureters, bladder and urethra on a diagram | 13.1 | | | |
| outline the structure of a kidney, including a nephron and its associated blood capillaries | 13.1 | | | |
| describe how urea is made by deamination of excess amino acids in the liver | 13.1 | | | |
| describe how filtration and reabsorption happen in a nephron | 13.1 | | | |
| describe how urine is formed, and what it contains | 13.1 | | | |
| define homeostasis | 13.2 | | | |
| describe the effect of insulin | 13.2 | | | |
| explain how negative feedback keeps values close to a set point | 13.2 | | | |
| describe how the liver and pancreas – which secretes insulin and glucagon – keep blood glucose concentration close to a set point | 13.2 | | | |
| identify structures on a diagram of the skin | 13.2 | | | |
| describe how the hypothalamus in the brain helps in temperature regulation | 13.2 | | | |
| describe how insulation, sweating, shivering, vasodilation and vasoconstriction help to keep body temperature close to a set point | 13.2 | | | |

# Chapter 14
# Reproduction in plants

**IN THIS CHAPTER YOU WILL:**

- learn about the differences between asexual and sexual reproduction
- find out how flowers are involved in sexual reproduction
- investigate seed germination

> learn about self- and cross-pollination and their potential effects on a population.

# CAMBRIDGE IGCSE™ BIOLOGY: COURSEBOOK

## GETTING STARTED

Look at the photographs in Figure 14.1. They both show a strawberry plant reproducing.

**Figure 14.1:** Two methods of reproduction in strawberry plants.

With a partner, discuss what is happening in each plant. How is each one reproducing?

## BANANAS

Bananas are one of the world's favourite fruits. Wild banana plants grow in Asia, and it is thought that people first began to grow them as crops in New Guinea, about 10 000 years ago.

The fruits of wild banana plants contain seeds. Reproducing by producing seeds is a type of sexual reproduction. The new plants that grow from the seeds are all a little bit different from each other. One of the advantages of this is that, if a new disease strikes, then at least some of the individual plants are likely to have resistance to it and will survive.

However, modern banana cultivars have been bred to be seedless. The only way of propagating the plants is to dig up suckers that grow from a mature plant, and plant them so that they will grow into new plants. A sucker is a stem, with roots, that grows out of the parent plant. Suckers are produced by asexual reproduction, and they have exactly the same genes as their parent.

One particularly popular variety of banana is called Cavendish. Half of all bananas grown, and 99% of those exported for sale, are Cavendish bananas. Because they are always propagated asexually, all Cavendish banana plants are genetically identical to one another. Every Cavendish banana plant is susceptible to a fungal disease called Panama disease. This fungus cannot be killed with fungicides. It is spreading rapidly across the world. Scientists and breeders are working hard to try to produce new varieties of banana to replace Cavendish.

They need to find ways of introducing new genes into the banana plants, so that some of them will have natural resistance to the fungus.

### Discussion questions

1. Could breeding varieties of bananas that are naturally resistant to the fungus have benefits other than increasing yields?

2. Is it a good thing that so many of the bananas grown and sold are the same variety? Why do you think this has happened? Should we try to avoid this situation in the future?

# 14.1 Asexual and sexual reproduction

Reproduction is one of the characteristics of all living things. Each kind of organism has its own particular method of reproducing, but all of these methods fit into one of two categories – **asexual reproduction** or **sexual reproduction**.

In reproduction, each new organism obtains a set of chromosomes from its parent or parents. Chromosomes are long threads of DNA found in the nucleus of a cell, and they contain sets of instructions known as genes. As you will find out in Chapter 17, these genes vary slightly from one another in different individuals.

> **KEY WORDS**
>
> **asexual reproduction:** a process resulting in the production of genetically identical offspring from one parent
>
> **sexual reproduction:** a process involving the fusion of the nuclei of two gametes to form a zygote and the production of offspring that are genetically different from each other

Asexual reproduction involves just one parent. Some of the parent's cells divide to produce new cells that contain exactly the same genes as the parent cell, and so they are said to be genetically identical. They grow into new organisms, which are all genetically identical to each other and to their single parent.

## An example of asexual reproduction

Many plants are able to reproduce asexually, and gardeners and farmers make use of this. Asexual reproduction can quickly and efficiently produce many new plants, all genetically identical to one another. This is advantageous to the grower if the original plant has exactly the characteristics that are wanted, such as large and attractive flowers, or good flavour, or high yield.

Potatoes, for example, reproduce using stem tubers (Figure 14.2). When it is warm enough, some of the plant's stems grow normally and produce leaves above ground, which photosynthesise. Other stems grow under the soil. Swellings called tubers form on them. Sucrose is transported from the leaves into these underground stem tubers, where it is converted into starch and stored. The tubers grow larger and larger. Each plant can produce many stem tubers.

The tubers are harvested, to be used as food. Some of them, however, are saved to produce next year's crop. These tubers are planted underground, where they grow shoots and roots to form a new plant. Because each potato plant produces many tubers, one plant can give rise to many new ones. To get even more plants, each tuber can be cut into several pieces. As long as each piece has a bud on it, it can grow into a complete new plant.

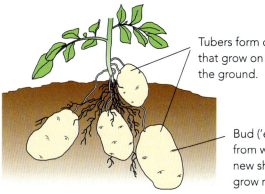

Tubers form on stems that grow on or under the ground.

Bud ('eye') from which new shoots will grow next year.

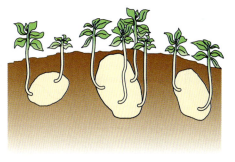

Next year, each tuber grows into a new plant.

**Figure 14.2:** Asexual reproduction in potatoes.

Plants are not the only organisms that can reproduce asexually. Bacteria, for example, reproduce asexually when one cell splits into two cells. Even some simple animals can reproduce asexually. A tiny animal called *Hydra*, which lives in fresh water and is related to sea anemones, reproduces asexually by growing 'buds', which develop into a young *Hydra* before breaking away from the parent (Figure 14.3).

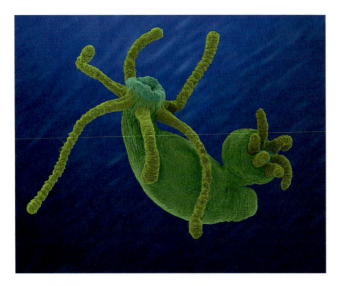

Figure 14.3: The bud on this *Hydra* is almost ready to break away and start an independent life.

The zygote contains chromosomes from both its parents. It can have any combination of their genes. Sexual reproduction therefore produces offspring that are genetically different from each other and from their parents.

> ### KEY WORDS
>
> **gamete:** a sex cell; a cell with half the normal number of chromosomes, whose nucleus fuses with the nucleus of another gamete during sexual reproduction
>
> **fertilisation:** the fusion of the nuclei of two gametes
>
> **zygote:** a cell that is formed by the fusion of two gametes

## Sexual reproduction

In sexual reproduction, the parent organism produces sex cells called **gametes**. Eggs and sperm are examples of gametes. Two of these gametes join and their nuclei fuse together. This is called **fertilisation**. The new cell which is formed by fertilisation is called a **zygote**. The zygote divides again and again, and eventually grows into a new organism.

### Gametes

Gametes are different from ordinary cells, because they contain only half as many chromosomes as usual. This is so that when two of them fuse together, the zygote they form will have the correct number of chromosomes (Figure 14.4).

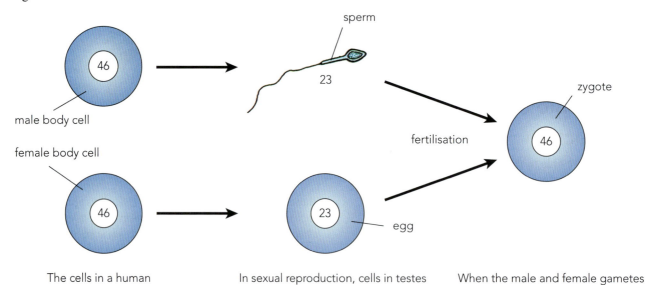

The cells in a human body each contain 46 chromosomes.

In sexual reproduction, cells in testes and ovaries produce gametes, with half the number of chromosomes.

When the male and female gametes join together, a zygote is formed which has the full number of chromosomes.

Figure 14.4: Chromosome numbers in sexual reproduction.

In most organisms that reproduce sexually, there are two types of gamete. Female gametes tend to be relatively large, and they do not move. In plants, the female gamete is a nucleus inside an ovule. In animals, it is called an egg. Male gametes are usually much smaller, and they can move. In plants, the male gamete is found inside the pollen grains. In animals, the male gametes are called sperm.

In humans, there are two sets of chromosomes in each cell. One of these sets came from the father, and one from the mother. Each set contains 23 chromosomes, so in total there are 46 chromosomes in each body cell. A cell or a nucleus that has two complete sets of chromosomes is said to be **diploid**.

But human egg and sperm cells only have 23 chromosomes each. They each have a single set of chromosomes. A cell or a nucleus containing a single set of chromosomes is said to be **haploid**. Gametes are haploid.

When an egg and sperm fuse together at fertilisation, the zygote which is formed will therefore have 46 chromosomes, the normal number. Zygotes are diploid.

It is important to realise that not all organisms have 46 chromosomes! For example, the cells of a eucalyptus tree have 22 chromosomes. Their male and female gametes each have 11 chromosomes. When these gametes fuse together they produce a zygote that has 22 chromosomes.

Gametes are made when cells in reproductive organs divide. For example, human sperm are made when cells in a testis divide. The gametes inside pollen grains are made when cells in anthers divide.

Normally, when cells divide, they do so by a process called **mitosis**, which produces new cells that contain exactly the same number and type of chromosomes and genes as the parent cell. But gametes must have only half as many chromosomes as their parent cell, so division by mitosis will not do. When gametes are being made, cells divide in a different way, called **meiosis**. Mitosis and meiosis are both described in Chapter 16.

In flowering plants and animals, meiosis only happens when gametes are being made. Meiosis produces haploid gametes from diploid parent cells.

> **KEY WORDS**
>
> **diploid:** having two complete sets of chromosomes
>
> **haploid:** having only a single set of chromosomes
>
> **mitosis:** division of a cell nucleus resulting in two genetically identical nuclei (i.e. with the same number and kind of chromosomes as the parent nucleus)
>
> **meiosis:** division of a diploid nucleus resulting in four genetically different haploid nuclei; this is sometimes called a reduction division

Often, one organism can only produce one kind of gamete. Its sex is either male or female, depending on what kind of gamete it makes. All mammals, for example, are either male or female.

Sometimes, though, an organism can produce both sorts of gamete. Earthworms and slugs, for example, can produce both eggs and sperm. An organism which produces both male and female gametes is a hermaphrodite. Many flowering plants are also hermaphrodites.

## Questions

1. The cells in a durian tree have 28 chromosomes. How many chromosomes will there be in a nucleus in an ovule of a durian tree?
2. a What is the haploid number of a durian tree?
   b What is its diploid number?
3. In a plant, the root grows when cells divide just behind its tip. Pollen grains are produced when cells divide in its anthers.

   Explain why cell division by meiosis happens in the anthers, but not in the root.

## 14.2 Sexual reproduction in flowering plants

### Flowers

Many flowering plants can reproduce in more than one way. Often, they can reproduce asexually and also sexually, by means of flowers.

The function of a flower is to make gametes, and to ensure that fertilisation will take place. Figure 14.6 illustrates the structure of an insect-pollinated flower. Figure 14.5 shows flowers of *Eucryphia* which makes both male and female gametes, so it is a hermaphroditic flower. Most, but not all, flowers are hermaphrodites.

**Figure 14.5:** Flowers on a south American tree called *Eucryphia*. Can you identify the different parts of the flower?

On the outside of the flower are the **sepals**. The sepals protect the flower while it is a bud. Sepals are normally green.

Just inside the sepals are the **petals**. These are often brightly coloured. The petals attract insects to the flower.

> The petals of some flowers have lines running from top to bottom. These lines are called guide-lines, because they guide insects to the base of the petal. Here, there is a gland called a nectary. The nectary is a gland at the base of a petal that secretes a sugary liquid called nectar, which attracts insects.

Inside the petals are the **stamens**. These are the male parts of the flower. Each stamen is made up of a long **filament**, with an **anther** at the top. The anthers contain **pollen grains**, which contain the male gametes.

### KEY WORDS

**sepals:** leaf-like structures that form a ring outside the petals of a flower

**petals:** coloured structures that attract insects or birds to a flower

**stamens:** the male parts of a flower

**filament:** the 'stalk' part of a stamen

**anther:** the structure at the top of a stamen, inside which pollen grains are made

**pollen grains:** small structures which contain the male gametes of a flower

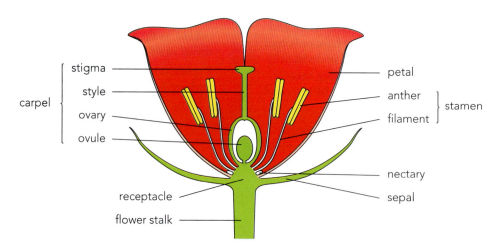

**Figure 14.6:** The structure of a simple flower.

## 14 Reproduction in plants

The female part of the flower is in the centre. It consists of one or more carpels. A **carpel** contains an **ovary**. Inside the ovary are many **ovules**, which contain the female gametes. At the top of the ovary is the **style**, with a **stigma** at the tip. The function of the stigma is to catch pollen grains.

### KEY WORDS

**carpel:** the female part of a flower

**ovary:** the part of the flower that holds the ovules

**ovules:** small structures that contain the female gametes

**style:** the part of a carpel that connects the stigma to the ovary

**stigma:** the part of a flower that receives pollen

The female parts of different kinds of flower vary. One of the differences is the arrangement of the ovules in the ovary. Figure 14.7 shows one arrangement.

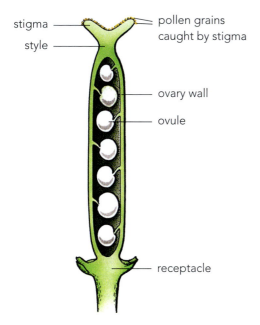

**Figure 14.7:** Section through the female part (carpel) of a flower.

## Pollen grains and ovules

The male gametes are inside the pollen grains, which are made in the anthers.

Figure 14.8a illustrates a young anther, as it looks before the flower bud opens. You can see in Figure 14.8b that the anther has four spaces inside it, which are called pollen sacs. Some of the cells around the edge of the pollen sacs divide to make pollen grains. When the flower bud opens, the anthers split open (Figure 14.8c). Now the pollen is on the outside of the anther.

**a** A young anther

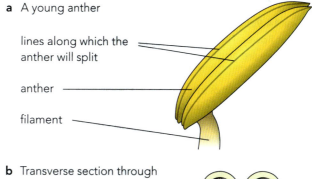

**b** Transverse section through a young anther

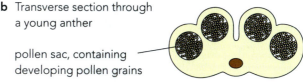

**c** Transverse section through a mature anther

**Figure 14.8:** How pollen is made.

Pollen looks like a fine powder. It is often yellow. Under the microscope, you can see the shape of individual grains (Figure 14.9). Pollen grains from different kinds of flower have different shapes – sometimes spiky, sometimes smooth. Each grain is surrounded by a hard coat, so that it can survive in difficult conditions if necessary. The coat protects the male gametes that are inside the grains, as the pollen is carried from one flower to another.

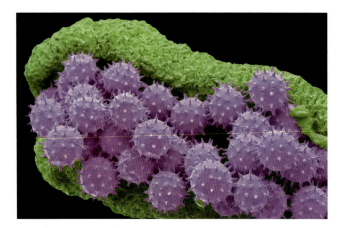

Figure 14.9: Pollen grains on the surface of an anther of a hibiscus flower. This is a scanning electron micrograph, and the colours are artificial – the pollen is not really purple.

The female gametes are inside the ovules, in the ovary (Figure 14.10). Each ovule contains a nucleus. Fertilisation happens when a pollen grain nucleus fuses with an ovule nucleus.

Figure 14.10: A section through the ovary of a daffodil flower. The green part is the wall of the ovary, and you can see part of the short style at the top left. Each little white structure is an ovule, and each ovule contains a nucleus that is a female gamete.

## Pollination

For fertilisation to take place, the male gametes must travel to the female gametes. The first stage of this journey is for pollen to be taken from the anther where it was made, to a stigma. This is called **pollination**.

Pollination is often carried out by insects (Figure 14.11). Insects such as honeybees come to flowers, attracted by their colour and strong sweet scent. The bee follows the guide-lines to the nectaries, brushing past the anthers as it goes. Some of the pollen sticks to its body. The bee then goes to another flower, looking for more nectar. Some of the pollen it picked up at the first flower sticks onto the stigma of the second flower when the bee brushes past it. The stigma is sticky, and many pollen grains get stuck on it. If the second flower is from the same species of plant as the first, pollination has taken place.

Figure 14.11: The bee has come to the flower to collect nectar. Pollen gets stuck to its body, and the bee will then carry this to the next flower it visits.

### KEY WORD

**pollination:** the transfer of pollen grains from the male part of the plant (anther of stamen) to the female part of the plant (stigma)

# 14 Reproduction in plants

> ### ACTIVITY 14.1
>
> **Investigating the structure of a flower**
>
> Work with a partner for this activity. You will need a flower, and perhaps also some transparent sticky tape.
>
> Look carefully at a simple flower – one that has a ring of petals, surrounding some anthers and ovaries.
>
> Using Figure 14.5, identify each part of the flower.
>
> Now take off the outer ring of flower parts – the sepals. You can stick them into your book if you like. Even better, you could construct a table with three columns. Name the part in the first column, stick the part into the next one, and write a description of its function in the third column.
>
> Work your way through to the centre of the flower, removing each ring of flower parts in turn.

> ### REFLECTION
>
> Do you find that doing something active, such as taking apart a real flower, helps you to understand it better than just looking at a flower or a picture of one? If you do, think about how you could use some kind of activity to try to help your brain to understand and remember other topics.

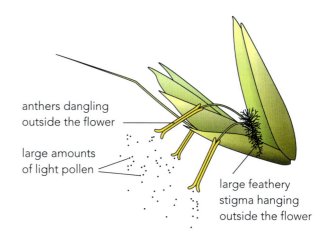

**Figure 14.12:** A grass flower – an example of a wind-pollinated flower.

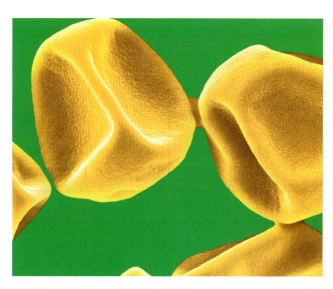

**Figure 14.13:** Pollen grains from a grass flower. These small, smooth grains are adapted to be carried easily by the wind.

# Wind pollination

In some plants, it is the wind which carries the pollen between flowers. Figure 14.12 shows a grass flower, which is an example of a wind-pollinated flower. Figure 14.13 shows pollen grains from a grass flower. You can see how smooth they are, compared with the spiky pollen grains in Figure 14.9.

Wind-pollinated flowers usually produce much more pollen than insect-pollinated flowers. This is because a lot of the pollen doesn't land on another flower, so huge amounts are wasted. Although insects do eat some pollen, they are still much more likely to deliver pollen successfully to another flower than the wind.

Wind-pollinated flowers usually do not have petals, as there is no need to attract insects. Their anthers and stigmas dangle outside the flower, to catch the wind. The filaments of the anthers are very flexible, so they can swing in the wind and release their pollen. The feathery stigmas have a large surface area, increasing the chances of catching pollen. In contrast, insect-pollinated flowers have anthers and stigmas that are enclosed within the petals, so that insects have to brush past them to reach the nectar.

Table 14.1 compares insect-pollinated and wind-pollinated flowers.

| Insect-pollinated flower | Wind-pollinated flower |
| --- | --- |
| large, conspicuous petals, often with guide-lines | small, inconspicuous petals, or no petals at all |
| often strongly scented | no scent |
| often have nectaries at the base of petals | no nectaries |
| anthers inside flower, where insect has to brush past them to reach nectar | anthers dangle outside the flower, where they catch the wind |
| stigma inside flower, where insect has to brush past it to reach nectar | stigmas large and feathery and dangle outside the flower, where pollen in the air may land on it |
| sticky or spiky pollen grains, which stick to insects | smooth, light pollen, which can be blown in the wind |
| quite large quantities of pollen made, because some will be eaten or will be delivered to the wrong kind of flower | very large quantities of pollen made, because most will be blown away and lost |

**Table 14.1:** A comparison between insect-pollinated and wind-pollinated flowers.

## Questions

4   Figure 14.14 shows a bee visiting a flower.

**Figure 14.14:** A bee visiting a flower.

Describe how the flower is adapted to make sure that bees will visit it, and also that the bees will pick up pollen and deposit it in the right place.

5   Figure 14.15 shows some grass flowers.
   a   Explain how these flowers are adapted for wind pollination.
   b   Many people suffer from an allergy to pollen, called hay fever. They are usually more badly affected by grass pollen than by pollen from insect-pollinated flowers. Suggest why.

**Figure 14.15:** Grass flowers.

## Self- and cross-pollination

Sometimes, pollen is carried to the stigma of the same flower, or to another flower on the same plant. This is called **self-pollination**.

If pollen is taken to a flower on a different plant of the same species, this is called **cross-pollination**.

If pollen lands on the stigma of a different species of plant, the pollen grain usually dies.

> **KEY WORDS**
>
> **self-pollination:** the transfer of pollen grains from the anther of a flower to the stigma of the same flower, or a different flower on the same plant
>
> **cross-pollination:** the transfer of pollen grains from the anther of a flower to the stigma of a flower on a different plant of the same species

## Fertilisation

After pollination, the male gamete inside the pollen grain is on the stigma. It still has not reached the female gamete. The female gamete is inside the ovule, and the ovule is inside the ovary. For fertilisation to take place, the male gamete (a nucleus inside a pollen grain) must fuse with a female gamete (a nucleus inside an ovule).

If the pollen grain has landed on the right kind of stigma, it begins to grow a tube. The pollen tube grows down through the style and the ovary, towards the ovule (Figure 14.16). It secretes enzymes to digest a pathway through the style.

The ovule is surrounded by several protective layers of cells called the integuments. At one end, there is a small hole, called the micropyle. The pollen tube grows through the micropyle, into the ovule.

The pollen nucleus (the male gamete) travels along the pollen tube, and into the ovule. It fuses with the ovule nucleus (the female gamete). Fertilisation has now taken place.

One pollen grain can only fertilise one ovule. If there are many ovules in the ovary, then many pollen grains will be needed to fertilise them all.

## Seeds

After the ovules have been fertilised, many of the parts of the flower are not needed any more. The sepals, petals and stamens have all done their job. They wither (dry and shrink), and fall off.

Inside the ovary, the ovules start to grow. Each ovule now contains a zygote, which was formed at fertilisation. The zygote divides by mitosis to form an embryo plant. The ovule is now a **seed**.

A seed contains very little water. When the seed was formed on the plant, the water in it was drawn out, so that the seed became dehydrated. Without water, almost no metabolic reactions can go on inside it. The seed is **dormant**. This is very useful, because the dormant seed can survive harsh conditions, such as cold or drought, which would kill a growing plant.

A seed must be in certain conditions before it will begin to germinate. You can find out what they are in the following investigation.

> **KEY WORDS**
>
> **seed:** the structure that develops from an ovule after fertilisation; it contains an embryo plant
>
> **dormant:** inactive, with metabolic reactions taking place very slowly or not at all

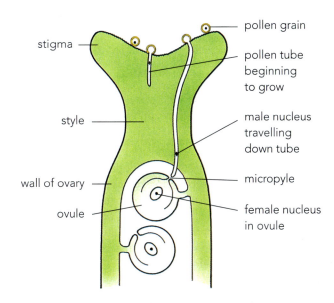

Figure 14.16: How a male gamete travels to a female gamete in a flower.

## EXPERIMENTAL SKILLS 14.1

### Investigating the conditions necessary for the germination of seeds

In this investigation, you will provide several sets of seeds with different combinations of conditions. This will enable you to work out which conditions they need before they will germinate. You will also practise constructing and completing a results table.

**You will need:**
- at least 50 small seeds, e.g. mustard seeds or tomato seeds
- the apparatus shown in Figure 14.17.

### Method

1  Set up five large test-tubes, as shown in Figure 14.17. If there is no suitable dark place to leave tubes B and C, you can cover the tubes with black paper instead. Make sure that you put the same number of seeds into each tube.

2  Check the tubes each day. Count how many seeds have germinated, and record this as a percentage in a results table.

3  Use your results to decide which conditions these seeds require, in order to germinate.

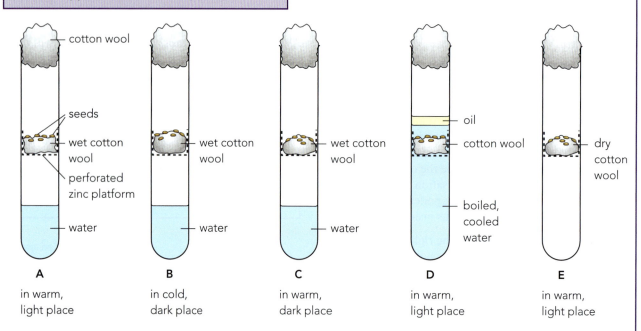

Figure 14.17: Apparatus for Experimental skills 14.1.

### Questions

1  Most seeds need water, oxygen and a warm temperature before they will germinate. (You probably found that your seeds needed these conditions.) When a seed germinates, there is a lot of metabolic activity inside the seed. Suggest why these three conditions are required for germination.

2  Although many seeds do not need light for germination, some do. For example, seeds of trees that grow in tropical rainforests will often only germinate if they have a lot of light. This could happen, for example, if a large tree fell over, leaving a gap in the forest. Suggest the advantage to these seeds of germinating only when they have light.

> **CONTINUED**
>
> **Self-assessment**
>
> How satisfied are you with the results table that you constructed?
>
> Does it clearly show the conditions in each tube?
>
> Does it clearly show the percentage of seeds that germinated in each tube?
>
> Is it easy to quickly see which conditions produced the highest percentage germination?

## 14.3 Advantages and disadvantages of different methods of reproduction

### Comparing asexual reproduction and sexual reproduction

Many plants, including the strawberries shown at the beginning of this chapter, can reproduce in two ways – asexually and sexually. Which is better?

We have seen that, in asexual reproduction, some of the parent's cells divide by mitosis. This makes new cells that are genetically identical to the parent cell. They are clones. Asexual reproduction does not produce genetic variation.

But in sexual reproduction, some of the parent's cells divide by meiosis. The gametes that are made have only half as many chromosomes as the parent cell, and the combination of genes on these chromosomes is not the same in every gamete. When two sets of chromosomes in two different gametes combine at fertilisation, a new combination of genes is produced. So sexual reproduction produces offspring that are genetically different from their parents.

Is it useful or not to have genetic variation among offspring? This depends on the circumstances.

Sometimes, it is a good thing not to have any variation. If a plant, for example, is growing well in a particular place, then it is clearly adapted to its environment. If its offspring all inherit the same genes, then they will be equally well adapted and are likely to grow well. This is especially true if there is plenty of space for them in that area.

However, if it is getting crowded, then it may not be a good thing for the parent to produce new offspring that grow all around it. It might be better for them to spread further away. In flowering plants, sexual reproduction produces seeds, which are likely to be dispersed over a wide area. This spreads the offspring far away from the parents, so that they are less likely to compete with them. It also allows them to colonise new areas.

Another advantage of asexual reproduction is that a single organism can reproduce on its own. It does not need to wait to be pollinated, or to find a mate. This can be good if there are not many of those organisms around – perhaps there is only a single one growing in an isolated place. In that case, asexual reproduction is definitely the best option. (Do remember, though, that even a single plant may be able to reproduce sexually, by using self-pollination.)

However, if the plant is not doing very well in its environment, or if a new disease has come along to which it is not resistant, then it could be an advantage for its offspring to be genetically different from it. There is a good chance that at least some of the offspring may be better adapted to that environment, or be resistant to that disease. In that case, sexual reproduction would be much more advantageous than asexual reproduction.

You will find out more about variation, and its importance for evolution, in Chapter 17.

Figure 14.18: All the tulips in each row are genetically identical to each other – they have been produced using asexual reproduction. The different varieties of tulips have been produced using sexual reproduction.

Figure 14.19: Flowers of many species of violet are able to self-pollinate, without any need for a pollinator. Some of the flowers open like this one, waiting for a pollinator to arrive. Other flowers do not open, keeping the stamens and stigmas covered over, and in contact with one another, so that their own pollen is transferred to their own stigma.

Farmers and other commercial plant growers also make use of these two possible methods of propagating their plants. For example, if a rose grower wants to produce many more rose plants that will have flowers exactly the same as the parent plant, they will use asexual reproduction (Figure 14.18). But if they want to produce a new variety of rose, they will breed together two different rose plants, using sexual reproduction. They can then grow the seeds that are produced, each of which will grow into a plant that isn't quite the same as any of the others. With luck, one of these might prove to be a commercial success.

We have seen that, if growers rely on producing new plants by asexual reproduction over long periods of time, they run the risk of all their plants becoming vulnerable to attack by a pest or disease. This has happened with some varieties of bananas. Breeders are now going back to wild banana plants, and trying new breeding programmes, using sexual reproduction, to try to produce new varieties to replace the old ones.

## Comparing self-pollination and cross-pollination

Both self-pollination and cross-pollination are methods of sexual reproduction. Both of them involve gametes and fertilisation.

Following self-pollination, a male gamete from a plant fuses with a female gamete from the same plant. The plant has, in effect, fertilised itself. You might think this would result in no variation in the offspring, because all the genes going into the offspring have come from a single parent. But that is not quite correct. When gametes are made, and fertilisation takes place, new combinations of genes can be formed. So there is some variation – though usually not very much – among the offspring. You will find out more about this when you study inheritance in Chapter 16.

In cross-pollination, there is much more variation, because each of the parent plants may be genetically different from one another. So fertilisation produces zygotes that can be very different from each other and from either of their parents.

The advantages and disadvantages of self-pollination and cross-pollination are very similar to the advantages and disadvantages of asexual reproduction and sexual reproduction. Self-pollination is good if there are advantages in keeping variation to a minimum (if the plant is already well adapted to where it is living). It is also useful if there might be difficulty in finding another plant nearby to exchange pollen with. Some flowers that self-pollinate can do so without pollinators such as bees (Figure 14.19), so that is really useful if there is a shortage of pollinators. Cross-pollination is good if there is a need for more genetic variation.

You can read more about the advantages of genetic variation in Chapter 17, where natural selection is described.

## Questions

6  Rank these three methods of reproduction in increasing order of the amount of genetic variation that they produce:
   A  sexual reproduction using self-pollination
   B  sexual reproduction using cross-pollination
   C  asexual reproduction.

7  Suggest the best method – using asexual reproduction or sexual reproduction – by which a gardener could produce new plants in each of the following situations. In each case, explain your answer.

   a  She has a single plant which has flowers in exactly the shade of red which she loves. She would like to grow a large number of plants just like this one.
   b  She has many individual plants of the same type, which all vary slightly from one another in the colour of their flowers. She would like to try to produce a plant that has a slightly different colour from any of the others.
   c  She has some vegetable plants which are all being attacked by a fungal disease, which is killing almost all of them. She wants to be able to grow plants which are resistant to the fungus.

## SUMMARY

Asexual reproduction involves a single parent and produces genetically identical offspring. Sexual reproduction may involve one or two parents, which produce gametes. The nuclei of the gametes fuse in the process of fertilisation, producing genetically different zygotes.

In flowering plants, male gametes are found inside pollen grains and female gametes inside ovules.

Gamete nuclei that have one set of chromosomes and are said to be haploid. Body cells have two sets of chromosomes, and are diploid.

An insect-pollinated flower has petals and nectaries to attract insects, which pick up pollen grains from the anthers and deposit them on a stigma.

Wind-pollinated flowers generally do not have petals. They have anthers and feathery stigmas that dangle outside the flower, so that pollen can easily be blown away by the wind, and land on a stigma.

Insect-pollinated flowers produce relatively small quantities of sticky or spiky pollen. Wind-pollinated flowers produce very large quantities of smooth, lightweight pollen.

Fertilisation happens when a pollen nucleus fuses with a nucleus in an ovule.

A pollen grain that has landed on a stigma of the same species of plant grows a tube that pushes down through the stigma to an ovule. The pollen nucleus travels down this tube to reach the nucleus in the ovule.

After fertilisation, an ovule becomes a seed. Seeds can only germinate when they have water, oxygen and a suitable temperature.

Asexual reproduction is useful to a species of plant that is well adapted to the current environmental conditions, or when there are not many other plants available that it could exchange gametes with. Sexual reproduction is useful to a species of plant that will benefit from genetic variation, such as to adapt to changing environmental conditions.

A grower can use asexual reproduction to propagate plants that are all identical to the original plant. They can use sexual reproduction to produce new varieties.

Self-pollination and cross-pollination are both types of sexual reproduction. Self-pollination produces less genetic variation than cross-pollination.

## PROJECT

### Seed banks

You are going to work in a group to research what a seed bank is and what happens there.

Seed banks are places that store millions of seeds of wild plants and crop plants, to make sure they are safe for the future. There are several seed banks in the world, which between them are attempting to store as many different kinds of seeds as possible (Figure 14.20).

**Figure 14.20:** A sample of cereal grain seeds stored in the Svalbard Global Seed Vault.

Seed banks that you could research include:

- the Svalbard Global Seed Vault, in Norway
- the Millennium Seed Bank, in England
- the Australian PlantBank
- the Singapore Botanic Gardens Seed Bank
- Navdanya Community Seed Banks, in India.

There are many others. You may like to find out if there is one in your country.

In your group, produce a display explaining the work of your chosen seed bank.

Here are some questions you could try to find answers to.

- What is the focus of the seed bank – what is it trying to do?
- Where and how are the seeds collected?
- How are the seeds prepared for storage?
- How are the seeds stored? Do different seeds need different types of storage?
- Some of the seeds are germinated every few years – why is this done?
- What are the major challenges faced by the seed bank?

**Figure 14.21:** These seeds were collected from an area of Brazil just before all the trees were cut down. They were saved in the Instituto Terra, and are now being used to replant trees in that area.

# 14 Reproduction in plants

## EXAM-STYLE QUESTIONS

1  The diagram below shows a flower.
   In which part are pollen grains produced? [1]

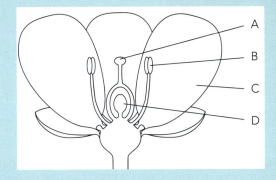

2  Which two words complete the sentence?
   Sexual reproduction involves the fusion of the nuclei of ___1___, producing ___2___.

   |   | 1 | 2 |
   |---|---|---|
   | A | gametes | zygotes |
   | B | ovules | seeds |
   | C | pollen | ovules |
   | D | zygotes | flowers |

   [1]

3  Which is a feature of wind-pollinated flowers?
   A  coloured petals
   B  enclosed anthers
   C  feathery stigmas
   D  spiky pollen grains [1]

4  A nucleus in a palisade cell in a jacaranda tree has 18 chromosomes. What correctly describes the number of chromosomes in a nucleus in a female gamete of a jacaranda tree?
   A  haploid, 9 chromosomes
   B  haploid, 18 chromosomes
   C  diploid, 36 chromosomes
   D  diploid, 9 chromosomes [1]

## CONTINUED

5 What is cross-pollination?
   A  the transfer of pollen grains from an anther on one flower to a stigma on the same flower
   B  the transfer of pollen grains from an anther on one plant to a stigma on another plant of a different species
   C  the transfer of pollen grains from an anther on one plant to a stigma on another plant of the same species
   D  the transfer of pollen grains from an anther on one plant to a stigma on a different flower on the same plant  [1]

6  Match each of these words with its definition.

   **fertilisation    gamete    pollination    seed    zygote**

   a  a sex cell; it can be male or female
   b  a cell formed by the fusion of the nuclei of two gametes
   c  the transfer of pollen from an anther to a stigma
   d  an ovule after fertilisation
   e  the fusion of the nuclei of two gametes  [5]

7  A student investigated the conditions that mustard seeds need, in order to germinate. This figure shows the apparatus he used.

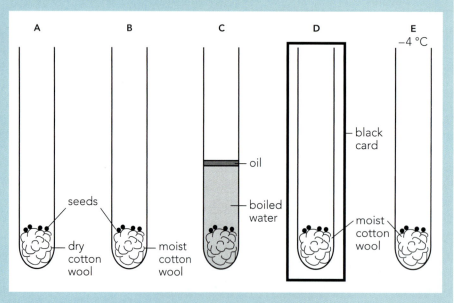

14 Reproduction in plants

### CONTINUED

a Copy and complete the table, to show the environmental conditions present in each tube.

The first row has been done for you.

| Tube | A | B | C | D | E |
|---|---|---|---|---|---|
| Water | ✗ | ✓ | ✓ | ✓ | ✓ |
| Oxygen | | | | | |
| Warm temperature | | | | | |
| Light | | | | | |

[2]

b Mustard seeds require water, a warm temperature and oxygen in order to germinate. **Predict** the tubes in which the seeds will germinate. [2]

c Seeds are produced after fertilisation happens in a flower.
   i **Describe** what happens during fertilisation in a flower. [2]
   ii Name the part of a flower that develops into a seed, after fertilisation. [1]

[Total: 7]

### COMMAND WORDS

**predict:** suggest what may happen based on available information

**describe:** state the points of a topic / give characteristics and main features

8 The diagram below shows a banana plant producing suckers.

a Name the type of reproduction that is shown in the diagram. [1]
b Describe the advantage to the growers of banana plants of using this type of reproduction to propagate their plants. [2]
c Banana plants can be killed by fungal diseases, such as black sigatoka and Panama disease.

Explain why a population of bananas produced by the method shown in the diagram could all be killed by the same disease. [2]

[Total: 5]

## CONTINUED

9 The diagram below shows two types of primrose flower.

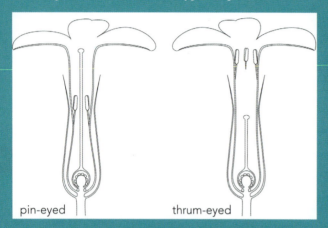

pin-eyed    thrum-eyed

These types of flower are often found growing close together. Any one primrose plant, however, only has one type of flower.

a  Describe the difference in the arrangement of the anthers and stigmas in the pin-eyed and thrum-eyed primrose. [2]

b  Primroses are pollinated by insects, which reach into the bottom of the flower to get nectar. Which part of the insect's body would pick up pollen in
   i   a pin-eyed primrose and [1]
   ii  a thrum-eyed primrose? [1]

c  Which part of the insect's body would touch the stigma in
   i   a pin-eyed primrose and [1]
   ii  a thrum-eyed primrose? [1]

d  Explain how this will help to ensure that cross-pollination takes place. [3]

e  Self-pollination does sometimes occur in primroses. Would you expect it to occur more often in pin-eyed or thrum-eyed primroses? Explain your answer. [2]

f  Explain the advantages of cross-pollination to a plant species. [2]

[Total: 13]

## 14 Reproduction in plants

### SELF-EVALUATION CHECKLIST

After studying this chapter, think about how confident you are with the different topics. This will help you to see any gaps in your knowledge and help you to learn more effectively.

| I can | See Topic... | Needs more work | Almost there | Confident to move on |
|---|---|---|---|---|
| describe asexual reproduction as a process that produces genetically identical offspring from one parent | 14.1 | | | |
| describe sexual reproduction as a process that involves fertilisation (the fusion of gamete nuclei), forming zygotes that are genetically different from one another | 14.1 | | | |
| explain what is meant by the terms *haploid* and *diploid*, and state that gametes are haploid and zygotes are diploid | 14.1 | | | |
| identify these parts on photographs or specimens of insect-pollinated flowers: sepals, petals, stamens, filaments, anthers, carpels, styles, stigmas, ovaries and ovules | 14.2 | | | |
| explain the functions of all of the parts of an insect-pollinated flower | 14.2 | | | |
| compare the structures of insect-pollinated and wind-pollinated flowers, including differences between their pollen grains | 14.2 | | | |
| describe how pollination takes place | 14.2 | | | |
| state that fertilisation in a flower happens when a nucleus from a pollen grain fuses with a nucleus in an ovule | 14.2 | | | |
| describe the growth of a pollen tube, and how this results in fertilisation | 14.2 | | | |
| investigate and describe the conditions that seeds need for germination (water, oxygen and a suitable temperature) | 14.2 | | | |
| compare the advantages and disadvantages of sexual reproduction and asexual reproduction, to a population of a species living in the wild | 14.3 | | | |
| compare the advantages and disadvantages to a gardener of using sexual reproduction and asexual reproduction to produce more plants | 14.3 | | | |
| compare the potential effects of self-pollination and cross-pollination | 14.3 | | | |

# Chapter 15
# Reproduction in humans

**IN THIS CHAPTER YOU WILL:**

- learn about the structure and function of the male and female reproductive systems
- consider how sperm and eggs are adapted for their functions
- find out how hormones are involved in reproduction
- study HIV as an example of a sexually transmitted infection.

# 15 Reproduction in humans

## GETTING STARTED

With a partner, think of a way to complete each of these two sentences. Try to include plenty of information in your sentences.

Gametes are …

Sexual reproduction is …

When you are happy with your own sentences, listen to the sentences suggested by other groups. Work together with all the other groups to construct a short paragraph that includes the best ideas from everyone's sentences.

## THE HOMUNCULUS THEORY

In 1654, a Dutch scientist, Anton van Leeuwenhoek, looked down his microscope at a sample of semen. He was the first person to see sperm, and he made careful drawings of them (Figure 15.1). However, he was too embarrassed to talk about his findings until a student, Johan Ham, spoke to him in 1677, about what he himself had seen when studying semen under the microscope. He said that he could see small animals with tails.

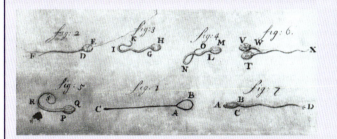

Figure 15.1: Leeuwenhoek's drawings of sperm.

Leeuwenhoek gradually overcame his reluctance to talk about his findings and shared them with other scientists. As more and more people continued these studies, various theories emerged about how human life began. One suggestion was that these 'small animals with tails' each contained a tiny human being – a homunculus. Indeed, in 1695 Nicholas Hartsoecker, a Dutch physicist, made a drawing of what he thought one might look like, though he made it clear that he never actually saw one through his microscope (Figure 15.2).

At this time, no one understood that an egg was also involved in creating a new life. This caused difficulties in explaining why children resembled both their father and their mother. One idea was the little developing homunculus gradually absorbed characteristics of its mother as it developed inside her uterus.

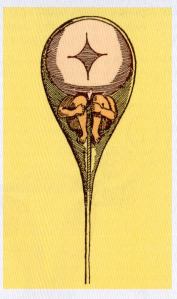

Figure 15.2: Nicholas Hartsoecker's drawing of a homunculus.

### Discussion questions

1 In the 17th century, scientists shared ideas by writing letters to each other, or by giving lectures. How do scientists share ideas today?

2 Nicholas Hartsoecker had no evidence for his drawing of a homunculus, yet many people believed his ideas. Even in the 21st century, ideas for which there is no evidence spread widely. Why do you think so many people are ready to believe these ideas?

## 15.1 The human reproductive systems

Humans, like all mammals, reproduce sexually. A new life begins when the nucleus of a male gamete fuses with a female one, forming a zygote. This is how every human being is formed.

### The female reproductive organs

Figure 15.3 shows the reproductive organs of a woman. The female gametes, called eggs or egg cells, are made in the two **ovaries**. Leading away from the ovaries are the **oviducts**, sometimes called Fallopian tubes. The tubes do not connect directly to the ovaries but have a funnel-shaped opening just a short distance away.

The two oviducts lead to the womb or **uterus**. This has very thick walls, made of muscle. It is quite small – only about the size of a clenched fist – but it can stretch a great deal when a woman is pregnant.

At the base of the uterus is a narrow opening, guarded by muscles. This is the neck of the uterus, or **cervix**. This narrow opening connects to the **vagina**, which then leads to the outside of the body.

The opening from the bladder, called the urethra, is a tube that is in front of the vagina, while the rectum is just behind it. These three tubes open quite separately to the outside.

### The male reproductive organs

Figures 15.4 and 15.5 show the reproductive organs of a man. The male gametes, called spermatozoa or sperm, are made in two **testes** (singular: **testis**). These are outside the body, in two sacs of skin called the **scrotum**.

> **KEY WORDS**
>
> **ovaries:** organs that produce female gametes (eggs)
>
> **oviducts:** tubes leading from the ovaries to the uterus; also known as Fallopian tubes
>
> **uterus:** the organ in which a fetus develops before birth; also known as the womb
>
> **cervix:** a narrow opening leading from the uterus to the vagina
>
> **vagina:** opening from the uterus to the outside of the body
>
> **testes** (singular: **testis**): organs in which the male gametes (sperm) are made
>
> **scrotum:** the sac that contains the testes

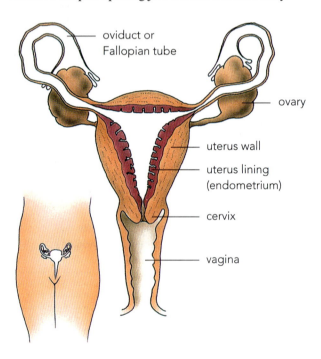

**Figure 15.3:** The female reproductive organs.

## 15 Reproduction in humans

## Human gametes

Eggs begin to be formed inside a girl's ovaries before she is born. At birth, she will already have thousands of partly developed eggs inside her ovaries.

When she reaches puberty (described later in this topic), some of these eggs begin to mature. Usually, only one develops at a time.

An egg is a single cell. Figure 15.6 shows the structure of an egg cell. When it is fully developed, it bursts out of the ovary and into the funnel at the end of the oviduct. This is called **ovulation**. In humans, it happens once a month throughout a woman's reproductive life.

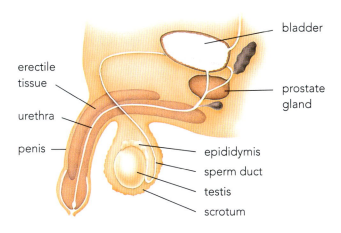

Figure 15.4: Side view of the male reproductive organs.

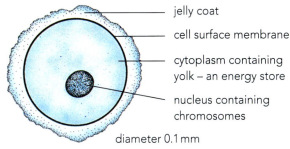

Figure 15.6: A human egg cell.

Figure 15.7 shows a section through a testis. It contains thousands of very narrow, coiled tubes or tubules. These are where the sperm are made. Sperm are then stored in the **epididymis**. Sperm develop from cells in the walls of the tubules. Sperm are made continually from puberty onwards. Figure 15.8 shows the structure of a sperm and describes how it is adapted for its function of fertilising an egg.

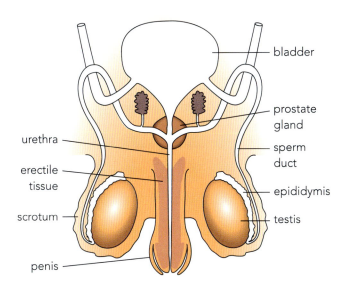

Figure 15.5: Front view of the male reproductive organs.

The sperm are carried away from each testis in a tube called the **sperm duct**. The sperm ducts from the testes join up with the urethra just below the bladder. The urethra continues downwards and opens at the tip of the **penis**. The urethra can carry both urine and sperm at different times.

Where the sperm ducts join the urethra, there is a gland called the **prostate gland**. This makes a fluid called semen, which the sperm swim in.

### KEY WORDS

**sperm duct:** a tube that transports sperm from the testis to the urethra

**penis:** organ containing the urethra, through which urine and sperm are carried

**prostate gland:** organ that produces a nutritious fluid in which sperm are transported

**ovulation:** the release of an egg from an ovary

**epididymis:** part of the testis in which sperm are stored

305

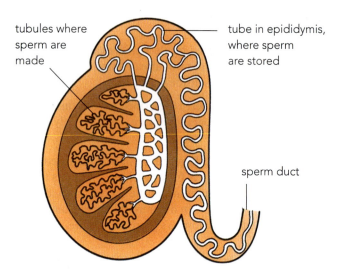

Figure 15.7: Section through a testis.

Sperm production is very sensitive to heat. If they get too hot, the cells in the tubules will not develop into sperm. This is why the testes are positioned outside the body, where they are cooler than they would be inside.

Eggs and sperm are haploid cells. Each human egg and each human sperm has a single set of 23 chromosomes in its nucleus. Eggs and sperm are made when cells in the ovaries and testes divide by meiosis.

> **KEY WORDS**
>
> **flagellum** (plural: **flagella**): a long, whip-like 'tail' structure found on sperm cells, used for swimming
>
> **acrosome**: a structure containing digestive enzymes, in the head of a sperm cell

## Fertilisation

After ovulation, the egg is caught in the funnel of the oviduct. Very slowly, the egg travels towards the uterus. Cilia lining the oviduct help to sweep it along. Muscles in the wall of the oviduct also help to move it, by producing gentle rippling movements.

If the egg is not fertilised by a sperm within 8–24 hours after ovulation, it dies. By this time, it has only travelled a short way along the oviduct. This means that a sperm must reach an egg while it is quite near the top of the oviduct if fertilisation is to be successful.

To bring the sperm as close as possible to the egg, the man's penis is placed inside the vagina of the woman. Sperm travel out of the penis into the vagina. This happens when muscles in the walls of the tubes containing the sperm contract rhythmically. The wave of contraction begins in the testes, travels along the sperm ducts, and into the penis. The sperm are squeezed along the tubes, out of the man's urethra and into the woman's vagina.

The fluid containing the sperm is called semen. The liquid part of semen is produced by the prostate gland, and it contains sugars and other nutrients to provide the sperm with energy. The semen is deposited at the top of the vagina, near the cervix.

The sperm are still quite a long way from the egg. They swim – using their flagella and energy released in their mitochondria – up through the cervix, through the uterus, and into the oviduct (Figures 15.9 and 15.10).

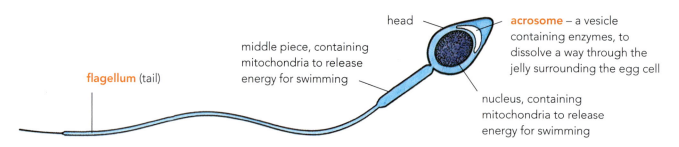

Figure 15.8: A human sperm. Sperm are motile (can move) and have adaptations to help them to swim.

# 15 Reproduction in humans

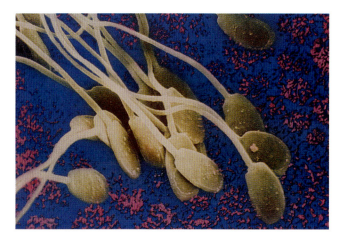

Figure 15.9: This photograph of human sperm swimming through an oviduct was taken using a scanning electron microscope.

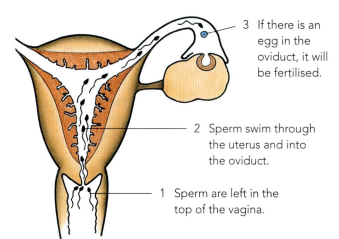

Figure 15.10: The route taken by sperm to get to an egg. The sperm are shown many times bigger than they really are, in relation to the female reproductive organs.

1. Sperm are left in the top of the vagina.
2. Sperm swim through the uterus and into the oviduct.
3. If there is an egg in the oviduct, it will be fertilised.

Sperm can only swim at a rate of about 4 mm per minute, so it takes quite a while for them to get as far as the oviducts. Many will never get there at all. But about a million sperm are deposited in the vagina at once, so there is a good chance that some of them will reach the egg.

When a sperm cell contacts the jelly coat surrounding an egg cell, the acrosome is activated. It releases its digestive enzymes, and these enzymes digest the jelly coat. This allows the head of the sperm to push through and get into the cytoplasm of the egg. Only the head of the sperm goes in; the flagellum is left outside. The nucleus of the sperm fuses with the nucleus of the egg. This is fertilisation (Figure 15.11).

As soon as the successful sperm enters the egg, the egg membrane and jelly coat become impenetrable, so that no other sperm can get in. The unsuccessful sperm will all die.

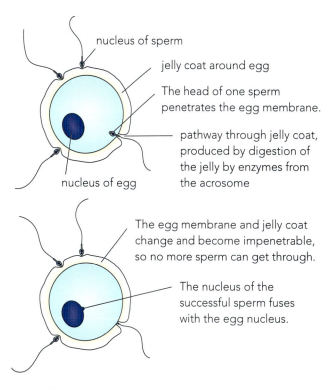

Figure 15.11: Fertilisation.

## Implantation

When the sperm nucleus and the egg nucleus have fused together, they form a zygote. The zygote continues to move slowly down the oviduct. As it goes, it divides repeatedly. After several hours, it has formed a ball of cells. This is called an **embryo**. The embryo obtains nutrients from the yolk of the egg.

> **KEY WORD**
>
> **embryo:** the ball of cells that is produced by repeated division of the zygote

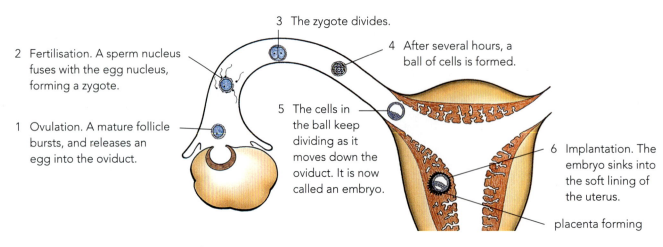

Figure 15.12: Stages leading to implantation.

It takes several hours for the embryo to reach the uterus, and by this time it is a ball of 16 or 32 cells. The uterus has a thick, spongy lining, and the embryo sinks into it. This is called **implantation** (Figure 15.12).

> **KEY WORD**
>
> **implantation:** attachment of the embryo to the lining of the uterus

## Questions

1. State precisely where eggs and sperm are made in a human.
2. Copy and complete each of these sentences.
   a. The liquid part of semen is produced in _____.
   b. Fertilisation happens in _____.
   c. Implantation happens in _____.
3. Construct a table to compare the structure of an egg and a sperm. Include a column which explains the reason for each difference.
4. Before fertilisation happens, both sperm and eggs are moving. Describe the differences in the way that the two types of gamete move.

## The placenta

The cells in the embryo, now buried in the soft wall of the uterus, continue to divide. As the embryo grows, a **placenta** also grows, which connects it to the wall of the uterus (Figure 15.13). The placenta is soft, dark red, and has finger-like projections called villi. The villi fit closely into the uterus wall. The placenta is where substances are exchanged between the mother's blood and the embryo's blood. It is the embryo's life support system.

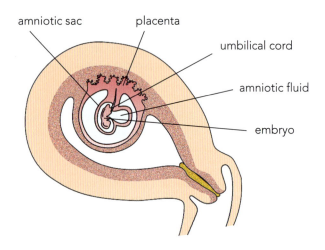

Figure 15.13: A developing embryo inside the uterus.

After 11 weeks, the embryo has developed most of its organs, and is now called a **fetus**. The placenta is joined to the fetus by the **umbilical cord**. Inside the cord are two arteries and a vein. The arteries take blood from the fetus into the placenta, and the vein returns the blood to the fetus.

## 15 Reproduction in humans

### KEY WORDS

**placenta:** an organ that connects the growing fetus to its mother, in which the blood of the fetus and mother are brought close together so that materials can be exchanged between them

**fetus:** an unborn mammal, in which all the organs have been formed

**umbilical cord:** a structure containing blood vessels that connects the fetus to the placenta

The placenta contains capillaries filled with the fetus's blood (Figure 15.14). The lining of the uterus contains large spaces filled with the mother's blood. The fetus's and mother's blood do not mix. They are separated by the wall of the placenta. But they are brought very close together, because the wall of the placenta is very thin.

Oxygen and dissolved nutrients in the mother's blood diffuse across the placenta into the fetus's blood and are then carried along the umbilical cord to the fetus. Carbon dioxide and other excretory products diffuse in the other direction and are carried away in the mother's blood.

Some unwanted substances can also cross the placenta. These include toxins such as alcohol and carbon monoxide. Some pathogens, such as the virus that causes rubella, can also pass across the placenta.

As the fetus grows, the placenta grows too. By the time the baby is born, the placenta is a flat disc, about 12 cm in diameter, and 3 cm thick.

### The amniotic sac

The fetus is surrounded by a strong membrane, called the **amniotic sac**. This makes a liquid called **amniotic fluid**. You can see these in Figure 15.13 and Figure 15.15.

Amniotic fluid helps to support the embryo, and to protect it from mechanical injury. The embryo floats in the fluid and is able to freely move its arms and legs, which helps the muscles and skeleton to develop correctly.

### KEY WORDS

**amniotic sac:** a tough membrane that surrounds a developing fetus in the uterus

**amniotic fluid:** liquid secreted by the amniotic sac, which supports and protects the fetus

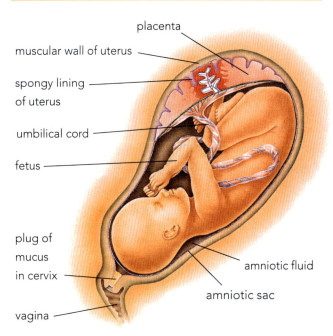

Figure 15.15: A fetus in the uterus, just before birth.

After nine months, when the fetus is ready to be born, contractions of muscles in the uterus wall often cause the amniotic sac to break, releasing the amniotic fluid so that it flows into the vagina. This is often the first sign that a woman is about to give birth.

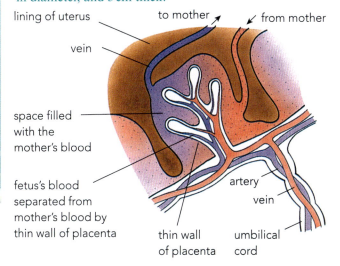

Figure 15.14: Part of the placenta. You can see how the placenta allows the mother's and fetus's blood to come very close to one another, without mixing.

## Questions

5. Explain the difference between a fetus and an embryo.
6. Make a list of **five** substances that are transferred from the mother's blood to the embryo's blood in the placenta.
7. State **two** substances that are transferred from the embryo's blood to the mother's blood.
8. Which human organ, other than the placenta, contains villi? Explain how the roles of the villi in this organ and the placenta are similar to one another.

## Testosterone and oestrogen

The functions of the reproductive organs are strongly affected by hormones. The main reproductive hormone produced in men is testosterone, while in women oestrogen and progesterone are secreted.

The time when a person approaches sexual maturity is called adolescence. Sperm production begins in a boy, and ovulation begins in a girl. The point at which sexual maturity is reached is called **puberty**. This is often a few years earlier in girls than in boys. A person is still not completely adult at this point, as there are still changes and development happening in the brain.

> **KEY WORD**
>
> **puberty:** the time at which sexual maturity is reached

The changes that happen during adolescence are brought about by hormones. In boys, testosterone is secreted by the testes. During adolescence, the quantity of testosterone that is secreted greatly increases, and this causes the secondary sexual characteristics to develop. These include growth of facial hair and pubic hair, broadening shoulders and general muscular development, and a deepening voice.

Oestrogen is secreted by the ovaries. It causes the breasts to grow larger, pubic hair to grow, and the hips to become wider.

## The menstrual cycle

Eggs develop in small structures called **follicles**, in the ovaries. After a girl reaches puberty, one egg is usually released from a follicle into the oviduct every month. Before the egg cell is released, the lining of the uterus becomes thick and spongy, so that it is ready to receive a zygote. It is full of tiny blood vessels, which will supply the embryo with nutrients and oxygen if it should arrive.

However, if the egg cell is not fertilised, the spongy lining is not needed. It gradually breaks down and is slowly lost through the vagina. This is called **menstruation**, or a period. It usually lasts for about five days. After menstruation, the lining of the uterus builds up again, so that it will be ready to receive the next egg, if it is fertilised.

Figure 15.16 shows what happens during the human menstrual cycle.

> **KEY WORDS**
>
> **follicle:** a structure within an ovary, in which an egg develops
>
> **menstruation:** the loss of the broken down uterus lining through the vagina

## Questions

9. State **one** function of testosterone, and **one** function of oestrogen.
10. Describe what is happening in an ovary during the menstrual cycle, when each of these events is happening in the uterus:
    a. The uterus lining is breaking down.
    b. The uterus lining is building up again.
    c. The uterus lining is remaining thick and well supplied with blood.

The recurring events of the menstrual cycle are controlled by four hormones – oestrogen, progesterone, **FSH** and **LH**.

Oestrogen and progesterone are secreted by the ovaries. FSH and LH are secreted by a small gland attached to the base of the brain, called the **pituitary gland**.

During the first part of the cycle, following menstruation, both FSH and LH are produced (Figure 15.17, top graph). FSH causes a follicle to develop in the ovary, with a developing female gamete (egg) inside it.

15 Reproduction in humans

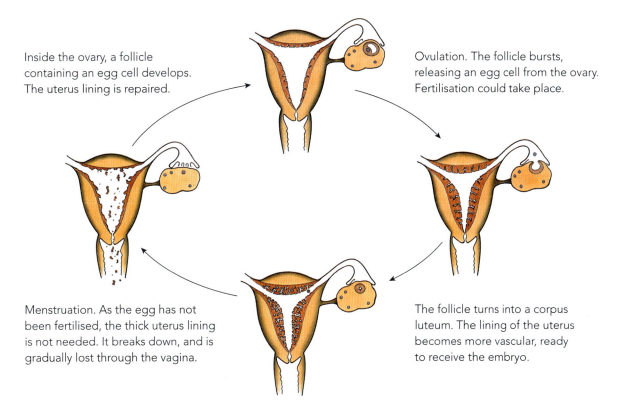

Inside the ovary, a follicle containing an egg cell develops. The uterus lining is repaired.

Ovulation. The follicle bursts, releasing an egg cell from the ovary. Fertilisation could take place.

Menstruation. As the egg has not been fertilised, the thick uterus lining is not needed. It breaks down, and is gradually lost through the vagina.

The follicle turns into a corpus luteum. The lining of the uterus becomes more vascular, ready to receive the embryo.

Figure 15.16: The menstrual cycle.

The developing follicle secretes oestrogen in increasing amounts (Figure 15.17, second graph). Oestrogen causes the lining of the uterus to become thicker and better supplied with blood (Figure 15.17, bottom graph).

When the follicle is fully developed, there is a surge in production of LH. This causes ovulation. When ovulation has taken place, the oestrogen level starts to fall.

The follicle from which the egg was released develops into a structure called a **corpus luteum**. This secretes progesterone, so the concentration of progesterone increases. Progesterone keeps the lining of the uterus thick and spongy, ready to receive a fertilised egg.

The increase in progesterone inhibits the pituitary gland, which causes FSH and LH production to decrease.

If the egg is not fertilised, the corpus luteum breaks down, so the secretion of progesterone drops, and menstruation occurs. Because progesterone is now not inhibiting their secretion, the levels of FSH and LH start to increase and the whole cycle runs through again.

However, if the egg is fertilised, progesterone levels stay high. This happens because the corpus luteum remains in the ovary and continues to secrete progesterone.

Progesterone helps to maintain the thick uterus lining, so that the embryo can implant into it. Once the placenta has developed, this takes over the role of secreting progesterone, which it does throughout pregnancy, until the baby is born.

The high levels of progesterone during pregnancy inhibit the secretion of FSH by the pituitary gland, so no more follicles develop in the ovary.

### KEY WORDS

**FSH:** follicle stimulating hormone, a hormone secreted by the pituitary gland which causes a follicle to develop in an ovary

**LH:** luteinising hormone, a hormone secreted by the pituitary gland that causes ovulation to happen

**pituitary gland:** a small endocrine gland attached to the underside of the brain

**corpus luteum:** a structure that develops from the empty follicle after an egg has been released from an ovary; also known as a yellow body

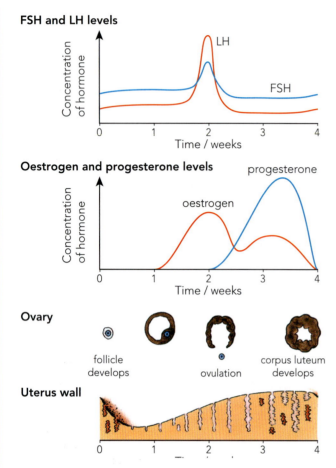

Figure 15.17: Changes in hormonal levels and the uterus lining during the menstrual cycle.

## 15.2 Sexually transmitted infections

**Sexually transmitted infections**, or STIs for short, are infections caused by bacteria or viruses that can be passed from one person to another during sexual contact. By far the most important of these infections is HIV/AIDS.

The disease **AIDS** (acquired immune deficiency syndrome) is caused by **HIV**. HIV stands for human immunodeficiency virus. Figure 15.18 shows this virus.

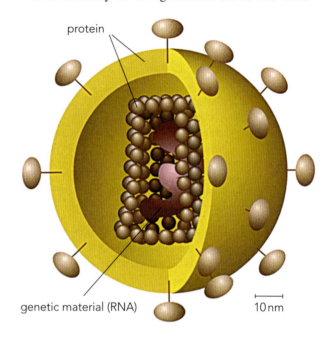

Figure 15.18: The human immunodeficiency virus, HIV. The letters nm stand for nanometre, and there are $10^6$ nanometres in one millimetre.

## Questions

11  Look at Figure 15.17.
   a  Explain what causes the lining of the uterus to remain thick, following menstruation.
   b  Explain why it is important that the lining of the uterus remains thick at this time.
   c  Describe the function of the corpus luteum.
   d  Compare what happens to the corpus luteum when an egg is **not** fertilised, and when an egg is fertilised.

> ### KEY WORDS
>
> **sexually transmitted infection (STI):** a disease caused by pathogens that are transmitted during sexual contact
>
> **AIDS:** acquired immune deficiency syndrome; a disease caused by HIV, which destroys white blood cells and therefore reduces the ability of the immune system to defend against other pathogens
>
> **HIV:** the human immunodeficiency virus

HIV infects white blood cells, and in particular a type called T cells. Over a long period of time, HIV slowly destroys T cells. Several years after infection with the virus, the numbers of certain kinds of T cells are so low that they are unable to fight against other pathogens effectively.

T cells are normally our strongest defence against viruses. Because HIV attacks the very cells which would normally kill viruses, it is very difficult for someone's own immune system to protect them against HIV.

About ten years after initial infection with HIV, an untreated person is likely to develop symptoms of AIDS. They become very vulnerable to other infections, such as pneumonia. They may develop cancer, because one function of the immune system is to destroy body cells that may be beginning to produce cancers. Brain cells are also quite often damaged by HIV. A person with AIDS usually dies from a collection of several illnesses.

Today, however, there are excellent drugs to control HIV, called antiretrovirals. They stop the virus from multiplying inside the person's cells. A person who takes these regularly is likely to live a healthy and normal life.

Researchers are working on the production of a vaccine against HIV infection, and there have been promising signs in early trials. By the time you read this, perhaps a vaccine will have become available.

# Preventing HIV transmission

The virus that causes AIDS cannot live outside the human body. In fact, it is an especially fragile virus – much less tough than the cold virus, for example.

In general, there is no danger of anyone becoming infected with HIV from normal contact with someone with AIDS. You can quite safely talk to the person, shake hands with them, drink from cups which they have used and so on.

A person can only become infected with HIV through direct contact of their body fluids with those of someone with the virus. A person with HIV is said to be HIV positive. A person can become HIV positive in one of the following ways.

## Through sexual contact

HIV can live in the fluid inside the vagina, rectum and urethra. During sexual intercourse, fluids from one partner come into contact with fluids of the other. It is very easy for the virus to be passed on in this way.

The more sexual partners a person has, the higher the chance of them becoming infected with HIV. Higher percentages of people have developed AIDS where it is common to have multiple sexual partners.

The best way of avoiding AIDS is never to have more than one sexual partner. If everyone did that, then HIV would immediately stop spreading. Using a condom (a sheath that covers the penis and prevents semen from escaping) is a good way of lowering the chances of the virus passing from one person to another during sexual intercourse – though it does not offer complete protection.

It is also important that anyone who is infected with HIV knows that they have this virus in their body, so that they can avoid passing it on to anyone else. If someone discovers that they are HIV positive, health workers will try to trace the people who they could have passed the infection on to, and make sure that they are all tested for the virus. This can reduce the spread of HIV through a population.

## Through blood contact

Many cases of AIDS have been caused by HIV being transferred directly from one person's blood to another. In the 1970s and 1980s, when AIDS first appeared, and before anyone knew what was causing it, blood containing HIV was used in transfusions. People being given the transfusions were infected with HIV, and later developed AIDS. Now all blood used in transfusions in most countries is screened for HIV before it is used.

The virus can also pass from a mother to her child during childbirth, when the blood of the mother comes into contact with the baby. The chance of this happening is greatly reduced if the mother takes antiretroviral drugs during her pregnancy.

Blood can also be transferred from one person to another if they share hypodermic needles. This most commonly happens in people who inject drugs. Many drug users have died from AIDS. It is essential that any hypodermic needle used for injection is sterile. People who have to deal with accidents, such as police and paramedics, must always be on their guard against HIV if there is blood around. They often wear protective clothing, just in case a bleeding accident victim is infected with HIV.

## Through breast feeding

If a woman is infected with HIV, the virus can get into her breast milk and so be passed on to her baby. The chance of this happening is greatly reduced if the mother takes antiretroviral drugs during her pregnancy and while breast feeding.

## ACTIVITY 15.1

### Breast feeding or not?

Work in a group of two or three for this activity.

In some countries, mothers who are HIV positive are advised not to breast feed their babies, but instead to feed them with formula milk in a bottle. In other countries, the advantages of breast feeding are considered to outweigh the risk of passing on HIV.

In your group, discuss why the advice may be different in different countries.

Listen to the ideas from other groups, and also share your own group's ideas.

Write a short summary of the possible reasons your class has thought of, to explain why the advice given in different countries may not be the same.

### Self-assessment

How well did you work with your group? Did you:

- contribute by giving your own points of view?
- listen to other people's points of view?
- think carefully about these, even if you did not agree with them to begin with?

## SUMMARY

| |
|---|
| The male reproductive system consists of the testes, scrotum, sperm ducts, prostate gland, urethra and penis. |
| Sperm are made and stored in the testes, which are enclosed in the scrotum. Sperm ducts carry sperm to the urethra in the penis. The prostate gland makes a liquid in which sperm are carried, forming semen. |
| The female reproductive system includes the ovaries, oviducts, uterus, cervix and vagina. |
| Eggs are made in the ovaries and released into the oviducts. |
| Sperm are motile. They have a flagellum which is used for swimming; many mitochondria to release energy by aerobic respiration; and an acrosome containing enzymes to help entry to an egg. |
| Eggs have a jelly coat to control the entry of sperm, and nutrient stores to provide energy for the first few days after fertilisation. |
| Sperm are produced in much larger numbers than eggs. Unlike eggs, sperm can swim actively, and they are much smaller than eggs. |
| Fertilisation happens when the nucleus of a sperm fuses with the nucleus of an egg. A sperm cell releases enzymes from its acrosome, which digests a pathway through the jelly coat of the egg, allowing the sperm head to enter the egg. The entry of the sperm head causes a change in the egg membrane and jelly coat, preventing more sperm entering. |
| The zygote formed at fertilisation divides repeatedly to form a ball of cells called an embryo. This implants into the lining of the uterus. |
| After implantation, a placenta develops, in which the blood of the fetus is brought close to the blood of the mother, but without mixing. Nutrients and oxygen diffuse from the mother's blood to the fetus's blood, and excretory products diffuse in the other direction. Blood vessels in the umbilical cord transport dissolved substances between the fetus and the placenta. |
| The amniotic sac secretes amniotic fluid which supports and protects the fetus. |

## CONTINUED

| |
|---|
| Testosterone is secreted by the testes and causes the development of male secondary sexual characteristics during puberty. Oestrogen is secreted by the ovaries and causes the development of female secondary sexual characteristics. |
| During the first five days of the menstrual cycle, the lining of the uterus breaks down and is lost through the vagina. At about day 14, an egg is released from an ovary, after which the follicle from which the egg came changes into a corpus luteum. The cycle lasts about 28 days, after which it begins again. |
| FSH secreted by the pituitary gland causes a follicle to develop in an ovary. When the follicle is fully developed, the pituitary gland produces a surge of LH, which causes ovulation. |
| Oestrogen concentrations increase during the first half of the menstrual cycle, after which they fall. Progesterone concentrations rise after ovulation, as the corpus luteum secretes this hormone. Progesterone is also secreted by the placenta during pregnancy. |
| STIs, such as HIV/AIDS, are transmitted through sexual contact. |
| HIV is a viral pathogen that causes AIDS. It can be transmitted by sexual contact, direct blood-to-blood contact, or through breast feeding. Tracing contacts, using condoms, using antiretroviral drugs and avoiding sharing needles can help to reduce its spread. |

## PROJECT

### Comparing plant and human reproduction

You are going to work with a partner or in a group of three, to produce a presentation or display about the similarities and differences between flowering plant reproduction and human reproduction.

**Figure 15.19:** Are there any similarities in the way that humans and plants reproduce?

Begin by brainstorming ideas. On two pieces of paper, or two pages in your notebook, write the headings 'Similarities' and 'Differences'.

Write down anything you can think of that fits into those two categories. Some of them will be quite general – for example plants can reproduce both asexually and sexually, but humans can reproduce only sexually. Both humans and plants produce haploid gametes. Others may be more specific, such as a comparison of the structures of the gametes, or how fertilisation takes place.

When you have your list, think about how you will organise the points and how you will present and/or display your comparison. You should be able to come up with several ideas, and then decide on the best one. It would be excellent if different groups in your class use different ways of presenting their comparison.

> REFLECTION
>
> Linking different parts of the syllabus can be tricky, but it can help you to understand each part a little better. How well do you think that you reviewed the plant reproduction topic, so that you could link it to human reproduction? Did you find that doing this helped you to understand the two topics better than you did before tackling this Project? If so, can you see ways in which you could use a similar approach for increasing your understanding of other topics?

## EXAM-STYLE QUESTIONS

1 What implants into the lining of the uterus, after fertilisation?
   A  a fetus
   B  an embryo
   C  a placenta
   D  a zygote [1]

2 In which organ does fertilisation take place?
   A  cervix
   B  ovary
   C  oviduct
   D  uterus [1]

3 Why is it almost impossible for more than one sperm to fertilise an egg?
   A  The jelly coat thickens after one sperm has entered the egg.
   B  There is not enough space for more than one sperm inside the egg.
   C  The sperm change after fertilisation, so their acrosomes do not function.
   D  The sperm stop swimming once one of them has entered the egg. [1]

4 Which is **not** a method of transmission of STIs?
   A  breast feeding
   B  sexual contact
   C  sharing a drinking cup
   D  sharing hypodermic needles [1]

5 Which row shows substances that pass from the fetus to the mother, and from the mother to the fetus, across the placenta?

|   | from fetus to mother | from mother to fetus |
|---|---|---|
| A | carbon dioxide | red blood cells |
| B | glucose | carbon dioxide |
| C | oxygen | amino acids |
| D | urea | oxygen |

[1]

## 15 Reproduction in humans

### CONTINUED

**6** Copy and complete these sentences about the male reproductive system. You can use each of the words in the list once, more than once or not at all.

**oestrogen   oviducts   primary   progesterone
prostate   secondary   sperm   sperm ducts
testes   testosterone   ureter   urethra**

Sperm are made in the _____ and can travel along the _____ _____ and then through the _____ to the outside world. The _____ gland adds fluid to the sperm.

The testes make a hormone called _____. This causes _____ production to begin, and also causes the development of _____ sexual characteristics. [7]

**7** This diagram shows a human sperm.

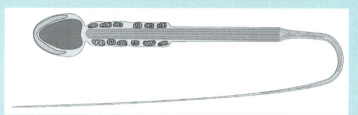

a Make a copy of the diagram. On your diagram label the following parts:

**cell membrane   cytoplasm   nucleus
mitochondrion   flagellum   acrosome** [3]

b With reference to your diagram, *explain* how the structure of a sperm adapts it for its function. [4]

c *Describe* how a human egg cell is adapted for its function. [3]

[Total: 10]

**8** The graph below shows the concentrations of oestrogen and progesterone in a woman's blood, during a 28-day menstrual cycle.

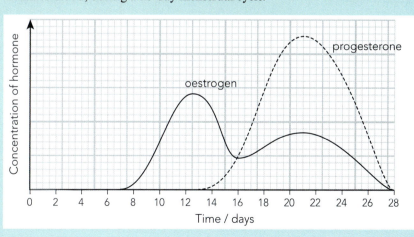

### COMMAND WORDS

**explain:** set out purposes or reasons / make the relationships between things evident / provide why and/or how and support with relevant evidence

**describe:** state the points of a topic / give characteristics and main features

## CONTINUED

a  Name the organ that secretes oestrogen and progesterone.  [1]

b  Describe what is happening in the following organs during the first 14 days of the cycle.

   i   the uterus  [2]

   ii  the ovaries  [2]

c  Describe the role of progesterone during the menstrual cycle.  [2]

[Total: 7]

9  The graph below shows the number of people in the world who became infected with HIV, who were living with HIV/AIDS and who died from AIDS, between 1990 and 2017. Note that, to **calculate** the numbers of people living with HIV, you have to multiply the number on the *y*-axis scale by 10.

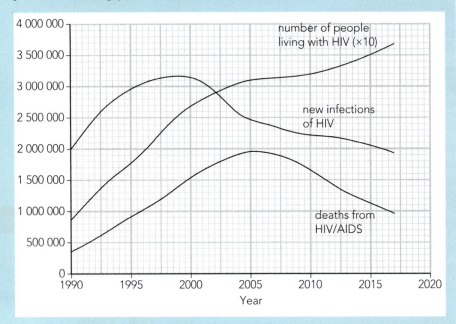

a  With reference to the graph, describe the changes in the number of new infections of HIV.  [3]

b  **Suggest** why the actual number of people infected with HIV could possibly be greater than the numbers shown on the graph.  [2]

c  Explain how infection with HIV leads to the symptoms of AIDS.  [5]

d  **Compare** the trends shown by the number of people living with HIV/AIDS with the number of deaths from HIV/AIDS. Suggest reasons for the differences that you describe.  [5]

[Total: 15]

**COMMAND WORD**

**calculate:** work out from given facts, figures or information

**COMMAND WORDS**

**suggest:** apply knowledge and understanding to situations where there are a range of valid responses in order to make proposals / put forward considerations

**compare:** identify/ comment on similarities and/or differences

# 15 Reproduction in humans

## SELF-EVALUATION CHECKLIST

After studying this chapter, think about how confident you are with the different topics. This will help you to see any gaps in your knowledge and help you to learn more effectively.

| I can | See Topic… | Needs more work | Almost there | Confident to move on |
|---|---|---|---|---|
| name the parts of the male reproductive system, and describe their functions | 15.1 | | | |
| name the parts of the female reproductive system, and describe their functions | 15.1 | | | |
| explain the adaptive features of eggs and sperm, and compare them | 15.1 | | | |
| describe what happens at fertilisation | 15.1 | | | |
| describe how the zygote forms an embryo, which implants into the uterus lining | 15.1 | | | |
| state the functions of the umbilical cord, placenta, amniotic sac and amniotic fluid | 15.1 | | | |
| describe how dissolved nutrients, gases and excretory products are exchanged between the blood of the mother and the blood of the fetus, in the placenta | 15.1 | | | |
| name a virus that can pass across the placenta | 15.1 | | | |
| describe the functions of testosterone and oestrogen at puberty | 15.1 | | | |
| describe the changes that take place in the ovaries and uterus during the menstrual cycle | 15.1 | | | |
| describe the sites of production of oestrogen and progesterone during the menstrual cycle and during pregnancy | 15.1 | | | |
| explain the roles of FSH, LH, oestrogen and progesterone in the menstrual cycle and pregnancy | 15.1 | | | |
| explain what is meant by a sexually transmitted infection (STI) | 15.2 | | | |
| state that HIV is a pathogen that can cause AIDS | 15.2 | | | |
| explain how HIV is transmitted, and how its transmission can be controlled | 15.2 | | | |

> # Chapter 16
# Chromosomes, genes and proteins

### IN THIS CHAPTER YOU WILL:

- learn about chromosomes and genes
- use genetic diagrams to predict how characteristics are inherited
- > find out about how and why cells divide by mitosis and meiosis
- > learn how genes determine the proteins that are made in a cell.

# 16 Chromosomes, genes and proteins

## GETTING STARTED

Earlier in your course, you have learnt about these structures or substances.

**chromosome    ribosome    DNA    protein    enzyme    gamete    zygote**

Choose one of these words, but do not tell anyone which one you have chosen.

Now ask a partner or the rest of your group, to ask you questions to try to find out which word you are thinking of. You can only answer 'yes' or 'no'. The questions have to be about the meaning of the word, not the word itself – so they cannot ask you if it begins with the letter c, for example.

## BREEDING CHINCHILLAS

Chinchillas are small rodents, with very soft and thick fur. In the wild, they live in the Andes mountains in South America. They make good pets.

Imagine that a breeder wants to produce some unusual types of chinchilla. These can be worth more when the breeder sells them.

All the chinchillas that the breeder has are the normal, pale grey colour. But the breeder has a customer who wants to buy some chinchillas with charcoal (very dark grey) coats.

The breeder buys a male chinchilla with charcoal fur. He breeds this with one of his grey females. To his disappointment, all the offspring are pale grey (Figure 16.1).

**Figure 16.1:** A cross between a normal, grey chinchilla and a charcoal chinchilla is likely to produce grey offspring.

The breeder reads up about the genetics of chinchilla fur colour. He learns that, although all of the offspring from his grey and charcoal chinchilla parents are grey, in fact they are carrying a 'hidden' gene for charcoal fur. To get more charcoal chinchillas, he needs to breed these offspring with their father or another charcoal chinchilla. He tries this and is successful – half of the offspring of this cross have grey fur, and half have charcoal fur.

### Discussion questions

1. What do you think determines the coat colour of a chinchilla?

2. Do you think that all the features of a chinchilla are determined in this way?

## 16.1 Chromosomes and cell division

The nucleus of every cell contains a number of long threads called **chromosomes**. Most of the time, the chromosomes are too thin to be seen except with an electron microscope. But when a cell is dividing, they get shorter and fatter so they can be seen with a light microscope. Figure 16.2 shows human chromosomes seen with a powerful electron microscope.

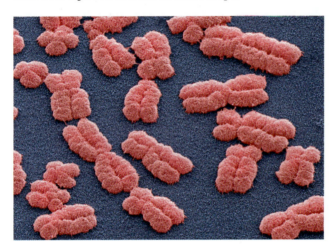

**Figure 16.2:** A scanning electron micrograph of human chromosomes, just before a cell divides. Each chromosome is made of two identical, thick threads joined together – these will split apart so that each cell gets a thread, when the cell divides.

Each chromosome in a cell contains one very long molecule of **DNA**. The DNA molecule carries a code that instructs the cell about which kinds of proteins it should make, and you can find out how it does this in Topic 16.3. Each chromosome carries instructions for making many different proteins. A part of a DNA molecule with the instructions for making one kind of protein is called a **gene**.

The genes on your chromosomes determine all sorts of things about you – for example, what colour your eyes or hair are, whether you have a turned-up nose or a straight one, and whether or not you have a genetic disease such as cystic fibrosis. You inherited these genes from your parents.

Most genes come in more than one form or variety. The different forms of a gene are called **alleles**. For example, the gene coding for a protein that determines the colour of a chinchilla's fur might have alleles for charcoal (very dark grey) or pale grey fur.

Each species of organism has its own number and variety of genes. This is what makes their body chemistry, their appearance and their behaviour different from those of other species. Humans have many chromosomes and tens of thousands of genes. We each have 46 chromosomes inside each of our cells, all with many genes on them. Every cell in your body has an exact copy of all your genes.

All humans have the genes for the same characteristics, but we all differ in the alleles of those genes that we have. No one in the world has exactly the same combination of alleles that you have – unless you have an identical twin.

> **KEY WORDS**
>
> **chromosome:** a length of DNA, found in the nucleus of a cell; it contains genetic information in the form of many different genes
>
> **DNA:** a molecule that contains genetic information, in the form of genes, that controls the proteins that are made in the cell
>
> **gene:** a length of DNA that codes for one protein
>
> **alleles:** alternative forms of a gene

## Questions

1. In which part of a cell is DNA found?
2. Arrange these in order of size, smallest first:

   cell    nucleus    DNA molecule    chromosome    gene

3. Explain why your appearance is not the same as the appearance of anyone else in the world.

# Chromosomes in haploid and diploid cells

We have seen that humans have 46 chromosomes in each cell. These 46 chromosomes are two sets of 23. One of these sets came from your mother, and the other set from your father.

You began your life as a single cell – a zygote – formed by the fusion of an egg cell and a sperm cell. The nuclei of each of these gametes contained a single complete set of 23 chromosomes. When they fused together, they produced a zygote with 46 chromosomes.

A cell with a single set of chromosomes, such as a gamete, is said to be haploid. The nucleus of the zygote that was formed when the egg cell and sperm cell fused together was diploid. The zygote was a diploid cell.

Figures 16.3 and 16.4 show the chromosomes in a cell of a woman and of a man. In each picture, the chromosomes have been arranged in order, largest first. They have also been arranged in pairs, with similar chromosomes from the two sets placed side by side. In each pair, one is from the person's mother and the other from their father. The two chromosomes of a pair are called homologous chromosomes.

> ### ACTIVITY 16.1
>
> #### Looking at chromosomes
>
> Work with a partner.
>
> First look carefully at the images in Figures 16.2, 16.3 and 16.4, and think about these questions on your own:
>
> - What similarities and differences can you see in the images of the chromosomes in Figure 16.2, compared with the images in Figures 16.3 and 16.4? (The colour has been added artificially to the photographs, so this is not a significant difference between them.)
> - In Figures 16.3 and 16.4, how do you think the numbers written underneath each pair of chromosomes have been decided on?
> - What differences can you see between Figures 16.3 and 16.4?
>
> Now turn to your partner and discuss your answers together.

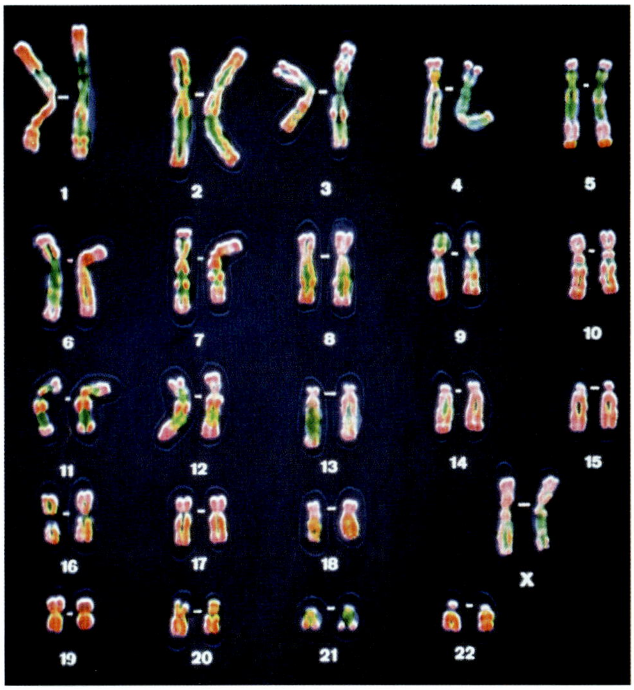

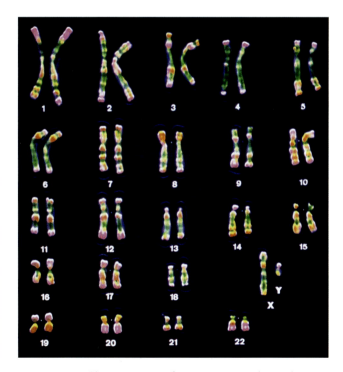

Figure 16.3: Chromosomes of a woman, arranged in order. The photograph was taken using a light microscope.

Figure 16.4: Chromosomes of a man, arranged in order.

## Mitosis

Think again about those two gametes fusing together in the very first moments of your life. Soon after the zygote was formed, it began to divide over and over again, producing a ball of cells that eventually grew into you. Each time a cell divided, the two new cells were provided with a perfect copy of the two sets of chromosomes in the original zygote. The new cells produced were all genetically identical.

This type of cell division, which produces genetically identical cells, is called mitosis. Mitosis is the way in which any plant or animal cell divides when an organism is growing or repairing a damaged part of its body. Mitosis produces new cells to make the body grow larger, or to replace damaged cells. For example, if you cut yourself, new skin cells will be made by mitosis to help to heal the wound.

Mitosis is also used in asexual reproduction. You have seen, for example, how a potato plant can reproduce by growing stem tubers which eventually produce new plants (Chapter 14). All the cells in the new tubers are produced by mitosis, so they are all genetically identical.

Just before mitosis takes place, each of the chromosomes in the parent cell are copied. This must happen so that there are enough chromosomes to be shared out into the new cells – for example, in a human, each cell needs to get 46 chromosomes of its own. Each copy remains attached to the original one, so each chromosome is made up of two identical threads joined together (Figures 16.2 and 16.5). The two identical threads are called chromatids, and the point where they are held together is called the centromere.

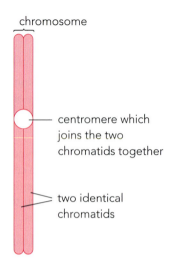

Figure 16.5: A chromosome just before cell division.

On the left of Figure 16.6, you can see a diagram of a cell with four chromosomes. There are two sets of two chromosomes – the blue ones belong to one set, and the pink ones belong to the other set. The rest of the diagram shows what happens when this cell divides by mitosis.

At the end of mitosis, two new cells have been formed from one parent cell. The new cells are sometimes called daughter cells. Each daughter cell has one copy of each of the four chromosomes. As the new cells grow, they make new copies of each chromosome, ready to divide again.

Strictly speaking, we should think of mitosis as being a division of the *nucleus* of a cell, not of the cell itself.

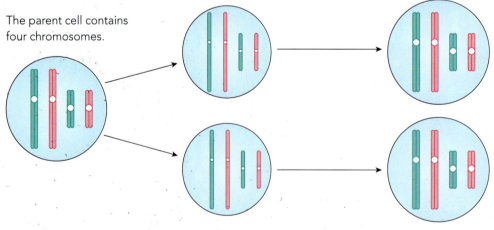

Figure 16.6: Chromosomes during the life of a cell dividing by mitosis.

This is because sometimes a nucleus divides to form two nuclei, which both stay inside the same cell. This happens, for example, when pollen grains develop. But normally the whole cell divides, not just the nucleus. So, we end up with new cells each with a nucleus containing perfect copies of the chromosomes that were present in the original cell.

## Questions

4  A cell that contains 32 chromosomes divides by mitosis. How many chromosomes are there in each of the two daughter cells produced?

5  Explain, in your own words, why it is important that the two chromatids in a chromosome each contain exactly the same genetic information.

6  Before a human cell divides by mitosis, the 46 chromosomes each form two genetically identical chromatids. Suggest why it is important that these two chromatids remain held together until the cell is ready to split into two.

## Meiosis

In Chapter 14, we saw that sexual reproduction always involves gametes. Gametes have only half the number of chromosomes of a normal body cell. They are haploid cells. Gametes have one set of chromosomes instead of two sets. This is so that when they fuse together, the zygote formed has two sets.

Human gametes are formed by the division of cells in the ovaries and testes. The cells divide by a special type of cell division called meiosis. Meiosis shares out the chromosomes so that each new cell gets just one chromosome of each homologous pair. The new cells therefore each have a single set of chromosomes. The diploid parent cell produces haploid daughter cells.

Meiosis is said to be a **reduction division**. This means that the number of chromosomes is halved – or reduced – as a result of meiosis. In humans, for example, a diploid cell with 46 chromosomes divides by meiosis to form haploid daughter cells each with 23 chromosomes.

### KEY WORDS

**reduction division:** a term used to describe what happens in meiosis, where the number of chromosomes is halved (reduced)

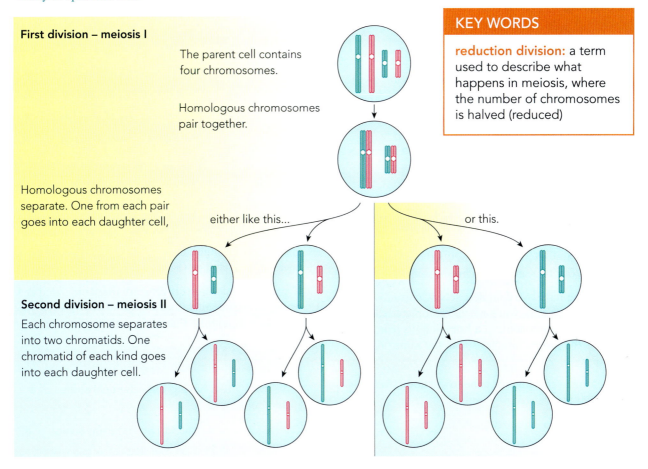

Figure 16.7: How meiosis produces haploid cells from a diploid cell.

> You do not need to know any details of what happens during meiosis. However, Figure 16.7 may help you understand how it works. This diagram shows how a diploid cell with four chromosomes can divide by meiosis to produce four haploid cells, each with two chromosomes. The cell actually divides twice – first to separate the chromosomes from their homologous partners (this is the reduction division) and then to split the chromatids in each chromosome apart.

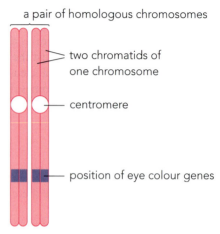

Figure 16.8: Homologous chromosomes have genes for the same characteristic in the same position. Here, the position of a gene that codes for eye colour is shown. There would be hundreds of other genes on each chromosome.

You may remember that one of each pair of homologous chromosomes came from the person's mother, and one from their father. During meiosis, the new cells get a mixture of these. So, a sperm cell could contain a chromosome 1 from the man's father and a chromosome 2 from his mother, and so on. There are all sorts of different possible combinations. This is one of the reasons why gametes are genetically different from the parent cell. Meiosis produces genetic variation in the gametes and in the offspring.

## Questions

7   Explain why meiosis is called a 'reduction division'.
8   A cell has a diploid number of 28. How many chromosomes will there be in each of the daughter cells produced by meiosis?
9   Explain why it is important that human gametes are produced by meiosis, and not by mitosis.

## 16.2 Inheriting genes

We have seen that chromosomes each contain many genes. We think there are about 20 000 human genes, carried on our two sets of 23 chromosomes.

Because you have two complete sets of chromosomes in each of your cells, you have two complete sets of genes. Each chromosome in a homologous pair contains genes for the same characteristic in the same positions (Figure 16.8).

Let us look at one kind of gene to see how it behaves, and how it is inherited.

## Genes and alleles

In chinchillas, genes determine the colour of the fur. The genes are sets of coded instructions for producing the proteins that cause different fur colours. We have seen that there are different forms of the fur colour gene, and that these different forms are called alleles.

We can refer to these alleles using letters as symbols. For example, we can call the allele that gives grey fur **G**, and the allele that gives charcoal fur **g**.

Because there are *two* of every kind of chromosome in each cell in a chinchilla's body, there are also *two* genes giving instructions about which kind of fur colour protein to make. This means that there are *three* possible combinations of alleles. A chinchilla might have two **G** alleles, **GG**. It might have one of each, **Gg**. Or it might have two **g** alleles, **gg** (Figure 16.9).

If the two alleles for this gene are the same – that is, **GG** or **gg** – the chinchilla is said to be **homozygous**. If the two alleles are different – that is, **Gg** – then it is **heterozygous**.

> ### KEY WORDS
>
> **homozygous:** having two identical alleles of a particular gene (e.g. GG or gg)
>
> **heterozygous:** having two different alleles of a particular gene (e.g. Gg)

# 16 Chromosomes, genes and proteins

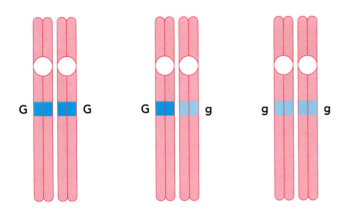

**Figure 16.9:** Genotypes for the fur colour gene in chinchillas.

This happens because the allele **G** is dominant to the allele **g**. A dominant allele has just as much effect on phenotype when there is only one of it as when there are two of it. A chinchilla that is homozygous for a **dominant allele** has the same phenotype as a chinchilla that is heterozygous. A heterozygous chinchilla is said to be a carrier of the charcoal colour because it has the allele for it but does not have charcoal fur.

The allele **g** is recessive. A **recessive allele** only affects the phenotype when there is no dominant allele present. Only chinchillas with the genotype **gg** – homozygous recessive – have charcoal fur.

> **KEY WORDS**
>
> **genotype:** the genetic makeup of an organism in terms of the alleles present (e.g. **GG**)
>
> **phenotype:** the observable features of an organism
>
> **dominant allele:** an allele that is expressed if it is present (e.g. **G**)
>
> **recessive allele:** an allele that is only expressed when there is no dominant allele of the gene present (e.g. **g**)

## Genotype and phenotype

The genes that that a chinchilla has are its **genotype**. Its genotype for fur colour could be **GG**, **Gg** or **gg**.

If its genotype is **GG**, then it has light grey fur. If its genotype is **gg** it has charcoal fur. If its genotype is **Gg** it has light grey fur.

The features the chinchilla has are called its **phenotype**. The phenotype of an organism can include what it looks like – for example, the colour of its fur – as well as things which we cannot actually see, such as what kind of protein it has in its cell membranes.

You can see that, in this example, the chinchilla's phenotype for fur colour depends entirely on its genotype. This is not always true. Sometimes, other things, such as what it eats, can affect its phenotype. However, for the moment, we will only consider the effect that genotype has on phenotype, and not worry about effects that the environment might have.

## Dominant and recessive alleles

We have seen that there are three different possible genotypes for chinchilla fur colour, but only two phenotypes. We can summarise this as follows:

| genotype | phenotype |
| --- | --- |
| GG | grey |
| Gg | grey |
| gg | charcoal |

## Questions

10 In a species of animal, the allele for brown eyes is dominant and the allele for green eyes is recessive.
   a Write down suitable symbols for these two alleles.
   b Using your symbols, write the three possible genotypes, and the phenotypes that are produced by each genotype.
   c Which of the genotypes you have written are homozygous, and which are heterozygous?

11 In a species of plant, there are two alleles of the gene that determines leaf shape. One allele produces round leaves, and the other produces oval leaves. Heterozygous plants have round leaves.
   Which allele is dominant? Explain how you can tell.

12 When we choose symbols for alleles, it is not a good idea to choose letters such as S or C. Letters like A or B are better choices. Can you suggest why?

## Codominance

Sometimes, neither of a pair of alleles is completely dominant or completely recessive. Instead of one of them completely hiding the effect of the other in a heterozygote, they both have an effect on the phenotype. This is called **codominance** (Figure 16.10).

> **KEY WORD**
>
> **codominance:** alleles that are both expressed in the phenotype when they are both present

Imagine a kind of flower that has two alleles for flower colour. The allele $C^W$ produces white flowers, while the allele $C^R$ produces red ones. If these alleles show codominance, then the genotypes and phenotypes are:

| genotype | phenotype |
|---|---|
| $C^W C^W$ | white flowers |
| $C^W C^R$ | pink flowers |
| $C^R C^R$ | red flowers |

Notice how we write the symbols for codominance. We cannot use a capital letter and a small letter, because this would suggest that one allele is dominant and the other one is recessive. Instead, we use the same capital letter for both, and then use a superscript (a small letter written above and to the right) to indicate which allele we mean. It's really important to remember to do this, when you are working with codominant alleles.

The inheritance of the ABO blood group antigens in humans is a good example of codominance. The gene that determines your blood group is represented with the capital letter **I**. It has three alleles – not two as we have worked with up to now. Alleles $I^A$ and $I^B$ are codominant, but both are dominant to $I^o$.

| genotype | phenotype |
|---|---|
| $I^A I^A$ | blood group A |
| $I^A I^B$ | blood group AB |
| $I^A I^o$ | blood group A |
| $I^B I^B$ | blood group B |
| $I^B I^o$ | blood group B |
| $I^o I^o$ | blood group O |

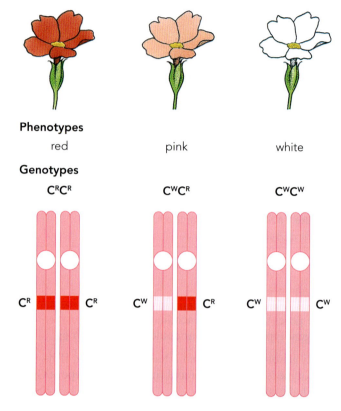

**Figure 16.10:** Codominance. Two alleles of the gene for flower colour are both expressed in a heterozygous plant.

## Questions

13 In one breed of cattle, the hair can be red, white, or a mixture of red and white called roan.
   a  Suggest suitable symbols for the two codominant alleles that determine coat colour. (Remember to use one letter for the gene, and then superscripts for the two alleles.)
   b  Using your symbols, write down the three possible genotypes and the phenotypes that each one produces.

14 Explain how the alleles for blood groups in humans demonstrate both dominance and codominance.

## Alleles in gametes

An understanding of genes and alleles can be used to study and predict how characteristics are passed on from one generation to the next. This area of study is called genetics. Geneticists study **inheritance** – the transmission of genetic information from generation to generation.

> **KEY WORD**
>
> **inheritance:** the transmission of genetic information from generation to generation

The genetic information is transferred in gametes. Each gamete has only one of each kind of chromosome instead of two, as in the body cells. So, for example, human egg and sperm cells have 23 chromosomes, not 46 as in other cells. These cells, therefore, only carry *one* of each pair of alleles of all the genes.

Imagine a male chinchilla that has the genotype **Gg**. He is a carrier for charcoal fur. In his testes, sperm are made by meiosis. Each sperm cell gets either a **G** allele or **g** allele. Half of his sperm cells have the genotype **G** and half have the genotype **g** (Figure 16.11).

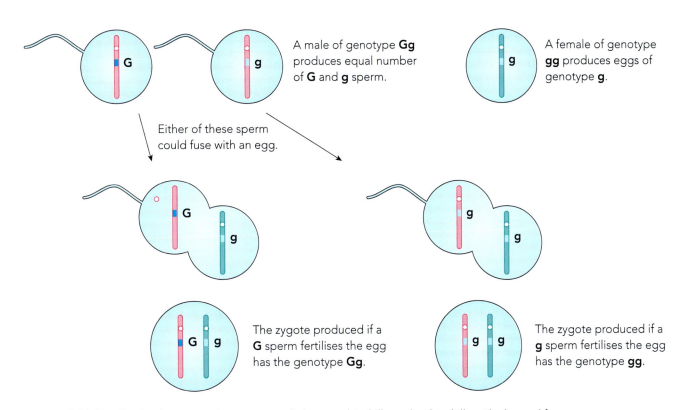

Figure 16.11: Fertilisation between a heterozygous light grey chinchilla and a chinchilla with charcoal fur.

## Genes and fertilisation

If this heterozygous chinchilla is crossed with a female with charcoal fur (genotype **gg**), will their offspring have charcoal fur?

The eggs that are made in the female's ovaries are also made by meiosis. She can only make one kind of egg. All of her eggs will carry a **g** allele.

When the two chinchillas mate, hundreds of thousands of sperm will begin a journey towards the egg. About half of these sperm will carry a **G** allele, and half will carry a **g** allele. If there is an egg in the female's oviduct, it will probably be fertilised. There is an equal chance of either kind of sperm getting there first.

If a sperm carrying a **G** allele wins the race, then the zygote will have a **G** allele from its father and a **g** allele from its mother. Its genotype will be **Gg**. When the baby chinchilla is born, it will have the genotype **Gg**.

But if a sperm carrying a **g** allele manages to fertilise the egg, then the baby will have the genotype **gg**, like its mother (Figure 16.11).

## Questions

15 Write down the genotypes of the different kinds of gametes that can be produced by organisms with each of these genotypes:

   a   **TT**
   
   b   **Tt**
   
   c   **tt**

16 Two organisms with the genotype **TT** breed together. Use your answer to 15a to write down the only possible genotype of their offspring.

17 An organism with genotype **TT** breeds with an organism with the genotype **tt**. Use your answers to 15a and 15c to write down the only possible genotype of their offspring.

18 An organism with genotype **TT** breeds with an organism with the genotype **Tt**. Use your answers to 15a and 15b to write down the two possible genotypes of their offspring.

## Genetic diagrams

There is a standard way of writing out all this information about how the alleles from two parents can be passed on to their offspring. It is called a **genetic diagram**.

First, write down the phenotypes and genotypes of the parents. Next, write down the different types of gametes they can make, like this:

| | | |
|---|---|---|
| **Parents' phenotypes** | grey | charcoal |
| **Parents' genotypes** | **Gg** | **gg** |
| **Gametes** | Ⓖ or Ⓖ | Ⓖ |

Notice that the genotypes of the gametes have circles around them. It's a really good idea to do this, as it makes the gametes stand out and helps you keep track of all the symbols in your genetic diagram.

The next step is to write down what might happen during fertilisation. Either kind of sperm might fuse with an egg:

**Offspring genotypes and phenotypes**

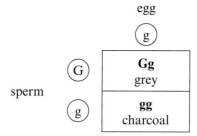

To finish your summary of the genetic cross, write out in words what you would expect the offspring from this cross to be. In this case, we would expect approximately half of the offspring to be heterozygous with grey fur, and half to be homozygous with charcoal fur. Another way of putting this is to say that the expected ratio of grey fur to charcoal fur would be 1 : 1.

> **KEY WORDS**
>
> **genetic diagram:** a standard way of showing all the steps in making predictions about the probable genotypes and phenotypes of the offspring from two parents

It is really important to understand that this genetic diagram does **not** mean that the chinchillas will have two offspring, one grey and one charcoal. What it means is that there are equal chances of having a grey offspring or a charcoal offspring.

This cross, and all the others in this chapter, are examples of *monohybrid crosses*. This means that we are looking at the inheritance of only one ('mono') gene.

## Another genetic cross

Here is a genetic diagram that we can use to predict the offspring that might be born if two heterozygous chinchillas mate with each other:

| **Parents' phenotypes** | grey | grey |
|---|---|---|
| **Parents' genotypes** | Gg | Gg |
| **Gametes** | G or g | G or g |

**Offspring genotypes and phenotypes**

|  | eggs | |
|---|---|---|
|  | G | g |
| sperm G | GG grey | Gg grey |
| sperm g | Gg grey | gg charcoal |

This looks more complicated than the first genetic diagram because this time both the parents can produce two different types of gametes. The set of boxes that show all the possible results of these gametes fusing together is called a *Punnett square*. It's a neat way of working out and showing the possible combinations of alleles that might occur. The boxes in the Punnett square are also the best place to write down the phenotypes that each of the genotypes produce.

We can use the entries in the Punnett square to work out the expected proportions of the different kinds of offspring that might be produced. We would expect about one quarter of the offspring to have charcoal fur, and three quarters to have grey fur.

> **KEY WORDS**
>
> **monohybrid cross:** a cross where we consider the inheritance of only one gene
>
> **Punnett square:** the part of a genetic diagram that shows the predicted genotypes and phenotypes that can result from the random fusion of the male and female gametes

## Probabilities in genetics

In the last example, there were four possible offspring genotypes at the end of the cross. This does not mean that the two chinchillas will have four offspring. It simply means that each time they have offspring, these are the *possible* genotypes that they might have, in those *probable* proportions.

The Punnett square tells us that, for any one offspring, there is a 1 in 4 chance that its genotype will be **GG**, and a 1 in 4 chance that its genotype will be **gg**. There is a 2 in 4, or 1 in 2, chance that its genotype will be **Gg**.

However, as you know, probabilities do not always work out. If you toss a coin up four times you might expect it to turn up heads twice and tails twice. But does it always do this? Try it and see.

With small numbers like this, probabilities do not always match reality. However, if you have the patience to toss your coin up a few thousand times, you will almost certainly find that you get nearly equal numbers of heads and tails.

The same thing applies in genetics. The offspring genotypes that you work out are only probabilities. With small numbers, they are unlikely to be exactly what we predict. With very large numbers of offspring from one cross, they are more likely to be accurate.

So, for example, we might use a genetic diagram to predict that one-quarter of the kittens born to a pair of cats would be expected to have black fur, one-quarter to have ginger fur and the remaining half to have grey fur. But the cats might actually have seven kittens (Figure 16.12) and the proportions might not work out exactly as we predicted. This is because which sperm fuse with which eggs is all due to chance.

**Figure 16.12:** Genetic diagrams don't give us any information at all about how many offspring will be produced, and the probable phenotypes that they predict are only probabilities, not certainties.

### ACTIVITY 16.2

#### Breeding beads

Work in a group of two or three for this activity.

> **You will need:**
> - two containers
> - approx. 150 beads of one colour, and 150 of another colour.

Each container represents a parent. The beads represent the alleles in the gametes they make. The colour of a bead represents the genotype of the gamete. For example, a red bead might represent a gamete with genotype **A**, for 'long tail'. A yellow bead might represent a gamete with the genotype **a**, for 'short tail'.

#### Method

1. Put 100 red beads into the first container. These represent the gametes of an animal that is homozygous for the long tail allele, **AA**.

2. Put 50 red beads and 50 yellow beads into the second container. These represent the gametes of a heterozygous animal with the genotype **Aa**.

3. Close your eyes, and pick out one bead from the first container, and one from the second. Write down the genotype of the 'offspring' they produce. Put the two beads back.

4. Repeat step 3 100 times, recording the genotype of the offspring each time.

5. Count how many of each genotype there are in the offspring. Write down the ratios of the different genotypes and phenotypes of the offspring that were produced.

6. Now try a different cross – for example, **Aa** crossed with **Aa**.

#### Question

1. How well do the ratios of the different phenotypes and genotypes of the 'offspring' match the ratios predicted by a genetic diagram? If they are not exactly the same, suggest why this is.

#### Self-assessment

A lot of patience is needed to complete this task. How well did you manage to concentrate?

## Pedigree diagrams

A pedigree diagram is a way of showing the phenotypes (and sometimes the genotypes, too) of the family members in several generations. All the individuals in one generation are shown in the same row. Males are shown with a square symbol, and females with a circle. Parents are connected with a horizontal line between them, and a vertical line leads down to their offspring.

Guinea pigs can have smooth hair or curlier hair that forms rosettes (Figure 16.13). Figure 16.14 is a pedigree diagram showing the phenotype for hair in three generations of guinea pigs.

**Figure 16.13:** The guinea pig on the left has a smooth coat, while the one on the right has rosettes.

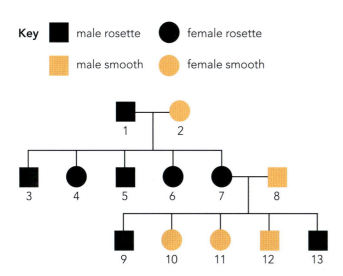

**Figure 16.14:** Pedigree diagram showing phenotype for smooth or rosette hair in three generations of guinea pigs.

What can we work out from this pedigree diagram? In the first row, there is a male rosette guinea pig that has mated with a female smooth guinea pig. They have had five offspring, all with rosette hair. This strongly suggests that the allele for rosette hair is dominant. We can therefore try using **R** to represent the rosette hair allele, and **r** for the smooth hair allele.

If we are correct, then all of the smooth-haired guinea pigs must have the genotype **rr**. So, we now know the genotypes of guinea pigs 2, 8, 10, 11 and 12 must all be **rr**.

But what about the others? Look at guinea pig 1. He has rosette hair, so he could be **RR** or **Rr**. If he is **Rr**, then he would be able to make some sperm with the **R** allele, and some with the **r** allele. If so, then we would expect at least some of his offspring to get an **r** allele from him, as well as from the female – which would make them smooth. But none of them are smooth, so it seems likely that he is **RR**, not **Rr**. But we cannot be sure – perhaps it is just chance that no **r** sperm met up with an **r** egg.

Now look at guinea pig 7. She has rosette hair, so again she could be **RR** or **Rr**. She has mated with a smooth male, and they have had five offspring. Three of these have rosette hair, so they must be **rr**. And this means that they have received an **r** allele from their mother, as well as from their father. So, guinea pig 7 must have the genotype **Rr**.

## Questions

19  Fruit flies can have normal wings or wings that are so small that they are useless. These are called vestigial wings. The allele for normal wings, **N**, is dominant, and the allele for vestigial wings, **n**, is recessive.

   a  Write down the three possible genotypes and their phenotypes.

   b  Construct a complete genetic diagram to show the offspring that are produced when a heterozygous fly mates with a fly that is homozygous for the normal wing allele.

20  In a species of animal, the allele for red hair is recessive to the allele for brown hair. Two animals have five offspring, three with red hair and two with brown hair. Use a genetic diagram to explain how this can happen.

21  A man of blood type A married a woman of blood type B. They had three children, with blood types O, B and AB respectively.

   What are the genotypes of the parents and children? Use genetic diagrams to explain your answer.

22 Figure 16.15 is a pedigree diagram showing the known blood groups in three generations of a family.

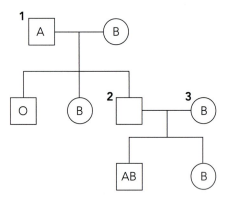

Figure 16.15: Blood groups pedigree diagram.

What are the genotypes of persons 1 and 2? What is the blood group of person 2?

## Test crosses

An organism that shows a dominant characteristic could have either of two possible genotypes. It could be homozygous for the dominant allele, or it could be heterozygous. For example, a grey chinchilla could have the genotype **GG** or **Gg**.

We can find out the genotype of an individual with the dominant phenotype for a particular gene by crossing it with one known to have the homozygous recessive genotype for the same gene. This is called a **test cross**.

### KEY WORDS

**test cross:** a cross used to try to determine the genotype of an organism showing the characteristic produced by a dominant allele; the unknown organism is crossed with one showing the recessive characteristic

For example, if we know that the allele for tallness is dominant to the allele for dwarfness in a certain species of pea, then the genotype of any tall plant could be determined by crossing it with a dwarf plant. If any of the offspring are dwarf, then this must mean that the tall parent had an allele for dwarfness. It must have been heterozygous.

If none of the offspring are dwarf, this almost certainly means that the tall parent was homozygous for the tallness allele. However, unless there are large numbers of offspring, this could also happen if the tall parent is heterozygous but, just by chance, none of its gametes carrying the recessive allele were successful in fertilisation.

### ACTIVITY 16.3

#### Explaining a test cross

Work with a partner. One of you is a chinchilla breeder, and the other is a genetics expert.

The breeder has a grey chinchilla. He or she wants to find out if it has the allele for charcoal fur or not.

If you are the genetics expert, explain to the breeder how he or she can find out. You could use some genetic diagrams as part of your explanation.

If you are the breeder, ask the genetics expert lots of questions, until you really understand what is being explained to you.

## Pure-breeding

Some populations of animals or plants always have offspring just like themselves (Figure 16.16). For example, a rabbit breeder might have a strain of rabbits which all have brown coats. If he or she interbreeds them with one another, all the offspring always have brown coats as well. The breeder has a pure-breeding group of brown rabbits. Pure-breeding organisms are always homozygous for the pure-breeding characteristics. Heterozygous organisms are not pure-breeding.

Figure 16.16: These chickens are pure-breeding for feather colour. When they reproduce, all their offspring have the same feather colour as themselves.

## 16 Chromosomes, genes and proteins

## Sex determination

Right at the start of this chapter, we looked at the complete set of chromosomes in a human cell. One of the pairs of chromosomes in Figures 16.3 and 16.4 is responsible for determining what sex a person will be. They are called the **sex chromosomes** (Figure 16.17).

A woman's sex chromosomes are both alike and are called **X chromosomes**. She has the genotype **XX**. A man, though, only has one **X** chromosome. The other, smaller one is a **Y chromosome**. He has the genotype **XY**.

> **KEY WORDS**
>
> **sex chromosomes:** chromosomes that determine sex
>
> **X chromosome:** the larger of the two sex chromosomes in mammals
>
> **Y chromosome:** the smaller of the two sex chromosomes in mammals

## Question

23  A couple have three children, all girls. What is the chance that their next child will be a boy?

## Sex linkage

The X and Y chromosomes do not only determine sex. They have other genes on them as well.

We have seen that, for most chromosomes, we have two copies of each one – a homologous pair. They contain the same genes in the same positions. This means that we have two copies of each gene.

But this isn't true for the sex chromosomes. The Y chromosome is tiny, and only has a few genes (Figure 16.18). The X chromosome is much larger and has many more genes. This means that, for most of the genes on the X chromosome, a man only has one copy. There is no second copy on the Y chromosome.

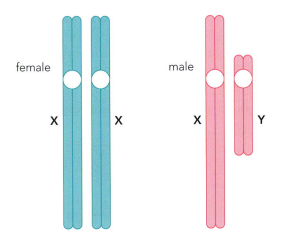

Figure 16.17: The sex chromosomes.

You can work out sex inheritance in just the same way as for any other characteristic, but using the letter symbols to describe whole chromosomes, rather than individual alleles.

| Parents' phenotypes | male | female |
|---|---|---|
| Parents' genotypes | XY | XX |
| Gametes | X or Y | X |

**Offspring genotypes and phenotypes**

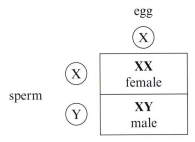

So, each time a child is born, there is a 1 : 1 chance of it being either sex.

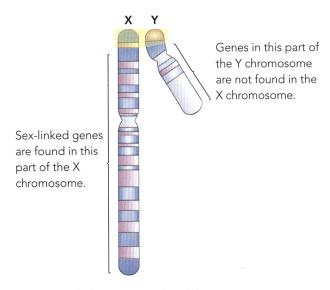

Figure 16.18: Genes on the X and Y chromosomes.

335

There are also a few genes on the Y chromosome that are not found on the X chromosome. This means that a woman never has a copy of these genes, and a man has only one copy. Genes that are found only on the non-homologous parts of the X or Y chromosomes are called **sex-linked genes**.

> **KEY WORDS**
>
> **sex-linked genes:** genes that are found on a part of one of the sex chromosomes (usually the X chromosome) and not on the other sex chromosome; they therefore produce characteristics that are more common in one sex than in the other

One of these sex-linked genes controls the production of the three different kinds of cone cell in the retina. A recessive allele of this gene, **b**, results in only two types of cone cell being made. A person who is homozygous for this allele cannot tell the difference between red and green. They are said to be red–green colour-blind. This condition is much more common in men than in women.

Figure 16.19 shows the various genotypes and phenotypes for this sex-linked condition. You can see that there are three possible genotypes that a woman might have, but only two possible genotypes for a man.

When we write genotypes involving sex-linked genes, we need to show the chromosome as well as the allele.

So, the five possible genotypes and their phenotypes for red–green colour blindness are:

| genotype | phenotype |
|---|---|
| $X^B X^B$ | woman with normal vision |
| $X^B X^b$ | woman with normal vision (who is a carrier) |
| $X^b X^b$ | woman with red–green colour blindness |
| $X^B Y$ | man with normal vision |
| $X^b Y$ | man with red–green colour blindness |

## Inheritance of sex-linked characteristics

We can use a genetic diagram to show how sex-linked genes are inherited. For example, what might happen if a woman who is a carrier for red–green colour blindness marries a man with normal vision?

**Parents' phenotypes**  normal man   carrier woman

**Parents' genotypes**   $X^B Y$          $X^B X^b$

**Gametes**              $X^B$ or $Y$     $X^B$ or $X^b$

**Offspring genotypes and phenotypes**

|  | eggs $X^B$ | eggs $X^b$ |
|---|---|---|
| sperm $X^B$ | $X^B X^B$ normal female | $X^B X^b$ normal female (carrier) |
| sperm $Y$ | $X^B Y$ normal male | $X^b Y$ red-green colour-blind male |

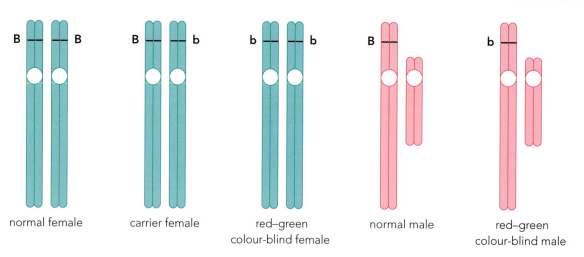

Figure 16.19: Genotypes and phenotypes for red–green colour blindness.

This genetic diagram predicts that about half of their male children will be red–green colour blind. All of the female children will have normal vision.

## Questions

24  a   A man who is red–green colour-blind marries a woman with normal vision. They have three sons and two daughters. One of the sons is red–green colour-blind. All the other children have normal colour vision. Draw a genetic diagram to suggest an explanation for this.

   b   What is the chance that the couple's next child will be a colour-blind boy?

> ### REFLECTION
>
> In a situation where time is limited, such as in an examination, it is tempting to take short cuts with your answers to genetic questions. For example, you might not bother to write a list of genotypes and phenotypes before you start, or you may decide to skip the Gametes row in the genetic diagram.
>
> Do you think there are circumstances where it is justifiable to take these short cuts? Or is better always to work thoroughly through each step?

# 16.3 Genes and protein synthesis

Chromosomes are made of DNA. In Chapter 4, we saw that a DNA molecule is made up of two long strands of molecules called nucleotides. There are four different nucleotides, each containing a different base – A, C, T or G. Figure 16.20 shows the structure of a very small part of a DNA molecule. (You have seen this diagram before, in Chapter 4.)

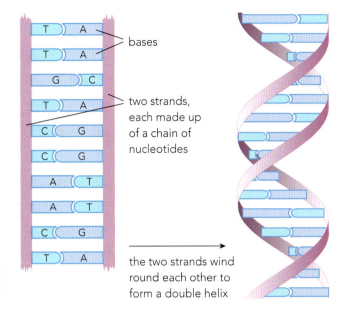

**Figure 16.20:** A small part of a DNA molecule. The letters A, C, G and T stand for the four different bases in the molecule.

You should also remember that protein molecules are made up of long chains of smaller molecules – amino acids (Chapter 4). There are 20 different amino acids and the sequence of the amino acids in a protein molecule determines the final shape of the molecule. This shape affects how the protein works. So, for example, the sequence of amino acids in an amylase enzyme determines the shape of the active site, into which a starch molecule can fit and form an enzyme–substrate complex. If the sequence of amino acids is not absolutely correct, then the shape of the enzyme will not be correct. Its active site may not be a complementary shape to a starch molecule, and it will not be able to catalyse the reaction in which starch is broken down to maltose (Chapter 5).

A gene is a length of DNA that codes for making a particular protein – for example, amylase. The code is in the form of the sequence of bases. The sequence of bases in the DNA molecule determines the sequence in which amino acids are linked together to produce a protein.

In this way, the DNA in the nucleus controls the functions of the cell. It does this by determining the shapes – and therefore the functions – of all the different proteins that the cell makes (Figure 16.21). These include not only enzymes, but also other proteins such as the carrier proteins in the cell membrane, and the receptor proteins onto which neurotransmitter molecules can bind at a synapse.

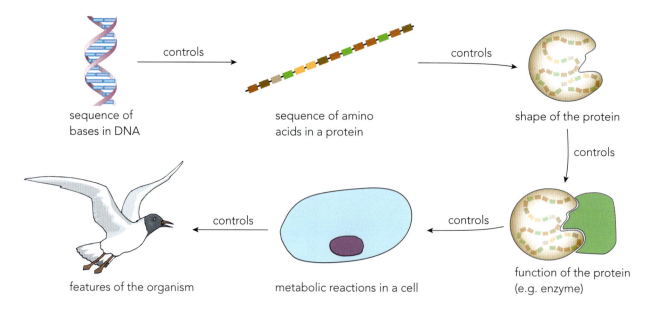

**Figure 16.21:** The sequence of bases in a DNA molecule determines the sequence of amino acids in the protein molecules made in an organism's cells – and therefore the features of the whole organism.

## Protein synthesis

DNA is found in the nucleus. Protein synthesis happens on the ribosomes, in the cytoplasm. To carry information from the DNA to the ribosome, a messenger molecule called **messenger RNA (mRNA)** is used (Figure 16.22).

When a protein is to be made, a carefully controlled sequence of events takes place. First, an mRNA molecule is made in the nucleus, copying the base sequence from the length of DNA that makes up a gene. The DNA stays in the nucleus.

The mRNA moves out of the nucleus and into the cytoplasm. The mRNA then attaches to a ribosome.

If you have been eating a good diet, then the cytoplasm in your cells will contain plenty of all the 20 different amino acids. As the long, thin mRNA molecule passes through the ribosome, the ribosome links amino acids together in exactly the right order to make the desired protein, following the code contained on the mRNA molecule.

## Specialised cells and stem cells

Every cell in your body contains tens of thousands of genes. All of your cells contain exactly the same genes, because they have all been produced by mitosis from the original zygote. They are all genetically identical.

But any one cell does not need to make all of the possible proteins that its genes code for. Each cell needs only a particular set of proteins. For example, a cell in your skin might need to use the gene to make keratin (the protein that hair is made of) and the gene to make the pigment that colours the keratin. But a neurone in your brain doesn't need to make either of those proteins. Instead, it makes proteins such as the receptors on its membrane, that allow neurotransmitters from other neurones to bind to it and set up nerve impulses in it.

When the information carried by a gene is used to synthesise a protein, we say that the gene is **expressed**. Each specialised cell expresses only the genes that it needs, in order to carry out its specific function.

> **KEY WORDS**
>
> **messenger RNA (mRNA):** a molecule that carries a copy of the information on DNA to a ribosome, to be used to synthesise a protein
>
> **expressed:** used to make a protein; a gene is expressed when the protein that it codes for is synthesised in a cell

Some cells, however, are not specialised. For example, when the zygote is first formed, it divides repeatedly to form a little ball of almost identical cells, which make up the embryo. At this stage, you cannot see any differences

16 Chromosomes, genes and proteins

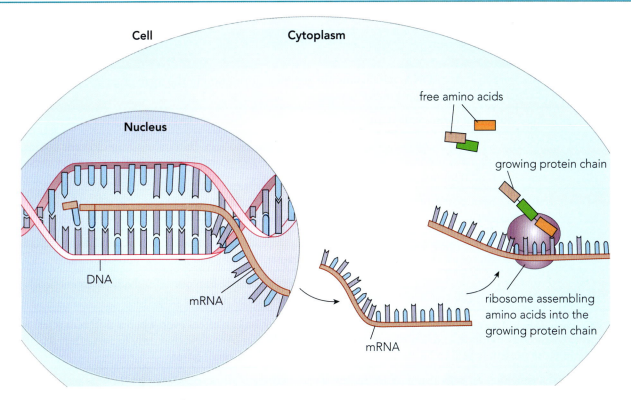

Figure 16.22: How proteins are made.

between the cells. Each cell is able to divide to produce other cells, which can then become specialised for different functions.

These unspecialised cells are called **stem cells**. A newly formed embryo contains nothing but stem cells. By the time we are adults, most of our cells have become specialised – but some stem cells still remain in our bodies. These are really important to us, because they are able to divide by mitosis to form other, specialised cells. For example, we have stem cells in our bone marrow that are always dividing to produce the specialised cells in blood – red blood cells, platelets, phagocytes and lymphocytes (Figure 16.23). Stem cells in the brain can divide to produce new neurones.

The range of stem cells that are present in an adult human has only recently been discovered by scientists, and we are still learning a lot about them. A better understanding of stem cells could lead to new treatments for medical problems that we currently cannot solve. For example, could stem cells be used to produce new heart muscle in someone with heart failure? Could they produce new nerve cells, for someone with a damaged spinal cord? Science is moving on quickly in this field of research. If you do the Project at the end of this chapter, you will be able to find recent information about some of the exciting developments taking place.

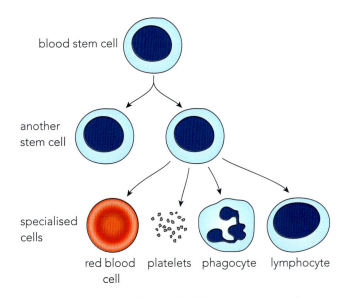

Figure 16.23: Stem cells can divide by mitosis to produce specialised cells.

### KEY WORDS

**stem cells:** unspecialised cells that are able to divide by mitosis to produce different types of specialised cell

339

## SUMMARY

Chromosomes are long strands of DNA, which contain genetic information in the form of genes. Each gene codes for the production of a particular kind of protein.

Most genes come in different forms, called alleles.

A haploid cell has one set of chromosomes, while a diploid cell has two sets. In humans, haploid cells contain 23 chromosomes and diploid cells contain 46 chromosomes, that is 23 pairs. The two similar chromosomes from the two sets are called homologous chromosomes.

Mitosis is a division of the nucleus of a cell, in which the two new nuclei contain exactly the same number and types of chromosomes as the parent nucleus. Usually, the whole cell divides after the nucleus has divided, producing two genetically identical daughter cells.

Mitosis is used in growth, repair of damaged tissues, replacement of cells and asexual reproduction.

Meiosis is a reduction division, in which a diploid cell divides to produce haploid cells. These are genetically different from their parent cell and from each other. Meiosis is used to produce gametes.

We can use letters to represent the alleles of a gene. An allele that has an effect even when a different allele is present is said to be dominant and is represented with a capital letter. An allele that only has an effect when no other allele is present is said to be recessive and is represented by a small letter.

The alleles of a gene that an organism has are its genotype, and the features produced by those alleles are its phenotype.

There are two copies of each gene in every body cell. If both copies are the same allele, the organism is homozygous. If there are two different alleles, the organism is heterozygous. Homozygous organisms are pure-breeding, but heterozygous organisms are not.

We can use genetic diagrams to show how alleles are passed from one generation to the next, which is called inheritance. If we consider the alleles of only one gene, then this is a monohybrid cross.

Each gamete contains only one allele of a gene. Any male gamete can fuse with any female gamete, and we can show the resulting genotypes and phenotypes of the offspring using a Punnett square.

A test cross is used to determine the genotype of an organism that shows the dominant feature, and could be either homozygous or heterozygous, by crossing it with an organism showing the recessive feature.

Codominant alleles both have an effect in a heterozygous organism.

Blood group is determined by a gene with three alleles, $I^A$, $I^B$ and $I^o$. $I^A$ and $I^B$ are codominant. Both are dominant to $I^o$, which is recessive.

Sex is determined by the X and Y chromosomes. In humans, a female is XX and male is XY.

Genes on the unpaired parts of the sex chromosomes are said to be sex-linked. Sex-linked characteristics, such as red-green colour blindness, are more common in one sex than the other.

The sequence of bases in a gene determines the sequence of amino acids in a specific protein. Different sequences of amino acids result in different shapes, and therefore functions, of proteins.

## 16 Chromosomes, genes and proteins

### CONTINUED

> During protein synthesis, the gene stays in the nucleus. mRNA carries a copy of the sequence of bases in the gene to a ribosome in the cytoplasm. Amino acids are then linked together in the sequence specified by the mRNA, to make the protein.

> All the cells in an organism's body contain the same genes, but only some genes are expressed in each type of specialised cell, depending on the proteins that are required by that cell.

> Stem cells are unspecialised cells, which are able to divide by mitosis to give rise to cells that are specialised to carry out particular functions.

### PROJECT

**Stem cells in medicine**

Figure 16.24: The researcher is holding a bottle containing stem cells. The cells are being cultured (grown) in a liquid that contains the nutrients that they need to survive and divide.

Stem cells were first discovered in the 1970s. Today, many different teams of scientists all over the world are carrying out research to try to find ways in which we might be able to use stem cells to improve people's health.

Work in a group of three or four for this project. You are going to write a short, scripted news piece on one aspect of the use of stem cells. You can include still pictures or video content if you wish. You may be able to present your completed news piece to the rest of the class.

Here are some topics that you could research. Choose one of them – or feel free to think of a different one of your own. Try to make sure that you are not researching the same topic as any other group in your class.

- What is a stem cell? Why are stem cells important in an organism?

- What are the differences between the stem cells in an embryo, and the stem cells in an adult person? How does this affect the way that these stem cells might be used in medicine?

- Most countries regulate the kind of research that scientists can do on stem cells. Why do they do this, and what kind of regulations do they impose? Do you agree with the regulations?

- Are stem cells being used today to treat any diseases in humans? If so, how are they being used, and how is the treatment being regulated?

- How do scientists think that stem cells might be used in the future?

## EXAM-STYLE QUESTIONS

1 In which structure in a cell is DNA found?
   A cell membrane
   B chromosome
   C ribosome
   D vacuole [1]

2 Which sex chromosomes are found in the gametes of a man and a woman?

|   | gametes from a man | gametes from a woman |
|---|---|---|
| A | X only | X or Y |
| B | X or Y | X only |
| C | Y only | X or Y |
| D | X or Y | Y only |

[1]

3 Two individuals with the same phenotype breed together. They always produce offspring with the same phenotype as themselves.
Which statement about these two individuals is **not** correct?
   A They are both heterozygous.
   B They are both homozygous.
   C They are pure-breeding.
   D They belong to the same species. [1]

4 How many pairs of chromosomes are there in a diploid human cell?
   A 2
   B 23
   C 46
   D 92 [1]

5 A man with blood group A, and woman with blood group B, have a son with blood group O.
What could be the genotypes of the man and the woman?

|   | genotype of the man | genotype of the woman |
|---|---|---|
| A | $I^A I^A$ | $I^B I^B$ |
| B | $I^A I^B$ | $I^B I^o$ |
| C | $I^A I^o$ | $I^B I^B$ |
| D | $I^A I^o$ | $I^B I^o$ |

[1]

## CONTINUED

**6** Choose the term that best fits each description. You will not need to use all of the terms.

**allele   dominant   heterozygous   phenotype   monohybrid
pure-breeding   genotype   recessive**

    **a** an organism that has two different alleles of the same gene [1]

    **b** a term used to describe organisms that produce offspring just like themselves when they are bred together [1]

    **c** the observable features of an organism [1]

    **d** a term used to describe an allele that only has an effect when a different allele is not present [1]

    **e** one of several different forms of a gene [1]

    [Total: 5]

**7** The leaves of tomato plants can have leaves with smooth or indented edges. The allele for indented edges, **E**, is dominant, and the allele for smooth edges, **e**, is recessive.

    **a** **Give** the genotypes of

        **i** a homozygous smooth plant [1]

        **ii** a homozygous indented plant. [1]

    **b** A pure-breeding (homozygous) smooth plant was crossed with a homozygous indented plant. All of the offspring had the genotype **Ee**. Several of these offspring were crossed together. There were 302 plants with indented leaves and 99 with smooth leaves.
Construct a complete genetic diagram to **explain** this result. [5]

    [Total: 7]

**8** A breed of domestic chickens can have black, grey or white feathers. These colours are produced by two alleles, $C^B$ and $C^W$.

    **a** Write down the genotypes that produce black, grey and white feathers. [2]

    **b** Explain why the alleles are written in this way, rather than as a capital letter for one allele and a small letter for the other. [2]

    **c** A cockerel (male chicken) with grey feathers was mated with a hen (female chicken) with white feathers.
Draw a complete genetic diagram to predict the ratio of the different colours of chicks that will be produced. [5]

    [Total: 9]

---

**COMMAND WORDS**

**give:** produce an answer from a given source or recall/memory

**explain:** set out purposes or reasons/make the relationships between things evident/provide why and/or how and support with relevant evidence

## CONTINUED

9 The figure below shows a pedigree chart for a family in which some of the members are red–green colour blind.

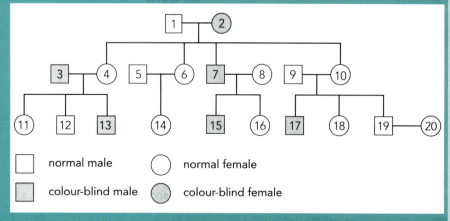

a Explain how the pedigree supports the idea that red–green colour blindness is a sex-linked characteristic. [2]

b Using the symbols $X^B$ for the allele for normal vision, and $X^b$ for the allele for colour blindness, state the genotypes of each of the following individuals. If there is more than one possible genotype, write down both of them.

　　2, 3, 11, 13, 19 [5]

c If individuals 3 and 4 have another son, what is the probability that he will be colour blind? Use a genetic diagram to explain your answer. [5]

d Explain why a colour-blind man cannot pass on this condition to his son. [2]

[Total: 14]

# 16 Chromosomes, genes and proteins

## SELF-EVALUATION CHECKLIST

After studying this chapter, think about how confident you are with the different topics. This will help you to see any gaps in your knowledge and help you to learn more effectively.

| I can | See Topic… | Needs more work | Almost there | Confident to move on |
|---|---|---|---|---|
| explain what is meant by the terms *chromosome*, *DNA*, *gene* and *allele* | 16.1 | | | |
| describe the roles of mitosis in organisms | 16.1 | | | |
| describe the role of meiosis in organisms | 16.1 | | | |
| use appropriate symbols to represent the alleles of a gene, and explain the meanings of the terms *dominant*, *recessive*, *homozygous* and *heterozygous* | 16.2 | | | |
| use the terms *phenotype* and *genotype* and relate the phenotype of an organism to its genotype | 16.2 | | | |
| construct genetic diagrams – including Punnett squares – to predict the genotypes and phenotypes in a monohybrid cross | 16.2 | | | |
| explain how to use a test cross | 16.2 | | | |
| describe codominance, and explain the inheritance of A, B, AB and O blood groups | 16.2 | | | |
| explain how sex is determined and inherited | 16.2 | | | |
| explain what a sex-linked characteristic is, and use genetic diagrams to show how sex-linked characteristics such as red-green colour blindness are inherited | 16.2 | | | |
| explain that the sequence of bases in a DNA molecule determines the sequence of amino acids in the proteins made in a cell, and how this controls the features of the organism | 16.3 | | | |
| describe how proteins are synthesised in a cell | 16.3 | | | |
| explain why not all genes are expressed in a cell | 16.3 | | | |
| explain what a stem cell is | 16.3 | | | |

# Chapter 17
# Variation and selection

**IN THIS CHAPTER YOU WILL:**

- find out about discontinuous and continuous variation, and what causes them
- identify and describe adaptive features in different species
- think about how selection can cause changes in the features of a species or population.

# 17 Variation and selection

> **GETTING STARTED**
>
> Think about the answers to these questions.
>
> - What is the difference between a gene and an allele?
> - What are genes and alleles made of?
> - How are alleles passed from one generation to the next?

## CONFUSING BUTTERFLIES

The two butterflies in Figure 17.1 look very different. Most people would assume they belong to two different species. But that is not the case. Both butterflies belong to the species *Papilio polytes*, the common mormon butterfly.

This species of butterfly is found in many different countries in Asia. The males always look the same – like the one at the top. Some of the females look just like the male. But some – such as the one shown at the bottom – have very different wing shapes and colours.

The butterfly at the bottom, with the pink colour on its wings, is called the *stichius* form of the common mormon. This form is found only where another butterfly that looks very similar, the common rose swallowtail, is found. The common rose swallowtail is poisonous, so predators quickly learn to avoid catching it. The common mormon is not poisonous. By pretending to be a common rose swallowtail, the female butterflies are much less likely to be eaten.

This pretence is called mimicry. It only works if there are large numbers of the genuinely poisonous butterfly, and much smaller numbers of the non-poisonous one – otherwise, predators would not learn to avoid them.

### Discussion questions

1 Why do you think that the *stichius* form of the butterfly is only found where the common rose swallowtail butterfly is found?

2 Can you think of any reasons why it might be more important for the female butterfly to avoid predation, than for the male?

**Figure 17.1:** Variation in shape and colour in the common mormon butterfly.

## 17.1 Variation

Look around your classroom. Everyone is different from everyone else. Some of the more obvious differences are in height or hair type. We also vary in blood groups, the shape of our ears, how good we are at sport, how sociable we are and many other ways. Differences between individuals belonging to the same species are called **variation**.

## Continuous and discontinuous variation

There are two basic types of variation. One type is **discontinuous variation**. Blood groups are an example of discontinuous variation. Everyone fits into one of four definite categories – each of us has group A, B, AB or O. There are no intermediate (in-between) categories.

Figure 17.2 is a graph showing discontinuous variation in blood groups. On the *x*-axis, because each blood group is a separate, distinct category, there is no continuous scale. The percentages of people in the **population** with each blood group are shown as bars with gaps between them. It would not be appropriate to use a line graph.

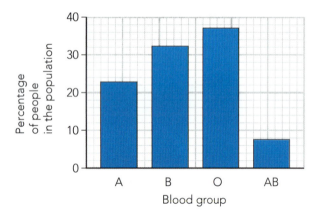

**Figure 17.2:** Percentages of people with the four blood groups in an Asian country. This is an example of discontinuous variation.

The other type of variation is **continuous variation**. Height in humans is an example of continuous variation (Figure 17.3). There are no definite height categories that a person must fit into. People vary in height, between the lowest and highest extremes. There is a complete range of phenotypes between these extremes.

**Figure 17.3:** Human height shows continuous variation. What characteristic here shows discontinuous variation?

Figure 17.4 shows continuous variation in height. We can show these data as a histogram (frequency diagram). Notice that the scale on the *x*-axis now goes up steadily, rather than having completely separate categories as in Figure 17.2. The bars in a histogram touch each other, because the scale is continuous.

We can also represent continuous variation as a line graph (Figure 17.5). Very often, we find that the data produce a bell-shaped curve. Most individuals come somewhere in the middle of the range, with smaller numbers at the extremes.

> **KEY WORDS**
>
> **variation:** differences between the individuals of the same species
>
> **discontinuous variation:** variation in which there are distinct categories of phenotype, with no intermediates
>
> **population:** a group of organisms of one species, living in the same area at the same time
>
> **continuous variation:** variation in which there is a continuous range of phenotypes between two extremes

17 Variation and selection

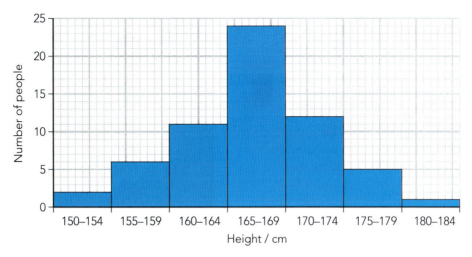

Figure 17.4: Histogram (frequency diagram) showing continuous variation in height.

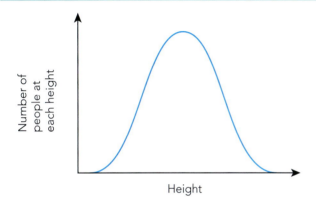

Figure 17.5: Line graph showing continuous variation in height.

## The causes of variation

One reason for the differences between individuals is that their genotypes are different. Blood groups, for example, are controlled by genes. There are also genes for hair colour, eye colour, height and many other characteristics. Discontinuous variation is almost always caused only by genes. Examples of discontinuous variation include the presence or absence of horns in cattle (Figure 17.6), and wrinkled and round seeds in peas (Figure 17.7).

Figure 17.6: The absence or presence of horns in cattle is an example of discontinuous variation, and it is controlled by a gene. The dominant allele of the gene causes horns to grow. Hornless cattle have two copies of the recessive allele of this gene.

Another important reason for variation is the difference between the environments of individuals. For example, you may have the genes to enable you to grow tall, but unless you eat a good diet, you will not grow to your full potential height. Features such as body mass and height in humans, which show continuous variation, are affected not only by genes, but also by environment.

Only features that are caused by genes are passed on to an organism's offspring. Variation caused by the environment is not passed on (Figure 17.8).

Figure 17.7: The shape of pea seeds is controlled by two alleles. The dominant allele produces round seeds, while the recessive one produces wrinkled seeds. There are no intermediates – the seeds are either wrinkled or round.

Variation caused by the environment is not inherited. A cutting from a bonsai pine tree would grow into a full size tree, if given sufficient space.

A bonsai pine tree is dwarfed by being grown in a very small pot, and continually pruned.

A dwarf pony, such as a Shetland pony, is small because of its genes. The offspring of Shetland ponies are small like their parents, no matter how well they are fed and cared for.

Figure 17.8: Some characteristics are caused by genes alone, but others are affected by the environment as well.

# Causes of genetic variation

## Mutation

Sometimes, a gene may suddenly change. This is called **mutation**. Mutation is how new alleles are formed. Mutations are the only source of brand-new characteristics that appear in a species. So, mutations are really the source of all genetic variation.

Mutations often happen for no apparent reason. They are random events – they can happen at any time, and the change in the gene is unpredictable. However, we do know of many factors that make mutation more likely. One of the most important of these is ionising radiation, such as X-rays, gamma radiation, beta radiation and alpha radiation. Radiation can damage the bases in DNA molecules. If this happens in the ovaries or testes, then the altered DNA may be passed on to the offspring.

Many different chemicals are known to increase the risk of a mutation happening. Heavy metals such as lead and mercury can interfere with the process in which DNA is copied. If this process goes wrong, the daughter cells will get faulty DNA when the cell divides. Chemicals which can cause mutations are called mutagens.

### KEY WORD

**mutation:** a random change in a gene, which can produce new alleles; mutation involves a change in the base sequence in DNA

## 17 Variation and selection

Mutations involve random changes in the base sequence of DNA. The base sequence in DNA determines the amino acid sequence in the proteins that are made in a cell. So, a mutation in DNA results in a change in the proteins that are made. Usually, the change will be harmful – if the protein is a different shape, it will not be able to carry out its function (Figure 17.9). But very occasionally the mutation may be beneficial. We will look at this in Topic 17.2.

## Meiosis

During sexual reproduction, gametes are formed by meiosis. In meiosis, pairs of homologous chromosomes exchange genes, and separate from one another, so the gametes which are formed contain different combinations of alleles.

## Random mating and random fertilisation

In most populations of animals and plants, any male individual and any female individual can potentially reproduce together. And any two male and female gametes can fuse together at fertilisation, so there are many possible combinations of alleles than can be produced in the zygote. In an organism with a large number of genes, the possibility of two offspring having identical genotypes is so small that it can be considered almost impossible.

**Figure 17.9:** Mutation of a gene controlling coat colour has produced a white coat in this tiger. It is unlikely that this tiger could survive in the wild, as it will not be camouflaged and will be unable to catch prey.

### EXPERIMENTAL SKILLS 17.1

**Measuring continuous variation in humans**

In this investigation, you will collect data about continuous variation in the people in your class. You will then practise recording these data in tables and graphs.

> **You will need:**
> - a ruler or tape measure.

**Method**

1. Measure the length of the third finger of the left hand of everyone in your class. (It's best if you can take measurements from at least 30 people, so if there are not that many in your class, perhaps you can also include measurements from another class.) Take the measurement from the knuckle to the finger tip, not including the nail.

2. Divide the finger lengths into suitable categories, and record the numbers in each category, like this.

| Length / cm | Number of measurements |
|---|---|
| 8.0–8.4 | 2 |
| 8.5–8.9 | 4 |

3. Construct a histogram to display your data. You can use Figure 17.4 for guidance.

**Questions**

1. The category, or class, which has the largest number of individuals in it is called the modal class. What is the modal class for finger length in your results?

2. The mean finger length is the total of all the finger lengths, divided by the number of people in your sample. What is the mean finger length of the sample?

3. Do you think that variation in finger length is affected by genes, the environment or both? Explain your answer.

## Questions

1 State whether each of these features shows continuous variation or discontinuous variation.
   a   blood group in humans
   b   foot length in humans
   c   leaf length in a species of tree
   d   presence of horns in cattle

2 For each of the examples in **a** to **d** above, suggest whether the variation is caused by genes alone, or by both genes and environment.

3 In peas, seeds can be either yellow or green. Plants grown from green seeds are pure-breeding, but plants grown from yellow seeds can produce some green seeds when they are bred together.
   a   Is this an example of continuous variation or discontinuous variation? Explain your answer.
   b   Explain how this variation is caused.

4 Figure 17.10 shows a maize cob. Each of the kernels (fruits) in the cob is a new individual.

**Figure 17.10:** A maize cob showing variation in kernel colour.

   a   Does colour in maize kernels show continuous variation or discontinuous variation? Explain your answer.
   b   Estimate the ratio of white : brown kernels in the maize cob.
   c   Suggest suitable symbols for the alleles that have produced these colours, and also suggest the genotypes of the parents that produced the offspring in this maize cob.

5  a   State how new alleles of genes are formed.
   b   List **four** ways in which genetic variation is caused.

## 17.2 Selection

Every organism has features that help it to survive in its environment. In this topic we will look at how the features of the organism can affect its chances of reproduction, and therefore the chances of its genes being passed on to the next generation.

### Adaptive features

A feature of an organism that is caused by its genes, and that helps it to survive and reproduce in its environment, is known as an **adaptive feature**.

> **KEY WORDS**
>
> **adaptive feature:** an inherited feature that helps an organism to survive and reproduce in its environment

Some adaptive features are very obvious. All fish, for example, have gills that allow them to obtain oxygen under water. Different species of fish have adaptations that help them to survive in different environments (Figure 17.11). For example, fish that live on sand in shallow water may have very flat, sand-coloured bodies, so that they are camouflaged from predators. Predatory fish that live in the open ocean have streamlined bodies for fast swimming, and teeth that they use to kill their prey.

Other adaptive features may not be so easy to spot. For example, the pygmy seahorse and the tuna might have different enzymes in their digestive systems so that they are efficient at digesting the nutrients in their different diets. The tuna might have more mitochondria in its muscle cells than the seahorse, to provide more energy through aerobic respiration, allowing it to swim faster.

## 17 Variation and selection

**Figure 17.11 a:** The pygmy seahorse is adapted to be perfectly camouflaged among the sea fans where it lives. **b:** Tuna are fast-swimming predators, with streamlined bodies and strong swimming muscles.

## Question

6   Figure 17.12 shows a small mammal called a tarsier. Tarsiers feed on insects, which they hunt in trees at night. What adaptive features can you see in the photograph?

**Figure 17.12:** A tarsier.

## Xerophytes

Plants that live in deserts can easily run short of water, especially if the temperatures are hot. Desert plants, such as succulents and cacti (Figure 17.13), must be well adapted to survive in these difficult conditions. Plants that are adapted to live in places where water is in short supply are called **xerophytes**.

All xerophytes have adaptations that help them to survive in a difficult dry environment.

**Figure 17.13:** Desert plants have adaptations that help them to conserve water.

> **KEY WORD**
>
> **xerophyte:** a plant that has adaptive features that help it to survive in an environment where water is scarce

### Closing stomata

Plants lose most water as water vapour, through their stomata. If they close their stomata, transpiration slows down to an almost complete stop. Figure 17.14 shows how changes in the guard cells can cause the stoma (the gap between them) to open or close.

However, if its stomata are closed, the plant cannot photosynthesise, because carbon dioxide cannot diffuse into the leaf. Stomata close when it is very hot and dry or when the plant could not photosynthesise anyway, such as at night.

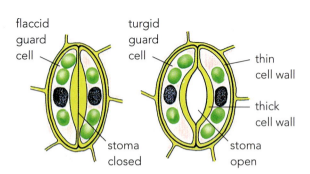

When a plant is short of water, the guard cells become flaccid closing the stoma.

When a plant has plenty of water, the guard cells become turgid. The cell wall on the inner surface is very thick, so it cannot stretch as much as the outer surface. So as the guard cells swell up, they curve away from each other, opening the stoma.

**Figure 17.14:** Osmotic changes in the guard cells cause a stoma to open or close.

## Waxy cuticle

The leaves of desert plants are often covered with a very thick waxy cuticle, made by the cells in the epidermis. The wax makes the leaf waterproof.

## Hairy leaves

Some plants that live in dry places have hairs on their leaves (Figure 17.15). These hairs trap a layer of moist air next to the leaf. The moist air reduces the diffusion gradient for water vapour from the leaf into the air, so less water vapour diffuses out of the leaf.

**Figure 17.15:** These *Sempervivum* plants have a thick waxy cuticle covering their fleshy leaves, to reduce the loss of water vapour. The hairs also help – they trap water vapour in the air among them, so that less water vapour diffuses out of the leaves and into the air.

## Sunken stomata on underside of leaves

In most leaves, there are more stomata on the lower surface than on the upper surface. The lower surface is usually cooler than the upper one, so less water will evaporate. In desert plants, there are often fewer stomata than usual, and the stomata may be sunk into deep pits in the leaf (Figure 17.16). When water vapour diffuses out through the stomata, it collects in the air trapped in the pits. This reduces the diffusion gradient, so less water diffuses out of the leaf.

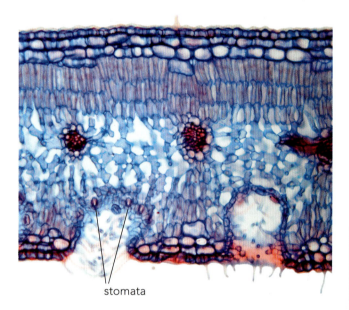

**Figure 17.16:** This is a transverse section through a leaf of an *Oleander* plant. On the underside of the leaf, there are two deep pits, and the stomata are inside these. This reduces water loss from the leaf. You can also see hairs on the underside of the leaf – how might these help the plant to survive?

## Reducing the surface area of the leaves

The smaller the surface area of the leaf, the less water vapour will diffuse out of it. Plants like cacti (Figure 17.17) have leaves that are so small they are just spines. These spines are also useful for preventing hungry and thirsty animals eating the cactus. Instead of using its leaves for photosynthesis, the cactus has chloroplasts in the outer cells in its thick stem. The cells deep inside the stem are adapted to be able to store water.

# 17 Variation and selection

Figure 17.17: This small cactus has spines instead of leaves, and a thick stem that can photosynthesise and store water.

## Having deep or spreading roots

Desert plants may have to seek water very deep down in the soil, or across a wide area. They usually have either very deep roots, or roots that spread a long way sideways from where the plant is growing. Some have both.

In fact, many plants – even those that do not live in deserts – have at least some of these adaptations. For example, a plant growing in your garden may have to cope with hot, dry conditions at least some of the time. Most plants have stomata only on the undersides of their leaves, which close when the need arises. Most of them have waxy cuticles on their leaves, to cut down water loss. Desert plants, though, show these adaptations to a much greater extent.

## Hydrophytes

Plants that live in very wet places, including those that live in water, are called **hydrophytes**. These plants have no problem of water shortage. They do not need adaptations to conserve water, as desert plants do.

> **KEY WORD**
>
> **hydrophyte:** a plant that has adaptive features that help it to survive in water

The water hyacinth, *Eichhornia crassipes*, is an example of a plant adapted to live in fresh water (Figure 17.18). The roots of water hyacinths do not attach to the bed of the river or pond where they grow but float freely in the water. The stems and leaf stalks have hollow spaces in them, filled with air, which help them to float on the top of the water where they can get plenty of light for photosynthesis.

Figure 17.18 a: Water hyacinth is so well adapted to living in fresh water that it can completely cover lakes and rivers. b: In this photograph, you can see the swollen stems and leaf stalks, filled with air to help them to float.

Unlike terrestrial (land) plants, water hyacinths have stomata on the upper surfaces of their leaves as well as on the lower surfaces. This is because the upper surface is in contact with the air, so this is where the carbon dioxide comes from that the plant uses for photosynthesis. There is no need for the stomata to be hidden underneath the leaf, away from the heat of the sun, because the plant does not need to conserve water. There is also no need to close stomata when it is hot. It has more water than it can possibly need.

Not all hydrophytes look like water hyacinth. Some, such as *Cabomba* (Figure 17.19), are adapted to live completely under water. (You may have used a plant like this for photosynthesis experiments.) These plants often have thin leaves that may be really feathery. Feathery leaves spread out easily in the water, so that each leaf gets plenty of sunlight.

355

They also help the plant to float, and allow strong water currents to flow over the plant without causing damage to its leaves or stems. Other hydrophytes may be attached to the bottom, with roots that penetrate into the mud. Unlike xerophytes, there is no need for these roots to grow very deep, or to spread very widely – they just need to go deep enough to hold the plant in position.

**Figure 17.19:** The feathery leaves and flexible stems of *Cabomba* are adaptations for living in water.

### ACTIVITY 17.1

**Describing adaptive features**

Work with a partner for this activity.

First, choose an interesting plant or animal. You may be able to study a live one, or you may have to use images on the internet or in books.

Now describe the environment in which the organism lives, and any features of its lifestyle that you think are important – for example, what it eats, what eats it, how it gets water and so on.

Take a really large sheet of paper (for example, from a flip chart) and make a large, clear diagram of your chosen organism in the middle of it. Write annotations around the diagram to describe and explain some of the adaptive features that the organism has. For each one, say what the feature is *and* explain how it helps the organism to survive and reproduce in its environment.

### CONTINUED

**Self-assessment**

Did you find at least five adaptive features on your organism?

How well do you think you *explained* how each feature helps the organism to survive and reproduce in its environment?

If you were asked to do a similar task in the future, how could you improve what you did?

## Question

7 Copy and complete this table, to compare adaptations of xerophytes and hydrophytes. One row has been done to start you off. Add another row for each feature you think of.

| Feature | Xerophyte | Hydrophyte |
|---|---|---|
| roots | spread widely, and/or penetrate deeply, into the soil | may hang in the water; sometimes grow into the mud, but not deeply |
| | | |

## Selection

In the first topic of this chapter, we saw that individuals within a population are not all the same – they show variation. Within a population of pygmy seahorses, perhaps some have slightly different colouration, so that some are slightly better camouflaged than others. Within a population of tuna, perhaps some individuals have more mitochondria than others, so they can release more energy and swim just a little bit faster than the rest of the population.

An animal or plant that is well adapted to its environment is much more likely to survive than one that is not. A pygmy seahorse that was bright blue instead of pink and white would not be camouflaged and would probably be killed and eaten by a predator long before it reached adulthood. Only well-adapted individuals have a good chance of living long enough to reproduce.

Adaptive features are caused by genes. Individuals whose alleles give them slightly better adaptive features are more likely to survive and reproduce than the other individuals in the population. So, their alleles are more likely to be passed on to the next generation.

Over time, this results in more and more of the population having these alleles. The better-adapted individuals survive and reproduce, while those that have alleles that do not provide quite as good adaptive features die. We say that the better-adapted individuals – those that have alleles that give them slightly better adaptive features – are selected.

This process is called **natural selection**. It is happening all the time, in all the populations of all the different species of organism in the world. We can summarise natural selection in four points:

1. **Variation.** There is variation within a population of organisms. Some of these variations are caused by having different alleles of genes. Some of the variation affects the adaptive features of the organisms.
2. **Overproduction.** Within a wild population, many more offspring are produced than will survive to become adults and reproduce. For example, only about half of all the zebra foals that are born will survive to become adults (Figure 17.20).
3. **Best-adapted individuals more likely to survive and reproduce.** Within the population, it is the individuals that have the best adaptive features that have the best chance of surviving and reproducing. We can say that there is a 'struggle for survival' (this does *not* mean that the organisms fight each other). Sometimes, for example, the individuals might have to compete for food if this is in short supply, and only the ones that have the best adaptations for getting food survive.
4. **Alleles that confer useful adaptations more likely to be passed on.** These better-adapted individuals are therefore the ones that pass on their alleles to the next generation (Figure 17.21). The alleles that confer the best chance of survival therefore increase in the population, while alleles that are not advantageous become less common.

> ### KEY WORDS
>
> **natural selection:** a process in which individuals with advantageous features are more likely to survive, reproduce and pass on their alleles to the next generation

**Figure 17.20:** Scientists are not sure why zebras have stripes, but some research suggests it makes them less attractive to blood-sucking flies. This spotty foal, however, has a mutation in the gene producing the pattern on its skin. This could make it less likely to survive long enough to reproduce.

Most of the time, natural selection does not make anything change. Zebras have stripes because this is a good adaptation that helps them to survive. A mutation that causes a different pattern is not selected for, because it reduces the chance of survival. The allele that causes the spotted pattern in the foal in Figure 17.20 will probably not be passed on to the next generation. The population of zebras will stay striped, not become spotty.

But sometimes, natural selection can cause change in a population. There are two reasons this might happen:

- A new allele could arise, just by chance, by mutation. If this allele gives an organism a better adaptive feature than any of the other individuals in the population, then this organism will be selected for – that is, it will have a good chance of surviving and reproducing. The new allele will be passed on to the next generation.

- The environment could change, so that features that once helped an organism to survive are no longer as useful. For example, as climate change progresses, species that now have plenty of plants to eat and water to drink may find that their environment has become drier. Individuals that have adaptive features that help them to survive in this new environment will pass on their alleles and, over time, there will therefore be change in the adaptive features of the species.

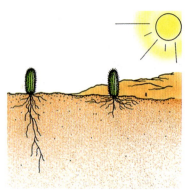
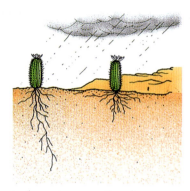
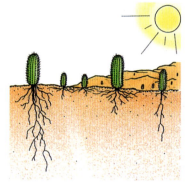

1 Genetic variation. In a population of cacti, some have longer roots than others.

In the wet season they flower.

2 Overproduction. The cacti produce large numbers of offspring.

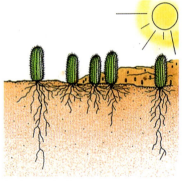

3 Struggle for existence. During the dry season, there is competition for water.

4 Survival of the fittest. The cacti with the longest roots are able to obtain water, while the others die of dehydration.

5 Advantageous characteristics passed on to offspring. The long-rooted cacti reproduce, producing offspring more likely to be long-rooted themselves.

**Figure 17.21:** How natural selection could affect a population of cacti.

## An example of natural selection

Natural selection can help us to understand some changes that took place in the features of a species of moth in Britain and Ireland.

The peppered moth, *Biston betularia*, lives in most parts of Great Britain and Ireland. It flies by night, and spends the daytime resting on tree trunks. It has speckled wings, which camouflage it very effectively on lichen-covered tree trunks (Figure 17.22).

**Figure 17.22:** Four peppered moths on a lichen-covered tree trunk. The two normal, speckled moths are at the left. The dark ones are a variation caused by a different allele of the gene for wing colour.

Moth collecting was a fashionable activity in the 19th century, so we know that up until 1849, all the peppered moths in collections were pale and speckled. But in 1849, a dark form of the moth was caught near Manchester. By 1900, 98% of the moths near Manchester were dark. By 1958, there were dark peppered moths in many parts of the country (Figure 17.23).

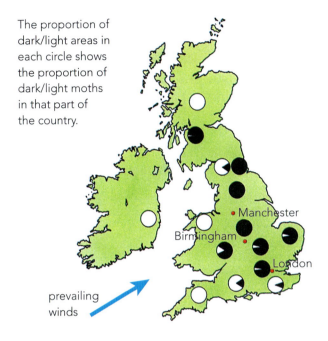

The proportion of dark/light areas in each circle shows the proportion of dark/light moths in that part of the country.

prevailing winds

**Figure 17.23:** The distribution of the pale form and the dark form of the speckled moth in 1958.

How can we explain the sudden rise in numbers of the dark moths, and their distribution today?

We know that the dark colour of the moth is caused by a single dominant allele of a gene. The mutation from a normal to a dark allele happens fairly often, so it is reasonable to assume that there have always been a few dark moths around, as well as pale speckled ones.

Up until the beginning of the Industrial Revolution, the pale moths had the advantage, as they were better camouflaged on the lichen-covered tree trunks. The pale moths were more likely to survive and reproduce, so the allele producing the pale colour was much more common than the allele for dark wings.

But in the middle of the 19th century, some areas of Britain became polluted by smoke. Because the prevailing winds in Britain blow from the west, the worst affected areas were to the east of industrial cities such as Manchester and Birmingham. The polluted air prevented lichens from growing. Dark moths were now better camouflaged than pale moths on trees with no lichens on them.

Proof that the dark moths do have an advantage in polluted areas has been supplied by several investigations. Figure 17.24 summarises one of them.

1 Equal numbers of dark and pale peppered moths were collected and marked with a spot of paint on the underside.

2 Equal numbers of each type of moth were released into a polluted wood and an unpolluted wood.

3 After a few days, flying moths were recaptured using a light trap.

4 Most of the recaptured moths in the polluted wood were dark, suggesting that the pale ones had been eaten by birds.

In the unpolluted wood, more pale moths had survived.

**Figure 17.24:** An investigation to measure the survival of dark and pale peppered moths in polluted and unpolluted environments.

The factor that gives an advantage to the dark moths, and a disadvantage to the pale moths in polluted areas, is predation by birds. This is called a **selection pressure**, because it 'selects' the dark moths for survival. In unpolluted areas, the pale moths are more likely to survive.

> **KEY WORDS**
>
> **selection pressure:** something in the environment that affects the chance that individuals with different features will survive and reproduce

## Questions

8   Look at the four numbered points summarising how natural selection happens, near the beginning of the section headed **Selection**.

    Use these four points to summarise how selection caused the proportion of dark peppered moths near Manchester to increase at the end of the 19th century.

9   Today, in the 21st century, air quality in Britain is much better than it was in the past. It is now very rare to see a dark peppered moth in Britain. Explain how selection has caused this reversal in the proportions of pale and dark peppered moths in the population.

## Antibiotic resistance in bacteria

In the previous topics, we have looked at adaptive features of organisms, and how these increase their ability to survive and reproduce. The process by which these features develop over many generations in a population, gradually making the population more suited to its environment, is called **adaptation**. In this section, we will look at how adaptation to a changing environment has resulted in bacterial populations becoming more suited to their environment, in ways that are very inconvenient to the human population.

When someone is ill, we can often use **drugs** to help to ease their symptoms, or to help them to recover. A drug is a substance that affects metabolic reactions in the body. Drugs that help us to stay healthy are called medicinal drugs.

**Antibiotics** are medicinal drugs that kill bacteria in the body, without harming our own cells. They are a very important tool in medicine. Antibiotics help to cure bacterial infections that could otherwise be very serious or even fatal. Antibiotics do not, however, affect viruses, so there is no point in using them to treat viral infections such as colds.

Over the last few decades, however, many populations of pathogenic bacteria have become resistant to antibiotics. This has happened by natural selection. These resistant bacteria are no longer killed by the antibiotics.

> **KEY WORDS**
>
> **adaptation:** the process, resulting from natural selection, by which populations become more suited to their environment over many generations
>
> **drug:** any substance taken into the body that modifies or affects chemical reactions in the body
>
> **antibiotic:** a substance that is taken into the body, and which kills bacteria but does not affect human cells or viruses

Penicillin is an antibiotic that stops bacteria from forming cell walls. When a person infected with bacteria is treated with penicillin, the bacteria are unable to grow new cell walls, and they burst open.

However, the population of bacteria in the person's body may contain several million individuals. Within that population, there are likely to be at least one or two individuals that have an allele that makes them resistant to penicillin. These individuals will have a tremendous selective advantage. They will be able to go on reproducing while all the others cannot. Soon, their descendants – all containing the allele that confers resistance to penicillin – may form a huge population of penicillin-resistant bacteria (Figure 17.25).

This does, in fact, happen quite frequently. This is one reason why there are so many different antibiotics available – if some bacteria become resistant to one, they can be treated with another.

Today, there are many populations of bacteria that have become resistant to more than one antibiotic. The bacterium *Staphylococcus aureus* lives on the skin of most of us and is normally completely harmless, but it can sometimes cause dangerous infections if it gets through the skin and into the body. In the past, it was easy to treat these infections, because *S. aureus* could be killed with many different antibiotics, including penicillin, oxacillin, amoxicillin and methicillin.

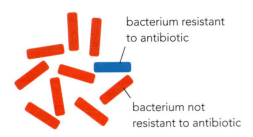  

In a population of bacteria, not every one is alike. By chance, one may have an allele that makes it resistant to an antibiotic.

Antibiotic is added, which kills the bacteria that are not resistant.

The resistant one multiplies and forms a population of resistant bacteria just like itself.

Figure 17.25: Populations of bacteria become resistant to antibiotics through natural selection.

These resistant populations are given the name **MRSA**, standing for *methicillin-resistant Staphylococcus aureus*. Doctors do still have a few antibiotics that can kill MRSA, but this bacterium is constantly adapting to its new environmental pressures. It is a kind of race – the bacterium develops, through random mutation and natural selection, a new adaptation that helps it to survive treatment with antibiotics, and we then find new antibiotics to treat it with. The bacterium then becomes resistant to the new antibiotic, and so on.

> **KEY WORD**
>
> **MRSA:** *methicillin-resistant Staphylococcus aureus*; bacteria that are resistant to the antibiotic methicillin

The more we use antibiotics, the more likely it is that resistant populations of bacteria will develop. It is very important to restrict the use of antibiotics as much as we can. Of course, if someone has a serious bacterial infection, they need antibiotics to help them to recover. But it is pointless to give someone antibiotics for a cold or for a minor bacterial infection that the body can fight off on its own. Reducing our use of antibiotics means that bacteria that have resistance to them have no selective advantage, so populations of resistant bacteria are much less likely to arise. Then, when someone really does need to be treated with the antibiotic, it will work.

## DNA sequences and classification

In Topic 17.1, we saw that a mutation produces a change in the base sequence of DNA. If this change is advantageous, natural selection may cause the change to become more common over time, as it is passed on to subsequent generations. Over very long periods of time, more and more mutations can occur, so the base sequence of the DNA in a population can become more and more different from their ancestors. Eventually, the DNA may become so different that the population can no longer breed with the one that it originated from. A new species has been produced.

Biologists can use this to work out how closely related different species of organisms are. DNA base sequences are now quite often used to help to classify organisms into species, genera, families and so on.

DNA is extracted from the cells of an organism of one species, and the base sequence of certain parts is determined. The same procedure is carried out for another organism and the two sets of base sequences are compared. If they are identical, then the two organisms probably belong to the same species. If they are different, this suggests that the organisms may belong to different species.

If there are a lot of differences in the DNA base sequences of the two species, this suggests that there has been time for many mutations to happen since the two species stopped breeding with one another. They are only distantly related to one another and share only a distant ancestor.

If there are only a few differences in the DNA base sequences, this could mean that the two species only stopped breeding with each other a relatively short while ago. They are quite closely related to one another and share a recent ancestor.

Figure 17.26 **a:** A wild mouflon – this is the wild species of sheep from which we think all the domesticated breeds have been developed. **b:** Selective breeding for thick, high-quality wool production has produced the Merino breed of sheep. **c:** Selective breeding for the ability to survive in harsh environments has produced the Damara breed of sheep.

## Selective breeding

Humans can bring about changes in living organisms, by selecting certain individuals for breeding. Figure 17.26 shows examples of the results of this kind of selection. For example, from the varied individuals among a herd of cattle, the breeder chooses the ones with the characteristics he or she wants to appear in the next generation. He or she then allows these individuals, and not the others, to breed. If this selection process is repeated over many generations, these characteristics will become the most common ones in the population.

The process of choosing only certain animals or plants to breed is called **artificial selection** or **selective breeding**. It has been going on for thousands of years, ever since humans first began to cultivate plants and to domesticate animals. It works in just the same way as natural selection. Individuals with 'advantageous' characteristics breed, while those with 'disadvantageous' ones do not.

> **KEY WORDS**
>
> **artificial selection** or **selective breeding:** choosing particular organisms with desired characteristics to breed together, and continuing this over many generations

Even when a particular breed has been produced, farmers will still continue to use selective breeding to enhance the characteristics that they choose. Imagine, for example, that a farmer has a herd of cows, which she keeps for milk production. She wants to improve her herd. She will follow these steps:

1. Choose only the cows that produce large volumes of high-quality milk.
2. Choose a bull whose mother, sisters and/or daughters produce large volumes of high-quality milk.
3. Breed the chosen cows with the chosen bull.

**4** Allow the calves to grow to adults. From this generation, select the cows that produce the greatest volumes of high-quality milk, and breed them with the chosen bull (which could be the same one, or a different one).

**5** Repeat for many generations.

Sometimes, the breeder may want to combine two useful characteristics. So, she might, for example, choose to breed a cow that produces high-quality milk with a bull that is very docile (calm and easy to handle). If she repeats this over several generations, she should be able to produce cows that are both easy to handle, and good milk producers.

## Questions

**10** Sheep produce methane, which is a greenhouse gas. In New Zealand, farmers are using selective breeding to produce flocks of sheep that produce less methane. Outline how they can do this.

**11** Wheat is a cereal crop that is attacked by many different pests, including a fungus called yellow rust. Some varieties of wheat have quite good resistance to yellow rust, but do not produce high yields.

   **a** Describe how you could use selective breeding to produce a new variety of wheat that has good resistance to yellow rust and produces high yields.

   **b** When resistant varieties of wheat are produced by selective breeding, it is often found that, after a few years, they are infected by yellow rust again.

   Explain how natural selection might cause the yellow rust to become able to infect the resistant varieties of wheat.

## Comparing natural selection and selective breeding

There are many similarities between natural selection and selective breeding. In both, only certain individuals survive and breed. However, there are also many differences between them – both in how they work, and their results.

- In natural selection, it is the environment that determines or 'selects' which individuals are able to survive and breed. In artificial selection, it is humans that do this.

- In natural selection, there is random mating between individuals – animals choose their own mates, while plants can receive pollen from any anthers onto any stigmas. In artificial selection, humans determine which individuals reproduce with each other.

- In natural selection, adaptive features that increase the chances of an individual surviving and reproducing are selected for. These adaptive features help the organism to survive in its natural environment. But in selective breeding, the features that are selected for are not adaptive features. They are the features that the breeder wants. These features might actually make it *less* likely that the organism could survive in the wild (Figure 17.27).

**Figure 17.27:** This Merino sheep got lost, so his wool was not removed by a farmer for many years. Merino sheep have been selectively bred to produce a lot of wool, and his wool weighed so much that he almost died. He was eventually found and his wool removed.

- In natural selection, the selective advantage of a particular feature can be quite small – there is only a slightly better chance of some individuals surviving rather than others, and even individuals that don't have the best adaptive features still have a chance of reproducing. In artificial selection, only the very 'best' organisms are chosen to reproduce.

- The relatively weak selection pressures in natural selection mean that the amount of variation that is present in a wild population is often much greater than in a population produced by artificial selection.

- With natural selection, the speed of change in a population is usually quite slow. In many cases, there is no change at all over time. With artificial selection, quite large changes in features can happen over quite short periods of time.

## SUMMARY

Differences between individuals of the same species are called variation.

Continuous variation occurs when an individual can have any phenotype in a complete range between the two extremes. There are no distinct categories. It is caused by genes and the environment. Human height and body mass are examples of continuous variation.

Discontinuous variation occurs when there is a limited number of phenotypes, such as the A, B, AB and O blood groups in humans. It is caused by genes alone. Other examples include wrinkled and smooth peas, and green and yellow peas.

Mutation is genetic change. It is the way that new alleles are formed. The chance of mutation happening is increased by ionising radiation and some chemicals.

Gene mutation is a random change in the base sequence of DNA.

Mutation, meiosis, random mating and random fertilisation are sources of genetic variation in populations.

An adaptive feature is an inherited feature that increases the chance that an individual will survive and reproduce.

Xerophytes are plants that have adaptive features that enable them to survive and reproduce where water is in short supply. Hydrophytes have adaptive features that help them to survive and reproduce in water.

Natural selection acts on variation among the individuals in a population. More offspring are produced than will survive to adulthood, and those individuals with the best adaptations to their environment are more likely to survive long enough to reproduce. We can say that there is a 'struggle for survival', including competition for resources such as food supply. The best-adapted individuals are therefore more likely to pass on their alleles to the next generation.

Adaptation is the process, resulting from natural selection, by which populations become better adapted to survive and reproduce in their environment, over many generations.

The development of antibiotic resistance in bacteria is an example of natural selection.

Differences in the DNA sequences of organisms, caused by mutation and natural selection over time, can be used to determine how closely related they are, and to classify them.

Selective breeding involves humans selecting individual animals or plants with desirable features to breed together, repeating this process with the offspring, and then repeating again for several generations. It is used to improve crop plants and domestic animals.

Natural selection is slower than artificial selection and maintains more variation in the population than artificial selection does. The features selected for in natural selection are those that adapt organisms for their environment, whereas in artificial selection the features are those chosen by humans, which may not be adaptive features.

# 17 Variation and selection

## PROJECT

### Using beads to investigate the effects of selection

Figure 17.28: Different types of brassica.

How do so many different types of vegetables arise from one type of plant? Specific selection pressures can lead to changes in phenotypes and produce a wide range of new breeds. In the case of these brassicas, artificial selection for specific characteristics has produced six different vegetables.

In this project, you are going to use beads to model natural or artificial selection. In Chapter 16, you may have used different colours of beans or beads to represent alleles in the activity *Breeding beads*. In this project, we are going to do something similar, but with some important changes to the procedure.

You will use the beads as in that activity, to model how alleles are passed on from one generation to the next, and to predict the ratios of the different genotypes and phenotypes in the next generation. However, this time, you are going to apply a selection pressure *against* a specific genotype to each 'generation' of beads.

Here is how to do this:

- Put 100 red beads and 100 yellow beads (or whatever colours you have) into a large beaker. This is your population of organisms. The beads represent the alleles in the gametes that they make. Red beads represent allele **A**, and yellow beads represent allele **a**.

- Without looking, pick out two beads from the container. These represent the result of two individuals in the population mating. Record the genotype of the offspring you have just produced. Put these beads into another container.

- Keep doing this until you have used up all the beads in your initial population.

- Write down the number of organisms of each genotype that you have produced in the next generation.

- Now let your new generation breed, just as the first one did. But this time, apply a selection pressure to the **aa** offspring. Let's say that one in five of them do not survive to reproduce. To model this, remove every fifth offspring with the genotype **aa** from your populations. (That is, put every fifth pair of yellow beads – **aa** – into a different container as soon as they appear and ignore them from now on – they are dead.) Record your results again.

- Keep going, repeating your one in five selection against the **aa** offspring, for several generations.

Other groups could try different selection pressures, like this:

| Selection pressure against homozygous recessive individuals | What you do |
|---|---|
| 5% | Remove every 20th **aa** offspring from the population |
| 10% | Remove every 10th **aa** offspring from the population |
| 20% | Remove every 5th **aa** offspring from the population |
| 25% | Remove every 4th **aa** offspring from the population |
| 50% | Remove every 2nd **aa** offspring from the population |
| 100% | Remove every **aa** offspring from the population |

When all the groups have collected results, discuss what you have found. Here are two issues you may like to discuss:

1. How do your selection pressures affect the proportion of homozygous recessive organisms in the population? Do they ever disappear completely?

2. How well do you think this model represents what really happens in a population of organisms?

365

> **REFLECTION**
>
> This is quite a time-consuming process for you, and it is easy to get the beads muddled up. What did you do to help to keep focused, and to avoid mistakes?
>
> Are there other activities that you regularly do in your Biology work where you have to work hard to stay focused? What tactics do you use to help you?

## EXAM-STYLE QUESTIONS

1. Which is an example of continuous variation?
   - A  ABO blood groups in humans
   - B  body mass in humans
   - C  seed colour in peas
   - D  seed shape in peas [1]

2. How are new alleles formed?
   - A  by artificial selection
   - B  by continuous variation
   - C  by discontinuous variation
   - D  by mutation [1]

3. What two words are missing from this description of an adaptive feature?
   An ____1____ feature that helps an organism to survive and ____2____ in its environment.

   |   | 1 | 2 |
   |---|---|---|
   | A | artificial | live |
   | B | artificial | reproduce |
   | C | inherited | live |
   | D | inherited | reproduce |
   [1]

4. Which process almost always results in adaptation to the environment?
   - A  artificial selection
   - B  mutation
   - C  natural selection
   - D  selective breeding [1]

5. What is a difference between natural selection and artificial selection?
   - A  Artificial selection produces more variation in a population than natural selection.
   - B  Natural selection happens more slowly than artificial selection.
   - C  Selection pressures in natural selection are generally stronger than in artificial selection.
   - D  The chance of mutation taking place in natural selection is greater than in artificial selection. [1]

## CONTINUED

**6** Copy and complete the following sentences, using words from the list. You may use each word once, more than once or not at all.

**adapted   continuous   discontinuous   environment   genes
genus   matched   mutation   selection   sex   species**

Variation can be defined as differences between individuals belonging to the same _____. Sometimes, the differences are clear-cut, and each individual fits into one of a small number of defined categories. This is called _____ variation. This kind of variation is caused by the organisms' _____. In other cases, the differences have no definite categories. This is called _____ variation.

New features can arise when new alleles are produced by _____. This is usually harmful because these changes make an organism less well _____ to its environment. [6]

**7** A farmer used selective breeding to try to improve the milk yield in her herd of cows.

The graph below shows the mean yield of milk per cow over the 11 years that the farmer carried out selective breeding.

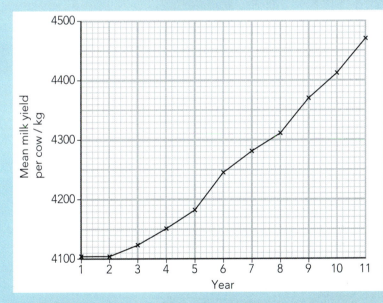

**a** **Describe** the changes in mean milk yield during the selective breeding programme. [4]
**b** Describe how the breeder would have carried out the breeding programme. [4]
**c** **Explain** why the breeder does not need to know anything about the genes that affect milk production, in order to carry out a successful breeding programme. [2]
**d** The mean percentage protein content of the milk in year 1 was 3.83. This steadily fell, reaching 3.79 in year 11. **Suggest** why this happened. [1]

[Total: 11]

### COMMAND WORDS

**describe:** state the points of a topic / give characteristics and main features

**explain:** set out purposes or reasons / make the relationships between things evident / provide why and/or how and support with relevant evidence

**suggest:** apply knowledge and understanding to situations where there are a range of valid responses in order to make proposals / put forward considerations

## CONTINUED

8 The graph below shows the number of deaths caused by MRSA and by non-resistant *Staphylococcus aureus* in a European country between 1993 and 2012.

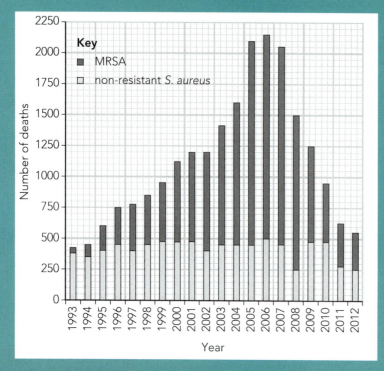

a Describe the changes in the number of deaths from MRSA between 1993 and 2012. [3]

b The percentage of deaths from *S. aureus* that were caused by MRSA in 1993 was 8.3%.

Calculate the percentage of deaths from *S. aureus* that were caused by MRSA in 2006. [2]

c In 2006, new procedures were introduced into hospitals to try to prevent the increase in cases of MRSA.

Suggest and explain **two** changes that could have helped to cause the subsequent change in the number of cases of MRSA shown on the graph. [4]

[Total: 9]

9 Gene mutation is a source of genetic variation in a population.
   a Explain what is meant by *gene mutation*. [2]
   b State **two** factors that can increase the rate of gene mutation. [2]
   c Explain how gene mutation results in changes in phenotype in an individual. [3]
   d Outline the sources of genetic variation, other than mutation, in a population. [6]

[Total: 13]

# 17 Variation and selection

## SELF-EVALUATION CHECKLIST

After studying this chapter, think about how confident you are with the different topics. This will help you to see any gaps in your knowledge and help you to learn more effectively.

| I can | See Topic… | Needs more work | Almost there | Confident to move on |
|---|---|---|---|---|
| describe variation as differences between individuals belonging to the same species | 17.1 | | | |
| explain the differences between continuous variation and discontinuous variation, and give examples | 17.1 | | | |
| investigate, record and analyse examples of continuous and discontinuous variation | 17.1 | | | |
| state that mutation is the way that new alleles are formed | 17.1 | | | |
| state factors that increase the rate of mutation | 17.1 | | | |
| describe gene mutation as a random change in the base sequence of DNA | 17.1 | | | |
| list the four sources of genetic variation in populations | 17.1 | | | |
| describe what an adaptive feature is, and interpret images to describe an organism's adaptive features | 17.2 | | | |
| explain how xerophytes and hydrophytes are adapted to their environments | 17.2 | | | |
| describe natural selection resulting from variation, overproduction of offspring, struggle for survival (including competition), reproduction by organisms with better adaptations, and the passing on of their alleles to the next generation | 17.2 | | | |
| explain how populations of bacteria resistant to antibiotics have arisen by natural selection | 17.2 | | | |
| explain how DNA sequences can be used to estimate how closely related two groups of organisms are | 17.2 | | | |
| describe how selective breeding is done, and how it can be used to improve crop plants and domesticated animals | 17.2 | | | |
| compare natural and artificial selection | 17.2 | | | |

# Chapter 18
# Organisms and their environment

### IN THIS CHAPTER YOU WILL:

- explain how energy is transferred through food webs and back to the environment
- practise using pyramids of number and biomass
- describe nutrient cycles in ecosystems
- use graphs and diagrams to describe and explain population growth

> explain why pyramids of energy or biomass provide more useful information than pyramids of number.

# 18 Organisms and their environment

## GETTING STARTED

Ask one person in your class to write the name of a plant or animal on the board.

Now, another person writes the name of a plant or animal that eats, or is eaten by, the first one, and adds an arrow to show how energy transfers from one to the other.

Continue like this, until your class has constructed a really big food web on the board.

## A FOSSIL FOOD CHAIN

About 250 million years ago, there was a huge supercontinent on Earth, called Pangaea. The centre of this enormous landmass was so far from the sea that rain rarely fell. Later, as the plates that make up the Earth's crust drifted apart, Pangaea broke up. Some of the northern areas became what is now Russia.

We know something about the animals that lived in this area at that time, because we have found their fossils. We know that there were herbivores that ate vegetation, and carnivores that fed on the herbivores. We can work this out from their skeletons and teeth. For example, if an animal has broad, flat teeth with ridges on them, this suggests it was adapted to feed on plants. If its teeth were pointed and sharp, this suggests it killed and ate other animals.

It's difficult, though, to be certain exactly what any one species ate, and we have only limited evidence about the food chains and food webs that might have existed 250 million years ago in this part of the world.

One strong possibility is that a carnivore called *Inostrancevia* preyed on a herbivore called *Scutosaurus* (Figure 18.1). Fossils of both of these dinosaurs are found in similar areas, and date from the same time. *Inostrancevia* was probably the apex (top) predator at the time – it was up to 3.5 m long and had a huge skull with upper canines that grew to 15 cm long.

### Discussion questions

1 How do you think scientists can work out food chains and food webs today? What evidence can they use, and how might they collect this evidence?

2 How does this differ from the kind of evidence that scientists can use to try to construct food chains and food webs in the distant past?

**Figure 18.1:** *Inostrancevia* and *Scutosaurus*.

## 18.1 Energy flow and food webs

One very important way of studying living things is to study them where they live. Animals and plants do not live in complete isolation. They are affected by their environment (surroundings). Their environment is also affected by them. The study of the interaction between living organisms and their environment is called **ecology**.

There are many words that you need to be able to use when you learn, talk and write about ecology. Here are some – and you will meet quite a few more as you work through this chapter.

The area where an organism lives is called its **habitat**. Each species of organism has adaptive features that enable it to live in its specific habitat (Figure 18.2).

The habitat of a tadpole might be a pond. There will probably be many tadpoles in the pond, forming a population of tadpoles. A population is a group of organisms of the same species, living in the same area at the same time.

Tadpoles will not be the only organisms living in the pond. There will be many other kinds of animals and plants making up the pond **community**. A community is all the organisms, of all the different species, living in the same habitat.

The interactions between the living organisms in the pond, the water in it, the stones and the mud at the bottom, make up an **ecosystem**. An ecosystem consists of the interactions between the organisms in a community and their environment.

> ### KEY WORDS
>
> **ecology:** the study of organisms in their environment
>
> **habitat:** the place where an organism lives
>
> **community:** all of the populations of all the different species in an ecosystem
>
> **ecosystem:** a unit containing all of the organisms in a community and their environment, interacting together

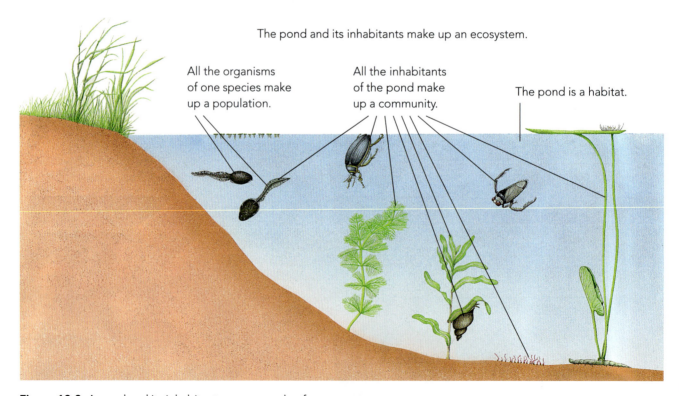

Figure 18.2: A pond and its inhabitants – an example of an ecosystem.

Within the ecosystem, each living organism has its own life to live and role to play. The way in which an organism lives its life in an ecosystem is called its **niche**. Tadpoles, for example, eat algae and other weeds in the pond; they disturb pebbles and mud at the bottom of shallow areas in the pond; they excrete ammonia into the water; they breathe in oxygen from the water, and breathe out carbon dioxide. All these things, and many others, help to describe the tadpoles' role, or niche, in the ecosystem.

## Energy flow

All living organisms need energy. All the energy in an ecosystem originates from the Sun. Some of the energy in sunlight is captured by plants, and used to make organic nutrients – glucose, starch and other organic substances such as fats and proteins. These contain some of the energy from the sunlight. When a plant cell needs energy, it breaks down some of this food by respiration.

Animals get their food, and therefore their energy, by ingesting (eating) plants, or by eating animals which have eaten plants. Again, when a cell needs energy to carry out a particular process, such as muscle contraction or active transport, the energy is released by respiration.

The sequence by which energy, in the form of chemical energy in food, passes from a plant to an animal and then to other animals, is called a **food chain**. Figure 18.3 shows one example of a food chain.

Many different food chains link to form a **food web**. Figure 18.4 shows an example of a food web.

> **KEY WORDS**
>
> **niche:** the role of an organism in its natural environment; the way in which it interacts with other organisms and with the non-living parts of the environment
>
> **food chain:** a diagram showing the flow of energy from one organism to the next, beginning with a producer
>
> **food web:** a network of interconnected food chains

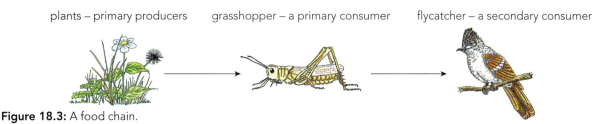

**Figure 18.3:** A food chain.

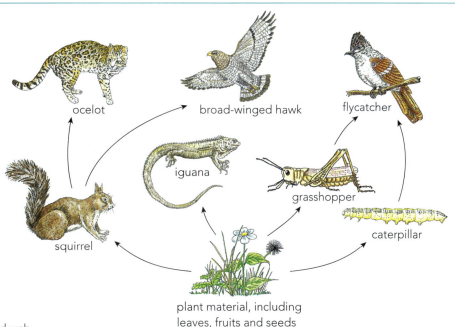

**Figure 18.4:** A food web.

## Producers and consumers

Every food chain begins with green plants because only they can capture the energy from sunlight. They are called **producers** because they produce the energy-containing organic nutrients that all the other organisms in the food chain need.

Animals are **consumers**. An animal that gets its energy by eating plants is a primary consumer, because it is the first consumer in a food chain. An animal which eats that animal is a secondary consumer. An animal that eats a secondary consumer is a tertiary consumer. Rarely, there may also be animals that get their energy by eating tertiary consumers, and they are called quaternary consumers. Primary consumers are also called **herbivores**, and consumers that eat other animals are called **carnivores**.

Fungi are also consumers. They get their energy by feeding on dead and decaying bodies and waste organic material from plants and animals. Consumers that feed like this are called **decomposers**.

> ### KEY WORDS
>
> **producer:** an organism that makes its own organic nutrients, generally using energy from sunlight, through photosynthesis
>
> **consumer:** an organism that gets its energy by feeding on other organisms
>
> **herbivore:** an animal that gets its energy by eating plants
>
> **carnivore:** an animal that gets its energy by eating other animals
>
> **decomposer:** an organism that gets its energy from dead or waste organic material

> ### ACTIVITY 18.1
>
> **Matching ecology terms**
>
> Work in a small group for this activity.
>
> You need 26 identical pieces of card. On one side of 13 of them, write one of the key words you have met in this chapter. On one side of the other 13, write the meanings of these key words.
>
> Shuffle the cards. Place them all upside down on the table and spread them out.
>
> **CONTINUED**
>
> The first person turns over a card, and reads what it says. Everyone in the group must be able to see that card. The same person then turns over another card and reads what that card says.
>
> If the two cards give a word and its meaning, the person keeps the cards and has another go. If the two cards do not match, then the cards are turned face down again, in their original positions. The next person then takes their turn.
>
> The winner is the person with the most cards when all 22 cards have been matched.

## Energy losses

As energy is passed along a food chain, some of it is lost to the environment. This happens in several ways (Figure 18.5).

- When an organism uses glucose and other organic compounds for respiration, some of the energy released from the glucose is lost as heat energy to the environment.

- When one organism eats another, it rarely eats absolutely all of it. For example, the grasshopper in the food chain in Figure 18.3 may eat almost all of the parts of the plant above ground, but it will not eat the roots. So not all of the energy in the plant is transferred to the grasshopper.

- When an animal eats another organism, enzymes in its digestive system break down most of the large nutrient molecules, so that they can be absorbed. But not all of the nutrient molecules are digested and absorbed. Some just pass through the alimentary canal and are eventually lost from the body in the faeces. These faeces contain energy that is lost from this food chain.

This means, the further you go along a food chain, the less energy is available for each successive group of organisms. In Figure 18.5, the plants get a lot of energy from the Sun, but only a fraction of this energy is absorbed by the grasshoppers, and only a fraction of that is absorbed by the flycatcher birds.

We can therefore think of energy as flowing from the Sun as energy in light, then through a food chain in the form of chemical energy in organic nutrients, and finally back to the environment as heat energy.

# 18 Organisms and their environment

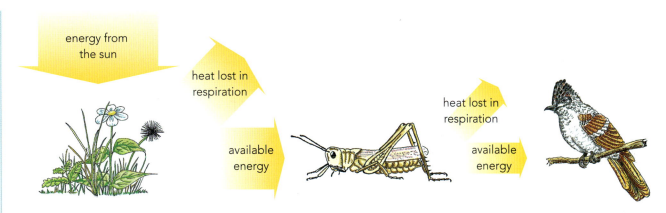

Figure 18.5: Energy is lost to the environment as it passes along a food chain.

## Questions

1 In a desert, kangaroo rats eat seeds of creosote bushes. Some of the kangaroo rats are eaten by kit foxes (Figure 18.6). Coyotes eat kit foxes.

Figure 18.6 a: A kangaroo rat. b: Kit foxes.

   a  Show this information as a food chain. (You do not need to draw the organisms – just write their names.)
   b  Name the producer in this food chain.
   c  Identify the primary consumer, secondary consumer and tertiary consumer in this food chain.
   d  Which organisms in the food chain are herbivores? Which are carnivores?
   e  Leaves of creosote bushes are also eaten by grasshoppers and jackrabbits. Kit foxes also eat jackrabbits. Grasshoppers are eaten by kit foxes and tarantulas.
      Add this information to your food chain, to make a food web.
2 Construct a food chain of your own, with a human at the end of it. Label your food chain to show the producer, and also the different levels of consumers.
3 Most food chains have only a few links, and it is very rare to find a food chain that has more than five links in it. Suggest an explanation for this.

## Trophic levels

If we count the numbers of organisms at different positions in a food chain, we usually find that there are more plants than animals, and more herbivores than carnivores. We can show this by drawing a kind of graph called a **pyramid of numbers** (Figure 18.7). In the pyramid, the area of each block represents the number of organisms at that step in the food chain. Each level in the pyramid is called a **trophic level** ('trophic' means feeding).

> **KEY WORDS**
>
> **pyramid of numbers:** a diagram in which the area of the bar at each trophic level shows the relative number of organisms at that level in the food chain
>
> **trophic level:** the position of an organism in a food chain, food web or pyramid of biomass or numbers

375

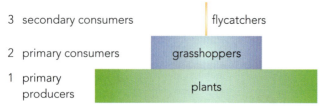

Figure 18.7: A pyramid of numbers.

The pyramid is this shape because there is less energy available as you go up the trophic levels, so there are fewer organisms at each level. There is a lot of energy for the plants in this ecosystem. The grasshoppers that eat the plants do not get all of this energy, because most is lost to the environment. This means that there cannot be as many grasshoppers as there are plants – there is simply not enough energy to support them.

In the same way, the flycatchers only receive a small proportion of the energy that the grasshoppers contain. Only enough energy reaches the flycatchers to support a small population of them.

Many organisms feed at more than one trophic level. You, for example, are a primary consumer when you eat vegetables, a secondary consumer when you eat meat or drink milk, and a tertiary consumer when you eat a predatory fish such as a salmon.

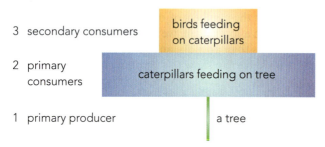

The pyramid is this shape because one tree may provide food for hundreds of caterpillars.

Figure 18.8: An inverted pyramid of numbers.

# Pyramids of biomass

Figure 18.8 shows a differently shaped pyramid of numbers. The pyramid is this shape because of the masses (biomass) of the organisms in the food chain. Although there is only a single tree, it is huge compared with the caterpillars which feed on it.

If you make the areas of the blocks represent the mass of the organisms, instead of their numbers, then the pyramid becomes the right shape again. It is called a **pyramid of biomass** (Figure 18.9). Pyramids of biomass are much better than pyramids of number, because they take the size of each organism into account. They give us a much better idea of the quantity of energy at each level than a pyramid of numbers does.

> **KEY WORDS**
>
> **pyramid of biomass:** a graph showing the relative quantity of biomass at each trophic level

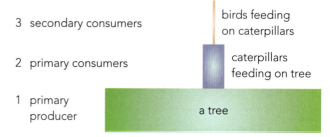

In this pyramid, the size of each box represents the mass of each kind of organism.

Figure 18.9: A pyramid of biomass.

## ACTIVITY 18.2

### Working with pyramids

#### Task 1

Look at the food chain that you drew for question 1a.

A scientist counted the number of creosote bushes, kangaroo rats, kit foxes and coyotes in an area of the desert. He found that for every 122 creosote bushes, there were 21 kangaroo rats, 5 kit foxes and 1 coyote.

Figure 18.10 shows the first part of a pyramid of numbers to show this information.

Copy and complete this diagram, using graph paper. Add labels to show the names of the organisms, and the trophic levels.

#### Task 2

The mean masses of the organisms in this food chain are:

creosote bush   24 kg

kangaroo rat   0.9 kg

kit fox   2.5 kg

coyote   15 kg

Use this information, and the pyramid of numbers that you have just drawn, to construct a pyramid of biomass.

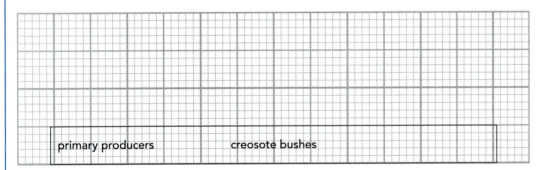

**Figure 18.10:** The start of a scale diagram of a pyramid of numbers.

### Peer assessment

Exchange your pyramid of biomass with a partner.

Assess how successful they have been in drawing the pyramid.

- Are the bars drawn carefully, with a ruler?
- Are the bars stacked symmetrically on one another?
- Is each bar the correct length?
- Are the bars clearly and fully labelled?

## Question

4   A food chain shows only one particular 'route' through a food web. For example, kangaroo rats eat the seeds of many different kinds of plants, not only creosote bushes. Explain how this could affect the shape of a pyramid of numbers or pyramid of biomass that is drawn for a single food chain.

## Pyramids of energy

Pyramids of numbers and pyramids of biomass are useful ways of visualising the numbers or masses of organisms at different levels of a food chain or food web. But, as we have seen, what actually determines the numbers or biomass of organisms at each trophic level is the quantity of energy that is available to them.

We can draw a **pyramid of energy** to show this. Figure 18.11 is a sketch of a pyramid of energy for a food web in a grassland ecosystem. (A sketch just shows the approximate proportions and is not drawn absolutely to scale.)

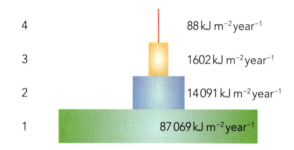

**Trophic level**

|  |  |
|---|---|
| 4 | 88 kJ m$^{-2}$ year$^{-1}$ |
| 3 | 1602 kJ m$^{-2}$ year$^{-1}$ |
| 2 | 14091 kJ m$^{-2}$ year$^{-1}$ |
| 1 | 87069 kJ m$^{-2}$ year$^{-1}$ |

**Figure 18.11:** A pyramid of energy for a food web in a grassland ecosystem.

> **KEY WORDS**
>
> **pyramid of energy:** a graph showing the relative quantity of energy at each trophic level

Notice that the units for the quantity of energy at each level are given in kJ per square metre per year. This measurement shows how much energy passes through each trophic level in one square metre of the grassland in one year. It is a good way of measuring the energy flow through the ecosystem.

How could these data be collected? It is really difficult and time-consuming to do. The researchers would first have to work out all the links in the food web. Then they would have to collect or capture samples of each organism. Then they would have to find out how much energy each organism, or each gram of an organism, contains. This is done by killing the organism, drying it, and then burning it to measure how much energy is released.

The researchers would need to count the numbers of each organism or measure their biomass. Then they can use their results for the energy content of each organism to work out the total quantity of energy at each trophic level.

Not surprisingly, this is not done very often. It is much easier to collect the data to draw a pyramid of numbers or even a pyramid of biomass.

So, although pyramids of energy are the best way of showing energy flow through an ecosystem, they are very difficult to produce. Pyramids of biomass are the next best type to use. They are not as informative as pyramids of energy, because we cannot be sure that one gram of biomass for one species contains the same quantity of energy as one gram of biomass of a different species.

## Efficiency of energy transfer

Understanding how energy is passed along a food chain can be useful in agriculture. Humans can eat a wide variety of foods, and can feed at several different trophic levels. Which is the most efficient sort of food for a farmer to grow, and for us to eat?

The nearer to the beginning of the food chain we feed, the more energy there is available for us. This is why our staple foods such as wheat, rice and potatoes are plants.

When we eat meat, eggs or cheese or drink milk, we are feeding further along the food chain. There is less energy available for us from the original energy provided by the Sun. It would be more efficient, in principle, for humans to eat the grass in a field, rather than to let cattle eat it, and then to eat them. But although there is far more energy in the grass than in the cattle, it is not available to us. We simply cannot digest the cellulose in grass, so we cannot release the energy from it. The cattle can; they turn the energy in cellulose into energy in protein and fat, which we can digest.

However, there are many plant products which we can eat. Soya beans, for example, yield a large amount of protein much more efficiently and cheaply than cattle or other animals. It is not energy efficient to feed soya beans to cattle, and then eat the cattle.

## Questions

5. Look at Figures 18.8 and 18.9. Sketch a pyramid of energy for this food chain.
6. Figure 18.12 shows a dairy farm. This is in a desert region, where there is no grass for cattle to graze. Instead, the cattle are fed on soya beans.

   Explain why this is not an energy-efficient way of producing food for humans.

Figure 18.12: A dairy farm.

## 18.2 Nutrient cycles

### Decomposers

One very important group of organisms which is easy to overlook when you are studying an ecosystem is the decomposers. As we have seen, decomposers feed on organic waste material from animals and plants, and on their dead bodies. Many fungi and bacteria are decomposers.

Decomposers are extremely important because they help to release substances from dead organisms. The released substances can then be used by other living organisms. Two of these substances are carbon and nitrogen.

### The carbon cycle

Carbon is a very important component of living things, because carbon atoms are part of the molecules of carbohydrates, fats and proteins.

Figure 18.13 shows how carbon circulates through an ecosystem.

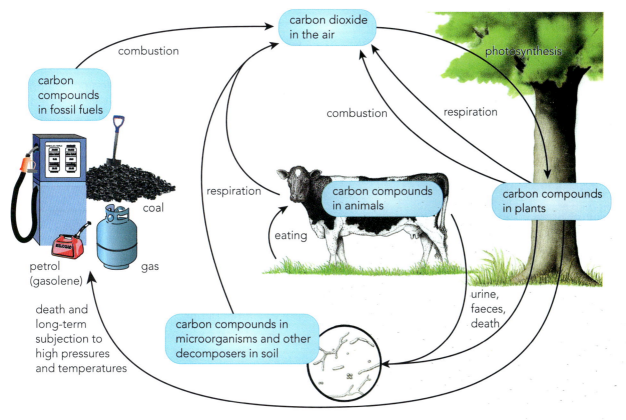

Figure 18.13: The carbon cycle.

About 0.04% of the air is carbon dioxide. When plants photosynthesise, carbon atoms from carbon dioxide become part of glucose and starch molecules in the plant. Some of the glucose is then broken down by the plant in respiration. The carbon in the glucose becomes part of a carbon dioxide molecule again, and is released back into the air. Some of the carbon-containing compounds in the plant will be eaten by animals. The animals respire, releasing some of it back into the air as carbon dioxide.

When the plant or animal dies, decomposers will feed on them. Decomposers also feed on waste materials, such as urine and faeces from animals. The carbon becomes part of the carbon-containing compounds in the decomposers' bodies. When the decomposers respire, they release carbon dioxide into the air again.

Sometimes, however, dead bodies and waste materials are not broken down by decomposers. For example, in places where there is little oxygen such as the seabed in the deep oceans or in waterlogged ground, decomposers may not be able to respire aerobically. Instead, these waste substances become buried in sediments. Over long periods of time, they are gradually changed into coal, oil or natural gas. These are called fossil fuels – not because they contain fossils, but because they were formed millions of years ago, from living organisms. (A true fossil is the remains of an organism that have been turned to stone.)

When these fossil fuels are burnt, the carbon in them combines with oxygen from the air, in a process called combustion (Figure 18.14). Wood can also undergo combustion. The carbon and oxygen combine to form carbon dioxide, which is released into the air again.

Figure 18.14: This coal is undergoing combustion.

> ### ACTIVITY 18.3
>
> #### Modelling the carbon cycle
>
> In this activity, you will use people to represent carbon atoms, and explore how a carbon atom can move around the carbon cycle. It's best to do this activity as a whole class.
>
> Start by looking at Figure 18.13. Choose five areas in the room to represent the five places that a carbon atom can be, shown in blue on the diagram. Label these areas in the room.
>
> Now choose some people to be carbon atoms. Put some carbon atoms in each labelled area.
>
> Someone who is not a carbon atom now calls out one of the processes on a labelled arrow. Some (it is best if it is not all of them) of the carbon atoms affected by this process move to a different place. For example, if the process is 'combustion', some of the carbon atoms in the 'fossil fuel' area move to the 'air' area.
>
> Carry on with this, using different processes at random.

> ### REFLECTION
>
> Did using this model help you to understand the carbon cycle? Can you explain why it helped or why it did not?
>
> How well do you think the model represents the carbon cycle? Can you think of any ways in which you could refine the model to make it easier to understand?

## Questions

7   Look at Figure 18.13.
    a   List the processes that remove carbon dioxide from the air.
    b   List the processes that add carbon dioxide to the air.
8   Describe how a carbon atom in a lion could become part of a grass plant.

## The nitrogen cycle

Living things need nitrogen to make proteins, and also to make DNA. There is plenty of nitrogen around. The air is about 78% nitrogen gas. Molecules of nitrogen gas, $N_2$, are made of two nitrogen atoms joined together. These molecules are very inert, which means that they will not readily react with other substances.

So, although the air is full of nitrogen, it is in such an unreactive form that plants and animals cannot use it at all. It must first be changed into a more reactive form, such as ammonia ($NH_3$) or nitrates ($NO_3^-$).

Changing nitrogen gas into a more reactive form is called **nitrogen fixation** (Figure 18.15). There are several ways that nitrogen fixation can happen.

## Lightning

Lightning makes some of the nitrogen gas in the air combine with oxygen, forming nitrogen oxides. They dissolve in rain, and are washed into the soil, where they form nitrates.

## Artificial fertilisers

Nitrogen and hydrogen can be made to react in an industrial chemical process, forming ammonia. The ammonia is used to make ammonium compounds and nitrates, which are sold as fertilisers.

> **KEY WORDS**
>
> **nitrogen fixation:** converting inert nitrogen gas into a more reactive form, such as nitrate ions or ammonia

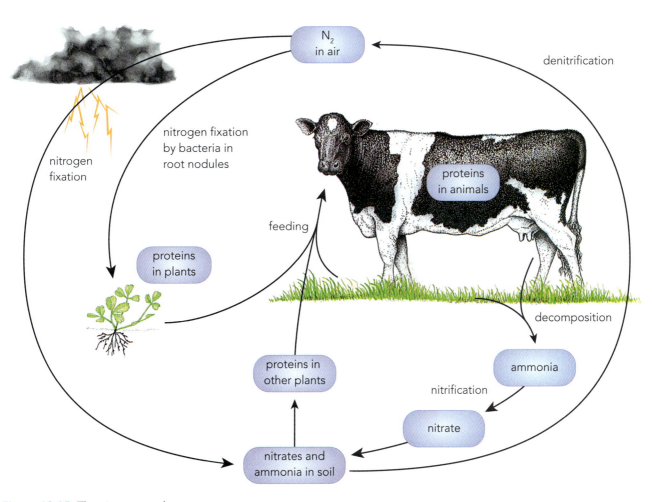

Figure 18.15: The nitrogen cycle.

### Nitrogen-fixing bacteria

These bacteria live in the soil, or in root nodules (small swellings) on plants such as peas, beans and clover. They use nitrogen gas from the air spaces in the soil and combine it with other substances to make ammonium ions and other compounds.

Once the nitrogen has been fixed, plants can use it to make amino acids, which can then be used to make proteins. Animals eat the plants, so animals get their nitrogen in the form of proteins.

When an animal or plant dies, bacteria and fungi decompose the body. The protein, containing nitrogen, is broken down to ammonium ions and this is released. Another group of bacteria, called nitrifying bacteria, turn these ions into nitrates, which plants can use again. Changing ammonium ions to nitrates is called **nitrification**.

Nitrogen is also returned to the soil when animals excrete nitrogenous waste material, which they have produced by deamination of excess amino acids (Chapter 13). The nitrogen may be in the form of ammonia or urea. Again, nitrifying bacteria will convert it to nitrates.

A third group of bacteria complete the nitrogen cycle. They are called denitrifying bacteria, because they undo the work done by nitrifying bacteria. They turn nitrates and ammonia in the soil into nitrogen gas, which goes into the atmosphere. This process is called **denitrification**.

> **KEY WORDS**
>
> **nitrification:** converting ammonium ions to nitrate ions
>
> **denitrification:** converting nitrate ions to nitrogen gas

## Questions

9   Outline the importance of each of these processes in the nitrogen cycle:
    a   nitrogen fixation
    b   nitrification

10  Microorganisms bring about four of the steps in the nitrogen cycle shown in Figure 18.15. What are these four steps, and how are microorganisms involved in each of them?

11  Deamination is not shown on Figure 18.15. Where does deamination happen, and what change takes place?

12  A soil is said to be waterlogged when there is so much water in it that there is not much room for air. In these circumstances, denitrifying bacteria work much faster than nitrogen-fixing ones. Carnivorous plants, such as sundews, often live in these places. These are plants that capture and digest insects, by producing proteases that they secrete onto the insect's body (Figure 18.16).

    Suggest why carnivorous plants are usually found growing in waterlogged soils.

Figure 18.16: A sundew leaf with a partly digested fly.

## 18.3 Populations

We have seen that a population is all the individuals of a particular species that live together in the same area at the same time. In this topic, we will look at how and why population sizes change.

Most populations tend to stay roughly the same size over a period of time. They may go up and down (fluctuate) but the average population will probably stay the same over a number of years. The population of greenfly in a garden, for example, might be much greater one year than the next. But their numbers will almost certainly be back to normal in a year or so. Over many years, the sizes of most populations tend to remain at around the same level.

Yet if all the offspring of one female greenfly survived and reproduced, she could be the ancestor of 600 000 000 000 greenfly in just one year (Figure 18.17). Why doesn't the greenfly population shoot upwards like this? Why isn't the world overrun with greenfly?

# 18 Organisms and their environment

**Figure 18.17:** Greenfly feed on plant juices. Each adult greenfly can produce huge numbers of young in a very short time.

The answers to those questions are of great importance to human beings, because our own population is doing just that; it is shooting upwards at an alarming rate. Every hour, there are more than 9000 extra people in the world. We need to understand why this is happening, and what is likely to happen next. Can we slow down the increase? What happens if we don't?

## Birth rate and death rate

The size of a population depends on how many individuals leave the population, and how many enter it.

Individuals leave a population when they die or when they migrate to another population. Individuals enter a population when they are born or when they migrate into the population from elsewhere. Usually, births and deaths are more important in determining population sizes than immigration and emigration.

A population increases if new individuals are born faster than the old ones die – that is, when the birth rate is greater than the death rate. If birth rate is less than death rate, the population will decrease. If birth rate and death rate are equal, the population will stay the same size.

This explains why we are not knee-deep in greenfly. Although the greenfly population's birth rate is enormous, the death rate is also enormous. Greenfly are eaten by ladybirds and birds, and sprayed with pesticides by gardeners and farmers. Over a period of time, the greenfly's birth and death rates stay about the same, so the population doesn't change very much.

## Factors affecting population growth

By looking at changes in population sizes in other organisms, we can learn quite a lot about our own. Many experiments on population sizes have been done on organisms like bacteria and yeast, because they reproduce quickly and are easy to grow. Figure 18.18 shows the results of an experiment in which a few yeast cells are put into a container of nutrient broth. The cells feed on the broth, grow and reproduce. The numbers of yeast cells are counted every few hours.

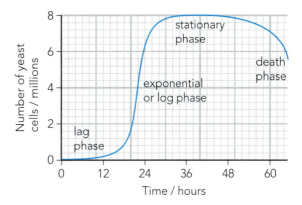

**Figure 18.18:** The growth of a population of yeast.

For the first 12 hours, the population grows only quite slowly, because there are not many cells there to reproduce. They also need time to adjust to the new conditions. This is called the **lag phase**.

But once they get going, growth is very rapid. Each cell divides to form 2, then 4, then 8, then 16. There is nothing to hold them back except the time it takes to grow and divide. This is called the **log phase**, or the **exponential phase**.

> ### KEY WORDS
>
> **lag phase:** the stage at the start of a population growth curve where the population remains small and grows only very slowly
>
> **log phase** or **exponential phase:** the stage in a population growth curve where the population grows at its maximum rate; birth rate exceeds death rate

As the population gets larger, the individual cells can no longer reproduce as fast, and begin to die off more rapidly. This may be because there is not enough food left for them all, so that there is competition for food. It could also be because they have made so much ethanol that they are poisoning themselves. The cells are now dying off as fast as new ones are being produced, so the population stops growing and levels off. This is called the **stationary phase**.

Eventually, the death rate exceeds the birth rate, so the number of living yeast cells in the population starts to fall. This is called the **death phase**.

This curve is sometimes called a **sigmoid growth curve**. 'Sigma' is the old Greek letter s, so 'sigmoid' means S-shaped.

> **KEY WORDS**
>
> **stationary phase:** the stage in a population growth curve where the population remains roughly constant; birth rate equals death rate
>
> **death phase:** the final stage in a population growth curve where the population falls; death rate exceeds birth rate
>
> **sigmoid growth curve:** an S-shaped curve showing the change in the size of a population through all the phases in population growth

## Limiting factors and population growth

Although the experiment with the yeast is done in artificial conditions, a similar pattern is found in the growth of populations of many species in the wild. If a few individuals move into a new environment, then their population curve may be very like the one for yeast cells in the flask. The population takes a while to settle in, then increases quickly, and then levels off.

We have seen that, in the log phase, the organisms are reproducing at their maximum rate. There is nothing slowing down their rate of reproduction other than their own capacity to reproduce. But eventually, some environmental factor comes into play, which slows down the population growth rate. This is a **limiting factor** – the factor that limits the rate of population growth even if everything else would allow it to increase.

In the case of the yeast in Figure 18.18 the limiting factor may be food supply, or it could be the build-up of toxins such as ethanol. The limiting factor for the greenfly in Figure 18.17 could be predation by ladybirds. The growth of other populations may be limited by disease, or the number of nest sites, for example.

It is usually very difficult to find out which environmental factors are controlling the size of a population. Almost always, many different factors will interact. A population of rabbits, for example, might be affected by the number of foxes and other predators, the amount of food available, the amount of space for burrows, and the amount of infection by a virus which causes a fatal disease such as myxomatosis.

> **KEY WORDS**
>
> **limiting factor:** a factor that is in short supply, which stops an activity (such as photosynthesis) happening at a faster rate

## Predator–prey relationships

Figure 18.19 shows an example of how the size of the population of a predator may be affected by its prey. This information comes from the number of skins which were sold by fur traders in Northern Canada to the Hudson Bay Company, between 1845 and 1925. Snowshoe hares and northern lynxes were both trapped for their fur, and the numbers caught probably give a very good idea of their population sizes.

Snowshoe hare populations tend to vary from year to year. No one is quite sure why this happens, but it may be related to their food supply. Whenever the snowshoe hare population rises, the lynx population also rises shortly afterwards, as the lynxes now have more food. A drop in the snowshoe hare population is rapidly followed by a drop in the lynx population. The numbers tend to go up and down, or oscillate, but the average population sizes stay roughly the same over many years.

## Age pyramids

When scientists begin to study a population, they want to know whether the population is growing or shrinking. This can be done by counting the population over many years, or by measuring its birth rate and death rate. But often it is much easier just to count the numbers of individuals in various age groups at one point in time, and to draw an **age pyramid**.

18 Organisms and their environment

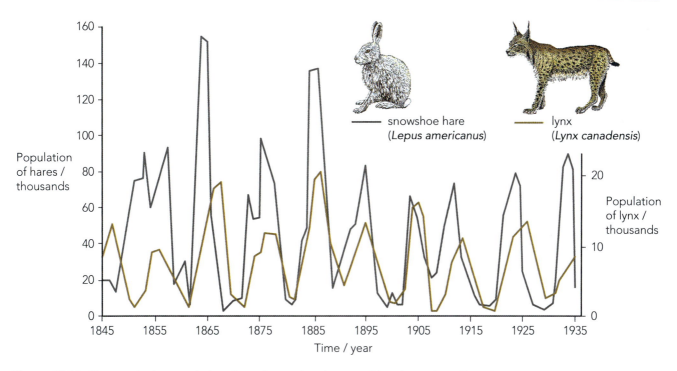

Figure 18.19: Changes in the population sizes of snowshoe hares and lynx in northern Canada.

Figure 18.20 shows two examples of age pyramids. The area of each box represents the numbers of individuals in that age group.

### KEY WORDS

**age pyramid:** a diagram showing the relative numbers of individuals of different ages in a population

Figure 18.20a is a bottom-heavy pyramid. There are far more young individuals than old ones. This indicates that birth rate is greater than death rate, so this population is increasing.

Figure 18.20b shows a much more even spread of ages. Birth rate and death rate are probably about the same. This population will remain about the same size.

a  An increasing population. If all the organisms in the younger age groups grow up and reproduce, the population will increase.

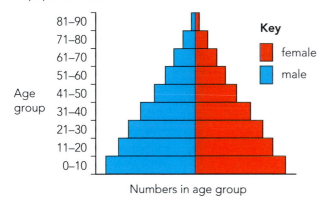

b  A stable population. The sizes of the younger age groups are only a little larger than the older ones, so this population should not change much in size.

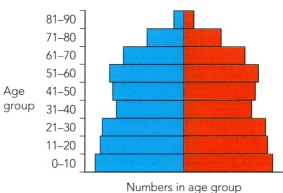

Figure 18.20: Age pyramids for two populations.

385

If an age pyramid is drawn for the human population on Earth, it is bottom-heavy, like Figure 18.20a. Age pyramids for many of the world's developing countries are also this shape, showing that their populations are increasing. But an age pyramid for a European country such as France looks more like Figure 18.20b. The human population in France is staying about the same.

## The human population

Figure 18.21 shows how the human population of the world has changed since about 4000 BC. For most of that time, human populations have been kept in check by a combination of disease, famine and war. Nevertheless, there has still been a steady increase.

There are two main reasons for this recent growth spurt. The main one is the reduction of disease. Improvements in water supply, sewage treatment, hygienic food handling and general standards of cleanliness have almost wiped out many diseases such as typhoid and dysentery in countries such as the USA and most European countries. Immunisation against diseases such as polio has made these very rare indeed. Smallpox has been totally eradicated. And the discovery of antibiotics has now made it possible to treat most diseases caused by bacteria.

Secondly, there has been an increase in food supply. More and more land has been brought under cultivation. Moreover, agriculture has become more efficient, so that in many parts of the world each hectare of land is now producing more food than ever before.

## Questions

13 Explain the difference between a population and a community.

14 List **three** environmental factors that affect the rate of a growth of a population of organisms.

15 Look at the two *y*-axis scales in Figure 18.19. Describe the difference between them, and explain why the numbers of lynx and snowshoe hares are so different from one another.

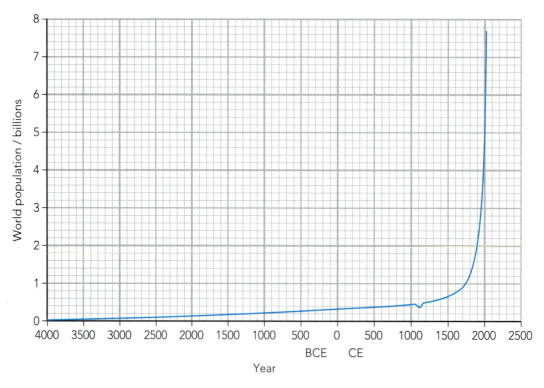

**Figure 18.21:** Changes in the human population in the last 6000 years.
Twice there have been definite 'spurts' in this growth. The first was around 8000 BC, not shown on the graph, when people in the Middle East began to farm instead of just hunting and finding food. The second began around 300 years ago and is still happening now. In 2020, the world's population reached 7.9 billion.

## SUMMARY

Biological systems depend on energy that originates from the Sun. A food chain shows how energy is transferred from one organism to another. A food web shows many interconnected food chains.

Energy flows through living organisms, and is eventually lost to the environment. Energy is lost at each step in a food chain.

Producers make their own organic nutrients from inorganic ones by photosynthesis, using energy from sunlight. Consumers get their energy by eating organic nutrients from other organisms. Consumers are classified as primary, secondary, tertiary or quaternary consumers, depending on their position in a food chain.

Herbivores are consumers that get their energy by eating plants, while carnivores get their energy by eating animals. Decomposers are consumers that get their energy by feeding on dead organisms, or their organic wastes.

A pyramid of numbers is a diagram that shows the relative numbers of organisms at each step in a food chain or web. A pyramid of biomass is similar, but shows the relative quantity of biomass rather than numbers. Each step in the pyramid is a trophic level.

A pyramid of energy shows the relative quantities of energy at each trophic level. Energy is normally measured in kJ per unit area per year.

Pyramids of biomass are more informative than pyramids of number, because they give a better picture of the quantity of energy that is present at each trophic level.

As energy passes along a food chain, some is lost within each organism, and at each transfer between organisms. The main reasons for loss are respiration (which releases some energy as heat), and some of the organisms at one level not being eaten or absorbed by the next level. Energy losses mean that there is rarely sufficient energy to support more than five links in a food chain.

It is more energy efficient for humans to eat crop plants than to eat livestock that have been fed on crop plants.

The carbon cycle summarises how carbon atoms move between organisms and their environment. Photosynthesis removes carbon dioxide from the air. Respiration and combustion return carbon dioxide to the air. Fossil fuels contain carbon atoms that were part of organisms that lived a very long time ago.

The nitrogen cycle summarises how nitrogen atoms move between organisms and their environment. Nitrogen gas, $N_2$, is very unreactive and must be converted to nitrate or ammonia before most living organisms are able to use it. This conversion is called nitrogen fixation, and is done by lightning and nitrogen-fixing bacteria. Nitrification converts ammonium ions to nitrate ions. Plants take up ammonium or nitrate ions, and use them to make amino acids and then proteins. Animals obtain their nitrogen by eating proteins from plants or other animals. Denitrification returns nitrogen gas to the air, by converting nitrates back to nitrogen.

The rate of growth of a population can be affected by food supply, predation and disease.

A population growth curve is often an S-shape, and is described as a sigmoid curve. It is made up of a lag phase, an exponential or log phase, a stationary phase and a death phase.

The environmental factor that limits the rate of growth of a population is called a limiting factor.

An age pyramid is a way of showing the age structure of a population at a point in time, and can be used to predict how the population size will change in future.

# PROJECT

**Using software to illustrate a food web**

You are going to use a computer or tablet to show a food web. You will then share what you have done with the rest of the class. This project is best done with a partner.

First, decide on your food web. You could research one in your own area, or you could find information about an interesting food web in a different part of the world.

Next, decide what you will do. This will at least partly depend on what software you have available, and your expertise in using it.

Here are some ideas:

- Simply draw a diagram of a food web, including pictures of the organisms in it. You could label each organism to show which trophic level it is at and whether it is a producer or a primary, secondary or tertiary consumer.

- Add animations to your food web diagram. For example, you could animate the arrows to show energy flowing through the web. You could make your labels interactive, so that they only pop up when the user does something.

- You could produce a series of slides to gradually build up the food web. You could animate some of the slides or the transitions between them.

- You could add an audio commentary explaining what the screen is showing.

You may have other ideas of your own. The aim is not to make things as complicated as possible, but to use what is available to you to produce an attractive and informative representation of a food web, and the ways that energy flows through it.

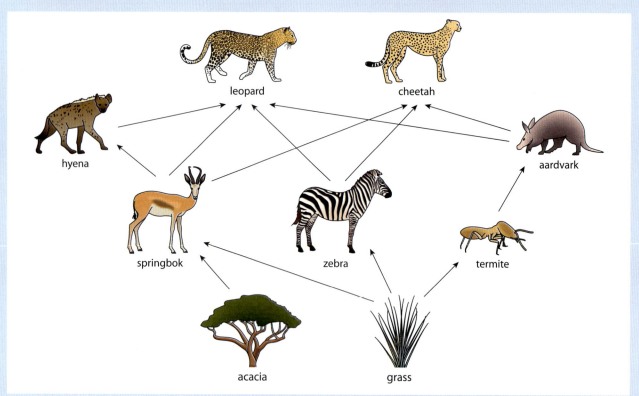

Figure 18.22: An illustrated food web.

## EXAM-STYLE QUESTIONS

1. What is a community?
   - A a group of organisms of the same species, living in the same area at the same time
   - B all the populations of different species living in the same area at the same time
   - C a unit containing organisms and their environment, interacting with one another
   - D the place where a group of organisms is adapted to live [1]

2. An organism obtains its energy by killing and eating animals that eat grass. Which terms describe this organism?
   - A carnivore, primary consumer
   - B carnivore, secondary consumer
   - C herbivore, primary consumer
   - D herbivore, secondary consumer [1]

3. How is carbon returned to the air?
   - A combustion and photosynthesis
   - B photosynthesis and feeding
   - C feeding and respiration
   - D respiration and combustion [1]

4. Organisms that feed at the fifth trophic level are rarer than those that feed at the fourth trophic level. What explains this?
   - A Energy is lost to the environment each time it is transferred from one trophic level to the next.
   - B The biomass of predators is generally larger than their prey.
   - C There is not usually enough space for large carnivores to survive.
   - D The populations of large predators are more likely to be limited by disease. [1]

5. Which term is used to describe the reactions that change ammonium ions to nitrate ions?
   - A deamination
   - B denitrification
   - C nitrification
   - D nitrogen fixation [1]

## CONTINUED

**6** The diagram shows a food web.

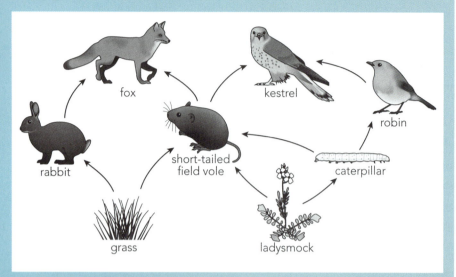

  a  **Explain** what the arrows represent. [1]
  b  Name **one** producer in this food web. [1]
  c  Draw a food chain containing four organisms, that is part of the food web shown above. [2]
  d  Use the food web to **predict** and explain **two** different ways in which a decrease in the population of short-tailed field voles could affect the population of rabbits. [4]

  [Total: 8]

**7  a**  Choose words or phrases from the list to complete the sentences about the carbon cycle.

  **0.04%   0.4%   decomposers   glycogen   herbivores
  photosynthesis   respiration   root hairs   starch   stomata**

  Approximately _____ of the air is carbon dioxide. This gas diffuses into plants through their _____, and is used to make glucose in the process of _____.

  Animals eat plants, and some of the carbon atoms in the glucose become part of molecules such as _____ in their bodies. When the animals die, their bodies are broken down by _____.

  Plants, animals and decomposers return carbon dioxide to the air through _____. [6]

  b  **Describe** how fossil fuels are formed, **and** how the carbon in them is returned to the air. [4]

  [Total: 10]

---

**COMMAND WORDS**

**explain:** set out purposes or reasons / make the relationships between things evident / provide why and/or how and support with relevant evidence

**predict:** suggest what may happen based on available information

**describe:** state the points of a topic / give characteristics and main features

## CONTINUED

**8** The table shows the numbers of eight different types of organism in a specified area of a marine ecosystem.

| Type of organism | Method of feeding | Number of individuals |
|---|---|---|
| phytoplankton (algae floating in the water) | producer | 10 000 |
| algae on the sea bed | producer | 700 |
| seaweed | producer | 500 |
| sea fans | herbivore | 7 000 |
| parrot fish | herbivore | 5 |
| surgeon fish | herbivore | 4 |
| grouper | carnivore | 3 |
| barracuda | carnivore | 1 |

    **a** Use the data in the table to sketch a pyramid of numbers. Label the trophic levels in your pyramid and indicate the number of organisms represented by each bar in the pyramid. [4]

    **b** Evaluate the extent to which this pyramid of numbers provides a true representation of the quantity of energy at each trophic level in this ecosystem. [2]

    **c** Explain why the numbers of carnivores are smaller than the numbers of herbivores. [4]

    [Total: 10]

**9 a** Proteins contain nitrogen atoms. List the **three** other elements found in all proteins. [1]

    **b** Describe how a nitrogen atom in the air can become part of a protein molecule in a human body. [6]

    **c** Seeds of a plant were carried by wind into a habitat where that species had not grown before. Over the next few years, the plants increased in number. The population then stabilised, as the plants had used up most of the nitrate ions in the soil.

       **i** Sketch a curve to show the changes in this plant population. Label the axes and include the names of the different stages shown by your curve. [4]

       **ii** Use this example to explain the term *limiting factor*, with respect to population growth. [2]

    [Total: 13]

# CAMBRIDGE IGCSE™ BIOLOGY: COURSEBOOK

## SELF-EVALUATION CHECKLIST

After studying this chapter, think about how confident you are with the different topics. This will help you to see any gaps in your knowledge and help you to learn more effectively.

| I can | See Topic... | Needs more work | Almost there | Confident to move on |
|---|---|---|---|---|
| explain the meanings of the terms *habitat*, *population*, *community* and *ecosystem* | 18.1 | | | |
| construct and interpret food chains and food webs, using arrows to show how energy is transferred through them | 18.1 | | | |
| describe the meanings of the terms *producer*, *consumer*, *herbivore*, *carnivore*, *decomposer* and *trophic level* | 18.1 | | | |
| identify producers and consumers in food chains and webs, and classify consumers as primary, secondary, tertiary and quaternary | 18.1 | | | |
| draw, describe and interpret pyramids of number and pyramids of biomass | 18.1 | | | |
| draw, describe and interpret pyramids of energy | 18.1 | | | |
| discuss the advantages of using pyramids of energy rather than pyramids of number or biomass | 18.1 | | | |
| explain why transfer of energy between trophic levels is inefficient, and use this to explain why food chains rarely have more than five trophic levels, and why it is more energy efficient for humans to eat plants rather than animals | 18.1 | | | |
| describe the carbon cycle, including photosynthesis, respiration, feeding, decomposition, formation of fossil fuels and combustion | 18.2 | | | |
| describe the nitrogen cycle, including decomposition and the conversion of protein to ammonium ions; nitrification; nitrogen fixation by lightning and bacteria; use of nitrate ions by plants to produce amino acids and proteins; feeding and digestion; deamination; denitrification | 18.2 | | | |
| state the roles of microorganisms in decomposition, nitrification, nitrogen fixation and denitrification | 18.2 | | | |
| state that food supply, predation and disease can affect the rate of population growth | 18.3 | | | |

## CONTINUED

| I can | See Topic… | Needs more work | Almost there | Confident to move on |
|---|---|---|---|---|
| identify the lag phase, log or exponential phase, stationary phase and death phase on a sigmoid curve showing population growth | 18.3 | | | |
| interpret other types of diagram showing population growth, e.g. age pyramids | 18.3 | | | |
| explain the factors determining each phase in the sigmoid growth curve, including reference to limiting factors | 18.3 | | | |

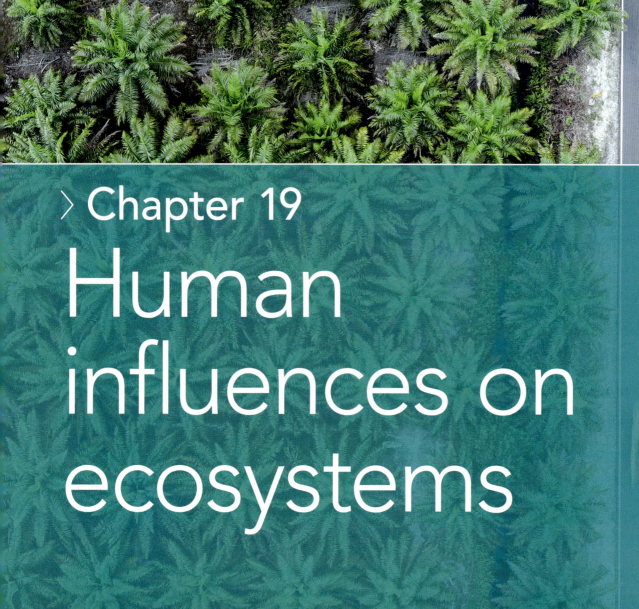

# Chapter 19
# Human influences on ecosystems

**IN THIS CHAPTER YOU WILL:**

- consider how humans have increased food production, and how this can affect the environment
- think about why habitats have been destroyed, including deforestation
- learn about some examples of pollution and their effects, including climate change
- discuss reasons for conservation, and some of the things that we can do to conserve species, habitats and ecosystems.

# 19 Human influences on ecosystems

## GETTING STARTED

With a partner, discuss how using the land in the way shown in Figure 19.1 could affect the organisms that might otherwise live there.

Make a list of your ideas, and then share them with the rest of the class.

Figure 19.1: This field is being used to grow lettuce plants.

## SAVING A SPECIES ON THE BRINK

Black-footed ferrets used to be common on the prairies of North America (Figure 19.2). But, as humans took over more and more land to graze cattle and grow crops, their habitat and food supply dwindled. Black-footed ferrets are predators that feed almost entirely on burrowing rodents called prairie dogs, and farmers killed large numbers of prairie dogs because they thought the rodents competed with cattle for grass. In 1974, the black-footed ferret was declared extinct in the wild.

But in 1981, in Wyoming, a dog brought a dead black-footed ferret to his owners. They notified wildlife officials, who leapt into action. Searches for the ferrets eventually discovered a small population of them living nearby.

The wild ferrets were given protection. But, as their numbers remained low, it was eventually decided that they needed more help. Some of the ferrets were taken to zoos, where they were given the right conditions to help them to breed. Many of the offspring were reintroduced into suitable habitats in several states, where their populations are gradually growing.

Today, the black-footed ferret is out of danger. Just in time, we managed to reverse a population decline that would have resulted in extinction.

### Discussion questions

1. Do you think it is important for humans to try to prevent species from becoming extinct? What are your reasons for your point of view?

2. Is it possible for us to grow enough food to support the growing human population, and also look after the natural environment?

Figure 19.2: Two black-footed ferrets.

# 19.1 Human pressures on ecosystems

As the human population continues to increase, we are using more and more land for making places to live and for producing food. Our activities are having negative effects on ecosystems all over the world. In this topic, we will look at some of these effects. The last topic in this chapter considers how we can conserve species, habitats and ecosystems, and why we should try to do this.

## Food production

Most of the world's supply of food is produced by growing crops or by keeping animals – although we do still harvest fish from the wild in large quantities.

During the last few hundred years, the quantity of food produced globally has greatly increased. Figure 19.3 shows the increase in one type of crop – cereal grains, such as wheat and rice – between 1950 and 2012.

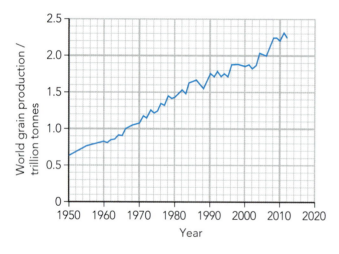

Figure 19.3: Increases in grain production since 1950.

It is important that we increase the quantity of food that we produce, because the world's increasing population needs to be fed. There are several ways in which this has been achieved.

## Agricultural machinery

Machinery such as tractors and combine harvesters have made a very big difference. A farmer can now cultivate a much greater area of land in a much shorter time than using manual labour and animals to pull machinery (Figures 19.4 and 19.5).

Figure 19.4: Ploughing with oxen and a simple wooden plough is very slow, and the plough cannot go very deep into the soil.

Figure 19.5: A tractor allows a farmer to plough much more land and to plough more deeply than without machinery.

## Agricultural chemicals

Farmers are also using agricultural chemicals to help to improve the growth of their crops, so that they can get more yield from the same area of ground.

- Chemical fertilisers add more mineral ions – such as nitrate ions – to soils that do not contain enough of them.

- Insecticides are sprayed onto crops to kill insect pests that might reduce yields or make the crop look less appealing to buyers.

- Herbicides are sprayed to kill weeds, which would compete with the crop plants and reduce their growth.

Although all of these chemicals are expensive, the cost is outweighed by the increased quantity and quality of the crops when they are harvested (Figures 19.6, 19.7 and 19.8).

## Selective breeding

Careful selection of plants and animals to produce new varieties has played an important part in increasing world food production. We have seen how breeders can choose parents, generation after generation, to produce new and improved varieties of animals and plants. For example, modern wheat varieties produce far more grain per plant than older ones did. Selective breeding has also produced crop plants that can grow in poor soils or that are resistant to diseases. Cattle now produce much more meat or milk than they did in the past, and hens lay more eggs – all as a result of selective breeding. The way that selective breeding is done, and some examples, are described in Chapter 17, Topic 17.2.

**Figure 19.6:** The men are spraying insecticides onto a rice crop, to kill insects and reduce the losses from insects such as leafhoppers.

**Figure 19.7:** Removing weeds from a crop reduces competition with the crop plants for water, mineral ions and light. However, weeding by hand is very labour intensive.

**Figure 19.8:** Spraying with selective herbicides, which kill weeds but not the crop plants, can cover a lot more ground much more quickly. Here the soya beans are unharmed, but the grass growing between the rows is dying.

**Figure 19.9:** This photograph shows ripe wheat that has been grown as a monoculture – a large area in which only wheat plants grow. All the wheat plants are the same variety, so they all tend to grow to the same height and ripen at the same time, making them easy to harvest.

## Monocultures

Crop plants are usually grown as large areas of a single variety (Figure 19.9). This is called a **monoculture**.

Monocultures make sowing, tending, harvesting and selling a crop more efficient for the farmer. This is because:

- using machinery to cultivate a large, uninterrupted area of land can be done more quickly and efficiently than tending several small, separate fields
- a uniform crop is likely to grow to the same height, and ripen at the same time, so it can all be harvested at once using specialised machinery
- a large area of the same crop can all be treated with the same herbicides or pesticides in the same way at the same time, increasing efficiency
- a monoculture will probably produce large quantities of seeds, fruit, or other harvestable parts that are all uniform in size and quality, making it easier for the farmer to market and more profitable to sell.

Monocultures do, however, also have some disadvantages.

### Reduction in biodiversity

Monocultures are very different from natural ecosystems. In a natural ecosystem, there are usually many different species of plants growing, which in turn support many different species of animals. We say that there is a high **biodiversity** (Figure 19.10). In a monoculture, biodiversity is low (Figure 19.11). Only a few species can live where the crop is growing.

> **KEY WORDS**
>
> **monoculture:** an area of ground covered by a single crop, with almost no other species present
>
> **biodiversity:** the number of different species that live in an area

**Figure 19.10:** The natural ecosystem in much of Indonesia is rainforest. It contains an enormous number of different species of plants and animals.

## 19  Human influences on ecosystems

**Figure 19.11:** Over huge areas of Indonesia, the rainforest has been cut down, and replaced with oil palms. The biodiversity here is very low in comparison with the natural forest.

### Increase in pests

Another problem with monocultures is that they can lead to an increase in the populations of organisms that are pests of the crop. For example, leafhoppers feed on the sap of rice plants, and can greatly reduce yields. They also transfer plant viruses to the rice, which cause serious diseases in the plants. If a large area of land is covered with only rice plants, then leafhoppers have so much food available to them that their population can become enormous.

Farmers can try to reduce the quantities of these pests by spraying insecticides onto the crop. However, this also kills other harmless insects – including predatory insects and spiders that would help to reduce the leafhopper population. It is also very expensive. And, in many places, leafhoppers have become resistant to the insecticides and are no longer killed by them.

Many farmers try to use other methods of controlling insect pests. One approach is to use mixed cropping, where only fairly small areas of ground are covered with the same crop at the same time of year. This makes it more difficult for insect pests to spread from one rice field to another.

### Reduction in soil fertility

Farmers sometimes grow the same crop on the same land for several years in succession. The crop plants all need the same mineral ions, so over time the minerals that they need are removed from the soil. The farmer has to keep adding fertilisers to replace these minerals or the yield from the crop will steadily reduce year by year. Growing a mixture of different crops and changing the crop that is grown on a particular piece of ground from one year to the next, helps to maintain a better balance of minerals in the soil.

## Intensive livestock production

In many parts of the world, cattle and other livestock are kept outside. They graze on grass, or are fed by people bringing freshly cut vegetation for them to eat (Figure 19.12). This is called extensive livestock production. The livestock do not take too much from their environment, and do not do much damage to it.

**Figure 19.12:** Extensive production of cattle in Africa. These Ankole-Watusi cattle have a large area in which they can feed.

In developed countries, livestock are often farmed intensively. This means that large numbers of livestock are kept in an area that would not normally be able to support more than a very small number of animals (Figure 19.13, and also Figure 18.12). The farmer uses high inputs to increase the production of milk, meat, or wool from his animals. This means, for example, using high-energy foods to feed the animals. Regular medication may be given to stop the development of disease. The animals may be kept in temperature-controlled buildings to maximise their growth rates.

399

**Figure 19.13:** These cattle are being kept to produce milk. They are farmed intensively, and are given supplementary feed when they come into the barn each day to be milked.

Intensive farming does have some advantages. It can help to provide more food for people, and can sometimes provide it more cheaply than extensive systems. This could mean that fewer people go hungry. Another possible advantage is that it takes up less land than extensive farming, which means that more land could perhaps be left in its natural state, providing habitats for other species.

However, intensive farming has some big disadvantages.

- There can be welfare issues for the livestock, which may suffer in the crowded conditions in which they are kept.

- Disease can spread easily among them. In some countries, this is dealt with by giving the animals regular doses of antibiotics – which, as we saw in Chapter 17, increases the risk that bacteria will develop resistance to the antibiotics.

- The waste from the intensive farming unit can pollute land and waterways nearby.

- Food for the animals is often produced from food that we could eat ourselves, such as soya beans. As we saw in Chapter 18, this is wasteful because we would get more energy from the beans themselves, rather than feeding them to cattle or other livestock.

- Energy is used to transport feed to the livestock, often over very long distances. If the animals are kept inside buildings, energy may also be used to maintain the temperature of the buildings in which they are kept, either by heating it or using air conditioning to keep it cool.

- Large quantities of water may need to be provided, if large numbers of animals are kept in one place. Sometimes, this takes badly needed water from the surrounding environment, so that other animals and plants cannot live there (Figure 19.14).

**Figure 19.14:** This satellite image shows the delta of the great Colorado River, in the south west of the USA. So much water is taken from the river upstream, for intensive livestock production and growing crops, that only a trickle of water actually reaches the sea.

## ACTIVITY 19.1

### Local farming practices

Work in a group of three or four to find out about some local farming practices. You could look at crops that are grown, or animals that are kept.

If possible, different groups in your class could find out about different types of farming.

Write a short, illustrated report on your findings. Try not to use more than 250 words in your report. Here are some issues you could think about. You do not need to report on all of them.

- Is the farming practice you are reporting on intensive or extensive?
- Does it involve the use of agricultural machinery, fertilisers, pesticides or herbicides?
- What are the advantages of this type of farming practice?
- How does the farming practice affect the local environment?
- How does the farming practice affect the quantity and quality of food that is produced?

## Questions

1 Choose the correct word or words to complete each sentence.

   agricultural machinery    fertilisers
   herbicides    insecticides    selective breeding

   a   Farmers add _____ to crops to provide nutrients so that the plants will grow faster.
   b   Farmers use _____ to kill weeds, reducing competition and increasing the yield of the crop.
   c   Farmers use _____ over many generations, to improve production by crop plants and livestock.
   d   Farmers use _____ to enable them to cultivate more land in a shorter period of time.
   e   Farmers use _____ to kill insect pests that would reduce the yield of their crops.

2   a   Outline **two** reasons why growing monocultures helps to produce more food.
    b   Outline **two** ways in which growing monocultures can harm ecosystems.

3   Figure 19.15 shows chickens being farmed intensively.

    Outline the disadvantages of this method of farming chickens.

**Figure 19.15:** Intensive chicken farming.

## Habitat destruction

We have seen that each species has adaptations that help it survive in its particular habitat. If humans destroy that habitat, then it is difficult for many species to survive in the new environment that results.

Habitats are destroyed when we use land for our own purposes. Here are some examples.

- We cut down native vegetation to make land available for growing crops, for farming livestock, for building houses and factories, and for building roads.
- We damage habitats when we mine for natural resources, such as metal ores, building materials such as sand or gravel, or fossil fuels (Figure 19.16). The mine itself destroys the habitats by removing the soil and vegetation, and toxic run-off (water that flows away from the mine) can enter rivers or the soil in the surrounding area.
- We add pollutants to land and water, which can kill the plants that normally live there, and so change the habitat.

**Figure 19.16:** This huge open pit copper mine is in Chile, in South America.

Habitats can also be damaged if we remove key species from them. For example, collecting live corals from coral reefs damages the whole coral reef habitat, endangering the hundreds of species of other animals that depend on corals (Figure 19.17). Corals contain tiny photosynthetic algae inside their bodies, which are the start of every food chain on the reef. This is an example of how, by damaging the food webs in a habitat, we can affect the habitats of all the plants and animals that live there.

**Figure 19.17:** All the organisms that live on this coral reef, in the Red Sea off the coast of Sudan, depend on the living coral animals to provide their habitat.

# Deforestation

Humans have always cut down trees. Wood is an excellent fuel and building material. The land on which trees grow can be used for growing crops for food, or to sell. One thousand years ago, most of Europe was covered by forests. Now, most of them have been cut down. The cutting down of large numbers of trees is called deforestation (Figure 19.18). Deforestation on a huge scale has happened in many countries recently and is still continuing in many places.

**Figure 19.18:** When rainforest is cut down and burnt, as here in Brazil, habitats are destroyed, large amounts of carbon dioxide are released and soil is eroded.

Rainforests occur in temperate and tropical regions of the world. Recently, most concern about deforestation has been about the loss of tropical rainforests. In the tropics, the relatively high and constant temperatures, and high rainfall, provide perfect conditions for the growth of plants (Figure 19.19). A rainforest is a very special place, full of many different species of plants and animals. More different species live in a small area of rainforest than in an equivalent area of any other habitat in the world. Rainforest has a high biodiversity.

19 Human influences on ecosystems

Figure 19.19: This rainforest is in the Royal Belum State Park in Malaysia, where it is protected from damage by humans.

When an area of rainforest is cut down, the soil under the trees is exposed to the rain. The soil of a rainforest is very thin. It is quickly washed away once it loses its protective cover of plants, and the roots that help to bind it together. This soil erosion may make it very difficult for the forest to grow back again, even if the land is left alone. The soil can also be washed into rivers, filling them with soil so that the water overflows and causes flooding (Figures 19.20 and 19.21).

Figure 19.20: The trees that used to cover this hillside were cut down so that people could grow crops. Instead, the rain is washing the unprotected soil down the hillside.

The loss of part of a rainforest means a loss of a habitat for many different species of animals (Figure 19.22). Even if small 'islands' of forest are left as reserves, these may not be large enough to support a breeding population of the animals. Deforestation threatens many species of animals and plants with **extinction**.

> **KEY WORD**
>
> **extinction:** the complete loss of a species from Earth

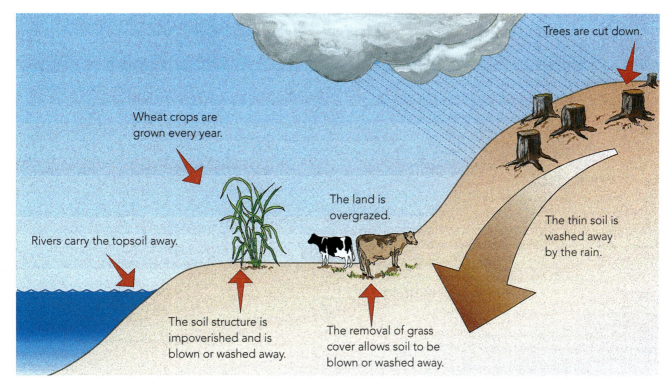

Figure 19.21: How human activities can increase soil erosion.

403

**Figure 19.22:** Many animals, such as these macaws, cannot survive if deforestation destroys their habitat.

The loss of so many trees can also affect the water cycle, and the amount of rain that falls nearby. While trees are present and rain falls, a lot of it is taken up by the trees, and transported into their leaves. It then evaporates, and goes back into the atmosphere in the process of transpiration. If the trees have gone, then the rain simply runs off the soil and into rivers. Much less goes back into the air as water vapour. The air becomes drier, and less rain falls. This can make it much more difficult for people to grow crops and keep livestock.

Most tropical rainforests grow in developing countries, and in some countries many of the people are very poor. The people may cut down the forests to clear land on which they can grow food. It is difficult to expect someone who is desperately trying to produce food to keep their family alive, not to clear land, unless you can offer some alternative. International conservation groups such as the World Wide Fund for Nature, and governments of the richer, developed countries can help. Money provided by these organisations can help to provide alternative sources of income for people. Many of the most successful projects involve helping local people to make use of the rainforest in a sustainable way.

In some countries, the greatest pressure on the rainforest may come from the country's own government, rather than the people living in or near the rainforest. For example, the government may be paid large amounts of money to allow logging companies to cut down forests and extract the timber.

## Questions

4   Explain why habitat destruction can lead to extinction of a species.

5   Explain why habitats such as coral reefs and tropical rainforests have a much higher biodiversity than a field in which a single crop is grown.

6   Outline **five** harmful effects of deforestation.

### ACTIVITY 19.2

**Deforestation poster**

Work with a partner to produce a poster illustrating the causes and effects of deforestation.

You could use pictures downloaded and printed from the internet or you can draw your own pictures.

You could use the internet to find some specific examples – such as how habitats have been damaged by deforestation, how deforestation has led to flooding or how deforestation has reduced soil cover.

Try to achieve a good balance of illustration and text, to keep people's interest as they look at your poster, and so that they can learn useful information from it.

**Peer assessment**

Ask another pair to explain their poster to you.

How well do you think their poster achieves these criteria?

- It is interesting to look at, and grabs your attention.
- It contains information about both the causes and the effects of deforestation.
- There are some good examples provided, which are interesting and help to make a clear point.
- There is plenty of genuine scientific information, containing correct facts.

## Pollution by greenhouse gases

Pollution means 'addition to the environment of something that harms it'.

The Earth's atmosphere contains several different gases that act like a blanket, keeping the Earth warm. They are sometimes called **greenhouse gases**. Carbon dioxide and methane are the two most important greenhouse gases in the Earth's atmosphere.

Carbon dioxide allows shortwave radiation from the Sun to pass through it. The sunlight passes freely through the atmosphere (Figure 19.23), and reaches the ground. The ground is warmed by the radiation, and emits longer wavelength, infrared radiation. Carbon dioxide does not let all of this infrared radiation pass through. Much of it is kept in the atmosphere, making the atmosphere warmer.

This is called the **greenhouse effect**, because it is similar to the effect which keeps an unheated greenhouse warmer than the air outside. The glass around the greenhouse behaves like the carbon dioxide in the atmosphere. It lets shortwave radiation in, but does not let out the longwave radiation. The longwave radiation is trapped inside the greenhouse, making the air inside it warmer.

> **KEY WORDS**
>
> **greenhouse gases:** gases such as carbon dioxide and methane that trap heat within the atmosphere
>
> **greenhouse effect:** the heating effect on the Earth of the trapping of heat by greenhouse gases; note that this is a natural and useful effect, as without it the Earth would be too cold to support life

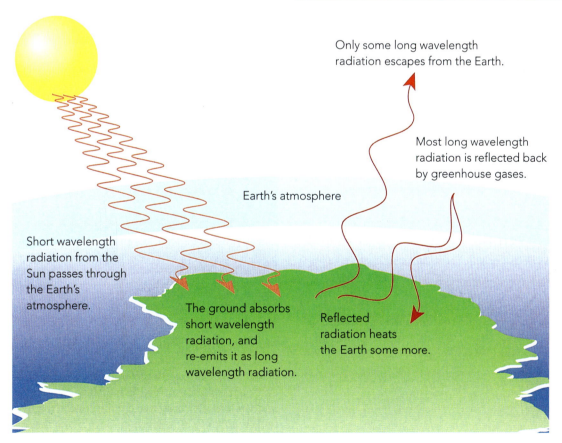

**Figure 19.23:** The greenhouse effect. Short wavelength radiation from the Sun passes through the atmosphere and reaches the ground. Some of it is absorbed by the ground, and is re-emitted as long wavelength radiation. Much of this cannot pass through the blanket of greenhouse gases in the atmosphere. It is reflected back towards the Earth, warming the atmosphere.

We need the greenhouse effect. If it did not happen, then the Earth would be frozen and lifeless. The average temperature on Earth would be about 33 °C lower than it is now.

However, the amount of carbon dioxide and other greenhouse gases in the atmosphere is increasing (Figure 19.24). This may trap more infrared radiation, and make the atmosphere warmer. This is called the **enhanced greenhouse effect**.

> **KEY WORDS**
>
> **enhanced greenhouse effect:** the increased heating effect caused by an increase of greenhouse gases in the atmosphere

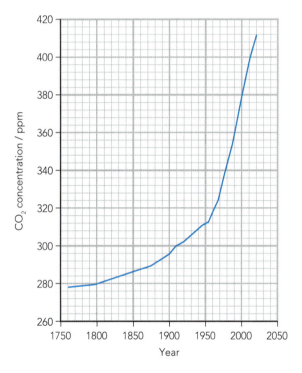

**Figure 19.24:** Changes in the concentration of carbon dioxide in the atmosphere since 1750. The carbon dioxide concentration is measured in parts per million (ppm). 400 ppm means 0.04%.

## Sources of greenhouse gases

Since the Industrial Revolution in the 18th century, the quantity of fossil fuels which have been burnt by industry, and in engines of vehicles such as cars, trains and aeroplanes, has increased greatly. This releases carbon dioxide into the atmosphere.

Deforestation can also result in an increased amount of carbon dioxide in the atmosphere. Cutting down rainforests leaves fewer trees to photosynthesise and remove carbon dioxide from the air. Moreover, if the tree is burnt or left to rot when it is chopped down, then carbon dioxide will be released from it by combustion, or by respiration of decomposers.

Other gases that contribute to the greenhouse effect have also been released by human activities. The most important of these is methane.

Methane is produced by farming activities (Figure 19.25). It is released by bacteria which break down organic matter in the mud in paddy fields (flooded fields which are used for growing rice), in the stomachs of animals which chew the cud (for example, cattle and sheep), and in some insects (for example, termites).

**Figure 19.25:** The mud in a flooded paddy field is a source of methane.

Methane is also produced by decomposers acting on decaying rubbish in landfill sites. We can reduce this problem by decreasing the amount of rubbish we throw away, and by preventing the methane escaping into the atmosphere. The methane can be collected and used as fuel (Figure 19.26). Although burning methane for fuel does release carbon dioxide, this carbon dioxide does not trap so much infrared radiation as the methane would have done.

## 19 Human influences on ecosystems

Figure 19.26: This landfill site has been covered with an impermeable sheet, and pipes collect the methane gas that is produced by bacteria inside the site. The gas can be used as fuel.

As the concentration of carbon dioxide and methane in the atmosphere increases, the mean temperature on Earth also increases (Figure 19.27). We are not able to predict just how large this effect will be. There are other processes, many of them natural, which can cause quite large changes in the average temperature of the Earth, and these are not fully understood.

### Sea level rise

As the Earth's temperature rises, we are already seeing big changes. For example, data from NASA's satellites show that the ice caps in both the Arctic and Antarctic regions have been losing mass since 2009, at an average rate of 127 gigatonnes per year in the Antarctic, and even faster in the Arctic. This melting ice releases a lot of extra water into the oceans, causing sea levels to rise. Sea level also rises because the volume of a liquid increases as its temperature increases. This is called thermal expansion.

The average sea level on Earth rose by 7.5 cm between 1993 and 2017, and there is evidence that the rate of rise is increasing. This is already affecting some low-lying countries, such as the Marshall Islands, where people are being forced to move inland. The government is considering building a new island, or artificially raising the height of the existing ones, so that people have somewhere to live. Other low-lying nations, such as Kiribati, Tuvalu and the Maldives, face similar problems. And many of the world's great cities, such as New York, Singapore and Mumbai, will be affected by rising sea water by 2060 (Figure 19.28).

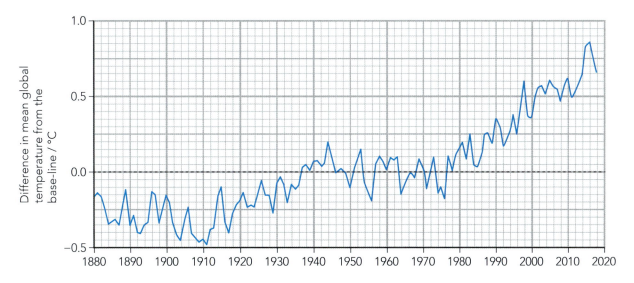

Figure 19.27: This graph shows changes in the mean global temperature since 1880. It uses the mean temperature between 1951 and 1980 as the base-line (0.0) and then plots the mean temperatures for other years to show how much they were above or below this base-line.

**Figure 19.28:** The coastal city of Venice, in Italy, has often experienced flooding from the sea, but the floods in 2019 lasted longer and were higher than all except one of the occasions in the past.

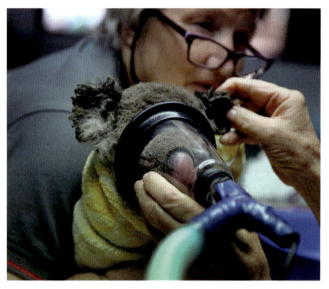

**Figure 19.29:** Rescuers help a koala that was affected by the bushfires raging close to Sydney in Australia in 2019. Many people think that the fires, and the drought that led to them, have been made worse by climate change.

## More extreme weather events

A rise in temperature will also affect the climate in many parts of the world. Higher temperatures mean that there is more energy in the atmosphere, which can lead to different wind patterns and the development of different weather systems.

There are too many variables for scientists to be able to predict the consequences, or even to be sure whether a particular event has been influenced by the rise in the Earth's temperature. But we should certainly expect more extreme weather events, happening more frequently. Hurricanes and tropical cyclones already seem to be happening more often, and to be stronger, than in the past. Droughts seem to be happening more often and lasting longer – this this can lead to more forest fires, which affect wildlife (Figure 19.29). Rainfall may also come at unexpected times of year, and be much heavier than usual, causing severe flooding. It is difficult to be absolutely sure, but as time goes on and we collect more data, it should be easier to see whether or not there really is an increase in the frequency and magnitude of these extreme weather events.

One obvious way to cut down the emission of greenhouse gases is to reduce the amount of fossil fuels that are burnt. This would reduce the amount of carbon dioxide we pour into the air. Agreements have been made between countries to try to do this, but they are proving very difficult to implement. Although many countries are increasing the use of renewable resources to produce electricity, such as solar and wind, some countries continue to rely heavily on coal.

## Questions

7 Explain the difference between the greenhouse effect, the enhanced greenhouse effect and climate change.

8 Each of the following has been suggested as a way of reducing climate change. For each suggestion, explain why it could work.
   a reducing the top speed limit for cars and trucks
   b improving traffic flow in urban areas
   c insulating houses in countries with cold climates
   d increasing the number of wind- and solar-powered electricity generating stations
   e encouraging people to recycle more of their rubbish

# 19 Human influences on ecosystems

## Eutrophication

Many organisms live in water. They are called aquatic organisms. Aquatic habitats include fresh water (streams, rivers, ponds and lakes) and marine environments (the seas and oceans).

Some pollutants, such as fertilisers and untreated sewage, can reduce the concentration of dissolved oxygen in water. This means that organisms that need dissolved oxygen for aerobic respiration (for example, fish) cannot survive. They either die or they have to leave the area.

Farmers and horticulturists use fertilisers to increase the yield of their crops. The fertilisers usually contain nitrates and phosphates. Nitrates are very soluble in water. If nitrate fertiliser is put onto soil, any that is not taken up by plant roots may be washed out in solution when it rains. This is called leaching. The leached nitrate ions may run into streams and rivers.

Algae and green plants in the river grow faster when they are supplied with these extra nitrate ions. They may grow so much that they completely cover the water. They block out the light for plants growing beneath them, which die. Even the plants on the top of the water eventually die. When they do, their remains are a good source of food for bacteria, which are decomposers.

The bacteria breed rapidly. As they decompose the remains of the plants and algae, the large population of bacteria respires aerobically, using up oxygen from the water. Soon, there is very little oxygen left for other living things.

This whole process is called **eutrophication** (Figures 19.30 and 19.31). Eutrophication can happen whenever food for plants or bacteria is added to water. As well as fertilisers, other pollutants from farms, such as slurry from buildings where cattle or pigs are kept, or from pits where grass is rotted down to make silage, can cause eutrophication.

> **KEY WORD**
>
> **eutrophication:** a chain of events caused by addition of extra plant nutrients to water, resulting in a decrease in the concentration of dissolved oxygen available for organisms that require it for aerobic respiration

**Figure 19.30:** Eutrophication of the water in this lake in Thailand has killed the fish.

**Water with few nutrients is rich in oxygen, and supports a variety of animal life.**

clear water

sunlight can penetrate deep into the water, allowing water plants to grow.

**Water with high concentrations of nutrients is low in oxygen, so few animals can live in it.**

run-off from fertilisers, animal waste and silage containing nitrates and other nutrients

No fish can live in this water.

Large populations of algae and bacteria grow.

No light gets through the water, so no water plants grow.

**Figure 19.31:** Eutrophication. Nutrients flowing into the water increase algal and bacterial growth. Aerobic respiration by the bacteria reduces oxygen concentration, killing fish.

Untreated sewage can also cause eutrophication. Sewage is waste liquid that flows from human toilets, kitchens and bathrooms. It also flows from industrial sites. It contains faeces, urine, detergents and many other substances. Good sewage treatment removes most of these harmful substances, but in many places untreated sewage is allowed to flow into rivers or the sea. Untreated sewage does not usually increase the growth of algae, but it does provide a good food source for many kinds of aerobic bacteria. Once again, their population grows, depleting the oxygen levels (Figure 19.32).

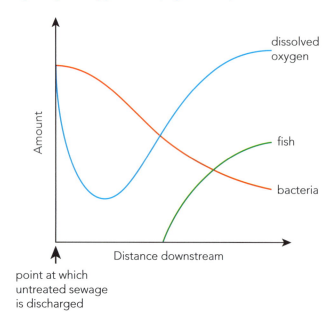

**Figure 19.32:** The effect of untreated sewage on a stream.

Can we reduce eutrophication? We should be able to treat all sewage before it is released into the environment. This would also reduce the risk of transmitting water-borne pathogens, such as the cholera bacterium. Could we stop using nitrate-containing fertilisers? It is not really sensible at the moment to suggest that we could. People expect to have plentiful supplies of relatively cheap food. Although fertilisers are expensive, they increase the yield of crops so much that farmers make more profit. If farmers did not use fertilisers at all, the yields would be much lower and they would have to sell their crops for a higher price, in order to make a profit.

Some farmers use organic fertilisers, such as manure. Organic fertilisers are better than inorganic ones in that they do not contain many nitrates that can easily be leached out of the soil. Instead, they release their mineral ions gradually, over a long period of time, giving crops time to absorb them efficiently. Nevertheless, manures can still cause pollution, if a lot is put onto a field at once, at a time of year when there is a lot of rain or when crops are not growing and cannot absorb the nutrients from the manure.

If nitrate fertilisers are used, there is a lot that can be done to limit the harm they do. Care must be taken not to use too much, but only to apply an amount which the plants can take up straight away. Fertilisers should not be applied to empty fields, but only when plants are growing. They should not be applied just before rain is forecast. They should not be sprayed near to streams and rivers.

## Non-biodegradable plastics

Plastics are human-made materials that we use for many different purposes. Most of them are made from fossil fuels. If you look around you now, you will almost certainly be able to see several items made from plastics. Plastics are cheap, lightweight and can be made into any shape and colour that we want.

One big problem with plastics is that most of them are **non-biodegradable**. This means that decomposers cannot break them down. When a plastic item is thrown away, it does not rot. Discarded plastic objects just accumulate (Figure 19.33).

**Figure 19.33:** Much of this rubbish that has been washed up onto a beach is plastic. Plastic causes pollution both on land and in water.

> **KEY WORD**
>
> **non-biodegradable:** not able to be broken down by decomposers

Litter is very unsightly. It can also be dangerous to other organisms. For example, plastic waste thrown away at sea is often mistaken for jellyfish by turtles. They eat it. As they eat more and more, it gradually collects up in their stomachs, because it cannot be broken down by their enzymes. Now they cannot eat their real food and eventually die.

On land, animals can also get trapped inside plastic containers, or may get plastic cords or bags wrapped around their bodies, which can kill them. Hermit crabs, which have no shell of their own, may choose a plastic container for their new home (Figure 19.34). This may be fine, but sometimes they crawl into a container that they cannot get out of, such as a smooth-sided bottle. When the crab eventually dies, other hermit crabs looking for homes pick up the scent of the dead crab and recognise a home that has just become available because its previous owner has died. They crawl into the same container. Researchers working on the Henderson Islands found 526 dead hermit crabs in one plastic container.

**Figure 19.34:** This plastic football has made a good home for a hermit crab, but many other plastic containers are lethal traps for them.

## Questions

9   List two substances that can reduce the oxygen concentration in aquatic ecosystems, if they are allowed to pollute waterways.

10  a   Explain what is meant by the term *non-biodegradable*.

    b   Outline why non-biodegradable plastics can cause more harm to ecosystems than biodegradable substances.

11  Look at the graph in Figure 19.32.
    Explain the shapes of the curves for:
    a   bacteria
    b   dissolved oxygen
    c   fish

# 19.2 Conservation

Conservation is the process of looking after the natural environment. Conservation attempts to maintain or increase the biodiversity of an area (the range of different species living in an area). We have seen that one of the greatest threats to biodiversity is the loss of habitats. Each species of living organism is adapted to live in a particular habitat. If this habitat is destroyed, then the species may have nowhere else to live, and will become extinct.

## Conserving forests

Tropical rainforests have a very high biodiversity compared with almost anywhere else in the world. This is one of the main reasons why people think that conserving them is so important. When tropical rainforests are cut down or burnt, the habitats of thousands of different species are destroyed.

Forests provide useful resources for humans. For example, we use them for timber to build houses and boats, and for fuel. If we use the forests carefully, then there will always be more trees for us to use in the future. They can provide a **sustainable resource** – a resource that will not run out, even if we keep on using it.

> **KEY WORDS**
>
> **sustainable resource:** one that is produced as rapidly as it is removed from the environment, so that it does not run out

We have already seen how deforestation in many parts of the world has caused severe problems. But it is possible to use forests sustainably:

- Governments can refuse to grant licences to companies who want to cut down valuable forests. This can be difficult, however, because governments can make large amounts of money from selling the rights to harvest timber from forests.

- Instead of cutting down all the trees in a forest (called clear-felling), just a small proportion of the trees are cut down. This is called selective felling. The remaining trees will hold the soil in place, and will continue to provide habitats for animals. New trees can regrow to replace those which have been cut down. In practice, however, selective felling often does a lot of damage to the forest because of:
    - the roads that are built to allow access
    - the large machinery that is used to drag the timber out
    - the disturbance caused by the people working in the forest.
- Many deciduous trees will regrow after they are cut down. Trees can be cut down to about one metre or less, and then left to regrow. This is called coppicing. Usually only part of a wood or forest is coppiced at any one time, and the rest of it remains untouched for many years. The coppicing can be done in a cycle over, say, 12 years, with different parts of the forest being coppiced each year.
- Where large numbers of trees are cut down, new ones should be planted to replace them (Figure 19.35). This is what happens with most of the trees used to make paper. However, planting new trees cannot replace primary forest. Primary forest is forest that has never been cut down. In the tropics, primary forest contains huge numbers of different species of trees, which provide habitats for many different species of animals. Primary forest should be conserved.
- Education can help to make sure that people understand how important it is to conserve forests. For example, in some places, local people cut down trees to use as fuel for cooking. If they understand the importance of conserving trees, then they can make sure that they replant new trees to replace the ones that they cut down. Better still, they may be able to use renewable sources of energy, such as solar energy, to reduce their need for wood.
- Some parts of a forest can be completely protected by law, so that people are not allowed to cut down trees or to hunt animals in them.

# Conserving fish stocks

Fish in the sea could be a sustainable resource, as long as we do not take so many that their populations fall to dangerously low levels.

Humans have probably always used fish as a source of high-protein food. However, there is increasing concern about the threat to fish populations from the large numbers of fish that are being caught. Figure 19.36 shows how fish catches have increased since 1950. The figures on this graph only include fish caught by people who then sell their catch. There are probably tens of millions of tonnes more that are caught by people who eat it within their own family or community.

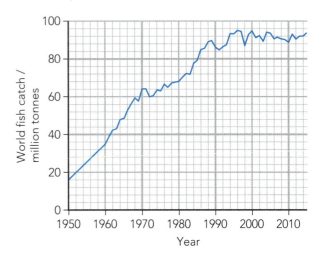

Figure 19.36: World fish catches since 1950.

Figure 19.35: These children in Nepal have grown young trees to plant in areas where trees have been cut down.

As a result of the great numbers of fish being caught, the populations of most of the species that are used for food are getting smaller. If we do not reduce catches, the populations will get so small that there will not be enough adult fish left to breed and sustain the populations.

Reducing the number of fish that are caught is not easy. Each country wants to make sure that it gets a fair share of the fish catch, so any international regulations are very difficult to draw up and to enforce. Everyone is worried that other countries are getting more fish than they are. Moreover, fish do not stay in one place in the sea. Even if a country manages to reduce fishing to reasonable levels around its own shores, the same fish may be under threat when they move to the seas around other countries.

There are a few ways that the number of fish being caught can be controlled:

- Quotas are agreed limits that allow countries, regions or fishermen to catch only a certain quantity of fish. Most quota systems specify different amounts for different species. For example, fishermen might be given quotas to catch large amounts of fish that are not under threat, but very low quotas – or none at all – for species whose populations have fallen to dangerously low levels. However, it is almost impossible for fishing boats to catch only one particular species of fish. They may accidentally catch fish of a different species, for which they have already passed their quota. They will not be allowed to land these fish, and will have to throw them back into the sea. It is unlikely that these fish will survive. Nevertheless, imposing and enforcing quotas can be very helpful in conserving threatened fish species.

- Some areas of the sea can be closed for fishing at certain times of year. These closures occur when fish are breeding and are called closed seasons. This allows the fish population to grow, as a new generation of fish is produced without disturbance from fishing boats.

- Some areas of the sea can be completely closed to fishing all the time. These are called protected areas. Protected areas act as refuges for fish, which can live and breed safely. The fish sometimes move into unprotected areas, where they can be caught. This means the fish can still be harvested and used by humans.

- Restrictions can be placed on the type of nets that are used to catch fish. For example, the use of bottom trawls or dredging nets, which are dragged over the sea floor, is completely banned in some areas. These nets scoop up everything that is living on the seabed, including all kinds of organisms that we do not want to eat. Dredging nets are very damaging to the seabed community.

- Restrictions can also be placed on the size of the mesh of the nets used to catch fish. If the mesh size is too small, then even very young fish are caught. These small fish will not have had time to grow and reproduce. If a larger mesh size is used, then only the biggest fish are caught. The smaller ones can grow and reproduce, adding new fish to the population.

- All of these rules are enforced by inspectors who visit fishing boats at sea, to monitor what is being done. Fishing vessels can also be required to fit electronic position sensors, which continually transmit information about where the boats are. Inspectors also check the catches that are brought to land. This monitoring is expensive to do, and is unpopular with fishermen.

# Endangered species

A species that no longer has any living individuals on Earth is said to be extinct. A species whose numbers have fallen so low that it is at risk of becoming extinct is **endangered**. Once a species has become extinct, it is gone for ever.

| KEY WORD |
|---|
| **endangered:** at serious risk of becoming extinct |

Through the history of life on Earth, millions of species have become extinct. Palaeontologists (people who study fossils) have identified several periods in the past when huge numbers of species seem to have become extinct. These are called mass extinction events (Figure 19.37).

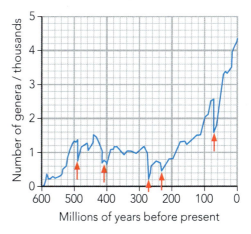

**Figure 19.37:** Mass extinction events have occurred five times in the last 500 million years.

Each of these mass extinctions was caused by a major change in the conditions on Earth. The most catastrophic event occurred about 251 million years ago, when 96% of all species disappeared. We are not sure what caused this event, but major climatic change may have played a part, perhaps brought about by the continuous eruption of huge volcanoes in Siberia. It is also possible that an asteroid hit the Earth at this time.

Another major extinction event is happening now. This time, no asteroid is involved. The cause of the mass extinction is us.

Species can become extinct for many different reasons. These include:

- climate change, habitat destruction and pollution – which are all described in Topic 19.1
- hunting by humans – either for food or sport
- overharvesting – such as a species of fish or a species of tree
- introduction of new species to an ecosystem.

We have seen that the addition of extra carbon dioxide and methane to the atmosphere is causing climate change. As temperatures rise on Earth, organisms with adaptations that allow them to live in a particular environment may no longer be so well adapted. This is especially true of species that require cold conditions, such as polar bears. Polar bears need large areas of sea ice on which to hunt seals. As the ice caps melt, they may be left without a habitat.

Humans have always hunted and harvested animals and plants for food, but sometimes this hunting or harvesting is so severe that it can destroy an entire species. There is much evidence that mammoths finally became extinct 5000 years ago because of hunting by humans. The dodo, a giant flightless pigeon that used to live on Mauritius, was destroyed by humans in the late 17th century, when its eggs were eaten and the adults killed.

The introduction of new species can disrupt food webs and cause changes in ecosystems that put native species (that is, species that naturally live in that area) at risk. For example, New Zealand has been separated from the other land masses on Earth for millions of years. There have never been any mammalian predators there, so many birds are flightless and nest on the ground (Figure 19.38). When the first settlers arrived in New Zealand, about 700 years ago, rats stowed away on their ships.

Later, people arriving from Europe brought rabbits to New Zealand to use as food, and then – when the rabbits bred out of control – they introduced stoats to try to reduce the number of rabbits. They also introduced possums from Australia, to farm for fur, but the possums escaped and now there are millions of them living wild in New Zealand. These introduced animals compete with the native ones for food, and also eat the eggs of the ground-nesting birds. Scientists think that 53 species of native birds in New Zealand have become extinct since humans arrived.

**Figure 19.38:** Many species of bird in New Zealand are flightless, because there have been no predators to exert selection pressures against birds that cannot fly.

# Conserving endangered species

Understanding why a species can become endangered or extinct can help us to prevent this happening. For example, in the 1970s, the Mauritian green parakeet, also known as the echo parakeet, was said to be the most endangered bird species in the world (Figure 19.39). Only about ten birds were known to exist. These parakeets live in forests and scrub habitats, but by 1996 only 5% of Mauritius was still covered with its native vegetation. The parakeets, which feed on fruits of native trees, had little to eat. They were also threatened by introduced species such as rats and monkeys, which took eggs from nests and competed with the parakeets for food. And the loss of old trees meant that there were few suitable nest sites available.

## 19 Human influences on ecosystems

**Figure 19.39:** Mauritian green parakeets in their natural habitat.

In 1973, an intensive conservation programme began. At first, it concentrated on helping the parakeets to survive and breed in their habitat. Nest boxes were put up, predators were controlled, and non-native trees and weeds were cleared from the forest. This helped, but numbers still remained very low, so some of the eggs were taken to be reared in captivity. Many captive-reared birds have now been released into the wild. The population stood at over 700 birds in 2020, so it looks as though this parakeet is now out of immediate danger.

Many local organisations and individuals have been involved in this conservation project. Visits to schools and other education initiatives have helped to make young people aware of the importance of taking care of this endangered species, and how their actions can help it to survive.

This conservation success story illustrates many of the different tactics that can be used to conserve endangered species. They include:

- monitoring and protecting the species in its natural habitat
- using **captive breeding** programmes
- educating local people about the importance of conservation, and what they can do to help.

Many zoos have captive breeding programmes. Animals are kept safe in the zoo, and encouraged to breed. This can build up the species' population. The hope is that some of the individuals can eventually be returned to the wild. However, this is only possible if the dangers that made them endangered in the first place – such as hunting or habitat destruction – can be reduced.

Animals are not the only organisms that are in danger of extinction. Many plant species are also under threat. We can use all of the same techniques that are used to conserve threatened animal species, but there is also another possibility – building up **seed banks** (Figure 19.40).

**Figure 19.40:** The Svalbard Seed Vault, in Norway, stores more than half a million different kinds of seeds deep under the frozen ground.

Seeds are often able to survive for many years in a dormant state, and then germinate when conditions are right. We can make use of that by collecting and storing seeds of as many different plant species as possible. These can be kept safe for long periods of time. In the future, if a species is threatened with extinction, we will have some of their seeds that can be used to grow into new plants, either to be kept 'in captivity' or reintroduced into their natural habitat.

Some of the seeds of each species are sown and allowed to grow into new plants from time to time. New seeds can then be collected, and stored. This makes sure that there are always seeds that have not been stored for too long, which could make them lose their ability to germinate.

> **KEY WORDS**
>
> **captive breeding:** keeping animals in captivity (e.g. in a zoo) and allowing them to breed, in order to increase the numbers in the population
>
> **seed banks:** facilities in which seeds of different plant species, or crop varieties, are stored for long periods of time, in order to conserve as many different species and varieties as possible

Many zoos, all over the world, are involved in captive breeding programmes for endangered species of animals. Zoos keep records of the pedigrees of their individual animals, and animals may be moved from one zoo to another so that males and females that are genetically different from one another can mate and produce offspring. This helps to maintain genetic diversity in the captive population. The aim is to be able to reintroduce some of the animals to the wild eventually, so that the wild population is increased. However, this can only work if the habitat for the animals is protected, so that whatever caused the species to become endangered in the first place is not repeated.

Animals in captivity do not always breed readily. Their unusual surroundings may not provide the correct environment for them to become ready to mate, or a particular male and a female may simply not respond to each other. This is often the case with giant pandas, for example. Males and females often show no interest in mating. In those cases, the zoo can help by using techniques called assisted reproduction. These include **artificial insemination** and **in vitro fertilisation**.

> ### KEY WORDS
>
> **artificial insemination (AI):** introducing semen, containing sperm, to the reproductive organs of a female; fertilisation occurs in her body in the normal way
>
> **in vitro fertilisation (IVF):** adding semen, containing sperm, to eggs in a container in a laboratory; fertilisation occurs in the container, and embryos can later be inserted into the body of a female

Artificial insemination (AI) involves taking semen from the male and inserting it into the vagina of the female. Hopefully, some of the sperm in the semen will find their way to an egg and fertilise it. The zygote will then develop into an embryo and implant into the uterus in the normal way.

Before AI is carried out, the female must be at the correct stage of her reproductive cycle, and there must be a good chance that there is an egg in her oviducts. In giant pandas, this happens only once a year, and the female only has an egg available for fertilisation for about 24 to 36 hours. She is monitored regularly, by testing the hormones in her urine, so that the perfect time for AI can be judged.

In vitro fertilisation (IVF) is a little bit more difficult. It involves collecting eggs from the female, placing them in a sterile liquid in a sterile container (such as a Petri dish) and then adding semen from the male. Fertilisation happens in the dish ('in vitro' means 'in glass') and several zygotes are formed. Some of these then divide to form tiny embryos. One or more of the embryos is then placed in the female's uterus, with the hope that it will implant in the normal way, grow into a fetus and eventually be born successfully.

Generally, it is necessary to wait until a female ovulates naturally before eggs can be harvested. She also needs to be in the correct stage of her reproductive cycle before the embryos produced in vitro can be implanted. But sometimes the female or male – or both – can be treated with hormones that cause them to produce gametes. It is so far proving difficult to achieve success with this in many species, largely because we still do not fully understand the hormonal control of reproductive cycles in most endangered species.

# Maintaining genetic diversity

In Chapter 17, we saw how important genetic variation is to a population. If there is variation between individuals, then the population as a whole has a better chance of surviving if they are threatened by a pathogen, or if their habitat changes in some way. At least some of the individuals may have variations that allow them to survive and reproduce, even if others are killed.

When the numbers of a species drop to very low levels, so that only a few individuals survive, then much of this genetic variation is lost. This makes the species much more likely to become extinct, especially if environmental conditions change.

Low levels of genetic variation also make it more likely that, when two individuals breed together, they may each carry the same harmful recessive allele of a gene. Some of their offspring may therefore inherit this harmful allele from each parent, and consequently have a homozygous recessive genotype which produces a phenotype making them less likely to survive.

This is a concern for the green parakeets in Mauritius. All the individuals now alive were bred from the ten birds that remained in the 1970s, so they are all quite closely related and share many of the same alleles. The breeding programmes are being organised to try to keep as much genetic diversity as possible.

Scientists at seed banks also work to maintain genetic diversity among the seeds that are stored. When seeds are collected from the wild, the collectors try to take them from different places, so that the plants that produced the seeds are not likely to be closely related. In the bank, some seeds are germinated every now and then, to produce fresh seeds for storage. When this is done, care can be taken to cross plants with different genotypes, to maintain genetic diversity among the seeds that are stored.

## Reasons for conservation programmes

So far, we have taken for granted that we want to try to stop species becoming extinct. But conservation programmes are expensive. They can cause conflict with people who want to use an area of land for a different purpose. So, what are the arguments for spending money and effort on trying to conserve endangered species and their habitats? Here are just a few of these arguments.

- For many of us, it is clear that we have no right to make any species extinct. We share the Earth with many different species and we have a responsibility to make sure that they can live successfully in their habitats. We are keeping them safe so that future generations can enjoy them.

- If we damage ecosystems, we can be doing harm to ourselves. Cutting down large numbers of trees, for example, can reduce the amount of water vapour that goes back into the air, which in turn can reduce rainfall. People who depend on locally collected wood for fuel may no longer be able to heat their homes or cook food.

- Losing species from an ecosystem, or introducing species that do not belong there, can have wide-reaching effects. The loss of one species may have harmful effects on other species that are part of the same food web, by reducing their food supplies. Conserving ecosystems can also help to maintain efficient recycling of nutrients such as nitrogen, through the nitrogen cycle.

- Many plant species contain chemicals that can be used as drugs. If we lose plant species, we may be losing potential new medicines.

- We have seen how selective breeding has been used to produce new varieties of crop plants. Wild relatives of our crop plants contain different alleles of genes that could be useful in future breeding programmes. Conserving wild plants, as well as all the different varieties of crop plants, is important if we are not to lose potentially useful alleles.

## Questions

12  List **five** reasons why species can become endangered or extinct.

13  Explain why introducing a new species to an ecosystem can cause native species to become endangered.

14  Describe what is meant by captive breeding and outline how it can help to save a species from extinction.

15  Explain why it is important to try to maintain genetic diversity when a captive breeding programme is undertaken.

## SUMMARY

Food production has been increased by using agricultural machinery, using chemical fertilisers, insecticides and herbicides, and selective breeding.

Biodiversity is the number of different species that live in an area.

Farmers gain efficiency by growing crops as monocultures, allowing them to sow, tend and harvest a big area in the same way at the same time. However, monocultures are not good for ecosystems, as they greatly reduce biodiversity.

Intensive livestock production enables large numbers of animals to be kept in a small area of land. However, there are welfare problems for the animals, high inputs of food and water are required, and local areas are at risk from pollution from the animal wastes.

Habitats for species are destroyed through humans using land for growing food crops, farming livestock and housing; through using land to extract natural resources such as mineral ores and fossil fuels; and through the pollution of land, fresh water and the sea.

Deforestation causes habitat destruction, reduces biodiversity, causes extinction of species, increases the risk of soil erosion and flooding, and increases the carbon dioxide concentration in the air.

Untreated sewage and fertilisers in waterways reduce oxygen concentration and therefore damage aquatic ecosystems.

An increase in nitrate ions in a waterway causes increased growth of producers, which then die. Aerobic bacteria decompose the remains of the producers, using up dissolved oxygen, so that not enough is left for aquatic animals such as fish, which require dissolved oxygen for aerobic respiration.

Non-biodegradable plastics accumulate in aquatic and terrestrial ecosystems, where they cause visual pollution and can harm animals that mistake them for food or places to live.

Carbon dioxide and methane are greenhouse gases, which contribute to the enhanced greenhouse effect and therefore to climate change. Increased levels of carbon dioxide are caused by the combustion of fossil fuels. Methane is released by cattle and sheep, and also from anaerobic mud in paddy fields.

Careful use allows us to conserve some resources, including forests and fish stocks.

Conservation of forests can be achieved through education, designating protected areas, applying quotas to logging companies and replanting trees.

Conservation of fish stocks can be achieved through education, closed seasons for fishing, designating protected areas, controlling the types and mesh size of nets used to catch fish, applying quotas to fishing boats and monitoring the fishing methods and catches of fishing boats.

Climate change, habitat destruction, hunting, pollution and introduced species can put species at risk of becoming extinct.

Monitoring and protecting species in the wild, and their habitats, as well as education, captive breeding programmes and seed banks, can help to conserve endangered species.

Conservation is important for: maintaining and increasing biodiversity; reducing extinction; protecting vulnerable environments; and maintaining ecosystem functions, including nutrient cycling, and provision of resources including food, drugs, fuel and genes for crop breeding.

19 Human influences on ecosystems

## PROJECT

### A conservation scenario

Conservation projects are often difficult to implement, because people may not always agree about the best thing to do.

Work in a group of five or six to write, produce and perform a short play involving a number of different people with differing viewpoints about a conservation project.

It is best if you use your own idea for a scenario. If you are stuck for ideas, here are three to start you off.

- A government wants to increase the tax on fuel, to reduce the use of cars and therefore reduce carbon dioxide emissions. Some people are strongly against the tax rise, because it will increase their costs and make it more difficult for them to travel for work or leisure.

- An international organisation proposes banning fishing in an area of the oceans, to allow fish stocks to recover. Fishermen from several countries, who normally fish in that area, strongly oppose the ban, as it will cause hardship for them and threaten the economy of the coastal towns where they live.

- A conservation organisation wants to kill predators that have been introduced to an island, where they are threatening native species with extinction. Some people are strongly opposed to this, as they like the introduced species (which happens to be cute and furry) and think it is cruel to kill them when the situation is not the fault of the introduced species.

**Figure 19.41:** Costa Rica is famous for its conservation efforts which have made it one of the most popular eco-tourism destinations in the world.

## REFLECTION

How pleased are you with your contribution to this project? Do you think that the role you took when helping to produce and perform the play was a good one for you? Did you find it easy, or was it challenging?

Would taking on an even more challenging role on a future occasion help you to develop your skills?

## EXAM-STYLE QUESTIONS

1. Increased carbon dioxide concentrations result in the enhanced greenhouse effect.

   Which other gas also contributes to this effect?

   A ammonia
   B carbon monoxide
   C methane
   D nitrogen [1]

2. What is an advantage of large-scale monocultures of crop plants?

   A decrease in biodiversity
   B increased efficiency of food production
   C increased use of chemical fertilisers
   D increase in pest populations [1]

3. Which does **not** increase the risk of extinction of species?

   A captive breeding
   B climate change
   C hunting
   D introducing non-native species [1]

4. What describes artificial insemination (AI)?

   A adding sperm to eggs in a dish in a laboratory
   B encouraging animals to breed in captivity
   C inserting semen into the reproductive system of a female
   D storing seeds in a seed bank [1]

5. What reduces oxygen concentrations in a river, after untreated sewage is added to it?

   A increased aerobic respiration by aquatic plants
   B increased aerobic respiration by bacteria
   C increased nitrogen fixation by bacteria
   D increased photosynthesis by aquatic plants [1]

6. Choose suitable words from the list to complete the sentences about deforestation.

   biodiversity    carbon dioxide    endangered    erosion    flooding
   food web    greenhouse effect    oxygen    polluted    yield

   Tropical rainforests contain a very large number of different species, so they are said to have high _____. The trees take _____ from the air when they photosynthesise. Their roots also help to hold soil in place.
   When large areas of trees are cut down, this causes habitat loss. Species of plants that are adapted to live in the forest, as well as animals, may become _____. The concentration of carbon dioxide in the atmosphere increases, which enhances the _____. Soil _____ increases. [5]

19 Human influences on ecosystems

CONTINUED

7 The hawksbill turtle has lost 90% of its population in the last 100 years. It is classified by the International Union for the Conservation of Nature (IUCN) as an endangered species. The photograph below shows a hawksbill turtle.

a **Explain** what is meant by an endangered species. [1]

b Hawksbill turtles spend most of their lives at sea. The females become ready to breed when they are 30 years old. They come to sandy beaches to lay their eggs in nests that they dig in the sand. The young hatch after about 60 days. The tiny turtles burrow out of their nest and make their way down the beach to the sea.
Use this information to **suggest** why hawksbill turtles are endangered. [5]

c Non-biodegradable plastics discarded in the sea may be mistaken by turtles for jellyfish and eaten. Explain how this could increase the threats to the turtle populations. [3]

[Total: 9]

8 The Iberian lynx, *Lynx pardinus*, is an endangered species. The photograph shows an Iberian lynx.

a State the genus of the Iberian lynx. [1]

b The main reason that the Iberian lynx has become endangered is loss of habitat.
Suggest **two** reasons why the habitat of the Iberian lynx has been lost. [2]

> **COMMAND WORDS**
>
> **explain:** set out purposes or reasons / make the relationships between things evident / provide why and/or how and support with relevant evidence
>
> **suggest:** apply knowledge and understanding to situations where there are a range of valid responses in order to make proposals / put forward considerations

## CONTINUED

c A captive breeding programme has been set up, to try to increase the numbers of this species. However, this has proved difficult because it is not easy to determine when a female lynx has become pregnant.

Researchers collected faeces from several individual female captive Iberian lynx, and measured the quantity of a chemical called PGFM. The results are shown in the graph below.

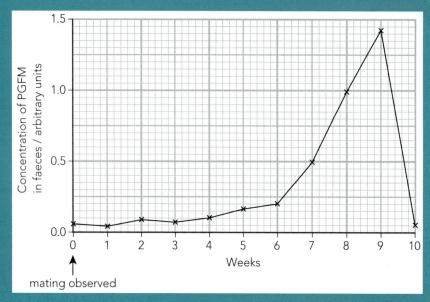

i Suggest why it is helpful to be able to determine when a female lynx in a captive breeding programme has become pregnant. [2]

ii Use the graph to explain how monitoring PGFM levels in faeces can help researchers to determine when a female lynx is pregnant, and when she is likely to give birth. [3]

iii In the captive breeding programme, animals are often moved from one breeding institution to another. Explain how this can increase the likelihood of the programme being successful. [3]

[Total: 11]

9 a Describe how seed banks can help to conserve endangered species. [6]

b Explain how the use of quotas can help to conserve forests and fish stocks. [6]

[Total: 12]

# 19 Human influences on ecosystems

## SELF-EVALUATION CHECKLIST

After studying this chapter, think about how confident you are with the different topics. This will help you to see any gaps in your knowledge and help you to learn more effectively.

| I can | See Topic... | Needs more work | Almost there | Confident to move on |
|---|---|---|---|---|
| describe how agricultural machinery, chemical fertilisers, insecticides, herbicides and selective breeding have helped to increase food production | 19.1 | | | |
| describe the advantages and disadvantages of large-scale monocultures of crop plants | 19.1 | | | |
| describe the advantages and disadvantages of intensive livestock production | 19.1 | | | |
| describe biodiversity as the number of different species that live in an area | 19.1 | | | |
| describe the reasons for habitat destruction, including increased area for food crop growth, livestock production, livestock housing, extraction of natural resources, pollution (freshwater and marine) | 19.1 | | | |
| explain how humans can have a negative impact on habitats by altering food webs | 19.1 | | | |
| explain the undesirable effects of deforestation: habitat destruction, reducing biodiversity, extinction, loss of soil, increased flooding, increase of carbon dioxide in the atmosphere | 19.1 | | | |
| describe the effects of untreated sewage and excess fertiliser on aquatic ecosystems | 19.1 | | | |
| explain how eutrophication takes place | 19.1 | | | |
| describe the effects of non-biodegradable plastics on aquatic and terrestrial ecosystems | 19.1 | | | |
| describe the sources and effects of excess methane and carbon dioxide in the air, including the enhanced greenhouse effect and climate change | 19.1 | | | |
| state that forests and fish stocks are resources that can be conserved | 19.2 | | | |
| explain how education, protected areas, quotas and replanting can help to conserve forests | 19.2 | | | |
| explain how education, closed seasons, protected areas, controlled net types and mesh sizes, quotas and monitoring can help to conserve fish stocks | 19.2 | | | |

423

## CONTINUED

| I can | See Topic... | Needs more work | Almost there | Confident to move on |
|---|---|---|---|---|
| explain that climate change, habitat destruction, hunting, pollution and introduced species can cause species to become endangered or extinct | 19.2 | | | |
| describe how monitoring and protecting species and habitats, education, captive breeding programmes and seed banks can help to conserve endangered species | 19.2 | | | |
| describe maintaining or increasing biodiversity, reducing extinction, maintaining nutrient cycling and the provision of resources such as food, drugs, fuel and genes, as reasons for conservation programmes | 19.2 | | | |
| describe the use of AI and IVF in captive breeding programmes | 19.2 | | | |
| explain why a decrease in population size of a species can lead to loss of genetic diversity, and why this increases the risk of extinction | 19.2 | | | |

# Chapter 20
# Biotechnology and genetic modification

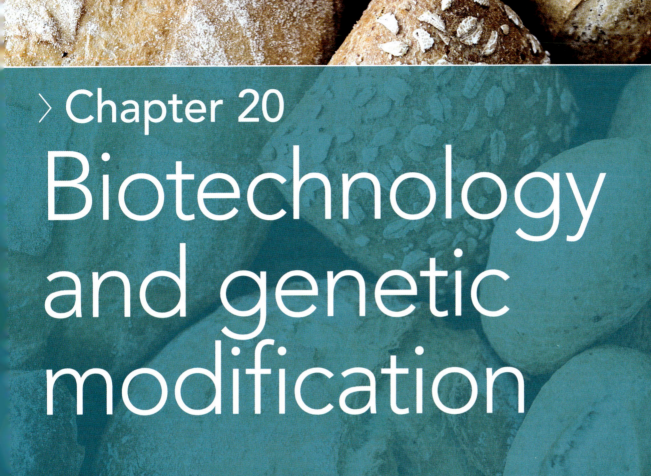

IN THIS CHAPTER YOU WILL:

- find out how we can use microorganisms and enzymes to make useful products
- learn about some examples of genetic modification
- explain how genetic modification is done
- discuss the advantages and disadvantages of genetic modification of crop plants.

# CAMBRIDGE IGCSE™ BIOLOGY: COURSEBOOK

## GETTING STARTED

With a partner, write down at least two facts about DNA.

Take turns with other pairs in your class to write one of your facts on the board. Keep going until all the different facts have been added.

## GOLDEN RICE

Humans have been altering the genetic makeup of organisms for thousands of years, long before we knew anything about chromosomes, genes or DNA. People began growing wheat and other cereal crops more than 11 000 years ago. Archaeological evidence shows how the crops changed over time, as people used the natural variation in the crop plants and selected the 'best' seeds to sow. They also used selective breeding to improve the animals they kept for meat, milk, skins and to pull their carts and ploughs.

In the 20th century, we learnt more about genetics, and began to use our knowledge of genes to plan how to breed plants or animals to get the particular features that we wanted. In 1953, Watson and Crick announced that genes are made of DNA. Since then, scientists have learnt how to move lengths of DNA from one cell to another. Now we are even able to alter the DNA in a cell.

Not everyone is comfortable with this. For example, in the 1990s, a project was begun to put DNA from other organisms into rice plants, so that the plants make an orange substance called carotene, which the human body can convert to vitamin A. Vitamin A deficiency causes an estimated 4500 deaths a day, mainly in children, and also causes blindness. The scientists successfully produced genetically modified (GM) rice, called Golden Rice, which contains much more carotene than normal rice (Figure 20.1). But so far, no one has used it, mostly because many governments and individuals have been worried about possible dangers of GM crops. Eventually, by 2019, Australia, Canada, New Zealand and the USA had registered this rice as safe, and many developing countries will probably follow their lead. The rice should be no more expensive for farmers to grow than ordinary rice, and it could save the sight and lives of huge numbers of people.

### Discussion questions

1. Why do you think that people are suspicious of genetically modified organisms, such as Golden Rice, but have no problem in accepting crops or animals that have been produced by selective breeding?

2. Do you think that governments concerned about the possible dangers of GM crops should ban them or are the potential life-saving benefits more important?

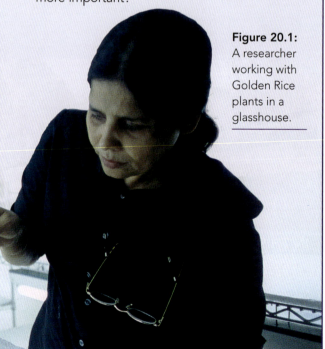

**Figure 20.1:** A researcher working with Golden Rice plants in a glasshouse.

# 20.1 Biotechnology

**Biotechnology** involves using living organisms to carry out processes that make substances that we want. Usually, the term is used only when microorganisms are involved, or when plants or animals are used to produce something other than food.

We have been using microorganisms to make various products for us for thousands of years. Yeast has been used to make bread and alcohol. Bacteria have been used to make yoghurt and cheese. Of course, people did not know that these microorganisms were involved in the processes they used because they are too small to see with the naked eye.

Today, we still use microorganisms to make these foods, but we now also use them to make many other substances, such as enzymes. And, in the 1970s, a new branch of biotechnology began when scientists first found out how to take a gene from one organism and put it into a different one. This is called **genetic modification**, and it has opened up entirely new possibilities for using microorganisms and other organisms.

> ### KEY WORDS
>
> **biotechnology:** using organisms, usually microorganisms, to produce required substances
>
> **genetic modification:** changing the genetic material of an organism by removing, changing or inserting individual genes

## Using microorganisms

Biotechnology and genetic modification often make use of microorganisms, such as bacteria. There are several reasons for this:

- Bacteria are very small and are easy to grow in a laboratory. They do not take up a lot of space.
- Bacteria reproduce very quickly. They are able to make a huge range of different chemical substances.
- Bacteria can make complex molecules that are useful to humans.
- No one minds what is done to bacteria and fungi. There are few ethical issues like those that might arise if we used animals.
- As well as their 'main' DNA – their 'chromosome' – bacteria also have little loops of DNA called plasmids. These are quite easy to transfer from one cell to another. We can use plasmids for moving genes from one organism's cells to another.

## Making use of anaerobic respiration in yeast

Yeast is a single-celled fungus. Figure 20.2 shows yeast cells seen using an electron microscope.

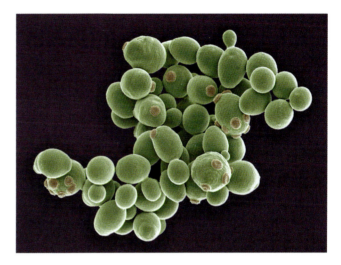

**Figure 20.2:** Yeast cells seen with a scanning electron microscope. You can see little buds growing from some of the cells – this is the way that yeast reproduces.

Yeast is able to respire anaerobically. When it does so, it produces ethanol and carbon dioxide.

$$\text{glucose} \rightarrow \text{ethanol} + \text{carbon dioxide}$$

### Making ethanol for biofuels

In Chapter 19, you saw that we need to reduce our use of fossil fuels. One alternative is to use plants to provide sugars, which yeast can then break down to form ethanol. The ethanol – sometimes called bioethanol – can then be used as a fuel.

Maize and sugarcane are two of the crops that are used in this process (Figure 20.3). Maize is first treated with amylase enzymes, which break down stored starch to glucose. Sugarcane does not need to be treated with enzymes because it stores most of its carbohydrate as sucrose rather than starch. Yeast is then added and allowed to use the glucose in anaerobic respiration. The ethanol that is produced can then be extracted from the mixture by distillation.

Although alcohol burns well, it does not contain as much energy per litre as fossil fuels. It is therefore normally mixed with gasoline (petrol) to make **biofuel** that is used in vehicle engines.

A possible advantage of using a biofuel like this is that the ethanol used is a sustainable resource. We can keep growing more maize to make more fuel. It also helps to reduce the amount of carbon dioxide that we add to the atmosphere. Although carbon dioxide is produced when the biofuel is burnt, the plants that are grown to make the fuel will have recently taken in carbon dioxide from the air during photosynthesis, using it to make the sugar and starch. This contrasts with burning fossil fuels, because then we are releasing carbon dioxide into the air that has been stored in the Earth for millions of years.

However, there are arguments against growing crops to make biofuels. These crops take up land that could otherwise be used to grow food for people. Using large quantities of maize and other crops to make biofuels puts up their price, making it more expensive for people to buy food. The land on which the crops are grown may originally have contained a biodiverse natural ecosystem, which was cleared to increase the area for growing the monoculture crop.

> **KEY WORD**
>
> **biofuel:** a fuel that is made by mixing ethanol (made by the anaerobic respiration of yeast) with petrol

**Figure 20.3:** Sugarcane being unloaded at a factory in Brazil. The sugarcane is used to make sugar, and the leftover waste material is used to make ethanol for biofuel.

> **ACTIVITY 20.1**
>
> **Thinking about biofuels**
>
> Some people think that using biofuels instead of fossil fuels can help to reduce climate change.
>
> Others think that biofuels are not a good answer to this problem.
>
> Take a few minutes to think about your own view on this issue. Then turn to a partner and share your ideas.
>
> When every pair is ready, take turns to share your point of view, and your reasons for it, with the rest of the class.

> **REFLECTION**
>
> How satisfied are you with your contribution to the discussion about biofuels?
>
> How clearly do you think you explained your point of view? Did you express yourself clearly? How successfully did you back up your argument with facts and examples?
>
> In future, what can you do to improve the way that you contribute to a discussion such as this?

**Making bread**

Bread is made from flour, which is made by grinding the grains (seeds) of cereal crops. Most bread is made from wheat flour.

Flour contains a lot of starch, and also protein – especially a protein called gluten. To make bread, the flour is mixed with water and yeast to make dough.

Amylase enzymes break down some of the starch in the dough to make maltose and glucose, which the yeast can use in anaerobic respiration. It produces bubbles of carbon dioxide. These get trapped in the dough. Gluten makes the dough stretchy, so the carbon dioxide bubbles cause the dough to rise (Figure 20.4).

Anaerobic respiration also makes alcohol, but this is all broken down when the bread is baked. Baking also kills the yeast.

## 20 Biotechnology and genetic modification

Figure 20.4: Yeast has been respiring anaerobically in this pizza dough. The carbon dioxide produced by the yeast made the dough rise.

## Questions

1. State two reasons why microorganisms, rather than animals, are often used in biotechnology.
2. Which product of anaerobic respiration by yeast is used to make biofuels?
3. Which product of anaerobic respiration by yeast is important in breadmaking?

## Making use of enzymes

Many different enzymes are used in industry. Most of them are obtained from microorganisms.

### Pectinase

Fruit juices are extracted using an enzyme called **pectinase**.

Pectin is a substance which helps to stick plant cells together. A fruit such as an apple or orange contains a lot of pectin. Pectinase breaks down pectin. This makes it much easier to squeeze juice from the fruit.

> **KEY WORD**
>
> **pectinase:** an enzyme that is used to digest pectin, increasing the quantity of juice that can be extracted from fruit, and clarifying the juice

Pectinase also helps to make the juice clear rather than cloudy (Figure 20.5). The cloudiness in fruit juice is often caused by insoluble carbohydrates that float in the juice. Pectinase and other enzymes such as cellulase (which breaks down cellulose) can be added to the cloudy juice. They break the insoluble substances to soluble ones, so the juice becomes clear.

Figure 20.5: The apple juice in the left-hand bottle has been treated with pectinase to break down insoluble pectin that makes the juice in the right-hand bottle look cloudy.

## Biological washing powders

Washing powders contain detergents. These help insoluble fats and oils mix with water, so they can be washed away.

Biological washing powders contain enzymes, as well as detergents. These enzymes help to break down other kinds of substances which can stain clothes. They are especially good at removing dirt which contains coloured substances from animals or plants, like blood or egg stains.

Some of the enzymes are proteases, which catalyse the breakdown of protein molecules to amino acids. This helps with the removal of stains caused by proteins, such as blood stains. Blood contains the red protein haemoglobin. The proteases in biological washing powders break the haemoglobin molecules into smaller molecules, which are not coloured, and which dissolve easily in water and can be washed away. Some of the enzymes are lipases, which catalyse the breakdown of fats to fatty acids and glycerol. This is good for removing greasy stains.

To prevent these enzymes from digesting proteins and fats in the skin of people handling them, the enzymes are packed into microscopic capsules (Figure 20.6). The capsules break open when the washing powder is mixed with water.

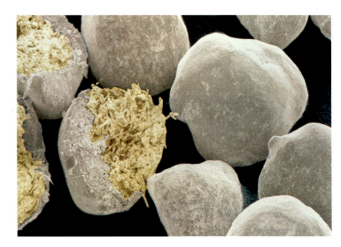

**Figure 20.6:** Scanning electron micrograph of granules of biological washing powder. The enzymes are packed inside the microscopic granules.

### EXPERIMENTAL SKILLS 20.1

#### Investigating biological washing powders

You are going to work in a small group to plan and carry out an experiment to investigate whether or not biological washing powders are better at removing stains than other washing powders. You will practise writing a careful plan, before you do your experiment. As you work, you will have the chance to make changes to your plan if you can see how it could be improved.

**You will need:**

- for writing the plan: a pencil and paper
- for your experiment: the apparatus and materials that you decide to use.

#### Method Part 1: Writing the plan

Here are some hypotheses that you could investigate. Choose **one** of them. Alternatively, you could write your own hypothesis. It is best if each group in the class investigates a different hypothesis.

- Biological washing powders remove egg stains better than non-biological washing powders.
- The optimum temperature for biological washing powders is lower than the optimum temperature for non-biological washing powders.
- Biological washing powders are better than non-biological washing powders at removing stains from cotton cloth.

## 20 Biotechnology and genetic modification

> **CONTINUED**
>
> Then, as you write your plan, think about these points:
>
> - What is your independent variable? How will you change it? How many different values will you use? What will be your highest and lowest value? Note: You may want to do some preliminary work, to decide on suitable concentrations or masses of washing powder to use.
> - What is your dependent variable? How and when will you measure it?
> - What variables do you need to keep the same (standardise)? How will you do this?
> - What apparatus will you need? What sizes of glassware will you use? What measuring instruments do you need? How many?
> - Are there any risks involved? What will you do to keep yourself and others safe?
> - What do you predict your results will show? Why do you think this will happen?
>
> Now make your list of what equipment you will need to carry out your plan.
>
> **Safety:** Make notes on any safety issues you can think of – remember you are dealing with biological washing powder.
>
> **Method Part 2: Doing your experiment**
>
> As you work, you may decide to make changes to your original plan. This is fine – it is a good thing to do.
>
> Record and display your results in the way that you think is best.
>
> **Questions**
>
> 1. What problems did you have in carrying out your experiment? How did you solve them?
> 2. How well did your results match your prediction?
> 3. If you did the same experiment again, would you expect to get exactly the same results? Explain your answer.
> 4. What do you think are the main sources of error (uncertainty) in your measurements and results? How could you reduce these sources of error if you did the experiment again?
>
> **Peer assessment**
>
> When everyone has completed their experiment, each group in the class should present a short description of their experiment, and their results and conclusion, to the rest of the class.
>
> As you listen to the first group's presentation, write down **two** things that you think they have done really well. Also write down **one** thing that you think they could improve and explain how they could improve it. The class can then give feedback to the group, before the next group gives their presentation.

# Questions

4. Explain why pectinase helps to obtain more juice from fruit.
5. What do biological washing powders contain, as well as detergents?
6. The first biological washing powders only worked in warm, rather than hot, water. Suggest why.
7. The enzymes that are used in modern biological washing powders are often obtained from bacteria which naturally live in hot water, in hot springs. Outline how natural selection may have resulted in the adaptation of these bacteria to live in hot springs.

## Lactase

Lactase is an enzyme that breaks down lactose, the sugar found in milk.

$$lactose \xrightarrow{lactase} glucose + galactose$$

All human babies produce lactase in their digestive systems. This is needed to help them to digest the lactose in the milk that is their only source of food for the first few months of their life. Some people – for example, those of European descent – continue to make lactase all of their lives. However, most people – for example, those of Asian descent – stop making lactase when they are adults. These people cannot digest lactose. They may feel ill if they eat or drink foods that contain lactose.

Milk can be treated with lactase to break down the lactose, so that people who don't make lactase themselves can drink milk or eat products made from the lactose-free milk (Figure 20.7).

**Figure 20.7:** Cow's milk that has been treated with the enzyme lactase can be safely drunk by people who do not make lactase in their digestive systems.

Another reason for treating milk with lactase is to produce the sugars glucose and galactose. These can be used for making sweets.

# Growing microorganisms in a fermenter

When bacteria or yeast are used to produce enzymes or other substances for our use, they are grown in a container called a **fermenter**. This allows production of the useful products on a large scale. Figure 20.8 shows a typical fermenter.

## Sterilisation

Before the fermenter is used, it is thoroughly washed and **sterilised**. This is usually done by passing steam through it. This kills all the microorganisms that are in the fermenter, so that they will not contaminate the **culture**. (A culture is the mixture of microorganisms and their nutrient supply.)

> ### KEY WORDS
>
> **fermenter:** a vessel, usually made of steel or glass, in which microorganisms can be grown in order to produce a required product
>
> **sterilised:** treated – e.g. with steam – to destroy all living cells
>
> **culture:** a population of microorganisms growing in a nutrient liquid or on agar jelly

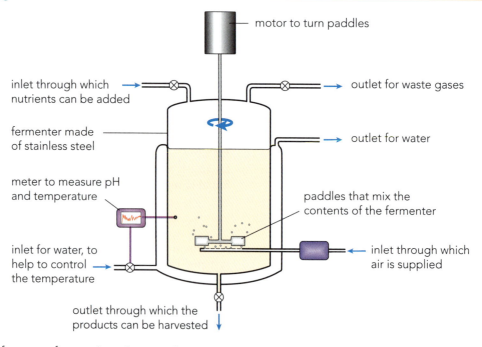

**Figure 20.8:** A fermenter for growing microorganisms.

## Providing nutrients

Water and the nutrients that the microorganisms need for growth are added to the fermenter. The exact nutrients required depend on the microorganism that is being cultured, and the product that we want. Glucose may be added, which the microorganisms can use in respiration to provide them with energy. Amino acids or nitrate ions may be added to provide a source of nitrogen, so the microorganisms can make proteins.

## Providing air

If the microorganisms will respire aerobically, air is bubbled through the contents of the fermenter. This provides oxygen. The fermenter has an outlet through which waste gases can escape, to make sure that the pressure inside the fermenter does not build up.

## Mixing the contents

In most fermenters, a motor turns paddles that keep the contents mixed. However, if the fermenter is being used to grow a fungus made up of long hyphae, there are usually no paddles, because they would get tangled up with the hyphae. Air bubbles also help with mixing the contents. This makes sure that the microorganisms in every part of the fermenter are supplied with nutrients and oxygen.

## Adding the microorganisms

When all this has been done, the microorganisms are added.

## Measuring and maintaining temperature

A temperature probe measures the conditions inside the fermenter. Temperature must be kept at the correct level, so that the enzymes in the microorganisms can work effectively, to produce the required product. As the microorganisms respire, they release heat energy, which can cause the temperature to increase above the optimum for their enzymes. Cold water is then passed around the fermenter to lower the temperature. If, however, the temperature falls below the optimum, then hot water or even steam can be passed around the fermenter.

## Measuring and maintaining pH

The pH of the fermenter contents is measured using a probe. It is important to keep the pH at the optimum level for the microorganisms' enzymes. If the microorganisms are producing carbon dioxide, this will lower the pH. pH is adjusted by adding small quantities of acidic or alkaline liquids to the contents of the fermenter.

## Harvesting the product

When the microorganisms have had time to produce the required product, the contents of the fermenter can be harvested. This may be done by allowing some of the contents to run out through an outlet tube or sometimes the whole fermenter is emptied at once.

## Purifying the product

The contents of the fermenter include the required product, but there will also be other substances, including the microorganisms themselves, which are not wanted. The required product is now separated from the unwanted substances, so that it can be used or sold.

Many different substances are now produced commercially using fermenters. These include:

- insulin, made by genetically modified bacteria
- the antibiotic penicillin, produced by the fungus *Pencillium*
- a food called mycoprotein, produced by a fungus called *Fusarium*.

# Questions

8   Explain why lactose-free milk is produced.

9   Explain why it is essential to sterilise a fermenter before it is used to make a product.

10  In what circumstances might it not be necessary to bubble air into a fermenter?

11  One product that is made in fermenters is the antibiotic penicillin. This is made by a fungus called *Penicillium*. The fungus is made up of long threads called hyphae.

   a   Explain what an antibiotic is used for.
   b   Carbohydrates and amino acids are added to the fermenter. Explain why both of these substances are added.
   c   The fermenters in which *Penicillium* is cultivated do not usually have paddles. Suggest why.

## 20.2 Genetic modification

We have seen that a gene is a length of DNA that codes for the production of a particular protein in a cell. Genetic modification involves changing the genetic material of a cell or of a whole organism. This can be done by removing genes, altering genes, or adding individual genes to cells.

Genetic modification was first carried out in the 1970s. Since then, many different uses have been found for this process.

### Making human proteins

Human genes can be inserted into bacteria. The bacteria follow the instructions on the gene to make a protein that is normally made in human cells.

For example, insulin is now produced by GM bacteria. The human insulin gene is inserted into the bacteria, and the bacteria are grown on a large scale. The insulin that they produce is purified. The insulin made by these bacteria can be used by people with type 1 diabetes, who need to inject insulin regularly. Before GM insulin was available, insulin had to be extracted from the pancreases of dead animals, such as pigs. Producing it from GM bacteria enables much more insulin to be produced in a short period of time, and also ensures that the insulin is pure and of a consistent quality.

### Making herbicide-resistant crop plants

Herbicides are sprayed on crop plants to kill weeds. However, this is no use if the herbicide also harms the crop plants. Some crop plants have been genetically modified to be resistant to herbicides or insect pests.

For example, soya plants have been genetically modified so that they are not harmed when a herbicide called glyphosate is sprayed onto them. This means that farmers can spray a field of these plants with the herbicide, and only the weeds are killed (as shown in the picture below).

### Making pest-resistant crop plants

Each year, huge quantities of crops are damaged by insect pests (Figure 20.9). This can greatly reduce yields. Farmers spray pesticides to kill the pests, but this is expensive, and the pesticides kill useful or harmless insects as well as the pests. Some crop plants have been genetically modified so that they are not damaged by insect pests.

For example, cotton plants have been genetically modified so that they contain a substance called Bt, which is toxic to insects. Insect pests, such as the cotton boll weevil, are killed if they eat the cotton plants. This reduces the use of pesticides.

**Figure 20.9:** Cotton boll weevils are beetles whose larvae live inside the fruits (bolls) of cotton plants. They are very destructive and can greatly reduce the harvest of cotton from the plants.

## 20 Biotechnology and genetic modification

## Improving nutritional qualities of crop plants

Some crops have had genes inserted into them that cause them to make larger quantities of nutrients that humans need.

At the start of this chapter, we saw that lack of vitamin A is a big problem for children in some parts of the world. This is especially so where the diet mainly consists of white rice (Figure 20.10). Severe vitamin A deficiency can cause blindness and is thought to kill more than one million people each year.

Genes from maize and bacteria have been inserted into rice, and the rice uses these genes to produce a substance called carotene. The human body can turn carotene into vitamin A. Carotene is the substance that makes carrots look orange, so the rice grains are yellow. This GM rice is called Golden Rice.

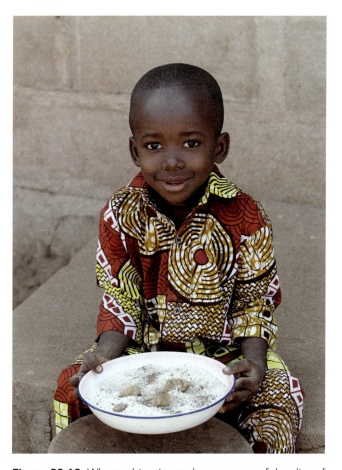

**Figure 20.10:** Where white rice makes up most of the diet of children, using Golden Rice instead could greatly reduce the risk of vitamin A deficiency.

### ACTIVITY 20.2

#### Should food containing GM crops be labelled?

In Europe, the USA and some other countries, food that contains nutrients derived from GM crops has to be labelled to show this (Figure 20.11).

**Figure 20.11:** Tins of tomato puree with a label telling consumers that the tomatoes are genetically modified.

Work in a small group to find out whether this is done in your country. If it is, you may be able to collect some labels with GM information on them.

Then discuss in your group whether or not you think it is important that foods containing GM products should be labelled. Identify your reasons for your point of view.

Your class can then take a vote on whether they think it is important to label GM foods or not.

## Question

12 Copy and complete this table, to summarise some examples of genetic modification.

| Type of genetic modification | One example | Comments |
|---|---|---|
| modifying bacteria to produce human proteins | | |
| modifying crop plants to confer resistance to herbicides | | |
| modifying crop plants to confer resistance to pests | | |
| modifying crop plants to improve nutritional qualities | | |

## Advantages and disadvantages of genetically modified crops

There are some concerns about the use of genetically modified crops, and it is important that these are carefully considered.

One argument against the use of GM crops is that we simply do not need them. For example, some people have argued that Golden Rice is not the way to solve problems caused by vitamin A deficiency. They say that it would be better to solve the real cause of these problems, which is that people do not have enough money or enough food in some parts of the world. Others argue that at least Golden Rice may be able to help some people now, whereas trying to get rid of poverty can be very complicated and take a long time.

Another argument against their use is that the seeds are more expensive for farmers to buy than non-GM seeds. This could mean that many farmers in developing countries cannot afford to buy the seeds, which could place them at a disadvantage compared with farmers who can afford these seeds. The companies that sell GM seeds generally prevent farmers from saving their own seed and insist that they buy new seed from the company each year.

A strong argument for growing GM crops that are resistant to herbicides is that it reduces the number of times that farmers need to spray herbicides onto their crops. This reduces the number of occasions on which the herbicide might cause harm to other plants growing nearby. Growing herbicide-resistant crops can also increase yields, because the spray that is used is very effective at killing all plants except the crop plants. This means that there is less competition from weeds, and the crop plants grow better. It also reduces labour costs, so it could mean cheaper food.

Arguments against growing GM herbicide-resistant crops include a concern that the herbicide resistance gene might spread from the crop plants into other plants growing nearby, producing 'superweeds' that can no longer be killed by herbicides. This could happen if pollen from the GM crop plant fell onto the stigma of a different plant, and the male gametes inside the pollen fertilised an ovule. This is very unlikely, however, because it is very unusual for pollen of one species to be able to grow on the stigma of another species. So far, despite millions of hectares of these GM crops being grown, no 'superweed' has yet appeared.

GM crops with resistance to pests have also been a source of concern. For example, some people think that eating Bt maize may harm their health, because the crops contain a toxin that kills insects. The Bt protein is a naturally occurring protein produced by a bacterium called *Bacillus thuringiensis*, which normally lives in soil – it is not something completely new. The Bt protein only works as a toxin when it binds with specific protein receptors that are found in the gut of the pest insects, but not in humans or other animals. Numerous tests have found absolutely no evidence that eating these crops causes any harm at all to people.

It is also possible that pesticide-resistant crops might harm insects other than those that eat the crop and cause damage – for example bees that eat nectar from the flowers, or ladybirds that are predators of insect pests such as aphids. However, so far studies show little or no effects on non-pest species of insects. Nevertheless, more studies need to be done before we can be sure that this is always true. Most evidence collected so far suggests that the use of the GM crops may benefit biodiversity, because the farmer does not have to spray the crop with insecticides that kill all kinds of insects, not just those that damage the crops.

One issue that is emerging is that some pest insects are evolving to become resistant to the Bt toxin. This is not a new problem, as resistance to ordinary pesticides has evolved on many occasions. A possible way of avoiding this problem is to plant only certain areas with the Bt-containing crop and grow non-Bt crops nearby. Insect pests will be able to feed on the non-Bt crop, and so the selection pressure for resistance to Bt will not be as great.

## How genetic modification is done

To explain the processes that are involved in genetic modification, we will look at the way in which bacteria can be genetically modified to produce a human protein. These proteins are made to use in medicine, to supply to people who are unable to make them in their own bodies. The first human protein made using GM bacteria was insulin, used to treat diabetes.

## 20 Biotechnology and genetic modification

Today, human proteins produced by GM microorganisms are widely used:

- blood proteins that are essential for blood clotting are used to treat people with the inherited disease haemophilia
- human growth hormone is used to treat people who would otherwise not grow fully
- interferon is used to treat some types of cancer.

All of these can now be manufactured quickly and in large quantities, using GM bacteria.

The process begins by identifying the length of DNA – the gene – that codes for the production of the desired protein. Enzymes called **restriction enzymes** are used to cut the DNA on either side of the gene (Figure 20.12). These enzymes cut DNA molecules at particular points. They leave short lengths of unpaired bases at either end of the cut DNA, called **sticky ends**.

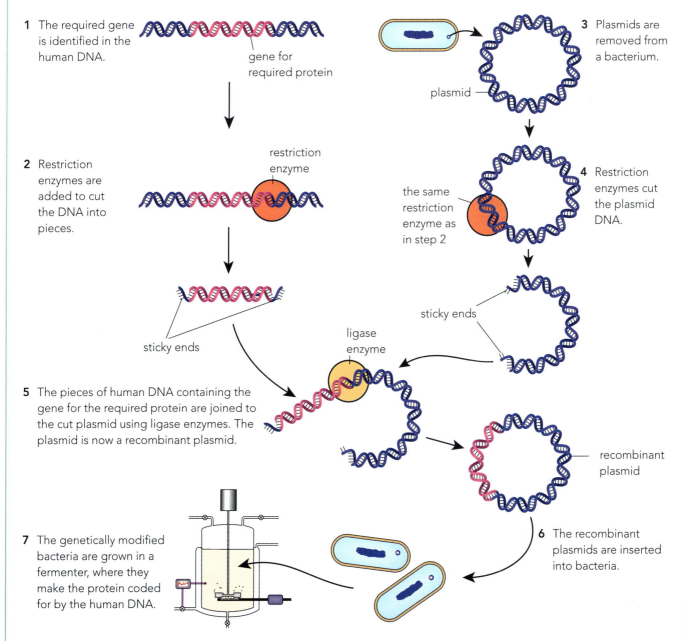

Figure 20.12: How bacteria can be genetically modified to make a human protein.

Next, plasmids are removed from bacteria. You may remember that a plasmid is a small circle of DNA that is found in many bacteria – it is not the main bacterial chromosome. The ring of DNA in the plasmid is cut, using the *same* restriction enzymes that were used for cutting the human DNA. The reason for using the same restriction enzyme is so that the sticky ends on the plasmid DNA are complementary to the sticky ends that were left on the human DNA.

The human DNA and the cut plasmids are now mixed together. The sticky ends (unpaired bases) on the human DNA pair up with the complementary sticky ends on the plasmid DNA. Another enzyme, called **DNA ligase**, links the two strands firmly together, closing the plasmid loop. Now we have plasmids that contain the human insulin gene. They are called **recombinant plasmids**, because they contain a combination of bacterial and human DNA.

Next, these genetically modified plasmids are added to a culture of bacteria. Some of the bacteria take up the plasmids into their cells. These are now genetically modified bacteria because they contain human DNA as well as their own. The GM bacteria are put into fermenters, where they reproduce asexually to form large populations. They express the gene for the human protein – that is, they use the code on the human DNA to make the human protein, which can be extracted from the fermenters and purified.

> **KEY WORDS**
>
> **restriction enzymes:** enzymes (biological catalysts) that cut DNA at specific points, and leave a short length of unpaired bases at each end
>
> **sticky ends:** lengths of unpaired bases on one strand of a DNA molecule; they are able to form bonds with complementary lengths of unpaired bases on a different DNA molecule
>
> **DNA ligase:** an enzyme that joins two DNA molecules together
>
> **recombinant plasmid:** a small circle of DNA, found in bacteria, which contains both the bacterial DNA and DNA from a different organism

## Questions

13  Outline the use of these enzymes in genetic modification:
    a  restriction enzymes
    b  DNA ligase

14  Explain the importance of using the same restriction enzyme on a plasmid, and on the DNA that is to be joined to the plasmid.

# 20 Biotechnology and genetic modification

## SUMMARY

- Bacteria are useful in biotechnology because they reproduce rapidly and can make complex molecules.
- Other reasons for using bacteria in biotechnology include the absence of ethical concerns and the presence of plasmids in their cells.
- Anaerobic respiration in yeast produces carbon dioxide that helps bread to rise.
- Anaerobic respiration in yeast produces ethanol, which can be used as biofuel.
- Pectinase is an enzyme that breaks down pectin that holds plant cells together. Using pectinase increases the quantity of juice that can be extracted from fruits and it can also be used to clarify the juice.
- Biological washing powders contain enzymes as well as detergents. The enzymes usually include protease and lipase, and sometimes also amylase. They break down proteins, fats and starches that can stain clothes, making them soluble in water so they can be washed off the fabric.
- Many people cannot digest lactose, because they do not produce lactase when they become adults. Lactase can be added to milk to break down the lactose to glucose and galactose. This makes the milk and products made from it safe for everyone to drink.
- A fermenter is a large container in which bacteria or yeast can be grown on a large scale in controlled conditions, to produce useful products. The fermenter is designed so that nutrients and air (to provide oxygen) can be added, and the temperature and pH can be controlled. Waste products such as carbon dioxide are removed.
- Genetic modification involves changing the genetic material of an organism by removing, changing or inserting individual genes.
- Bacteria have been genetically modified by inserting human genes for making proteins such as insulin and human growth hormone, so that these proteins can be produced on a large scale for use in medicine.
- Crop plants have been genetically modified to make them resistant to herbicides, so that spraying a herbicide on the crop kills weeds but not the crop plants.
- Crop plants have been genetically modified to make them resistant to insect pests, so that the farmer does not need to spray pesticides on the crop.
- Rice has been genetically modified to produce more carotene, which helps to prevent blindness or death resulting from vitamin A deficiency in people whose diet contains mostly rice.
- There are arguments for and against the use of genetically modifying crops such as soya, maize and rice.
- The first step in genetic modification of a bacterium to make a human protein involves cutting out the required human gene with restriction enzymes, leaving sticky ends.
- Bacterial plasmids are cut with the same restriction enzymes, leaving complementary sticky ends.
- The gene and cut plasmids are mixed, so that the complementary sticky ends join together. The strands of DNA are joined using DNA ligase. This forms a recombinant plasmid containing both bacterial DNA and human DNA.
- The recombinant plasmids are inserted into bacteria. The bacteria multiply to make a large population of genetically modified bacteria.
- The genetically modified bacteria express the human gene and synthesise the human protein.

## PROJECT

### Debating the use of genetically modified crops

You are going to take part in a debate about whether your class agrees or disagrees with this statement:

**This class believes that growing genetically modified crops does more good than harm.**

Half of your class should help to construct arguments to support the statement. The other half should help to construct arguments against the statement. You may be able to choose which side you are on but be prepared to have to argue for a point of view that you do not agree with! The aim of the debate is to help you to organise your ideas and to understand the arguments for and against the statement, so even if you have to argue for something you do not believe in, you will gain from the experience.

**Figure 20.13:** Students taking part in a debate.

### Structuring the debate

- The first speaker for one of the sides presents their team's case. They should put forward two or three strong arguments, with supporting evidence if necessary.
- The first speaker for the other side now does the same. They should use their prepared arguments but should also try to rebut (argue against) whatever the first speaker said.
- Next, the second speaker for the first side presents their case.
- Next, the second speaker for the second side does the same.

### Things for your class to decide on before you begin

- Depending on the size of your class, and how long you have, you could also have a third speaker for each side.
- You should limit the length of time that each speaker is allowed. This will depend on how long you have, but in general about four or five minutes will be sufficient.
- Will you allow people to ask questions of the person who is speaking?

### Structuring your arguments

Here are some things to think about as you build your presentation of your case.

- Start with a clear statement about your argument, which says exactly why you are for or against the statement.
- Next, present some evidence for your point of view.
- Finish by explaining how the evidence supports your claim.
- Make sure that the second (and third) speaker for each side uses arguments that are not just repeating those of the first speaker.

Here are some things to think about as you think of ways of rebutting an earlier speaker's arguments.

- How strong is their evidence? Is it just a few isolated stories or is there good scientific research behind it?
- Have they confused correlation with causation? Just because two things seem to be linked, it does not mean that one causes the other.
- Are things really as simple as the speaker suggested or is it more complicated in real life?

### The final vote

When each speaker has finished, the class should vote on the original statement. At this point, you are free to vote however you wish. You can vote against the argument that your team was putting forward, if you want to!

## EXAM-STYLE QUESTIONS

1 What is pectinase used for?
   A digesting food for babies
   B producing carbon dioxide for breadmaking
   C obtaining more juice from fruit
   D removing stains from clothing [1]

2 What is a reason for using bacteria in biotechnology?
   A They can cause disease.
   B They do not photosynthesise.
   C They have cell walls.
   D They reproduce rapidly. [1]

3 What is an example of genetic modification?
   A crossing two animals with different genotypes together
   B putting a gene from one species into an organism of a different species
   C selectively breeding cattle to produce more milk
   D using yeast to make biofuel [1]

4 What is used to join two DNA strands together, during genetic modification?
   A amylase
   B ligase
   C pectinase
   D restriction enzyme [1]

5 What is **not** an advantage of inserting genes into soya plants to make them resistant to insect pests?
   A Higher yields are obtained.
   B Less insecticide is used.
   C Nutritional quality of the crop is improved.
   D Populations of insect pests are reduced. [1]

6 Yeast is used in breadmaking.
   a  i  Name the process that occurs in yeast cells, which produces a gas that helps the bread to rise. [2]
      ii Name the gas that is produced by yeast during breadmaking. [1]
      iii Name one other substance that is produced by the yeast during this process. [1]
   b Yeast is also used for making biofuel.
      i  What is biofuel? [2]
      ii **Describe** how yeast is used to make biofuel. [2]
   [Total: 8]

> **COMMAND WORD**
>
> **describe:** state the points of a topic / give characteristics and main features

### CONTINUED

**7** **a** **Outline** one example of using genetically modified bacteria to produce a human protein. [3]

**b** **Suggest** one advantage of using bacteria to make this protein. [1]

**c** **State** two differences between selective breeding and genetic modification. [2]

[Total: 6]

**8** Lactase is an enzyme produced in babies, which digests lactose in milk. The enzyme is present in the cell membranes of the cells covering the villi in the small intestine.

In most adults, lactase is not secreted. People who do not secrete lactase may suffer from gut pain and diarrhoea.

**a** Undigested lactose causes an increase in the water content of the gut lumen. Suggest how this is caused. [4]

**b** Undigested lactose is usually broken down by bacteria in the small intestine. This produces hydrogen. Testing for hydrogen in the breath after consuming lactose is one method of diagnosing intolerance to lactose.

Explain how hydrogen produced in the gut can become a component of exhaled air. [3]

**c** Lactase can be made commercially using the bacterium *Lactobacillus*. The graphs below show how temperature and pH affect the quantity of lactase that the bacterium synthesises during the time the bacterium is grown in a fermenter.

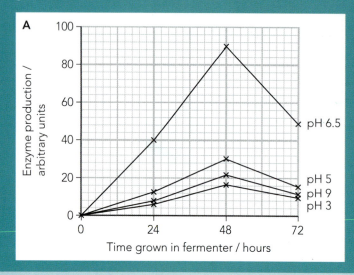

### COMMAND WORDS

**outline:** set out main points

**suggest:** apply knowledge and understanding to situations where there are a range of valid responses in order to make proposals / put forward considerations

**state:** express in clear terms

## CONTINUED

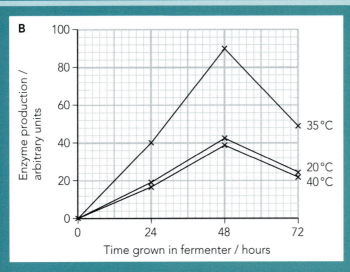

Use the information in the graphs, and your own knowledge, to suggest how *Lactobacillus* should be grown in a fermenter **and** explain how optimum conditions for its growth should be maintained. [6]

[Total: 13]

9 This graph shows how the use of two genetically modified (GM) crops changed in the USA between 1996 and 2019.

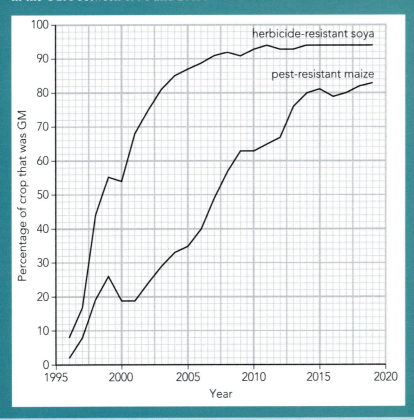

## CONTINUED

a Compare the changes in the use of herbicide-resistant soya and pest-resistant maize. [4]

b Explain why growing maize that is resistant to insect pests can be advantageous to both the farmer and the environment. [3]

c Evaluate the advantages and disadvantages of growing herbicide-resistant soya rather than non-GM soya. [4]

[Total: 11]

# 20 Biotechnology and genetic modification

## SELF-EVALUATION CHECKLIST

After studying this chapter, think about how confident you are with the different topics. This will help you to see any gaps in your knowledge and help you to learn more effectively.

| I can | See Topic… | Needs more work | Almost there | Confident to move on |
|---|---|---|---|---|
| list reasons why bacteria are useful in biotechnology and genetic modification | 20.1 | | | |
| discuss why bacteria are useful in biotechnology and genetic modification | 20.1 | | | |
| describe the role of anaerobic respiration in yeast during production of ethanol for making biofuel | 20.1 | | | |
| describe the role or anaerobic respiration in yeast in making carbon dioxide to help bread to rise | 20.1 | | | |
| describe how pectinase is used in the production of fruit juice | 20.1 | | | |
| investigate and describe the use of biological washing powders | 20.1 | | | |
| explain how and why lactase is used to make lactose-free milk | 20.1 | | | |
| describe and explain how bacteria and yeast can be grown in controlled conditions in a fermenter | 20.1 | | | |
| describe genetic modification as changing the genetic material of an organism by removing, changing or inserting individual genes | 20.2 | | | |
| outline examples of genetic modification, including: using bacteria to make human proteins; making crops resistant to insect pests or to herbicides; improving the nutritional qualities of crops | 20.2 | | | |
| describe how genetic modification is carried out, with reference to sticky ends, plasmids, restriction enzymes, DNA ligase and recombinant plasmids | 20.2 | | | |
| discuss the advantages and disadvantages of genetic modification of crops, including soya, maize and rice | 20.2 | | | |

# Glossary

## Command Words

Below are the Cambridge International definitions for command words which may be used in exams. The information in this section is taken from the Cambridge International syllabus (0610/0970) for examination from 2023. You should always refer to the appropriate syllabus document for the year of your examination to confirm the details and for more information. The syllabus document is available on the Cambridge International website www.cambridgeinternational.org.

**calculate:** work out from given facts, figures or information

**compare:** identify/comment on similarities and/or differences

**define:** give precise meaning

**describe:** state the points of a topic / give characteristics and main features

**determine:** establish an answer using the information available

**evaluate:** judge or calculate the quality, importance, amount, or value of something

**explain:** set out purposes or reasons / make the relationships between things evident / provide why and/or how and support with relevant evidence

**give:** produce an answer from a given source or recall/memory

**identify:** name/select/recognise

**outline:** set out main points

**predict:** suggest what may happen based on available information

**sketch:** make a simple freehand drawing showing the key features, taking care over proportions

**state:** express in clear terms

**suggest:** apply knowledge and understanding to situations where there are a range of valid responses in order to make proposals / put forward considerations

## Key Words

**absorbed:** soaked up; nutrients are absorbed from the alimentary canal into the blood, through the walls of the small intestine

**absorption:** the movement of nutrients from the alimentary canal into the blood

**accommodation:** changing the shape of the lens to focus on objects at different distances from the eye

**acrosome:** a structure containing digestive enzymes, in the head of a sperm cell

**active immunity:** long-term defence against a pathogen by antibody production in the body

**active site:** the part of an enzyme molecule to which the substrate temporarily binds

**active transport:** the movement of molecules or ions through a cell membrane from a region of lower concentration to a region of higher concentration (i.e. against a concentration gradient) using energy from respiration

**adaptation:** the process, resulting from natural selection, by which populations become more suited to their environment over many generations

**adaptive feature:** an inherited feature that helps an organism to survive and reproduce in its environment

**adrenaline:** a hormone secreted by the adrenal glands, which prepares the body for fight or flight

**aerobic respiration:** chemical reactions that take place in mitochondria, which use oxygen to break down glucose and other nutrient molecules to release energy for the cell to use

**age pyramid:** a diagram showing the relative numbers of individuals of different ages in a population

# Glossary

**AIDS:** acquired immune deficiency syndrome; a disease caused by HIV, which destroys white blood cells and therefore reduces the ability of the immune system to defend against other pathogens

**alimentary canal:** the part of the digestive system through which food passes as it moves from the mouth to the anus

**alleles:** alternative forms of a gene

**alveoli** (singular: **alveolus**): tiny air-filled sacs in the lungs where gas exchange takes place

**amino acids:** substances with molecules containing carbon, hydrogen, oxygen and nitrogen; there are 20 different amino acids found in organisms

**amniotic fluid:** liquid secreted by the amniotic sac, which supports and protects the fetus

**amniotic sac:** a tough membrane that surrounds a developing fetus in the uterus

**amylase:** an enzyme that catalyses the breakdown of starch to maltose

**anaerobic respiration:** chemical reactions in cells that break down nutrient molecules to release energy, without using oxygen

**antagonistic muscles:** a pair of muscles whose contraction has opposite effects; when one contracts, the other relaxes

**anther:** the structure at the top of a stamen, inside which pollen grains are made

**antibiotic:** a substance that is taken into the body, and which kills bacteria but does not affect human cells or viruses

**antibodies:** molecules secreted by white blood cells, which bind to pathogens and help to destroy them

**antigen:** a chemical that is recognised by the body as being 'foreign' – that is, it is not part of the body's normal set of chemical substances – and stimulates the production of antibodies

**anus:** the exit from the alimentary canal, through which faeces are removed

**aorta:** the largest artery in the body, which receives oxygenated blood from the left ventricle and delivers it to the body organs

**aquatic:** living in water

**arbitrary units:** these are sometimes used on a graph scale to represent quantitative differences between values, instead of 'real' units such as seconds or centimetres; this is usually because the real units would be very complicated to use

**artery:** a thick-walled vessel that takes high-pressure blood away from the heart

**arthropod:** an animal with jointed legs, but no backbone

**artificial insemination (AI):** introducing semen, containing sperm, to the reproductive organs of a female; fertilisation occurs in her body in the normal way

**artificial selection** or **selective breeding:** choosing particular organisms with desired characteristics to breed together, and continuing this over many generations

**asexual reproduction:** a process resulting in the production of genetically identical offspring from one parent

**assimilation:** the uptake and use of nutrients by cells

**atria** (singular: **atrium**): the thin-walled chambers at the top of the heart, which receive blood

**atrioventricular valve:** a valve between an atrium and a ventricle in the heart, which allows blood to flow from the atrium to the ventricle but not in the opposite direction

**auxin:** a plant hormone made in the tips of shoots, which causes cells to elongate

**axon:** a long, thin, fibre of cytoplasm that extends from the cell body of a neurone

**bacteria:** unicellular organisms whose cells do not contain a nucleus

**balanced diet:** a diet that contains all of the required nutrients, in suitable proportions, and the right amount of energy

**base:** one of the components of DNA; there are four bases, A, C, G and T, and their sequence determines the proteins that are made in a cell

**Benedict's solution:** a blue liquid that turns orange-red when heated with reducing sugar

**bile:** an alkaline fluid produced by the liver, which helps with fat digestion

**bile duct:** the tube that carries bile from the gall bladder to the duodenum

**binomial system:** a system of naming species that is internationally agreed, in which the scientific name is made up of two parts showing the genus and the species

**biodiversity:** the number of different species that live in an area

**biofuel:** a fuel that is made by mixing ethanol (made by the anaerobic respiration of yeast) with petrol

**biotechnology:** using organisms, usually microorganisms, to produce required substances

**biuret reagent:** a blue solution that turns purple when mixed with amino acids or proteins

**blind spot:** the part of the retina where the optic nerve leaves, and where there are no receptor cells

**breathing:** using the muscles in the diaphragm, and the intercostal muscles, to change the volume of the thorax so that air is drawn into and pushed out of the lungs

**bronchiole:** a small tube that takes air from a bronchus to every part of the lungs

**bronchus:** one of the two tubes that takes air from the trachea into the lungs

**buffer solution:** a liquid that has a known pH, and that keeps that pH steady all the time

**canines:** pointed teeth at either side of the incisors, used in a similar way to incisors; in carnivores, they are used for killing prey

**capillary:** a tiny vessel with walls only one cell thick, that takes blood close to body cells

**captive breeding:** keeping animals in captivity (e.g. in a zoo) and allowing them to breed, in order to increase the numbers in the population

**carbohydrases:** enzymes that break down carbohydrates

**carbohydrates:** substances that include sugars, starch and cellulose; they contain carbon, hydrogen and oxygen

**carnivore:** an animal that gets its energy by eating other animals

**carpel:** the female part of a flower

**carrier proteins** (or **protein carriers**): protein molecules in cell membranes that can use energy to change shape and move ions or molecules into or out of a cell

**catalase:** an enzyme that catalyses the breakdown of hydrogen peroxide to water and oxygen

**catalyst:** a substance that increases the rate of a chemical reaction and is not changed by the reaction

**cell membrane:** a very thin layer surrounding the cytoplasm of every cell; it controls what enters and leaves the cell

**cell sap:** the fluid that fills the large vacuoles in plant cells

**cell wall:** a tough layer outside the cell membrane; found in the cells of plants, fungi and bacteria

**cells:** the smallest units from which all organisms are made

**cellulose:** a carbohydrate that forms long fibres, and makes up the cell walls of plants

**cement:** the material that holds a tooth in the gum

**central nervous system (CNS):** the brain and spinal cord

**cervix:** a narrow opening leading from the uterus to the vagina

**chemical digestion:** the breakdown of large molecules in food into smaller molecules, so that they can be absorbed

**chlorophyll:** a green pigment (coloured substance) that absorbs energy from light; the energy is used to combine carbon dioxide with water and make glucose

**chloroplasts:** small structures found inside some plant cells, inside which photosynthesis takes place

**chromosome:** a length of DNA, found in the nucleus of a cell; it contains genetic information in the form of many different genes

**cilia:** tiny projections from some of the cells in the lining of the respiratory passages; the cilia of many adjacent cells beat rhythmically in unison

**ciliary muscle:** a circle of muscle surrounding the lens, and joined to it by the suspensory ligaments; when it contracts, it slackens the ligaments so that the lens becomes fatter

**circulatory system:** a system of blood vessels with a pump and valves to ensure one-way flow of blood

**codominance:** alleles that are both expressed in the phenotype when they are both present

**colon:** the first part of the large intestine

**common ancestor:** a species that lived in the past, and is thought to have given rise to several different species alive today; for example, all mammals share a common ancestor

**community:** all of the populations of all the different species in an ecosystem

**complementary:** with a perfect mirror-image shape

**complementary base pairing:** the way in which the bases of the two strands of DNA pair up; A always pairs with T, and C with G

**compound:** a substance formed by the chemical combination of two or more elements in fixed proportions

**concentration gradient:** an imaginary 'slope' from a high concentration to a low concentration

**cones:** receptor cells in the retina that are sensitive to light of different colours, but only function in bright light

# Glossary

**consumer:** an organism that gets its energy by feeding on other organisms

**continuous variation:** variation in which there is a continuous range of phenotypes between two extremes

**control:** a standard sample that you use as a comparison, to find the effect of changing a variable

**coordination:** ensuring that the actions of different parts of the body work together

**cornea:** a transparent layer near the front of the eye, which refracts light rays entering the eye

**coronary arteries:** vessels that deliver oxygenated blood to the heart muscle

**coronary heart disease (CHD):** disease caused by blockage of the coronary arteries

**corpus luteum:** a structure that develops from the empty follicle after an egg has been released from an ovary; also known as a yellow body

**cortex:** the tissue making up the outer layer in a kidney

**cross-pollination:** the transfer of pollen grains from the anther of a flower to the stigma of a flower on a different plant of the same species

**culture:** a population of microorganisms growing in a nutrient liquid or on agar jelly

**cuticle:** a thin layer of wax that covers the upper surface of a leaf

**cytoplasm:** the jelly-like material that fills a cell

**DCPIP:** a purple liquid that becomes colourless when mixed with vitamin C

**deamination:** the removal of the nitrogen-containing part of amino acids to form urea

**death phase:** the final stage in a population growth curve where the population falls; death rate exceeds birth rate

**decomposer:** an organism that gets its energy from dead or waste organic material

**decomposers:** organisms that break down organic substances outside their bodies, releasing nutrients from them that other organisms can use

**dendrites:** short fibres of cytoplasm in a neurone

**denitrification:** converting nitrate ions to nitrogen gas

**dentine:** a living tissue that lies just beneath the enamel of a tooth

**deoxygenated blood:** blood containing only a little oxygen

**dependent variable:** the variable that you measure, as you collect your results

**destarching:** leaving a plant in the dark for long enough for it to use up its starch stores

**diaphragm:** a muscle that separates the chest cavity from the abdominal cavity in mammals; it helps with breathing

**dichotomous key:** a way of identifying an organism, by working through pairs of statements that lead you to its name

**dicotyledons:** plants with two cotyledons in their seeds

**diet:** the food eaten in one day

**diffusion:** the net movement of particles from a region of their higher concentration to a region of their lower concentration (i.e. down a concentration gradient), as a result of their random movement

**digestion:** the breakdown of food

**digestive system:** the group of organs that carries out digestion of food

**diploid:** having two complete sets of chromosomes

**discontinuous variation:** variation in which there are distinct categories of phenotype, with no intermediates

**DNA:** a molecule that contains genetic information, in the form of genes, that controls the proteins that are made in the cell

**DNA ligase:** an enzyme that joins two DNA molecules together

**dominant allele:** an allele that is expressed if it is present (e.g. G)

**dormant:** inactive, with metabolic reactions taking place very slowly or not at all

**double circulatory system:** a system in which blood passes through the heart twice on one complete circuit of the body

**drug:** any substance taken into the body that modifies or affects chemical reactions in the body

**dry mass:** the mass of an organism after it has been killed and all water removed from it

**duodenum:** the first part of the small intestine, into which the pancreatic duct and bile duct empty fluids

**ECG:** a graph showing the electrical activity of the heart plotted against time

**ecology:** the study of organisms in their environment

**ecosystem:** a unit containing all of the organisms in a community and their environment, interacting together

**effectors:** parts of the body that respond to a stimulus; muscles and glands are effectors

**egestion:** the removal of undigested food from the body as faeces

**electron micrograph:** an image made using an electron microscope

**embryo:** the ball of cells that is produced by repeated division of the zygote

**emulsifies:** breaks down large drops of fat or oil into smaller droplets, increasing their surface area and allowing them to mix with watery liquids

**emulsion:** a liquid containing two substances that do not fully mix; one of them forms tiny droplets dispersed throughout the other

**enamel:** the very strong material that covers the surface of a tooth

**endangered:** at serious risk of becoming extinct

**endocrine glands:** glands that secrete hormones

**enhanced greenhouse effect:** the increased heating effect caused by an increase of greenhouse gases in the atmosphere

**enzyme–substrate complex:** the short-lived structure formed as the substrate binds temporarily to the active site of an enzyme

**enzymes:** proteins that are involved in all metabolic reactions, where they function as biological catalysts

**epidermis:** the outer layer of tissue on a plant; also the outer layer of an animal's skin

**epididymis:** part of the testis in which sperm are stored

**epithelium:** a tissue that covers a surface in an animal; for example, an epithelium covers the inside of the wall of the human alimentary canal

**eutrophication:** a chain of events caused by addition of extra plant nutrients to water, resulting in a decrease in the concentration of dissolved oxygen available for organisms that require it for aerobic respiration

**excretion:** the removal of the waste products of metabolism and substances in excess of requirements

**exoskeleton:** a supportive structure on the outside of the body

**expressed:** used to make a protein; a gene is expressed when the protein that it codes for is synthesised in a cell

**extinction:** the complete loss of a species from Earth

**fats:** lipids that are solid at room temperature

**fermenter:** a vessel, usually made of steel or glass, in which microorganisms can be grown in order to produce a required product

**fertile:** able to reproduce

**fertilisation:** the fusion of the nuclei of two gametes

**fetus:** an unborn mammal, in which all the organs have been formed

**fibrin:** an insoluble protein that is formed from fibrinogen when a blood vessel is damaged

**fibrinogen:** a soluble protein, present in blood plasma

**filament:** the 'stalk' part of a stamen

**flaccid:** a description of a plant cell that is soft

**flagellum** (plural: **flagella**): a long, whip-like 'tail' structure found on sperm cells, used for swimming

**follicle:** a structure within an ovary, in which an egg develops

**food chain:** a diagram showing the flow of energy from one organism to the next, beginning with a producer

**food web:** a network of interconnected food chains

**fovea:** the part of the retina where cone cells are very tightly packed; this is where light is focused when you look directly at an object

**FSH:** follicle stimulating hormone, a hormone secreted by the pituitary gland which causes a follicle to develop in an ovary

**fully permeable:** allows all molecules and ions to pass through it

**fungus:** an organism whose cells have cell walls, but that does not photosynthesise

**gall bladder:** a small organ that stores bile, before the bile is released into the duodenum

**gamete:** a sex cell; a cell with half the normal number of chromosomes, whose nucleus fuses with the nucleus of another gamete during sexual reproduction

**gas exchange:** the diffusion of oxygen and carbon dioxide into and out of an organism's body

**gas exchange surface:** a part of the body where gas exchange between the body and the environment takes place

**gastric juice:** a liquid secreted by the walls of the stomach; it contains pepsin and hydrochloric acid

**gene:** a length of DNA that codes for one protein

**genetic diagram:** a standard way of showing all the steps in making predictions about the probable genotypes and phenotypes of the offspring from two parents

**genetic modification:** changing the genetic material of an organism by removing, changing or inserting individual genes

**genotype:** the genetic makeup of an organism in terms of the alleles present (e.g. **GG**)

**genus:** a group of species that share similar features and a common ancestor

**glomeruli** (singular: **glomerulus**): a little 'network' of blood capillaries, where the blood is filtered in a kidney

# Glossary

**glucagon:** a hormone secreted by the pancreas, which increases blood glucose concentration

**glucose:** a sugar that is used in respiration to release energy

**glycogen:** a carbohydrate that is used as an energy store in animal cells

**goblet cells:** cells found in the lining (epithelium) of the respiratory passages and digestive system, which secrete mucus

**gravitropism:** a response in which part of a plant grows towards or away from gravity

**greenhouse effect:** the heating effect on the Earth of the trapping of heat by greenhouse gases; note that this is a natural and useful effect, as without it the Earth would be too cold to support life

**greenhouse gases:** gases such as carbon dioxide and methane that trap heat within the atmosphere

**growth:** a permanent increase in size and dry mass

**guard cells:** a pair of cells that surrounds a stoma and controls its opening; guard cells are the only cells in the epidermis that contain chloroplasts

**habitat:** the place where an organism lives

**haemoglobin:** a red pigment found in red blood cells, which can combine reversibly with oxygen; it is a protein

**haploid:** having only a single set of chromosomes

**hepatic artery:** the blood vessel that supplies oxygenated blood to the liver

**hepatic portal vein:** the blood vessel that carries blood from the small intestine to the liver

**hepatic veins:** the blood vessel that carry blood away from the liver

**herbivore:** an animal that gets its energy by eating plants

**heterozygous:** having two different alleles of a particular gene (e.g. **Gg**)

**high water potential:** an area where there are a lot of water molecules – a dilute solution

**HIV:** the human immunodeficiency virus

**homeostasis:** the maintenance of a constant internal environment

**homozygous:** having two identical alleles of a particular gene (e.g. **GG** or **gg**)

**hormones:** chemicals that are produced by a gland and carried in the blood, which alter the activities of their specific target organs

**host:** an organism in which a pathogen lives and reproduces

**humidity:** how much water vapour is present in air

**hydrophyte:** a plant that has adaptive features that help it to survive in water

**hyphae:** microscopic threads, made of cells linked in a long line, that make up the body of a fungus

**hypothalamus:** part of the brain that is involved in the control of body temperature

**ileum:** the second part of the small intestine; most absorption takes place here

**immune response:** the reaction of the body to the presence of an antigen; it involves the production of antibodies

**implantation:** attachment of the embryo to the lining of the uterus

**in vitro fertilisation (IVF):** adding semen, containing sperm, to eggs in a container in a laboratory; fertilisation occurs in the container, and embryos can later be inserted into the body of a female

**incisors:** chisel-shaped teeth at the front of the mouth, used for biting off pieces of food

**independent variable:** the variable that you change in an experiment

**infection:** the entry of a pathogen into the body of a host

**infertile:** not able to reproduce

**ingestion:** the taking of food and drink into the body

**inheritance:** the transmission of genetic information from generation to generation

**insulin:** a hormone secreted by the pancreas, which decreases blood glucose concentration

**intercostal muscles:** muscles between the ribs, which raise and lower the rib cage when they contract and relax

**internal environment:** the conditions inside the body

**iodine solution:** a solution of iodine in potassium iodide; it is orange-brown, and turns blue-black when mixed with starch

**iris:** the coloured part of the eye; it contains muscles that can alter the size of the pupil

**iris reflex (pupil reflex):** an automatic response to a change in light intensity; the receptors are in the retina, and the effector is the muscles in the iris

**keratin:** the protein that forms hair

**kinetic energy:** energy of moving objects

**kingdom:** one of the major groups into which all organisms are classified

**lacteals:** small vessels that absorb fatty acids and glycerol in the small intestine; their contents are eventually emptied into the blood

**lag phase:** the stage at the start of a population growth curve where the population remains small and grows only very slowly

**large intestine:** a relatively wide part of the alimentary canal, consisting of the colon and rectum

**lens:** a transparent structure in the eye, which changes shape to focus light rays onto the retina

**LH:** luteinising hormone, a hormone secreted by the pituitary gland that causes ovulation to happen

**lignin:** a hard, strong, waterproof substance that forms the walls of xylem vessels

**limiting factor:** a factor that is in short supply, which stops an activity (such as photosynthesis) happening at a faster rate

**lipases:** enzymes that break down lipids (fats and oils)

**lipids:** substances containing carbon, hydrogen and oxygen; they are insoluble in water and are used as energy stores in organisms

**liver:** a large, dark red organ that carries out many different functions, including production of bile and the regulation of blood glucose concentration

**log phase** or **exponential phase:** the stage in a population growth curve where the population grows at its maximum rate; birth rate exceeds death rate

**low water potential:** an area where there are not many water molecules – a concentrated solution

**lubricated:** made smooth and slippery, to reduce friction

**lumen:** the space in the centre of a tube, through which substances can move

**lymphocytes:** white blood cells that secrete antibodies

**magnification:** how many times larger an image is than the actual object

**maltase:** an enzyme that catalyses the breakdown of maltose to glucose

**maltose:** a reducing sugar made of two glucose molecules joined together

**mammary glands:** organs found only in mammals, which produce milk to feed young

**medulla:** the tissue making up the inner layers in a kidney

**meiosis:** division of a diploid nucleus resulting in four genetically different haploid nuclei; this is sometimes called a reduction division

**memory cells:** long-lived cells produced by the division of lymphocytes that have contacted their antigen; memory cells are able to respond quickly to subsequent contact with the same antigen

**menstruation:** the loss of the broken down uterus lining through the vagina

**messenger RNA (mRNA):** a molecule that carries a copy of the information on DNA to a ribosome, to be used to synthesise a protein

**metabolic reactions:** chemical reactions that take place in living organisms

**metabolism:** the chemical reactions that take place in living organisms

**metamorphosis:** changing from a larva with one body form to an adult with a different body form

**microvilli:** tiny folds on the surfaces of the cells of the epithelium of the villi in the small intestine

**mitochondrion:** a small structure in a cell, where aerobic respiration releases energy from glucose

**mitosis:** division of a cell nucleus resulting in two genetically identical nuclei (i.e. with the same number and kind of chromosomes as the parent nucleus)

**molars:** teeth similar to premolars but usually larger, with broad, ridged surfaces, found towards the back of the mouth; they are used for grinding food to increase its surface area

**monocotyledons:** plants with only one cotyledon in their seeds

**monoculture:** an area of ground covered by a single crop, with almost no other species present

**monohybrid cross:** a cross where we consider the inheritance of only one gene

**motor neurone:** a neurone that transmits electrical impulses from the central nervous system to an effector

**movement:** an action by an organism or part of an organism causing a change of position or place

**MRSA:** methicillin-resistant *Staphylococcus aureus*; bacteria that are resistant to the antibiotic methicillin

**mucus:** a smooth, viscous fluid secreted by many different organs in the body

**multicellular:** made of many cells

**mutation:** a random change in a gene, which can produce new alleles; mutation involves a change in the base sequence in DNA

**natural selection:** a process in which individuals with advantageous features are more likely to survive, reproduce and pass on their alleles to the next generation

**nectar:** a sweet liquid secreted by many insect-pollinated flowers, to attract their pollinators

**negative feedback:** a mechanism that detects a move away from the set point, and brings about actions that take the value back towards the set point

**nephron:** one of the thousands of microscopic tubes inside a kidney, where urine is made

**nerve:** a group of neurone axons lying together (like an electrical cable containing many wires)

**nerve impulse:** an electrical signal that passes rapidly along an axon

**net movement:** overall or average movement

**neurone:** a cell that is specialised for conducting electrical impulses rapidly

**neurotransmitter:** a chemical stored in vesicles at the end of neurones, which can be released to diffuse across the synaptic gap and set up an electrical impulse in the next neurone

**niche:** the role of an organism in its natural environment; the way in which it interacts with other organisms and with the non-living parts of the environment

**nitrification:** converting ammonium ions to nitrate ions

**nitrogen fixation:** converting inert nitrogen gas into a more reactive form, such as nitrate ions or ammonia

**non-biodegradable:** not able to be broken down by decomposers

**nucleotides:** molecules that are linked together into long chains, to make up a DNA molecule

**nucleus:** a structure containing DNA in the form of chromosomes

**nutrition:** taking in materials for energy, growth and development

**oesophagus:** the tube leading from the mouth to the stomach

**oils:** lipids that are liquid at room temperature

**optic nerve:** the nerve that carries electrical impulses from the retina to the brain

**optimum:** best; for example, the optimum temperature of an enzyme is the temperature at which its activity is greatest

**organ:** a group of tissues that work together to perform a particular function

**organ system:** several organs that work together to perform a particular function

**organic substances:** substances whose molecules contain carbon; in biology, we normally consider organic compounds to be ones that are made by living things

**organism:** a living thing

**osmosis:** the diffusion of water molecules through a partially permeable membrane

**osmosis (in terms of water potential):** the net movement of water molecules from a region of higher water potential (dilute solution) to a region of lower water potential (concentrated solution) through a partially permeable membrane

**ovaries:** organs that produce female gametes (eggs)

**ovary:** the part of the flower that holds the ovules

**oviducts:** tubes leading from the ovaries to the uterus; also known as Fallopian tubes

**ovulation:** the release of an egg from an ovary

**ovules:** small structures that contain the female gametes

**oxygen debt:** extra oxygen that is needed after anaerobic respiration has taken place, in order to break down the lactic acid produced

**oxygenated blood:** blood containing a lot of oxygen

**palisade mesophyll:** the layer of cells immediately beneath the upper epidermis, where most photosynthesis happens

**pancreas:** a creamy-white organ lying close to the stomach, which secretes pancreatic juice; it also secretes the hormones insulin and glucagon, which are involved in the control of blood glucose concentration

**pancreatic duct:** the tube that carries pancreatic fluid from the pancreas to the duodenum

**partially permeable:** allows some molecules and ions to pass through, but not others

**partially permeable membrane:** a membrane (very thin layer) that lets some particles move through it, but prevents others passing through

**particles:** (in this context) the smallest pieces of which a substance is made; particles can be molecules, atoms or ions

**passive immunity:** short-term defence against a pathogen by antibodies acquired from another individual, such as from mother to infant

**pathogen:** a microorganism that causes disease

**pathogens:** microorganisms that cause disease, such as bacteria

**pectinase:** an enzyme that is used to digest pectin, increasing the quantity of juice that can be extracted from fruit, and clarifying the juice

**penis:** organ containing the urethra, through which urine and sperm are carried

**pepsin:** a protease enzyme secreted in gastric juice; it has an optimum pH of 2

**peripheral nervous system (PNS):** the nerves outside the brain and spinal cord

**peristalsis:** rhythmical muscular contractions that move food through the alimentary canal

**petals:** coloured structures that attract insects or birds to a flower

**phagocytes:** white blood cells that destroy pathogens by phagocytosis

**phagocytosis:** taking bacteria or other small structures into a cell's cytoplasm, and digesting them with enzymes

**phenotype:** the observable features of an organism

**phloem:** a plant tissue made up of living cells joined end to end; it transports substances made by the plant, such as sucrose and amino acids

**photosynthesis:** the process by which plants synthesise carbohydrates from raw materials using energy from light

**phototropism:** a response in which part of a plant grows towards or away from the direction from which light is coming

**physical digestion:** the breakdown of food into smaller pieces, without making any chemical changes to the molecules in the food

**pinna:** a flap on the outside of the body that directs sound into the ear

**pituitary gland:** a small endocrine gland attached to the underside of the brain

**placenta:** an organ that connects the growing fetus to its mother, in which the blood of the fetus and mother are brought close together so that materials can be exchanged between them

**plasma:** the liquid part of blood

**plasmids:** small, circular molecules of DNA, found in many prokaryotic cells in addition to the main, much larger circle of DNA

**plasmolysed:** a description of a cell in which the cell membrane tears away from the cell wall

**platelets:** tiny cell fragments present in blood, which help with clotting

**pollen grains:** small structures which contain the male gametes of a flower

**pollination:** the transfer of pollen grains from the male part of the plant (anther of stamen) to the female part of the plant (stigma)

**population:** a group of organisms of one species, living in the same area at the same time

**premolars:** teeth with broad, ridged surfaces, found between the canines and molars; they are used for grinding food to increase its surface area

**producer:** an organism that makes its own organic nutrients, generally using energy from sunlight, through photosynthesis

**product:** the new substance formed by a chemical reaction

**prokaryote:** an organism whose cells do not have a nucleus

**prokaryotic cells:** cells with no nucleus; bacteria have prokaryotic cells

**prostate gland:** organ that produces a nutritious fluid in which sperm are transported

**protease:** an enzyme that catalyses the breakdown of protein to amino acids

**protein:** a substance whose molecules are made of many amino acids linked together; each different protein has a different sequence of amino acids

**protoctist:** a single-celled organism, or one with several very similar cells

**puberty:** the time at which sexual maturity is reached

**pulmonary artery:** the artery that carries deoxygenated blood from the right ventricle to the lungs

**pulmonary veins:** the veins that carry oxygenated blood from the lungs to the left atrium of the heart

**pulse rate:** the number of times an artery expands and recoils in one minute; it is a measure of heart rate

**Punnett square:** the part of a genetic diagram that shows the predicted genotypes and phenotypes that can result from the random fusion of the male and female gametes

**pupil:** a circular gap in the middle of the iris, through which light can pass

**pyramid of biomass:** a graph showing the relative quantity of biomass at each trophic level

**pyramid of energy:** a graph showing the relative quantity of energy at each trophic level

**pyramid of numbers:** a diagram in which the area of the bar at each trophic level shows the relative number of organisms at that level in the food chain

**range:** the lowest to the highest value

**reabsorption:** in a kidney nephron, taking back required substances into the blood

**receptor proteins:** proteins on the membrane of the second neurone at a synapse, which have a complementary shape to the molecules of neurotransmitter

**receptors:** cells or groups of cells that detect stimuli

**recessive allele:** an allele that is only expressed when there is no dominant allele of the gene present (e.g. g)

**recombinant plasmid:** a small circle of DNA, found in bacteria, which contains both the bacterial DNA and DNA from a different organism

**rectum:** the second part of the large intestine, where faeces are produced and stored

**red blood cells:** biconcave blood cells with no nucleus, which transport oxygen

**reducing sugars:** sugars such as glucose, which turn Benedict's solution orange-red when heated together

**reduction division:** a term used to describe what happens in meiosis, where the number of chromosomes is halved (reduced)

**reflex action:** a means of automatically and rapidly integrating and coordinating stimuli with the responses of effectors

**reflex arc:** a series of neurones (sensory, relay and motor) that transmit electrical impulses from a receptor to an effector

**refraction:** bending light rays

**relay neurone:** a neurone that transmits electrical impulses within the central nervous system

**reproduction:** the processes that make more of the same kind of organism

**respiration:** the chemical reactions in cells that break down nutrient molecules and release energy for metabolism

**restriction enzymes:** enzymes (biological catalysts) that cut DNA at specific points, and leave a short length of unpaired bases at each end

**retina:** a tissue at the back of the eye that contains receptor cells that respond to light

**ribosomes:** very small structures in a cell that use information on DNA to make protein molecules

**rods:** receptor cells in the retina that respond to dim light, but do not detect colour

**salivary glands:** groups of cells close to the mouth, which secrete saliva into the salivary ducts

**scrotum:** the sac that contains the testes

**secrete:** make a useful substance and then send it out of the cell where it is made, to be used in another part of the body

**seed:** the structure that develops from an ovule after fertilisation; it contains an embryo plant

**seed banks:** facilities in which seeds of different plant species, or crop varieties, are stored for long periods of time, in order to conserve as many different species and varieties as possible

**selection pressure:** something in the environment that affects the chance that individuals with different features will survive and reproduce

**self-pollination:** the transfer of pollen grains from the anther of a flower to the stigma of the same flower, or a different flower on the same plant

**semilunar valves:** valves close to the entrances to the aorta and pulmonary artery, which prevent backflow of blood from the arteries to the ventricles

**sense organ:** a group of receptor cells that are able to respond to a specific stimulus

**sensitivity:** the ability to detect and respond to changes in the internal or external environment

**sensory neurone:** a neurone that transmits electrical impulses from a receptor to the central nervous system

**sepals:** leaf-like structures that form a ring outside the petals of a flower

**septum:** the structure that separates the left and right sides of the heart, keeping oxygenated blood separate from deoxygenated blood

**set point:** the normal value or range of values for a particular parameter – for example, the normal range of blood glucose concentration or the normal body temperature

**sex chromosomes:** chromosomes that determine sex

**sex-linked genes:** genes that are found on a part of one of the sex chromosomes (usually the X chromosome) and not on the other sex chromosome; they therefore produce characteristics that are more common in one sex than in the other

**sexual reproduction:** a process involving the fusion of two gametes to form a zygote and the production of offspring that are genetically different from each other

**sexually transmitted infection (STI):** a disease caused by pathogens that are transmitted during sexual contact

**sigmoid growth curve:** an S-shaped curve showing the change in the size of a population through all the phases in population growth

**single circulatory system:** a system in which blood passes through the heart only once on one complete circuit of the body

**sink:** part of a plant to which sucrose or amino acids are being transported, and where they are used or stored

**small intestine:** a long, narrow part of the alimentary canal, consisting of the duodenum and ileum

**source:** part of a plant that releases sucrose or amino acids, to be transported to other parts

**species:** a group of organisms that can reproduce to produce fertile offspring

**specificity:** of enzymes, only able to act on a particular (specific) substrate

**sperm duct:** a tube that transports sperm from the testis to the urethra

**sphincter muscles:** rings of muscle that can contract to close a tube

**spongy mesophyll:** the layer of cells immediately beneath the palisade mesophyll, where some photosynthesis happens; this tissue contains a lot of air spaces between the cells

**spores:** very small groups of cells surrounded by a protective wall, used in reproduction

**stamens:** the male parts of a flower

**starch:** a carbohydrate that is used as an energy store in plant cells

**starch grains:** tiny pieces of starch, made of thousands of starch molecules, that are stored in some plant cells

**stationary phase:** the stage in a population growth curve where the population remains roughly constant; birth rate equals death rate

**stem cells:** unspecialised cells that are able to divide by mitosis to produce different types of specialised cell

**sterilised:** treated – e.g. with steam – to destroy all living cells

**sticky ends:** lengths of unpaired bases on one strand of a DNA molecule; they are able to form bonds with complementary lengths of unpaired bases on a different DNA molecule

**stigma:** the part of a flower that receives pollen

**stimuli** (singular: **stimulus**)**:** changes in the environment that can be detected by organisms

**stomach:** a wide part of the alimentary canal, in which food can be stored for a while, and where the digestion of protein begins

**stomata** (singular: **stoma**)**:** openings in the surface of a leaf, most commonly in the lower surface; they are surrounded by pairs of guard cells, which control whether the stomata are open or closed

**style:** the part of a carpel that connects the stigma to the ovary

**substrate:** the substance that an enzyme causes to react

**sucrase:** an enzyme that breaks down sucrose

**sucrose:** a sugar whose molecules are made of glucose and another similar molecule (fructose) linked together

**sugars:** carbohydrates that have relatively small molecules; they are soluble in water and they taste sweet

**suspensory ligaments:** strong, inelastic fibres that hold the lens in position; when they are under tension, they pull the lens into a thinner shape

**sustainable resource:** one that is produced as rapidly as it is removed from the environment, so that it does not run out

**sweat gland:** a structure found in the skin of mammals, which secretes a watery fluid onto the skin surface to reduce body temperature

**symptoms:** features that you experience when you have a disease

**synapse:** a junction between two neurones

**synaptic gap:** a tiny gap between two neurones, at a synapse

**target organs:** organs whose activity is altered by a hormone

**terrestrial:** living on land

**test cross:** a cross used to try to determine the genotype of an organism showing the characteristic produced by a dominant allele; the unknown organism is crossed with one showing the recessive characteristic

**testes** (singular: **testis**)**:** organs in which the male gametes (sperm) are made

**thorax:** the chest; the part of the body from the neck down to the diaphragm

**tissue:** a group of similar cells that work together to perform a particular function

**toxin:** a poisonous substance; a chemical that damages cells

**trachea:** the tube through which air travels to the lungs; it has rings of cartilage in its walls, to support it

**translocation:** the movement of sucrose and amino acids in phloem from sources to sinks

# Glossary

**transmissible disease:** a disease that can be passed from one host to another; transmissible diseases are caused by pathogens

**transmission:** the movement of a pathogen from one host to another

**transpiration:** the loss of water vapour from leaves

**transpiration pull:** a force produced by the loss of water vapour from a leaf, which reduces the pressure at the top of xylem vessels

**trophic level:** the position of an organism in a food chain, food web or pyramid of biomass or numbers

**tropism:** a growth response by a plant, in which the direction of growth is related to the direction of the stimulus

**trypsin:** a protease enzyme secreted by the pancreas; it works in the duodenum

**turgid:** a description of a plant cell that is tight and firm

**turgor pressure:** the pressure of the water pushing outwards on a plant cell wall

**type 1 diabetes:** a condition in which insufficient insulin is secreted by the pancreas, so that blood glucose concentration is not controlled

**umbilical cord:** a structure containing blood vessels that connects the fetus to the placenta

**unicellular:** made of a single cell

**urea:** a waste product produced in the liver, from the breakdown of excess amino acids

**ureter:** one of a pair of tubes that carries urine from the kidneys to the bladder

**urethra:** the tube that carries urine from the bladder to the outside

**urine:** a solution of urea and other waste materials in water, produced by the kidneys

**uterus:** the organ in which a fetus develops before birth; also known as the womb

**vaccine:** a harmless preparation of dead or inactivated pathogens that is injected into the body to induce an immune response

**vacuole:** a fluid-filled space inside a cell, separated from the cytoplasm by a membrane

**vagina:** opening from the uterus to the outside of the body

**valves:** structures that allow a liquid to flow in one direction only

**variation:** differences between the individuals of the same species

**vascular bundles:** collections of xylem tubes and phloem vessels running side by side, which form the veins in a leaf

**vasoconstriction:** narrowing of arterioles, caused by the contraction of the muscle in their walls

**vasodilation:** widening of arterioles, caused by the relaxation of the muscle in their walls

**vein:** a thin-walled vessel that takes low-pressure blood back to the heart

**venae cavae** (singular: vena cava): the large veins that bring deoxygenated blood to the right atrium

**ventilation:** the movement of air into and out of the lungs, by breathing movements

**ventricles:** the thick-walled chambers at the base of the heart, which pump out blood

**vesicle:** a very small vacuole

**vestigial:** description of a structure that has evolved to become so small that it is no longer useful

**villi** (singular: **villus**): very small finger-like projections that line the inner surface of the small intestine, greatly increasing its surface area

**water potential gradient:** a difference in water potential between two areas

**white blood cells:** blood cells with a nucleus, which help to defend against pathogens

**wilting (of a plant):** losing more water than it can take up, so the cells lose their turgidity

**X chromosome:** the larger of the two sex chromosomes in mammals

**xerophyte:** a plant that has adaptive features that help it to survive in an environment where water is scarce

**xylem:** a plant tissue made up of dead, empty cells joined end to end; it transports water and mineral ions and helps to support the plant

**Y chromosome:** the smaller of the two sex chromosomes in mammals

**zygote:** a cell that is formed by the fusion of two gametes

# Index

absorbed nutrients 132
absorption (digestion) 132, 133, 140–1
accommodation (focusing) 245
acquired immune deficiency syndrome (AIDS) 312–13
acrosomes 306
active immunity 205
active sites 85
active transport 61–2
adaptive features 352–3, 356–7, 363
adipose tissue 129
adolescence 310
adrenal gland 246, 247
adrenaline 246, 247
aerobic respiration 37, 61, 217, 218, 226–7
age pyramids 384–6
agricultural chemicals 397
agricultural machinery 396
AI (artificial insemination) 416
AIDS (acquired immune deficiency syndrome) 312–13
air, inspired and expired 224–5
alimentary canal 83, 84, 131, 133–5
alleles 322, 326, 327–9
alveoli 221, 222
amino acids
    deamination 263
    in meteorites 69
    in plants 102
    in proteins 75, 337, 338
    translocation 159–60
amniotic fluid 309
amniotic sac 309
amphibians 16
amylase 84, 134, 136, 138, 428
anaemia 130
anaerobic respiration 217, 218, 226, 427

animal cells 33–8, 58
animal fats 175
animal kingdom 10
animals, and food hygiene 198
antagonistic muscles 243
anthers 286, 287, 288, 289, 290
antibiotic resistance 360–1
antibiotics 360, 400
antibodies 75, 203–4, 205–6
antigens 203–4
anus 133
aorta 172, 173
aquatic organisms 20, 409
arachnids 20
arteries 172, 173, 178, 179, 180, 222
arterioles 271, 272, 273
arthropods 19–21
artificial blood 169
artificial fertilisers 381, 397, 409, 410
artificial insemination (AI) 416
artificial photosynthesis 98
artificial selection 362–3
asexual reproduction 283, 293–4
assimilation (digestion) 132, 133
athlete's foot 196
atria 172, 173, 176
atrioventricular valves 173, 176
auxin 252–3
axons 236, 237

Bacillus thuringiensis 436
bacteria
    in biotechnology 427
    cell structure 14, 40
    evolution 32
    in food 196
    genetically modified 434, 436–8
bacterial cells 14, 40

bacterial diseases 195, 360–1
    see also cholera
bacterial growth 199
balanced diets 128
bananas 282, 294
baobab trees 160
base pairing 77
base sequences 337–8, 361
bases 77
bees 288
Benedict's solution 71
bicuspid valve 176
bile 135, 139–40
bile ducts 135
binomial system 7
biodiversity 398
biofuels 98, 427–8
biological classification 5–7
biological washing powders 430
bird droppings 261
birds 17
    flightless 414
birth rate 383, 385
black-footed ferrets 395
bladder 266
blind spot 242
blood
    composition 182–5
    glucose concentration 267–8, 269–70
    in the placenta 308–9
    transmission of HIV through 313
    urea removal from 264–5
blood cells 182, 183–4
blood clots 174, 184
blood groups 169, 328, 348
blood plasma 182, 185

# Index

blood transfusions  169, 313
blood vessels  178–81
    see also arteries; capillaries; veins
body defences against pathogens  197
body temperature  266–7, 270–3
bones, brittle  130
bonsai pine trees  350
bran  131
bread  428
breast feeding  205, 313
breathing
    movements  224–5
    during sleep  216
breathing rate, exercise and  226–7
breathing system, human  221–3
breeding, selective  362–3, 397
brittle bones  130
bronchi  222
bronchioles  222
Bt protein  436
buffer solutions  87
buiret reagent  75
butterflies  347

cacti  354–5, 358
calcium in food  130
camouflage, and natural selection  358–60
canines  137
capillaries  178, 179, 180, 222, 271, 272, 273
captive breeding  415, 416
carbohydrases  85
carbohydrates
    in blood plasma  185
    and diabetes  270
    molecular structure  70–1
    in plants  101–2
    as a source of food  128
    see also cellulose; starch; sugars
carbon cycle  379–80

carbon dioxide
    in aerobic and anaerobic respiration  217
    in blood plasma  185
    and the carbon cycle  379–80
    diffusion  52, 53
    excretion  262
    gas exchange  220
    as a greenhouse gas  405
    in inspired and expired air  224
    in photosynthesis  99, 115–16
carnivores  374
carotene  435
carpels  287
carrier proteins  62
catalase  84, 92
catalysts  84
    see also enzymes
Cavendish banana  282
cell division  285, 324–5
cell membranes  35, 52–3, 58, 59
cell sap  35
cell walls  35, 59, 101
cells
    animal  33–8, 58
    bacterial  14, 40
    energy in  217
    plant  33–8, 59–60
    specialised  41–2
cellulose  11, 35, 70, 84
cement, tooth  137
central nervous system (CNS)  237
centromere  324
cervix  304
characteristics of organisms  3–5
CHD (coronary heart disease)  174, 175
chemical digestion  132, 133, 136, 138
chemical fertilisers  381, 397, 409, 410
chinchillas  321, 326, 327, 329–30
Chlamydomonas  13
chloride ions  202

chlorophyll  10, 11, 99, 102
chloroplasts  36, 106
cholera  202
cholesterol  174, 185
chromatids  324
chromosomes  36, 284, 285, 322–6, 335–6
cilia  221
ciliary muscle  245
circulatory systems  170–1
classification of organisms  5–7, 361
clear-felling  412
clots, blood  174, 184
CNS (central nervous system)  237
coastal redwoods  148
codominance  328
collagen  130
colon  134, 135
colour blindness  336–7
combustion  380
common ancestor  5
communities (ecosystems)  372
complementary base pairing  77
complementary shapes  85
compounds  55
concentration gradients  51–2
condoms  313
cones  242
conjunctiva  242
conjunctivitis  242
conservation  411–17
conservation programmes  417
consumers (food chains)  374
containers, plastic  410–11
continuous variation  348–9
control samples  109–10
cooking food  199
coordination  236, 247–8
coppicing  412
coral reefs  402
cornea  244
coronary arteries  174

coronary heart disease (CHD) 174, 175
coronaviruses 207–8
corpus luteum 311
cortex (kidney) 264
cotton, genetically modified 434
cotton boll weevils 434
cotyledons 22–3
coughing 196
Covid-19 207–8
cows, selective breeding of 362–3
crabs 411
crop plants
    genetically modified 426, 434–6
    monocultures 398–9
cross-pollination 291, 294
crustaceans 20
cultures 432
cuticle 104, 105, 354
cytoplasm 35, 131

dairy products 83
daughter cells 324
DCPIP 76
deamination 263
death phase 384
death rate 383, 385
decomposers 13, 374, 379, 380
defences against pathogens 197
deficiency diseases 130
deforestation 402–4, 406
denaturation 91
dendrites 236, 237
denitrification 382
dentine 137
deoxygenated blood 170, 173
dependent variables 54
desert plants 353–5
destarching 109
diabetes 269–70
dialysis 50
dialysis tubing 55

diaphragm 18, 224, 225
diarrhoea 202
dichotomous keys 7
dicotyledons 22–3, 103
diets 128–31
diffusion 51–3
    see also osmosis
digestion 84, 132, 133, 136–40
digestive system 132–5
dinosaurs 16
diploid cells 285, 323
direct pathogen transmission 196
discontinuous variation 348, 349
diseases 195–202
DNA 36, 77, 322, 337–8, 361
DNA ligase 438
dominant alleles 327
donkeys 6
dormant seeds 291
double circulatory systems 171
double helix structure of DNA 77
dredging nets 413
droughts 408
drug users and AIDS 313
drugs 360
dry mass 4
duodenum 134–5
dwarf ponies 350

Earth, origin of life on 69
ECGs (electrocardiographs) 175–6
echo parakeet 414–15, 416
ecology 372
ecosystems 372–3
education, and conservation 412
effectors 236
egestion 132, 133
egg cells 305, 306, 307, 329, 330
eggs, bird 261
electrocardiographs (ECGs) 175–6
electron micrographs 34
electron microscopes 34

embryo 307–8
emulsification 139–40
emulsions 73, 139
enamel, tooth 136, 137
endangered species 413–16
endocrine glands 246
    see also adrenal gland; ovaries; pancreas; testes
endocrine system 247
energy flow in food chains 373, 374–5, 378
energy requirements, human 128
enhanced greenhouse effect 406
environmental change, and natural selection 357
environmental effects on variation 350
enzyme specificity 86
enzyme-substrate complexes 86
enzymes 84–6, 138–40, 429–32
    see also amylase; carbohydrases; catalase; DNA ligase; lactase; lipases; maltase; pectinase; proteases; sucrase
epidermis 104, 105, 106
epididymis 305
epithelium 138
erector muscles 271, 272, 273
ethanol 427–8
ethanol emulsion test 73–4
eucalyptus trees 161
eutrophication 409–10
excretion 3, 5, 262–6
exercise 175, 217, 226–7
exoskeleton 19
expiration 225
expired air 224
exponential phase 383
expressed genes 338
extensive livestock production 399
extinction 403, 413–14
extreme weather events 408
extremophiles 32
eye 241–5

faeces 374
fat layers 271
fats 73, 129, 136, 175
fatty acids 73, 185
female reproductive organs 304
fermenters 432–3
ferns 22
ferrets, black-footed 395
fertile organisms 6
fertilisation 284, 291, 306–7, 330, 351
fertilisers, artificial 381, 397, 409, 410
fetus 308
fibre (roughage) 128, 131
fibrin 184
fibrinogen 184–5
fight or flight response 247
filaments 286
filtration of blood 264–5
fish 15, 171, 352
fish stock conservation 412–13
flaccid cells 59
flagella 306
flies 198
flightless birds 414
floods 408
flour 428
flowering plants 22–3
flowers 248, 286–7, 289–90, 328
focusing, eye 244–5
follicle-stimulating hormone (FSH) 310, 311, 312
follicles 310, 311
food, as a source of energy 217
food chains 373, 374–5, 378
food hygiene 198–9
food poisoning 196
food production 396–7
food webs 373
forest conservation 411–12
fossil fuels 98, 380, 406, 408
fovea 242
fronds 22

fructose 160
FSH (follicle-stimulating hormone) 310, 311, 312
fully permeable membranes 35
fungal diseases 282
fungi 12
fungus kingdom 12–13

gall bladder 135
gametes 284–5, 291, 294, 325, 329
gas exchange 220–3
gas exchange surfaces 220
gases
    diffusion 51, 52–3
    see also carbon dioxide; hydrogen sulfide; methane; oxygen
gastric juice 127, 139
gene expression 338
genes 322, 326–39
genetic diagrams 330–1
genetic diversity 416–17
genetic modification 426
genetic probabilities 331
genetic variation 293, 294, 350–1, 416–17
genetically modified (GM) bacteria 434, 436–8
genetically modified (GM) crops 426, 434–6
genetics 329
genotypes 327, 330, 334, 349
genus 7
glomeruli 264
glucagon 246, 267, 268
glucose
    in blood 185, 267–8, 269–70
    molecular structure 70
    in plants 99, 101
    produced by digestion 138
    in respiration 217
glycerol 73
glycogen 70
glyphosate 434

goblet cells 133, 221
Golden Rice 426, 435
grass flowers 289
gravitropism 247, 248, 253
greenhouse effect 405–8
greenhouse gases 405, 406–7
growth 3, 4
guard cells 106, 354
guide-lines 286
guinea pigs 333

habitats 372
    destruction of 401–2
haemoglobin 75, 183
hair erector muscles 271, 272, 273
hairy leaves 354
haploid cells 285, 306, 323
hares, snowshoe 384, 385
Hartsoecker, Nicholas 303
heart 170, 171, 172–6
heart valves 173
heartbeat 175
height variations, human 348
hepatic artery 180
hepatic portal vein 141
hepatic veins 180
herbicide-resistant crop plants 434, 436
herbicides 397
herbivores 374
herd immunity 207
hermaphrodites 285, 286
hermit crabs 411
heterozygous alleles 326, 329, 330
high water potential 56
HIV (human immunodeficiency virus) 195, 196, 312–13
homeostasis 266–8
homologous chromosomes 323, 324, 325, 326
homozygous alleles 326
homunculus theory 303
honeybees 288

hormones 185, 246–7
    see also adrenaline; auxin; FSH; glucagon; insulin; LH; oestrogen; testosterone
horns, in cattle 349
horses 6
hosts (organisms) 195
houseflies 198
human breathing system 221–3
human immunodeficiency virus (HIV) 195, 196, 312–13
human nervous system 236–9
human population 386
human reproductive system 304–12
humidity 159
hunting 414
Hydra 283–4
hydrochloric acid 127, 134, 197
hydrogen peroxide 84
hydrogen sulfide 51
hydrogencarbonate indicator 114
hydrophytes 355–6
hygiene 198–200
hyphae 12
hypodermic needles 313
hypothalamus 271–2

ice caps 407, 414
ileum 134, 135
immune response 203–8
immunity, active and passive 205–6
implantation 307–8
in vitro fertilisation (IVF) 416
incisors 136, 137
independent variables 54
indirect pathogen transmission 196–7
infection 195
infertile organisms 6
ingestion 132, 133
inheritance, genetic 329
Inostrancevia 371
insect pests 434, 436
insect pollination 288, 290

insecticides 397, 399
insects 19, 102
inspiration (breathing) 224
inspired air 224
insulin 246, 267, 268, 270, 434
intensive livestock production 399–401
intercostal muscles 224, 225
internal environment 266
iodine solution 71
ionising radiation 350
iris 243
iris reflex (pupil reflex) 243
iron
    in food 130
    in haemoglobin 183
islets 267
IVF (in vitro fertilisation) 416

jelly coat, egg cell 305, 307
jointed limbs 7

keratin 75
kidneys 50, 264, 266
kinetic energy 51, 91
kingdoms 10–14
knee jerk reflex 239

lactase 83, 431–2
lacteals 142
lactic acid 217, 226–7
lactose 431–2
lactose intolerance 83
lag phase 383
landfill sites 200–1, 406–7
large intestine 135
larynx 222
leafhoppers 399
leaves 59, 103–6, 154, 354
Leeuwenhoek, Anton van 303
lens, eye 244

LH (luteinising hormone) 310, 311, 312
life on Earth, origin of 69
light intensity 115
light microscopes 33
light rays, focusing 244–5
lightning 381
lignin 148, 149, 150
limiting factors 115–16, 384
lipases 85, 89, 136, 138, 430
lipids 73, 185
    see also fats; oils
liquids 51
litter, plastic 410–11
liver 132, 135, 142, 268
livestock production 399–401
living organisms
    characteristics 3–5
    classification 5–7
log phase 383
low water potential 56
lubricated food 133, 134
lumen 134, 180
lungs 170, 221, 222
luteinising hormone (LH) 310, 311, 312
lymphocytes 184, 203–4
lynx 384, 385
lysozyme 242

magnesium ions 102
magnification 42
maize, biofuels from 427–8
male reproductive organs 304–5
maltase 85, 138
maltose 84, 138
mammals 2, 18, 171
mammary glands 18
manures 410
mass extinction events 413–14
mating, random 351
Mauritian green parakeet 414–15, 416

# Index

measles 194, 207
meat 199
medulla (kidney) 264
meiosis 285, 325–6, 351
membranes, cell 35, 52–3, 58, 59
memory cells 204
menstrual cycle 310–12
menstruation 310
Merino sheep 362, 363
mesophyll cells 104–5, 154, 156
messenger RNA (mRNA) 338
metabolic reactions 35, 84, 131
metabolism 4, 272
metamorphosis 16
methane 200, 406
microscopes 33
microvilli 141
milk 83, 362–3, 432
mimicry 347
minerals 130, 185
mining 401–2
mitochondria 37, 61, 217, 306
mitosis 285, 324–5
mitral valve 176
mixed cropping 399
molars 137
molecular diffusion 51
monocotyledons 22–3, 103–4
monocultures 398–9
monohybrid cross 331
moths, peppered 358–60
motor neurones 236, 237
mouth 134, 221
movement 3
mRNA (messenger RNA) 338
MRSA (methicillin-resistant Staphylococcus aureus) 360
mucus 133, 134, 197
mules 6
multicellular organisms 13, 33
muscle contraction and blood flow 179

muscle walls, heart 173, 176
muscles and exercise 217
mushrooms 12
mutagens 350
mutations 350–1, 357
myelin 237
myriapods 21

naming system, binomial 7
natural selection 356–61, 363
nectar 102, 286
nectaries 290
negative feedback 267, 268
nephrons 264
nerve impulses 236, 237
nerves 236
nervous system 236–9, 247
net movement 51
nets, fishing 413
neurones 236, 237
neurotransmitters 240, 241
niche 373
nitrate fertilisers 409, 410
nitrate ions 62, 102, 409
nitrification 382
nitrogen cycle 381–2
nitrogen fixation 381–2
nitrogen-fixing bacteria 382
non-biodegradable plastics 410–11
nose 197, 221
nucleotides 77, 337
nucleus 36, 324–5
nutrient cycles 379–86
nutrients 128–31
nutrition 3, 5

oesophagus 134
oestrogen 246, 310, 312
oils 73, 129
optic nerve 242
optimum temperature 86, 91
organ systems 42

organic fertilisers 410
organic substances 11
organisms
    characteristics 3–5
    classification 5–7
organs 42
osmosis 55–6, 58–60, 354
ovaries 246, 287, 288, 304, 310
overproduction 357
oviducts 304
ovulation 305, 311
ovules 287, 288, 291
oxygen
    in aerobic respiration 217
    diffusion 52, 53
    gas exchange 220
    in inspired and expired air 224
oxygen debt 227
oxygenated blood 170, 173
oxyhaemoglobin 183

palisade mesophyll 104, 105
pancreas 132, 134, 135, 246, 267
pancreatic ducts 134, 135
pancreatic juice 134
panda, giant 416
Pangaea 371
parakeet, echo 414–15, 416
Paramecium 13
partially permeable membranes 35, 55, 58, 59
particles 51
passive immunity 205–6
pathogens 75, 195–202
    see also bacteria; viruses
peas, wrinkled and smooth 349–50
pectin 429
pectinase 429
pedigree diagrams 333
penicillin 360
penis 305, 306
peppered moths 358–60

pepsin 139
peripheral nervous system (PNS) 237
peristalsis 131, 133
permeable membranes 35, 55, 58, 59
personal hygiene 199–200
pest-resistant crop plants 434, 436
pests, crop 399
petals 286, 290
pH
    of blood 227
    and enzyme activity 86, 91, 138, 139
    in fermentation 433
phagocytes 184
phagocytosis 183, 184
phenotypes 327, 330
phloem 149
photomicrographs 34
photosynthesis 98, 99, 103, 107
phototropism 247, 252
physical digestion 132, 133, 136
pinna 18
pituitary gland 310
placenta 18, 308–9
plant cells 33–8, 59–60, 104
plant kingdom 10–11
plasma, blood 182, 185
plasmids 40, 427, 438
plasmolysed cells 60
plastics 410–11
platelets 182, 184
platypus 2
PNS (peripheral nervous system) 237
poliomyelitis 206
pollen grains 286, 287, 288, 290, 291
pollen sacs 287
pollination 288–91
pollinators 102
pollution
    by greenhouse gases 405–8
    and natural selection 359–60
ponies, dwarf 350

population growth 383–4, 386
populations 348, 372, 382–6
potatoes 283
potometers 157
predator-prey relationships 384
pregnancy, diet in 128
premolars 137
probabilities, genetic 331
producers (food chains) 374
product molecules 85
progesterone 310, 311, 312
prokaryote kingdom 14
prokaryotes 12
prokaryotic cells 14, 40
prostate gland 305
proteases 84, 134, 136, 138, 430
protein coat, viral 24
protein synthesis 337–9
proteins
    in blood plasma 185
    digestion 136, 263
    functions 75
    molecular structure 75
    in plants 102
    as a source of food 129
    see also amino acids; Bt protein; receptor proteins
protoctist kingdom 12, 13–14
puberty 310
pufferfish 4
pulmonary artery 172, 173, 222
pulmonary system 171
pulmonary veins 172, 173, 222
pulse rate 175
Punnett squares 331
pupil 243
pupil reflex (iris reflex) 243
pure-breeding 334
pygmy seahorse 352–3, 356
pyramids of biomass 376
pyramids of energy 378
pyramids of numbers 375–6

radiation
    ionising 350
    solar 405
rainforests 402–4, 411–12
random fertilisation 351
random mating 351
ranges 87
raw meat 199
raw sewage 200
reabsorption 265, 266
reaction times 235
receptor cells, eye 242
receptor proteins 240, 241
receptors 236, 237, 241
    skin 271–2
recessive alleles 327
recombinant plasmids 438
rectum 135
red blood cells 182, 183
red-green colour blindness 336–7
reducing sugars 71
reduction division 325
reflex actions 238–9, 243
reflex arcs 237–9
refraction 244
reheating food 199
relay neurones 237
replanting 412
reproduction
    as a characteristic of living organisms 3, 4
    in humans 304–12
    in plants 102, 282–4
reptiles 16–17
resistance to antibiotics 360–1
respiration 3, 4, 217–18
restriction enzymes 437, 438
retina 241
rib cage 224, 225
ribosomes 37, 338
rice 426, 435
rickets 130

# Index

rods 242
root hairs 62, 152–3
roots 247, 248, 355
running 235

salivary glands 134
SARS-CoV-2 207–8
saturated fats 175
scrotum 304
scurvy 130
Scutosaurus 371
sea level rise 407
seahorse, pygmy 352–3, 356
secretion 104, 105
seed banks 415, 417
seedless bananas 282
seeds 291, 293
selection, natural 356–61, 363
selection pressures 359–60
selective breeding 362–3, 397
selective felling 412
self-pollination 291, 294
semen 303, 306
semilunar valves 173, 176
sense organs 241–5
sensitivity 3, 4
sensory neurones 237
sepals 286
septum 172
Sequoia sempervirens 148
set points 267, 272
sewage 200–1, 410
sex chromosomes 335–6
sex-linked genes 335, 336
sexual reproduction 102, 283, 284–91, 293–4
sexually transmitted infections (STIs) 312–13
Shaw, Dr George 2
sheep, selective breeding of 362, 363
shivering 272
shoots 247, 248

sigmoid growth curves 384
single circulatory systems 171
sink part of plants 159
skin 197, 199, 270–1
sleep apnoea 216
small intestine 134, 135, 141
smallpox 206
smoking 175
sneezing 196
snowshoe hares 384, 385
soap, washing with 199–200
soil erosion 403
soil fertility 399
solar radiation 405
solids 51
solutes, diffusion 53
solvents 53
source part of plants 159
specialised cells 41–2
species 6
specificity of enzymes 86
specimen sizes 42
sperm 304, 306, 307, 329, 330
sperm ducts 305
sphincter muscles 133, 134
spongy mesophyll 105, 156
spores 13
sprinting 235
stamens 286
Staphylococcus aureus 360–1
staple foods 128
starch
    digestion 84, 136, 138
    molecular structure 70, 71
starch grains 36, 101
stationary phase 384
stem cells 339
sterilisation 432
sticky ends 437, 438
stigmas 287, 289, 290
stimuli 236

STIs (sexually transmitted infections) 312–13
stomach 134, 197
stomach cells 41
stomata 106, 116, 154, 353, 354
style 287
substrate molecules 85
suckers 282
sucrase 85
sucrose 101, 159–60
sugar solutions 55
sugarcane, biofuels from 427–8
sugars 70
    see also fructose; glucose; lactose; maltose; sucrose
sunlight 99, 103, 106, 373, 405
superweeds 436
surface area, leaf 354
suspensory ligaments 245
sustainable resources 411
sweat 199
sweat glands 270–1, 273
symptoms of disease 195
synapses 240, 241
synaptic gaps 240, 241
systemic system 171

T cells 313
tadpoles 373
target organs 246
tear glands 242
teeth 130, 134, 136, 200
temperature
    body 266–7, 270–3
    and diffusion 51
    and enzyme activity 86, 91, 138
    in fermentation 433
    and food hygiene 199
    global 407
    and photosynthesis 115–16
    and transpiration 159
temperature receptors 271–2

terrestrial organisms  19
test crosses  334
testes  246, 304, 305
testosterone  246, 310
thermal expansion  407
thorax  222, 224, 225
thymolphthalein  89
tissues  41, 104–6
toadstools  12
tongue  134
tooth decay  136
toxins  195
trachea  134, 221, 222
translocation  159–60
transmissible diseases  195
transmission of pathogens  195–201
transpiration  154–9
transpiration pull  156
transpiration rates  157, 159
trees  148, 160, 161
tricuspid valve  176
trophic levels  375–6
tropical rainforests  402–4, 411–12
tropisms  247
trypsin  139
tubers  283
tuna  352–3, 356
turgid cells  59
turgor pressure  59
type 1 diabetes  269–70

umbilical cord  308
unicellular organisms  13, 14, 33
urea  185, 262, 263
ureter  262
urethra  262, 304, 305
urine  261, 262, 264–5, 269–70
uterus  304, 308, 309

vaccination  194, 205–7
vaccines  205
vacuoles  35
vagina  304, 306
valves  170, 173, 179
van Leeuwenhoek, Anton  303
variables, dependent and independent  54
variation  293, 294, 348–51, 416–17
vascular bundles  103, 151
vasoconstriction  273
vasodilation  273
veins  141, 172, 173, 178, 179, 180, 222
venae cavae  172, 173
ventilation (breathing)  223
ventricles  172, 173, 176
Venus flytrap  4
vertebrates  15–18
vesicles  35, 240, 241
vestigial structures  19
villi  141, 308
viral diseases  195, 360
    see also AIDS; Covid-19; measles; poliomyelitis; smallpox
viruses  24, 195, 196
    see also HIV
vitamin A  426, 435
vitamin C  76, 130
vitamin D  130
vitamins  130
vocal cords  222

washing, and personal hygiene  199–200
washing powders, biological  430
waste disposal  200–1, 410–11

water
    in blood plasma  185
    in the body  70, 131, 266
    disease transmission by  197
    in plants  152–9
    as a solvent  55
    see also osmosis
water-baths  89
water consumption, in intensive farming  400
water cycle, effect of deforestation on  404
water hyacinth  355
water potential  56
water supply  198
water vapour  154, 156, 159, 217, 224
waxy cuticle  354
weather events, extreme  408
white blood cells  182, 183
wilting  159
wind pollination  289, 290
wind speed, and transpiration  159
windpipe  222
wisdom teeth  137
wool  362, 363

X chromosomes  335–6
xerophytes  353–5
xylem  103, 148, 149–50, 153

Y chromosomes  335–6
yeast  217, 427

zebras  357
zoos  415, 416
zygotes  284, 291, 307, 323

**Acknowledgements**

*The authors and publishers acknowledge the following sources of copyright material and are grateful for the permissions granted. While every effort has been made, it has not always been possible to identify the sources of all the material used, or to trace all copyright holders. If any omissions are brought to our notice, we will be happy to include the appropriate acknowledgements on reprinting.*

*Thanks to the following for permission to reproduce images:*

Twomeows/GI; Leonello Calvetti/GI; Oxford Scientific/GI; Rowell Porrad/GI; Antagain/GI; Volschenkh/GI; Elfi Kluck/GI; Benedek; Mary Jones (x4); Sheila Creighton/GI; Guenterguni/GI; Dantesattic/GI; Orenda Randuch/GI; Benedek/GI; PhotoTalk/GI; Manuel Rubio/GI; Ed Reschke/GI; Michael Stephan/GI; YS graphic/GI; Laguna Design/GI; Ktsdesign/Science Photo Library/GI; Dennis Kunkel Microscopy/SPL; Wildestanimal/GI; Jean Tresfon/GI; Reptiles4all/GI; Holger Langmaier/GI; SeaTops/GI; Jacobs Stock Photography Ltd/GI; Janetteasche/GI; Witthaya Prasongsin/GI; Fabian von Poser/GI; Alexis Rosenfeld/GI; Antagain/GI; Peter Dazeley/GI; Efilippou/GI; Don Farrall/GI; Gavriel Jecan/GI; Loridambrosio/GI; Eve Livesey/GI; Photo used with permission of Dr Gwilym Lewis; Eduard Muzhevskyi/Science Photo Library/GI; Russell Pearson/Barcroft Media/GI; Cimmerian/GI; Geoff Jones; Alanphillips/GI; Dr.Jeremy Burgess/SPL; Biophoto Associates/SPL; Alanphillips/GI; Dr Jeremy Burgess/SPL; Cnri/SPL; Jack0m/GI; Biophoto Associates/SPL; NNehring/GI; Cnri/SPL; Tara Moore/GI; Santiago Urquijo/GI; Naphtalina/GI; Callista Images/GI; Christoph Burgstedt/Science Photo Library/GI; Ed Reschke/GI; Amriphoto/GI; Sinhyu/GI; Guifang jian/GI; Martyn F.Chillmaid/SPL; Ye Aung Thu/GI; Andrew Lambert Photography/SPL; Martyn F.Chillmaid/SPL; Martyn F.Chillmaid/SPL; Andrew Lambert Photography/SPL; MB Photography/GI; Andrew Lambert Photography/SPL; Craftsci/Science Photo Library/GI; Carlos Clarivan/SPL; Konrad Wothe/GI; Bloomberg/GI; Martyn F.Chillmaid/SPL; Andrew Lambert Photography/SPL; Martyn F.Chillmaid/SPL; Alexandre Dotta/Science Source/SPL; Kei Uesugi/GI; Monash University/Tribune News Service/GI; Simonlong/GI; NNehring/GI; Fauzan Maududdin/GI; Nigel Cattlin, visuals unlimited/SPL; Simon Gakhar/GI; Thomas Winz/GI; Eye of Science/SPL; Dr Keith Wheeler/SPL; NNehring/GI; Nature Cutout's/Alamy; Mischa Keijser/GI; Ann Winterbotham/GI; Photo by author, Mary Jones; Claudia Totir/GI; David M.Martin, Md/SPL; Robynmac/GI; Maximilian Stock Ltd/GI; Education Images/GI; Philip Wilkins/GI; Science Photo Library-Pasieka/GI; Christoph Burgstedt/Science Photo Library/GI; Franckreporter/GI; Steve Gschmeissner/SPL/GI; David Arky/GI; Ingram Publishing/GI; Dr David Furness, Keele University/SPL; Steve Gschmeissner/SPL; Steve Gschmeissner/SPL; Tunart/GI; Steve Gschmeissner/SPL; Dr Keith Wheeler/SPL; Nigel Cattlin, visuals unlimited/SPL; Biophoto Associates/SPL; Jialiang Gao/GI; Pierre-Yves Babelon/GI; Yvonne Van der Horst/GI; Herve Conge,ism/SPL; Nnehring/GI; Kateryna Kon/SPL/GI; SDI Productions/GI; LeoPatrizi/GI; Yoshiyoshi Hirokawa/GI; JGI/Jamie Grill/GI; Prof.P.Motta/Dept. Of Anatomy/University "La Sapienza",Rome/SPL; Xia yuan/GI; Don W.Fawcett/Science Source/SPL; Steve Gschmeissner/SPL/GI; Track5/GI; Dennis Kunkel Microscopy/SPL; Kateryna Kon/SPL/GI; D.Jiang/; Callista Images/GI; Peter Dazeley/GI; John Lawson/GI; Peeterv/GI; Hadynyah/GI; FangXiaNuo/GI; Bashir Osman's Photography/GI; PeopleImages/GI; Robert Nickelsberg/GI; Noemi Cassanelli/GI; Callista Images/GI; Christoph Burgstedt/SPL/GI; Karl Tapales/GI; Niaid-Rml/National Institutes Of Health/SPL; RealPeopleGroup/GI; Morsa Images/GI; Lane Oatey/Blue Jean Images/GI; Xavierarnau/GI; Kuniharu Wakabayashi/GI; Cdc/SPL/GI; Digital Vision/GI; Drbimages/GI; Martin-dm/GI; Surya Fachrizal Aprianus/Anadolu Agency/GI; Magicmine/GI; Ucsf/GI; Mike Hill/GI; Jeff Pachoud/GI; Tongpatong/GI; JGI/Tom Grill/GI; Omikron/SPL; Ondacaracola photography; Martin Shields/SPL; Redmal/GI; Martin Shields/SPL; Fabio Nodari/GI; Wu Swee Ong/GI; Evelyn Joubert/Shutterstock; Steve Gschmeissner/SPL; Science Photo Library/GI; Bsip/Uig/GI; Jason Butcher/GI; Klaus Vedfelt/GI; Steve Gschmeissner/SPL; Jacky Parker Photography/GI; Volodymyr Nikitenko/Shutterstock; Xuanyu Han/GI; Fitri Iskandar Zakariah/GI; Dennis Kunkel Microscopy/SPL; Redzaal/GI; Steve Gschmeissner/SPL/GI; Jerome Wexler, visuals unlimited/SPL; Viktoria Rodriguez/GI; Clouds Hill Imaging Ltd/SPL; Martin Siepmann/GI; Alexandr Naumov/GI; Eye Of Science/SPL; Ichauvel/GI; Carole Gomez/GI; Massimo Brega/SPL; Christian Ender/GI; Raycat/GI; R.W.Horne/Biophoto Associates/SPL; Science Source/SPL (x2); Kathrin Ziegler/GI; Science Photo Library-Sciepro/GI; Blickwinkel/Alamy; Power And Syred/SPL; Cnri/SPL (x2); Cat'chy Images/Alamy; Science Photo Library; Andrew Greaves/Alamy; Westend61/GI; Jeanne Morgan/GI; Slowmotiongli/GI; Robbie Ross/GI; Nick White/GI; Eve Livesey/GI; Fabiano Strappazzon/GI; Martyn F.Chillmaid/SPL; Seng Chye Teo/GI; Philippe Psaila/SPL; Navith Yasasindhu/GI; Tony Chan/GI; Peter Pokrovsky/GI; Bob Gibbons/SPL; Archie Young/SPL; Dr Keith Wheeler/SPL; Tareq Saifur Rahman/GI; Agefotostock/Alamy; Science Photo Library; Abdelrahman Hassanein/GI; Ian_Redding/GI; Steve Allen/SPL; Agefotostock/Alamy; Edwin Remsberg/Alamy; Stephen Dorey/GI; Creativ Studio Heinemann/GI; Shikhei Goh/GI; Mauricio Anton/SPL; John Cancalosi/GI; Robert Shantz/Alamy; Pete Mcbride/GI; Dom Hart/GI; Auscape/Universal Images Group/GI; Danita Delimont/GI; Joakimbkk/GI; Guenter Fischer/GI; Fws/Alamy; Hal Beral/GI; Paulo Sousa/GI; Kampee Patisena/GI; Dennisjim/GI; Nigel Cattlin/SPL; Pixelda Picture License/GI; Smerindo_Schultzpax/GI; Anton Petrus/GI; TorriPhoto/GI; Hans Neleman/GI; Planetobserver/SPL; ChooChoo-ca-Chew/GI; Robas/GI; Bearacreative/GI; Luoman/GI; Hagens World Photography/GI; Science Photo Library; Christian Declercq/GI; Wiratgasem/GI; Walter Zerla/GI; NurPhoto/GI; Nathan Edwards/GI; Nigel Cattlin/Alamy; Nora Carol Photography/GI; Paulo Oliveira/Alamy; David Woodfall Images/SPL; Robin Bush/GI; Danita Delimont/Alamy; Arterra/Universal Images Group/GI; Thomas Winz/GI; Mark Newman/GI; Brian Laferte/GI; Javier Dez/GI; Vicki Jauron/GI; Westend61/GI; Joerg Boethling/Alamy; Steve Gschmeissner/SPL/GI; Yves Soulabaille/Look At Sciences/SPL; Mikroman6/GI; Westend61/GI; Power And Syred/SPL; Martin Lee/Alamy; Bill Barksdale/Agstockusa/SPL; Peggy Greb/US Department Of Agriculture/SPL; Riccardo Lennart Niels Mayer/Alamy; Robert Brook/SPL; Noah Berger/Bloomberg/GI; Hill Street Studios/GI.

**Key:** GI= Getty Images, SPL= Science Photo Library.

Popart

Mask

2 Position to loot with pop up pic and another in the top corner

on the "something" do a circle wipe to have a coloured background